PLANT MANAGER'S MANUAL AND GUIDE

Charles H. Becker

Prentice-Hall, Inc.
Englewood Cliffs, New Jersey

Prentice-Hall International, Inc., *London*
Prentice-Hall of Australia, Pty. Ltd., *Sydney*
Prentice-Hall Canada, Inc., *Toronto*
Prentice-Hall of India Private Ltd., *New Delhi*
Prentice-Hall of Japan, Inc., *Tokyo*
Prentice-Hall of Southeast Asia Pte. Ltd., *Singapore*
Editora Prentice-Hall do Brasil Ltda., *Rio de Janeiro*
Prentice-Hall Hispanoamericana, S.A., *Mexico*

© 1987 by

Charles H. Becker

"This publication is designed to provide accurate and authoritative information in regard to the subject matter covered. It is sold with the understanding that the publisher is not engaged in rendering legal, accounting, or other professional service. If legal advice or other expert assistance is required, the services of a competent professional person should be sought."

—From the Declaration of Principles jointly adopted by a Committee of the American Bar Association and a Committee Of Publishers and Associations.

> **This book was prepared entirely by the author, who is solely responsible for its content. Nothing in it should be construed to represent any policy, procedure, or opinion of the Export-Import Bank of the United States.**

Library of Congress Cataloging-in-Publication Data

Becker, Charles H.
 Plant manager's manual and guide.

 Rev. ed. of: Plant manager's handbook, 1974.
 Includes bibliographies and index.
 1. Production management. I. Becker, Charles H.,
date   . Plant manager's handbook. II. Title.
TS155.B39 1987   658.5   86-30545

          10 9 8 7 6 5

This book was previously published as *Plant Manager's Handbook*.

ISBN 0-13-680703-8

9 780136 807032

PRINTED IN THE UNITED STATES OF AMERICA

To Anne

About the Author

CHARLES H. BECKER is Deputy Vice President–Engineering of the Export-Import Bank of the United States, a federal government agency which provides financial assistance to facilitate exports of American goods and services. The Engineering Division evaluates the technical feasibility of projects for which financing is sought, and Mr. Becker's thirteen years of experience in it have brought him into contact with a number of America's major manufacturing and engineering firms. He has traveled to many parts of the world to observe projects under construction and in operation. In 1986 he led a U.S. Department of Commerce Trade Mission for Engineering and Construction Services to India and Pakistan.

Mr. Becker's background in the private sector covers twenty-three years of industrial production management, with assignments as shift foreman, department supervisor, assistant plant manager, and plant manager. His responsibilities included production, engineering, maintenance, quality control, collective bargaining, facilities management, and others during this period.

The author holds bachelor's and master's degrees in chemical engineering, and is a registered professional engineer in Pennsylvania.

Acknowledgments

A special word of appreciation goes to my colleagues at the Engineering Division of the Export-Import Bank, who have expanded my understanding of the applied sciences in many directions.

I would like to thank also the following manufacturers, associations, and publishers who provided and/or permitted use of their information and materials:

Akron Gear and Engineering, Inc.

American Iron and Steel Institute

Cincinnati Milacron Inc.

Cleaver-Brooks

Conveyor Equipment Manufacturers Association

Dodge Manufacturing Division, Reliance Electric Company

Dow Jones & Company, Inc.

Falk Corporation, Subsidiary of Sundstrand Corporation

FMC Corporation, Material Handling Systems Division

Hardinge Brothers, Inc.

Harper & Row, Publishers, Inc.

John Wiley & Sons, Inc.

Louis Allis, a Division of MagneTek, Inc.

Micro Control Systems, Inc.

Mixing Equipment Co., Inc.

Modine Manufacturing Company

National Electrical Manufacturers Association

National Fire Protection Association

National Safety Council

Proctor & Schwartz, Inc.

PT Components, Inc., Link-Belt Bearing Division

The American Society of Mechanical Engineers

What This Book Will Do for You

This book is a comprehensive guide specifically geared to plant managers and for all those who are involved with manufacturing and service operations. It's a handy manual for quick and profitable advice on sound plant management techniques. You'll find practical advice for organizing and operating the plant, and fundamental guidelines for improving relationships between employees and management. And it provides you with all the illustrations, tables, and checklists you need for adapting them to your own operations.

Here are some of the key areas covered in this book:

- The six steps to take in planning the plant organization, and the choices you have in building it.
- How to set up shift operations.
- How to evaluate Maintenance Department performance.
- How to establish an all-encompassing quality control program, and statistical techniques you can use to measure quality.
- What you must include in an operating cost system.
- How to take control of plant costs.
- Five steps you can take to establish a permanent cost reduction program.
- Four places to look for major energy cost savings.
- Five ways to achieve smooth industrial relations while maintaining plant discipline.
- Eight things you can do to keep the plant nonunion.
- Seven ways to develop more capable first-line supervisors.
- When to use robots, how to plan their installation, and what you should expect to pay for them.
- How to manage a construction project from the feasibility study through the post-completion audit.

- How to calculate return on investment, payback period, and discounted cash flow rate of return for a proposed project.
- The four basic ways in which computers are applied to manufacturing, and how computer intergrated manufacturing is achieved.

HOW THIS BOOK IS ORGANIZED

Plant Manager's Manual and Guide is divided into three main parts, and features operating examples throughout the book to show you just how the basic principles of plant management are applied in the plant.

Part I provides a thorough treatment of the management skills you will need to organize and operate the plant. Chapters 1 and 2 outline proven management techniques, describe the responsibilities of a plant manager, and outline the steps you must take to establish leadership. Chapter 3 sets out the choices you can make in building the plant organization. Chapters 4, 5, and 6 show how to schedule and implement procedures for production, maintenance, and quality control operations. Chapters 7 and 8 tell how capital and operating cost systems are established, and explain the methods used to implement permanent programs for cost control and cost reduction. Energy conservation has risen to such importance in American industry that it deserves and is given separate treatment in Chapter 9.

Part II is designed to help plant managers in their relationships with people who work for them. Chapter 10 is a guide to industrial relations, and is followed by two chapters dealing with unions. Chapter 11 discusses methods of keeping the plant nonunion, and takes you through an organizing campaign. Chapter 12 is a manual for collective bargaining; it starts with preparations for negotiations and covers all the phases of bargaining right through a possible strike. Chapter 13 is devoted to development of the first-line supervisor. Chapter 14 shows how to establish safety and housekeeping programs that work, while Chapter 15 deals with the requirements of the Occupational Safety and Health Administration (OSHA) and the Environmental Protection Agency (EPA).

Part III explains the technical aspects of plant facilities. Chapter 16 covers the basic principles and equipment encountered in the electrical, mechanical, fluid handling, and heating/ventilating/air conditioning systems of the plant. Chapter 17 tells how to build efficient materials movement systems. Chapter 18 explains the techniques for specifying and selecting plant equipment. Chapters 19 and 20 show how to involve the production staff in plant design, and how to proceed with construction projects. Chapter 21 is a basic guide to the application of computers in manufacturing. The Appendix offers useful tables of metric conversion factors, sheet metal and wire thicknesses, electric motor dimensions, and more.

Whether your intent is to brush up on topics or explore new techniques, *The Plant Manager's Manual and Guide* can help you achieve top performance in the many activities that fall within the responsibilities of a plant manager.

Charles H. Becker

Contents

Contents

PART II
MANAGING PLANT EMPLOYEES 157

PART III
PLANT FACILITIES AND EQUIPMENT *281*

Contents

PART I

Plant Management: Techniques for Organizing and Operating the Plant

Chapter 1

Proven Management Techniques for Corporate and Personal Reward

As a plant manager, you are a member of the corporate management team. You are expected to understand the language of management, to have a grasp of its basic concepts, and to take an active part in the management plan of action established by the company's chief executive. This chapter will help you become a more professional manager. It begins with a definition of management, then examines management as a science, outlines the fundamentals common to all management operations, and explains some current trends in the application of management techniques.

HOW TO CLASSIFY MANAGEMENT

There is no universally accepted definition of the word "management." Dictionaries speak vaguely of "direction," "control," and even "governing," but they do not offer definitions that include all of the essential elements of management. Basic courses in foremanship usually inform their students that "Management is getting things done through other people." Although it is a good reminder to the former machine operator that he can no longer turn out the production himself, the statement doesn't stand up as a full definition of management. (After all, if I take the bus downtown I am getting something done through other people, but we would hardly want to class that as management.)

Any definition of management should include these five elements: (1) directing the efforts (2) of a group of people (3) toward the accomplishment of one or more purposes, (4) evaluating the results, and (5) adjusting the efforts to improve performance.

Where do you look for guidance in directing the efforts of a group of people toward a common goal? How do you learn to evaluate the results and adjust performance? The answers lie in the fact that for the past hundred years industrial managers and researchers have gradually built up a body of knowledge and methods from which general principles can be derived for application to specific situations—in other words, a science. Like other sciences, management has separate branches of knowledge and techniques, such as planning, organizing, controlling, and decision making. Because this group of topics comprises specific skills that can be learned in a methodical way, it might well be called the *objective sciences* of management. A second group that includes communication, motivation, and performance appraisal might well be called the *social sciences* of management because more subjective approaches and direct contact with other people are involved. All of these topics will be discussed in this book.

HOW THE MANAGEMENT CYCLE WORKS: A THREE-PHASE PROCESS

Most managers have been exposed to bits and pieces of the management cycle throughout their careers. They have heard of "budgetary controls." They have submitted "organization charts." They have attended "planning seminars." And they have been through periodic campaigns emphasizing some part of the management cycle—"management by objectives," "management by exception," "management by *total* objectives," and so on. These are useful concepts, but they can be misleading to the extent that they fail to capture the full scope of the management function.

Management consists of three essential phases—*planning, organizing,* and *controlling.* No activity requiring management can be successful without them; they are always present, to a greater or lesser degree, in every organized enterprise carried on by groups of people. Together they constitute the *management cycle,* a term that implies, quite accurately, that the work done in any of the three functions is never complete in itself, but must be adjusted on a continuing basis to accommodate changes in each of the other two. Let's examine the elements of the management cycle more closely.

Planning is the first step you take as a manager. You approach a task assigned to you and develop a plan by pursuing two highly disciplined activities. You begin by developing an exact statement of the objective you want to reach, including not only *what* is to be accomplished, but *when* it is to be completed.

The second step you take is to determine exactly what activities must be carried out to reach your objective. These activities must be defined clearly in terms of their cost, manpower demands in numbers and skills, requirements for tools and materials, and the order in which they will be executed.

Organizing is the management process by which groups of people are assigned to the activities stated in the plan. As you structure the organization, you assemble the appropriate number of people with the required skills, and establish lines of authority and responsibility between yourself and the working groups. You coordinate their activities to avoid conflict and duplication of effort. And you see to it that no one reports to more than one superior, and no supervisor has more people reporting to him or her than he or she can reasonably handle.

Controlling completes the management cycle. In this step, you evaluate the progress of the organization toward its goal. You establish methods of measuring and evaluating the difference between the goal and the accomplishment at appropriate times. You set up checkpoints that warn you the effort is going off target before the situation gets too serious. When the warnings are received, you take corrective action in time to bring the effort back on target.

Now we come to an understanding of why planning, organizing, and controlling are called the *management cycle*. When you evaluate the signals you receive in the control phase, you may decide that the proper corrective action is to change the organization, or even go back to the planning stage and add or detract activities. In some cases the objective itself may have to be changed. When that happens, organization and control must be reviewed again, and the cycle may be repeated many times before success is achieved.

Operating Example 1-1: The Management Cycle in Action: Setting Up a Safety Glasses Program. This is how a plant manager, who has decided that he must establish a safety glasses program in the plant, goes about applying the principles of the management cycle.

He starts with the **planning** phase, and his first step is to define the objective as clearly as he can: "After March 31, 19XX, safety glasses will be worn by all employees and guests of the company in production, maintenance, and shipping areas of the plant."

His next planning move is to decide what activities must be carried out to reach the objective, and he writes down the following list:

A. Conduct an Educational Program

   1. Assemble facts about effectiveness of safety glasses, including eye injury case histories and statistics for the nation, the industry, and this plant.

   2. Conduct safety meetings with each plant work group, stating the reasons for requiring safety glasses, and presenting the information assembled in 1.

   3. Support the campaign with a series of articles in the company newspaper.

B. Provide Safety Glasses for All Personnel

   1. Plano glasses for personnel who do not wear glasses regularly.

   2. Prescription glasses for those who do. Each employee to submit his own prescription.

C. Establish Plant Regulations

   1. Draft a plant safety rule requiring safety glasses, and publish.

   2. Make it a condition of employment that safety glasses be worn.

   3. Establish disciplinary procedures for failure to comply.

   4. Post signs in appropriate areas.

With the planning phase completed, the plant manager moves next to the **organizing** step. In this case the plant manager won't even look at his organization chart. He knows that he can find on it groups of people who can operate the steam boilers, perform processing operations, and ship finished goods. But nowhere on the chart will he find a group of people set up to work on a safety glasses program. He will have to organize a group to carry out the program.

His first step in organizing is to decide what abilities are needed. Reviewing the activity list reveals the need for (1) researching the information required for the educational program, and developing it into a presentable form for worker meetings; (2) communicating the information to the employees and enforcing rules developed by the program; and (3) measuring and fitting each employee with a suitable set of frames and lenses.

The second step is to hire or assign people with these abilities. This plant manager feels that his personnel director has the skills required for (1) above. The production superintendent meets the requirements for (2). But there is no one in the organization who can accomplish (3). This skill will have to be acquired outside the company by engaging the services of an optometrist.

The third step in organizing is to establish lines of authority and responsibility. Our plant manager feels that many of the decisions to be made by the group need not involve him directly, so he delegates his authority by putting the personnel director in charge. The production superintendent is made accountable to the personnel director for matters relating to this project.

The fourth step is to establish the relationships between the elements of the organization. In this case, the plant manager decides that the personnel director will assume responsibility for hiring the optometrist, and conducting the research and publicity work. The production superintendent is made responsible for the meetings with plant personnel, for drafting the safety regulation, and posting of signs. By assigning the activities carefully, the plant manager avoids conflicts between the two supervisors over who is to do what.

Now that the organization is complete and ready to start work, the plant manager turns his attention to the **controls** he will use to satisfy himself that the program is proceeding according to plan.

He arranges monthly meetings with the personnel director to receive a verbal report on the program's progress. He notes on his calendar the dates when the accident statistics and publicity material are due, and he asks to see them. He requires written reports from the production superintendent on the plant meetings, and asks for them when the meetings are due. Several days after the March 31 deadline he walks through the plant to see if safety glasses really are being worn. At each control point, he takes corrective action if the goals of the program are not being met.

Our manager may have to go through the cycle several more times before his program can be called complete. He may get halfway through the planning and organizing stages only to realize that the development laboratory, which is located on the plant site but does not report to him, has been left out of the program; quick consultation with higher management reveals that the lab should indeed be included. This new circumstance compels the plant manager to go back to the planning stage and revise his objectives to include the lab and to review the educational program, which now must be tailored to meet the needs of a group whose work is quite different from that of the plant. Changes will also have to be made in the organizing phase—people from the lab will have to be brought into the task force, and new lines of authority established so that compliance with the new program is assured in the laboratory as well as the areas directly under the plant manager's control.

Application of the management cycle by the manager in the operating example never ends, nor should he, as a professional manager, expect it to. Once the program is firmly established, then control—evaluating the results of the program and adjusting it to be sure the original objectives are being met—is the main activity. As time goes on the original plans and objectives might have to be changed, perhaps because of a new government regulation. The organization originally developed for the task may well be in for changes—for example, if a safety director is hired, or if the task force is disbanded altogether and its residual functions included in the responsibilities of several managers. Even the control phase may undergo changes, such as intensified compliance enforcement as new laws make management more directly responsible for the prevention of plant injuries.

Operating Example 1-1 also shows how the social sciences of management could be used to help achieve the objective of the program. **Communication** with the affected employees would be achieved through the safety meetings, articles in the company newspaper, and the posted signs. **Motivation** might be established by dramatic presentations (through safety films, or talks by persons actually blinded in industrial accidents) and by putting in force the new plant regulations. **Performance appraisal** would no doubt be employed by you, the plant manager, as you evaluate the progress of your subordinate managers with the program, both short term and later in annual reviews.

Management by Exception (MBE): A "Commonsense" Approach

MBE is not a complete system of management, but it is based on sound principles. It is also deceptively simple. You announce to your subordinates that you will not become involved in the things that are going well; only those problems that cannot be solved at a lower level are to be brought to your attention. Application of this system demands two prerequisites: first, you must have in place operating procedures good enough to allow the day-to-day routine activities to proceed smoothly without your attention, and second, you must be willing to delegate authority and to insist that problems be handled at the lowest possible level. "Lowest possible level" is defined as that level in the organization where the skills and knowledge needed to solve the problem first appear.

There are four main advantages of management by exception: (1) you (or any manager) can apply it in your own department without reference to its application in other units of the company, (2) it allows you more time to concentrate on future progress and those activities and problems that need your special attention, (3) it is a "commonsense" method readily understood by subordinates and superiors alike, and (4) it develops subordinates by requiring them to make decisions on the problems that are within their competence. It also has some disadvantages, the most important being that the manager does not hear about the problem until the last step before it goes out of control, and has not been given the opportunity to take preventive measures earlier.

MBE is a method which many managers adopt intuitively; it is seldom accorded the dignity of being installed as a companywide system with the accompanying seminars, training sessions, and top management attention that more elaborate methods receive.

Management by Objectives (MBO):
Setting Performance Goals

One of the problems faced by the top management of a corporation is to find a system for applying sound management principles throughout the company, in a way that will be understood by all managers down to the lowest levels. Management by objectives (MBO) is a method designed to do just that. It requires every manager throughout the company to sit down with each of his or her subordinate managers and develop a set of goals which the subordinate is expected to meet over a particular time period—usually one year. These goals are stated in objective, measurable terms so that at the end of the time period the manager's performance in reaching them can be appraised without personal bias. In most applications of MBO the system is set in motion by the chief executive officer of the company, and his or her objectives are supported by and coordinated with each successive lower level of management as the process cascades down through the organization.

> **Operating Example 1-2: The MBO System in Action.** The President of XYZ Manufacturing Company, in setting the corporation's objectives for the upcoming fiscal year, decides that pretax profit must be increased by 6 percent. In consultation with her four divisional vice-presidents, she finds that goals can be set for the Marketing Division to increase sales so as to yield 2 percent; for the R&D division to complete work on a new product in time to provide another 2 percent; and for reduction of costs by the Administrative and Manufacturing Divisions so as to contribute 1 percent each.
>
> The vice-president of Manufacturing is now ready to discuss next year's goals with the plant manager of Plant 3, and informs him that if the division objective is to be met, plan 3 will have to reduce its costs by $50,000. The plant manager has been working on a plan for reducing off-grade production that would result in annual savings of $25,000; he is willing to commit to that as a goal for the ensuing year, and the vice-president accepts. The debugging of recently installed machinery has progressed to the point where the plant manager feels that he can drop a permanently assigned maintenance mechanic from the third shift and realize cost savings of $20,000; he is willing to commit to that figure as a goal, and the vice-president accepts. To find the additional $5,000 in needed savings, the plant manager brings up an idea he has been considering for some time: eliminate the breakfast meal served at the plant cafeteria and save $10,000 per year. The vice-president rejects this proposal, however, because he believes the ill-will it will engender more than offsets the potential savings. The two finally agree on the first two objectives for expected savings of $45,000; the vice-president will look elsewhere for the remaining $5,000 in savings. Of course, the plant manager will have objectives of his own to incorporate in the MBO program; this year he has decided to reduce

the number of grievances filed by the hourly rated group by one-third. He plans to do this by (1) reviewing last year's grievances to see if there is any pattern that might suggest remedial action on his part, and (2) to revise the complaint handling procedure used by the first-line supervisors so that fewer complaints become grievances.

One year later the two executives meet to review the performance of the plant manager against his objectives. Cost records show a drop in the amount of off-grade product resulting in savings of \$28,632. The third-shift mechanic was replaced but emergency call-ins were more frequent than predicted, and the cost savings from this move were slightly under target at \$18,459. The combined savings totaled \$47,091, exceeding the target of \$45,000 by 4.6 percent. Grievances dropped by 39 percent as a result of the plant manager's study and revision of the procedures. In all, a good performance by the plant manager for Plant 3, and the basis of his performance appraisal for the year.

The operating example not only illustrates, in a simplified way, how the MBO system works but also points up some of its advantages:

1. By the establishment of a network of coordinated goals throughout the several levels of management, the efforts of all of them are directed toward a common objective.
2. Through the commitment to stated goals the efforts of managers are focused on improving the business, rather than just "running the shop."
3. The MBO system brings with it a method of performance appraisal for the individual manager based on measurable standards that he helped to create, and allows him to develop his own strategies to meet the standards.

DECISION MAKING IN THE PLANT: TWO VALUABLE TECHNIQUES

Plant managers make many decisions, most of them without any hesitation. After all, if you have worked your way up through an industry you could probably respond quickly and decisively when asked how a piece of defective work might be corrected. But there are other situations where making a choice is not so easy, especially when it must be made among options that look pretty much alike. Further, as every manager, you know that decisions made by you do not always "stick," but set in motion chains of events requiring still further decisions, with the ultimate outcome hard to foresee. In such situations, you can use some help, and management science has provided two valuable techniques: decision trees and ranking of options.

How to Use Decision Trees

When the decisions that did not "stick" result in unpredicted outcomes that require still more decisions to be made in haste, the situation is described as "out of hand," and your critics will say that you did not think your problems through. Most managers, of course, do try to think their decisions through and predict their consequences several steps ahead; in a complicated situation, however, this is impossible to do, without a system for putting the problem down on paper and examining it in an organized way. A valuable tool for use in this process is the *decision tree,* which is a way of displaying in graphic form decision options, their possible outcomes, and the effect of uncontrollable events on them. The workings of this method are illustrated in the following example.

Operating Example 1-3: Using the Decision Tree to Analyze a Hiring Situation. Things are happening all at once in the Shipping Department. The foreman's job has just become vacant, and a decision must be made whether to promote from within or hire from the outside. A new automated stacking and retrieval system is to be installed in the warehouse within the next six months, and work has already started on the construction of a railroad siding so that shipments by boxcar can begin. The plant is unionized. The department has been handling export shipments for some time and will continue to do so.

In mulling over the situation, the plant manager realizes that the new foreman will need some special skills; he must be accustomed to a union environment, must have some experience with export shipments, must be capable of working with an automated stacking system, and must know how to handle rail shipments. Undue delay in the application of these skills will result in monetary losses caused by the return and rehandling of misdirected or damaged shipments, and intangible (but very real) losses from customer dissatisfaction. With all this in mind, the plant manager is inclined to hire from the outside; but what if the new foreman is resented and resisted by the department's employees? Or, if the plant manager promotes from within, what if the promotee doesn't acquire the needed skills in time to prevent severe losses? To help him examine the foreseeable ramifications of his decision, the plant manager draws up a decision tree such as that shown in Figure 1-1. In this diagram squares with check marks inside are used to depict decisions over which the plant manager has control; circles with question marks indicate events and consequences over which he does not have control. Opposite each terminal branch of the tree (at the far right of the diagram) are shown the results that would be obtained if decisions and events were carried to that point. Starting at the left with his first decision, let us suppose that the plant manager chooses to promote from within; he draws a line toward the top of the page, and inserts the first event over which he does not have control—will the promotee pick up the needed skills quickly on his own, or will he have to undergo a training program?

He draws two branches leading from that event; the upper branch is for the outcome that the promotee picks up the skills for the job quickly and on his own, and leads to the final result shown at the far right. The lower branch is for the outcome that the promotee needs additional training, and that in turn leads to another uncontrollable event—either the training is effective and the promotee is successful in the job, or the training does not work well and he is unable to master the job. The latter case leads to a new decision: fire the employee or demote him back to the ranks of the Shipping Department. The plant manager's estimate of the results each branch of the tree would bring are again listed on the right. A similar series of events and decisions for hiring from the outside is diagramed in the lower half of the figure.

Note that the decision tree in the example does not urge a particular decision upon the plant manager but merely shows the likely consequences of a series of decisions and events, leaving it up to the plant manager to decide which results are the most preferred, and which are the least acceptable. Some of the "uncontrollable events" are not as uncontrollable as they at first seem; if the plant manager in the example hires from the outside, for instance, there may be steps he can take to help the new person gain acceptability from the work force, and in so doing, avoid the negative consequences of the lower branches of the tree. The decision tree thus not only helps in the decision process, but is also a valuable tool for showing the manager where his efforts can affect the outcomes to his advantage.

In more sophisticated versions of the decision tree method, numerical probabilities are assigned to each of the event branches. This procedure gives the manager a more precise idea of the likelihood that a particular outcome will occur. If the results can be expressed in some quantitative measure such as dollars—as would be the case with investment decisions—then the most advantageous result can be quickly identified and decisions taken to reach it.

Ranking Your Options from Specific Choices

Not all management decisions require the open-ended type of exploration to which the decision tree is suited; often the manager makes a selection from clearly defined choices, as would be the case in choosing one of several applicants to fill a job, or selecting a piece of equipment from several competing makes. One way of making these decisions as objectively as possible is to use the *option table,* which is sometimes called a *decision matrix,* or even a *selection screen.* To construct the table, list the criteria by which you wish to judge your options, giving each criterion a numerical weight. Then give each option a numerical rating showing how well it meets each criterion. Multiplying the rating by the weight yields a score, and the scores are added up for each option; the option with the highest score is the best choice. The option table differs from the decision tree method of the previous example by clearly indicating which option the manager should choose.

> **Operating Example 1-4: Ranking of Options.** The plant manager of the previous operating example has decided to fill the foreman's position in the Shipping Department by hiring from the outside. He informs the Personnel Department that there are three qualifications which all candidates must have, and any who do not have them are to be rejected without further consideration: (1) a high school diploma, (2) three years of experience as a shipping department foreman, (3) one of which must be in a unionized plant. Following this determination of the qualifications which the candidates *must* have, the manager turns his attention to the qualifications which he would like them to have, and develops the list in the left-hand column of Table 1-1, under the heading "Desirable Qualifications." Opposite each of these desirable qualifications he puts a number representing the weight of importance he

Basic Situation

Vacancy in
Shipping
Foreman's
Position

Decisions and Uncontrollable Events

Results

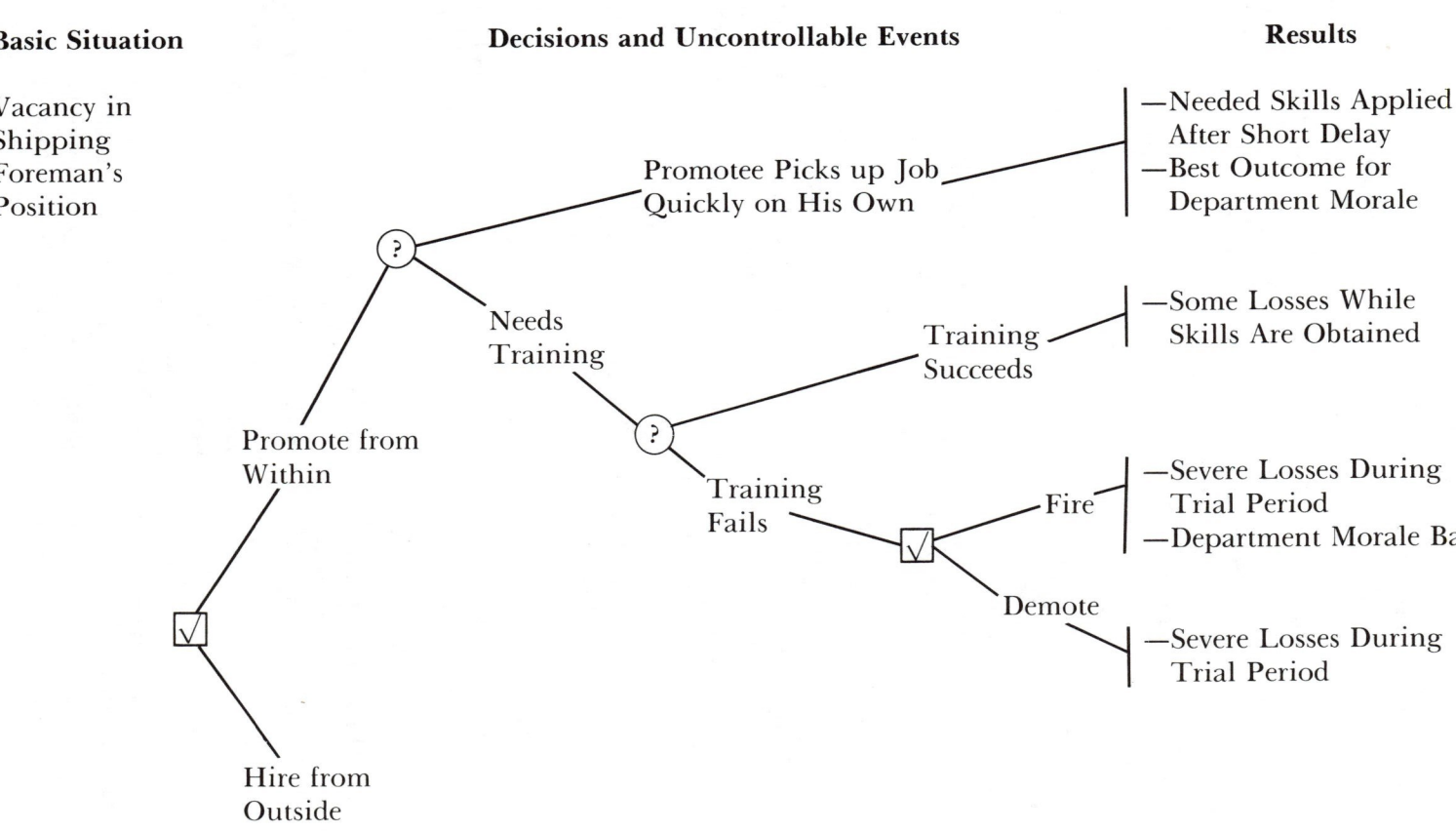

Promotee Picks up Job
Quickly on His Own

—Needed Skills Applied
  After Short Delay
—Best Outcome for
  Department Morale

Needs
Training

Training
Succeeds

—Some Losses While
  Skills Are Obtained

Promote from
Within

Training
Fails

Fire

—Severe Losses During
  Trial Period
—Department Morale Bad

Demote

—Severe Losses During
  Trial Period

Hire from
Outside

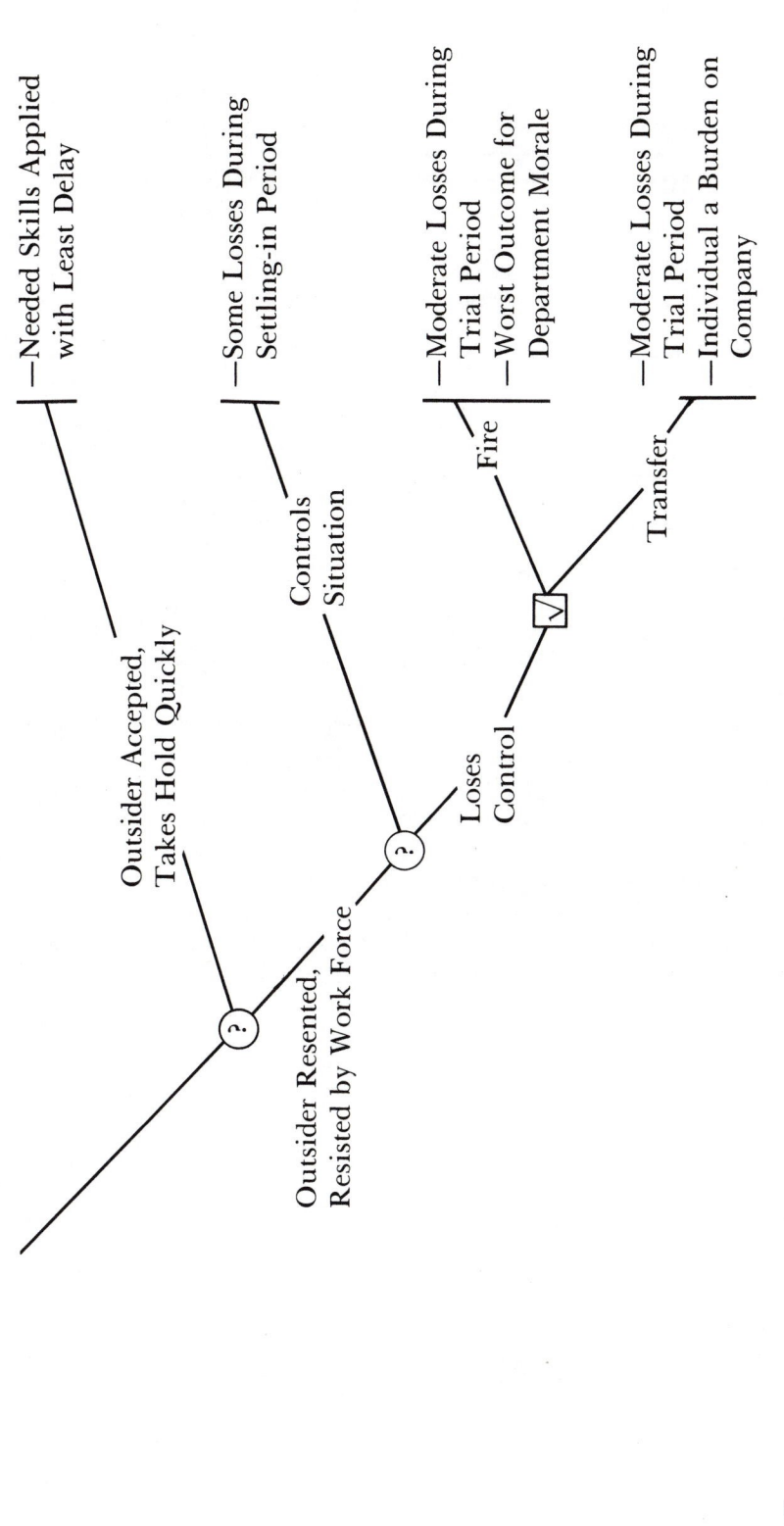

FIGURE 1-1: Decision Tree

TABLE 1-1: Option Table

Desirable Qualifications	Weight	Michael J. Rating	Michael J. Score	Janet C. Rating	Janet C. Score	William R. Rating	William R. Score
Familiar with Automated Stacking Systems	10	3	30	7	70	9	90
Good at Cost Control	8	10	80	5	40	2	16
Experienced in Rail Car Shipment	4	5	20	9	36	3	12
Experienced in Export Shipment	5	8	40	2	10	7	35
Total Score			170		156		153

attaches to it, usually on a scale of 10. In this case the manager feels that being good at cost control should be weighted at 8, while experience in loading boxcars would be worth only 4. (Although the manager used different weights for each of the criteria in the example, there is no requirement that he do so; another manager might have decided that the two qualifications were both worth 8. Also other scales than 1–10 could be used, especially if there are many criteria, or there is reason to make finer distinctions between them.) The Personnel Department comes up with three candidates, all of whom have the three "must" qualifications. The plant manager reviews their applications, interviews them, and then fills out the rest of Table 1-1. For familiarity with automated stacking he rates Michael J. 3 (again on a scale of 10), and multiplies that by the weight of 10 to give him a score of 30 for that criterion; he carries this same process out for each of the candidates and all of the qualifications. When he is done he totals the scores for each of the applicants, and in this case Michael J., with a total score of 170, emerges as the logical choice for the position.

Chapter 2

How to Recognize and Better Control Your Key Responsibilities as Plant Manager

Your job as plant manager is to turn your company's corporate plans into action. The success or failure of those plans depends on the energy and ability with which you apply the corporate resources of people, money, raw materials, and equipment to the task of producing the company's products and services.

As the complexity and pace of our economy increase, so do the demands upon you. New products move from the laboratory and design stage to full-scale production faster than before. Corporate management, caught in the profit squeeze, requires closer compliance with the budget and preplanned cost reductions. New plant processes require extra steps, more complicated equipment, and tighter quality controls. Employees anticipate ever greater financial rewards, security, and opportunities for advancement.

This chapter is designed to help you put your sometimes bewildering array of duties and assignments into a comprehensive whole, to understand the relationships between them, and to specify the management tools you will need to cope with them. In it, we will examine the basic responsibilities of your job as plant manager, some of the additional assignments you are likely to have, and your relationships with other departments of the company. Techniques of leadership and motivation will be presented, along with valuable ideas for self-improvement and conserving managerial time.

WHAT IS EXPECTED OF THE MANUFACTURING DEPARTMENT

The job of the Manufacturing Department is usually given in the simplified statement, "To make a quality product on time at lowest possible cost." Sometimes the phrase, "safely, and with good employee relationships," is added. There is nothing wrong with this old definition, except that it does not go far enough in describing the larger role present-day corporations expect the manufacturing group to play.

Let's look at "production." Of course the Manufacturing Department must produce the company's products in required quantities on time to meet customer demands. But, more than that, it is expected to communicate knowledge developed by its operations which may lead to new products or substantially improved old ones. It helps guard the company against obsolescence by responding quickly to meet changes in markets, technology, and intensity of competition.

Consider "cost." Manufacturing at lowest possible cost is a taken-for-granted objective. But the corporation looks for broader cost activities by its Manufacturing Department. It expects manufacturing to make profitable application of capital funds; it looks for wise use of money in the purchase of equipment which is labor-saving, maintenance-free, reliable, and offers maximum flexibility for future operations. The company must rely on the manufacturing people to protect its investment by proper maintenance and physical protection of plant property. And it expects the manufacturing group to help gain a competitive edge by continuously reducing costs.

The maintenance of good employee relationships is no longer considered a fringe activity by any serious manufacturing manager. But the company may expect more than just a low incidence of grievances and strikes in its plants; it may require the active development of good relationships with the entire communities in which they are located, including neighbors, civic authorities, the business and professional community, minority groups, and those concerned with the environment, as well as its employees.

SIX BASIC RESPONSIBILITIES OF THE PLANT MANAGER

While you occupy an important place in the broader development and operation of the company, you must continue to meet your basic responsibility for the operation of the plant. The "plant" may range from a small unit with ten or twelve workers to a mammoth complex with thousands of employees. No matter what the size, you are expected to produce results in six essential areas: production, quality, cost, safety, housekeeping, and employee relationships.

Production Output:
Your Greatest Chance for Success—or Failure

This is the job of manufacturing the required quantity of finished goods in time to meet customer demands. It is the most fundamental demand, and the one with the most obstacles to success. Late raw materials, absenteeism, strikes, bad weather, power outages, equipment breakdowns—all conspire to prevent your reaching the goal. It is the function which calls for you to exert your greatest powers of leadership, to foresee and overcome the obstacles to meeting production deadlines, and to motivate your people to get the work out in spite of the difficulties. You do this by refusing to yield to obstacles and exhibiting a tough-minded approach in fighting for the way to get the job out on time no matter what the difficulties. You have no choice—failure in this area of responsibility is a fundamental flaw that cannot be tolerated by higher management.

A second responsibility is to determine accurately the production capacity of the plant, so that the corporation can make profitable decisions regarding sales and marketing strategy. When you must develop an estimate of production capacity, be sure to include the time the equipment must be out of service for repairs, cleaning, and preventive maintenance. Report the additional capacity available if the number of shifts are increased.

Quality: Why Product Integrity and Profit Go Together

Most manufactured products are subjected to quality tests before they are declared ready for shipment. Material that does not meet specifications has to be scrapped, sold at a fraction of the price for prime material, or returned to the process for reworking—costly alternatives to making the product right in the first place.

Occasionally the quality goal is very simple—as when a machined shaft is made of a specified grade of steel to a length and diameter of so many inches plus or minus definite tolerances. Any shaft meeting these standards is shippable and will satisfy the customer. More often, however, the quality problem is much more complicated. The quality tests may not cover all of the possible product properties of interest to the customer. And the quality tests may not be capable of uncovering every possible error made in the manufacture of the product. Customers buying these products must depend on the manufacturer to make the product in exactly the same way every time it is produced.

Faced with this situation, you must establish an attitude in your organization which reaches far beyond the passing of quality tests; you have to establish a program of *product integrity*. This means that the entire organization is committed to making the product according to standard process instructions every time it is made, without shortcuts or individual deviations. Instilling this respect for total quality places heavy demands upon your leadership abilities, but it is a responsibility you cannot ignore in an economy where customers steadily grow more demanding in quality performance, more sophisticated in evaluating supplier's quality, and more willing to hold the supplier legally liable for losses caused by defective materials.

In the quest for quality, you cannot afford to lose sight of your profit responsibilities, as the following Operating Example demonstrates.

> **Operating Example 2-1: Quality and Profit.** The Resinous Products Plant of Talldrum Corporation is turning out 480,000 pounds per month of Resin A, which sells at $2.18 per pound. The quality standards under which the product is sold call

for a maximum water content of 0.5 percent. The newly appointed plant manager, in reviewing the production records, finds that Resin A has been consistently produced and shipped with an average moisture content of 0.1%. He realizes that the plant is shipping extra resin for which there is no monetary return, and that a higher moisture target, such as 0.4 percent, could be set and still keep the product safely inside the quality standard. If this were done, the company could recover $(.004-.001) \times 480,000$ lb/mo $\times$ 12 mo/yr = 17,280 lb/yr. At a cost of $2.18/lb, this amount of resin represents $37,670 in annual savings.

The most direct route to these savings is to order the Drying Department to aim at 0.4 percent rather than 0.1 percent moisture. Before taking action, however, the plant manager is likely to investigate the situation further; he may find that a sudden increase in moisture content would upset customers' operations, or that the plant has been shipping resin at 0.1 percent moisture for so long that it is now a de facto standard. This does not mean that the value of his effort is lost; if a new quality standard can be published, say at 0.15 percent, it may give Resin A a selling edge over competing products. Or, the marketing division might find that customers prefer to continue receiving the resin at 0.1 percent but would be willing to pay for the extra material.

Cost: Meeting the Challenge of Maximum Production with Minimal Expense

Producing a product at standard cost is the most obvious element of your cost responsibilities. When the plant cannot produce at the cost that has been previously agreed upon by sales, manufacturing, and engineering, the company may find its profits dangerously reduced, or eliminated altogether.

A second responsibility is to prepare annual operating budgets for all plant functions such as production, maintenance, and shipping—controlling expenses within the limits of those budgets throughout the year. Since you cannot personally approve each expenditure, you face the leadership task of creating a cost and value consciousness throughout your organization, and a system of workable controls.

Corporate managements are no longer willing to accept the once-a-year crash program for cost reduction, but expect plant managers to set up result-producing, continuing programs. The cost reductions predicted from a carefully planned and executed program are included in the company's profit projections.

You participate in the corporate capital expenditure program by the very nature of your job. You make recommendations for new plants and equipment to expand production, reduce cost, and improve quality. And you carry a continuing responsibility to protect the investment in existing facilities with sound maintenance practices.

Safety: Four Steps to an Improved Program

Any human being worthy of the name will do whatever he or she can to prevent injury to another in the work environment, and plant managers are no exception. But humanitarian feelings do not go far enough, and you must realize that you cannot meet your production schedules or cost commitments in a plant where accidents are frequent. In addition, federal and state laws require close adherence to specified safety standards, and your performance in terms of the number and severity of injuries to plant employees is reported not only to higher management, but to government entities as well.

Here are four steps to an effective safety effort:

1. Establish a continuing program of safety education conducted primarily by the line supervisors.
2. Include a safety section at the beginning of every standard operating procedure, and intersperse safety directions throughout the operating instructions.
3. Design new installations with the safety of the people who must operate and maintain them in mind.
4. Maintain a no-nonsense enforcement of safety regulations.

Housekeeping: An Ongoing Process

Safety is impossible in a plant that allows spilled materials and debris to accumulate. Dirty surroundings threaten product quality. Morale and efficiency of the work force deteriorate if the plant is not clean. Plant managers who once thought of housekeeping as a sporadic "cleanup" function—performed only when there isn't much else to do—are coming to understand that it has to be an ongoing activity for which they assume full responsibility. Corporate managements are also taking this view, and in some cases conduct competitive interplant housekeeping inspections.

Plants are often visited by members of higher management who may know little or nothing about technical operations. But they do know a clean plant when they see one, and base judgments about the ability of the plant manager on the physical conditions they observe. When these people later confront important decisions about where the company's capital is going to be invested, their recollections cannot help but influence the decisions.

Employee Relationships: Four Ways to Judge Your Performance

Throughout your career, you are exposed to all sorts of materials dealing with employee relations. Books, articles, seminars, company meetings and memoranda—all tell how to conduct employee relationships, but rarely tell you what results are expected from your efforts. Here are four result areas (three of them measurable) in which to judge your performance:

1. Plant operations are not interrupted by events arising from poor employee relationships.
2. The prevailing atmosphere in the plant is not one of laxness, but of a sense of purpose. Admittedly this is a subjective evaluation, but one very real to those experienced in plant operations.
3. When company-employee relationships are put to the test by complaint or grievance procedures, the plant manager will be found to have taken sound

positions. The plant manager should not be rated on the number of grievances filed—after all, that is up to the union—but on the number he loses in arbitration.

4. Absenteeism, lateness, and accident frequency are all at low levels.

It is not your job to keep everybody happy; that's an impossible task anyway. It is your job to keep your employee relationships on a businesslike basis, with the overall goals of the corporation in mind.

The Total Job: Each Area Counts

Plant managers sometimes make the mistake of attempting to do a good job in one or two of these result areas, while neglecting the others. Management people who are in a position to observe numerous plants agree on one point: Those plants that consistently meet their production, quality, and cost targets turn out to be the plants where safety, housekeeping, and employee relationships are also in good order. Avoid slogans like "Safety first, quality second, production third." They oversimplify and obscure the real fact of life in an industrial plant: A good job has to be done on *all* of these responsibilities.

THE PLANT MANAGER'S BROADER RESPONSIBILITIES

Corporations vary so widely in size, organizational structure, and management style that no single list of responsibilities will fit every plant manager's job. One or more of the following functions is likely to appear on the individual list of responsibilities.

Engineering

The plant manager who does not bear responsibility for some kind of engineering function is a rarity. In a small plant or a small company, you and one or two subordinates may constitute the entire engineering capability; when this is the case, you rely on outside engineering firms to handle the detailed engineering and to draw up the blueprints and specifications for major projects.

In a large corporation the services of a central Engineering Department with hundreds of employees may be available. Even so, the local plant may still have its own engineering staff to take care of smaller projects not suitable for assignment to a large department. Engineering responsibilities of the plant manager fall in one or more of these categories:

1. *Plant engineering and maintenance.* You are always expected to take responsibility for keeping the buildings, grounds, and equipment in good condition. An uninterrupted flow of utility services must be maintained, and a preventive maintenance program instituted to prevent surprise outage of production equipment.

2. *Process engineering.* You may have a process engineer (or engineering section) reporting to you whose function is to troubleshoot bottlenecks and problem areas in the manufacturing process. The effectiveness of this activity is judged on the basis of quantitative results—increased production output, statistical measures of quality improvement, and cost reductions that can be translated into lower budgets.

3. *Project engineering.* Once the decision has been made to expand the plant, add new equipment, or replace old equipment, an engineering project begins. It should have clearly defined goals in terms of the equipment to be installed, the cost of completing the project, and the date at which it is to be turned over to the operating work force. Good performance is required in all three phases of a project; the company's position in a new market or its profit performance for the year can depend on the successful completion of its important capital projects.

Purchasing

Corporations assign the purchasing function in a variety of ways. In some small organizations, the plant manager *is* the purchasing agent. In other, larger companies, the purchasing agent reports to the plant manager. In still others, the purchasing function does not report to the plant manager, but is part of a materials management group reporting to a different management echelon.

If you are in charge of the purchasing function, you are expected to

1. Assure the company of a continuing supply of raw materials and supplies of acceptable quality
2. Arrange for delivery of materials in time to meet the requirements of the manufacturing process
3. Reduce the cost of buying, moving, and storing raw materials

If you are not accountable for the purchasing function, your responsibilities shift to the area of communication—keeping the Purchasing Department fully informed of late deliveries or substandard quality. Close cooperation with the Purchasing Department is required in the scheduling of plant trials for the evaluation of materials submitted by new suppliers offering lower prices.

Traffic

When this responsibility is yours, you are expected to provide for movement of the company's incoming and outgoing shipments on time and at the lowest available cost. Like purchasing, the traffic function offers strong possibilities for cost reduction, ranging from the simple selection of cheaper routings all the way up to company ownership of its own means of transportation. Traffic activities include scheduling shipments, selecting routes, choosing the mode of transportation, reviewing bills and charges, and the pursuit of damage claims.

Community Relationships

Seldom is this aspect clearly spelled out in the plant manager's job description, and the way it is handled is set forth in less formal communications from top management. At the minimum the company wants its plants to enjoy good relations with the communities in which they operate, and expects you to maintain those relations with the long-range interests of the company in mind. Your job can involve you in these facets of community relations:

1. Liaison with municipal authorities—fire, police, public works, planning and zoning, water resources, and pollution control departments.
2. Participation in trade, civic, and professional organizations.
3. Handling complaints from neighboring residents and businesses concerning noise, traffic, air and water pollution.
4. Sociopolitical activities. Some companies encourage their managerial employees to engage in political work. Others are deeply involved in joint business-government-community programs to train and employ the handicapped or the disadvantaged.
5. Cooperation with charity drives—usually the United Fund or a similar give-once-for-all type.

WORKING WITH OTHER DEPARTMENTS

Your company cannot survive unless its divisions and departments form a smooth-working team. Customers don't care whether the Manufacturing Department gets along well with Engineering, or R & D with Accounting—they want quality merchandise delivered on time and will make no allowances for internal bickering. Within the company, however, the interests and objectives of the various departments differ so much that sometimes conflicts are inevitable. This section is designed to help you put into proper perspective your relations with other departments, and to sort out the important factors affecting them.

When handling situations of actual or potential conflict, keep two points in mind: if you agree to every special request made, you will find yourself saddled with so many inefficient procedures that operating costs are increasing without corresponding return. On the other hand, if you blindly refuse to consider the requests of other departments, the entire company may suffer in such important areas as customer relations, new product development, and the effective completion of major engineering projects.

Sales

There is one overriding aspect of the relationship between the Sales and Manufacturing Departments which may seem—and sometimes is—unfair to Manufacturing: If Sales has committed the company to deliver a product at a specified time to a customer, there is no choice but for everyone in the company, including Manufacturing, to strive to meet the requirement. Again, the customer views the company as one unit, and is not interested in its internal problems.

This is not to say that the Sales Department has no responsibility for maintaining contact with its accounts, avoiding "rush" deliveries, and manufacturing surprises. The Sales Department that makes promises to customers without first checking with Manufacturing is living dangerously indeed. Similarly, Manufacturing must keep Sales advised of actual or potential interruptions of production, and problems affecting quality.

Accounting

The points of contact between the Accounting and Manufacturing Departments lie in the areas of cost reporting and cost control. Manufacturing expects the Accounting Department to develop cost-reporting systems that allow Manufacturing managers to make the optimum financial decisions in day-to-day operations. It also expects Accounting to issue cost reports promptly—a monthly report issued three weeks after the month has ended is useless as a tool for controlling costs.

The Accounting Department expects to find a climate of cost consciousness in the manufacturing operation, and a willingness to cooperate in cost-control projects. To render prompt reports, it must have speedy submission of the Production Department records on which they are based—production totals, off-grade reports, receiving and shipping documents, and inventory totals.

Engineering

The Engineering Department's largest projects usually deal with the installation or modification of production facilities, and the relationship between the two departments is a close and continuing one.

The degree of independence which Engineering has in designing plant equipment and layout differs from company to company, but at the minimum the Manufacturing Department looks for Engineering to

1. Design equipment and installations with operating problems in mind—ease of maintenance, safety, convenient access to operating controls, and housekeeping, as well as production rate and quality.
2. Make use of the experience acquired by the Manufacturing Department with present plant and equipment.
3. Submit its preliminary plans and specifications to the Manufacturing Department for review and comment.

The Engineering Department should expect Manufacturing to

1. Supply complete and accurate data on the performance of existing equipment, including special studies when the regular process records do not contain the information needed.
2. Review plans and specifications promptly.

3. Keep in mind Engineering's responsibility for the cost of the project.

4. Participate in the post-completion audit to determine whether the project is generating the profit it was designed for.

Financial justification of engineering projects can fall to either department. When corporate practice calls for the Engineering Department to prepare the economic justification, it will need the help of Manufacturing in projecting labor and operating costs. When the Manufacturing Department justifies the project, it needs accurate cost and completion date estimates from Engineering.

Research & Development

Some plant managers hardly ever see a research worker, especially in those companies where the Engineering Department bridges the gap between development and full-scale production. In companies and industries where products must move from the research stage to manufacturing very quickly, the association can be very close.

When R & D approaches the Manufacturing Department, it usually wishes to make arrangements for experimental production of a new development on plant equipment. Manufacturing should expect R & D to come in with a carefully thought-out proposal, and to present a detailed operating procedure for the experiment in advance of the work. It will also want to see evidence that sufficient laboratory and pilot work has been done to justify a full-scale attempt on plant equipment and time.

Manufacturing's requests to R & D are usually for assistance in solving technical plant problems. R & D will look for clearly stated objectives and sound reasons (preferably financial) for devoting its time to the problem. It will also expect that manufacturing has applied all of its own resources to the problem before approaching R & D.

The two departments can help each other by keeping a two-way communication going:

1. Manufacturing should keep R & D supplied with up-to-date copies of all operating procedures. It should inform R & D of changes in manufacturing capabilities, and pass along any technical information discovered in the plant that might not turn up in laboratory or pilot plant investigations.

2. R & D should keep the Manufacturing Department informed on the progress of new development projects, especially those that may require new machinery or new personnel skills.

FIVE STEPS TO MORE EFFECTIVE LEADERSHIP

The management cycle discussed in Chapter 1, and the plant organization to be dealt with in Chapter 3, do not set themselves in motion. The spark that gets them moving is the leadership provided by one person—you.

There are volumes of information and advice available concerning motivation and leadership. While it is a good idea to become familiar with this literature, and to select from it those techniques which seem to best fit your personality and situation, it is also wise to avoid the excesses of some of the more faddish attempts to apply the principles of psychology to the industrial environment. Here are the five most important steps to leadership for the plant manager.

Step 1:
Seize the Initiative

There are really two parts to your job. In the first part you respond to forces outside your control: customer orders, union grievances, assignments from your superior, equipment breakdowns, and many more. This work is necessary and important, but its successful completion will earn you only a reputation for competence.

The second part of your job consists of the work which you assign to yourself. It consists of the improvements you make and the programs you carry out which are *not* required by outside forces. It is based on your assessment of the opportunities open to your organization, and the objectives which you set to take advantage of them. It can be in the area of cost, safety, technical improvement, or in many others. Whatever the area, the work which you do on your own is the work which sets you apart from the competent caretaker, and establishes you in the eyes of your subordinates and superiors as a leader.

Step 2:
Set the Right Example

You can rely on one key principle: the example you set in energy applied to the job, your determination to reach objectives, and the wisdom and ability with which you carry out the management cycle will not be exceeded by your organization. You are fortunate if it is matched. Therefore, if you expect high standards of performance from your subordinates, you must set even higher standards for yourself. Your example determines the tone of the work climate in the plant.

Step 3:
Fulfill the Needs of Your Workers

One concept of motivation is that people are prompted to action by an ascending order of physical and psychological needs. The lowest needs on the scale are those of physical survival—food, clothing, shelter. Higher on the scale are recognition, security, belonging, and self-fulfillment.

When the nation's economy is healthy, the lower needs are taken for granted. A plant employee can acquire food, clothing, and shelter by working almost anywhere, and sometimes by not working at all. Therefore, an employee's willingness to stay and to work hard at a particular plant depends upon the degree to which the needs for recognition, for belonging, for feeling that he or she is involved in something worthwhile are filled.

Sometimes the needs of the employee and those of the company are in conflict, and you must realize that not all psychological needs can be provided by employment. Your task in motivation is to identify those areas where the needs of each coincide (as in safety) and use this fact to the greatest advantage of both; and having identified the areas of conflict (as in absenteeism), to face them squarely so that employees know where they stand.

Step 4:
Spread the Work

The plant manager who entrusts as little as possible to subordinates, but tries to handle all the problems and projects him- or herself, is missing an important element of leadership. If employees are to feel that they are growing and developing in their jobs, they need to take on more challenging assignments; as these are successfully completed their self-confidence and sense of participation increase. The manager who develops such subordinates not only has a stronger team working with him or her, but opens up valuable blocks of time in which to pursue the initiative on his or her own job.

Step 5:
Be Yourself

Management styles are often described as "autocratic vs. democratic," or "production-oriented vs. people-oriented," or in other this-versus-that expressions. Studies of managers indicate that there is no one type of personality or set of personality traits attributable to the successful manager. The important points in developing your leadership style are: (1) study your own personality and adopt those leadership techniques that suit you best, (2) modify those personality traits that will bring you into conflict with the objectives of your job or with the company's approach to management, and (3) don't try to imitate someone else's style of management. You'll be unconvincing and appear insincere.

Modifying your personality is easier said than done; every manager must continually wonder, "What sort of traits should I have to get ahead in this organization?" The answer, of course, varies from company to company, but at least a general idea can be obtained from the following results of a survey taken by the Gallup Organization* in which corporate chief executives were asked to identify those traits in managers most important for advancement, and those most often cited as failings:

---

*Reprinted by permission of *The Wall Street Journal*. © Dow Jones & Company, Inc., 1980. All rights reserved.

HIGH ACHIEVERS			
Some Traits Chief Executives Cite as Most Important for Advancement			
	Large Firms	Medium Firms	Small Firms
Integrity	36%	27%	24%
Ability to Get Along With Others	32	36	34
Industrious-ness	25	23	24
Intelligence	25	14	10
Business Knowledge	23	25	24
Leadership	15	12	10
Education	5	7	1

WEAK MANAGERS			
Some Traits Chief Executives Cite as Failings of Subordinates			
	Large Firms	Medium Firms	Small Firms
Limited Point of View	23%	24%	9%
Inability to Understand Others	21	14	11
Inability to Work with Others	18	14	14
Indecisiveness	16	12	10
Lack of Initiative	9	9	10
Failure to Take Responsi-bility	7	6	6
Lack of Integrity	3	5	4

KEY TECHNIQUES FOR CONSERVING MANAGERIAL TIME

One of the most pressing problems that probably confronts you is how to divide your time among the many demands for your attention. The following techniques are designed to make more time available for you:

Delegate Work to Subordinates

Delegation is not only a sound principle of leadership, it is an essential device for gaining time. It is a simple axiom of cost efficiency that every job should be performed at the lowest possible level in the organization. Constantly review the tasks you perform to see if they can be assigned to subordinates. If you can recover 30 minutes per day, you will free 125 hours per year for "initiative" work.

Get Rid of Crises

Every plant has emergencies that legitimately demand the attention of the plant manager. But when the same crisis occurs again and again, an opportunity exists to reduce this erosion of time by establishing routine procedures to prevent (or take care of) the emergency. The production equipment which breaks down every seven or eight months, creating an "emergency," can be taken out of service on a planned schedule for repairs twice a year.

Analyze Your Use of Time

If you keep a record of how you spend your time for a month, you may be in for some surprises. You will find that your time is not really being spent where you thought it was, and that much of it is consumed in activities that will not further your objectives at all.

The techniques of personal time management are not complicated, but they do require self-discipline. Here are some suggestions:

1. Plan your time. Obtain an "executive planner" or similar booklet from the stationery store, and use it to block out the time you want to spend on each activity. Even if the unexpected interferes with the schedule, you will at least know what you deviated from, and can adjust to the change with the minimum loss of time.

2. Minimize the pleasantries. Subordinates, associates, even your boss—all seem to have unlimited time for social talk. You do not want to offend these people, but there is a lot you can do within that limitation to keep these conversations short, allowing you to get back to the work that counts.

3. Control your availability. Not every salesperson who shows up in the reception room should be admitted to your office by merely asking for the privilege. If it appears that you might be interested in a product or service, talk to him on the inter-office phone before inviting him in. You can then quickly terminate the contact if it is not worthwhile.

   You want your subordinates to bring certain matters to your attention. Without further guidance, they will bring a great deal more than you are interested in. Steadfast refusal by you to handle matters which should be taken care of elsewhere is your only defense against this waste of time.

4. Match the time period to the job. If you can depend on having two solid hours alone next Tuesday morning between 10:00 A.M. and noon, that's the time to tackle a two-hour job (perhaps review the blueprints for the new building addition). Don't waste that good block of time by handling four half-hour jobs which could be fitted into smaller time slots available throughout the week.

Seek Professional Help

The importance of conserving managerial time is evidenced by the growing number of professional management seminars devoted to the subject; in a recent year one organization held seminars devoted exclusively to this topic in 16 cities covering the entire United States. Entire books are being written on the subject; two useful volumes are *Managing Management Time* by William Oncken, Jr. (Prentice-Hall, 1984) and *Mastery and Management of Time* by S. Love (Prentice-Hall, 1982).

KEEPING UP WITH THE TIMES

If you have a written job description for your position, it will undoubtedly contain a section on self-improvement, calling upon you to increase your knowledge and ability in your field. This requirement is hardly necessary; any manager attempting to operate today with only the knowledge and skills he or she had ten years ago is headed for failure. Time and the economy do not stand still; the person or company who does not move ahead inevitably falls behind.

There are three areas in which you need to keep abreast of the times. One is the technical field of the plant operation—metal fabricating, plastics molding, electronic assembly, chemical processing, or whatever. Another is the field of management science—the continuing development of management as a body of knowledge in itself, and the development of new techniques for applying it. The third area is that of social and economic trends—developments in labor law, union organization, pollution control, employment trends, and civil rights legislation, for examples, have potential impact on the plant operation. You must be fully aware of all of these trends in order to adjust successfully to them.

If you wish to keep up with changes in the technical field, you have a number of methods from which to choose. Most colleges and junior colleges offer evening courses in a wide range of technical subjects, but with emphasis on those of interest to local industry; they may also offer intensive seminars lasting from one day to two weeks on technical topics. The major technical and engineering societies hold annual conventions around the country (and some hold regional meetings even more frequently) at which a great deal of information on recent developments can be acquired in a short time; their journals and magazines report technical advances throughout the year. Even unsolicited mail can be a source; as a plant manager you will probably sooner or later find yourself on mailing lists for free publications in fields ranging from general science through packaging and data processing to material handling.

Similar resources are available in the field of management science, with many colleges offering semester-long evening courses and the shorter, intensive daytime seminars. The American Management Associations conduct workshops, orientation seminars, and management courses up to a week in length in many cities; private management consulting firms also conduct seminars on similar topics. Some organizations, such as the National Management Association, organize local chapters of people interested in keeping up with the management field; they meet periodically to discuss management topics in much the same manner as the technical societies.

Keeping up with social and economic trends is largely a matter of reading. Newspapers and general circulation magazines are a good source. Some technical publications do a good job of keeping their readers advised on these matters as well as technical developments. A wide variety of commercially published bulletins and newsletters are also available for the price of a subscription.

Organizational Choices for Maximum Productivity

The plant manager who has had the opportunity to build an organization from the beginning of its existence is both fortunate and rare; most managers find themselves in charge of one established by others and evolved over a long period of time. No matter how long your organization has been in existence, it must be capable of adapting to external change by changing itself; organizations lacking this ability are doomed first to failure and finally to extinction. For that reason it is essential that you look periodically at the organizational structure as though it were being set up for the first time.

The fundamental aim of organization is to provide a system of relationships in which people can obtain the best results from their combined efforts, while minimizing the negative influences of conflict, confusion, and frustration. Choosing the optimum structure for your organization is one of the most important responsibilities you have. Your success in this effort will take you far down the road toward a smooth-running efficient operation, while a poor job of organizing will lead you toward a never-ending series of problems and failing plant performance.

This chapter shows how to build an organization starting from the goals to be met and the work that must be performed, describes the important options in organization structure and hourly pay systems, and offers useful methods for handling such organizational problems as setting up shift operations, upgrading existing organizations, and preserving an organization during slow periods. Its principles are equally applicable to starting a new organization or improving an existing one.

BUILDING THE ORGANIZATION FROM THE BOTTOM UP

Start with the Objectives

Among the first questions to ask are, "What am I trying to accomplish with organization structure?" and "How will I know when I have a good structure for my plant?" The broad answer is clear: The organization structure must make its full contribution to the plant goals of quantity, quality, and cost. The specific answer is contained in this list of objectives for the plant organization. It must:

1. **Accomplish the work.** Not only must it provide sufficient numbers of people with the ability to carry out the production tasks, but it must also furnish support personnel to move materials, judge quality, repair equipment, and supervise the operation.

2. **Minimize cost.** Good organization structure can contribute mightily to reducing costs. It avoids wasting labor just as a good production process avoids wasting material. Every task performed should be assigned to the lowest wage or salary level at which it can be performed competently. And while the organization is providing sufficient numbers of people to do the work, it must not provide excessive numbers.

3. **Maintain flexibility.** Every industrial plant experiences peaks and valleys of production output. Changes will occur in equipment, processes, and kinds of products manufactured. Key people may be absent for periods of time ranging from a few days to months, or may suddenly leave the organization altogether. The organization structure must provide maximum ability to meet these changing situations without losing the ability to continue production, and without incurring excessive cost.

4. **Provide clear-cut lines of authority and responsibility.** Unless each individual and group within the organization understands what his or her job is and where his or her authority begins and ends, group performance will be damaged by confusion and internal friction.

5. **Offer maximum opportunity for advancement.** People will leave when they see no chance to achieve higher positions and earnings. The organization structure can be built to encourage employees to broaden their skills, and to reward those who do; in return it gains employee loyalty and greater flexibility.

6. **Harmonize with the physical layout of the plant.** An existing arrangement of buildings and heavy machinery dictates to a large extent the shape of the organization that will run it; to ignore the boundaries of departments and sections so determined is to create administrative problems for the foremen and supervisors who must later lead them. When a new plant is to be built, the physical layout should be adjusted to meet the requirements of good organization structure; at this stage changes can be made at little or no cost, which will save many thousands of dollars in operating costs over the life of the plant.

SIX STEPS TO A MORE STRUCTURED ORGANIZATION

To build your organization from the ground up, follow the six steps listed below *in sequence*. Don't make the mistake of starting with a list of jobs to be filled; instead go back into the most basic tasks that must be accomplished and work upward for them:

1. List the tasks that must be performed by the organization.
2. Combine the tasks into jobs which will be filled by workers.
3. Group the workers into sections and departments.
4. Develop the supervisory and managerial structure.
5. Assign responsibilities to the sections and departments.
6. Coordinate the activities of the sections and departments.

The subsections that follow show you how to carry out these steps.

Step 1:
Determine the Tasks to Be Done

The starting point for the development of any organization is to examine the tasks that have to be performed. The use of the word "tasks," rather than "jobs," is deliberate; make no decisions about job content until you have made a complete list of all the tasks (large and small) that you expect the organization to accomplish. Working from this list, you can consider combining the tasks in many different ways into jobs, thus giving yourself the maximum opportunity to find the best combinations for your plant. Operating Example 3-1 shows how it works.

> **Operating Example 3-1: Listing Organization Tasks.** An organizational structure must be developed for the Shipping Department of a plant that receives raw materials and supplies in cartons and 100-pound bags, and liquids in 55-gallon drums and 5-gallon pails. It ships out both solid and liquid products in 50-pound bags, 5-gallon pails, and 55-gallon drums. The plant manager, working to develop the organization structure for this department, begins by listing, in no particular order, the tasks which the department must perform:

> Unload boxes, bags, and barrels from incoming trucks.
>
> Transfer finished goods from production area to warehouse.
> Sweep floors.
> Transfer raw materials from shipping dock to warehouse.
> Collect broken pallets.
> Transfer outgoing materials from warehouse to shipping dock.
> Take daily inventory of bulk storage tank levels.

> Take completed receiving reports to Accounting Department.
> Compare incoming bills of lading against purchase orders.
> Move broken pallets to Maintenance Department for repair.
> Attach labels to each piece of outgoing shipments.
> Draw small quantities of products to fill sample orders.
> Unload bulk liquid receipts into storage tanks.

Repackage outgoing shipments to meet customer requests.

Complete customer order form and return to office after shipment.

Unload incoming supplies.

Sign receipts for incoming shipments.

Remove trash to pickup bins.

Type labels for shipments.

Package samples in appropriate containers for parcel post.

Take weekly supply inventory.

Prepare bills of lading for outgoing shipments.

Call trucking companies to arrange shipment pickups.

Fill 55-gallon barrels from bulk storage tanks.

With this list completed, the plant manager is in a good position to decide what workers are needed.

Step 2:
Combine Tasks Into Jobs

The next step in the organization process is to combine the tasks that must be performed into jobs which will be filled by workers. What you are trying to achieve in this step is to find the most efficient combinations for your plant—those that will yield the greatest output at the lowest operating cost. No handbook can tell you what those combinations are; that must be decided on the basis of the particular conditions prevailing in your operation. The next three Operating Examples show how managers in three separate plants can combine the tasks in Operating Example 3-1 into different jobs in order to meet their respective operating constraints.

Operating Example 3-2: Using Minimum Cost to Combine Job Contents. Plant Manager 1 runs a medium-sized shipping operation with the requirement that, above all else, he is to keep labor costs to a minimum. He combines the tasks into just three jobs:

Shipping Clerk

Complete customer order form and return to office after shipment.

Compare incoming bills of lading against purchase orders.

Attach labels to each piece of outgoing shipments.

Sign receipts for incoming shipments.

Type labels for shipments.

Package samples in appropriate containers for parcel post.

Prepare bills of lading for outgoing shipments.

Call trucking companies to arrange shipment pickups.

Materials Handler

Unload boxes, bags, and barrels from incoming trucks.

Transfer finished goods from production area to warehouse.

Transfer outgoing materials from warehouse to shipping dock.

Draw small quantities of products to fill sample orders.

Unload incoming supplies.

Unload bulk liquid receipts into storage tanks.

Take daily inventory of bulk storage tank levels.

Transfer raw materials from shipping dock to warehouse.

Fill 55-gallon barrels from bulk storage tanks.

Utility Worker

Sweep floors.

Collect broken pallets.

Take completed receiving reports to Accounting Department.

Move broken pallets to Maintenance Department for repair.

Repackage outgoing shipments to meet customer requests.

Remove trash to pickup bins.

Take weekly supply inventory.

To keep his costs low, this plant manager has examined the task list for the simpler operations, and combined them into the job of Utility Worker. He can pay a lower rate for this job, and hire relatively unskilled people for it. By keeping the number of levels down to three he avoids the upward pressure on the Shipping Clerk's wage rate, which might result from having to include wage differentials for too many levels.

Operating Example 3-3: Dividing Job Contents to Offset Crowded Facilities. Plant Manager 2 has a larger shipping operation that has been growing by leaps and bounds. It now threatens to outstrip its physical facilities, which cannot be expanded at this location. The yard is so small that incoming trucks must be unloaded almost immediately. Dock space is limited, and the warehouse aisles are always crowded. Not pressed quite so hard on costs, this manager's problem is to get the day's work done in a limited amount of space; to do so she divided up the same task list differently:

Shipping Clerk

Complete customer order form and return to office after shipment.

Compare incoming bills of lading against purchase orders.

Sign receipts for incoming shipments.

Type labels for shipments.

Prepare bills of lading for outgoing shipments.

Call trucking companies to arrange shipment pickups.

Dock Loader

Unload boxes, bags, and barrels from incoming trucks.

Repackage outgoing shipments to meet customer requests.

Attach labels to each piece of outgoing shipments.

Unload incoming supplies.

Remove trash to pickup bins.

Warehouse Worker

Transfer finished goods from production area to warehouse.

Sweep floors.

Transfer raw materials from shipping dock to warehouse.

Collect broken pallets.

Transfer outgoing materials from warehouse to shipping dock.

Move broken pallets to Maintenance Department for repair.

Storage Tank Operator

Unload bulk liquid receipts into storage tanks.

Fill 55-gallon barrels from bulk storage tanks.

Take daily inventory of bulk storage tank levels.

Sampler

Draw small quantities of products to fill sample orders.

Take weekly supply inventory.

Package samples in appropriate containers for parcel post.

Take completed receiving reports to Account Department.

This is a somewhat more expensive system than used by Plant Manager 1, because it has more job levels, and a greater degree of specialization in each job category. The Utility Worker is gone, and his chores have been distributed among the more skilled and higher paying positions of this organization system.

Plant Manager 2 has accomplished her objective of covering each major activity with a specific job, so that the activity can be accomplished quickly without holding up the rest of the operation. For instance, she established the position of Dock Loader, so that there would always be workers at the shipping dock to load and unload trucks quickly, avoiding a pileup of materials there. She did the same with the position of Storage Tank Operator, so that a worker would always be available whose primary duty is to unload bulk liquids, avoiding delays at the bulk liquid station. Obviously, a high level of activity is required to provide economic justification for establishing such specialized positions.

Operating Example 3-4: Determining Job Content for Maximum Flexibility. Plant Manager 3 approaches the problem very differently. He runs a small shipping operation which employs less than ten people. It is subject to wide variations in work load distribution—heavy on truck loading one day, tank farm work the next, and sample preparation on the third day. If this manager adopts the job content used by Plant Manager 2, he runs the risk of having the Dock Loader partially idle on the day when tank farm work is heavy, and so on. He also realizes that with a small number of people it is risky to have too much specialization. If there is only one Shipping Clerk, and that person is absent or quits unexpectedly, there is no one trained to take over his duties quickly; similar reasoning applies to the other job categories. Plant Manager 3 clearly needs maximum flexibility in his organization structures.

To obtain this flexibility, he uses a system in which every worker is trained to perform every job in the department. Instead of combining the tasks into jobs as in the previous examples, he groups them into work areas or "fields:"

Shipping Desk   Tank Farm

Loading Dock   Warehouse

Sample Preparation

Individual tasks are grouped exactly as in the previous example, and therefore not repeated here. As each worker is hired, he or she is gradually trained in each of the fields. For instance, a new employee might be assigned to learn the Tank Farm and Sample Preparation work; as spare time allows he might help with and learn the simpler tasks of Warehouse and Loading Dock fields. The key point is that whenever he reports to work he can be assigned to any of the fields and be expected to perform the work at a level consistent with his experience in them. As the worker continues this training he passes through a series of grade levels on the basis of his demonstrated competence, with a higher wage rate attached to each grade level. The schedule of advancement might look like this:

	Time Required in Previous Level	*Qualifications for Advancement*
Beginner	—	—
Warehouse Worker	2 months	Automatic
Warehouse Worker	4 months	Automatic
Warehouse Worker	12 months	Performance Review and Examination
Warehouse Worker	18 months	Performance Review and Examination

(This method of organization is called the Operator Grade system, and it is discussed more fully on pages 49-50.)

Plant Manager 3 is using a more expensive system, because if there is no turnover in the department in 36 months then everyone will probably have risen to Warehouse Worker A and will be earning the top rate. But the plant manager gets some things of value in return. Gone are the jurisdictional arguments—"I'm a Dock Loader. You can't ask me to prepare samples." If, on a given day, too few dock loaders report for work, or the shipping clerk is absent, then any of the workers who are present can be assigned to those jobs. (Under other systems, some people might have to be paid overtime in order to get the work done.) No worker need be idle because there is too little to do in his or her area—he or she can always be assigned to help out in the fields where the load is the heaviest. For these reasons, Plant Manager 3 feels that the Operator Grade System gives him the lowest cost organization in the long run.

Step 3:
Build Up the Units

Now the agenda of organization moves to combining the workers into sections and departments. Some groupings seem obvious—after all, doesn't every plant have a maintenance department and a quality control group? Perhaps, but it may pay you not to accept the obvious too quickly. To achieve the greatest cost effectiveness in your organization consider the following issues, whether you are reworking an old structure or building a new one.

Choose between process and product orientation. The manager of a plant (somewhat simplified for this example) producing refrigerator cabinets, wastebaskets, and metal storage bins might decide to organize *by process*. If he does, he will establish these departments: Stock Preparation, Cutting, Metal Forming, Painting, and Trim. Each department will carry out its process on all the products made—whether cabinets, baskets, or bins. Or he can decide to organize *by product*, setting up a Cabinet Department, Wastebasket Department, and Storage Bin Department, and each department would perform all of the steps required to make its product.

How to make this choice? By finding the system that requires the least number of people. Under the heading *process orientation*, write down the names of the departments required. Opposite each department put down the total number of people required to run it. Do the same for *product orientation*. (The usefulness of his procedure can become quickly apparent; in our metal products plant example the manager found that under product orientation he would need a cutting machine in each department plus an operator, for a total of three machines and operators. In process orientation he discovered that two machines and operators could handle the total plant needs.) Choose the system that requires less people, but verify your decision by looking for offsetting cost factors: Would the chosen system require such highly skilled people that the total labor cost will be higher? Does it require additional support functions such as quality control or materials movement, which wipe out the labor savings? If so, a thorough cost analysis may be the only way to settle the question.

Centralization versus decentralization. This question applies most often to the support functions. Should a central department be set up to handle all material movements throughout the plant? It would have advantages: maximum use of equipment, better training of lift truck drivers, better control of safety and maintenance practices. Or would it be better to give each department its own material handling equipment and personnel? This method has advantages too: smoother operation within the Production Department, no material pileups while waiting for help to arrive, no time wasted in sending verbal or written communications to get material moved. Partial decentralization might be useful; would it be more efficient to have the production departments perform their own in-process quality controls, leaving the final checks to the Inspection Department? Would it be better to assign a pair of mechanics to a production department that can fully utilize its services, rather than have it report to the Maintenance Department every morning, only to be sent out to the same production area?

There is no "book" answer to these questions. The point is that they should be considered when departments are being set up or reorganized.

Conform to physical layout. Large buildings and major units of process equipment create natural outlines for sections and departments, and it is wise to follow these outlines. To ignore them—perhaps by establishing a department with most of its personnel in one building but with a small group in a different building at some distance away—is to invite coordination and supervisory problems that may seriously interfere with operating efficiency. Sometimes equipment is so specialized it requires a high degree of centralization and even its own organization; an example is a battery of distillation columns in a chemical plant. Although the battery may serve several different departments of the plant, it is nevertheless assembled in one area with its own operating personnel because of its unique size and mode of operation.

Step 4:
Develop the Supervisory and Managerial Structure

Some describe free enterprise simply as "competition between managerial teams." This may be an oversimplification, but it does emphasize the fact that performance of the managerial group often makes the difference between a profitable plant operation and one which barely gets along. Naturally you will hire and promote the best people available to fill your supervisory and managerial positions. The purpose of this section is to help you provide these people with an organizational structure that not only does not get in their way, but gives them a positive boost toward top performance.

Figures 3-1 and 3-2 provide the basis for what follows in this section and the remainder of the chapter. They are typical organization charts for a small manufacturing plant and a much larger one. In both cases they are for plants that operate twenty-four hours a day, seven days a week, and require four shifts (A, B, C, and D). The horizontal double line across each chart separates hourly from salaried employment levels; in Figure 3-1 it was possible to show all the hourly production workers on the chart, in Figure 3-2 they are indicated below the solid lines to conserve space.

Comparing the two charts brings out some of the points that must be considered when building the managerial structure. As we go from the small plant chart to the large plant chart, we see that the two production supervisor positions have been expanded to include a production manager, department superintendents, and general foremen. The post of Personnel Director-Office Manager has been expanded to Director of Industrial Relations with a personnel manager and safety director reporting to him. The quality control group is now part of a larger Technical Department. A Materials Management Department, which did not appear in the smaller plant, incorporates such functions as purchasing, inventory control, and freight traffic. In this comparison we can see how the management structure becomes more complex as the organization expands, and how the scope of the various managers' jobs increases. The precise point at which the management structure must be changed in a growing organization cannot be determined by some rule; it must be determined by the circumstances of the individual plant. For example, even a small plant might require a technical director or a materials manager if it is dealing with high technology processes or handles unusually complex materials. No matter what the size of your organization or its stage of growth, you should apply these principles when developing the management structure:

Keep it lean. Provide no more than the minimum number of supervisors and managers you foresee will be needed. If you must add help later on, it is easier to increase the staff than to cut it back. You do not want to get into the position of one company, threatened with bankruptcy, which called in a management consultant. Among other strong recommendations, the consultant advised the dismissal of half of the plant foremen; his advice was followed with disastrous results for a number of innocent people.

Provide unity of command. This is the principle that every worker in the organization reports to and takes orders from one superior only. This is plain common sense and plant managers will be naturally inclined to follow it, but there are occasions when it must be violated to a degree. In Figure 3-1 the Shift Leaders are hired, trained, promoted, fired, and receive their primary work instructions from the Department Supervisors. When on shift, however, they are accountable to and take instructions from the Shift Supervisors regarding certain work situations and emergencies. The chart shows this by a dotted line. When "dotted line" relationships are necessary, it is essential to spell out clearly where the authority of one manager ends and another begins.

Determine span of control. An often used rule of thumb for the number of people one person can supervise is 8 to 12, but this number can be sharply reduced or increased by the conditions of the job. When the workers are spread out over a large area, or are engaged in complex operations, a smaller number may be in order. When they are all in the same room, or on the same floor, or handling relatively simple tasks, the supervisor may be able to handle 20 to 35 people or more.

Specify the line-staff relationship. At one end of the spectrum of thinking on this subject the philosophy is to hire strong, versatile managers, and give them whatever help they need within the line organization; the view at the other end is that the line organization should merely carry out the procedures and ideas generated by the staff groups, where the really creative work is done. In Figure 3-2, a line-oriented company might place the Director of Materials Management under the Production Manager; a staff-oriented company might have the Director of Industrial Relations reporting to a corporate vice-president instead of the Plant Manager. Wherever your thinking or the philosophy of your company puts you on the spectrum, it is important that you determine exactly what you expect of line and staff, and build the organization accordingly.

Step 5:
Assign Responsibilities

The basic responsibilities of most plant sections are self-evident, if only from their titles—Screw Machine Department, Coil Winding Department, Powerhouse—and you need no elaborate schemes to help decide what these responsibilities are. Where you make a real contribution is in the adjustment of the fine points of assigning responsibility, so that a smoothly functioning organization is the result:

Responsibilities must add up. The sum of the responsibilities assigned to the departments must equal the total carried by the plant, without a "dropped

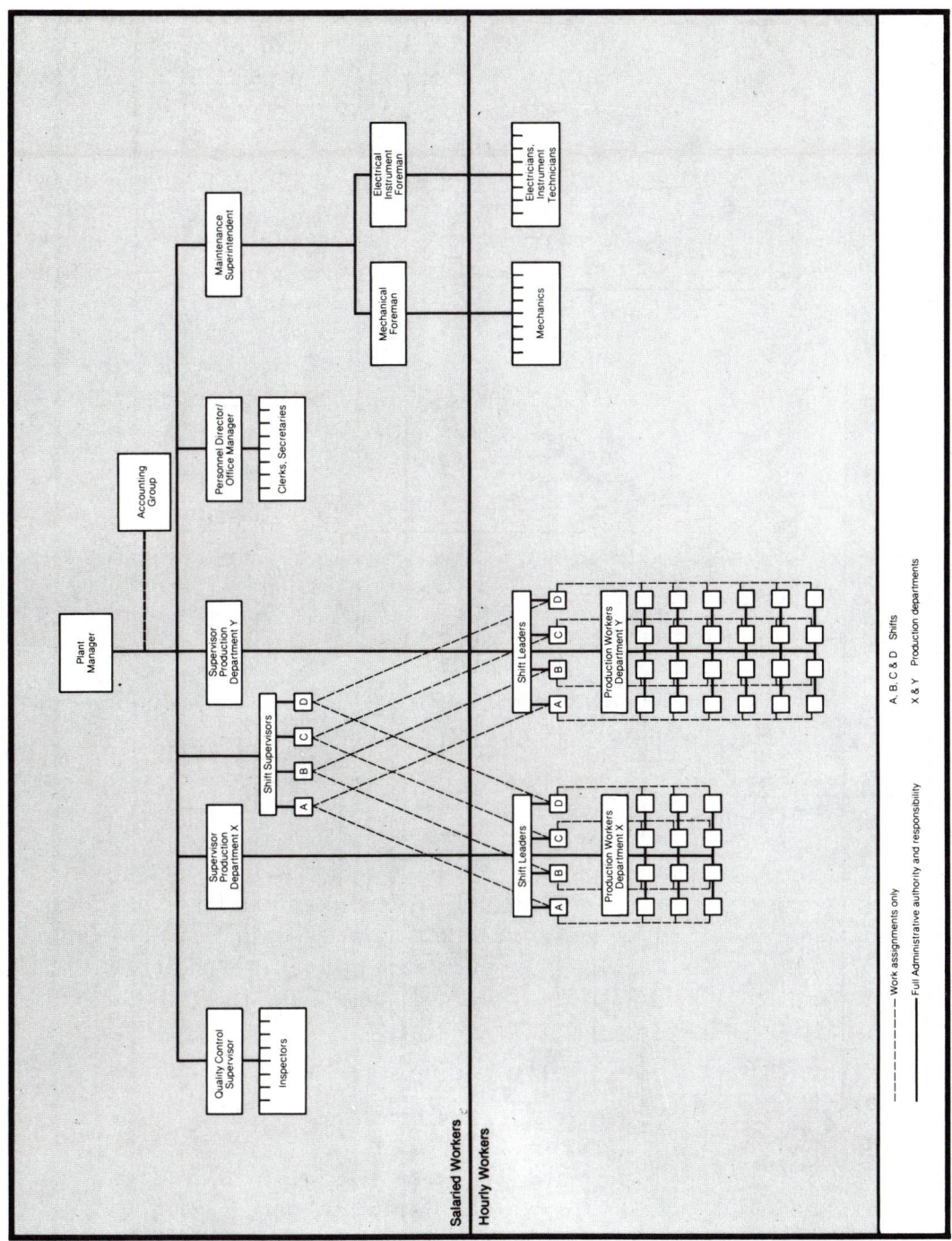

FIGURE 3-1: A Small Plant Organization

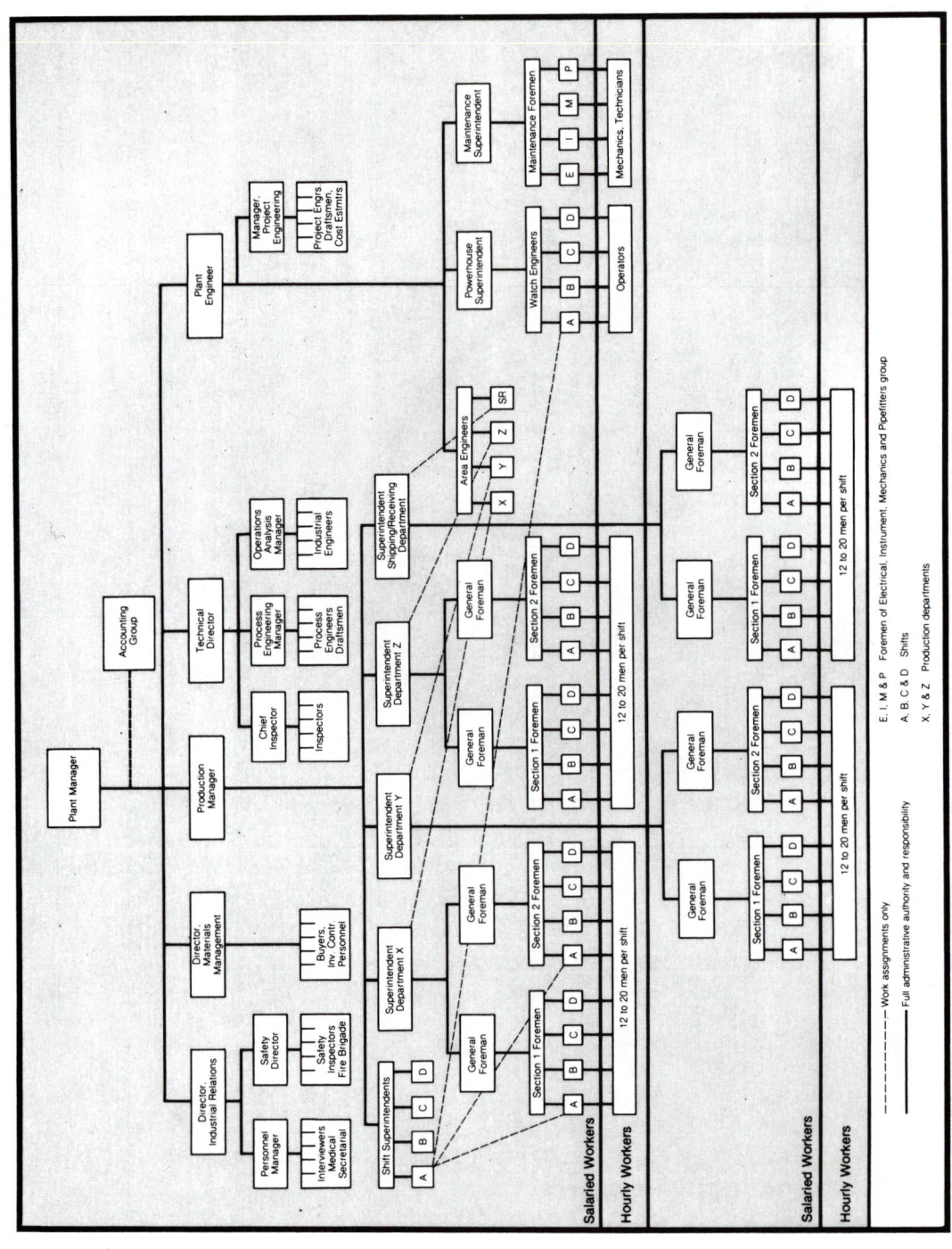

FIGURE 3-2: A Large Plant Organization

ball'' somewhere in the organization. Major responsibilities are not likely to be overlooked, but minor ones can be troublesome. For instance, will the Shipping Department be responsible for receiving *all* supplies including those of the Office and the Maintenance Department, or will vendors be required to deliver separately to those departments? If you opt for separate delivery, then you must provide the Office and Maintenance Department with the people required to handle this work. Whatever your decision, it must be made clear to all of the affected departments.

Put it in writing. Verbal instructions in a matter of this importance are inadequate; they are too easily confused, misinterpreted, or forgotten altogether. The most complete and elaborate format for the written assignment of responsibilities is the Plant Operations Manual, and plant management should develop one as soon as possible. Usually made up on printed forms and distributed in bound copies, the manual is a complete statement of the procedures to be followed and the responsibilities assigned to the plant departments. Figure 3-3 is an example of one such procedure.

If you do not have the time, resources, or personnel to develop a full-scale Operations Manual right away, there is an alternative. Issue each supervisor and manager a looseleaf binder labeled "Procedure Manual." Each time you handle a problem or establish a new system involving department responsibilities, write a procedure memorandum and distribute it to all manual holders for insertion in the appropriate section. Figure 3-4 is an example of a procedure memorandum that could have been put on a dictating machine in less than fifteen minutes. As these memoranda are collected over a period of time, they will constitute a useful operations manual that can be easily converted to a more formal volume when resources are available.

Match the responsibilities assigned to a group with its numbers, skills, and physical facilities. Don't overassign, giving it more responsibilities than its resources can handle; there is no point in assigning the repair and maintenance of a new computer-controlled milling machine with elaborate electronic gear to a maintenance department having only the traditional electrical and mechanical skills. Either the organization must be changed so that it has the necessary skills, or the responsibility assigned elsewhere. It can be just as bad to underassign, leaving the group with more equipment and people than needed for its mission; sloppy work practices and featherbedding are likely to be the results.

Keep up to date. Responsibilities must be reassigned as process methods, equipment, and available labor skills undergo change; these reassignments should be as clear-cut and as formal as the original assignments, and made prior to or at the same time as the changes requiring them.

Keep the appraisal system in mind. As we have already seen to some extent in the *Management by Objectives* section of Chapter 1 and will see again in the *Appraising Performance* section of Chapter 13, you will be making a serious effort to establish objective criteria against which the performance of department foremen and managers in meeting their responsibilities will be judged. In assign-

PLANT OPERATIONS MANUAL

SUBJECT   Receiving Reports   PROCEDURE NO. SR-4

                                          PAGE 1 OF 1

DEPARTMENT   Shipping and Receiving   DATE ISSUED _____

OTHER DEPTS.   REVISES PREVIOUS ISSUE
CONCERNED   Purchasing, Accounting   DATED None

WRITTEN BY   S. Jones   APPROVED BY   T. Vilani

Purpose of this procedure: To establish a method of and assign responsibility for the reporting of incoming shipments.

Background information: The standard Purchase Order form will contain one blue copy imprinted "Receiving Report." At the same time the Purchasing Department mails an order to a vendor, it will send the blue copy to the Shipping and Receiving Department (see Procedure PG-11, this manual).

1. When a shipment arrives, the Shipping Department Foreman will compare the Bill of lading with the appropriate Receiving Report. If he cannot identify the Receiving Report concerned, he will seek assistance from the Purchasing Department.

2. The foreman will compare the Bill of Lading with the Receiving Report. If they match exactly in type and quantity of material, he will instruct his personnel to unload the vehicle. If they do not, he will notify the Purchasing Department, who will provide instructions to unload all, part, or none of the shipment.

3. During the unloading, the foreman will have a check made of the actual contents of the shipment against the Bill of Lading. If they do not match exactly, he will ask the vehicle driver to remain while he obtains a decision from the Purchasing Department concerning unordered material.

4. If the contents do match the Bill of Lading, the foreman will have the material stored in the warehouse and sign the Receiving Report in the space marked "Received By."

5. When the material actually received differs from that listed on the Receiving Report, the foreman will note the differences in writing.

6. When a shipment arrives for which there is no Receiving Report, the foreman will notify the Purchasing Department. If their decision is to unload the material, they will make up a Purchase Order immediately and send the blue copy to the Shipping Department. Under no circumstances is material to be unloaded without a Receiving Report.

FIGURE 3-3: Specimen Page, Plant Operations Manual

TO: Maintenance Foreman   **Date**

FROM: Plant Manager

SUBJECT: Procedure Memorandum: Minor Work Orders

1. Effective June 1, 19XX all requests for maintenance jobs estimated to cost less than $200 must be made in writing on a Minor Work Order form (except in bona fide emergencies).
2. A supply of Minor Work Order pads will be maintained in the office supply locker by the office manager. Work orders are to be made out in two copies, with the originator keeping the pink copy and forwarding the white copy to the maintenance foreman.
3. Please assess the cost of completing each Minor Work Order you receive. If you estimate it to be more than $200, return to the originator requesting him to resubmit it on a Major Work Order form.
4. If you estimate the work to cost less than $200, please complete the job as soon as manpower and equipment are available. If it must be placed on the Maintenance Schedule, bring it up during our weekly scheduling meeting.
5. Please maintain files of completed work orders, and those awaiting action for my review. Notify me when there is a backlog of more than two weeks.

Distribution: All Production Foremen, Office Manager, R & D Section Leaders.

FIGURE 3-4: Typical Procedure Memorandum

ing department responsibilities it is important to do so in a way that will enhance, not conflict with, the establishment of objective performance criteria.

Step 6:
Coordinate to Prevent Problems

The organization chart clearly shows the vertical structure of an organization, but it has one weakness—it says nothing about the horizontal relationships between people and groups within the organization. These horizontal relationships constitute the problem of *coordination,* which requires careful adjustment to keep the organization running smoothly. To make these adjustments:

Arrange the use of buildings, equipment, and vehicles to avoid conflict between groups trying to use them at the same time.

Spell out clearly the responsibility for the care, cleaning, and maintenance of equipment used by more than one group.

Specify exactly the condition in which materials completed by one department are to be passed on to the next department.

Settle materials handling problems. Who moves process material from

Department A to Department B? Exactly where is it to be dropped off? How much materials is Department A allowed to accumulate before it must be moved to Department B?

Demand lateral cooperation. You must make it clear that you will not tolerate squabbling between departments and shifts, but that you expect full cooperation between them all of the time. Make cooperation a stated policy in operations manuals and written procedures.

Help the departments in their lateral communications. Verbal communications are often confused and misunderstood; a simple printed form, such as the Minor Work Order mentioned in Figure 3-4, can eliminate the difficulty. Other examples are requisitions for materials, samples, tools, quality checks, and transportation service.

CHOOSING THE RIGHT STRUCTURE FOR THE HOURLY WAGE FORCE: FOUR BASIC SYSTEMS

Although the hourly rated work force in the plant may not contain levels of authority and reporting relationships like those of the management structure, there is, nevertheless, a system of job levels associated with the difficulty of performing each job and the rate of pay which it commands. This structure deserves no less careful attention than the management organization; not only does it have major impact on the cost of operating the plant and the morale of the hourly employees, but once installed it may be very difficult to change at a later date. Choose from these four basic systems:

Flat Rate

Everyone receives the same rate of pay, and all do the same kind of work. While not found very often in industrial manufacturing plants, it does have application to specialized situations such as the assembly of novelties or the loading and unloading of freight in a truck terminal.

Advantages

1. The simplest system to administer.
2. The easiest to adjust in a tight labor market. The single rate can be raised to attract job applicants when necessary, in contrast to the difficulty of raising the bottom rate of a spread system to the same level and finding the top rate impossibly high.

Disadvantages

1. Very limited application.
2. No opportunities for advancement within the hourly ranks.

Merit System

In the most basic form of this system, the new worker is hired at a standard beginning rate, and his or her performance reviewed semiannually or annually by his or her supervisor. Any wage increase is based on the results of the supervisor's evaluation. In a modified form wage ranges are assigned to various classes of jobs, and merit increases awarded within the established ranges.

Advantages

1. The most management-oriented system. Management is in complete control of the individual's wage rate, and compensation is based entirely on performance.
2. The morale of the superior employee is kept high, since he or she is rewarded more than the less capable or industrious employee.

Disadvantages

1. The most vulnerable system to conscious or unconscious favoritism on the part of the foremen and supervisors.
2. Results in a very unequal wage structure after several years of operation.

Classification

This is the type of structure encountered in most industrial plants. The work content of each plant job is described precisely (see "Step 2: Combine Tasks Into Jobs" on page 34) and the job given a title descriptive of the work performed. The jobs are then classified in an ascending order according to a number of objective factors—skill and experience required, severity of working conditions, physical and mental effort called for, and the degree of responsibility for materials and machines. The higher rated jobs, of course, carry higher rates of pay. A typical classification system is shown in Part I of Figure 3-5.

The number of positions in each classification is firmly fixed; for example, the plant in Figure 3-5 may have ten Punch Press Operator positions. An employee in the Cutting Machine Operator classification must wait until a Punch Press Operator leaves his job before he can be promoted. This promotion will usually be awarded to the most senior Punch Press Operator who can perform the work. The frequency of advancement for any individual employee in this system depends, therefore, upon the chance openings that occur in the classifications above him.

Advantages

1. The pay rate for each job is closely matched to the work performed; this should result in the lowest average rate of pay for the plant work force.
2. It is the system best adapted to organizations with a wide range of skills required between the top and bottom jobs. Because it is encountered so often, it is the system best understood by hourly workers and labor unions.

Disadvantages

1. Employees may resist being assigned to jobs or being asked to work overtime outside their job classifications. The result is an inflexible work force that

I. Typical Classification System Job and Rate Structure

Production Department

	Step 1	Step 2	Maximum
Production Welder	11.56	11.96	12.35
Lathe Operator	10.93	11.32	11.72
Punch Press Operator	10.52	10.92	11.31
Cutting Machine Operator	10.05	10.42	10.80
Polisher	9.70	10.09	10.48
Helper	9.26	9.65	10.04

Maintenance Department

	Step 1	Step 2	Maximum
Machinist	12.17	12.58	13.00
Welder (Maintenance)	12.01	12.41	12.81
Electrician	11.85	12.25	12.65
Pipefitter	11.85	12.25	12.65
Helper	10.24	10.66	11.07
Lead Janitor	9.89	10.30	10.72
Janitor	9.45	9.86	10.28

II. Typical Operator Grade System Job and Rate Structure

Production Department

Grade	Qualification	Time Period (After Hiring)	Rate
Beginner	(Hired)	—	10.20
Operator D	Automatic	3 months	10.67
Operator C	Automatic	6 months	11.14
Operator B	Performance Review and Examination	12 months	11.93
Operator A	Performance Review and Examination	18 months	12.88

Maintenance Department

Helper	(Hired)	—	11.02
Mechanic C	Automatic	6 months	11.81
Mechanic B	Performance Review and Examination	14 months	12.76
Mechanic A	Performance Review and Examination	20 months	13.86

FIGURE 3-5: Comparison of Classification and Operator Grade Systems (All figures in dollars per hour.)

cannot cope with absenteeism, labor shortages, or sudden changes in workload within specific classifications.

2. The new employee faces an uncertain schedule of advancement; when jobs are plentiful he may become frustrated and leave if he cannot foresee his next move up.

A further note about the classification system shown in Figure 3-5. Within each classification three rates are shown—Step 1, Step 2, and Maximum. Progression to the higher steps can be made either after the passage of a fixed period of time of satisfactory performance, or preferably, after a fixed time and formal merit review. In this way some of the advantages of the merit system can be retained in the classification system. The wage table in Part I of Figure 3-5 is typical in that it embodies a wage overlap between the classifications. Thus, a Lathe Operator at the maximum rate of his classification, $11.72 per hour, earns more than the starting rate of $11.56 for the next higher classification, Production Welder. When a promotion is to be made in such a situation, it is common practice to pay the promoted employee his old rate plus a fixed amount (e.g., 20¢ per hour), or the midpoint wage of the new classification, whichever is lower.

Operator Grade System

This system is not encountered as often as the classification system, but it is found in smaller plants and those requiring a high degree of flexibility in the work force. A typical progression and rate schedule is shown in Part II of Figure 3-5.

The work tasks are not combined into "jobs" in the usual sense, to be held indefinitely by a particular person. Instead they are combined into work areas or "fields," and any employee can be assigned to any field at a given time. Each employee is ultimately expected to learn to perform in all of the fields and, after several automatic raises, promotions are based upon performance reviews by the supervisor, and the administration of a written examination to be sure he knows the job content. At the Operator B level he might be expected to know the routine procedures of three out of five fields and to be able to perform them with normal supervision. At the Operator A level he would be expected to qualify in all five fields, to demonstrate his ability to handle unusual or complicated situations, and to perform the job with a minimum of supervision. The opportunity to take the examination and undergo the performance review are offered each employee at a stated time interval after hiring. The supervisor undertakes an obligation to train and rotate every new employee through the work areas so that each will be prepared to meet these tests. The end result is a highly flexible work force, in which any employee can do any job. No limit is placed upon the number who can reach the top grade.

Advantages

1. Maximum flexibility. Training each employee in all of the jobs in a department produces a strong work force, capable of meeting the problems of

absenteeism, sudden separations, or shortages of help. Plant process and equipment can be changed with less upset, since no "jobs" are eliminated, only work activities. There are no arguments about work assignments or ability and obligation to perform overtime work.

2. Maximum opportunity. Since there is no limit on the number who can reach the top grade, the individual employee does not have to wait until someone in a higher grade leaves, creating an opening. Promotion is attained on a definite time schedule, and on the employee's own merits.

Disadvantages

1. This system can result in a higher average wage rate. When every employee has reached the top rate (as in periods of low labor turnover), the simpler tasks will be performed at wage rates higher than might be the case in classification or merit systems.

2. Once an employee reaches the top rate in a department, incentive for further personal development is minimized and based only on transferring to other departments or the hope of promotion to salaried ranks.

Should Hourly Workers Supervise?

Some companies establish a first level of supervision within the hourly work force, designating a "shift leader," "leadman," or "chief operator" at the top of the hourly rate structure. This employee takes charge of the work performed by his group, including the assignment of tasks to other workers. He does not have the right to hire or fire, or to discipline; his supervisory relationship is of the "dotted line" type shown in Figure 3-1 where the hourly work groups are headed by Shift Leaders.

This method has the advantage of providing supervision at lowest possible cost, but there are some major disadvantages. One is the problem of split loyalty, which occurs when this employee is called upon to report an operating error committed by one of his fellow workers. A second is the tendency for the post to be filled by the most senior employee in the group, as opposed to a candidate carefully chosen for supervisory ability. Some plant managers hold as a basic philosophy that all supervision should be within salaried management ranks.

MEETING SOME SPECIAL CHALLENGES

Upgrading an Existing Organization

If you are taking over an existing organization, you may be dismayed by what you find. Years of neglect in the procedures for hiring, training, and weeding out substandard employees can produce an organization incapable of efficient performance or future progress. When you are faced with this situation, use these tools to improve the caliber of the organization.

Raise the hiring standards. Decide what levels of education, experience, and quality of previous work record you need, and insist that those doing the hiring meet them. Require the foreman to interview every applicant coming into his department; if he approves, he has a commitment to help the employee make good. If he disapproves, the chances for success are low, and the employee should not be hired.

Separate the inadequate employee. This can seem like a formidable task, especially when a union is present to challenge your moves. But you have two basic factors working to your advantage:

Attrition itself. The inept and unconcerned employee tends to drift from job to job. When he leaves, replace him with a better one.

Enforcement of plant rules. Incompetent employees usually have bad absence and lateness records. By enforcing the plant rules rigidly in these areas, you can weed out some of the ineffective people. In some plants you can apply established rules for work output and quality performance in the same way. (Of course, you must apply all these rules fairly to all your employees, and you run the risk that once in a while a "good" employee will have to be discharged. It is a small risk, and well worth taking.)

Salvage what you can. Many substandard employees got that way because management permitted sloppy and careless habits to develop. With firm handling and close attention, these employees can be restored to a higher level of performance, and the advantages of upgrading an employee you know over hiring a new one you don't are many.

Start training programs. If you take over an organization which seems incapable, it may be that its people do not know what they are expected to do, or how they are expected to do it. Training is the answer. The most effective training is accomplished with compulsory, in-house programs using instructors recruited from the plant staff. When it is not possible to set up such a program, company-sponsored off-hour courses are another way of filling the need.

Steps for Preserving the Organization During Slow Periods

Temporary layoffs can result from a number of conditions beyond your control—a protracted sales decline, disabling fire in all or part of the plant, shortage of essential raw material, major change in product line. Such layoffs can offset your achievements in building a capable organization, especially when employees can find permanent jobs in other companies in the area. Take these steps to lessen the impact of a temporary slow period on your organization:

Forecast the length of the slow period. You will need an accurate estimate to make sound decisions on the cost break-even point between retaining and laying off employees and to plan the interim programs listed below. Make your own estimate, then compare it with those of the Sales Department, corporate planners, engineers, Purchasing Department, or any appropriate corporate group.

Compare the cost of layoff with the cost of retention. It will be simple to calculate the cost of keeping any given number of employees for the duration of the slow period, but don't forget that there are direct dollar costs incurred by laying off. Unemployment insurance rates go up, severance pay may be involved, and there will be the cost of hiring and training the replacements for the predicted number of laid-off employees who will be lost to the company for good. When these costs are calculated you will be able to establish a break-even point in time; how long you retain people beyond that point depends on the dollar amount you convince yourself and your superiors should be spent as an investment in the organization.

Find other work to do.   During periods of high production a number of useful jobs may have to be postponed because of the press of business. Performing these jobs during slow periods can provide the economic justification needed to keep the organization intact. Here are some suggestions:

Take inventory—finished goods, raw materials, capital equipment, fixtures and furnishings.

Use production personnel to assist with equipment repairs and preventive maintenance activities.

Paint equipment and buildings.

Housekeeping.

Training. Train or retrain workers in plant procedures, equipment care, safety, quality procedures, new technical developments, or general background of the company and its products.

Try to find substitute operations. A top quality printing house may offer to print cheap handbills when business is slow. A processing plant with a tunnel dryer does contract drying for outside firms. A plastics manufacturer supplying industry makes toy novelties.

Take vacations.   Employees may be willing to take their vacations at odd times of the year rather than go on layoff.

Use the "key person" concept in layoff.   This requires establishing a procedure that protects some proportion—say one-third—of the employees in the top classifications of any department from being bumped out during a layoff. The idea is keep the more qualified and ambitious employees who have sought the top jobs from being pushed out by less able employees who happen to have more seniority. If you operate a nonunion plant, you should carefully establish and announce this provision well ahead of time; if the plant is unionized, press for a contract clause at the next collective bargaining.

Organizing for Shift Operations

When the plant operates a second or third shift, some special problems of coordination, assignment of responsibility, and communication arise. The daytime managerial staff wants to maintain as much control as possible, but must relinquish some of its authority to shift supervision. Department foremen become uneasy when it appears that instructions from the shift superintendent conflict with those of their daytime superiors. The separate shifts, using the same buildings and equipment and frequently working on the same materials, can fall to bickering over who left what in poor condition.

You can minimize these problems by taking pains with the following aspects of shift operation:

Spell out the shift supervisor's duties and responsibilities. This should be done precisely and in writing. Figures 3-1 and 3-2 depict plant organizations with four shifts for 24-hour, seven days per week operation. Consider the small plant organization in Figure 3-1. The B Shift Supervisor is shown having a dotted line relationship to the Shift Leaders of B Shift in Departments X and Y, although these shift leaders normally report to the day supervisors of the two departments. Of course, the shift supervisor will have the authority to keep order, to react to emergencies, and to maintain a smooth flow of production materials through the plant. But does he have the authority to shut the plant down when quality is off? Can he fire an hourly worker on the spot? Can he order the shift leaders to switch product lines? Does he give the shift mechanic routine assignments, or only emergency work (leaving the routine work to be assigned by the daytime maintenance foreman)? At exactly what point in process difficulties is he required to call a daytime supervisor? Unless his position and authority in such matters are clearly understood by everyone involved, confusion and conflict are inevitable.

Clarify lines of communication. In the small plant organization of Figure 3-1, it is feasible to require that the Shift Leaders make no calls outside the plant (to day supervisors) except through the Shift Supervisor; in the organization of Figure 3-2 with eight foremen and a watch engineer on each shift it may not be possible to have every question about the technical details of shop orders passed on through the Shift Superintendent. If the foreman is allowed to call his General Foreman directly, what matters is he allowed to refer in this way, and which ones must go through the Shift Superintendent? Technical questions only? Shutdown decisions when quality is poor? Alternate production when raw materials are not available for scheduled runs? To whom does a foreman refer when he feels that he cannot carry out the General Foreman's night instructions? Even if you do nothing these questions will be answered somehow; the results will be far better if you answer them in advance with clear procedures.

Require the keeping of shift logs. The Shift Leaders or Foremen, and the Shift Supervisors or Superintendents, should be required to keep a written log of all significant events occurring on the shift, the condition of plant and materials at the end of the shift, and precautions and warnings for the oncoming shift. Attempting to transfer this information orally can lead only to misunderstanding, contention, and denial. On the positive side, written records are important not only to the oncoming shift, but can serve to keep the daytime supervision fully informed of plant conditions.

Beware of "shift wars." It is a common phenomenon for the operating shifts to begin criticizing each other. Complaints and perhaps sarcastic comments will appear in the shift logs, or tales carried personally, that "D Shift left the plant dirty,'' or ''A Shift did not set up materials properly,'' and so on. This kind of bickering can be the result of simple competition—the foreman feels he can get ahead by running the other person down. When this is the case, you can correct the situation by stating directly that you want cooperation, not contention, and by rewarding those who cooperate and censuring those who do not.

The problem may not be one of simple competition. It may be the result of poorly conceived procedures, or no procedures at all, or misunderstandings about responsibilities and authority. When organizational principles have been neglected, the symptoms may very well be the complaints and bickering mentioned above. The cure is to straighten each confused situation out with a well-defined procedure.

The Challenge of Change

The conditions that lead you to build your organization in a particular way are not static, and you must be prepared to revise your organization as changes occur. Some changes are so obvious and dramatic that they cannot be ignored: a new product is introduced, new equipment is purchased, and a new building erected to house them. But there are many gradual, subtle changes that also affect organization: employees leave and are replaced; sales competition requires higher quality and better service at the same or reduced cost; the supply of skilled people in the labor market expands and contracts. When you begin to see symptoms of organizational trouble—production delays, missed schedules, departmental squabbling—it is time to review the organizational structure, adjusting it to the new conditions.

Getting into Operation Smoothly: Schedules, Shifts, and Procedures

Plant managers preside over an incredibly large variety of process operations; their plants produce everything from toy dolls to mammoth presses, from potato chips to petrochemicals. Some operate continuous flow processes, others produce assembled units for stock, some manage custom job shops. Yet within this multiplicity of processes there are problems common to all—how to schedule the plants most efficiently, how best to utilize manpower, how to handle start-ups and shutdowns, how to meet emergencies, how to keep track of materials produced.

It is with these universal concerns of production operations that this chapter deals, offering an analysis of each problem and a choice of solutions.

THREE MAIN OBJECTIVES OF PRODUCTION SCHEDULING

As you begin to work on the scheduling function, you need an understanding of the objectives of the process, the information that goes into it, and the techniques of developing and using plant schedules.

There are three main objectives of scheduling:

1. To meet customer delivery requirements. The only reason for the plant to exist is to give the customer what he wants when he wants it. Meeting this objective is the primary goal not only of scheduling, but of most other plant activities as well.

2. To satisfy inventory requirements. It is not practical to wait until a customer

order is received before starting production. Instead, the customer is served from inventory, and the plant is scheduled to maintain inventory levels set to provide the most effective service.

3. To maximize plant efficiency. The object is to load the plant as evenly as possible with long production runs; to minimize interruptions for setups, tool changes, and cleaning equipment; and to utilize machinery and equipment as fully as possible, thus enhancing return on capital investment.

These objectives can be mutually exclusive. If you operate only for maximum efficiency by scheduling production runs without regard for customer needs, you will soon have no customers. On the other hand, if you accept repeated disruptions of the production process to satisfy every vagarious customer demand or are willing to bear the cost of such high inventory levels that the warehouse could never be out of stock in any product, you will soon find that you have no plant to run—excessive costs will have driven it out of business. Scheduling often turns out to be the art of striking a compromise among goals that may be mutually conflicting.

The information base for scheduling includes the following:

1. *Firm customer orders.* They take precedence over all other contenders for position in the schedule, can be scheduled far in advance with certainty, and form the backbone of the production schedule.

2. *Sales forecasts.* They vary widely in accuracy. If your Sales Department provides consistently reliable projections, you can safely schedule production on them. If not, you may still be able to use them by making adjustments on the basis of past experience—if salesperson Jones has a history of underestimating actual sales by 10 percent, you can adjust the numbers she submits to obtain more accurate figures.

3. *Inventory requirements.* When product stock levels fall below minimum, or when distribution pipelines must be filled for a new product, some of the plant's production capacity is scheduled to replenish inventory. Scheduling to inventory, when done well in advance and combined intelligently with actual customer orders and sales forecasts, offers the best opportunity to schedule for maximum plant efficiency and strike the optimum compromise among the mutually conflicting goals discussed previously. The key here is advance planning; inventory production delayed too long suddenly turns into customer requirements that must be produced hastily, and therefore, inefficiently.

4. *Crisis events.* When a strike, or any foreseeable event that can cripple production, is impending in your plant or your suppliers', or in local or national transportation systems, you must adjust production schedules to minimize the effects of these emergencies on customers. Operating Example 4-1 shows how such an adjustment can be made deliberately, in advance, and without the customary panic reaction.

Operating Example 4-1: Production Scheduling for a Crisis Event. The manager of a plant, which has a production capacity of 1,000 units per week of a product that must ship by rail, learns on April 2 that a nationwide rail strike is likely to occur June 1 and last for one week. Current production is at the rate of 850 units per week and is expected to stay at that level for the next two months. The Sales Department manager says that in order to protect the plant's customers, extra shipments should be received during the interim period equivalent to a week's production, or 850 units. To be sure that this material will reach customers before the strike begins, it must be shipped by May 20. The plant manager calculates that if he operates the plant at full capacity, each week he will produce $1,000 - 850 = 150$ units to assign to the emergency inventory. Dividing 850 by 150, he realizes that it will take 5.7 weeks to turn out the needed extra production, and schedules the plant to start producing at 1,000 units per week on April 7. This means that the emergency production will be completed by May 15, with an extra five days available to be sure that shipment can be completed by May 20. This manager also realizes that the job is not done simply by changing the schedule, but that he must coordinate the effort with the materials manager and the production superintendent to assure that sufficient additional raw materials and manpower are available as needed to handle the extra production load.

Nonforeseeable events such as fire, explosion, flood, severe weather, and earthquake can also disrupt the regular flow of raw materials from suppliers or the transportation systems that take finished goods to customers. These events come with little or no warning, and the scheduling process is reduced to reacting to the disruptions as they occur, usually by reducing the level of production, or inserting substitute work and cleanup activities into the production schedule.

Key Scheduling Techniques

1. Put the schedule on paper. Have it typewritten and duplicated for distribution, or filled in on a printed form. If a larger size is required for posting, it can be reproduced on a blueprint machine or a big electrostatic copier. Blackboards or peg boards that are changed as the schedule is completed are good for display purposes, but they leave no permanent record; such a record is invaluable to the manager who must make plant production capacity estimates based on operating experience.

2. Use the schedule as a control device. Next to every increment of production shown on the schedule, leave a space for the actual amount produced. This converts the schedule into a control tool, which shows management whether production is on schedule, and if not, how far it is off.

3. Communicate the schedule to all who can use it. Maintenance, Purchasing, Order Departments, and others in your organization will benefit from knowing what the plant is planning to do. See that they get copies of the schedule and are kept up to date on changes.

4. Devise a schedule format appropriate to the type of production operation:

   Continuous process. This is characterized by a main process stream that produces one or several products. The process may be initiated as a continuous stream or by successive identical batches. Typical operations would be petroleum refining, food processing, and chemical manufacturing. Figure 4-1 is an example of a schedule format for this type of plant. In this case the process starts with a batchwise operation and turns later to a continuous stream. Because it takes a number of days before material charged to the start of the process ends up as finished product, the manager who devised the schedule decided to keep track of both "Material Charged to Process" and "Production Completed." By adding columns for scheduled and actual production and grouping them into "Today" and "Month-to-Date" sections, the manager has not only provided the plant with instructions as to how

MONTHLY PRODUCTION SCHEDULE AND COMPLETION REPORT

Month of _____October_____ 19 _85_

Department _____Batch Plant_____

(All figures in pounds)

Date	Material Charged to Process				Production Completed			
	Today		Month-to-date		Today		Month-to-date	
	Schedule	Actual	Schedule	Actual	Schedule	Actual	Schedule	Actual
1	84,194	83,260	84,194	83,260	79,142	80,721	79,142	80,721
2	84,194	80,179	168,388	163,439	79,142	78,635	158,284	159,356
3	84,194	84,108	252,582	247,547	79,142	79,444	237,426	238,800
4	84,194	85,622	336,776	333,169	79,142	79,632	316,568	318,432
5	84,194	85,428	420,970	418,597	79,142	79,158	395,710	397,590
6	84,194	85,774	505,164	504,371	79,142	79,007	474,852	476,597
7	84,194	83,729	589,358	588,100	79,142	80,131	553,994	556,728
8	84,194	79,622	673,552	667,722	79,142	78,914	633,136	635,642
9	84,194	82,518	757,746	750,240	79,142	81,002	712,278	716,644
10	84,194	82,491	841,940	832,731	79,142	79,415	791,420	796,059
11	84,194	84,006	926,134	916,737	79,142	78,917	870,562	874,976
12	84,194	85,981	1,010,328	1,002,718	79,142	79,510	949,074	954,486
29	84,194	78,553	2,441,626	2,423,235	79,142	80,211	2,295,118	2,306,674
30	84,194	83,998	2,525,820	2,507,233	79,142	81,565	2,374,260	2,388,239
31	84,194	85,371	2,610,014	2,592,604	79,142	79,452	2,453,402	2,467,691

FIGURE 4-1: Process Plant Schedule

much to produce, but himself with a control tool that shows what was accomplished on any day and up to any point in the month.

Series Operations. In this type of operation material is produced in discrete units or pieces, and moved from one work station to the next for further processing or combination with other pieces until a finished product is obtained. Examples would be machine shops, assembly operations, and clothing manufacture. Figure 4-2 is a schedule for a stamping and small assembly operation with six machines, and shows for Job 2019 how material flows through the shop for a period of one week. Opposite each machine number is shown the block of time during the week when it is working on Job 2019, and within each block the scheduled and actual number of pieces produced. The lines ending in arrows show how materials flow through the shop; for example, the stampings made on Machines 1 and 2 on Monday and Tuesday are sent to Machine 3, while the stampings made on Wednesday and Thursday are sent to Machine 6. Note that Job 2019 does not occupy all the machines for the whole week. This situation can be remedied by adding more jobs and extending the schedule vertically; this is shown on Figure 4-2 below the double line near the bottom, where a new job is started. It shows Machine 1 scheduled for late Tuesday and early Wednesday when it has available time not occupied by Job 2019. The schedule can be extended in this fashion until all the machines are shown as occupied for the full week. The use of Figure 4-2 as a control tool is limited by the fact that actual production is not entered until the completion of the machine run; it could be improved by enlarging the format so that scheduled and actual production could be shown for each day or half-day.

Single Unit Manufacture. Each unit produced is so different in design and materials of construction that it must be handled as though it were a separate project. An example would be a shop that makes process vessels—one job might be an open top tank made of carbon steel while the next would be a closed pressure vessel made of stainless steel and having a set of nozzles specified in size and location by the customer. Others might include aircraft manufacturing or shipbuilding, where customer specifications may vary so much that each unit produced must be regarded as a separate project. For these one-of-a-kind situations, a scheduling technique called Program Evaluation and Review Technique, better known by its acronym PERT, is widely used.

How the Program Evaluation and Review Technique Works

Figure 4-3 illustrates the use of a PERT diagram for the manufacture of a unique process vessel for a new customer. The first step in development of the schedule is to set down the following list of landmark events which must transpire from start to finish of the job:

PRODUCTION SCHEDULE FOR WEEK OF <u>April 7</u> **19** <u>86</u>

DEPARTMENT <u>Stamping & Small Assembly (SSA)</u>

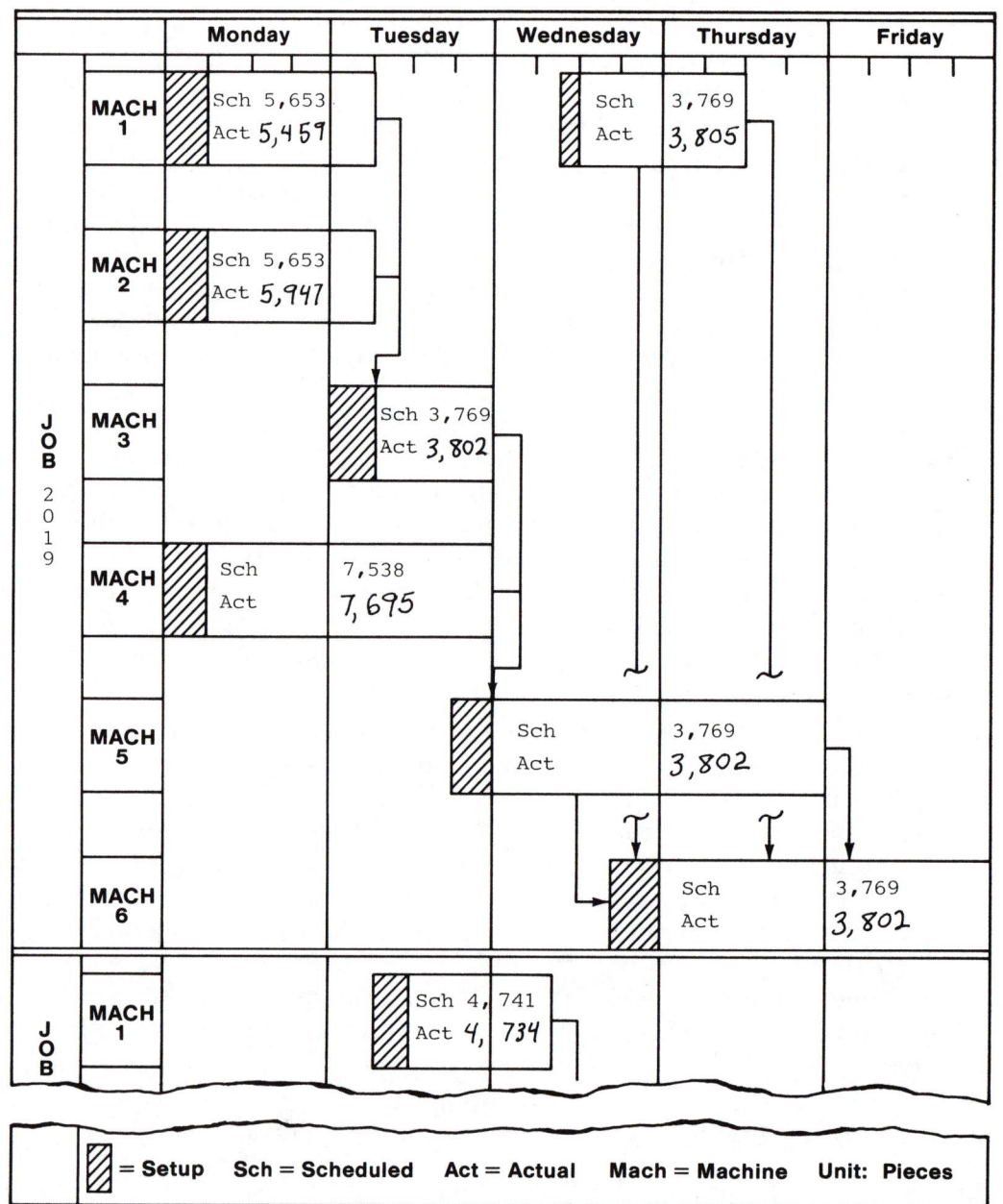

FIGURE 4-2: Series Operations Schedule

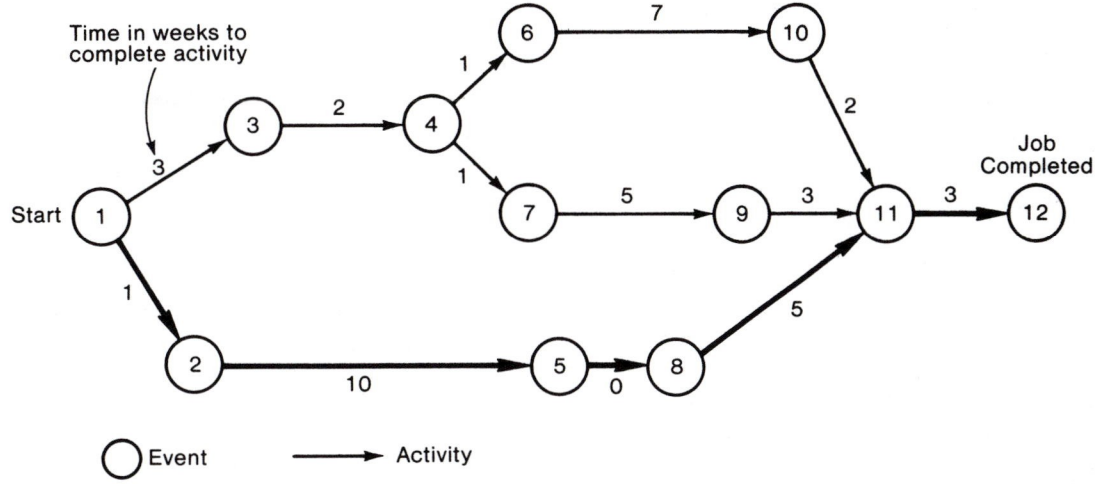

FIGURE 4-3: PERT Diagram for Production Scheduling

1. Order received
2. Unique raw materials ordered
3. Engineering completed
4. Drawings approved by customer
5. Unique raw materials received
6. Subassembly A ordered
7. Subassembly B ordered
8. Fabrication started
9. Subassembly B received
10. Subassembly A received
11. Subassemblies incorporated into main structure
12. Fabrication done, job completed

The events are represented by numbered circles on the diagram, arranged in logical sequence with time running from left to right. Thus, events 6 and 7, ordering of subassemblies, must follow event 4, approval of the engineering drawings by the customer. Events on a PERT diagram take no time in themselves, but are usually the culmination of activities which are represented by arrows connecting the events. The scheduled time for each activity (measured in weeks in this case) is marked next to the arrow representing it; in Figure 4-3 it takes 10 weeks from the ordering of certain unique raw materials (Event 2) for their manufacture by a supplier and their receipt at the plant (Event 5). An important advantage of this type of schedule is that it shows (for this case) three sequences of events leading to completion of the job: 1-3-4-6-10-11-12, 1-3-4-7-9-11-12, and 1-2-5-8-11-12. If the time in weeks it takes to pass through each sequence is added up, it is found that the last sequence takes 19 weeks, longer than either of the other two. This sequence is called the *critical path* because a delay in any of its activities will result in a delay of the same magnitude in completion of the job. Note that it is not always necessary for time to elapse between two events; in the figure it requires zero weeks from the receipt of unique raw materials, Event 5, to the start of fabrication, Event 8.

Keeping Schedule Changes Down

Once the schedule has been established, materials ordered, or work begun, sudden changes can have the following negative effects on plant operation:

> **Crowding** of operating floor with materials assembled for prior orders, which must now wait while the rush order is processed
>
> **Overtime** costs
>
> **Increase** of production and quality errors
>
> **Reduced plant efficiency** in output per man-hour
>
> **Wasted time** of schedulers, foremen, and managers
>
> **Worker resentment** of sudden changes in assignment, especially when they result in waste of previous work

You bear a double responsibility when schedule changes are demanded of your plant. It is your duty—as well as everyone else in the company—to serve legitimate customer needs. On the other hand, it is also your duty to point out the additional costs of the negative effects listed above, and to probe the reasons for schedule changes. Often the reasons are poor—someone "forgot" an order, "lost a paper," or a clerk was absent and no one did his work. When such cases occur frequently, you can rightfully demand that these deficiencies should not be redeemed by increased plant costs.

MANAGING OTHER OPERATING FUNCTIONS

Guidelines on When to Use Overtime

Premium rates charged for overtime range from one and one-half to three times the base hourly rate, making a prima facie case for very close control and even elimination of overtime. Nevertheless, you know that you cannot simply do away with overtime by issuing an edict, and the cost decisions are not as simple as they first appear. Here are some guidelines to use in making overtime decisions:

1. Use overtime to keep the organization lean. When your man-hour calculations call for 9.5 people to staff a section, hire 9 and make up the difference with overtime. Assuming that you pay for the 0.5 man at time and a half, your cost liability is 0.75 at straight time rates, rather than the 1.0 you would

have paid had you hired the tenth man. Equally important, you will avoid hiring more people than you need, a practice which inevitably leads to loose work habits and hidden costs much higher than the overtime incurred.

2. Base overtime decisions on hard economic facts whenever possible. If holding a freight car another day will cost $75.00 but four man-hours of overtime at $10.50 times 1.5 can get it unloaded, then the decision is in favor of the overtime. If it will require a thousand dollars worth of overtime to meet a deadline on a job that will only return seven hundred dollars in profit, the economic decision is against the use of overtime.

3. The cost of fringe benefits affects the economics of overtime decisions. Often the cost of these benefits, such as vacations, holidays, work clothing, and insurance, will total 30 percent of the base hourly rate, but does not increase because of overtime. Thus when a choice must be made between having the existing force work overtime or hiring new workers at straight time, it is really between 1.5 times the base rate for the overtime work, and 1.3 times the base rate for the new workers.

4. Include unavoidable overtime in the budget. Sometimes you are required by forces beyond your control—sales policy, clerical mistakes in order handling, bad weather, the need to clean up for important visitors—to use overtime work. Although the individual occurrences cannot be foreseen with much accuracy, over a year their total costs tend toward a repetitive annual figure which can be predicted. You should insist that these costs be included in the budget.

Managing Start-Ups and Shutdowns

Throughout the year you are faced with a number of occasions requiring the planning of a shutdown or a start-up: holidays, slow production periods, vacations, maintenance turnarounds, and bringing new facilities on stream. It is imperative that these operations be carried out from written procedures, not only to prevent the omission of an important step, but also because the mere act of planning will uncover problems of coordination that must be answered ahead of time.

Shutdowns. Use this checklist of special preparations for a plant closing:

- Building security—windows and doors locked, heating and ventilating systems adjusted properly.
- Electrical systems—switches off, fuses pulled, breakers locked out.
- Fluid systems—valves closed, vessels and pipes drained, depressured, or vented.
- Sprinklers and other fire protection systems—in working order, provisions for last-minute checks.
- Freeze-ups—special protection not only for outdoor equipment, but for pipes that pass through or run close to cold walls.
- Preparation for maintenance work—if equipment repairs and overhauls are

planned for the shutdown, be sure that the work area is cleaned up, process materials removed, and potentially dangerous conditions offset by safety precautions.

Start-ups. The object is to get the plant running again quickly and smoothly. Consider these points in planning the start-up:

- Bring maintenance and utility crews in early—to have buildings, machines, and services ready when the production personnel start work.

- Coordinate material flow—plan operations, especially in continuous and series-type production, so that production crews are neither idle nor swamped by excessive work coming from previous steps in the process.

- Beware of pressure systems—steam, gas, and water lines may be carrying unusually high pressures because of zero demand during the shutdown period; valves must be opened more slowly and carefully than usual.

- Expect equipment problems—lubricants will have drained from metal surfaces, pumps lost suction, fluid systems become airbound, and instruments off calibration or stuck in one position.

Emergency Procedures

As in the case of start-ups and shutdowns, emergency procedures must be thought out ahead of time, reduced to printed form, and widely disseminated to those who will actually put them into practice. It is an excellent idea to conduct drills and problem exercises in the use of power failure, flood, and fire emergency procedures to be sure that plant personnel will react promptly and effectively when actual emergencies occur.

Power Failure (Loss of electricity or steam)

- Prior to any actual emergency examine all instruments and control devices to be sure that they are set for *fail-safe,* that is, when they are deprived of power they will cause cooling rather than heating, low rather than high pressure, to occur.

- Shut off electrical start-stop switches. Some types of electrical equipment can be damaged by a partial return of electric power, and in any event, the main breakers may cause a second power failure if they are overloaded with all equipment on when the power returns.

- If the failure is in the steam system, take steps to protect the building against freezing—close windows and doors, turn on emergency electric heaters if electricity is available. Decide at what building temperature workers will be sent home. Close steam valves at points in the system where process materials can be drawn into the pipes by vacuum, and where air can be drawn in.

- Provide for emergency cooling. If your plant has a cooling tower for heat removal from process equipment, its fans and pumps will be shut down in an electrical failure. Arrange for emergency tie-ins to city water mains to accomplish enough cooling for safety purposes.

Fire

- The first step in preparing an emergency procedure for fire is to decide what you want your employees to do first. Turn in the alarm? Evacuate the building? Fight the fire with hand equipment until it is out or too big to handle? The answers to this question will vary with the type of plant you operate and the prevailing safety philosophy in your company. The important point is that the decisions be made ahead of time and incorporated into well-rehearsed procedures.

- Shutdown decisions can be more complicated than they first appear. If there is a fire in one section of the plant, it would seem sensible to shut down operations in all other sections until the situation is under control. But if a part of the plant is handling flammable liquids or gases, a sudden shutdown can cause venting of these materials, or perhaps spills, increasing the danger of fire. It may be safer to keep a department of this type running unless the fire is very close to it.

- The fire procedure will contain a description of the plant alarm system, its signals, and what to do if it fails. It should also spell out who is authorized to deal with the press and public in an emergency situation.

Flood

- Flooding usually gives more warning of its arrival than other types of emergencies, and the decision process can be spread out over a long period of time. If your plant is in the flood plain of a river your state flood control agency or the U.S. Army Corps of Engineers can probably give you detailed data on the depth of water to expect and the frequency of flooding in the area.

- Develop the procedure for evacuation. The primary questions are who makes the shutdown decisions, on what criteria, which sections shut down first, and the composition and duties of emergency crews, if any.

- Provide for protection of property. Doors and windows are closed, and if there is time, sealed. Electrical equipment is de-energized, delicate apparatus moved out of danger, materials which can catch fire when exposed to water relocated.

Snow Emergency

- The decision-making process is the key to a successful procedure, and should be detailed carefully in advance. Who makes the final decision on running or shutting down? With whom must he consult? Who feeds the first information and warnings to him? How will the information be disseminated to employees?

- Beware of hourly pay squabbles. Some union contracts (and even non-union plant rules) require that prior notice be given of a cancelled shift, or the workers are paid for the day anyway. Situations can arise in which one worker stays home and gets paid, while another reports, does a day's work, and gets the same pay; obviously the second worker will feel he is owed some kind of premium. To avoid such situations, one plant stays open if at least one supervisor can make it to the plant to assign workers; those who do report get paid for the work they do, while the absentees are not paid.

- Communications. If the plant is to be shut down, employees must be notified in advance. Make arrangements with one or more local radio stations to broadcast your emergency announcements. Each fall post a notice telling employees which stations to listen to for emergency instructions.

Holiday Operations

Some operations must run on holidays, either because their outputs cannot be stored or because they are too costly or complicated to shut down. Others which have the option of shutting down will usually do so unless urgent customer needs or exceptional economic conditions dictate keeping the plant open. In either case, give special attention to these points when considering holiday operations:

1. "Double time and a half" is not what it seems. You pay an employee eight hours straight time pay whether he works the holiday or not; therefore, when he works the holiday your incremental cost is at time and a half.

2. In prosperous times employees will generally resist holiday work, unless the nature of the operation obviously requires it. If the entire plant does not have to operate, it may be wiser to recruit a skeleton crew from among those who wish to volunteer for holiday work.

3. Holidays may bring increased incidence of drinking, sleeping on the job, and absenteeism; at these times the rules need to be firmly announced and impartially administered. Plant rules or the union contract should provide that an employee must work the day before and the day after the holiday in order to receive holiday pay.

4. Prepare for a lack of supporting operations both inside and outside the plant. The office is closed, clerks are gone, truck terminal dispatchers and railroad agents not available, fuel and food deliveries may not take place.

PUTTING THE PLANT ON SHIFT

Because of the many problems that face employees and management alike, the decision to schedule shift work for the plant is not made lightly—but for many operations the need is compelling. This section examines such needs, the problems encountered, and what is involved in setting up shift operations.

Four Reasons for Establishing Shift Operations

1. Utilization of capital equipment. When the cost of a machine is very high

compared to profit realized on each unit of production, the machine may have to be operated for more than eight hours a day in order to justify its cost.

2. High sales and production levels. When they exceed one-shift capacity the workday must be extended to second and third shifts. Because it is time-consuming to recruit and train supervision and operating personnel for additional shifts, this decision is usually made to run on more than a short-term basis—at least a matter of months.

3. Processes that cannot be shut down easily or economically. High heat furnaces, which take several days to reach operating temperatures, and complicated chemical processes in which a raw material does not emerge as the finished product until a week after it has entered the process, are examples of operations that require shift work. Plant personnel will be more receptive to the idea of working shifts when the process itself makes the need obvious.

4. Products that cannot be stored. Transportation terminals and electric power plants are examples of plants whose "products" must be used at the instant they are created, and their need for shift work is obvious. Plants that make products for a daytime market—such as bakeries and dairies—are similarly affected.

Management Problems with Shift Operations

Communications. Direct contact between the upper levels of plant management and personnel of second and third shifts is limited to brief periods in the early morning and late afternoon; with some shift schedules direct contact can be almost nonexistent. To overcome the problem written communications are used to a greater extent; the daytime superintendent or general foreman may leave a handwritten "night sheet" in which he gives detailed instructions for the work to be performed that night, any safety hazards he foresees, and minor notices of interest to the shift personnel. The shift foremen, in turn, keep a written log of their activities for the use of daytime supervision.

Management control. It is much more difficult for daytime plant management to be sure its procedures and plant rules are being observed when its members are not physically present to see what is going on. The use of rotating rather than fixed shift schedules can help management to overcome this problem.

Labor shortages. When employment rates are high in the surrounding area, it becomes difficult or impossible to staff night shifts. It may be necessary to offer very high wages and shift differentials to attract workers, and even these are not guaranteed solutions.

Cost of shift premiums. When shifts are instituted the cost of labor rises through the payment of a shift differential. Five percent of base wage is a typical level, but premiums in excess of 10 percent are not unheard of.

Reduced worker efficiency. Many third-shift workers do not get full, satisfying rest; there are too many daytime household noises and distractions to permit uninterrupted sleep. The second-shift worker fares better, but he is tempted to take a second job or become absorbed in home projects during the day, showing up for work with a day's activity already behind him. In either case the worker may not be inclined or able to work with as much efficiency as the daytime worker.

How to Set Up Shift Operations

Assign workers. This can be the knottiest problem of all. Workers usually feel that they should be allowed to choose their shift assignments on the basis of seniority, while management feels that it should have the right to assign workers so as to give each shift a balance of experience, skills, strengths, and weaknesses. One answer is to set a schedule of rotating, rather than fixed, shifts so that each group takes its turn at night work.

Assign supervision. When shifts must be added, the problem of finding adequate supervision can be acute. Most plants promote from within, feeling that it is easier to train an employee familiar with the company's products and procedures to be a foreman than it is to hire a foreman from outside and teach him or her new operational techniques. Whichever plan is chosen, the new foreman will need at least four to six weeks break-in period on days under the eyes of the plant superintendent or manager.

Rotating shifts can be used to achieve supervisory balance on the night shifts as well as worker balance. Some companies use different schedules for supervision from those of the workers; the idea is to have each supervisor work with all of the shifts over a period of time, avoiding the "ingrown" effect of having the same workers and supervisor together for long periods of time.

Keep operations at a minimum. The fewer tasks carried out on the night shift, the smaller the problems of staffing, communications, and management control. Unit cost of production may be higher on the night shifts because of shift premiums paid to employees.

Provide support services. When the combined cost of lost production and maintenance call-ins caused by equipment breakdowns on the night shifts approaches the wages of a maintenance worker, it is time to assign a shift mechanic to each of the night shifts. This employee should report administratively to the daytime maintenance supervisor, but should receive work assignments on breakdowns from the night superintendent.

Provision must be made for emergency food service. While employees will generally bring their own lunches to the night shifts, depending upon the plant only to provide vending machines for beverages, candy, and cigarettes, a problem arises when a worker stays over from one shift to another and has no opportunity to have lunch. There are three solutions to the problem: (1) send the employee out to a restaurant, (2) arrange for a caterer to bring the required number of meals in on each shift, or (3) maintain a stock of frozen dinners and a quick-heat oven at the plant so that employees can serve themselves. The last mentioned method offers the best combination of employee satisfaction and management control of the situation.

Establish shift schedules. There are two basic types—fixed and rotating:

(1) Fixed shifts. Personnel are permanently assigned to either the first shift (7 A.M. to 3 P.M. or 8 A.M. to 4 P.M. are typical hours), second shift (3 P.M. to 11 P.M. or 4 P.M. to midnight), or third shift (11 P.M. to 7 A.M. or midnight to 8 A.M.). Advantages of this system are that it is easier to follow for both workers and management, and is probably less fatiguing to personnel than the rotating shift system. Disadvantages are that the night shifts are out of contact with daytime supervision, and there will be heavy pressure on you to award preferred shift assignments on the basis of seniority. The latter can lead to a serious unbalance in shift capability.

For a five-day week, simply assign personnel to the first, second, and third shift. The one basic question to be answered concerns the start and end of the work week: should it begin at 11 P.M. Sunday and end at 11 P.M. Friday, or should it begin at 7 A.M. Monday and end at 7 A.M. Saturday? In the absence of any overriding technical requirement which affects starting time, choose the former system because it avoids having two full shifts in operation after daytime supervision has left for the week.

For a seven-day week, when the plant operates twenty-four hours per day for seven days per week, four shifts are required, usually designated by the letters A, B, C, and D. A typical fixed-shift, seven-day schedule is shown in Figure 4-4. The three lettered shifts A, B, and C have permanent assignments on the first, second, and third shifts, respectively. D is the "swing shift," which fills in on the days off for the other three shifts, and therefore has a rotating schedule of its own.

The seven-day schedule has a basic problem: four groups working five days per week can cover only 20 shifts, but there are 21 shifts in the calendar week. There are two ways to make up the difference. One is to schedule one of the groups to work six days per week on a regular basis, and in Figure 4-4 Shift A was chosen for this assignment. Another is to train one "relief" worker to handle the jobs of each group of five workers on the shift, and let the relief worker relieve them a day at a time.

(2) Rotating shifts. Personnel are assigned to lettered shifts—A, B, C, and D—which take turns working the first, second, and third shifts. Advantages are that each shift shares equally in the inconveniences of night work, making assignment of personnel to the various shifts far less controversial; and daytime management is assured of meeting each shift regularly for a series of full days. Disadvantages are more complex work schedules, and the greater difficulty experienced by workers in adjusting to the constantly changing hours of work.

For a five-day week, assign personnel to three lettered shifts (A, B, and C),

	M	T	W	T	F	S	S
1st Shift (7–3)	A	A	A	A	A	A	D
2nd Shift (3–11)	B	B	B	B	D	D	B
3rd Shift (11–7)	C	C	D	D	C	C	C

FIGURE 4-4: Fixed Shift, Seven-Day Schedule

and schedule each group on first, second, and third shifts in weekly rotation. Some plants prefer to rotate every two or three weeks to give employees a better chance to become acclimated to the different working hours.

For a seven-day week, the most complicated of all the schedules, four lettered shifts are needed (just as in the fixed seven-day schedule), but there is no "swing shift." There is an almost endless variety of rotating shift schedules in use, with cycles ranging from four to twenty weeks.

Figure 4-5 shows a four-week, seven-day, rotating cycle. Each lettered shift is scheduled for an extra day when it comes on the 8-4 shift, but a "relief worker" can be set up for every five positions on the shift to avoid having anyone work overtime. Note that although the other three shifts work only five days in the calendar week, they actually work seven days in a row; because of this their days off keep advancing through the week until they finally achieve a long weekend. For example, C shift is off Sunday of the third week and Monday and Tuesday of the fourth week. The calendar for three months of the particular year has been superimposed on this schedule to show how a printed card or mimeographed sheet can be made up to help employees keep track of their assignments.

HOW TO ESTABLISH A PRODUCTION REPORTING SYSTEM

Every manufacturing plant needs a record of its production activities; this information is essential to the making of routine decisions such as when to replace raw material inventory, and when and how to ship orders to customers. Accurate production records are also required for the calculation of product manufacturing costs. With such simple resources as a clerk working with raw production data

Jul				1	2	3	4		5	6	7	8	9	10	11 Jul
Jul	26	27	28	29	30	31	1		2	3	4	5	6	7	8 Aug
Aug	23	24	25	26	27	28	29		30	31	1	2	3	4	5 Sep
Sep	20	21	22	23	24	25	26		27	28	29	30	1	2	3 Oct
	M	*T*	*W*	*T*	*F*	*S*	*S*		*M*	*T*	*W*	*T*	*F*	*S*	*S*
12-8	C	C	D	D	D	D	D		D	D	A	A	A	A	A
8-4	A_1	A_2	A_3	A_4	A_5	A	B		B_1	B_2	B_3	B_4	B_5	B	C
4-12	B	B	B	B	C	C	C		C	C	C	C	D	D	D
Jul	12	13	14	15	16	17	18		19	20	21	22	23	24	25 Jul
Aug	9	10	11	12	13	14	15		16	17	18	19	20	21	22 Aug
Sep	6	7	8	9	10	11	12		13	14	15	16	17	18	19 Sep
	M	*T*	*W*	*T*	*F*	*S*	*S*		*M*	*T*	*W*	*T*	*F*	*S*	*S*
12-8	A	A	B	B	B	B	B		B	B	C	C	C	C	C
8-4	C_1	C_2	C_3	C_4	C_5	C	D		D_1	D_2	D_3	D_4	D_5	D	A
4-12	D	D	D	D	A	A	A		A	A	A	A	B	B	B

FIGURE 4-5: Rotating Shift, Seven-Day Schedule, with Calendar Superimposed. Subscripts indicate "relief days" for each shift position.

and a desk calculator, you can obtain the information you need to take action on trends in productivity, inventory levels, product quality, and costs. Finally, production records enable you to take the first step in the control phase of the management cycle by asking the question: Where are we compared to where we ought to be?

What to Include in Production Reports

For designated time periods (hour, shift, day) record the following:

The quantity of material produced.

The quantities of finished goods produced that are salable, require reworking, or must be scrapped.

The total quantities of raw materials consumed.

The process conditions prevailing at stated intervals—number of lines operating, number of machines in use, pressures, temperatures, flow rates.

Inventory levels of raw materials, finished goods, and supplies.

Usage of man-hours, supplies, and utilities.

How to Collect Production Data. A *job ticket* (or batch card, work ticket, job order, batch sheet, and many other names) is a printed form that accompanies the work as it is processed from stage to stage through the plant. It carries the lot, job, or batch number and gives instructions on what raw materials are to be used and how they are to be processed. It becomes a production record when spaces are provided for the operators to sign off operations as they are completed, and to enter the quantities of material used, the time spent in each operation, and the quality results at each step.

As job tickets are collected from the end of the process, they are tabulated to build a picture of the plant's production rate, quality record, and cost performance. Once filed, they can be used at any time later for tracing the history of any production lot—especially when customer complaints arise.

A *shift log* is used at the end of each shift. The foreman makes a written record of the shift activities—the routine (units produced, machines in operation, people present), the unusual (absences, equipment breakdowns, late raw materials), and problems he or she foresees for the relieving shift.

Have the printer make up a log book with perforated pages (for easy tear-out) and carbon paper, so that when the foreman writes the shift log a copy is automatically made. The original is forwarded to the production superintendent or you, but the copy is left in the book to become a valuable reference, not only for the relieving foreman, but especially for one who has been away on a long shift changeover or on vacation.

An *operator's log* is another helpful tool. Ask the print shop to make up an 18-by-24-inch sheet. The horizontal lines will be for each hour of the day; the vertical columns will represent various pieces of equipment or instruments to be read. As the shift progresses, readings are taken of process conditions by the hour, and the completed sheet is sent to the production manager in the morning. This method is especially well adapted to continuous operations.

MAKING EFFECTIVE USE OF MANPOWER

Chronic shortages of labor and the high cost of available people make compelling reasons for any manager to avoid wasting manpower in operations. Follow these lines of action:

1. Keep the work force flexible. The more kinds of work each employee can perform, the better the manpower utilization.

2. Have plans ready for slow periods. Cleanup, painting, repairs, scrap rework—all can be used to utilize manpower effectively when production operations are at an ebb.

3. Develop and maintain the attitude that all employees are expected to be engaged in useful activity during working hours.

4. If flexibility is not a prime consideration, then be sure that all plant work is performed at the lowest possible skill level.

5. Consider the use of manpower pools for the entire plant, rather than duplicate reserves of workers within each department.

6. Provide sufficient supervision. When the ratio of supervisors to workers drops too low, even the best motivated workers waste time trying to find someone to give them new assignments or to whom they can report a production holdup.

7. Provide effective support services. Materials should be on time, machines in good repair, and tools and supplies readily available.

How to Control Outside Personnel Working in the Plant

It is inevitable that there will be people working in your plant who do not belong to your organization—truck drivers, utility company workers, sales and delivery people, cleaning service personnel. While deliberately hostile acts—theft, industrial spying, disturbing regular employees—are rare, there is a significant danger from outside personnel not knowing the safety hazards and precautions required on the premises. Use these methods to keep control of the situation:

1. Designate one of your supervisors to be responsible for each kind of outside employee—maintenance foreman for utility workers, project engineer for contractors' personnel, personnel supervisor for vending machine servicemen. Your employees should know when outside personnel enter the plant, when they leave, and what they do while in it.

2. Identify visitors clearly. Use special visitor's badges; if safety hard hats are required in the plant, use a special color for visitors.

3. Issue written instructions to outside personnel. One company has a printed card—about 8 by 10 inches—which the gate guard hands to every truck driver

and picks up from him as he leaves. It tells the driver where he can and cannot go in the plant, what facilities (lunchroom, rest room, smoking area) he may use, whether he can leave his engine running, and any safety precautions he must take.

When outside contractors' personnel first enter the plant to begin work, the project engineer should give them a one-page set of safety instructions and review them with each outside worker. All too often newspaper accounts of a serious plant fire end with "... authorities believe the blaze was ignited by an outside welder's torch."

CONCLUSION

In this chapter we have dealt with the problems common to all manufacturing plants—production scheduling, the use of overtime, start-ups and shutdowns, emergency procedures, holiday and shift operations, the utilization of manpower, and outside personnel working in the plant. Throughout the techniques developed to handle these varied problems runs the basic theme of the management cycle: the need to make plans and prepare for contingencies, to organize the work group and assign its members to the mutual advantage of themselves and the company, and to establish reliable methods of monitoring and controlling the operation.

Chapter 5

How to Develop a Cost-Effective Maintenance Operation

The list of functions performed by the maintenance department is truly imposing: it repairs inoperable equipment, maintains equipment so as to prevent break-downs, handles small-to-medium sized capital projects, operates equipment (boilers, compressed air systems, cooling towers) to supply some utilities and monitor the receipt of others, provides or purchases painting, cleaning, trash removal and other services, and keeps track of the capital equipment inventory. The way it handles these responsibilities affects overall plant performance in five major areas—production, quality, cost, safety, and housekeeping.

The successful fulfillment of these functions, however, is not accomplishment enough. The cost of maintenance, like all other plant costs, ends up in the price of the plant's products which must make their way in the competitive marketplace. This chapter is designed not only to help you develop a maintenance organization that gets its assigned work done competently but also uses manpower efficiently and controls its own costs closely.

FLEXIBILITY—KEY TO ORGANIZING THE MAINTENANCE DEPARTMENT

Depending upon the size of the plant and the nature of its operations, several or more of the following crafts and skills will be needed in the maintenance group:

Rigging	Insulating	Firefighting and Safety
Pipefitting	Machining	Painting

Millwright	Electrical Repair and Installation	Custodial Work
Machining		Welding
Masonry–Plastering	Instrument Repair and Installation	Lubrication
Mechanics		Carpentry
Heating-Ventilating-Air Conditioning Operation and Repair	Motor Vehicle Repair	Stockroom Operation
	Tool and Die Work	

This list is awkwardly worded because it deliberately avoids terms like "Carpenters," "Pipefitters," or "Riggers," to drive home the point that one of the manager's chief goals in organizing a Maintenance Department is to achieve flexibility—the right to assign a single maintenance employee to a number of different jobs. More and more management is refusing to go along with the notion that when an electrician needs to put up a few boards to support temporarily a stretch of conduit he must call a carpenter to do it; instead the maintenance worker is asked to perform tasks related to the job but not necessarily included in a narrow definition of his craft.

The plant manager who chooses to organize a Maintenance Department along traditional lines would hire craftsmen with the skills shown above and divide them into groups like these, each led by a foreman:

Group 1	*Group 2*	*Group 3*	*Group 4*
Riggers	Insulators	Electricians	Machinists
Millwrights	Pipefitters	Instrument Mechanics	Mechanics
Masons	Firemen		Oilers
Carpenters	Janitors	Welders	Motor Vehicle Mechanics
Painters	Tool Crib Attendance	Air Conditioning Mechanics	Tool & Die Makers

This structure would be suitable to a large maintenance organization where many craft skills are required and enough work available to keep the craftsmen employed in their specialized areas. But such conditions are rare, and most plant managers are better advised to seek a more flexible structure like the Operator Grade System described on pp. 48–50 and in Figure 3-5, in which there are no craft position titles but everyone is described only as a mechanic and in moving upward through the grade structure is rewarded for acquiring a diversity of skills. The result is a much more cost-effective organization, in which manpower is used at maximum efficiency.

A further step toward complete flexibility is a system in which all plant hourly employees are first hired into the maintenance group. Those with long experience in high grade maintenance skills can be quickly and permanently assigned to work using their specialties. The remainder are given a combination of training and work assignments in basic maintenance. When those who do not remain permanently with the maintenance group take up assignments in the production and warehousing units, they will be able and expected to perform some maintenance work themselves—especially valuable on second and third shifts. Because of their experience these employees will better understand how to operate equipment so as to avoid maintenance problems.

HOW TO SET UP A SCHEDULING SYSTEM IN THREE SIMPLE STEPS

The key to a cost-effective maintenance operation is establishing management control, and the first step in control is the scheduling of maintenance activity. Follow these steps to get a maintenance scheduling system started:

1. Convene a weekly meeting of the plant manager, maintenance superintendent and foremen, and appropriate production supervisors. The meeting should be held late in the week (Thursday or Friday) to take advantage of the latest possible information concerning the amount of work that must be carried over from the current week and the extent of new work orders received.

2. Schedule all maintenance work that requires two or more man-hours to complete for the following week.

   Figure 5-1 is an example of a maintenance schedule for a plant with six maintenance workers. It shows how their time is to be allocated to a series of planned maintenance jobs during a particular week. All 48 hours of worker time available each day is accounted for, although the last assignment on the list, "Minor Work Orders," provides some time for jobs too small to schedule and for emergencies. This schedule can be developed into an even more useful form by adding columns showing the actual hours expended on each job, and by listing below the scheduled items the backlog of jobs waiting to be scheduled in future weeks.

3. Have the schedule duplicated, posted, and distributed to foremen, supervisors, and managers of interested or affected departments—production, shipping, engineering, office and laboratory.

Four Benefits of Maintenance Scheduling

These are the benefits you should expect to derive from maintenance scheduling:

1. It guides the maintenance foreman into better planning practices. If he knows early in the week that on Thursday leaks in the hydraulic system of #2 Stamping Machine are going to be repaired, he will be asking himself questions like "Who is the best mechanic for that job?" "What special materials or tools will be needed?" "When should I see the production foreman about preparing the machine for maintenance work?" Without a scheduling system no such "thinking ahead" may occur.

2. Supervisors of the departments in which the work is to be performed are given ample notice and time in which to shut down the affected equipment and have it prepared properly for maintenance work. They also gain the opportunity

THE XYZ CORPORATION

Beaver Falls Plant

Maintenance Schedule for Week of April 29, 19X7

	MON	TUES	WED	THURS	FRI
Clean and Overhaul #2 Boiler	3/8	3/8	3/8		
Replace Battery, Lift Truck #5	2/2				
Clean Cooling Tower Suction Screens and Test Sump for Leaks	1/4				
Replace Motor #2 Conveyor		2/4			
Replace Blades, Sheet Metal Shear		2/3			
Electric Chain Hoists—Safety Inspection and Preventive Maintenance			1/8	1/8	
Repaint Parking Lot Stripes			1/6	1/6	
Main Office Air Conditioning System—Inspection, Cleaning, Leak Testing				2/8	
Repair Hydraulic System Leaks, #2 Stamping Machine				1/8	
Replace Space Heater, NW Corner of Warehouse					3/4
Repair Steam Trap Leaks, Main Plant Heating System					2/4
Move Accounting Department File Cabinets					2/2
Instrument Calibration and Scale Testing					2/8
Routine Lubrication Program	1/2	1/2	1/2	1/2	
V-Belt Inspection	1/8				
Minor Work Orders	1/6	1/8	1/8	1/8	1/8

Symbols: 3/4 = three workers assigned for four hours

FIGURE 5-1: Sample Maintenance Schedule

to schedule production activities around the planned equipment outage, avoiding the use of costly overtime.

3. You will have—and should take advantage of—the ready-made chance to participate in the preparation of the maintenance schedule and thus be sure that *your own order of priority* is used in programming the work. You will be aware of the man-hours planned for each job, and can keep track of the backlog of jobs awaiting action. The file of completed schedules becomes a handy source of information for your reports and for studies you may want of trends in maintenance activity and performance.

4. The first important step toward the development of a preventive maintenance program has been taken. The basic concept of preventive maintenance—taking equipment out of service for routine overhaul on a preplanned basis—virtually requires a maintenance scheduling system.

MAJOR AND MINOR WORK ORDERS

The first step in keeping track of the work performed by the Maintenance Department is to establish a work order system and insist that every job performed be covered by a major or minor work order. The term "minor" indicates a job estimated by the originator to cost less than $300 (or any appropriate figure set by you).

Figure 5-2 shows a minor work order form which can be printed and bound in pads, with alternate white and yellow copies. The originator uses a carbon, forwards the white copy to the maintenance foreman, and keeps the yellow copy for follow-up. Have the printer number the forms serially; it will help the originator, the Maintenance Department, and the Accounting Department (if the completed form is used for charging out costs) locate filed orders more easily.

You should have the maintenance supervisor bring the file of uncompleted work orders to the weekly schedule meeting. In this way you can keep yourself informed of the size of the maintenance backlog and the priorities observed by the maintenance supervision.

The major work order form shown in Figure 5-3 is used for projects whose cost falls between the maximum allowed on a minor work order and the minimum for which a special capital appropriation request is required. (Some plants use the major work order form even when a capital request is submitted, as a means of keeping track of the work in a uniform filing system.)

THE XYZ CORPORATION

Beaver Falls Plant

No. 89463

MAINTENANCE JOB ORDER (MINOR)

Date Written _____ Date Required _____ Charge Account No. _____

Describe Work to be Done _____

_____

_____

_____

Signed_____
(Originator)

FIGURE 5-2: Minor Maintenance Work Order

THE XYZ CORPORATION

Beaver Falls Plant

No. 3649

MAINTENANCE JOB ORDER (MAJOR)

Date Written _____ Date Required _____ Dept. _____ Page _____ of _____

Building _____ Location _____ Ref. Maps _____

Charge Costs to: Account No. _____ Capital Approp. No. _____

DESCRIPTION OF WORK (Include sketch of equipment.)

REASONS FOR WORK (Include economic justification when appropriate.)

Signed _____

(Originator)

COSTS	ESTIMATED	ACTUAL	REQUIREMENTS	APPROVALS
Matls. Labor Contr.			Equipment Downtime	Dept. Supv. _____
				Maint. Fmn. _____
TOTAL			Equip. Preparation	Plant Engr. _____
				Proj. Engr. _____
			Safety Permits	Plant Mgr. _____

FIGURE 5-3: Major Work Order Form

The originator of the major work order form is asked, in keeping with the larger expenditure of money, to supply more information about the project he or she is requesting. A more complete description of the work is required, as well as a statement of the reasons for doing it and the economic justification. The originator must obtain a series of approvals, and is asked to outline the requirements of equipment preparation, downtime, and safety permits. The maintenance supervisor or the project engineer estimates the cost of the job before the approvals are given, and inserts the actual costs when it is completed.

The form for Figure 5-3 should be made up by a printer and numbered serially; it can be printed on "carbonless" carbon paper, or if that system will not produce enough copies, on plain stock and the completed form duplicated on an office copier and distributed to those concerned with the work.

HOW TO DEVELOP A PREVENTIVE MAINTENANCE PROGRAM

The object of the preventive maintenance (PM) program is to inspect and repair equipment *before*, rather than *after*, its sudden breakdown impairs production, quality, safety, or cost performance. The program involves deciding what pieces of equipment are to be taken out of service periodically, which components of that equipment are to be repaired, replaced, or adjusted, and how often it is to be done. The format can be as simple as the handwritten reminders in a foreman's notebook or as elaborate as a computerized system that compiles a record of past PM activities and projects them for months and even years into the future.

Advantages of a Preventive Maintenance Program

A preventive maintenance program appropriate to the size and complexity of the operation is a must if you are to meet your overall performance goals. Look for these advantages from your PM program:

- **Fewer unplanned outages of equipment.** Sudden breakdowns interfere with timely delivery to customers, waste managerial time, and impair employee morale.
- **Better control of repair costs.** Emergency breakdowns are usually repaired on overtime and may involve expensive transportation arrangements and high prices for repair parts and services. Production overtime and extra transportation costs to serve customers must be added to this bill.
- **Improved safety conditions.** The sudden collapse of operating equipment may be accompanied by severe safety hazards such as flying debris, overheating, high pressure, discharge of flammable or hazardous material, high electrical currents, fire, or explosion.
- **Extended equipment life.** Equipment that is routinely inspected, lubricated, and overhauled can be counted on to sustain a longer operating life.
- **Better product quality.** Process equipment that has gotten out of adjustment but is still running can cause a high quality reject rate. This is especially true of equipment with cutting edges, closely calibrated mechanisms, and control instruments. The preventive maintenance program can be designed to ensure that critical equipment is kept in top operating condition.

Guidelines for Determining Timing of PM Activities

Carried to its logical extreme, the idea of preventive maintenance would involve periodically shutting down and overhauling everything from the office pencil sharpener to the largest hydraulic press. This is neither physically possible nor economically optimum. Instead, use these guidelines to determine the selection and timing of PM activities:

1. Decide what is critical. Will downtime on a given piece of equipment subject the plant to severe safety hazards? Shut down other processing departments? Seriously delay customer deliveries? Cause product spoilage? If so, preventive maintenance is clearly indicated; if not, it may not be worth the expense.

2. Include PM in purchasing decisions. Consult present owners of proposed brands of equipment to determine incidence of breakdowns, frequency and extent of preventive maintenance required, and whether it is subjectable to PM procedures.

3. Make use of manufacturer's recommendations. They can be especially helpful for new equipment on which there is no plant history.

4. Conduct inspections. Periodic inspection of equipment will reveal not only whether it needs to be taken out of service for repair of expected defects, but the nature and extent of unexpected defects as well.

5. Use plant experience and history. If a pump bearing in rough service repeatedly wears out between 12 and 15 weeks, schedule it for preventive maintenance once a quarter.

6. Solicit the advice of mechanics, operators, and production supervisors. The people who work most closely with the equipment will have valuable ideas about what is likely to go wrong and when.

What to Include in Your PM Program

What are the specific techniques to be used in establishing a preventive maintenance program? They will vary from plant to plant because the choices are influenced by the type of equipment to be serviced, the hazards involved in equipment failure, plant economics, and the degree of production reliability that the plant must maintain to satisfy its customers. The following fundamentals, however, are common to all PM systems:

1. The heart of a preventive maintenance program is its record-keeping system. For each piece of equipment covered by the program a record must be established; it can be a page in a foreman's notebook, a record card with such information as the make and model of the machine, serial number, date of installation, and relevant technical specifications, or a computerized record with the same information (see Chapter 21, p. 438). Whichever form is used, it should also show the inspection and maintenance procedures to be followed when the equipment is down for PM, provide spaces for entering scheduled and actual dates

of maintenance, and have a section for remarks by the inspecting personnel. Both computerized records and the equipment cards (by use of punched holes around the edges) can be set up to allow sorting by useful classifications, such as frequency of maintenance, type of equipment, or plant departments.

2. PM goes hand and glove with maintenance scheduling. The weekly scheduling meeting provides a convenient forum in which to discuss plans for PM activities; those not scheduled for the week immediately ahead are listed in the backlog section of the maintenance schedule where they cannot be forgotten and provide maximum notice to those concerned of upcoming events in the PM program.

3. Get the most out of equipment downtime. Mechanics should not only perform the routine inspections and parts replacement called for in the PM procedures, but should look for all signs of possible trouble. If they are found and there is not time to repair them immediately, production and maintenance supervisors can work out a future schedule for repair before the equipment is likely to fail.

How far to go in replacing parts while the machine is down? It is a matter of experience and economics; in a plant where repair labor and production downtime are expensive it may pay to replace all or most of the minor, inexpensive parts of a machine that could cause failure. The price of a $15.00 part is certainly worthwhile insurance against a $2,000 outage.

4. Follow-up is an indispensable ingredient. In addition to your weekly involvement through the scheduling procedure, you will want maintenance supervision to draw up comprehensive annual plans for the program and to submit periodic reports on its progress and findings. These reports should be structured so as to bring out the cost comparison between the PM program and the old "fix 'em when they fail" methods. In the absence of such follow-up the program may simply fade away, with plant personnel finding all sorts of reasons for postponing PM activities until the point of extinction is reached.

BEYOND PREVENTIVE MAINTENANCE:
THE BENEFITS OF PREDICTIVE MAINTENANCE

Why Periodic Shutdowns May Not Be Possible for Your Operation

As valuable as the results of a good preventive maintenance program may be, some managers may still find that periodic shutdowns are not feasible. Their situations have the following characteristics:

1. Intervals between equipment failures vary considerably. Setting the correct PM interval for a machine which ran for three years on one occasion but broke down at seven months on another can be a puzzle; a six-month period would prevent any surprise outages, but would result in five unnecessary inspections during the three-year period.

2. The equipment is complicated and requires delicate adjustments. Disassembly and routine parts replacement may cause such machinery to run worse after inspection than before. A long run-in period may be required, with attendant off-grade production.

3. The equipment is large, shutdown is expensive, and it is part of a process train with equipment arranged in series. A good example is an ammonia plant: when its main gas compressor is shut down, the whole plant is out of service. The capacity of such plants has gradually been increased to 1,100 tons per day; when ammonia sells at $200 per ton the cost of a 24-hour outage in lost revenue alone is $220,000.

Monitoring Devices for Predictive Maintenance

Managers with problems of this type, which call for inspection methods that do not require shutdown and disassembly, are turning to the techniques of *predictive maintenance*. Its tools are monitoring devices that measure various physical conditions of equipment while it is running; sudden changes in the measurements provide the signals to arrange for shutdown and repair. Vibration testers are prime examples of predictive maintenance devices; they can measure the amplitude and frequency of vibrations in rotating machinery in three dimensions. If they are connected to electronic analyzers, the combination is a sophisticated tool that not only warns something is wrong, but may be able to tell what is causing the trouble. That knowledge reduces costs by permitting the Maintenance Department to prepare more effectively for the shutdown and to limit the scope of maintenance work to be performed.

More ordinary instruments are also used for this work; ammeters and watt-meters can be connected to the motors that power machinery. Operators soon become accustomed to their readings under normal conditions, and can notify the Maintenance Department when abnormal readings occur indicating changes in a machine's condition. Recording thermometers can be attached to bearings; a rise in temperature can indicate lubrication failure or excessive wear. Radiographic equipment that uses gamma rays to measure wall thickness can be installed to follow the progress of corrosion in pipe, tubing, and tanks; repair or replacement of the metal structure can be delayed until a point safely short of critical reduction of the metal thickness is reached.

Predictive maintenance devices such as ammeters and recording thermometers are usually installed permanently on one machine so that base readings can be established. More expensive devices and those that might not withstand plant conditions, such as radiographic equipment, are kept in protected areas and brought into the plant for periodic tests on a number of different machines.

THREE STEPS TO DESIGNING MORE FUNCTIONAL SHOP FACILITIES

From the plant manager's point of view, the key to successful development of maintenance shop facilities is to be sure that they match the needs of the plant precisely. You should require that requests for maintenance equipment be accompanied by economic justification just as cogent as you would require for production equipment. The cost of production losses must be carefully weighed against the cost of specialized maintenance equipment with full consideration of an important third factor: the availability and cost of outside repair services in the plant area.

There are three distinct steps to take in the design and specification of maintenance facilities.

Step 1: Lay Out the Functional Areas

Work benches, storage, machine groupings, welding and painting facilities will each claim separate areas of the shop.

The storage area will need suitable shelves and racks to hold minimum inventories of parts and supplies—pipe and fittings, fasteners, sheet metal, gaskets, seals, lubricants, wood, and electrical parts.

Welding and painting areas will require curtains, partitions, and ventilating equipment to protect the safety and comfort of workers using them and those in the general area.

Work benches should not be assigned to individual employees, but should be functional for the type of work performed—one for mechanical work, another for electrical work, sheet metal operations, and so on. In this way attention is focused on the work performed, and no one lays a claim to a particular part of the shop.

Step 2: Select the Major Shop Tools

Your shop may need highly specialized tools for maintaining the particular equipment of your industry; in addition, the typical shop will need grinders, pipe threaders, bench saws, lathes, welders, and drill presses. The number, size, complexity, and degree of automation of each should be economically justified.

Step 3: Provide Auxiliary Equipment

This includes hydraulic lift tables, automatic hoists, roller conveyors, and lift trucks for easy handling of equipment to be worked on; wheeled toolboxes, and motorized carts for moving individuals quickly to and from jobs in the plant. Other examples of auxiliary equipment would include a pickup truck or station wagon for moving small loads and making trips to hardware stores and supply points outside the plant, as well as instruments, testers, and gauges.

TIME RECORDS AND CHARGING OF COSTS

The Maintenance Department is a service department, and all of its expenses should be charged out to the plant departments which use its services. Expenditures to maintain the shop itself are overhead costs that are included in the charges to the departments. The major and minor work order forms provide the most convenient means for distributing maintenance costs. The originator of either document is required to include the operating account expense number or the capital appropriation number to which the cost of the work is to be charged. (Maintenance supervision should be instructed not to accept a work order without a suitable account number, and to raise questions if they doubt that the originator has the authority to charge costs to the account number given.) When the job is completed the total costs of labor and materials can be entered on the work order, which is forwarded to the Cost Department for posting to the proper accounts.

Individual time records have a dual purpose—they record the proportion of a mechanic's time applied to each of the jobs worked on, and therefore provide a way of costing out all of the mechanic's time. They are also used to compare the time expended on a particular job with established standards or previous executions of the same job.

There are several ways of keeping individual time records. One is to print a form on the back of the work order. Each mechanic who works on the job enters his name or clock number, the time he spends on the job, and any materials he uses. A maintenance department clerk or someone in the Accounting Department can cross-total the hours listed to be sure each mechanic's time is fully accounted for.

Another way is to have each mechanic fill out a separate card for each day's work, showing the time spent on each job. Maintenance supervision collects these cards at the end of each day, checks to see that each person's time is fully accounted for, and forwards them to the Cost Department for posting to the appropriate account numbers.

No matter what system is used, the collected papers—completed work orders, time cards, and material requisitions associated with the job—should be forwarded to the originator after they have been through the Accounting Department. The originator has a right to check out the charges, to see that they have been properly allocated, and to discuss with maintenance supervision any question he or she may have about the costs charged to the account.

PURCHASE, STORAGE, AND CONTROL OF MAINTENANCE SUPPLIES

You need to assure yourself of four results from your maintenance stores program: (1) that supplies are purchased at the lowest available price; (2) that they are used economically in the plant with little waste, (3) that they are charged out to the jobs and departments that actually use them; and (4) that critical supplies are available when needed.

Techniques for Stores Purchasing

Obtain competitive bids before choosing suppliers. There is a tendency for maintenance supervision to buy from the nearest suppliers and those that offer the most convenient service. Usually, however, competitors can be found who will match the best service available in order to get the business.

Write annual contracts to get the largest discounts.

Whenever possible have the supplier, rather than your storeroom, maintain inventories.

Involve members of the Purchasing Department in the stores program. They can offer professional assistance in dealing with suppliers on the three previous points.

How to Control Stores Usage

These are the basic principles in the control of stores usage in the plant:

1. Keep small, valuable, and "popular" items in specially locked compartments.
2. Very inexpensive items (nuts, bolts, small pipe fittings) may not be worth the expense of cataloguing and following with paper work. They can be declared "free stock" and kept in bins in the shop for general usage without requisitions.
3. Conduct periodic inventories and audits, just as you would for production materials and supplies.
4. Control the issuance of supplies:
   a. The large plant may use several storerooms, with a trained storekeeper manning each one. All items are listed in a printed catalogue with a control number suited to electronic data processing. Stores are issued only by written requisition showing the job or account number to be charged. Information from the requisition slips is fed into a computer to charge out costs, keep a perpetual total inventory in dollars, and remind the storekeeper when a reorder point is reached for any item.
   b. In a medium-sized plant, there will generally be one storeroom with a full-time storekeeper. It may not have a printed catalogue, but requisitions are required; posting of charges to job numbers and accounts is done manually, as well as the monitoring of inventory for reorder.
   c. In a small plant, storekeeping may be a part-time job for a maintenance foreman, clerk, or other Maintenance Department employee. The requisitioner may be simply required to sign out for materials in a log book. The maintenance clerk or someone from the Accounting Department charges out costs periodically from the log book to the using department. Reordering is based on visual inspection.

To be sure that supplies will be on hand when needed:

Classify all stores items into critical and noncritical categories. Critical items are those that would result in unacceptable production delays or safety hazards if they are not on hand.

Establish maximum and minimum stock levels and reorder points for the critical items. The reorder point is set far enough above the minimum level to allow for anticipated usage during the period between reorder and delivery of the material.

WHEN TO EMPLOY OUTSIDE CONTRACTORS

All manufacturing plants use outside contractor services for various maintenance and project jobs from time to time, for these reasons:

They can handle peak loads without disrupting the normal work of the regular plant maintenance staff.

They complement plant forces, supplying skills which the latter may not have.

They can do some (or possibly all) of the maintenance work more cheaply.

Outside contractors are used to supply these services:

1. Maintenance operations that are sporadic, seasonal, or require specialized skills: painting, cleaning, window washing, vermin control, landscaping, testing and adjustment of scales, servicing control instruments, boiler cleaning, and railroad track repair.

2. Major equipment overhauls and capital projects.

3. All or part of regular mechanical maintenance operations. This is the famous "contract maintenance" question, and in deciding whether to have some or all of the maintenance work performed by outside contractors keep these points in mind: If yours is a new plant you can start out with all contract maintenance and change to regular maintenance forces later, but you probably can't do it the other way around. The cost charged per hour of contract labor will seem high compared to the base rate of your own workers, but the cost of fringes, supervision, and other types of overhead must be added to your workers' base rates. There is a high cost penalty for having permanent personnel on the payroll during slack periods.

When outside help is being considered or is actually in the plant, take these precautions:

1. Satisfy yourself that the contractor under consideration is capable of maintaining administrative and working control over his own forces. Featherbedding and sloppy work practices in your plant are going to cost you money, no matter whose employees are involved.

2. If either his shop or yours is nonunion, and the other unionized, iron out any possible problems with all parties concerned before any outside forces report to work.

3. Make sure that all outside personnel are trained in, understand, and actually follow plant safety rules.

4. There is a natural tendency for outside personnel to use or borrow your tools and supplies. Clarify the question of who supplies these items beforehand, and instruct your people to refuse requests outside of those arrangements.

HOW TO MEASURE MAINTENANCE DEPARTMENT PERFORMANCE

In this chapter we have given the Maintenance Department its organizational structure, established work order and cost recording systems, and installed preventive and/or predictive maintenance programs. The big question remaining is this: How well is the department performing? To provide the answers take the following steps:

Establish work standards for maintenance labor. This can be as simple as the foreman estimating that it will take two workers a half day to perform a certain job—in fact, the mere act of scheduling requires him to make such a judgment. When the same job is repeated many times through the course of a year (such as the replacement of filter elements in a dust collection system), a standard number of man-hours for the completion of the job can be readily established and all future executions of the job measured against standard. When it is undesirable to wait until a substantial history can be built up, or when there are too many tasks and not enough people to gather the past history, standards can be obtained from outside sources, such as the U.S. Navy Department Maintenance Standards.

Develop numerical indexes to follow trends. The simplest measures of performance would be the total dollars spent per month to run the department, the cost of labor, or supplies, or the number of overtime hours. For these figures to have any useful meaning, however, the important plant operating conditions—volume of production, number of machines, hourly wage rates—would have to remain the same from month to month. Because this is so rarely the case, managers can select from the following list of ratios to measure various aspects of maintenance department performance:

For Overall Department Performance

> Maintenance Costs: Manufacturing Costs
>
> Maintenance Costs: Units of Production
>
> Maintenance Costs: Sales Volume in Dollars
>
> Maintenance Costs: Capital Cost of Plant

For Performance Within the Department

> Actual Job Time: Standard Job Time
>
> Maintenance Job Orders (MJO) Received: MJOs Completed
>
> Maintenance Labor Costs: Maintenance Material Costs
>
> Overtime Hours: Total Hours
>
> Cost of Supervision: Total Maintenance Costs

For Effectiveness of Preventive Maintenance Programs

> Scheduled Maintenance Hours: Total Maintenance Hours
>
> Emergency Maintenance Hours: Total Maintenance Hours
>
> Machine Downtime Hours for Maintenance: Hours Scheduled for Operation

Most plants will not find it feasible to use all of these ratios, and might find it too confusing to attempt to follow so many trends even if they could. Choose those ratios that seem the most appropriate to the circumstances in your plant, then follow their trends and, as shown in the following Operating Example, interpret them *in relation to each other* to derive their most cogent meaning.

Operating Example 5-1: Using Maintenance Ratios to Pinpoint a Problem. A plant manager who follows the ratio of total maintenance costs to plant capital cost is disturbed at what appears to be an alarming trend in this index over the past year. The monthly ratio figures (multiplied by 1,000 to make them easier to work with) are

JAN	1.67	JUL	1.97
FEB	1.83	AUG	2.08
MAR	1.75	SEP	2.10
APR	1.91	OCT	1.99
MAY	1.94	NOV	2.11
JUN	2.01	DEC	2.09

Not only does the ratio show a definite upward trend through the year, but it stands 31 percent higher at the end of the year than at the beginning. Knowing that labor accounts for 80 percent of her maintenance costs, the manager is inclined to feel that the maintenance crews are not performing as well as they should, and that perhaps sloppy work practices are beginning to creep in. Before taking action on this conclusion however, she decides to review another index that is routinely reported—the ratio of actual job time to standard job time. The figures for this ratio over the same period are

JAN	1.02	JUL	.97
FEB	.99	AUG	1.01
MAR	1.01	SEP	1.01
APR	1.03	OCT	.97
MAY	.98	NOV	.94
JUN	1.06	DEC	1.02

These data present a very different picture: they fall within a narrow range, and if there is any discernible trend it is slightly downward. Therefore, sloppy work practices by the maintenance crews are not the answer to the upward trend in the ratio of maintenance costs to capital costs. By comparing trends in the two ratios the manager is able to avoid a morale-damaging confrontation and is guided to look elsewhere for the cause of the problem. In this case, she reviews the problem with the maintenance superintendent and discovers that four of the plant's eleven production machines have been breaking down with increasing frequency; the maintenance crews, however, have been responding promptly and getting the repairs done in standard time. When the two review the equipment records they realize that these machines have reached the age where they are prime candidates for replacement.

Chapter 6

How to Establish a Pervasive Quality Control Plan

Putting out a product that maintains existing quality levels by routinely meeting specifications is no longer enough. The relentless pressure of competition from other manufacturers, domestic and foreign, creates a demand for product integrity (see page 17) and ever-increasing customer expectations for improved quality which must be met if the company is to survive. This chapter deals with the technical details of establishing a quality control program. It starts with the broadest aspects of quality—the whole array of concerns, values, and activities by which the plant organization is imbued with concepts of quality performance and improvement.

BUILDING THE ORGANIZATION FOR QUALITY

Where Does Quality Begin?

The effort to build quality into the product begins long before a single piece or pound is manufactured. If the Production Department is to have any chance at all of achieving the company's goals for quality, these elements of the manufacturing system must be put in order before production begins:

Product design. If the blueprints, formulas, or job orders are so drawn that you believe the products made from them will not meet specifications, you must register an objection and obtain resolution of the problem before production begins.

Raw material purchase. Often raw materials are purchased without any specifications, or so loosely specified that there is no assurance that finished goods specifications can be met. You must assure yourself that raw material quality is capable of meeting required finished goods quality.

Equipment procurement. When manufacturing tools and equipment are purchased, you must satisfy yourself that the materials of construction will not detract from product quality, that there will be no contamination of product by lubricants, that designs for sampling devices are included, that control instrumentation is adquate for quality needs, and that the performance warranty covers quality of finished product.

> **Operating Example 6-1: Removing Process Equipment as a Source of Poor Quality.** The manager of a specialty products plant had a problem with one process that involved cutting sheets of rubber into thin strips and dissolving them in a solvent to make an adhesive. The cutting was done on a machine known to the trade as a "guillotine," which had a vertically mounted blade driven downward by a hydraulic cylinder located directly above the blade and cutting table. Hydraulic oil (not easy to detect because of its light color) often leaked from the cylinder, running down the blade and contaminating the rubber strips. Since oil is the enemy of adhesion, the quality of the final product suffered and customer complaints began to come in. Attempts to solve the problem by replacing the seals more often and admonishing operators to keep the blade clean were helpful but did not eliminate it.
>
> In his search for a replacement cutter, the manager found a relatively simple solution to the problem—he was able to purchase a machine with double hydraulic cylinders, one mounted on each side of the blade rather than above it. Oil leaking from these cylinders would run off to the side without contaminating the process material, and the equipment was eliminated as a source of poor quality.

Sales vs. manufacturing specifications. As illogical as it may sound, cases have occurred in which the sales literature for a product contained specifications different from those used by the Manufacturing Department in making it. When manufacturing specifications are tighter than sales specifications, money is wasted in producing unnecessarily high quality; when the situation is reversed customer complaints and rejection of shipments are the inevitable result.

Operating procedures. General shop orders and plant operating procedures should spell out not only the steps for carrying out process operations, but should also instruct the operator in the precautions he or she must take to protect product quality.

How to Set Up the Quality Control Department

Smaller plants may require only a basic testing group; larger plants and those with more complicated technology need more elaborate quality organizations. Follow these steps in setting up a quality control department that can develop with a growing plant:

Establish the basic testing group. It is the nucleus of the department, and in many plants it is the entire department. It consists of inspectors or quality control technicians who perform a series of standard tests on raw materials, in-process work, and finished goods. They pass or reject the material tested on the basis of objective, predetermined specifications; display test information for the benefit of the plant operators; maintain sample files; and report the results of accumulated quality records to you.

Specialize and add. As the plant grows, the basic group can be divided into sections that specialize in raw material, in-process, and finished goods testing. More fundamental changes come when the department branches out by establishing sections for Statistical Methods, Value Analysis, Vendor Evaluation, and Quality Engineering.

Choose between salaried and hourly personnel. The present trend in industry is toward salaried personnel for inspectors and quality control technicians. While some economies may be realized by the use of hourly employees, there is a problem of split loyalty and peer pressure when they are called upon to reject material produced by their associates.

Fix reporting relationships. The quality control department usually reports to some level of production management for two reasons: quality of line product is the responsibility of production management, and the speed and accuracy with which testing is performed affects the flow of production material through the plant.

Quality Circles for Greater Involvement

Quality circles are voluntary groups of five to twelve workers from the same department who meet once a week on company time to identify and find solutions to quality problems. They are based on the idea that the people actually doing the work will have good ideas on what is impeding it and how it can be improved. Each circle chooses the problems to be worked on, devises its own solutions to those problems, and presents them to management for implementation. The benefits to be derived from a quality circle program can be great—large cost savings (sometimes in the hundreds of thousands of dollars per year), significant improvements in product quality, increased productivity, a heightened sense of involvement on the part of the workers, and a new mutual respect between them and management.

To encourage the free flow of ideas, organizational details are kept to a minimum. A management member of the circle can serve as "leader" to help keep discussion on the track, and to provide continuity and follow-up from previous meetings. In larger organizations the circle may include a "facilitator," a person from a central group who can help with logistics and provide technical support. In conducting its meetings the circle may borrow some techniques from brainstorming; negative criticism is discouraged, while positive criticism—in the form of a suggestion to improve on a pending proposal—is encouraged. All ideas are kept under consideration until the best solution emerges.

Setting up a quality circle program requires preparation. Participants must be given some basic instruction in the collection and interpretation of production data and in developing presentations for management consideration. Decisions must be made as to what levels and which individuals from management will participate in the circles. The question is whether to give cash awards for solutions that result in cost savings, or to emphasize the psychological rewards of recognition, an increased sense of participation and improved job satisfaction.

Pitfalls to avoid.   If not properly coached, first-line and middle managers may resent the program, fearing a loss of control over events in their departments or being embarrassed by the emergence of solutions to problems they never knew existed. Union officials may see the program as a device to go around them in dealing with the workers, or may claim that since the circles ultimately affect working conditions, setting them up should be the subject of collective bargaining. If the distribution of awards and recognition is perceived as unfair, resentments and jealousies can arise that will seriously damage the program's effectiveness.

Quality circles are a relatively recent development in American industry, but at least one organization has been formed for pursuing the subject more intensely: The International Association of Quality Circles, P.O. Box 30635, Midwest City, Oklahoma 73140, which publishes *The Quality Circle Journal* as well as other materials on the subject.

DEVELOPING EFFECTIVE TEST PROCEDURES

Quality cannot be tested into a product; it must be built into it. Nevertheless, testing is essential to the discovery of defective material early in the manufacturing process and for ensuring that the customers are getting the properties they are paying for in the final product. Use these techniques to set up the testing program:

Take a Representative Sample

In most quality control work judgments of quality are based on tests done on samples which are only a tiny portion of the shipment, lot, batch or production run being checked. It is essential that the sample by truly *representative* of the body of material it comes from; use the following techniques to be sure that it is.

Select material at random from various parts of the batch, lot, or production run.

If the system to be sampled is a fluid or a bulk granular material, be sure it is **well mixed** before sampling.

When the process is continuous **take samples at evenly spaced intervals** throughout the shift.

Entrust the taking of samples only to reliable, well-trained personnel who are instructed to label the sample clearly with the date, time, lot number and any other information important to later interpretation of the test results.

Decide how many samples to take. In some situations common sense can be the guide, for instance, in a batch process involving a fluid or flowing solid it seems reasonable to take one sample per batch. In others more sophisticated techniques are called for, as would be the case in deciding how many pieces to test in a production lot of 3,000 pieces. Such determinations involve statistical methods that are beyond the scope of this book, but are explained in standard texts on industrial statistics.

What to Test—and When

Start with the **raw materials,** but before the test program begins you must reach agreement with the supplier on the specifications of the material and the test methods to be used (much fruitless debate over the quality of a shipment will result if the supplier is using a different test method from yours). If shipments consist of a large number of pieces you must reach agreement on the acceptable quality level: do you return, at the supplier's expense, a shipment of 5,000 pieces when one is defective? 10 are defective? 100?

When the plant cannot afford to test all of the raw materials received, establish priority on the basis of importance to the quality of the finished product, value of the material, and relative quantities received. Reliable suppliers will often perform the quality tests and report the results to you at no charge, but you will probably want to back this system up with an occasional spot-check of your own.

In-process materials. The purpose of in-process testing is to remove defective material early in the production process, before money is wasted on subsequent steps. Beyond that it provides a basis for corrective action, so that material which is off-grade at an early stage can be restored to an acceptable quality level. Economy can often be achieved by training process operators to perform these tests, and there is a growing trend to instrumentation which automatically monitors the process—thickness gauges, dielectric testers, chromatographs, and viscosimeters, which put out continuous readings.

Finished goods. These are the most important tests of all because they offer the last opportunity to prevent defective product from getting to the customer. Ordinarily the Quality Control Department is empowered to release finished goods for shipment if all test results are within specification limits. The principle of *product integrity* must not be forgotten at the time of final qualification of product (see Chapter 2). If any foreman or supervisor knows of any significant processing deviation or adverse quality attribute, he or she should be empowered and encouraged to suspend shipment of the material until you can render a decision, *even though it meets standard quality specifications.*

Where to Find Test Methods

Suppliers and customers. When you buy from or sell to a large organization, its technical staff may have standard quality tests that they will make available to you. Besides being an inexpensive way to acquire test methods, it eliminates disagreement over what tests are to be used in quality evaluation.

National organizations. The American Society for Testing and Materials (ASTM) publishes a wide variety of quality standards and test methods. A catalog can be obtained by writing to the society at 1916 Race Street, Philadelphia, PA

19103. The American National Standards Institute (formerly the United States of America Standards Institute) at 1430 Broadway, New York, NY 10018, offers similar services.

Manufacturers' associations and technical societies. The National Electric Manufacturer's Association (NEMA) is an outstanding example of the many industrial associations that develop and publish quality standards for their products. The American Society of Mechanical Engineers (ASME) and the American Society of Heating and Ventilating Engineers (ASHVE) are examples of technical societies that publish product codes and test methods for materials and equipment.

Develop your own. Employees of the Quality Control Department should be encouraged to devise test methods where none exist, and to suggest simpler and cheaper versions of existing tests.

STATISTICAL TECHNIQUES USED IN QUALITY CONTROL

The Normal Distribution

The science of statistics has placed in the hands of the quality control manager very powerful tools for the analysis and interpretation of quality measurements collected in the plant. The most important of them is the curve of the normal distribution. When a large number of measurements of a single attribute are made (the weights of 1,000 children in the seventh grade, the diameters of 600 shafts turned out in a plant, the viscosities of 900 resin batches made in a chemical plant), a graph of the individual measurements against the frequency with which they occur often approximates the bell-shaped curve known as the normal distribution, one example of which is shown in Figure 6-1. Measurements are plotted along the horizontal axis, and the frequency with which they occur on the vertical axis. The average value is at the center of the curve and occurs most frequently. The spread of the data around the average is measured by the value of σ, which is the distance from the average to the point of inflection of the curve. The area under the curve and within the span of σ on either side of the average, known as the "one sigma limits," will include 68.3 percent of all the values; 95.4 percent of the values will fall within the two sigma limits, and 99.7 percent within the three sigma limits as shown in the figure.

In statistical terminology, when all of the individuals in a population are measured and plotted in the frequency distribution, the average is designated by the Greek letter mu (μ), and, as we have seen, the spread of the data, or the *standard deviation* by the Greek letter sigma (σ). It is seldom possible to measure all of the individuals in a population, and the average and standard deviation are often estimated from a sample of the population; when this is done they are designated as $\overline{X}$ (pronounced "X-bar") and s respectively. The way in which average and standard deviation are estimated from a group of measurements is shown in Operating Example 6-2.

Operating Example 6-2: Calculating Average and Standard Deviation. Twenty pieces were taken from a manufactured lot and measured. The process manager would like

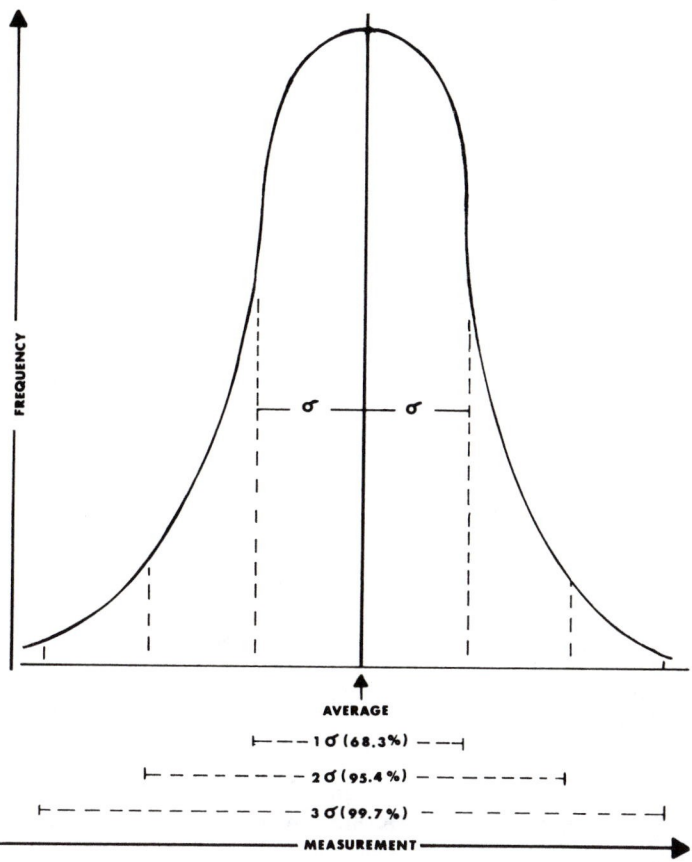

FIGURE 6-1: The Normal Distribution

an estimate of the average and standard deviation of the entire lot. The first step is to list the measurements as shown in the left-hand column of the table under the heading "X."

X	$X - \overline{X}$	$(X - \overline{X})^2$
2.935	−.063	.003969
3.083	.085	.007225
3.082	.084	.007056
3.086	.088	.007744
3.003	.005	.000025
3.003	.005	.000025
2.998	.000	.000000
2.972	−.026	.000676
2.965	−.033	.001089
3.006	.008	.000064
2.903	−.095	.009025
2.958	−.040	.001600
2.968	−.030	.000900
3.095	.097	.009409
2.928	−.070	.004900

(continued)

X	$X - \overline{X}$	$(X - \overline{X})^2$
2.981	$-.017$	.000289
3.024	.026	.000676
2.919	$-.079$	.006241
3.022	.024	.000576
3.038	.040	.001600
$\Sigma X = 59.969$		$\Sigma(X - \overline{X})^2 = .063089$

The 20 measurements are added up, and their total indicated at the base of the left hand column by the symbol ΣX (the upper case Greek letter sigma, Σ, denotes summation, and can be read "sum of"). The average is the sum of the measurements divided by their number, N, and in statistical notation becomes

$$\overline{X} = \frac{\Sigma X}{N}$$

In our example, ΣX is 59.969 and N is 20. The average is therefore

$$\overline{X} = \frac{59.969}{20} = 2.998$$

The standard deviation is calculated by the formula

$$s = \sqrt{\frac{\Sigma (X - \overline{X})^2}{N - 1}}$$

In the table the figures in the column marked $X - \overline{X}$ are obtained by subtracting the average from each of the individual measurements. In the third column this quantity is squared, yielding $(X - \overline{X})^2$. By adding the figures in the third column we obtain $\Sigma (X - \overline{X})^2$, or in the example given, .063089. Since $N - 1 = 19$, the standard deviation becomes

$$s = \sqrt{\frac{.063089}{19}} = .0576$$

Using this sample of 20 measurements as an approximation of the entire population from which it is drawn, we would expect the lot to have an average measurement of 2.998, and that 99.7 percent of the pieces will fall within $\pm 3 \times .0576$ or $\pm .173$ of the average. The larger the number of measurements N in the sample, the more closely $\overline{X}$ will approximate the true average μ, and s the true standard deviation, σ.

The Quality Control Chart

If the quality measurements of the output from an industrial process follow the normal distribution, the parameters of that distribution can be used to develop a very useful monitoring device called the Quality Control Chart. The straight-line axes of the normal distribution (see Figure 6-1) are rotated 90 degrees to the right, and the average line becomes a horizontal solid line, while the 3 σ limit lines are drawn above and below it (as dotted lines). The measurement axis is now vertical rather than horizontal. Samples taken from the process are numbered successively, and the quality result for each sample is plotted on the chart.

This process is illustrated in Figure 6-2, which depicts some of the important features of an industrial quality control chart. In this case the solid center line is the average line, but on some charts the center line is placed at the quality target rather than the actual average of the process. The positive and negative 3 σ dotted lines are labeled "Upper Control Limit" (UCL) and "Lower Control Limit" (LCL) in control chart terminology. The samples are numbered consecutively, and the quality measurement for each represented by a round circle; the circles are connected by straight lines to aid in visualizing what the process is doing.

One very important benefit to be derived from the control chart is the intelligent setting of product specifications. If they are set at the upper and lower control limits, the process can be expected to produce 99.7 percent acceptable quality. If they are set narrower than the control limits, plant personnel are doomed to struggle indefinitely to satisfy quality standards which the process is incapable of meeting. If specifications are set too far outside the natural limits of the process, sloppy production practices will begin to appear in the plant; in addition, a competitive advantage is lost in the marketplace if the product specifications are set at a wider range than the process can normally produce.

The use of the control chart in monitoring the production process is shown in these interpretations of the quality patterns in Figure 6-2.

1. From points 1 through 10 the process is in good control. The points fall above and below the average line in random pattern (if seven points fell on one side of the line it would indicate a shift in process average), and there are no disturbing trends.

2. Point 11 and the seven points following constitute a trend; the chart is telling us that something has happened in the process to push quality measurements

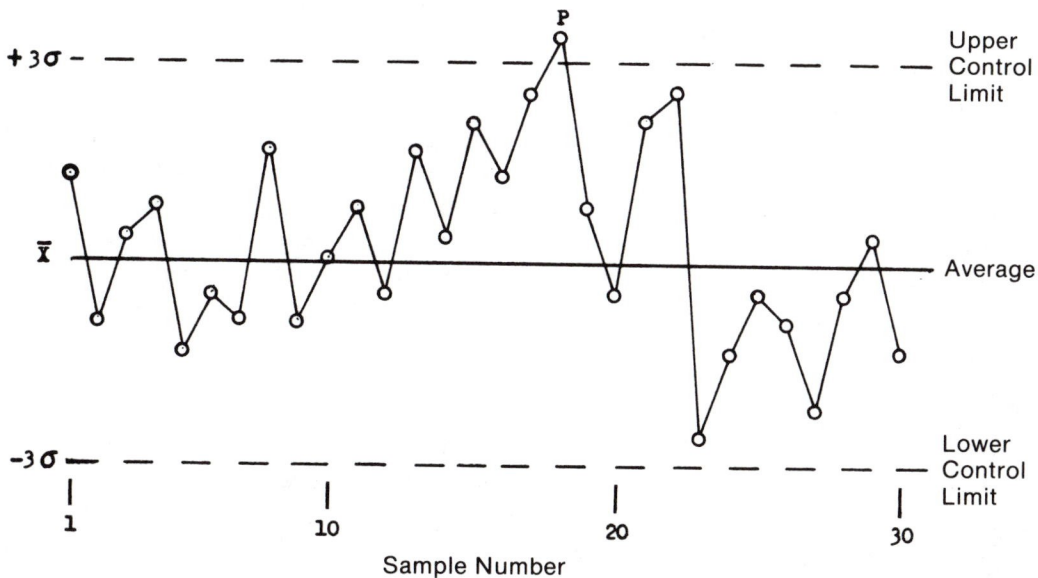

FIGURE 6-2: Industrial Quality Control Chart

toward the high side, and if left unchecked, will eventually result in off-grade quality.

3. Point 18, labeled "P," lies above the upper control limit and is the culmination of the trend we saw starting at Point 11. Even if point P were not at the end of a trend it would still be significant. We expect that 99.7 percent of the material produced will lie within the 3 σ limits, or that only 3 measurements out of 1,000 will lie outside. Another way of putting it is to say that the odds are 333 to 1 that point P is not part of the normal variation of the process, but is the result of an *assignable cause*—some factor that changed the process. Whatever the factor turns out to be, it may or may not affect the points on either side of P.

4. The spread between points 22 and 23 could be a case of "overcontrol." Someone became nervous when point 22 approached the upper control limit (even though it may have been part of the normal process variation) and ordered a major adjustment of process controls. The result was a sudden shift to the low side, with seven of the last eight points falling below the normal process average; it will probably require another adjustment to bring it back up to desired levels. Had the process been left alone at point 22 the second adjustment would not be necessary, and a more satisfactory quality level would have been achieved.

Many industrial quality control departments use a refinement of the quality control chart called the Shewhart chart for averages and ranges. In this system individual measurements from the process are not plotted as in Figure 6-2, instead the measurements are grouped together in samples of n individuals. The average of each sample is plotted as one point on a chart for averages; the range, that is, the difference between the highest and lowest measurement in each sample, is plotted on another chart. Special statistical tables are used to find the control limits for each of these charts. The Shewhart system offers these advantages: (1) When averages of samples are plotted in a frequency distribution the resulting curve is closer to a normal distribution than if individual measurements are plotted, (2) control limits for both the averages chart and the range chart are readily calculated from a table of constant numbers, (3) both the level of quality (average chart) and the variability (range chart) of the process are constantly monitored, and (4) upward or downward trends in either level or variability stand out more clearly. For detailed instructions on the use of the averages and range charts see *Statistical Quality Control* by Eugene L. Grant and Richard S. Leavenworth (New York: McGraw-Hill, Inc., 1980).

Assorted QC Methods

Statisticians have ventured far beyond the control chart in developing techniques for solving common industrial quality problems. The description of some of the more useful methods here is brief; managers intending to apply them to their own operations will want to consult the standard texts on industrial quality control for more complete descriptions and tables of critical values.

Student t Test

The *Student t* test is used to determine whether the average of a sample (say a week's quality measurements) is significantly different from the averages of the total population (overall plant output).

Operating Example 6-3: Applying the Student t Test—Is This Average Significantly Different? Let's assume that the data presented in Operating Example 6-2 are from a new production run. The average quality for all previous runs was 2.960 (but the standard deviation is not known). The production manager wants to be sure that the new run will have the same average quality as the previous runs, and will make a process change when there is at least a 95% probability that it is not. Looking at the new average $\overline{X} = 2.998$, derived from $N = 20$ samples with a standard deviation of $s = .0576$, the statistical question becomes: Is it likely that this sample came from a larger population whose average is 2.960?

To answer this question, the manager calculates a new statistic from the data

$$t = \frac{(\overline{X} - \mu)\sqrt{N - 1}}{s}$$

in which μ is the overall average of the process, and $(N - 1)$ is a quantity referred to as "degrees of freedom," or D.F. For this problem the manager calculated t at

$$t = \frac{(2.998 - 2.960)\sqrt{20 - 1}}{.0576} = 2.875$$

Consulting a standard reference on statistics, the manager finds that the critical values of t for 19 D.F. at various levels of probability are: 95%, 2.09; 98%, 2.54; 99%, 2.86. Because the calculated value of 2.875 exceeds the critical value of 2.09 the manager acts to correct the process with the 95% probability of being right; in fact since the calculated t exceeds 2.86, the manager's assumption that the new lot represents production with a different average from the previous runs has a 99% probability of being correct.

F Test

The *F test* is used to determine whether the variances of two samples are significantly different so that it can be assumed, at a given level of probability, that they did not come from the same population.

Operating Example 6-4: Applying the F Test—Are These Variances Significantly Different? The supervisor of a Process Department has just bought a new agitator for a 10,000-gallon tank in which batches of resin dissolved in a solvent are mixed. Each batch is characterized by the percent of resin in it, or the total solids content (TS). The supplier of the agitator has guaranteed that if batches differing by as much as 2.0% TS are charged to the tank, they will be completely mixed within one hour. The supervisor wishes to conduct a test of the newly installed agitator to see if it meets the guarantee.

The supervisor decides on the following plan. He will take a single control sample of the product and divide it into five parts. Each part will be sent to the laboratory for a TS analysis; since the five readings are from the same material, this will establish the variability of the lab's testing procedure. Next he will have the plant produce two batches of the product, one aiming at a TS of 35%, the other at 37%. They will be charged to the tank, and after an hour of mixing the agitator will be stopped and the contents pumped out. Five evenly spaced samples will be taken from the pipeline as the contents are pumped; if the agitator has thoroughly mixed the two batches, the variability of the five pipeline samples should not be significantly greater than that of the control sample.

When the results for the control sample come back from the lab, the supervisor arranges the data and makes calculations exactly as shown in the table in Operating Example 6-2, labeling each quantity with the subscript c to show it is from the control sample:

X_c	$(X - \overline{X})_c$	$(X - \overline{X})_c^2$
35.9	−.1	.01
36.3	.3	.09
35.7	−.3	.09
36.2	.2	.04
36.0	.0	.00
$\Sigma X_c = 180.1$		$\Sigma(X - \overline{X})_c^2 = .23$
$N_c = 5$		
$\overline{X}_c = 36.0$		

At this point, however, he does not calculate the standard deviation s, but the square of the standard deviation, a quantity known as the *variance*. This is done by simply leaving the square root sign off the quantity shown for s in Operating Example 6-2:

$$\text{Variance} = s^2 = \frac{\Sigma (X - \overline{X})^2}{N - 1} \qquad s_c^2 = \frac{.23}{4} = .0575$$

Calculating the data from the pipeline samples in the same way, he obtains:

X_p	$(X - \overline{X})_p$	$(X - \overline{X})_p^2$
36.1	−.1	.01
35.8	−.4	.16
36.4	.2	.04
36.5	.3	.09
36.2	.0	.00
$\Sigma X_p = 181.0$		$\Sigma(X - \overline{X})_p^2 = .30$
$N_p = 5$		and the variance $s_p^2 = \frac{.30}{4} = .075$
$\overline{X}_p = 36.2$		

Now, the statistic F, which is the ratio of the two variances, is calculated:

$$F = \frac{s_p^2}{s_c^2} = \frac{.0750}{.0575} = 1.30$$

He consults the table of F ratios in a standard reference text on statistics, and finds that the critical value is 6.39 when there are four degrees of freedom $(N - 1)$ for each sample. Since the calculated value does not exceed the critical value the supervisor concludes that (at the 95% level of probability) there is no reason to believe that the variability of the pipeline samples is greater than that of the control sample, and therefore no reason to believe that the agitator has not done its job.

Regression and Correlation Techniques

These techniques are used to study the relationship between a process variable and its suspected effect. For instance, a production engineer might use these methods to determine whether there is a statistical correlation between the hardness of copper wire and the adhesiveness of a particular insulation coating to it. If data from a series of tests are plotted on a graph and the trend of points suggests a straight line, regression analysis is used to find the line that best fits the data.

Analysis of Variance

A number of techniques under the general heading of *analysis of variance* are used when you wish to design experiments to reveal the effects of a number of variables on a process result. An example would be the study of the effect of both temperature and time of heat treatment upon the ductility of a particular metal. Not only do these techniques reduce the number of experiments needed to determine the effect of each variable, but they also reveal interactions between the variables, such as when a particular combination of temperature and treatment time produces an effect on ductility beyond the sum of the effect of each variable acting alone.

QUALITY CONTROL AS A COST CENTER

Quality control is not an end to be served in itself, but an interrelated function that must make its contribution to the overall plant operation. Money spent on it must be included in production costs; it is no more privileged in this respect than any other phase of plant operation. When a new product is being considered, its quality costs must be added to the estimates of other operating costs if a true picture of profitability is to be obtained. When proposals to add quality control personnel, facilities, or equipment are being considered, they should have an economic justification in one or more of these areas:

Reduction or elimination of the **cost of material** that must be discarded, reworked, or sold at distress prices because of poor quality.

Reduction or elimination of costs associated with **customer dissatisfaction, lawsuits, or warranty replacement** of goods.

Competitive advantage and increased sales resulting from improved quality performance.

Compliance with government regulations regarding the quality or safety of the product, or requiring control of environmental and safety hazards associated with its manufacture.

Nor is the quality control function exempt from the cost reduction program; quite the contrary, it can often make substantial contributions to plant profitability in areas such as these:

Reducing the number of tests performed on a product; perhaps the needs of the customer and the manufacturer could be served as well by measuring four attributes as measuring six.

Finding simpler ways of conducting tests or reducing the complexity of apparatus used to make them.

Reducing the frequency of testing. One hundred percent testing is not always necessary, and statistical techniques can be applied to allow testing a fraction of the output while still maintaining a reliable evaluation of quality.

Installing in-line quality evaluation and testing equipment in the production line, eliminating the labor needed for taking, transporting, and testing samples.

Pinpointing areas in procurement and manufacturing where changes could result in cost savings.

Chapter 7

Establishing Capital and Operating Cost Systems to Measure Plant Performance

The corporate profit and loss statement is like the scoreboard at a baseball game—it tells the local team how well it is doing against the competition, when it has scored successes, and when it has made errors. If the scoreboard is to be of any value the information on it must be accurate, up to date, and contain all the facts the manager needs to make winning decisions.

Your involvement in the scorekeeping effort is with operating and capital costs, and you have two major responsibilities in these areas: to see that accurate cost reporting systems are in place that provide utilizable information, and to mount a consistent effort to control and reduce manufacturing costs. This chapter deals with the first of these responsibilities and is designed to help the plant manager who must structure his own cost systems as well as the manager who operates under systems framed by others. It opens by showing where manufacturing costs fit in the P&L statement, then identifies the cost elements manufacturing people must deal with, and shows how to collect and report costs and build them into cost systems. Ways of predicting future costs are developed, and illustrations of an operating budget and capital budget are provided, including a description of depreciation methods.

WHERE PLANT COSTS FIT IN THE P&L STATEMENT

Most corporate profit and loss statements will look much like this:

FINEWORK MANUFACTURING COMPANY, INC.
Statement of Income
(000's Omitted)

	Year Ended June 30
Gross Sales	51,512
Less: Returns and Allowances	614
Net Sales	50,898
Less: Cost of Sales	15,976
Depreciation	2,981
Gross Profit (or Loss)	31,941
Less: General and Administrative Expenses	3,395
Selling Expenses	2,726
Net Operating Profit (or Loss) Before Taxes	25,820
Less: Taxes	13,426
Net Income	12,394

The Manufacturing Department contributes to only two of the items on the income statement: cost of sales and depreciation (although on some statements returns and allowances include the cost of customer return of goods made defective by errors in the manufacturing process). In cost of sales the company adds up all of its manufacturing costs and charges them against the income from sales. Under depreciation the company deducts from sales income that portion of the cost of its tangible capital assets allocated to the current income period; in a manufacturing enterprise the bulk of these assets are represented by production equipment and buildings.

If these costs are not properly collected and accurately reported, the Statement of Income will be in error, and the company will not be able to provide its top managers with financial information upon which sound decisions can be based, nor will it be able to represent truthfully its fiscal condition to stockholders, employees, the investing public, and government.

ELEMENTS OF OPERATING COSTS

The starting point for any cost system is the type of expenditure that will be reported and charged to the plant, department, or other cost center for which the system is devised. Table 7-1 lists the most common manufacturing cost elements that should be considered for inclusion in plant cost reporting.

Not all of these costs will be included in every report used throughout the company. A cost report that will be used for making decisions about product pricing or plant location should be all-inclusive. Another report intended for cost control by general foremen would omit items like depreciation, taxes, and insurance in order to focus their attention on items over which they have more control.

How to Collect and Report Costs

Any cost system is meaningless unless all the expenditures made by the plant, department, or other cost center are recorded and charged back to it on the periodic cost report. This is a complicated job, and requires use of the following techniques:

Labor: The hourly time card is the base record. A space should be provided for the account number to which the employee's wages are charged; several spaces will be needed if he works for different cost centers. (This arrangement will be useful for the person who completes a day in one department and then works overtime in another.)

Salaried personnel do not ordinarily punch time cards, but may keep time sheets; account numbers can be inserted as for hourly time cards. If the time distribution of either type of employee is very complicated, a separate card can be used for time distribution alone. The time card may also be used to record the employee's output, such as number of pieces produced.

Raw materials and containers: Purchase price and freight charges are readily available from suppliers' invoices and freight bills. Handling and yield losses are determined by charging the quantities of material delivered to a cost center and comparing them to the amount in inventory and consumed in finished

TABLE 7-1: Elements of Plant Costs

LABOR	RAW MATERIALS
Production	Purchase price
Shipping	Freight in
Maintenance	Handling and yield losses
Materials movement	CONTAINERS FOR FINISHED GOODS
Quality control	SUPPLIES
Fringe benefits	Production
Training	Shipping
Supervisory and administrative	Maintenance
UTILITIES	Janitorial
Water	Office
Fuel	TAXES AND LICENSES
Electricity	INSURANCE
Telephone	SUPPORT SERVICES
DEPRECIATION	Fire protection
Buildings	Guard service
Equipment	Waste disposal
Vehicles	Lunch/cafeteria
CUSTOMER RETURNS OF	Cleaning
DEFECTIVE GOODS	

goods at the end of a fixed time period. Use job tickets, shift logs, and intra-plant receipts to keep track of material consumed and transferred. (See *How to Establish a Production Reporting System* in Chapter 4.)

Supplies: Purchase orders and suppliers' invoices are the key records. Establish a policy that nothing is to be bought without a written purchase order; then insist that the originator furnish the account number to which the material is to be charged.

Utilities: Monthly bills make it easy for the Accounting Department to keep track of the total sums spent; the difficulty lies in distributing the charges among the various cost centers within the plant. The most accurate method is to put meters on steam, air, and water lines to the several departments and distribute the charges according to usage. Often this is prohibitively expensive and offers no overall return on the investment. Many plants, therefore, have their engineers estimate the proportion used by each department, and charge the costs out on that basis.

Depreciation: Tax regulations require precise segregation of funds spent for current operating expenses from those spent on capital investments. The best place to start is with a Capital Expenditure form (also called Appropriation Request, Project Justification, etc.) which must be filled out by the originator of the project before any purchases are made. On it the originator is required to show the cost of the capital acquisition, its classification (land, buildings, fixtures, machinery, vehicles, etc.) and its depreciable life. The Accounting Department will need this information to apportion depreciation charges properly, from both a legal and a cost analysis standpoint.

Support services: If these services are supplied by plant employees the methods of allocating labor and supplies charges already shown will suffice; if the services are obtained outside the company, purchase orders or service contracts will be the basic documents used for cost distribution.

Taxes, licenses, and insurance: These charges are billed annually or less frequently, and are usually handled by the central accounting office without special documentation from the plant.

HOW TO BUILD A COST SYSTEM

Characteristics of the Major Cost Systems

The purpose of a cost system is to display the collected cost information in the best form for managers who must make economic evaluations and decisions. Any system devised for a particular manufacturing operation should be adapted to its special characteristics, but in general the choices are between these major types of approach:

Job order and process costing.   The job shop produces "one-of-a-kind" products to specific customer order; if it is to know whether a given order was profitable or not, it must keep track of and charge all the costs to the job. Material and labor usages can be recorded on the job ticket (see Chapter 4). Manufacturing overhead is often apportioned on the basis of the number of hours of labor consumed, or the hours of machine time allotted to the project. This is called *job order* costing.

When the plant operates a continuous process or produces discrete items that are all alike, the costs of labor, materials, and overhead are collected for a definite time period (usually one month) and divided by the number of units produced in that period to find the unit cost. This is called *process* costing.

Job order costing provides detailed, up-to-date information on each order turned out, and identifies inefficiencies and cost overruns early; it may be required on cost-plus contracts. It has the disadvantages of being costly to operate and requiring strict control to achieve accuracy. Process costing is cheaper to administer, but local deviations tend to be hidden in the "average" cost of production.

Actual and standard costing.   In an actual cost system all of the expenses actually incurred in making the particular finished piece are collected and charged to the cost of the final product. Collecting and charging these costs for components such as labor and materials is straightforward, but when it comes to such overhead costs as depreciation or administrative services, some sort of allocation system is normally required. For example, all of the costs of utilities, supplies, depreciation, and support services could be added up and divided by the number of machine hours used during the same period; the resulting figure would be multiplied by the number of machine hours consumed by each product made during the period and that cost charged to the product.

In the standard cost system expenses for labor, material and overhead items are predicted for an ensuing time period—one month, a quarter, six months—on the basis of the best available estimates of wages, raw material prices, and volume of production for the period. These costs are established as *standard costs* and set out as such in the operating budget. During the cost reporting period, usually one month, actual costs are collected and compared with the standards; any differences are reported as *variances,* which may be either positive or negative.

Actual costing gives the most accurate value of goods produced. It is valuable in industries whose raw material (or other) costs fluctuate rapidly and that tend to produce a variety of custom-made items. It has the disadvantage that costs are not known until the work is finished and the costs have been collected and tabulated. Standard costing allows much earlier valuation of goods (even before they are made), provides better control of costs by giving department supervisors cost targets to aim at, gives the manager a yardstick with which to measure the cost performance of the operation, and permits the marketing organization to do a better job of setting selling prices and submitting job bids.

Absorption and direct costing.   The distinction is based on the difference between *variable* and *fixed* costs. *Variable* costs are those that fluctuate with the amount of product turned out; the acid test of a variable cost is that it goes to zero when no product is produced. Variable costs can be in materials, labor, *and* overhead. *Fixed* costs do not fluctuate with the amount of product made, and include such items as depreciation, taxes, insurance, and some utility and support services. In absorption costing (sometimes called conventional costing) all of the fixed and variable manufacturing expenses are included in inventory valuation and reported on the cost center's statement. In direct costing only the variable expenses are included, and the fixed expenses are listed as a separate item on the overall P & L statement.

Absorption costing gives an all-inclusive cost of goods produced, and assures that fixed costs are not forgotten. Direct costing, by focusing on the variable cost elements only, is more useful for cost control by managers, for judging profitability of alternative products, and for make-or-buy decisions.

The cost systems described in this section are seldom found applied in their pure forms, and there is no reason why the manager building a cost system for his or her plant cannot combine various elements from each of them. The only limitations are that government tax and securities authorities may require certain bookkeeping practices when direct costing is used, and customers may insist on certain procedures for cost plus fee contracts.

Charge Out Service Department Costs

Every plant has operating departments that produce no product, but supply services to the departments which do. Examples are the maintenance department, power house, water treatment plant, storeroom, and materials handling department. Some of these departments are users of services themselves—the power house, for instance, requires maintenance services.

There are two reasons why it is important to collect the costs of these service departments and charge them back to the manufacturing sections: (1) the true cost of manufacturing a product will never be fully known unless the costs of services that it requires are charged to it, and (2) intelligent decisions about discontinuing an operation or relocating it require a good historical record of service costs as well as direct costs.

Follow these steps to develop the allocation system:

1. Establish a cost account number for the service department.

2. Charge all of the costs that the service department incurs to its account number.

3. Establish a method of assessing the proportion of the service department's output that each using department consumes. A method for the Maintenance Department has already been suggested (see Chapter 5). In the case of a power plant producing steam or electricity, meters can be installed at each of the consuming departments. If such installations are too expensive, or the service cannot be measured, a standard percentage allocation can usually be arrived at from basic engineering information using the method described in Operating Example 7-1.

4. At the end of each cost period (one month is typical) charge back *all* of the costs of the service departments to the consuming departments.

Operating Example 7-1: Allocating Powerhouse Costs. The Turndown Manufacturing Company's plant has three production departments, a shipping and receiving department, and maintenance, laboratory and administrative facilities. It also has a powerhouse which generates and supplies electricity to the other departments. For the month of June the powerhouse incurred the following costs:

Fuel	$346,275
Labor	31,176
Maintenance	34,139
Supervision	4,022
Supplies	12,164
Depreciation	77,667
Total	$505,893

The using departments have no meters on their incoming lines for measuring electrical consumption. To establish a basis for allocation, the plant's engineers (1) estimated the connected load in each department from blueprints of the electrical system, and (2) estimated the number of hours per month each connected load is turned on by examining machine logs and production reports. For instance, if Production Department A has a 5,000-watt electrical heater that is used 50 hours per month, the department is rated as using 250 kilowatt-hours for that piece of equipment. The department's other usages are similarly calculated and added up to provide an estimated total consumption; this process is repeated for the other departments and when the sum total is obtained a percentage of total usage is calculated for each department. Using this method, Turndown arrived at the following breakdown of average electrical usage among its departments:

Department	Average Monthly Consumption Estimated by Engineers (kilowatt-hours)	Percentage
Production A	1,330,000	28%
Department: B	902,500	19
C	1,425,000	30
Shipping and Receiving	760,000	16
Maintenance, Lab, and Administration	332,500	7
Total	4,750,000	100%

This breakdown is used to distribute powerhouse costs month by month unless (1) there is a significant event during the month, such as one department shutting down for a week, which requires an adjustment, or (2) important changes are made in the connected load, such as adding or removing major pieces of equipment, which requires a recalculation of the allocation percentages. Application of the percentages given above resulted in the following distribution of powerhouse costs for the month of June:

Department	Application of Percentage	Allocated Power-house Costs
A	$505,893 × .28 =	$141,650
B	.19 =	96,120
C	.30 =	151,768
Shipping and Receiving	.16 =	80,943
Maintenance, Lab, and Administration	.07 =	35,412
Total		$505,893

Predicting Operating Costs: Four Sources of Information

Every time you are asked to submit an expense budget you are, of course, called upon to predict operating costs for some period in the future. Between budgets you must often predict costs for proposed new processes, or estimate the cost effects of important changes on existing processes. Use these sources of information as the basis for making cost predictions:

Activity forecasts. The amount of material which is to be manufactured in a future period is the most significant determinant of the total costs that will be incurred. Furthermore, the level of activity is likely to have an effect on the unit cost of production—a product that costs $0.83 per unit to manufacture at a level of ten million units per year may cost only $0.69 per unit to make at an annual activity level of twenty million units. The prediction of next year's production rate may come in the form of an assignment from higher headquarters, be based on the sales forecast, or derived from historical production data by you and your staff.

Cost history. Any cost item for which records have been kept over a period of years can be plotted on a sheet of graph paper to see if a trend is discernible. Projections into the future should be limited to 20 percent of the base time period; beyond that they tend to become unreliable. A refinement of the graphical technique is to use a sheet of semilogarithmic paper—plot years or months on the arithmetic scale, and the cost to be studied on the log scale. If the points fall along a straight line the cost is rising or declining at a fixed percentage rate.

Price fluctuations can often obscure trends in usage, and it is better for some purposes not to plot dollars but units consumed. Consider the case of an operating department in which the consumption (and therefore the conservation) of electric power is important. A graph of kilowatt-hours consumed per unit of production may show a definite trend over a period of years which will allow a reliable projection; if the same data were plotted in terms of dollars spent on electricity the curves could be seriously distorted by rate raises granted to the utility company, or by the kilowatt-hour charge dropping into a lower bracket because other departments are consuming more electricity.

Foreseeable effects. When major factors affecting manufacturing costs are known in advance they can be added to or substituted for the trends of historical data. Look for predictable changes in these areas:

Labor rates. If the plant has a union contract, labor rates can be predicted with great precision for as long as three years. If the contract expires in the current year, the size of wage settlements in other companies can be used as a guide. The nonunion plant can use wage surveys of its area and its industry to foretell the labor rates it will have to pay to remain competitive.

Materials and supplies. The plant that uses only a few materials can have its Purchasing Department research possible price fluctuations intensively, usually with accurate results. If a large variety of materials and supplies is consumed it may not be feasible to fully probe the cost future of each of them; historical plots of total costs (especially the semilog type) can be a reliable substitute.

Utilities. Applications for rate increases by public utility companies usually must be filed well in advance of the effective date and are covered in the local news media; the utility companies themselves, or even the commission to which they must apply, may be willing to answer inquiries about pending rate increases. *Depreciation* charges for new equipment can be predicted from the capital budget; proposed changes in *taxes* at all levels of government are usually known well in advance of their enactment and are covered in the news media.

Cost reduction efforts. Projects that are fully defined and certain of implementation can be included in cost predictions; it is dangerous, however, to include overall goals or "blue sky" savings in budget preparation.

THE OPERATING BUDGET

The operating budget and its corollary, the monthly budget report, are the end result of the expense reporting methods selected, cost systems chosen, and predictions generated according to the previous sections of this chapter. Its appearance and final form will depend upon the choice between absorption and direct costing, job order and process costing, the way in which service department costs are allocated, and so on. But there are two basic elements in any budget, no matter what its form: (1) it is a plan for spending money on specified items for a definite period in the future, and (2) its monthly report is a device for measuring how close to the plan the actual spending comes.

There are also variations in the way companies use their operating budgets. For some, they are general guides to plant spending, and the only requirement is that major variances be explainable. For others they are a very closely followed control tool, and the manager's performance rating is closely tied to his control of budget expenses. In some situations the budget is the authorization for the manager to spend funds, and he is not allowed to exceed its limits without prior approval.

How to Construct a Budget

Figure 7-1 is an example of an operating budget monthly report. A detailed examination of its features will shed light upon the ways in which a budget can be constructed:

Choice of cost center. A cost center is a collection of personnel and equipment to which charges are assigned and which generates a measurable output. In this example Department Z is the cost center; it could have been a subsection of a department, or it could have been the whole plant.

Production level. This plant's experience had been that the cost of producing a unit (100 lbs. in this case) varied with the total amount produced in a month; therefore, budgets were developed for 1.0, 1.5, 2.0, and 2.5 million lbs. Because the actual production fell at 1,603,410 lbs., the budget standards for 1,500,000 (the closest budgeted figure) were used. The use of different production level budgets explains why the budgeted cost of Raw Material A is $2.23 for March, but only $2.18 for the year to date.

Figures reported. The designers of this budget chose to report in terms of dollars spent per 100 lbs. of product. Thus the figure of $1.50 in the Actual column for Raw Material B means that $1.50 × 1,603,410 lbs./100 lbs. = $24,051.15 was spent for this raw material by the department. They felt that since production fluctuates from month to month, ratio reporting would iron out the effects of the fluctuations. If the production rate were constant from month to month, they might have chosen to report total dollars. If the price of the raw material fluctuates widely, they might have preferred to report pounds of Raw Material A consumed rather than dollars, especially on those copies used by manufacturing supervisors.

Cost system. This is a budget for a process cost system, with only one product produced by this department. If the department manufactured a great number of products during the year, separate budgets might have been developed for each product, or a job order cost system devised.

The report is designed for both direct and absorption costing. It is broken down into sections marked "Variable Costs" and "Fixed Costs." In a pure direct costing system only the variable cost section would be shown, and only the costs shown in it would be used to valuate finished good inventory. In absorption costing, the fixed cost section would be added, and included in value of inventory. "Fixed Costs" might even be included on a direct costing report as a matter of interest and guidance to the managers using it.

A word about "variable utilities" and "fixed utilities": Let's say that a process uses steam to manufacture its product. The steam used for actual manufacture would be costed under "variable utilities." If the plant were shut down, however, the steam used to keep the building warm would be classed under "fixed utilities." Similar comments apply to "variable maintenance" and "fixed maintenance." The former would include the cost of maintenance work to keep the production machinery going; the latter would include the building repair work or any other maintenance services required even when there is no production.

MANUFACTURING COST REPORT. Dept.: Z Product: Y Month: March 19___						
Budget Quantity: 1,500,000 lbs. Quantity Produced: 1,603,410 lbs.						
Cost Basis: 100 lbs. Figures in: Dollars						
	This month			**Year to date**		
Cost Category	**Budget**	**Actual**	**Var.**	**Budget**	**Actual**	**Var.**
Variable Costs						
Materials						
Raw Matl A	2.23	2.20	.03	2.18	2.19	(.01)
Raw Matl B	1.49	1.50	(.01)	1.47	1.40	.07
Containers	2.37	2.37	—	2.36	2.35	.01
Scrap Reworked	.27	.32	(.05)	.29	.28	.01
Scrap Discarded	.01	—	.01	.01	.03	(.02)
Labor						
Straight Time	.98	.96	.02	.95	.95	—
Overtime	.14	.17	(.03)	.11	.13	(.02)
Fringe Benefits	.21	.21	—	.20	.18	.02
Variable Supervision	.09	.08	.01	.08	.09	(.01)
Supplies	.74	.78	(.04)	.72	.75	(.03)
Variable Maintenance	.16	.17	(.01)	.15	.13	.02
Quality Control	.12	.12	—	.12	.11	.01
Variable Utilities	.07	.06	.01	.06	.04	.02
Subtotal	8.88	8.94	(.06)	8.70	8.63	.07
Fixed Costs						
Fixed Supv. & Admin.	.08	.07	.01	.07	.07	—
Fixed Utilities	.03	.03	—	.02	.03	(.01)
Depreciation	.83	.85	(.02)	.81	.80	.01
Fixed Maintenance	.04	.04	—	.03	.05	(.02)
Taxes & Insurance	.11	.12	(.01)	.10	.10	—
Subtotal	1.09	1.11	(.02)	1.03	1.05	(.02)
Grand Total	9.97	10.05	(.08)	9.73	9.68	.05
( ) indicates unfavorable variance.						

FIGURE 7-1: Operating Budget Monthly Report

Four Steps to Better Budget Preparation and Zero-Base Budgeting

Operating budgets are usually prepared for one year ahead in a series of steps similar to these:

1. Several months before the fiscal year begins top management requests forecasts of sales, raw material prices, and wages and salaries from the Marketing, Purchasing, and Personnel Departments.

2. These forecasts are modified if thought necessary and combined with top management's policy changes and decisions for the next year's business; the resulting guidelines are then sent to those managers in the company concerned with budget preparation.

3. The operating managers use the forecasts and guidelines to revise their existing budgets.

4. The revised figures are returned to top management where any final adjustments are made and the resulting budget officially adopted.

In this traditional method of budget preparation operating managers start with the cost of ongoing operations and add or subtract costs as foreseeable circumstances dictate; for instance if a manager has 400 hourly workers in his unit and they are to get a 40¢ per hour raise next year, he simply adds the calculated additional cost to this year's figure for labor to arrive at next year's budget. This system has the advantages of being readily understood, requiring minimum effort, and producing acceptably accurate projections of next year's costs of doing business.

It does not, however, address some very fundamental questions: Why are we spending money on this item at all? Can this activity be performed in a more cost-effective way? Does the system provide management with clear-cut budget choices so that it can make the most effective allocation of money resources?

How Zero-Base Budgeting Works

To provide answers for such questions a method called *zero-base budgeting* has been developed and applied both in industry and government; it is described in a book by Peter A. Pyhrr entitled *Zero-Base Budgeting* (New York: John Wiley & Sons, 1973). It works this way:

1. As before, top management issues the general assumptions, forecasts, and policy changes under which it plans to conduct next year's business.

2. Each manager in the company down to a chosen level (usually department head or perhaps general foreman) then examines the various activities and functions performed under him or her, and groups them into a series of *decision packages*. The subject of a decision package can be any separate activity associated with identifiable costs. It does not necessarily follow organizational lines, and may involve people, projects or services, or any combination of them; the "rules" for making up packages are purposely kept

simple to give managers the widest possible scope in the way they look at their operations. (An example of a decision package subject might be three maintenance mechanics who are permanently assigned to repairing drill bits.) The package itself is a written statement that describes the activity and the purposes it is expected to accomplish, tells what would happen if the activity were not performed at all, describes other course of action that could be taken to accomplish the same purposes, and states the costs and benefits associated with the activity and the suggested alternatives. In developing the list of other possible courses of action the manager not only looks for different ways to perform the function (should we do away with the janitorial staff and contract the work out?), but also considers different levels of carrying out the activity (should we keep the number of computer runs at the existing level, raise it by 50 percent, or cut it by a third?).

3. The manager next prepares a list of all packages ranked in order of priority, with the highest priorities at the top. Opposite each package listed is its estimated cost for the budget period and the cumulative cost of it and all the packages above it on the list. Alternative courses of action are listed separately on the ranked order, and not necessarily shown adjacent to the base package because they may have very different levels of priority.

4. The ranked list of packages then goes to the next higher level of management. Action can be taken at that point to approve the items on the list, or cut them back to fit within a realistic availability of funds. Or, they can be combined with packages from other managers and sent to still higher management; how far up the organization the lists go would depend upon how many packages must be reviewed; there is no point in swamping upper management with so many packages that they couldn't possibly study them all. At any stage of the process upper management can discuss the proposed activities to be funded with lower management. If it must limit the funding of a given unit to a certain number of dollars it can quickly go down the list to the cumulative total equal to that number of dollars and see clearly what activities it is continuing (all those above it) and what activities it is eliminating (all those below it).

The advantages to all concerned now become evident. The lower-level manager gets the opportunity to decide what are the most and least important activities under his direction and if reductions must be made, to have them carried out on the basis of his priorities. Beyond that, he not only has an opportunity to show the effect of budget cuts on his operation, but conversely, to show the benefits of expansion of particular activities. Finally, his outlook is broadened and his managerial skills improved by being required to take an overall look at his organization periodically and answer some fundamental questions about the activities he supervises. Upper management also receives some important advantages: all current activities of the company are periodically reviewed for cost effectiveness; a valuable tool is provided for deciding where the company's funds should be spent to obtain the greatest return, and if cuts have to be made they are done so on the basis of recommendations of the people closest to the work.

THE CAPITAL BUDGET

Just as the company formalizes its plans for operating expenditures in the expense budget, so must it establish a definite program for spending on capital projects. Here are the reasons why:

1. The company's financial managers need to be informed in advance of the dates on which they will have to supply the very large sums of money required for capital projects.

2. The capital budget is a planning tool. It requires responsible managers to clearly define their projects, estimate their costs accurately, and predict their times of completion.

3. The capital budget is a control tool. When issued in a periodic (monthly, quarterly, or even annual) report form, it highlights the comparison between the actual progress of a project and its original goals, offering the manager a first basis for corrective action. It can be combined with the post-completion audit discussed in Chapter 20, to achieve beginning-to-end control of capital projects.

4. It provides a method of first approval. Most companies require detailed cost estimates and economic justification calculations before *final approval* of capital projects. But the manager with a capital proposal can submit a *budget estimate* for her project; if the proposal is not approved for inclusion in the budget, she need spend no further time and money on detailed analysis.

Figure 7-2 illustrates one way in which a capital budget and its report form can be constructed. The report is issued quarterly, this one covering the first quarter of the year. Each project is listed by title with a project number (which can also be used as the Engineering Department's project number) followed by a letter suffix indicating whether the capital item is an addition of new equipment or replacement of old.

The cost and expenditure columns are divided into "Estimated" and "Known" or "Actual" categories. In project 803R the exact cost was known at the time it was included in the budget, so no estimate is given. Project 804A was estimated at $54,300, but actually cost $57,500 when built; both figures are shown in the "Total Cost" section.

Spending projections for the current year are shown in the "Expenditures" section. There are no entries in the "1st Quarter-Estimated" column because the period is ended, and any money spent would be shown in the "Actual" column. Taking Project 801A as an example, we find that $76,000 was spent in the first quarter, $231,000 is planned for the second quarter, $95,000 for the third and $14,000 for the fourth quarter. The last column shows that completion of the project is anticipated by November 1 (projects already completed are marked

ZZZ Corporation   Denver Plant   CAPITAL BUDGET QUARTERLY REPORT   Date Issued: March 31, 19___

Proj. No.	Title	Total Cost		Spent to Date	Expenditures 19___								Est'd Compl. Date.
					1st Qtr.		2nd Qtr.		3rd Qtr.		4th Qtr.		
		Est'd	Known		Est'd	Act.	Est'd	Act.	Est'd	Act.	Est'd	Act.	
803R	Replace Lift Truck 3	—	21.7	-0-			21.7						5/15
801A	Warehouse Expansion	416	—	76		76	231		95		14		11/1
796A	Welding Machine-Maintenance Dept.	—	3.5	3.5		3.5							Compl.
800A	New Screw Machines-Fastener Dept.	282	291	219			72						6/30
802A	Land Acquisition (Parcel "C," South Side of Plant)	270	—	-0-					270				9/15
799A	Fire Alarm System	—	83	28			55						4/23
798A	Warehouse Racks	42	—	-0-					42				8/31
804A	New Electrical Service to Main Building	54.3	57.5	57.5		57.5							Compl.
806R	Replace Boring Machine-Gear Housing Dept.	72.9	—	-0-							72.9		12/15
805A	New Press Brake-Sheet Metal Dept.	33.4	—	-0-							33.4		11/30
	TOTALS	1,170.6	456.7	384.0		137.0	379.7		407		120.3		

NOTES: 1. All figures in thousands of dollars.   2. Project Number Code Letters: A = Addition   R = Replacement

FIGURE 7-2: Capital Budget Quarterly Report

"Compl." in this column). As new reports are issued through the year the figures are updated to reflect the latest cost information.

This report has been held down to a simple one-page affair, but there is no reason why it could not be expanded to show additional information needed by those who use it. For instance, columns could be added showing the capital appropriation number, whether or not the project has final approval, salvage value of old equipment, anticipated cost overruns, depreciable life of new equipment, and financial criteria such as percent return on investment and payback period.

DEPRECIATION OF CAPITAL EQUIPMENT

When the plant buys a piece of equipment that costs $50,000 and is expected to last 10 years, an accounting problem is created. If the entire $50,000 is charged as a cost to the profit and loss statement in the year the equipment is purchased, profit will be distortedly low for that year, but unaffected in the other nine years of productive life. Since the equipment will be contributing to profit for the full 10 years, it would make more sense to distribute its cost over the entire period.

Depreciation is an accounting system that does just that—it provides a method of charging some portion of the cost of capital equipment to current expenses in each year of the equipment's life. It is a fictitious charge because the $50,000 really was expended in the first year, and therefore it is added back to net income to calculate *cash flow* for the period. In the case of Finework Manufacturing Company whose P&L statement is shown on page 106, cash flow for the year ended June 30 is the sum of net income of $12,394,000 plus depreciation of $2,981,000, which equals $15,375,000; it is this sum which is available to management to distribute as dividends, reinvest in the business, or set aside as reserves.

Because depreciation is deducted from profit before income taxes are calculated, the Internal Revenue Service has established rules affecting the way annual depreciation rates are determined for tax purposes. Land cannot be depreciated at all, nor can raw material and finished goods inventories. For the various kinds of depreciable assets—vehicles, office furniture, manufacturing equipment, buildings—the IRS publishes guidelines for determining the depreciable life. The following describes some of the currently used methods of figuring depreciation.

Four Ways to Calculate Depreciation

Going back to our example of a piece of manufacturing equipment with a first cost of $50,000 and a 10-year life, let's add the assumption that it has a salvage value of $5,000 at the end of its depreciable life. Using these figures, depreciation could be calculated by one of these methods:

1. *Straight Line Method*

The original cost less the salvage value is divided by the years of depreciable life to give the annual depreciation amount. In our example the result would be

($50,000 − $5,000)/10 = $4,500. In the straight line method the depreciable amount is the same for all years of depreciable life.

The remaining methods are all designed to allocate higher depreciation amounts to the earlier years of equipment life, tracking the profile of its actual value more closely than the straight line method.

2. Declining Balance Method

First calculate the straight line annual factor by dividing 1 by the number of years of depreciable life; in our example, $1/10 = 0.1$. Then take a multiple of this factor to obtain the annual depreciation rate; for manufacturing equipment the multiple is 2, but for other kinds of assets it could be 1.25 or 1.50. In our example the annual depreciation rate would be $0.1 \times 2 = 0.2$. Apply this rate to the original cost to obtain the first year's depreciation; subtract that from the original cost and multiply by the same rate to get the second year's depreciation. Continue the process until the salvage value is reached or until a switch is made to the straight line method because the annual depreciation amounts have fallen below the straight line values. In our example:

Year	Calculation		Depreciation Amount
1	$50,000 × 0.2	=	$10,000
2	($50,000 − $10,000) × 0.2 =		$8,000
3	($40,000 − $8,000) × 0.2 =		$6,400
4	($32,000 − $6,400) × 0.2 =		$5,120
5	($25,600 − $5,120) × 0.2 =		$4,096
6	($20,480 − $4,096) × 0.2 =		$3,277
7	($16,384 − $3,277) × 0.2 =		$2,621
8	($13,107 − $2,621) × 0.2 =		$2,097
9	($10,486 − $2,097) × 0.2 =		$1,678
10	($8,389 − $1,678) × 0.2 =		$1,342
		Total	$44,631

A deficiency in this method is immediately obvious: the total depreciation amount of $44,631 does not equal the full depreciable amount of $45,000 (original cost less salvage value). To get around this problem a switch is made to the straight line method some time in the later years, usually after the annual depreciation amount falls below that which the straight line method alone would yield. In our example the switch would be made after the eighth year; at that point the depreciated value of the equipment would be $10,486 − $2,097 = $8,389. Subtracting the salvage value of $5,000 leaves a remaining depreciable value of $3,389; dividing that by the remaining two years of depreciable life gives a depreciation amount of $1,694 for each of those years, bringing the total depreciation amount to the full $45,000.

3. *Declining Rate or Sum of Digits Method*

The depreciation amount for each year is obtained by applying a progressively decreasing fraction to the original cost less salvage value. The denominator of this fraction remains constant and is the sum of the digits representing the years of depreciable life; for 10 years it is $10 + 9 + 8 + 7 + 6 + 5 + 4 + 3 + 2 + 1 = 55$. The numerator for any year is the remaining number of years of depreciable life at the start of the year; for the first year the fraction would be 10/55, for the second year 9/55, and so on down to 1/55 in the tenth year. In our example:

Year	Calculation		Depreciation Amount
1	$10/55 \times (\$50,000 - \$5,000)=$		$8,182
2	$9/55 \times \$45,000$	=	$7,364
3	$8/55 \times \$45,000$	=	$6,545
4	$7/55 \times \$45,000$	=	$5,727
5	$6/55 \times \$45,000$	=	$4,909
6	$5/55 \times \$45,000$	=	$4,091
7	$4/55 \times \$45,000$	=	$3,273
8	$3/55 \times \$45,000$	=	$2,455
9	$2/55 \times \$45,000$	=	$1,636
10	$1/55 \times \$45,000$	=	$818
		Total	$45,000

4. *Tax Code Methods*

The IRS sets depreciation rules for tax purposes according to current tax law. Both the law and the rules change frequently, and a detailed example presented in a book of this type would soon become obsolete. As a matter of general information, however, the 1986 tax law sets the depreciable life of most industrial equipment at seven years, and requires calculation of depreciation using the declining balance method with a multiple of 2 (sometimes expressed as 200 percent). Other types of equipment have depreciable lives ranging from five to twenty years, and some use the 1.5 multiple in the declining balance method.

The law may require the corporation to use certain depreciation methods for tax purposes, but it may choose to use other systems for its own internal bookkeeping. The company may feel that depreciating a pump over a 7-year period is fine for tax purposes but does not reflect the actual useful life of the equipment for purposes of calculating profit, making investment decisions, or facilities planning; in such situations the company may choose a much different depreciation period for its own use.

In the discussion so far there has been an implicit assumption that the depreciable life of assets is measured in terms of calendar years, but there are other criteria which can be used: hours of operating time, number of units produced, or, for vehicular equipment, miles driven. For example, a company may choose to depreciate its corporate airplane on the basis of hours flown rather than years owned.

We have been working with another tacit assumption—that at the end of its useful life equipment is worn out and worth only its salvage value. Actually, equipment can reach the end of its useful life while it is still in excellent working order by the operation of the process of *obsolescence*, in which the appearance of newer and better equipment on the market renders existing equipment so inefficient that it can no longer keep the plant competitive in cost or quality.

Chapter 8

How to Improve Budget Performance with Permanent Cost Control and Cost Reduction Programs

At the beginning of Chapter 7 the two main cost responsibilities of the plant manager were set out: to see that serviceable cost systems are in place, and to mount a consistent effort to control and reduce manufacturing costs. The systems described in that chapter are the tools the manager uses to meet his second responsibility. This chapter will show how to get results in the major areas of plant cost control, how best to utilize cost reporting systems, and how to set up and operate a permanent cost reduction program.

TIPS ON CONTROLLING COSTS

Control, as part of the management cycle, is the process of finding out where you are compared to where you want to be and closing the distance. When it comes to costs, this means measuring actual costs and comparing them to standard costs. But before that process can begin you must look out for the first pitfall in the road to cost control: if the careless use of labor time or sloppy handling of materials is tolerated by plant management, the cost of these poor practices will gradually become imbedded in the standard costs, rendering them useless as a means of control.

Major Areas of Cost Control: The Plant Manager's Big Four

The corporation is interested in controlling the costs of many items—everything from the salespeople's expense reports to the consumption of office supplies. For you as the plant manager, however, there are four basic areas where your efforts will do the most good. This section will look at those areas, discuss aspects of their routine control, and tell how to go beyond routine surveillance to get maximum effect.

Labor.   First decide how much of a variance from standard you are willing to accept; then request an explanation of each deviation beyond that amount from the foreman or supervisor involved. It helps greatly to have the labor account broken down into its component parts—as is the case in Figure 7-1, where costs are reported for straight time, overtime, fringe benefits, and supervision—because the corrective action for a deviation in any one of these components will be quite different from the others. If you find recurring variances in a particular category, set up additional routine reports that highlight the problem area. For instance, if overtime charges repeatedly exceed standard on the monthly budget report, establish a weekly overtime report so that all managers and supervisors concerned can follow the situation more closely.

But control of labor costs requires much more than checking monthly reports. Walk around the plant. Are employees habitually late in returning from breaks and lunch periods? Are there obvious labor-saving operational changes that could be made? Have someone above the level of foreman review the weekly time-clock cards. Are there strike-overs, erasures, and write-ins of missing time punches? If so, dishonest and illegal practices may be getting started; they must be controlled immediately. Absenteeism is a prime cause of excessive labor and overtime costs; insist that each foreman keep an absentee log on each employee (rather than rely on distant personnel department files) so that the foreman can quickly identify overtime problems arising from that source and take the required action.

Materials.   Detailed knowledge of the cost of materials going into the finished product is essential to the running of any business, and every manufacturing plant will have some kind of materials accounting system. You will want to satisfy yourself that these costs are reported in sufficient detail for item-by-item control; this point is illustrated in Figure 7-1 where the materials used by the department are broken down into raw materials, containers, off-grade material reworked, off-grade material scrapped, and supplies. A significant negative variance for any one of these items will put the investigating supervisor on the right track quickly; a large positive variance (if it is not a record-keeping error) may lead to an important cost reduction.

Even that cost breakdown may not be detailed enough; for instance, the "Supplies" category may be too broad to be of much use to the investigator when costs are out of line, and he would be greatly helped if all the individual supplies used were listed separately. The growing use of computers for turning out cost reports makes a detailed breakdown more feasible, but if the list is still too long try breaking out the top 20 percent of the supplies ranked in order of money spent on them; you will probably find you have accounted for 80 percent of the total supply costs.

Visual inspection by the plant manager will be as rewarding in this cost area as it is in that of labor. Are raw materials and supplies carelessly handled by employees? What is going into the sewer? What is going out of the plant in trash containers? Again, poor practices, if accepted or ignored by management, wind up in "standard" costs.

Equipment. Cost control with respect to major pieces of equipment makes two demands upon the manager: to prevent costly unplanned breakdowns, and to keep the capital investment fully utilized. The first is achieved by an active preventive maintenance program whose operational details and cost implications are described in Chapter 5. The second is met by the use of utilization reports that compare the actual hours of operation and downtime with established standards; they can be developed for any time period from one shift up to a month—for most plants one week is a good choice.

Put equipment costs in perspective. Find out how much it costs per hour to keep a critical piece of equipment in operation—the sum of depreciation, repairs, and electrical or other energy to run it. If it costs $40 per hour for the equipment and the cost of labor is $8 per hour, you can sacrifice labor efficiency to keep the equipment running. If the equipment costs $4 per hour, you can sacrifice its utilization to gain labor efficiency.

Utilities. Be sure that utilities are included on the cost reports that first-line supervisors receive; without their knowledge and cooperation control of utilities usage is impossible. Managers at *all* levels must be involved and constantly checking to see that steam leaks are repaired, lights and other electrical equipment are turned off when not in use, heaters and air conditioners are not running in rooms with doors and windows open, engines are turned off when motor vehicles are not in motion, and the use of vehicles is planned to minimize the number and duration of trips. Not only should utility consumption and energy conservation be matters of regular cost control, but projects that further those ends should be included in the plant cost reduction program.

Cost Reports: Steps for Getting Out the Message

The primary tool for cost control is the Manufacturing Cost Report, shown in Figure 7-1. To get the greatest return from the effort that goes into preparing it, follow these steps:

Distribute to first-line supervisors. Just above every decision they make affects costs; their ability to take cost factors into account depends on their knowledge of the plant's cost standards and its current performance in relation to the standards. Merely handing them the cost reports will not be enough—they will need your counseling and direction in applying the information to cost control.

Decide the frequency of issue. One month is the most common, but don't hesitate to issue them more frequently, or to abstract especially important sections and publish them at shorter intervals, when quicker response to deviations in certain costs is called for.

Issue special editions for supervisors. A dilemma is created when the decision is made to pass cost reports on to the first-line supervisor: much of the information on it is either confidential, or sensitive, or both. Supervisors frequently have desks and offices in locations where it is hard to keep papers concealed, and the company may not want its hourly employees to know the cost of producing Product A or how much money was spent on overtime last month.

One way out is to publish a version of the report in terms of units consumed, rather than in dollars. In Figure 7-1 for instance, raw materials could have been reported as pounds, tons, or number of pieces; labor as man-hours; and quality control in terms of units of test work.

Act on deviations. The cost report is just another interesting piece of paper until it becomes the basis for action taken on cost deviations. Your goal is to be sure that your supervisors and managers know why the cost deviations occurred and have plans for correcting or taking advantage of them. You do this through personal contact, holding cost meetings, or even requiring written cost control reports.

Cost Control in the Purchasing Function

The purchase of raw materials and supplies accounts for a very large share of the cost dollar in most companies, and is the logical place for intensive cost control efforts to begin. Whether you supervise the purchasing function directly or it is a staff service, you will want to be familiar with the application of these purchasing cost controls:

Economic order quantity. It costs money to process an order, and the fewer raw material orders processed the lower this cost. But if fewer orders are placed, more material must be purchased, and it costs money to carry inventory. This formula gives the optimum balance between the two factors:

$$Q = \sqrt{\frac{2AC}{I}}$$

Where Q is the economic order quantity in dollars, A is the annual requirement in dollars, C is the cost of processing an order in dollars, and I is the annual cost of carrying inventory expressed as a decimal fraction of the purchase price.

Special arrangements with suppliers. You may be able to obtain more favorable pricing and delivery arrangements from a supplier if you offer to contract for a whole year's needs. With or without a contract, he may be willing to take on the job of maintaining inventory in order to get your business.

ABC analysis. Make a list of all the materials and supplies purchased, ranking them in order of total dollars spent on each per year. Chances are that you will see a distribution somewhat like this: The top 10 percent of the items will account for 60 percent of the money spent (Class A), the next 25 percent will account for 30 percent of the money spent (Class *B*), and the bottom 65 percent will account for only 10 percent of the total expenditures (Class *C*). Class *A* materials offer the greatest rewards for effort in price reduction and inventory control; Class *B* materials should be carefully watched; and Class *C* items can be managed with less control because they have so little impact on total cost.

Cost Control by Payment Authorization

This is a simple, effective device for cost control, but somehow ignored in many companies. It consists of having the appropriate supervisor, superintendent, or manager initial each invoice or bill for purchases ordered by his or her department before the Accounting Department makes payment. Although it adds some "paper-work" to the jobs of each of these people, it has the following advantages:

1. It keeps the manager informed of expenditures as they occur, rather than having him confronted with an accumulated total of bills too numerous to investigate.
2. It helps the manager to recognize differences between what she was told an item "would cost" and what is actually charged for it.
3. Because of his special knowledge of the department and the circumstances surrounding the purchase, the manager may be able to correct erroneous charges.
4. As the manager monitors the incoming bills, she can caution her subordinates and put the brakes on her own spending if she sees the totals climbing too high.

What to Do When Costs Go Out of Control

Despite the most carefully designed cost control systems and the best efforts of the people who use them, the plant manager will eventually receive a cost report showing large unexpected deviations from budget. When this happens, use these guidelines to discover the causes and to develop corrective action:

Inform everyone concerned. You will need their observations, knowledge, and opinions to arrive at the causes. Ask for help from outside the Production Department—engineering, accounting, purchasing, and inventory control personnel may have valuable insights into the problem. It is especially true of cost problems that the more eyes and ears focused on the investigation, the better its chances of success.

Temporarily shorten the intervals of reporting. If the normal reporting period is one month and you are in trouble with high raw material usage, have inventory counts and usage reports weekly or every two weeks until the trouble is cleared up.

Attack a complex cost problem with a **priority system.** If it is not possible to investigate several out-of-control cost components at once, an obvious method is to take the costliest ones first. Or, it may result in quicker payoff to handle first those which appear easiest to solve.

Look for unrealistic cost standards. If the standard cost of manufacturing an item is based on 1,000 pieces per day, but the process is actually run on a machine which can produce only 500 pieces per day, there is little hope of meeting the standard, and it must be changed. Newly developed standards are more suspect than older ones.

Look for cost reporting errors. If labor charges, material requisitions, or vendors' invoices are charged to the wrong accounts, the cost report can be seriously unbalanced. There should be a clear-cut trail leading back from the cost report through postings in the Accounting Department to the original cost documents.

SYSTEMATIC COST REDUCTION

How to Set Up a Permanent Cost Reduction Program

Peter Drucker has aptly stated the situation in many companies: "The annual cost reduction drive . . . is as predictable in most businesses as a head cold in spring. It is about as enjoyable."*

The annual cost reduction drive is really not cost reduction at all; it is usually an attempt to get people to do what they should have been doing all along—exercise proper cost *control. Cost reduction* is something far different—it is the continuing development and application of *ideas* that eliminate or favorably modify specific cost-generating activities. To be effective, it must be as formal as the cost reporting system, i.e., it must have stated objectives and a means of measuring actual performance against those objectives.

To set up a permanent cost reduction program in your plant, take the following steps:

1. Develop the concept of the formal cost reduction project for implementing a single cost reduction idea. For each project the sponsor describes in writing the idea he plans to implement, states when it will go into effect, and the investment in capital and operating costs which must be made to achieve the savings.

2. Decide at what level in the organization projects are to be sponsored. For most plants the appropriate level is the one at which capital and operating budgets are maintained. For example, if the plant is divided into operating and service departments that have their own cost budgets, then the department would be the level at which cost reduction projects are sponsored, and the department head would be the sponsor.

---

*Peter F. Drucker, *Managing for Results* (New York: Harper & Row Publishers, Inc., 1964), p. 68. Used by permission.

3. Establish a project approval step. When the sponsor submits a written proposal it should be approved by higher authority, normally his immediate superior, who will have a broader idea of whether or not the proposal fits the plant's operations, and whether or not the company is prepared to commit the required resources. You must also decide whether or not approval of the project constitutes authorization to go ahead with the capital and operating expense increases required, or whether such expenditures must still go through their normal approval steps (see Chapter 20, page 410).

4. Appoint a Program Coordinator who will set up the program's record-keeping system and issue periodic reports on its progress. In a plant oriented toward the line organization one of the department heads themselves might be selected for the job; in other situations the choice might be someone from the Accounting Department.

5. Motivate the department heads to contribute. The plant manager will want to explain the program and its purposes at an introductory meeting, and give the Program Coordinator an opportunity to spell out the procedure for project approval and the reporting system. In many plants the fact that the plant manager (and quite likely his or her superior) is following the progress reports is enough to keep the department heads interested and active. In others it may be appropriate to develop a competitive atmosphere among the department heads. In most situations the plant manager will want to make cost reduction performance one of the topics discussed in the supervisor's annual salary review.

Project Approval and the Program Reporting System

We have already seen that the sponsor is required to make project commitments in writing, and Figure 8-1 is an example of how a cost reduction proposal can be reduced to specific terms, approved for implementation, and entered on the program's books. This particular form assumes that the plant is divided into departments, but any cost center designation could be used instead. Spaces are provided for a description of the project, the expected savings it will produce, a date for its inception, and the cost of any investment required. When the project is approved it is given a number, and copies are sent to the originator and the Program Coordinator.

Figure 8-2 illustrates a format the Program Coordinator can use to summarize the performance of the entire plant. Its frequency of issue is determined by the needs of the individual plant—the level of activity in the program, the importance of reporting its accomplishments, and keeping motivation and interest at a high level. This report happens to be issued quarterly; some plants would prefer a monthly report.

This example is made up for a Production Department and a Maintenance Department; most plants will have more than two cost centers, and the report would be enlarged to include all of them. Each project is identified by the cost

THE RTZ CORPORATION
Dudley Plant

COST REDUCTION PROJECT

DATE 1/7/87

PROJECT TITLE Motorized Tool Carts for Remote Jobs

DEPARTMENT Maintenance   PROJECT NO. 1026

DESCRIPTION OF PROJECT:

   Purchase 1 Taylor-Dunn Model SS Electric Truck for transporting maintenance personnel to and from the shop to jobs in remote areas of the plant. It is estimated that use of the cart will save an average 0.416 hours of maintenance time per shift, or 454.3 hours per year (3 shifts per day, 7 days per week, 52 weeks per year) at $12.65 per hour.

EXPECTED SAVINGS: $ 5,747   PER — (UNITS OF PRODUCTION)

PER Year (MONTH OR YEAR)

BEGINNING 2/20/87 (DATE)

INVESTMENT REQUIRED: $ $2,993   CAPITAL (APPR. NO. C87-1)

$ — EXPENSE

DESCRIPTION OF INVESTMENT Truck purchase

plus installation of electrical wiring to charging

station.

APPROVALS: *C. D. Williams* (SUPERINTENDENT)

L. R. Santi (PLANT MGR.)

FIGURE 8-1: Cost Reduction Project Approval Form

THE RTZ CORPORATION

Dudley Plant

COST REDUCTION PERFORMANCE REPORT

4th Qtr., 1987

Dept.	Proj. No.	Project Title	Forecast Savings	Actual Savings	Capital Spent
A	931	Improved Scrap Recovery Method	$29,058	25,340	60,588
A	932	Steam Condensate Return System		-Expired-	
A	933	Consolidation of Second Shift	4,058	4,058	-0-
A	934	Replacement of Wooden Storage Pallets with Steel	1,098	1,185	8,030
A	935	Use of Smaller Size Grinding Wheels	295	295	-0-
		Total	34,509	30,878	68,618
Maint.	1026	Motorized Tool Carts for Remote Jobs	1,437	1,905	2,993
Maint.	1027	Use of Precut Pump Packing	465	448	-0-
Maint.	1028	Open Stock Issue of Small Fittings	142	142	-0-
Maint.	1029	Automatic Pipe Threader	570	542	3,035
		Total	2,614	3,037	6,028
		Grand Total	37,123	33,915	74,646

FIGURE 8-2: Cost Reduction Program Period Performance Report

center sponsoring it, and by project number and title. The forecast savings are taken from the project approval form, and the actual savings and capital spent during the period reported by the cost centers. Project 1026 appears in both Figures 8-1 and 8-2 and shows how the important information tracks from one form to the other. Project 932 illustrates the point that cost reduction projects should have a finite life (one year is a common choice), after which it is marked "expired" and included in the basic cost structure of the plant.

Figure 8-1 identifies the plant manager as the final approving authority for projects submitted; in the very large plants this function may have to be delegated further down in the line organization. In either case the approving authority and those participating in the program need a set of criteria for judging proposed projects. Use these guidelines for establishing your own standards:

1. Set a minimum level of cost savings to keep the program from being bogged down in the "we saved twelve paper clips per week" type of project. One

hundred dollars per month is a suggested level for a plant doing $20 million per year in sales, but local factors may require raising or lowering this figure.

2. Each project must have a definite, demonstrable financial return. "We should spread salt on the sidewalk in winter because it may save the cost of an accident," while a worthy idea, is not a cost reduction project.

3. Avoid confusion between cost reduction and cost control. "We will put the lights out every night and save $700 per year" is not a cost reduction project; it is a form of cost control that should have been exercised right along.

4. Don't hesitate to accept projects which depend wholly or largely on labor savings. Some managers object to this on the grounds that a project which saves two man-hours per day doesn't allow a reduction in the number of people employed, and therefore doesn't really save money. The answer is threefold: the saving of two hours per day may immediately reduce the use of overtime; although one project saving two hours does not permit a reduction in force, several projects totaling eight hours do; and the cost center that has been working at labor savings for a period of time can handle additional duties or expanded production capacity without adding people.

Where to Look for Cost Reduction Opportunities

The whole program depends upon the number and quality of the cost reduction ideas generated, and when the program is first announced plant personnel will need some coaching in where to look for possible projects. Here are some ideas they should examine:

All capital appropriation requests. Capital improvements are most often justified on the basis of a financial return that comes from expanded capacity or reduced costs. The latter type are very legitimate projects for inclusion in the cost reduction program.

The major cost categories. Production departments control costs in four major areas: labor, materials, supplies, and utilities. They should be encouraged to search each of these areas methodically for cost reduction opportunities.

The highest cost elements. When studying supplies, for instance, list the individual items purchased in order of the dollars spent on them annually; those at the top of the list offer the greatest opportunities for cost reduction.

Ongoing efforts. Production departments characteristically strive to make their work easier, more productive, and less costly. Many of these efforts will meet the criteria for cost reduction projects, and should be included in the program. Encouraging department heads to develop projects out of these routine efforts can be a big help in developing their enthusiasm for the program, particularly when it is first being organized.

Purchases and activities that can be eliminated altogether. There is no surer way of achieving a cost reduction than to eliminate the activity which generates the cost; although the rewards are great, it is the most difficult kind of cost reduction for most department heads.

How Purchasing and Accounting Departments Can Help

Purchasing and accounting are staff functions, and it must be remembered that the primary responsibility for cost reduction in the production organization is not theirs—indeed, they have major responsibilities for cost reduction in their own departments. But they can offer assistance to the production group in its search for cost reduction opportunities:

Purchasing. Because of their continuing contacts with the outside world of suppliers and salespeople, the personnel of this department are in a good position to collect and transmit suggestions for improved operating methods and reduced costs to the operating departments. Those departments should inform the purchasing people of the areas in which they are seeking improvements, no matter how vague the requests might be in the early stages, so they can be alert for solutions to the cost problems.

Accounting. These people are in the best position to discern trends in costs, to identify the cost categories that offer the greatest opportunity for cost reduction, and to make specific suggestions for cost reduction projects. Their ideas should be solicited; in return they will usually work very hard to help the cost program. They may also provide important staff services in evaluating cost reduction proposals—gathering cost data and calculating rates of return.

Chapter 9

Cost-Saving Measures for Conserving Energy

AMERICAN ENERGY SOURCES: AN OVERVIEW

Americans are accustomed to plentiful supplies of energy. Their agricultural society was first supported by wood fuel from immense forests, and its simple machines driven by wind and water power. As the industrial revolution took hold, coal became the dominant and plentiful fuel. By the middle of the twentieth century oil and gas had become the fuels of choice because they burned cleanly, required little storage space, and could readily be transported through pipelines.

During this period of ample supply, designers of American manufacturing plants did not have to give the highest priority to energy efficiency. With fuel abundant and cheap, the cost savings to be gained from elaborate energy-saving schemes were too small to justify the necessary equipment to carry them out.

Today the outlook for American energy sources is different. American gas and oil reserves are no longer sufficient to meet demand, and an ever-increasing share of energy supplies comes as imports. These imported supplies may, at times, be controlled by a group of countries small enough to form a cartel, raise prices to 15 times their previous levels in a short time, and withhold supplies to achieve foreign policy goals.

The effect on American industry has been immediate and profound. Methods of conserving energy, not economically feasible with oil at $2 a barrel, suddenly become financially attractive at $30 a barrel. Faced with actual and potential shortages of oil and gas, industrial managers have begun searching for alternate fuels, notably a return to coal. But this creates a conflict with public demand for a clean environment—the fuel must be burned cleanly and particulates and noxious gases removed from the stack emissions.

How does a plant manager find his bearings in such turmoil? This chapter presents some important fundamentals, pointing out places to look for conservation opportunities, showing how to set up an energy conservation program and examining alternate sources of energy, all while keeping an eye on the bottom line. While delving into the particulars of these topics, you are advised to keep some basic truths in mind:

- *Conservation* is the most powerful tool. Almost every manufacturing plant abounds with opportunities to reduce energy consumption without switching fuels, and without making major changes in equipment or process.

- Oil and gas are fuels of *convenience,* and when the price of the convenience exceeds its value there should be no hesitation to replace them.

- Energy problems have not changed the *rules* of economics, only the numbers. Equipment additions that will cut the use of energy must still be economically justified (Chapter 20, page 410), and proposed operating changes must be shown to enhance, not reduce profitability.

WHAT YOU NEED TO KNOW ABOUT HEAT TRANSFER

Manufacturing plants usually purchase energy in the form of fossil fuels (coal, gas, and oil) or as electricity. Fossil fuels are burned to produce heat energy carried by steam, hot water or other fluids, and heated gases. Electricity is mostly converted into illumination or mechanical energy, but some is transformed into heat in resistors, induction coils, and arc furnaces. Because most energy losses in the typical plant occur as heat losses it will be useful to review some of the basic technical concepts of heat transfer.

Heat is a form of energy that is measured in *British thermal units* or *Btu.* One Btu is the quantity of heat required to raise the temperature of one pound of water by one degree Fahrenheit. (The metric system employs *calories, kilocalories,* or *joules.*) Heat flows from one point in a system to another when there is a temperature difference between them, and flows from the point of high temperature to the point of low temperature.

How Heat Is Transferred: Three Methods

Heat transfer in any system occurs by one or more of the following methods: *conduction, convection,* and *radiation.*

Conduction is the flow of heat from one point to another in a body, or between bodies in direct contact. This concept is illustrated in Figure 9–1, which depicts a brick wall with its left side at temperature t_A, and the right side at lower temperature t_B. The wall has a thickness of L feet, and a

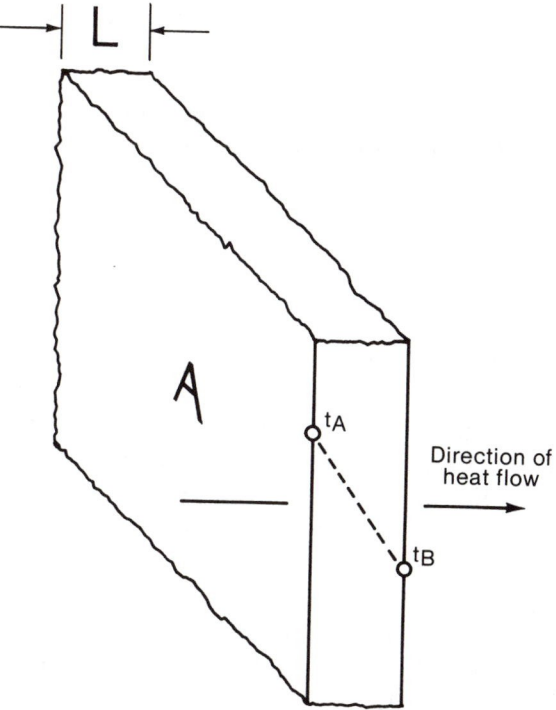

FIGURE 9-1: Heat Transfer by Conduction

heat flow of Q Btu per hour is passing through the wall over an area of A square feet. Before we can calculate the heat flow through the wall, we must know the value of a specific property of the brick called *thermal conductivity,* represented by the letter k. (We instinctively recognize the difference in thermal conductivities of different materials when we grasp a metal cup containing hot coffee much more carefully than a ceramic or foamed plastic cup.) The flow of heat in Figure 9-1 is given by the equation

$$Q = k(t_A - t_B)\frac{A}{L}$$

If we assume that the brick has a k value of 0.5, that the area A through which the heat is passing is 300 square feet, that the temperature at point A is 70° F and at point B is 28° F, and that the wall is 0.5 feet thick, then for the situation shown

$$Q = 0.5(70-28)\frac{300}{0.5} = 12,600 \text{ Btu per hour}$$

In situations where we want heat to transfer quickly, such as through the tubes of an industrial heat exchanger, we use materials with high thermal conductivities; metals, for example, have k values ranging from 8 for stainless steel to 242 for silver. When we want to slow down the transfer of heat we use insulating materials, which typically have k values varying from .02 to .08. For various types of wood the range is .06 to .12, and for concrete from 0.4 to 1.0.

Convection is the transfer of heat by the motion of a fluid. In a room warmed by a baseboard heater the air in contact with the hot surface is heated, expands, and rises. As it does so, cool air moves in to replace it, is heated, and also rises; the repetition of this process sets up a convection current, which eventually transfers heat from the unit throughout the room. When the fluid moves by virtue of changes in density caused by temperature changes, the process is called *natural convection;* when the fluid carrying heat is moved by a mechanical device (fan, blower, pump, compressor) the process is called *forced convection.*

Consider Figure 9-1 again. If we imagine that the brick wall is the wall of a building and that the surface marked A is in contact with the warm (70° F) air of a room, while the opposite side of the wall is in contact with the outside atmosphere (at 30° F), then heat will flow from the air of the room to surface A by convection, through the wall by conduction, and from the outside surface of the wall to the atmosphere by convection again. The equation for heat transfer given in the previous section on conduction cannot be used for this situation because, in addition to the conduction of heat through the wall, we have the transfer from the warm air of the room to surface A and from the outside surface of the wall to the cold atmosphere. The rate at which heat passes through these interfaces is affected by the physical properties of the fluids (warm and cold air) and the velocities at which they pass the surfaces. Therefore the thermal conductivity k, which is only a property of the wall itself, is replaced by the overall coefficient of heat transfer U, which includes all of the factors mentioned above as well as k. If the temperature in the room is t_r and the outside temperature is t_o, the heat transfer equation becomes

$$Q = U(t_r - t_o)A$$

U is expressed in Btu per hour per square foot per degree Fahrenheit of temperature difference. L, the width of the wall, is not seen in the overall equation because it is also included in the factors that make up U. A typical value for U in the example given might be 0.6. For forced convection inside an industrial heat exchanger where warm water is heating cool water, the value might be 200; if steam is heating the water, the value could be on the order of 1,000. In industrial heat exchangers the temperatures of the fluids change continuously along the length of the exchanger, posing a question as to what temperature difference to use in the equation. One method is to take the arithmetic average of the temperature differences at the inlet and outlet ends of the exchanger. Industrial designers, however, often find it more useful to use the *logarithmic mean temperature difference,* which is obtained by taking the temperature difference, or Δt, between the hot fluid and the cold fluid at one end of the exchanger and subtracting from it the Δt at the other end, and dividing the remainder by the natural logarithm of the ratio of the first Δt to the second.

Radiant heat transfer occurs by the emission of electromagnetic waves that are transmitted through space and do not require solid or fluid media for transmission (although the radiation may pass through them). The science of radiant heat transfer is built upon the concept of the *black body*, which is defined as a body that absorbs all of the radiant energy impinging upon it, emits the maximum amount of radiant energy at a given temperature, and emits radiation with an intensity which varies only with the fourth power of its absolute temperature. The equation for radiant heat interchange is developed from a highly theoretical model in which a black body with a surface area A and at absolute temperature T_1 is completely surrounded by a black body enclosure whose surface is at absolute temperature T_2. In this situation the net interchange of energy is given as

$$Q = \sigma A(T_1^4 - T_2^4)$$

where Q is in Btu per hour, A is in square feet, T is in degrees Rankine (= degrees Fahrenheit + 459), and σ is the Stefan-Boltzmann constant which always has the value 17.13×10^{-10} when expressed in Btu per hour per square foot per (degrees Rankine)^4.

The conditions of the theoretical model are rarely met in industrial practice, and various factors are introduced into the equation to accommodate the deviations. A geometric factor F is used, which takes on different values with changing configurations—parallel planes, perpendicular planes with a common side, rows of tubes receiving radiant energy from one side, and so forth. Actual materials usually do not behave as black bodies, and the actual energy emitted by a body divided by the energy emitted by a black body at the same temperature gives a ratio called *emissivity;* it is usually represented by the letter e when inserted into the equation. It can range from .02 for highly polished metals to above 0.90 for brick, asbestos board, or surfaces coated with oil paints.

Absorptivity is the ratio of the energy absorbed by an actual body to that which would be absorbed by a black body under the same conditions; it is usually represented by the letter a. Absorptivities may vary from a low of .07 for polished aluminum to above 0.95 for asbestos slate. The wavelength of the radiation may also enter into the equation. The development of these factors and their incorporation into the heat transfer equation is a complicated process, beyond the scope of this book.

The discussion so far has centered on the ability of materials to emit or absorb radiation, but it should be remembered that in some materials impinging radiation simply passes through them (as in the case of visible light passing through glass), and in still others impinging radiation is partly reflected away. This latter property can be of value when you want to hold the radiant energy entering a system to the minimum, as in the case of a building or other structure that is exposed to sunlight but must be kept as cool as possible.

WHERE TO LOOK FOR ENERGY SAVINGS IN THE PLANT STRUCTURE

Plant buildings may house offices, laboratories, warehouses, and production operations. Heating will usually be required in the winter months and, for some of the building space, air conditioning in the summer. Look for energy conservation opportunities in the following key areas.

How to Stop Unwanted Air Movement

Reduce the infiltration of outside air (or flows between parts of a building) by

1. Applying caulking and weatherstripping to holes in the building walls and to poorly sealing windows and doors. Look for holes around window and door frames and where pipes and conduit pass through walls.

2. Installing strip curtains in doorways and wall openings, such as those for a conveyor, which must be left open for traffic but at the same time allow unwanted air currents to move. The strip curtains will part to allow personnel and objects to pass, but close up again as soon as they are through.

3. Sealing off doorways in plant areas that must handle frequent traffic by installing impact doors consisting of two flexible sections, each covering half of the opening. The sections part when contacted by a moving object such as a lift truck, automatically resealing after it passes.

4. Installing dock seals and shelters at the warehouse loading docks. They consist of blocks of flexible foam insulation covered with a resistant fabric, and placed on the outside wall of the dock in an inverted U at the dock opening. The truck is backed up to the dock so that the edges of its sidewalls and roof contact the blocks, sealing off air flow from the outside while the truck is being unloaded.

Techniques for Blocking Solar Radiation

When buildings must be kept as cool as possible by natural means or when they require expensive energy for air conditioning, use these techniques to reduce the heat load imposed by incident sunlight:

1. Change the color of exterior surfaces exposed to sunlight. Light colors reflect more of the sun's radiation, with aluminum and white-colored surfaces reflecting most of all. One building owner in the Southwest found that the use of white roof gravel would reduce absorbed heat from sunlight by 42 percent.

2. Be sure that windows are provided with shades or blinds, that their reflecting surfaces are kept clean, and that they are used.

3. Provide exterior shading of walls and windows with awnings, canopies, overhangs, and plantings.

4. Install reflective or tinted glass in windows to reflect incident sunlight or to block those wavelengths that produce the greatest heating effect.

5. For larger buildings, adjust the responses of heating and cooling systems to the variation in loads in different parts of the building. As the sun moves through the sky in a normal workday, various parts of the building receive different amounts of solar heat. People working in the north end of the building may complain, winter and summer, that they are "always cold"; those on the south side may have just the opposite complaint. Concentrations of people and the activities they perform may vary in different parts of the building at different times of the day. The solutions can be as simple as putting separate zone controls in those parts of the heating and cooling systems serving various parts of the building and as sophisticated as installing entirely new control systems operated by computers which constantly monitor changing conditions and direct the most economical response to them.

Tips for Using Solar Radiation

In those areas, and at those times of the year when heating loads are the most important energy consumers, the sun's energy can be used in these ways to help carry the loads:

1. Reverse as many as practicable of the techniques mentioned above to block solar radiation—use darker exterior colors, remove exterior and interior shading of windows and doorways.

2. Install skylights so that sunlight can help with the lighting load. A refinement is to add light-sensitive dimmer switches to the artificial lighting controls so that they contribute more light when the sunlight is weak and less when it is strong, maintaining a constant level of light in the illuminated areas.

3. More elaborate passive solar heating systems can be installed. Their fundamental components are (a) an unoccupied area of the building, (b) a large roof or wall section fitted with glass or other transparent material through which the sun's rays can pass to heat the air in the unoccupied section, creating a "greenhouse effect," and (c) a means of circulating the air thus warmed to the occupied sections of the building. Control systems can be as simple or as complex as desired.

How to Reduce Conduction/Convection Losses

The object here is to cut down the losses or gains of heat through walls, roofs, and floors—the "building envelope"—primarily through the use of insulation.

1. *Roofs:* The upsurge in fuel costs which occurred the early 1970s have caused building designers to take a more careful look at the amount of roof insulation provided. One owner of an industrial building complex built on the U.S. Gulf Coast found that by increasing the standard one inch of roof

insulation to three inches he could cut heat gain or loss by 20 percent, and thus achieve the best balance between additional construction cost and fuel savings.

2. *Walls and floors:* Uninsulated concrete floors laid on ground can be expected to have a heat loss of about 2 Btu per hour per square foot, assuming room temperature at 70° F and the ground at a constant 50° F. Uninsulated brick and concrete walls exposed to outside temperatures down to 0° F can be expected to lose 15 Btu per hour per square foot; insulation thicknesses of 1½ inches, once considered adequate for industrial buildings, have been increased in some cases to two or three times that amount, depending upon the cost of fuel and the severity of the climate.

3. *Windows:* Ordinary window glass comes in thicknesses of 1/16 or 1/8 inch. Even if the thermal conductivities of glass and building brick are roughly the same, a 1/8 inch thickness of glass will conduct 96 times as much heat as the same area of a 12-inch brick wall. That is why many newer industrial buildings (especially if they are conditioned) are designed without any windows at all. "Double glazed" or *thermal pane* windows, which consist of two (sometimes three) sheets of glass separated by dead air space, can be used (when the building must have windows) to reduce heat loss or gain, but their high cost has tended to limit industrial applications.

4. *Ceiling height:* In buildings (particularly older ones) with high ceilings a great deal of energy can be wasted in heating successive layers of warm air, which rise to the ceiling, until they fill the air space down to the level at which personnel are comfortable. One way to avoid this loss is to install a false ceiling at normal room height, cutting off the space above from the flow of air. If this cannot be done for some reason, another solution is to install fans in the upper air space to direct the warm air back to the lower levels.

Lighting Conservation Measures

Look for energy savings in these areas:

1. *Reduced illumination.* Do you really need all that light? One company found that it could reduce the "normal" standard of illumination of 100 foot-candles to 70 without interfering with worker effectiveness; it also provided three levels of lighting in office and general work areas, and added "task lighting" at specific work stations. The drop from 100 to 70 foot-candles resulted in a reduction of 30 percent in energy consumption.

2. *Fluorescent lighting.* Fluorescent lamps will provide the same illumination as incandescent types for about one-third of the energy consumption.

3. *Windows:* Ordinary window glass comes in thicknesses of 1/16 or 1/8 inch. Even if the thermal conductivities of glass and building brick are roughly the same, a 1/8 inch thickness of glass will conduct 96 times as much heat as the same area of a 12-inch brick wall. That is why many newer industrial additional savings, and manual override added for unusual situations.

4. *Heat from lights.* In buildings that have extensive lighting systems, advantage can be taken of the heat given off by the lamps. Blowers are set up to move air across the banks of lights, and the air thus warmed is distributed for space heating. Economies are realized not only in the reduction of heat that must be supplied from other sources, but also in the prolonged life of the lamps resulting from their operation at lower temperatures. In the cooling season this warm air is diverted to the exterior of the building, reducing the load on the air conditioning system.

Three Ways to Save Energy with Heating and Cooling Systems

Here are three ways you can work with the system you have to save energy:

1. Adjust temperature settings in unoccupied spaces. There will be a number of areas of the plant not occupied at all during some parts of a 24-hour day, or occupied only sparsely and intermittently. Heat control settings should be lowered and cooling control settings raised in such areas, and automatic controls are usually the cheapest method of adjustment. Of course, nothing beats shutting them down altogether—there is no greater energy saving than zero consumption—but the savings must be compared with the costs of wear and tear caused by frequent start-ups and the extra energy required to bring the space back to its normal controlled temperature.

2. Lower control settings in winter, raise them in summer. In times of energy shortages, Americans are asked to heat occupied buildings only to 68° F, and cool them to 78° F. While these temperatures may not be comfortable for everyone, you can set up a test program to see how closely these settings can be approximated without an undue number of complaints.

3. Establish adjustment and preventive maintenance programs. Make sure that fuel-air ratios, dampers, vanes, and valves are properly adjusted on a regular basis; that heat exchange surfaces are cleaned; and that filters and belts are replaced or adjusted.

WHERE TO LOOK FOR ENERGY SAVINGS IN PLANT OPERATIONS

In Steam Generation and Distribution

Conservation in the steam system starts with the question: How much of the energy paid for in the purchased fuel is lost? Look for ways to recover it in the answers to the following questions.

How much energy is going up the stack?

Losses can start right off with the improper burning of fuel, and combustion engineers have found some boiler stack gases with oxygen content as high as 8 percent. By reducing air supply to the burner so as to get the stack gas concentration down to 2 to 4 percent, an almost equal percentage reduction in fuel consumption can be obtained. When fuel prices are high, the cost of elaborate, computerized control systems based on the measurement of either oxygen or carbon monoxide/carbon dioxide in the discharged gases may be justified.

Substantial energy losses can occur when the stack gases are discharged to the atmosphere at too high a temperature. When the temperature is much above 400° F, it may be cost effective to install an *economizer*, a heat exchanger in which the incoming boiler feedwater is heated by the stack gas. Less fuel is then consumed in the boiler firebox.

How much energy is lost in steam leaks and malfunctioning steam traps?

Steam leaking through a gap or opening equivalent to a 1/8 inch diameter hole can lose the heat equivalent of a barrel of fuel oil in 30 hours. For every doubling of the hole size, the amount of steam loss is *quadrupled*. Facts like these should be enough to convince any plant manager that frequent inspection for and prompt repair of steam leaks is an absolute must.

The steam trap is a device designed to discharge liquid water that has condensed inside a steam system. When working properly, it will open when condensate has collected behind it and close as soon as the water is gone, preventing the escape of steam. A trap that is stuck open, or one that is improperly sized, can allow substantial quantities of steam to blow through to the atmosphere. One company found that 12.9 percent of its traps were blowing through, and that they were losing an average of 58 pounds of steam per hour. When this company set about a repair/replacement program it saved $11 for every $1 spent. At a minimum your program should consist of (a) an initial survey to determine which steam traps are malfunctioning or are not the proper type of adequate size for the job, (b) replacement or repair of the substandard traps found in (a), and (c) periodic inspections, which, if carried out semiannually, will probably hold the level of malfunctioning traps to around 7 percent. For an excellent report on how to set up a steam trap program see S. J. Vallery, "Are Your Steam Traps Wasting Energy?" *Chemical Engineering*, Feb. 9, 1981, pp. 84-98.

How completely is the steam you generate used?

When fuel was cheap plants that had generated steam for process use at say 200 pounds per square inch (psi) might use it at successively lower pressure stages until at 5 or 10 psi it was discharged to the atmosphere; condensate collected at various points in the system might simply be discharged to the sewer. High fuel prices make such practices prohibitively expensive, and you will want to consider installing heat exchange equipment so that the wasted heat can be used for process or space heating purposes, or to heat boiler feedwater. The cost savings can be very high, and the cost of capital equipment often recovered in only one or two years. If your steam system generates more than 50,000 pounds per hour you may want to consider *cogeneration*—installing an electric generator driven by a steam turbine, and letting the steam pressure down through the turbine (instead of through a reducing valve), thus generating electric power as well as process steam. Power generation systems standing alone will have a fuel efficiency of around 35 percent, while process steam generating systems will be much higher—75 to 85 percent. Combining them can produce efficiencies of 65 to 85 percent, and fuel savings of 8 to 30 percent.

How much energy is lost through poor insulation?

Here are the steps to take in a four-pronged attack to cut those losses: (a) Inspect the insulation you have. It is subject to deterioration through mechanical abuse, failure of the coverings and the cements and mastics that hold them in place, and becoming soaked with water. The first step is to replace or repair the insulation you already have. (b) Deterioration is not always visible to the naked eye, and the use of insufficient insulation almost never is. The answer lies in the use of heat detection instruments—heat flow meters for measurement of heat losses at precise locations, and infrared thermographic scanners which give a qualitative idea of the relative heat losses along an insulation system. When the energy conservation program is big enough to justify the cost of these instruments, they can provide a great deal of valuable information on just how effective your insulating techniques are. (c) Choose the best insulation for your system. For steam systems with temperatures up to 1200° F, calcium silicate is regarded as an excellent all-around insulation. In addition to good thermal properties, it has high mechanical strength and resistance to physical abuse. For higher or lower temperatures, or for application to metal surfaces other than carbon steel, other insulations such as glass block and fiber, rock wool, or perlite may be needed. Your insulation manufacturer or supplier will be glad to make recommendations. (d) Decide how much insulation is optimum. When fuel is cheap or the size of the system does not justify more sophisticated methods, you might consult a handbook and find that for a 3-inch pipe carrying steam at 600° F you should install 2½ inches of calcium silicate; the handbook will have a table showing recommended thicknesses for other pipe sizes and temperatures. When fuel is expensive or larger systems are involved, you will want to calculate the *economic thickness of insulation*, which is based on the following concept: as the amount of insulation applied is increased, the annual cost of its installation and maintenance will plot as a rising curve. On the other hand, the annual cost of heat lost from the system will be plotted as a falling curve as the insulation is increased. The sum of these two curves is the final cost to the owner, and the idea is to find at what thickness of insulation this total cost curve goes through a minimum point. Finding this optimum point requires making calculations involving over twenty variables, a tedious process if performed manually; to make the job easier a computer program has been prepared in FORTRAN and is available from the Thermal Insulation Manufacturer's Association, Seven Kirby Plaza, Mt. Kisco, New York, 10549.

In the Electrical System

The plant electrical system is nothing more than a means of distributing energy, and it was inevitable that rising energy prices would cause changes in the way electricity is generated, distributed, used, and controlled. If you are planning a new installation, your electrical design team should be prepared to explain the tradeoffs between increased capital costs for devices to increase efficiency and the cost of energy saved over the life of the equipment.

But most plant managers are not building new plant and must address the problem of conserving electrical energy in an existing installation. The first and probably most remunerative action to take is to look at the plant *power factor*, which is the ratio of the electric power utilized in the plant to that supplied by the power company. If the power factor is low the addition of capacitors to raise it may well be justified; if it is very low, the power company may be imposing a penalty charge because they have to provide larger distribution equipment to handle the load. See Chapter 16 for a more complete description of power factor and how to correct for it. Another area that may yield results is the efficiency of the plant's electric motors, especially the squirrel cage induction motors. As energy prices began their rise, motor manufacturers developed more efficient versions; the price is higher, and only cost calculations can show whether buying them to replace existing motors is worth it.

In Plant Processes

No matter what industry your plant is a part of, it probably has its own literature—books, trade magazines, and technical journals. Your technical staff should review the literature for energy conservation ideas specific to your industry. At the same time here are some general lines of attack that can be pursued in most plants.

1. **Don't throw away energy you have already paid for.** Too often a hot process stream at the end of the production process is cooled with water or air, and its heat rejected to the atmosphere. With heat exchange equipment this energy can be recovered and used profitably, e.g., to preheat cold feed streams or provide hot water for various purposes. And don't forget that heat can be reclaimed from hot solid products as well as from fluids—usually by air (or other gas) streams which, when warmed, can be fed to furnaces and burners, cutting their energy consumption, or for space heating. The same idea applies to energy in the form of pressure; one plant which operates a large air compressor for process use achieved flow control by blowing off some of the compressed air to the atmosphere. As part of an energy conservation program it connected the compressor vent to the plant's utility air system, allowing it to shut down completely that system's smaller compressor, and found a process use for the remaining vented air. In the first year alone cost savings were four times the capital costs incurred in making the necessary changes.

2. **Keep heat transfer surfaces clean.** Process streams can deposit undissolved solids on heat exchanger surfaces by a silting process, or dissolved materials can precipitate on them along with decomposition products. More efficient use of these heat transfer surfaces may be achieved by more thorough cleaning of the stream before it starts through the process, or, if the product can tolerate

it, addition of antifouling chemicals to resist deposition on heat transfer surfaces. If neither of these works, periodic shutdowns to permit physical scraping and brushing may be necessary. If one of the heat transfer surfaces consists of fins exposed to the air, they should be periodically washed or blown to remove dust and grease accumulations.

3. **Consider energy consumption when purchasing new process equipment.** Makers of industrial equipment have been giving more attention to the energy efficiency of their products since the high-priced energy era began. Request energy consumption information from the manufacturers whose equipment you are considering, and include energy usage per unit of output in the purchasing decision.

4. **Look for energy saving opportunities in the way process and utility flow streams are controlled.** Prior to the arrival of expensive energy, industrial practice was to pump liquids and gases at higher pressure than needed, and insert a throttling valve in the line to reduce flows to desired levels. Although not as obvious to the naked eye as a steam leak blowing to the atmosphere, throttling valves waste energy by converting it to heat, which is dissipated in the flow stream or lost to the atmosphere. One way to reduce these losses is to install variable speed motors on the pumps and blowers in the system, whose output can then be adjusted to changing flow demands, reducing the need for throttling. For an elaboration on this and other ideas for saving process system energy, see F. G. Shinskey, *Control Systems that Save Energy*, Elias P. Gyftopoulos and Karen C. Cohen, eds., *Industrial Energy Conservation Manuals: No. 2*, (Cambridge, Mass.: MIT Press, 1982).

In the Use of Heat Pumps

To understand how heat pumps work it will be necessary to refer to Figure 16-19 (page 357), which is a diagram of the vapor compression refrigeration cycle, and its accompanying explanation. Note that both the evaporator and the condenser are heat exchangers, with the working fluid absorbing heat in the evaporator, and thus creating a cooling effect in the space to be air conditioned, and transferring this heat to the atmosphere or cooling water in the condenser. The net effect is that the system is pumping heat from the space to be cooled to the outside environment, which is what we would want to do in warm weather. If the flow of the working fluid is reversed, however, the heat exchanger shown on the diagram as the evaporator becomes the condenser, while the exchanger shown diagrammatically as the condenser now becomes the evaporator. In this mode the system is absorbing heat from the outside environment and pumping it into the air conditioned space, which is what we would want to do in cool weather. A refrigeration system designed to switch direction in this fashion is called a *heat pump*. Under favorable conditions the heat pump can deliver four times as much energy as it absorbs in running the compressor, which makes it an attractive energy conservation device. In the winter mode, however, when it absorbs heat from the outside air, its efficiency drops off rapidly if the outside temperature falls below freezing. An ideal situation for the heat pump exists when a large supply of noncorrosive underground water is available (which will have a steady temperature close to 50° F) for the external heat exchanger. Then the working fluid can reject heat to the water (summer) or absorb heat from it (winter) at good efficiencies.

Although heat pump systems have been designed and built since the 1930s, they did not come into widespread use until the era of high energy prices, and their application has been mostly for residential and commercial space heating and cooling. Some industrial applications have been reported in low-level heating processes, and in distillation and evaporation.

In Switching Fuels

A recent U.S. Department of Energy survey found that 70 percent of large industrial boilers in the United States were capable of burning more than one fuel, and the most popular combination was the ability to burn natural gas or fuel oil.

Natural gas is the most widely used industrial boiler fuel because it is clean-burning, requires the least operator attention, and the least capital investment in burning equipment. However, industrial users may find that for economic reasons or through a requirement of the gas supplier, they must contract for gas on an "interruptible" basis. This means that during periods of peak demand the gas company may require industrial users to stop using it, forcing plants either to shut down or switch to an alternative fuel.

For boilers capable of using only natural gas, the addition of an alternative fuel is easiest when the new fuel is oil. Although gas-only and oil-only boilers are built somewhat differently, the design parameters are usually within 20 percent, and only minor modifications to the internal structure of the boiler are needed as the alternate burning equipment is added. But the process is not entirely without complications: fuel oil tanks will have to be installed; soot blowers may have to be installed to remove ash deposits from the boiler tubes; and the smokestack may have to be lengthened to reduce the air pollution effects at ground level.

Converting a gas boiler to use coal as an alternate fuel is a much more difficult problem. Here the design parameters vary by 50 percent, and extensive changes to the furnace and the boiler tubes will be required. Installation of a soot blower will be mandatory. Before proceeding very far with such a project, a thorough study should be undertaken by a competent engineering group; they may ultimately recommend installing a second coal-fired boiler alongside the gas boiler rather than trying to modify it. Another possibility would be to consider a coal-water slurry as the fuel, rather than dry coal; conversion to this fuel might involve much less modification of the original boiler.

HOW TO SET UP A SUCCESSFUL ENERGY CONSERVATION PROGRAM

Essential Elements of an Energy Conservation Program

By looking back through this chapter you can see that energy conservation is: (1) an *engineering* problem that involves replacing and redesigning equipment, (2) a *maintenance* problem in keeping insulation, steam systems and other possible energy-loss sources in good repair, (3) an *operating* problem requiring energy conservation discipline among the people who throw the switches and open the valves that control energy flow, (4) a *cost* problem because so much capital and operating expense is involved, and (5) a *management* problem because all these elements must be combined into a coordinated effort to achieve visible results.

Five Steps to Take in Beginning Your Program

These are the five basic steps to take in setting up an energy conservation program:

Step 1: Make an energy survey of the plant. This step readily breaks down in two phases. Phase one will consist of a physical inspection of the plant and an examination of its records to answer the following kinds of questions:

- How much energy is being used?
- What kinds of energy are consumed?
- Where in the plant is it being consumed?
- Are there leaks, sloppy operating practices, or other energy-losing situations readily observable?

Phase two consists of examining the information obtained in phase one to answer these questions:

- Which units are operating at the lowest levels of efficiency and therefore offer the greatest opportunities for energy conservation?
- Are there cost saving or security of supply benefits to be obtained by changing or adding to the types of energy purchased by the plant?
- What additional electric meters, steam flow meters, and other types of instrumentation must the plant install to be able to measure the effects of energy conservation measures?

Step 2: Identify capital projects that will improve the plant's energy position. Typical projects would include (a) modification of existing equipment such as adapting boilers to use alternate fuel, (b) replacement, such as retiring production equipment that may be still operable but is obsolete in terms of energy consumption, and (c) installing new equipment, such as heat exchangers and electric capacitors to make more efficient use of energy.

Step 3: Identify operating changes. These are the measures that can be taken without changes to plant equipment, and might include shutting down certain energy-consuming units for part of the day, operating equipment at lower temperatures and pressures, and modifying operating procedures and rules so that a higher degree of energy conservation discipline is actually obtained.

Step 4: Establish goals for energy improvement. Steps 1 through 3 provide the tools for making things happen to improve the plant's energy situation. Now it is up to management to establish the goals which the program is expected to accomplish. They must be expressed in clear, measurable terms (preferably units of energy consumption), have a stated time period for accomplishment, and be realistic—too difficult, and a sense of frustration will set in; too easy, and no one will be motivated to work very hard.

Step 5: Train and motivate plant personnel at all levels. Everyone in the plant must understand what it is you are trying to accomplish, why you are conducting the program, and what it means to them to contribute all they can, if the program is to be successful.

How to Organize Your Plant's Energy Program

This job cannot be accomplished by appointing a "plant energy committee," having it meet once a month, and hoping that something comes of it all. The job of upgrading the plant to optimum efficiency with respect to energy consumption is clearly one for the line organization, and only that group can be expected to accomplish the program's goals.

In a small plant the plant manager himself may head up the energy conservation group. In larger plants, an assistant plant manager or operations manager may be available to take charge; if so, he must carry the full delegated authority of the plant manager to implement the program. Each production, utility, and staff department head is automatically a member of the conservation group, and is responsible for carrying the program in his department.

None of this is to say there should not be staff assistance. A Plant Energy Coordinator can be appointed whose job is to assist the line organization by keeping records of progress, disseminating information and new ideas on conservation techniques, reminding line managers of upcoming deadlines, preparing reports of the program's progress, and participating in the training effort; in the larger plants this may constitute a full-time job. Some plants have found it useful to have each department head appoint a subordinate to handle the working details of the conservation effort, and to have these people form a liaison group that meets regularly to exchange ideas, identify problems, and report progress. The important point is to not allow the Coordinator or the liaison committee to become bogged down in trying to carry out conservation projects themselves.

Keeping Track of Progress

The program will require its own special record-keeping system in order to provide a coherent picture of past performance and provide a justification for future activity. Follow these steps in setting up the system:

Step 1: Adopt a standard energy use statistic for all departments of the plant. The unit that probably has the widest applicability is Btu per unit of production (pounds, tons, or item count). Users of various forms of energy such as steam, electricity, and natural gas, would convert all their consumption rates to Btu and divide the number of Btu by the production units. A cautionary note is in order here, however, which is best illustrated by an analogy from ordinary life. If an automobile is driven over a 50-mile course at 65 miles per hour, it will consume considerably more gasoline per mile than if it were driven over the same course at 40 mph. Production equipment may react in much the same way—consuming more energy per unit produced if it is driven harder to meet special time or quality requirements. Provisions must be made for these variations in the record-keeping systems if valid performance comparisons are to be made.

Step 2: Establish uniform recording methods for all departments. Not only should they report for the same time periods and in the same units, but they should use the same energy conversion factors and the same formulas for calculating such measures as boiler and process equipment efficiency. The record-keeping system may also have to conform to rules issued by corporate headquarters, if the company owns more than one plant.

Step 3: Establish a baseline for energy consumption before undertaking energy improvement projects. The energy survey mentioned above should provide sufficient data to establish the preprogram energy consumption levels of the various plant units.

Step 4: Computerize. The number of items to be kept track of, the calculations and data manipulation required, and the frequency of reporting all make the energy reporting system a natural application for the computer, especially for the mini-computer. An undue amount of energy reporting in industry is still being done manually—in small manufacturing units because no computer is available, and in large operations because access to the mainframe is not readily available and sufficiently informal. The declining costs and rapidly expanding power of mini-computers make them a tool for energy management programs that should not be overlooked.

Inform the Players

General support for the program will lag if only a few insiders know what is going on. Management will demand matter-of-fact reports that report the energy usage and dollar value achievements of conservation measures employed by the program, as well as any progress made toward security of operation—the ability to keep the plant running if one of its sources of energy is suddenly cut off or curtailed.

The general plant population will want something more informal and easier to understand. Some useful ways of communicating to keep interest alive are monthly newsletters, plant billboards, signs in each department showing past usage and future goals, foremen's meetings, and department- or plantwide general meetings.

NEWER DEVELOPMENTS IN ENERGY SUPPLY

Solar Energy

Some very broad definitions of solar energy have appeared, including not only the direct energy received from sunlight but extended to include indirect effects such as wind, ocean waves, and biomass conversions. This section will deal only with the direct use of sunlight.

The main limitations on the application of solar energy to industrial uses have not been technological factors but cost. Although a number of pilot units have been constructed that demonstrate the technical feasibility of generating hot water and steam, industrial development has awaited very large reductions in the capital cost of the required equipment. The following are main types of solar devices which may find ultimate industrial/commercial use.

Flat-plate-solar collector: This which resembles a large window frame lying on its side, usually mounted on a roof or similar structure so that it faces the sun. At the top of the frame are one or two sheets of glass or plastic, through which the sun's rays pass. Below that is a flat metal plate painted black. If water is the working fluid to be used, the metal plate is attached to pipes or tubing containing water. Below them is a thickness of insulation supported by a base plate. The radiant energy is received by the blackened plate and converted into heat, which is transmitted to the water; the transparent plates prevent the loss of this heat back to the atmosphere by convection and to some extent, by radiation. Flat-plate collectors have been commercially applied to residential hot water heating, and could be applied for the same purpose in industrial situations where they are cost effective. They are generally limited to producing fluid temperatures below 200° F, however.

Thermal power central receiver system: This system consists of a steam boiler mounted on an outdoor tower. It is surrounded by a field of mirrors shaped to focus the sun's rays on the boiler and equipped with mechanisms that allow them to follow the sun as it moves through the sky. Steam is generated in the boiler and can be used for process purposes or to drive an electric power generator. Much higher temperatures—up to 2000° F—can be generated. These systems require a great deal of land space and will probably find their greatest use in the Southwest.

There is an obvious gap between the need of a manufacturing plant for a steady supply of energy and the fluctuation of energy available from sunlight caused by changes in the length of day and variable cloud cover. Solar power systems therefore usually require a conventional backup system (electric power from a utility or fossil fuel burning equipment), or a means of storing surplus solar energy for later use (electric batteries, or, in a hydroelectric system, a pumped storage facility).

Fuel Cells

Basic courses in chemistry often include a demonstration in which an electric current is passed through water, decomposing the water into its constituent elements, hydrogen and oxygen. The fuel cell works in just the opposite way—hydrogen is passed over one electrode of a cell, oxygen over the other, and electricity is produced. Thus, the fuel cell is a means of converting chemical energy into electrical energy, and in practical applications it produces heat as well. The oxygen can be supplied pure or contained in an air stream. The hydrogen is obtained from natural gas, oil refinery products (naphtha), or coal; since this brings us right back to the use of fossil fuels, the question may well be asked, "Why bother with the fuel cell—why not just burn the fuel directly?"

The answer lies in efficiency of the process. The efficiency of fuel utilization in a fuel cell will run from 10 to 40 percent higher than in a conventional system. The higher number applies when both the electricity and heat generated in the cell are used. The electricity is generated as direct current (usually at less than 500 volts), and for plants using that kind of power there is an additional saving over the efficiency loss suffered when alternating current purchased from a utility is converted to direct current.

These devices are expensive, and widespread application will await steep declines in the capital cost of the cells.

ECONOMICS:
THE BOTTOM LINE STILL COUNTS

Throughout this chapter we have dealt with the two basic goals of the energy conservation program, the first goal being to find ways of reducing the suddenly very high costs of supplying fuel to the plant. This is a cost reduction effort, and its projects are expected to generate a return on capital investment at least competitive with, if not superior to, other possible cost reduction opportunities requiring capital. Although the search for new energy conservation methods is challenging and often fascinating, money is the yardstick that tells us when we have gone far enough.

The second goal is to protect the company against going out of business altogether if the primary form of energy used by the plant is threatened with interruption or curtailment for any length of time. When survival is the issue the rules can be bent rather sharply, but even in this situation there are economic limits. If, for instance, the annualized cost of installing a backup fuel system is greater than the company's expected earnings for the next eight years, then the risk of being shut down for a period may have to be borne. In a less extreme situation, if the cost of the backup system is not actually prohibitive but would preclude a very attractive investment in production equipment that would increase the company's market penetration, then a more careful study of the risks must be made. It would involve making estimates such as the probability of an energy supply failure occurring and its length, and its severity expressed in dollars—loss of sales, diminished competitive position.

Operating Example 9-1: Determining the Cost Effectiveness of an Energy Conservation Proposal. Following the plant energy survey, a plant manager was presented with the following proposal from his powerhouse superintendent: An economizer (see page 146) can be installed on the main boiler to heat the incoming feedwater and thus recapture some of the heat now going to the atmosphere in stack gases. The installed cost of the equipment is estimated at $302,000. The area engineer estimates that approximately 18,000 barrels of fuel oil will be saved per year, yielding annual cost savings of $223,560. For investment analysis purposes the plant manager assumes that the economizer will have a useful life of 10 years with no salvage value and, using the economic justification method described on pages 410–412, makes the following evaluation:

Return on Investment

Total pretax profit over life of project (10 × $223,560)	$2,235,600
Less depreciation	302,000
Taxable profit	1,933,600
Income tax at 34%	657,424
After-tax profit	1,276,176
Average annual after-tax profit (Divide by 10 years)	127,618
Return on investment (127,618 ÷ 302,000)	42.2%

Payback Period

After-tax profit	1,276,176
Plus depreciation	302,000
Cash flow	1,578,176
Average annual cash flow (Divide by 10 years)	157,818
Payback period (302,000 ÷ 157,818) (Investment ÷ Annual cash flow)	1.91 yr

With a 42 percent return and a payback period of two years, this might be an attractive investment to management. But there could be other economic considerations that would create serious second thoughts about proceeding with it. For instance, if capital funds are very hard to obtain for some reason and only enough money is available for this project or for the installation of new production machines needed to keep the company competitive in its business, then the company may have to forego the energy savings as a matter of survival.

PART II

Managing Plant Employees

Chapter 10

Time-tested Methods for Improving Industrial Relations

Industrial workers have long sought more from their employment than just the opportunity to trade a day's work for a day's pay; they have also wanted job security, safe conditions, fair treatment, opportunity for advancement, and financial protection against disability and old age. A newer generation has added more concerns—greater participation in deciding how their jobs are to be performed, protection against long-term effects of toxic materials, equality of the sexes in the workplace, and flexible working hours to accommodate changing social and family patterns.

But the new demands are mixed with new anxieties. As the American worker watches plant after plant in basic manufacturing industries close or sharply reduce operations, he realizes as never before that he is working in direct competition with foreign labor. Out of this realization grows a sincere desire to improve productivity and quality, and a resolve to keep his plant from closing so strong that he may agree to "givebacks" in wages, fringe benefits and work rules in exchange for a company's promise to keep the plant operating.

A work force in foment? Perhaps, but with elements that are not all bad. Whenever workers genuinely want to improve output and quality, and are ready to make economic sacrifices to assure survival of the plant, the plant manager has an excellent foundation upon which to build or improve the industrial relations program. And he can take further encouragement from the results of recent surveys reported which show that despite widely held perceptions, job satisfaction and commitment to the job has not declined among American workers.

The total relationship between employees and the company—much more than publishing the company magazine or planning the annual picnic—is the subject of industrial relations. This chapter will deal with those aspects of the subject that closely involve the plant manager, whether he is in complete charge of industrial relations or is assisted by a department or section which reports elsewhere.

CRITICAL ASPECTS OF COMMUNICATION IN ALL PLANTS

Two Key Requirements of Downward Communications

The company is continuously communicating with its employees. Verbal communications include instructions and information from the first-line supervisor; meetings with personnel or industrial relations people on safety, insurance, pensions, and so forth; and occasional meetings with higher plant management to receive information on the progress of the plant and company. Written communications take the form of bulletin board notices, employee handbooks and union contract booklets, operating procedures and plant regulations, the house organ, and letters sent to the employee's home.

There are two vital requirements for all these communications. First, they should be straightforward, and mean what they say. I have always been puzzled by the ability of some work groups to stage a slowdown by following all the procedures in the operating manual. If an instruction isn't meant to be followed, it shouldn't be in the manual at all; if it is important enough to be there, it should be followed all the time. Second, communications must be consistent. A loyal employee will soon turn into a cynic if he attends a safety meeting to learn a safety practice and then is told to ignore that practice when he returns to his work area.

Workers have not given management good marks on the amount and quality of the information reaching them. In one survey taken about half said the information coming down to them was insufficient to enable them to perform their jobs well. This adds a third requirement to those downward communications which an employee will use to do his job: they must be complete.

Four Steps to Upward Communications

Why should a plant manager have to discover what workers are thinking through surveys taken elsewhere—probably remote from his area and outside his industry? There is no good reason; his own workers will tell him what they are thinking provided the plant atmosphere is conducive to upward communication. Here are some steps to take to assure that it is:

Step 1: Train the supervisors to be receptive to comments and ideas from workers. This includes communication between you and the plant work force, especially the first-line supervisors. If the prevailing atmosphere around the plant is that whoever speaks up is likely to be regarded as a "troublemaker," not much communication is going to flow. That will also be true if the first-line supervisor suspects that passing a worker's good idea up the line will somehow reflect poorly on him for not having thought of it himself. Everyone below you in the plant management structure must feel comfortable that no penalty will ensue if he or she passes information up the line.

Step 2: Use worker groups. We have already seen this idea at work in the section on quality circles in Chapter 6. But fostering upward communications does not have to await the installation of quality circles—there are other gatherings where workers' ideas can be heard, such as department and section meetings, safety meetings, and meetings with representatives of the Personnel Department. To go more directly to the source, many plant managers find it valuable to hold their own meetings, usually on a quarterly basis, with the work force to discuss matters of mutual interest (provided the size of the work force is not so large as to render the idea impractical).

Step 3: Develop informal contacts. As the foremen, the intermediate supervisors, and the plant manager walk around the plant they are going to make contact with workers, usually one at a time or in small groups. These are good opportunities to find out what workers are thinking in a less formal atmosphere than that of a meeting. Again, the information received must be handled so as not to embarrass those who provided the information or any intermediate level of supervision which might not have been present.

Step 4: Recognize contributions. The recognition may consist of nothing more than going back to an employee and saying "I remembered what you said the last time we talked, and it was discussed at the last management meeting." It may consist of handing the worker a check for several thousand dollars, if his idea was a cost-saver. Or it may be what is possibly the best form of recognition of all: seeing his idea adopted in the workplace, with management freely acknowledging to him and his peers where the idea came from. Whatever the form, management must give some convincing signal that it finds upward communications useful and wants them continued. They will die very quickly without such a signal.

Maintaining the Work Environment

The company says more about what it thinks of its people by the way it builds and maintains its plants than in almost any other form of communication. A good foundation for industrial relations is established when work areas and personnel facilities are clean, attractively painted, well-maintained, and properly lighted and ventilated.

Using Performance Appraisal

To meet the need of employees to know how their work is rated, most plants use some form of performance appraisal. The method may range from simply having the foreman call in the employee once or twice a year and "tell him how he is doing," to the use of an elaborate printed form which is filled out by the foreman and reviewed by one or more higher level of supervision. Whatever system you use, include these characteristics: Choose rating factors that can be measured in terms of results, such as quantity and quality of work, and attendance. Avoid rating factors that are subject to bias on the part of the supervisor, such as "personality" and "judgment." Review the results of the rating with the employee, with emphasis on how it can help him to improve performance.

Safety as an Industrial Relations Tool

The prime objective of any safety program is the prevention of accidents but the plant manager should also be aware of its immense value in developing and maintaining good industrial relations. This value is enhanced even further in an era when employees, as noted in the introduction to this chapter, are more knowledgeable and more concerned about the toxic effects of materials to which they are exposed in the workplace. Employees will be favorably impressed by the willingness of the company to spend time and money to protect them from injury; despite some initial grumbling, they will respect the company for insisting on obedience to safety rules. And the company which has a good safety record and reputation for safety in the community has a valuable edge in hourly recruiting if the labor supply should ever become tight.

How to Handle Employee Suggestions

There are two basic approaches to handling employee suggestions. One is to establish a formal suggestion system, in which employees write their ideas on a printed form and drop them in a suggestion box. Each suggestion is reviewed by a committee, and if accepted, the employee is given a lump sum cash award, or a percentage of the cost savings for a fixed period.

The second approach is informal. Supervisors are trained to be alert for employee suggestions, and to include them in upward communications. Suggestions are given as careful consideration by all levels of management as in the formal system; the reply to the employee is more personal and direct. Rewards for accepted suggestions are in the form of praise, recognition, and the employee's satisfaction in seeing his idea actually applied in the plant.

I favor the second approach. When properly handled, it establishes a deeper sense of involvement of the employee in his or her company than can be achieved by cash awards. And it avoids some of the unpleasant side effects I have observed in cash award systems: dissatisfaction with the size of an award, suspicion that another employee was rewarded for one's own idea, claims that the company used the suggestion without paying for it.

A Three-Step Disciplinary Action Procedure

In either the union or nonunion plant, keep the disciplinary system as simple as possible. Here is a simple three-step progression of disciplinary action for a repeatedly offending employee:

> **Verbal warning.** The first-line supervisor tells the employee what he has done, why it is wrong, and what may happen if he does it again. A written record of the warning is placed in the employee's personnel file, and the union is notified of the action (if there is a union).

Disciplinary letter. Written and signed by the foreman, with copies to personnel file and union. Refers to the verbal warning, states what has happened since then, and warns the employee that the next step will be discharge.

Discharge. The third infraction represents a serious challenge to the rules of the plant or the authority of the supervisor, and discharge is usually called for. It should always be carried out by the supervisor—no one else. To avoid embarrassing reversals, have the supervisor put the offending employee on suspension as a matter of policy. The discharge can then be reviewed the next day by all concerned to be sure that the facts of the case warrant termination.

Such a progression is clear to everyone involved, and will stand up under an arbitrator's scrutiny.

Two essential points: While it is a good idea to publish a set of plant rules which you expect employees to observe, don't let the list become too long or picayune. If it does, a rule that is not listed may be unenforceable. Avoid writing long lists of punishable offenses into the union contract. Arbitrators and courts expect employees to know the basic rules of industrial conduct on their own. Above all, don't publish a rule unless you mean it; if you publish it, enforce it impartially.

Disciplinary layoff is sometimes added to the disciplinary progression shown above. It is being abandoned by more and more companies for two reasons: It always penalizes the company, which has to replace the absent employee at overtime rates, or by some rearrangement of work schedules. And it is downright silly to attempt to penalize a chronic absentee by giving him days off; the penalty is the same as the offense.

Controlling Absenteeism

To tolerate a high rate of casual absenteeism (as opposed to legitimate absences such as sickness and funerals) is inexcusable on the part of any management. Using the disciplinary procedure in the previous section, you can control casual absenteeism this way:

Publish the absenteeism rule—on the bulletin boards if it is not already in your employee handbook. If you have a rule but have not been enforcing it, restate your intention to enforce it.

Enforce it rigidly. You can't penalize one worker and ignore the absenteeism of another. Don't buy the "he's a good worker when he's here" approach— the person who doesn't show up for work is worth zero to you that day.

Keep good records. A special absence record can be kept by the foreman or by the personnel office. When a disciplinary case comes up, you don't want to have to search through a stack of old time cards. Unions are usually reluctant to press an absenteeism case through the grievance procedure if the record is unassailable and the rule has been impartially enforced.

Determine an acceptable rate of absenteeism. There is no pat answer for your organization. A plant with an excellent attendance record would not want to loosen its control to allow absenteeism to come up to some "national average." A manager who is bringing the rate down would not want to relax her efforts simply because she has achieved such a level. But it is valuable to have a statistical reference point by which to judge whether the overall rate in your facility requires stronger enforcement action.

As a very rough guide, workers in manufacturing industries may be expected to be absent about 4 percent of the time. Three percent is for illness and injury, and 1 percent for miscellaneous reasons.

WHAT TO DO WHEN THERE IS A UNION

The basic principles of good management and effective industrial relations do not suddenly change when the plant becomes unionized. Employees continue to want the same returns from their employment as their nonunion colleagues; they will still respect good leadership from the plant management. What is different is the formality of a written contract, the intervention of a third party, and the threat of strikes to enforce employee demands.

The Union Contract

This document is a statement of the agreements reached by company and union negotiators during collective bargaining, on such subjects as wages, fringe benefits, grievance procedure, and may cover a wide range of industrial relations topics. Frequently there is a "management rights" clause and very often a preamble recognizing the duty of both parties to establish peaceful labor relations and to operate the plant safely and economically. Remember these points when you must deal with a union contract:

It is a legal agreement. You should expect to live up to the company's commitments under it, and should expect the union to do the same.

It does not cover every detail of industrial relations. When the contract is silent on a given matter, an opportunity exists for management to establish its own practices.

It does formalize the relationship between you and your employees, and you will have to live by the letter of its provisions even when it seems eminently fair to do otherwise.

Operating Example 10-1: Observing the Letter of the Union Agreement. One of your hourly workers has been out sick for a long period, and today is his first day back at work. You require four hours of overtime in that department. The contract says that overtime must be offered to the employee with the lowest accumulated hours, and charged against his total if he refuses it. Operating from common sense, you would prefer not to offer this overtime to a worker just returned from sick leave, nor to penalize him for refusing it. But you must offer it. If you don't, the next employee in line may object to having the hours charged against him, and file a grievance. Even if you get by with it, the union can use the incident as precedent for some future case which you might want to handle differently.

When Is a Complaint a Grievance?

The typical union contract defines a grievance as "any dispute or controversy arising out of the meaning of interpretation of this agreement," and then proceeds to spell out a series of steps involving ever higher levels of authority within the union and the company through which the complainant can take his case. If agreement is not reached in one of these steps, the dispute may ultimately go to an outside arbitrator whose decision is binding upon both parties.

The situation differs from that of the nonunion plant in two significant respects. The first is that the question may be ultimately settled by an outside authority, and therefore every management decision on it must be judged on how it will stand up before that authority. The second is the extreme formality of the procedure, which creates a dangerous pitfall: that management will tend to ignore those employee complaints which do not technically qualify as grievances.

> **Operating Example 10–2: How a Complaint Becomes a Grievance.** An hourly employee doesn't like and doesn't get along with the employee working next to him. He complains in a general way to his foreman, who realizes that the complaint hardly qualifies as a "dispute . . . arising out of this agreement," and may be inclined to ignore it rather than resolve it. Therein lies the danger. The unresolved complaint may be followed by a request for transfer to another department. If that is denied, the employee and his shop steward may find all kinds of grounds for filing a grievance—interpretation of the seniority clause, contract clauses regarding transfer, preferential assignment, what the company has done in previous cases. If the company should lose such a grievance, the whole system of work assignment in the plant could be badly undermined.

How to Handle Grievances in a Unionized Plant

Follow these fundamental principles for handling grievances and complaints in the unionized plant:

Train the entire managerial staff to recognize the difference between a complaint and a formal grievance, and to understand the importance of each. Make sure that first-line supervisors do not ignore complaints simply because there is no contractual basis to consider them grievances.

Prepare the first-line supervisor to handle his part in the grievance procedure. When a grievance is presented, he should know how long he has to answer it, what form his answer should be in, and who should be present when he gives it. It is essential that he review his decision on the grievance and the way he will present it with you before replying to the employee and the union.

Do your homework on each case. Obtain all of the "facts" available; challenge their validity until you are satisfied they will stand up as facts. Then assess your chances of winning the case if it should go to arbitration. Consult your labor attorney, check up on "past practice," review the grievance files for decisions on similar cases, and study current publications.

If you can't win, get out early in the grievance procedure. Fighting a losing grievance through the higher levels, "as a matter of principle," simply makes it harder for management people, especially first-line supervisors, to accept the inevitable defeat gracefully.

Insist that the union follow the rules. If the contract states that the grievance must be taken to Step 3 within four days after the decision in Step 2, don't accept it six days later. If the contract limits the number of union representatives who can leave their jobs to attend grievance meetings, don't allow the limits to be exceeded. To do so is to jeopardize the handling of future cases, and to introduce a great deal of uncertainty in the procedure.

Tips for Keeping the First-Line Supervisor an Effective Leader

The management person who feels the impact of a union in the plant most consistently is the foreman; that is to be expected because he works at the point of contact between management and the hourly work force. It is he who sometimes must make decisions in a hurry, only to have them become the source of union grievances and possibly second-guessing from his own management. Every move he makes comes under the scrutiny of union stewards who may only be waiting for him to make a mistake. Take these steps to keep your first-line supervisor effective while operating under a union contract:

Don't let him become intimidated. He can be plagued into almost complete inaction by fears—the fear of losing a grievance, the fear of organized opposition, the fear of having to defend his action in formal proceedings, the fear of being criticized by his superiors for having "too many" grievances. Faced by opposition from below and second-guessing from above, he may simply decide it is easier to avoid decisions than to make them.

You can help him. Make sure he understands that all of the agencies concerned with the development and administration of labor law—managements, unions, the National Labor Relations Board, arbitrators, the legislative bodies which passed the laws—all expect the foreman to assert and use his authority to manage his operation. Of course he runs into trouble when he makes a mistake, but he will run into more trouble by failing to make decisions and to take consistent, authoritative action.

Operating Example 10-3: Inconsistent Enforcement. A foreman who had repeatedly failed to enforce the rules on lateness now realizes the situation is getting out of hand, and wants to "put on the brakes." He comes to you with a proposal to apply disciplinary action to an hourly employee who happens to be the latest in a long line of violators. You want to back up the foreman as a general management principle, and at the same time clean up a messy lateness problem. Should you support his proposal?

Probably not. If you apply the disciplinary penalty the union is likely to file a grievance pointing out that people have been coming in late for months with no notice or action taken by management, and claiming that the foreman is probably using "selective enforcement" to discriminate against this employee on the basis of some real or imagined animosity. If the grievance goes to arbitration the company may be in for a difficult time; the arbitrator may have as much trouble as the union trying to understand why the company suddenly chose this moment and this employee to start enforcing the rule after ignoring it for so long.

What to do next? As noted in the earlier section on absenteeism (page 163), the best procedure is to restate the rule, make sure that everyone is notified that compliance will be expected, and then begin enforcing it equitably. If a grievance is filed at some later time, the company, with a background of clear and consistent enforcement of the rule, will be in a much better position to win.

Make sure that your first-line supervisor knows the union contract thoroughly. He or she should understand your interpretation of any of its unclear provisions. Require him to review the decisions he makes under it with you whenever possible, especially if those decisions have plantwide implications.

Keep him informed. When you have negotiated a new contract, made a supplementary agreement on an existing one, or simply held a meeting with the union to discuss problems, inform your first-line supervisors immediately. It is essential to their morale that they hear the results first from you, rather than from their employees or shop stewards. When you settle a grievance in one department, notify the supervisors in all the other departments—one of them may have a similar case. And if you have changed your interpretation of some part of the contract, or know of new developments in state or federal labor law which affect supervisory functioning, you should explain the situation to them.

Be realistic with him. Don't tell him you will "always back him up." You can't do that. Tell him you will back him up when he is right, will help him to be right, and will help him get out of trouble gracefully when he is wrong

The Danger of Establishing a Precedent

No matter what the union contract says, if both parties to it have permitted a particular practice to prevail over the life of the contract, that practice may become the rule. For instance, a company which had always permitted its employees to leave their workplace five minutes before lunch time to wash up would probably find that it cannot withdraw that privilege even though the contract is silent on it. The union might have a great deal of trouble in requiring the company to follow contract rules on overtime assignment if it has consistently looked the other way when the company awarded overtime outside those rules.

Although this is a tricky area legally, the message is clear: Be sure that those plant rules and contract provisions which are important to you are regularly enforced. If you don't, they may turn out to be ineffective when you do decide to enforce them.

Use the Probationary Period Wisely

Under most union contracts new hourly employees are hired for a probationary period lasting anywhere from thirty days to six months. During this period the employee can be discharged at the discretion of the company, without recourse to the grievance procedure.

Train your supervisors to observe the new employee very carefully during this probationary period. He knows he is on probation and his performance will be as good or better than at any later time. If there are latent signs of trouble—incipient absenteeism, lateness, not getting along with other employees, inability to learn the work—it will be better to discharge the employee than to live with a host of troubles generated by him later on. Once he gets past the probationary period he becomes a full union member and cannot be discharged except for cause, and that is subject to challenge by the union.

You can help the supervisor in two ways. Have the Personnel Department send him a written notice of the expiration of the probationary period in time to make a deliberate judgment of the employee. Then require him to fill out a rating form which covers all the qualities you consider important in a new employee.

How the International Representative Operates

Sometimes called the "business agent," this individual is a paid professional probably working out of a regional headquarters of the international union of which your unit is a local. He is the "third party" in your industrial relations; he will advise your shop stewards on matters at issue between them and the plant management, he will help them decide whether or not to file a grievance over a given management action and you will be dealing with him when either the company or the union has a special request to make of the other. He will be a key figure in collective bargaining, and in any strike situation that may develop. The grievance procedure usually calls for him to enter the discussions at the third or fourth step. Most contracts give him the right to enter plant property "for purposes of administering the contract."

Here are three key points to cover in your relationship with the international representative:

1. Assess the degree of his influence with your local union leaders. If it is strong, he may be able to make agreements for the local on his own. If his position is weak, he must constantly refer decisions to the local leaders, who will challenge and sometimes reject his ideas. If you are not sure where he stands on this scale of control, test the situation on some relatively unimportant matter at the first opportunity.

2. Try to estimate his position within the international union. He may aspire to higher office. He may be fighting the loss of his job because of a union merger. He may be part of a faction pressing some particular point of view within the international union. He may be trying to negotiate uniform clauses on a specific subject into all the contracts in his area. This kind of knowledge will explain many of the moves he makes, and allow you to predict his future positions and actions.

3. Insist that the formalities of the contract be observed regarding visitation. If it states that he must obtain permission of the plant manager before entering the plant, be sure that he does. You will always want to know when he is in the plant, and if possible, whom he is talking to and why.

Chapter 11

What You Need to Know to Keep Your Plant Nonunion

Workers in industrial plants have the right, under American law, to decide whether or not they will be represented by a union. That same law gives management the right to try to convince its workers—as long as it does not commit certain unfair practices—that their interests would be better served by not having a union. This chapter answers the question of why it is important to try to keep the plant nonunion, and then deals with the most significant steps management must take to accomplish that end. It is not written from the standpoint that unions are inherently evil and must be kept out of the plant by any means fair or foul, but from the position that a well-intentioned, professional plant management can do better for its employees (and all concerned with the plant) without a union.

One precaution: The chapter touches upon some of the management do's and don'ts prescribed by labor law. It is not, however, written by a lawyer, nor is it intended to provide any legal interpretations, and you are advised to obtain professional counsel when questions of law arise.

WHY NOT A UNION?

The ambivalence of some managers who wonder whether "a union might be a good thing" for their plants is surprising. Perhaps they are tempted to think that by the presence of a union and a union contract the scrambled mix of personnel problems requiring management policy decisions will somehow be codified and taken care of. They may feel that a union will help shoulder the responsibilities of controlling absenteeism and dealing with complaining workers. Or they may be lured by the prospect of having to deal with the adjustment of wages and fringe benefits only at the formalized intervals of contract renewal—from one to three years.

These can be dangerous delusions. No union will (nor should it be expected to) handle any portion of management's responsibilities; it has serious and important responsibilities of its own which it frequently considers as opposing those of management.

Three Disadvantages of Having Unions

Personnel problems do not lie dormant during negotiation intervals; management has the job of administering the contract, and its administration is continually probed and challenged by the union's complaints, grievances, slowdowns, and even work stoppages. Not only will the benefits of having a union in the plant prove illusory, but there will be three major areas of disadvantage in addition:

Strikes. When the union chooses to use its economic weapon, the plant may be shut down and its output reduced to zero while many of its costs continue, customers look for other sources of supply, and employees are stirred to a bitterness against the company that may have long-lasting effects.

Interference of a third party. The direct, one-to-one relationship between a company and its employees ends when a union enters the picture. A third party, which may have no interest in the success or even continuation of the business, must now be consulted on every major matter affecting employees. Union headquarters may decree that settlements at your plant must conform to some regional or national pattern that has nothing to do with your company's particular situation. The union has its own regulations and discipline for employees, and demands that they split their loyalty. Politics and factionalism within the union can create unwanted tension and divisiveness among your employees. And they may be promised benefits by the third party which the company has no ability or intention to grant.

Diversion of managerial effort. Huge amounts of managerial time at all levels of the company are devoted to preparing for and handling union negotiations, demands, and grievances. The difference between this effort and that required to do a good, responsible job of labor relations in the nonunion company could be better devoted to improving operations and conditions for all concerned. The ultimate security of the plant's employees rests not with the union, but with the combined efforts of management and labor to improve those factors that make their product competitive: quality, cost, and output.

Why Keeping the Plant Nonunion Is an All-Management Problem

Let's assume that you are manager of a nonunion plant which you would like to keep that way. You will be faced with three special problems:

Irresolution at other management levels. Consider the lower management levels—the foremen, supervisors, and superintendents who report to you. They may have lingering feelings that a union isn't too bad an idea, and it might get us all another holiday or two. You will want to call these people together, and explain carefully the reasons for your position with emphasis on what is at stake for them—the constant challenge to their authority, the necessity of handling every situation so that it will later stand up under the grievance procedure, strike duty, and the deterrent to higher management's placing new or expanded failities at the unionized site. And you will want to drive home the point that the union can't grant anything; only the company can grant additional benefits from the income generated by the business.

With higher levels of management, your best persuasive powers are called for. If you present the same reasons which led to your position in a cogent manner, you can usually win support; in most cases it will be there anyway. One thing is certain: without that support, your task is virtually impossible.

The temptation to take employees for granted. Managers, especially those in older plants, can falsely assume that there is a mystical bond of loyalty between themselves and their employees that a union can never break. This is the "good old Jim would never vote for a union," or "our employees are perfectly happy," school of thought.

Look out.

"Good old Jim" may never have heard the word *paternalism,* but he'll support a union if he thinks you feel you own him. And those "happy" employees may be harboring a nest of hidden grievances and frustrations just waiting for a chance to come out in the open.

Your employee relationships in the nonunion plant should never reflect a feeling on your part that your employees will support you no matter what you do. And your entire management team must be constantly sensitive to hidden complaints and grievances which do not come out in the open as quickly as in the unionized plant.

Sensitivity of the work force to major moves in industrial relations. When wages are increased, fringe benefits expanded, layoffs carried out, or major disciplinary action taken, the plant communications to its employees should be handled in such a way that they will not feel that they would have come out better with a union. If they are working in an area where they can easily make comparisons with practices in nearby plants, the reasons offered for such moves should take account of these comparisons.

PREVENTIVE ACTIONS YOU CAN TAKE

Maintaining your plant's nonunion status cannot be left to chance. A conscious, sustained effort to prove to the plant employees that their needs and expectations can best be met by the plant management, without the interference of a third party, must be mounted.

The first phase of this effort, and by far the most important, consists of everything you do to establish sound industrial relations before a particular union knocks on the door, claiming to represent the plant employees. Concentrate on these aspects to give the union organizer as little as possible to work with:

Wages and fringe benefits. Keep them at least equal to and preferably ahead of the surrounding plants in your labor market. If your workers feel that they are enjoying greater rewards than unionized plants can provide, you have a long head start.

Job security. People want two things: Continuity of employment, and fair treatment when layoff becomes inevitable. The manager of a nonunion plant ought to do everything he can to avoid layoffs (see"Preserving the Organization During Slow Periods," page 51) which, at best, upset employee morale. If layoff cannot be avoided, each employee will want to know exactly where he or she stands and why. Meet these expectations by establishing and publishing a detailed layoff procedure well before the need to use it arises.

Individual self-respect. Your employees want to feel that they are doing important work, that opportunities for advancement exist for them, and they they will be treated with respect. Management has sole control over these areas, and therefore has unique opportunities to reach its people which are not open to the union. Use all appropriate means of communication to show each employee the importance of the company's products, and where his or her contribution fits into the larger picture. Promote from within whenever possible, interview all qualified employees, explain to all the reasons for the final decision. Ensure that employees are treated courteously by their supervision and in their dealings with personnel, insurance, and payroll departments.

Complaint handling. There must be an active, trusted, and workable grievance procedure.

Phase two begins when one of your employees seeks out or is contacted by a union representative. This marks the start of a union campaign which usually ends in a secret ballot election to determine whether your employees want that union or no union. To survive this phase, plant management must

1. Be alert for the first signs of organizing activity and be prepared to deal with it calmly and effectively.

2. Take advantage of all legal means open to it to win the campaign. In general, management has the right to communicate with its employees, to present its case under certain rules of fairness, and to challenge illegal conduct by the union.

3. Avoid handing the election to the union by the commission of unfair labor practices. You cannot offer rewards or promises of benefits to "buy off" the employees, nor threaten, discipline, or discriminate against those attempting to organize.

How to Set Up a Successful Grievance System

The employee who works in a plant where there is no set procedure for handling complaints, where the foreman's word is "law," or where his complaints go unanswered for long periods or are forgotten altogether, is fair game for the union organizer. Plant management, busy with its production problems, perhaps uneasy about dealing with such a negative feature of its employee relations, and possibly feeling that complaints only come from "troublemakers" anyway, may hang back from establishing a definite grievance procedure. The result is a big gap in the relations between the company and its employees, a source of frustration to the latter, and a golden opportunity for the organizer.

Setting up a grievance procedure which employees of a nonunion plant will really trust is not easy. But you must do it if you would hope to have your employees vote "No union" in a representation election. Meet these key requirements for your complaint system:

Make it formal. Every employee should have the right to have his or her complaint heard in a succession of explicit steps, starting with the first-line supervisor and proceeding up through the management chain to the personnel department, the plant manager and on to the highest level included—perhaps the president of the company. The procedure should spell out the employee's right to have another employee accompany him and present the case, the point at which the complaint is reduced to writing, and the number of days allowed for an answer at each level before the complaint automatically goes to the next level.

Publish it widely. Give a copy to every new employee, and make it part of the introduction procedure. Make copies available to all in the personnel office. Post it on the bulletin boards. If there is an employee handbook, this will be one of its most important sections.

Train foremen, supervisors, and department managers to use the procedure effectively. Not only should they be thoroughly familiar with each step of the procedure, but they must be more sensitive to real or imagined complaints than their counterparts in unionized plants. Make it clear that unless they handle this part of their jobs well, a union will soon do it for them. And they should understand that you will rate their skill in grievance handling in your reviews of their performance.

Avoid token provisions and insincere statements of the "my door is always open" type. Your door isn't always open, and obviously can't be. Tell the employee how he or she really can get in contact with you—what levels of the complaint procedure must be previously exhausted, whom to see to make the appointment, who else must be notified. The employee can understand and accept these provisions without feeling that he has been fooled by a bland statement which really means nothing.

Make sure it is legal. Labor law forbids setting up company-dominated, quasi-union organizations. For instance, it may be illegal to have employees in the nonunion plant elect representatives to handle their grievances. Let your labor attorney review the procedure before you publish it.

The Employee Handbook

Publish an employee handbook in about the same size and format as a union contract. Make it more attractive in appearance, and less legalistic in language. Involve line management as well as the Industrial Relations Department in writing its sections. In it explain the wage system, fringe benefits, holiday schedule, sick leave provisions, plant rules, disciplinary action, and the grievance procedure. Not only is this a good way to communicate such important matters to employees, but it will give them a sense of security to see them spelled out in a printed book with the company's name on it. And it can be an important psychological offset when the union organizer arrives brandishing copies of union contracts from other plants.

Dealing with Wages and Benefits

This can be a baffling problem. If you have to pay wages and benefits above those of the area, why don't you just forget the whole thing and have a union? Because you can afford to use some of the money which having a union will cost. Keep the situation under control by handling it this way:

1. Find out exactly where your plant stands in wages and benefits. Exchange detailed information with other plants in the area, and participate in surveys conducted by employers' associations. See "Sources Outside the Company," Chapter 12, for additional ways to gather information.

2. Decide how far above the prevailing level you can afford to go. Remember that if you have a union you will have to pay for hourly workers' time consumed in union business or for their replacements when they are absent but unpaid, for managerial time spent on union matters, for strikes, for expenses of contract negotiations—hotel rooms, secretaries, recording, printing of contracts, for grievance arbitration and the legal help you will need in them. Your colleagues in union plants can help you estimate these costs; you can then decide how much can be allotted to keep wages and benefits above surrounding levels.

3. Beware of attempting to match the wages of every plant in town. If you are assembling electronic components, you probably can't afford to pay the wages offered in an oil refinery. You will have to be honest in explaining to your employees that wage levels are different from industry to industry, and that there are usually compensating factors for these differences.

Keep the Lines of Communication Open

Nothing can hurt plant management more than to be unaware of the problems and issues on the minds of its employees. It must know exactly where the rough spots are in its employee relationships; which of its moves work well and which do not; when organizing activity begins; what the issues are between the pro-union and anti-union groups among the employees.

How are communications kept open? As we saw in Chapter 10, it starts with the first-line supervisor who, of all management people, is closest to the work force and in the best position to know what questions and problems are on employees' minds. Train him to be sensitive to issues affecting plant workers, to be a good listener, to pass information upward without bias or editing. The upward flow of communication will stop, of course, unless higher levels of management—department heads, superintendents, assistant plant managers and the plant manager himself—are interested in what the foreman has to say, and are available for him to say it. These people should be seen frequently in the plant, and available to employees for informal chats. Continue the flow of information by including a discussion of the state of employee relationships in the daily production meetings.

WHAT TO DO WHEN THE UNION APPEARS

Sooner or later you can expect the union organizer to appear, either on his own or in response to a call from some of your employees. His arrival marks the start of the campaign, and it calls for these actions by you:

Make no moves in panic, rashness, or from emotion. Your actions are now covered by a complicated body of law, and a wrong move can hurt your cause in any legal battles to follow. (If you don't have a labor attorney or consultant it is very late; hire one immediately.)

Report the organizing activity to other concerned elements of the corporation— headquarters, other plants, industrial relations, your immediate superior.

Call together your management people, including first-line supervisors. Bring them up-to-date on the facts of the situation. Instruct them on what they can and cannot do; tell them you will meet with them later to outline the campaign and their part in it in full.

How to Handle the Union's Organizing Campaign

The union representative may present you with authorization cards signed by a majority of your employees, and ask you to recognize his union without an election conducted by the National Labor Relations Board (NLRB). At this point you have four choices:

1. Agree to recognize the union and begin making plans to enter into collective bargaining. This is a poor choice because some of the employees may have signed the authorization cards under peer pressure (after all, it isn't done in secret), and the cards may not really represent a majority. Beyond that, any arrangements you make might be later upset if it turns out that the union has no legal right to do business, the composition of the bargaining unit is not legally appropriate, or a rival union appears claiming that *it* represents the employees.

You will be better protected against such potential problems if the union is certified through an NLRB election procedure, rather than merely recognized by you.

2. Refuse to recognize the union. Then either the union or the company can petition the NLRB to decide whether the organization claiming to represent the employees (or one of several so claiming) is entitled to be certified as their collective bargaining agent. The usual response, although there are variations, is that the Board orders an election to be held. (The union also has the right to request certification even if the company has *not* refused to recognize it.)

3. Agree to a consent election. Under the general direction of the regional office of the NLRB, the company and the union agree upon the composition of the bargaining unit, the date and place for the election to be held, the choices to appear on the ballet (usually the name of the union and "no union"), and a way of determining who is eligible to vote—usually those employees in the proposed bargaining unit who are on the payroll as of an agreed date.

4. Insist upon the Board's full procedure. If the parties do not agree to a consent election, the regional NLRB office will conduct an examination of the situation and hold a hearing at which both the union and the company may present facts and their views on the questions at issue. (The issue which is often the hardest to settle is the composition of the bargaining unit.) Following the hearing(s) the regional director of the NLRB either dismisses the petition, or, after defining the appropriate bargaining unit, orders an election.

Putting Your Own Campaign into Action

By the time the election date is set, the campaign is in full swing. Plan the campaign you will conduct, working with your attorney or consultant to develop the message you want to convey to your employees, and the arguments you will use to try to convince them to vote "no union." Outline the means of communication open to you—employee meetings, letters home, the line organization, Industrial Relations department, and the company newspaper. Set a timetable for the moves you want to make. Be sure to decide in advance what the tone of your response will be to the various types of union criticism of you and the company, which are sure to be a part of the campaign.

A word about the outside attorney or consultant. You will need sound advice on labor law and on handling the issues of the campaign. But it is best that providers of this advice be kept in the background and not thrust into a visible role in the campaign. Management should be careful not to delegate its authority or responsibility to its advisers, nor to regard advice that would take it outside the law.*

---

*For a quick review of what the law is, obtain a copy of the latest revision of the very useful *A guide to basic law and procedures under the National Labor Relations Act* (Washington, D.C.: Office of the General Counsel, National Labor Relations Board, rev. 1978). Available from the Superintendent of Documents, U.S. Government Printing Office, Washington, D.C. 20402.

Put the campaign plan into effect. Remember that you cannot intimidate, coerce, threaten, or make promises of rewards to keep a union out. You do, however, have the right to communicate with your employees, to state your case, and to challenge the union when it commits unfair labor practices. The legal details will have to be answered by your attorney; you will be asking him such questions as these: Can I prohibit union organizers from entering plant property? Can I prohibit distribution of union literature by my own employees inside the plant? How far am I, my managers, and the first-line supervisors allowed to go in discussing the campaign with individual employees? What information am I required to supply to the union?

The Representation Election

The regional director's order for an election will give the date (usually within 30 days of the order), time, and place (normally on the employer's premises). Following issuance of the order, the employer is required to supply a list of the names and addresses of the employees in the designated bargaining unit for use by all parties to the election. The Regional Office will also send to you, the employer, election notices and sample ballots which you must post in conspicuous places at least 72 hours before the election. Be careful not to change the sample ballots in any way, nor mark them with what you consider to be the right choice.

The voting is by secret ballot. There must be no campaign speeches to assembled groups of employees on company premises during working hours within the 24 hours preceding the election; violation of this rule may result in the election being set aside, even if the content of the speech was not coercive or threatening. The rule applies to both union and employer.

On the day of the election the Board will have an agent present at the polls. Both the union and the employer are permitted to have observers at the polls—usually one each—who identify those eligible to vote, assist the agent in the conduct of the election, and certify the results. They are not allowed to handle ballots, however—only the agent may do that.

A booth is set up to assure secrecy of the ballot. Voters appear, identify themselves, and are checked off the list of those eligible. Each is given a ballot, which is marked and placed in the ballot box. If a voter is challenged his ballot is sealed in a special envelope for later consideration.

When the voting time is up, the ballots are counted by the agent in the presence of the observers. First the agent attempts to get agreement on whether the challenged ballots should be counted; if so, they are mixed with the others. If not, the unchallenged ballots are counted to determine a tentative outcome; then the regional director investigates to see whether there are enough challenged ballots to change the tentative outcome; if not, it stands as the final outcome, but if so, further hearings are held to pass upon their validity.

To win an election, a union must obtain a majority vote of *those voting;* in a tie vote between a union and "no union," "no union" wins, because the union failed to get a majority. When there are two or more unions and "no union" on the ballot and none obtains a majority, a run-off election is held between the two choices with the most votes.

If there are no objections to the conduct of the election, the regional director certifies the results to the interested parties and a winning union (if any) as the representative of the employees in the bargaining unit. If there are objections further investigations, hearings and possibly lawsuits may result. Objections by any of the parties must be filed with the regional director within five days after receipt of the vote tally. Although elections may be set aside because the NLRB representatives themselves fail to conduct the election properly, most often the cause is improper conduct by the employer or the union. This conduct is not limited to, but often arises from, the commission of unfair labor practices.

Unfair Labor Practices

Either union or management can commit unfair labor practices at any time, but the vast majority of charges arise during organizing campaigns. This is a complicated legal area in which you will need professional advice, but the following summary of unfair labor practices as identified in the National Labor Relations Act will help you to better understand that advice, and perhaps keep you from making a serious error while waiting for it to arrive.

By an employer:

1. To interfere with, restrain, or coerce employees in the exercise of their rights to self-organization; to form, join or assist labor organizations; to bargain collectively through representatives of their own choosing; or to refrain from such activities.

2. To dominate or interfere with any labor organization, or contribute financial or other support to it.

3. To discriminate in regard to hire or tenure of employment, or any condition of employment, in order to encourage or discourage membership in any labor organization (the law specifically exempts a union shop agreement, however).

4. To discharge or otherwise discriminate against an employee because he or she has filed charges or given testimony under the Act.

5. To refuse to bargain collectively with representatives of employees.

By a union:

1. To restrain or coerce (a) employees in the exercise of their rights (listed in 1. above) (b) an employer in the selection of his or her representatives for collective bargaining or the adjustment of grievances.

2. To cause, or attempt to cause an employer to discriminate against an employee, or to discriminate itself against an employee whose union membership has been denied or terminated on some ground other than failure to pay regular initiation fees and dues.

3. To refuse to bargain collectively with an employer.

4. To engage in a strike or refusal to handle goods or perform services, or encourage other employed individuals to do so, or to coerce or threaten any person engaged in commerce (including employers) where the object is to (a) force an employer or self-employed person to join any labor or employer organization, or to enter into a "hot cargo" agreement,* (b) force anyone to boycott the goods or business of another, or forcing another employer to recognize or bargain with a union which is not certified to represent his employees, (c) force an employer to recognize or bargain with a union when a different union has been certified as the representative of his employees, (d) force an employer to assign work to employees in a particular union, trade, or class rather than those in another union, trade, or class.

5. To charge an excessive or discriminatory initiation fee.

6. To cause or attempt to cause an employer to pay for services which are not performed.

7. To picket an employer to force him to recognize or bargain with a union, or force his employees to select that union (unless the union is currently certified as the representative of his employees) if the employer has lawfully recognized another union, a valid election has been held within the past 12 months, or the picketing has continued for 30 days without the union filing a petition for an election. (However, the law exempts truthful informational picketing which does not induce a boycott or a strike.)

When the Board determines that there is sufficient interference with the rights of employees to organize freely, and that a fair election cannot be held under the prevailing climate, it can certify a union as the representative of a group of employees without an election and require the employer to bargain collectively with it.

Decertification Elections and Union Shop Deauthorization

The law gives employees the right to shed themselves of a union they no longer want through a process called *decertification*. If enough employees sign a petition for decertification (usually 30 percent), the NLRB will order an election to determine whether or not the union shall continue to be their bargaining representative.

I was once approached by several union employees who wanted to know how they could go about having their union decertified. Unsure as to what to tell them, I asked for some time to look into it and called the company's labor attorney. His reply was immediate and firm: "Don't touch it with a ten-foot pole. Give them the address and phone number of the nearest office of the Department of Labor and go no further."

---

*A "hot cargo" agreement is one in which a union and employer agree to refrain from handling the goods of another employer and from doing business with him. Hot cargo agreements are forbidden by the act (with certain exceptions in the construction and apparel industries), whether or not they were entered into voluntarily.

Whether he would give that same advice today I can't say (and it's still a good idea to get in touch with him if you receive such a request). But it is true that over the last two decades the number of decertification elections has risen dramatically, and the proportion of union victories in those elections has steadily declined. Employees are obviously exercising their rights to be free of union representation when they so desire.

The employer is more restricted in the period leading up to the filing of a decertification petition than in an ordinary representation election, and there must be no indication that the move to decertify was somehow inspired by him. The petition cannot be filed by the employer, his representative, any of his supervisory or confidential employees, or by any employee acting for or assisted by him; it must be filed by one or more employees, or an individual or labor organization acting on their behalf. Once the petition is granted and the campaign begins, however, the rules are essentially the same as for representation elections, and management has the same right to join the campaign and try to convince the employees to vote "no union."

A union shop is one in which employees are required to join the union after they are hired; this requirement may be negotiated into the union contract by the employer and the union except where it is forbidden by state law. The National Labor Relations Act, however, gives employees the right to withdraw the authority of the union to continue such a union security agreement, and upon petition by 30 percent or more of the employees the NLRB will order a *union-shop deauthorization election*. If they vote to deauthorize, the employees would still be represented by the union but any union security agreement, even an existing one, requiring union membership would become invalid. There is a difference in what is required to win the election, however: A majority of employees in the unit, not just those voting, must be obtained to deauthorize the union shop.

Chapter 12

Guidelines for a Successful Collective Bargaining Campaign

In the unionized plant, such matters as wages, working conditions, fringe benefits, and the manner of settling complaints are not determined by the management alone but are specified in a union contract produced by collective bargaining. Bargaining teams (or sometimes individuals) representing both the management and union sides meet to exchange proposals and counterproposals dealing with these and other issues. This exchange normally takes place in the 60 days prior to the termination of the present union contract, but many companies start the process earlier, and some make arrangements to continue the bargaining process throughout the life of the contract. Most plants come under state and federal laws requiring participation in the collective bargaining process, and managements or unions that refuse to meet and consider proposals and make counterproposals are subject to charges of unfair labor practice.

Each side comes to the bargaining table with its own weapon to force the other side into agreement. The union's weapon is the threat of a strike, and ultimately the strike itself. The company can use the lockout but rarely does because its best interests are usually served by keeping the plant running if employees are willing to work. The company's real weapons are its ability to withstand a strike longer than the union can carry it on and its right to hire permanent replacements for economic (as opposed to unfair labor practice) strikers.

This clearly is an adversarial process, rooted in the concept that the interests of the two parties are in direct conflict, and the solution is to hammer out a set of rules (the union contract) both parties can accept. The legalities of this system and its operating rules are not expected to change very much during the remainder of this century, but some observers of the industrial scene predict that management and labor will be forced by foreign competition to emphasize more strongly in collective bargaining those subjects in which their interests coincide. If that happens, union contracts of the future will put more stress on mutual-interest clauses and deal with such subjects as greater worker participation in determining job content, quality circles, and flexibility in work rules and work assignment procedures.

In this chapter, all phases of the collective bargaining process from the management side will be presented, beginning with the responsibilities of the plant manager and the organization of the company bargaining team, proceeding on to preparation for and conduct of the bargaining sessions, and ending with actions to be taken in the event of a strike. Followed closely, it will be an effective guide to the conduct of a successful collective bargaining campaign.

KEY RESPONSIBILITIES OF THE PLANT MANAGER

As Chief Negotiator

By the very nature of the job, the plant manager is intimately associated with matters concerning both sides in collective bargaining. Your ability to meet responsibility for the profitability of the plant is directly tied to the cost of wages, fringes, and work practices specified by the union contract. For these reasons the plant manager is very often chosen to be the chief negotiator for the company, and the remainder of this chapter is written from this point of view. As chief negotiator, you will have the multiple jobs of recruiting, organizing, and directing the management bargaining team; preparing for and conducting bargaining sessions; and developing and executing plans for action in the event of a strike.

As Supporting Member

In some companies a member of the industrial relations department is designated as chief negotiator, and the plant manager joins him or her as a supporting member of the team. In very large companies when multiplant bargaining is conducted at company headquarters, you may be asked to participate as a team member. In these situations you are in a unique position to supply valuable information about the day-to-day operations of the plant and the effect of union proposals on product cost, customer service, and management control. Even as a supporting member, you will want to become familiar with the bargaining techniques and strategies developed in the remainder of this chapter.

Not on the Team

In some situations the plant manager will not be present in the bargaining room at all; this usually happens when a lawyer or labor consultant is hired or assigned to negotiate alone for the company. Such a professional negotiator will look to the plant manager for much of the information used in the bargaining sessions. The negotiator should be required to maintain close contact with the plant manager to keep you informed of the progress of negotiations.

PUTTING THE MANAGEMENT TEAM TOGETHER

Size of the Team

A bargaining team of four or five members represents the best compromise of the conflicting factors that influence team size. Smaller teams may not be able to provide sufficient coverage in depth of all the subjects to be discussed in the bargaining sessions. Individual members may become overloaded in attempting to handle larger shares of the bargaining work in addition to their regular duties. If one or more members are lost to the team during the negotiations (illness, transfer, separation), it may become too small to handle the load. Hasty recruitment of new members during the course of the negotiations is not likely to produce the desired results.

Larger teams may have the undesirable effect of diverting too much of the plant staff from its regular duties. They may prove unwieldy in reaching strategy decisions when meeting alone, and difficult to control in the bargaining room.

Selection of Members

Because the results obtained by the bargaining team cannot be expected to surpass the combined capabilities of its members, their selection requires great care. Failure may not always be the fault of the team, but success cannot be obtained without a highly capable group. Look for these qualities:

1. Enthusiasm for and an interest in collective bargaining
2. General knowledge of the plant and detailed knowledge of one of its operational or administrative functions
3. A stake in the outcome
4. Good health
5. Ability to function as part of a team
6. Alertness and sensitivity

Once the selections are made, the plant manager often finds one more hurdle to clear: some of the people you want may not report to you, and you will have to convince another executive that it is in the company's best interests to detach that employee from part or all of her regular duties for a period of time. Presented with the consequences of a bad contract or a strike, the executive will usually respond favorably; when this is not the case, the help of higher management should be sought immediately.

From Which Departments?

The departments from which the team members are chosen is a matter of importance. In its proposals and bargaining discussions, the union will bring up a wide variety of issues requiring thorough analysis by the company representatives. It will often raise specific points requiring immediate rebuttal for best effect. In these situations the company needs bargainers who can respond from a close association and a detailed knowledge of the topics at issue.

Several of the members will be selected from the Manufacturing Department, since their knowledge of plant operations is essential in evaluating union proposals on work rules, shift assignments, distribution of overtime, seniority in work assignments, and the like. They should come from as many different sections of the manufacturing operation as possible—production, maintenance,shipping—to have the widest coverage available in the bargaining room.

The plant that has a Personnel or Industrial Relations Department will invariably place a member from that group on the bargaining team because of their close contact with grievances, insurance, transfers, seniority lists, pensions, and many other matters directly governed by the union contract.

Less obvious is the very important need to have a member of the Accounting Department on the bargaining team, and many companies overlook the two essential services that member can provide: (1) Cost information supporting the company's position on wages, fringes, vacations, insurance, sick leave, and so on; (2) The impact of the union's proposals on plant finances, especially those proposals that may contain hidden costs. All too often a company will sign a union contract without fully understanding how much it will cost. And it is a depressing sight to watch a company negotiator armed with vague, incomplete, and possibly inaccurate cost information attempting to maintain his position against the onslaughts of a union negotiator who detects the weakness.

First-Line Supervisors

It is a good idea to bring the first-line supervisors into the bargaining sessions. They do not need to be assigned as permanent members but can rotate. In the bargaining room they can be very helpful in preventing the union's representation of what goes on in a particular department from becoming too one-sided (it is valuable to have the maintenance foreman at the bargaining table the day the discussion turns to problems of overtime distribution in the Maintenance Department), and they will develop a greater appreciation of the problems faced by management in negotiations and a more positive identification with management positions on various issues. Once back in the plant, they will be less subject to distorted rumors about the course of the bargaining.

Whom to Keep Out

Who should *not* attend the bargaining sessions? In a word, all outsiders. When the bargaining is conducted by a union team consisting of workers from the local plant (and perhaps an international representative), the introduction of strange faces into the bargaining room simply forces them into a period of suspicious waiting. Avoid the temptation to have a lawyer sit in on or conduct the negotiations; the union team may conclude that the company is trying to fool them with tricky legalistic maneuvers and become impossible to convince of anything.

In the branch plant or subsidiary company, the idea may be advanced that a representative of headquarters management should come and sit in on the bargaining sessions. The local negotiator should hold out against this idea as long as possible. The message to the union here is that there is a higher authority it can appeal to, and its best strategy is to bypass the local management team and bring in higher management as soon as possible. If the union is successful in this ploy, the local management team will have great difficulty in ever conducting serious bargaining again.

CONTRACT NEGOTIATIONS: GETTING STARTED

Early Answers to Tough Questions

Union contract negotiations are going to force the company to make some very hard decisions. How much money can it afford to grant in wage and benefit increases? At what wage level will it take a strike rather than go higher? How far is it willing to go in yielding management rights to the union? Will it accept a strike rather than grant another holiday?

All too often the chief company negotiator finds it harder to obtain early decisions on these questions from management than it is to bargain with the union. While the reluctance of top management to contemplate the worst is understandable, the chief negotiator must make clear to higher management that his position is badly weakened unless he has these answers. The union will be probing the company bargainers all through the negotiations for signals—what they say, tone of voice, facial expressions—telling it where the company really intends to draw the line. The company negotiator who doesn't know whether the company will take a strike rather than grant another holiday is unable to put it convincingly that another holiday isn't possible. Both sides can blunder into an unncessary strike under these conditions.

No Time to Lose

The company that makes its final decisions under the pressure of a contract expiration in a few days or hours, or worse yet under the pressure of a strike, is putting itself at an unnecessary disadvantage. It has forfeited the time needed to make a thorough examination of the consequences of yielding on a particular issue. If the issue is of such importance to both sides that a strike is inevitable, the company is better off knowing this early in the negotiations.

HOW TO PREPARE FOR BARGAINING:
TEN ESSENTIAL STEPS

Success at the bargaining table cannot be achieved without extensive preparation by the management team. There are no shortcuts, no quick and easy methods. An ill-prepared team in the bargaining room is headed for disaster.

There is nothing mysterious about preparing for collective bargaining, and the following list gives ten essential steps in the general sequence in which they should be taken.

1. Select the management bargaining team members.
2. Arrange for legal aid.
4. Begin regular management team meetings.
4. Collect factual data needed—cost of proposals, other contracts, general economic information.
5. Draw up company demands.
6. Develop a bargaining manual.
7. Obtain higher management decisions on strike issues.
8. Notify union of intention to amend contract.
9. Notify Federal Mediation and Conciliation Service and appropriate state agencies of expiration of contract.
10. Make arrangements with union representatives for the first bargaining session.

When Preparation Begins

Preparation for the next contract starts the day after the previous contract is signed. The first order of business after a contract completion is for the chief negotiator to write a critique of the just-finished bargaining while it is still fresh in her memory. The report will contain a narrative history of the negotiations and an objective evaluation of the company's strategy. What was done right? What features of the company's approach should be retained and enhanced in the next negotiations? What features should be dropped? Improved? What were the union weaknesses, and how can they be turned to the company's advantage next time?

Negotiating File

The next order of business is to establish a bargaining file for the *next* negotiations. Over the life of the contract, material on such subjects as cost of living, contract settlements in other companies, reports of strikes, changes in union leadership, National Labor Relations Board rulings, and court decisions can be collected from newspapers, trade magazines, and government publications. As plant situations occur that suggest new or improved contract provisions, they should be written up and inserted in the file. Incidents of this kind are easily forgotten over a two- or three-year contract period; reduced to writing and collected in one place, they are valuable in developing company demands at the next negotiations.

When to Start Team Meetings

Start holding private meetings of the company bargaining team about six months before the expiration of the contract. A quiet location and freedom from interruptions is required; since these ideal conditions are hard to come by during the regular business day, some committees have found a solution in having dinner together at the end of the day and meeting for several hours in the early evening once a week. Each meeting should have an agenda prepared by the chief negotiator, covering a specific topic such as company goals, anticipated union demands, information needed and assignments for collecting it, company demands, location and timing of the bargaining sessions, bargaining room strategy, and strike preparation. While a definite agenda is used (to avoid wasting the time of the committee members), an atmosphere of free and open discussion should be maintained. It is in these meetings that the most valuable ideas for company strategy will be developed and the team shaken down into a well-disciplined and smoothly functioning unit.

WHAT YOU NEED TO KNOW TO BEGIN BARGAINING

The company bargaining team will need to have at its fingertips full and accurate information on a wide variety of subjects. Before it can adopt sound bargaining positions on wages, fringe benefits, and working conditions, it must have complete cost information. Not only will this information be required to convince higher management of the correctness of the team's position, but it will also be used to back up the company's position in the bargaining room. Here the data presented by the company will be subject to challenge by the union and will have to stand up to adverse examination. (There is a reverse benefit to be gained here: If the company's information is repeatedly found to be accurate and complete, the union will spend correspondingly less time in challenge.)

The gathering of this information cannot be left to chance. It should be the subject of an early bargaining team meeting at which a list of the required data is developed and individuals assigned the responsibility for collecting it.

Six Key Cost Items to Be Aware of

While it is not possible to list every conceivable type of information required for a particular bargaining situation, these items represent the major proportion of the cost data needed:

Wages: Total annual dollars paid in total payroll, straight time, overtime, and shift differential. Average individual hourly rate, straight time, and overtime.

Hours worked: Total annual straight time and overtime hours. Average hours per employee, straight time, and overtime. Overtime hours as a percentage of total hours.

Fringe benefits: Total annual dollar cost *and* cents per hour cost of holidays, vacations, insurance, sick leave, pensions, funeral leave, jury duty, military leave, special bonuses, work clothing, and safety equipment.

Economic background: Cost of living index for the area, with recent trends; business outlook for the year ahead for the company and industry; recent contract settlements in major industries; average wages paid and hours worked in your specific industry.

Other companies: As much detailed information as can be obtained on wages, fringe benefits, and contract provisions and work rules from companies in your area and in your industry. This information should be collected for the categories just listed.

Lost time and absenteeism: Fifty-two weeks times forty hours per week amounts to 2,080 hours. Deduct holidays and vacation time; then compare the average straight-time hours worked per employee with this figure. The difference is lost time from all sources, and it can be broken down into sick leave, jury duty, and so on. Casual absenteeism can be derived from these calculations or worked up from the individual time records. Calculate Monday and Friday absenteeism as a percentage of the total.

Sources from Within the Company

Plant time records: Many companies prepare daily or weekly compilations of actual time worked and time lost by hourly personnel in each section of the plant. Records are often kept of overtime worked and overtime refused by each employee. Individual summaries of time worked and lost may be kept for each employee on an annual basis.

Such records will provide the information required in the "Hours Worked" category. If ready-made compilations are not available, however, the bargaining team will have to take action to have them prepared, going all the way back to the time cards themselves if necessary.

Cost reports: The monthly cost report, issued in some form in virtually all manufacturing plants, contains a great deal of information useful to the negotiator. It will provide much of the basic data on wages, overtime, and fringe benefits, and will show the time trends for these items. Caution must be exercised in deciding how much and in what form this data can be revealed to the union during the negotiations.

Accounting Department: The Accounting Department can provide a great deal of help in assembling and analyzing the data discussed so far. More importantly, it can handle the more complicated calculation projects such as determining the future cost of anticipated or actual union proposals (what will it cost in the coming year to raise holiday overtime pay from double time and a half to triple time?), the total cost of various settlement packages, and the effect of a total settlement on company profits and prices. The chief negotiator will want to establish a close working relationship with the Accounting Department early in the preparations; this task will be made easier if a member of the Accounting Department has joined the bargaining team.

Personnel Department: Much of the discussion at the bargaining table will concern aspects of the work force that cannot be measured in dollars and cents. The files of the Personnel Department will give the average age of the work force, distribution of seniority among its members, labor turnover, interdepartmental transfers, number and size of insurance claims, and safety statistics. Managers in this department can offer valuable insights into the morale and attitudes of the plant work force.

Outside Sources to Consider

Other companies: It is essential that the company bargaining team enter the negotiations with full, up-to-date information on wages, fringes, and work practices of other companies in the same labor market area. Exchanges of union contracts are relatively easy to arrange with neighboring plants. The nonunion plant may be more reluctant to divulge information about its pay practices. In either case, a personal visit is the most effective way of establishing a good mutual information exchange. The Personnel Department may be perfectly capable of handling area surveys, but it is a good idea to assign some of the contact work to members of the bargaining team to give them a better perspective on the local labor picture.

Regional and trade associations: Regional groups such as the local Chamber of Commerce, Management Council, or state Association of Manufacturers frequently act as statistical collection agencies for their members and may issue reports on wages and fringe benefits paid in the area. Often these groups will provide forums for personal exchange of experiences and discussion of problems of common interest. Trade associations, made up of companies engaged in a specific industry, perform similar services for their members, but application of their data requires caution because of the wide geographical area covered.

Publications: As a plant manager you will sooner or later find yourself on the advertising mailing list of a number of periodicals covering continuing developments in the labor relations field. It is a good idea to subscribe to one or two of these bulletins, and to pass them on to all members of the bargaining team.

Of special interest is a monthly magazine published by the U.S. Department of Labor called *Monthly Labor Review*. The editorial content consists of articles about such subjects as employment outlook in various industries, developments in insurance and pension plans, union conventions, and reviews of decisions by the courts and the National Labor Relations Board. The Bureau of Labor Statistics uses the magazine to publish about forty pages of data on hours worked, earnings, labor turnover, and employment in various industries, as well as the familiar cost of living index. Subscriptions are obtained from the Superintendent of Documents, U.S. Government Printing Office, Washington, D.C. 20402, for about thirty dollars.

Several publishing firms offer continuing services in the labor relations field. Prentice-Hall publishes a two-volume series called *Labor Relations Guide*. The purchaser pays an annual fee in addition to the original purchase price and receives a current set of volumes in looseleaf binder form, as well as periodic replacement sheets to keep the books up to date. These volumes cover labor law changes, NLRB and court decisions, arbitration awards, government executive orders, cost of living statistics, and changes in state labor laws. Similar services are offered by Commerce Clearing House in *Labor Law Guide* and the Bureau of National Affairs in *Collective Bargaining Negotiation and Contracts*.

WHEN LEGAL HELP IS NEEDED

The management bargaining team should have at its disposal the services of an attorney skilled in labor law and contract negotiations. Often the choice of an attorney is made by higher management; if the chief negotiator makes the choice, it should be someone who not only has sound legal qualifications but is currently active in the labor field. Additional values would include a knowledge of the industry, international union, and possibly the international representative.

It has already been recommended that the attorney not be present in the bargaining room. However, the attorney should be available by telephone on very short notice once the bargaining sessions begin. Have him or her review all contract clauses before they are included in the final document and check the completed contract before it is signed, for possible conflict between the various articles and clauses. A very valuable orientation session can be provided for the entire negotiating team by having the attorney come to one of the preparation meetings to give his or her views on bargaining in general and the upcoming negotiations in particular. If legal complications develop during the negotiations, such as charges and countercharges of refusal to bargain or unfair labor practices, the attorney's services will be indispensable.

SCOUTING THE INTERNATIONAL REPRESENTATIVE AND THE SHOP COMMITTEE

Just as a baseball team scouts the opposition before an important game, it will pay the company bargaining team to learn as much as it can about the work-related factors affecting the thinking of the representatives on the other side of the bargaining table. Such factors as age, education, seniority, pay, ratings by supervisors, and jobs held within the company and prior to employment by it may help to explain or predict the thinking of various individuals on the bargaining issues. Any information that can be obtained about the political situation within the union and the aspirations of the union bargainers will be of assistance in understanding their motives in the bargaining room.

Scouting the international representative is a more difficult task. If anyone in the company has previously negotiated with him, this person would be the first to contact. Talk to bargainers from other companies who have bargained with him; they will be able to discuss his style of bargaining, weak points, issues he gives priority, objectives in recent negotiations, and political aspirations in the international union. Your labor attorney may be able to supply similar information.

WHEN TO NOTIFY THE OTHER PARTY OF CONTRACT EXPIRATION

If the plant is covered by federal labor law, either party to the union contract must notify the other party 60 days before contract expiration of its desire to amend or change the contract. The party taking this action must notify the Federal Mediation and Conciliation Service *and* any state mediation service which may exist, 30 days later if a settlement has not been reached, that a dispute exists.

The services of the federal mediator are available at no cost to the parties on a completely voluntary basis. He or she will usually meet separately with the parties, try to find the causes of deadlock, and search for areas of agreement. Suggestions may then be made to both sides of the ways in which they might move toward agreement. Both sides may be called together in a joint meeting to get the bargaining going again. The federal mediator will not assume the role of an arbitrator or try to judge the merits of the dispute. The company negotiator will make the decision to accept or reject the services of the mediator on a number of local factors: ability of the mediator, the confidence of the union side in that particular mediator, nature of the issues at stake, and the degree to which communication between the parties has broken down. Mediation can be a very valuable tool in reaching a contract settlement; it should not be rejected without the most careful consideration.

HOW TO CONDUCT PRODUCTIVE BARGAINING SESSIONS

Decide Where to Hold the Bargaining Sessions

The first step is to decide where the bargaining sessions are to be held—on company property or away from it. The union may insist on meeting off the company premises; in any case, the advantages lie with making arrangements for meeting rooms at a local hotel, motel, or other facility. The management team will be better able to concentrate on the job at hand, free from the many interruptions which seem inevitable when they are on the plant site. The union team will feel freer to involve themselves in the give and take of bargaining if they are not subjected to questioning by their own membership every time they emerge from the bargaining room.

If bargaining arrangements are not already determined by long practice, it is worthwhile to discuss with the union the sharing of the cost of the rooms. One survey has shown that the union pays some portion of the room cost in about 25 percent of the bargaining situations studied.

Have at least two rooms available—one for meetings, the other for team caucuses. The furnishings need not be elaborate, but the rooms should not be so small as to be crowded. They should be provided with a large table, water pitcher and glasses, pads and pencils, and a chalkboard or chart pad.

Take Charge of the Meetings—Informally

In many bargaining situations, especially when union personnel are relatively new to negotiating, the chief company negotiator may be able to assume a kind of informal chairmanship of the meetings—open them, adjourn them, call for breaks, determine the order in which topics are discussed. While this isn't quite the same thing as being elected president of the local Rotary Club, it does offer some opportunities to guide and control the course of the negotiations, and the company negotiator should go as far as possible in this direction.

Maintain a Businesslike Tone

Insist that the negotiations be conducted in a businesslike manner. Emotional outbursts should be minimized and must never come from the management side. If the union takes the occasion to go back over all of the individual complaints that have come up during the life of the contract, they should be reminded that such matters are not the subject of the negotiations and should be handled by the grievance procedure.

The company negotiator should present the arguments for management's proposals and their responses to the union's proposals in a straightforward, unruffled manner. If you can develop a reputation early in the negotiations for complete honesty and having your facts straight, it will pay off handsomely in the latter stages of the bargaining. This is the point where exhaustive preparations begin to pay back the time and effort invested in them.

Above all, the management team should never allow itself to become the target of personal abuse or profanity. If faced with this kind of behavior, the chief company negotiator should remind all present of their obligation to conduct themselves in a civil manner; if this fails, postpone further negotiations until a calmer atmosphere can be restored.

Operate Under Tight Discipline

The management team should operate under tight discipline in the bargaining room, with the chief negotiator controlling the management strategy. Team members can unwittingly cut the ground out from under the chief negotiator with casual remarks or side conversations which have not been thought out carefully in advance. Set up a system of signals for the team members to get the attention of the chief negotiator when they wish to speak. Simply passing written notes is one system and has the advantage of notifying the chief negotiator of what the speaker wants to say.

Good use can be made of the caucus as a strategy device. When tempers are rising across the table or the management side seems boxed in or a question of fact needs to be researched or the management team is divided on a subject, simply call a caucus to get the time needed to adjust the situation.

Avoid Late Hour Bargaining

Physically tired negotiators cannot give the full, careful scrutiny to contract changes which they require. Whenever possible, schedule negotiating sessions during regular business hours; a fully rested management team will do a better job, and if it does need additional review and strategy meetings, the evenings are left open for them.

WHY YOU NEED TO KEEP ACCURATE AND UP-TO-DATE RECORDS OF BARGAINING SESSIONS

It is important that a complete and accurate record of the bargaining sessions be kept. As contract language is agreed to during the progress of the sessions, it may later become the subject of controversy if an unassailable record is not kept. The management team will often want to refer to exact statements made by either side in earlier sessions. And if a dispute arises during the life of the contract as to the intent of a particular clause, an arbitrator may decide the issue on the basis of what was said during the negotiations. The company that has an accurate record of the bargaining sessions can approach such a problem with confidence that the record will support its position, or if this is not the case be able to get out of the situation gracefully at an early stage.

There are several ways to obtain a complete record. One is to have a tape recorder running in the bargaining room and give the tapes to a professional stenography firm for transcription into a written record. This is probably the best system, not only for the current negotiators but for the team that will handle the next negotiations several years from now. It is also the most expensive, and transcribing ten sessions may run up a bill in the thousands of dollars. Another method is simply to keep the raw tapes as a record. It has the disadvantages that after several months or years, identification of the speakers may be difficult; and if the tapes must be played back in the presence of union representatives, any heated exchanges or unpleasant outbursts are revived exactly as they occurred. A third approach is simply to assign one member of the management team to take notes. This is the least satisfactory method because the note-taker will be preoccupied with that job and will not function effectively as a bargainer. Also, the notes may be incomplete or unconsciously edited, and their accuracy and objectivity are certain to be challenged by the union.

HOW TO EVALUATE UNION DEMANDS

The end product of all collective bargaining is a new or revised union contract, a document which is written in precise, matter-of-fact, and often legal language.

The demands submitted by the union at the first bargaining session may look like anything but formal contract language. They may be delivered verbally. They may be delivered in a variety of written forms ranging all the way from carefully typewritten, precisely worded clauses down to crudely scrawled pencil lists. The first job of the company negotiator in the bargaining sessions is to review them one by one with the union, translating them into specific contract clause changes. When this is completed, ask if these are all the demands the union has—no surprises are wanted later in the negotiations.

The union list is likely to be long and to include many items that will not be included in the completed contract. The company bargaining team will meet alone shortly after the union demands are in to try to determine which are important to the union and which are not. This evaluation necessarily contains a large element of guesswork and will be subject to continuing review as the negotiations proceed.

The team now proceeds to assess the union's demands from the company's point of view. It will decide, or seek decisions from higher management, which union demands are acceptable, which can be tolerated, and which are completely unacceptable. If all of the information needed to make these decisions is not at hand, assignments can be made to the team members to research the proposals in terms of their effects on cost, management rights, conflict with corporate policy, ability to serve customers, and impact on salaried personnel. Then the company team will be ready to prepare its counterproposals.

PREPARING COMPANY DEMANDS

The company should *never* enter collective bargaining without a set of demands of its own. In most contract settlements the company ends up giving a great deal; it should get something in return. Without company demands, the bargaining takes on a one-sided atmosphere. With them, the company team has some points to trade off against union proposals. If the union unexpectedly accedes to some of them, the company is that much farther ahead.

The company's demands will find their sources in the overall corporate objectives, future plans for the plant whose contract is being negotiated, and experiences—good or bad—with the existing contract. In drafting the company demands, exercise caution on two points: (1) Be sure that the company demand will have real value to the company if the union agrees to it; otherwise you may wind up trading an important concession to the union for a worthless gain for the company; (2) If either side bargains for a contract change but fails to achieve it, its position on the subject may be weaker than if it had never been mentioned (with respect to law and arbitration proceedings). For example, if the contract is silent on interdepartmental transfers and present practice favors the company, it would be unwise to bring the subject up in collective bargaining. If the company demand is not included in the final contract, the union may be able to restrict the company's right to administer transfer by showing that the company had failed to gain its right in the collective bargaining.

Many of the union proposals will deal with sections of the contract that the company also would like to see changed. In some cases the company will go in the same direction as the union but not quite as far. In others, it will want to go in the exact opposite direction. Rather than confuse the issue by stating its position in brand-new proposals, the company submits counterproposals to those put forth by the union. For example, the union may have proposed that the new contract provide for two additional holidays. The company, desiring to grant only one additional holiday, would submit a counterproposal calling for a single holiday addition.

HOW TO WORK UP A BARGAINING MANUAL

As the negotiations proceed, the bargaining team will find that it has been amassing a large amount of information. Cost data, area surveys, economic background, company demands and the reasons supporting them, union proposals and the arguments supporting the company's position on them—all are being gathered in the company's file. The entire bargaining team will need to have instant access to all of this information in the bargaining room.

This objective is met by developing a bargaining manual, which contains the collected information in readily accessible form. While in some very large companies it may reach the proportions of a fully bound and printed volume, in most medium-sized plants it will be in typewritten looseleaf form, with a copy for each permanent member of the bargaining team. Work should begin on the bargaining manual as soon as the negotiating team starts its regular meetings. Cost data and other factual background information can be included before the actual negotiations begin.

Figure 12-1 is a sample page from the bargaining manual of a fictitious corporation preparing for collective bargaining. Actual cost data for the entire payroll costs for all the previous year are shown in terms of dollars paid, dollars per hour worked, and the percentage each item represents of the total. Another section provides handy cost factors which can be used for quick mental or written calculations. The negotiator who has this book handy can quickly respond to union arguments and avoid costly pitfalls.

As the union demands are received and evaluated, a separate bargaining manual page should be devoted to each one. Figure 12-2 is an illustration of how John Doe Manufacturing decided to handle Union Proposal No. 11. Most of the entries on this page are self-explanatory, but the section "Company Reasons" deserves comment. In it are shown the fundamental reasons for the company's position. They may or may not be reasons the company wishes to expose to the union. The section "Bargaining Arguments" gives the points that can be used in the bargaining room and are worded for maximum persuasive effect.

DRAFTING CONTRACT LANGUAGE

The completed union contract is a document that attempts to set forth the intentions of the parties who agreed to it. During its life it will be subjected to interpretation by people who were not present when it was drafted, and to the strains of grievance and arbitration procedures. While it is definitely recommended

THE JOHN DOE MANUFACTURING COMPANY
Union Contract Negotiations
Bargaining Manual

BASIC COST DATA

I. Actual Wages and Fringe Benefits, Previous Year

		Cost in Dollars	*% of Total*	*Dollars per Hour*
A. Wages				
	1. Straight Time	1,377,539	63.0	10.34
	2. Overtime	204,346	9.3	
	3. Shift Differential	7,850	.4	.06
	Total Wages	1,589,735	72.7	10.40
B. Fringe Benefits				
	1. Holidays	57,501	2.6	.43
	2. Vacation	73,373	3.4	.55
	3. Sick Leave	27,414	1.3	.20
	4. Funeral Leave	1,514	.1	.01
	5. Break & Washup Time	114,839	5.2	.86
	6. Group Insurance	68,650	3.1	.52
	7. Social Security, Unemployment Tax	127,179	5.8	.95
	8. Workmen's Compensation	64,941	3.0	.49
	9. Work Clothes	61,616	2.8	.46
	Total Fringes	597,027	27.3	4.47
	Grand Total	2,186,762	100.0	14.87

II. Useful Cost Data

A. Average Hourly Rate — 10.34

B. Average Overtime Hours — 180

C. Cost of an Additional Holiday

    1. Total Dollars — 6,038
    2. Cents per Hour — 4.5

D. Annual Value of Increases/Decreases in Hourly Wage

    1. 1% — $15,178
    2. 1¢/hr. — 1,531
    3. 20¢/hr. — 30,608
    4. 35¢/hr. — 53,564
    5. 50¢/hr. — 76,519
    6. 65¢/hr. — 99,475

FIGURE 12-1: Sample Bargaining Manual Page—Cost Data

THE JOHN DOE MANUFACTURING COMPANY
19___ Union Contract Negotiations
Bargaining Manual

UNION PROPOSALS

UNION PROPOSAL No. 11. Article V, Section D 4.

Work performed on a holiday or on the day on which the holiday is celebrated shall be paid for at twice the regular rate in addition to the holiday pay.

COUNTERPROPOSAL: None

COMPANY POSITION: Retain present contract provision.

COMPANY REASONS:

Labor costs become prohibitive if future developments in customer requirements or process changes should require holiday work on a regular basis. Average triple time rate would become $31.02 per hour—$10.34 for straight time, plus $20.68 for the premium.

BARGAINING ARGUMENTS:

1. We do not work holidays often. Keep contract on those items that have more meaning.

2. Proposed language tends to benefit only a few people and, of course, would have to come out of the total economic package granted by the company. It is better to provide benefits everyone can share.

3. Object of the business is to run at a profit. If we have to operate the plant on a holiday to accommodate a customer, we cannot triple the cost of labor and still make a profit. The company is therefore left with two very poor choices: Fail to serve the customer or serve him at a loss. Neither of these choices is good for anyone.

SECOND LINE OF DEFENSE:

If it becomes necessary to grant this proposal, be sure to eliminate the words ''. . . on a holiday or . . .'' Otherwise, if the Fourth of July falls on a Sunday and is celebrated on Monday, we will have to pay triple time for hours worked on both days.

AREA PRACTICE: Of 9 local companies: 2 pay triple time
                                         5 pay 2½ time
                                         2 pay double time

FIGURE 12-2: Sample Bargaining Manual Page—Union Proposal

that the contract not be studded with legalistic "whereases" and "wherefores," the wording of each clause accepted or proposed by the company should be carefully considered. For instance, an incomplete street address in the very first sentence of the contract may mean that the new plant being built on the other side of town will automatically be unionized the day it opens. Many clauses can be strengthened or weakened from the management point of view by simple changes in the wording. Use these techniques to obtain the best wording:

Compare Contracts

In the course of bargaining preparations, obtain copies of union contracts from a number of other companies. When preparing wording of a vacation clause change, review the vacation clauses in all of the other contracts. Then select the best combination of phrases for your clause.

Use Published Versions

Obtain a published contract language guide. Several publishers in the labor relations field have one or more books on this subject. They point out pitfalls in drafting contract language and offer specimen clauses designed to maximize management rights. Of special interest are publications of the Bureau of National Affairs, Washington, D.C.

Seek Legal Help

The company's labor attorney should review every clause change before it is written into the final contract. During preparation he or she will be able to suggest or obtain good clauses on the subjects you anticipate dealing with and should review the entire contract before it is signed to be sure (1) that the various clauses do not conflict with each other, and (2) that the contract does not violate any federal or state laws.

WHERE TO INVOLVE THE FIRST-LINE SUPERVISOR

As the plant manager, you should decide exactly what you want from your first-line supervisors during contract negotiations and explain their part in the proceedings to them in a clear, unmistakable manner. It is a serious error to neglect them during the bargaining period; not only will their positive contributions be lost, but since they are in continuous contact with union members it could not be considered unhuman of them if, hearing nothing from their management, they come to agree with the union's point of view on some issues. No company negotiator wants to hear from the union side of the bargaining table, "Your own foremen agree that we should have two more holidays."

The first-line supervisor's participation as a member of the bargaining team has already been discussed. Here are some additional ways that person can contribute:

Contribution to Company Demands

Operating at that point in the organization where the union contract provisions are translated into action, the foreman is in a unique provision to discover what parts of the contract are unworkable or detrimental from a management point of view. Solicit these ideas when drawing up the list of company demands.

Keeping a Calm Shop

Plant operations can be seriously affected by the high degree of excitement that can develop among the hourly workers at contract negotiation time. There will be discussion, disagreement, and arguments among the workers and between them and their union leadership. If this activity is allowed to become a major occupation of the work force, production output may suffer at a time when it is most needed. The first-line supervisor should be instructed to do everything during this period to maintain a calm, businesslike atmosphere in the plant. Since plant management is likely to be tied up in negotiating sessions, the supervisor is often very much alone in carrying out this responsibility and needs guidance.

This is a period when the rumor mill is at its most active, and the wildest versions of what the company wants and is doing in the negotiations will not only circulate among the plant workers but will pervade the lower salaried ranks as well. One of the company's best weapons against the most outrageous misrepresentation is a well-informed foreman, who can scotch a wild story before it gets started. Clearly, it is to the advantage of the company to keep the first-line supervisor well informed.

Maintaining Upward Communication

Closeness to the union membership puts the first-line supervisor in a very good position to collect scraps and bits of information which may be of value to the bargaining team and which provides a means to pass information along. While the law forbids his engaging in spy-like activities designed to intimidate the workers or interfere with their right to organize and run a union, in the normal course of work he will hear and see things about union politics, the relative importance of union demands, and the mood of the membership which can help the plant management chart a better course for all involved.

HOW TO MINIMIZE THE IMPACT OF A STRIKE WITH ADVANCE PREPARATION

As the plant manager you can do a great deal to minimize the effects of a strike on your company by careful preparation in advance of the contract expiration.

Sales Planning

At least six months prior to the strike deadline, work out a program with the Sales Department to protect the company's customers. The salespeople may want to contact their customers to inform them of a possible strike situation, and to ask them to place protective stock-up orders early in the negotiation period. A plan to stock outside warehouses might be developed, so that deliveries to customers could still be made if the plant is struck. Whatever system is devised, you should measure the difference between normal production and total capacity, and start early enough so that the difference can be used to amass the desired protective stock.

Decide Whether or Not to Operate

The company must decide whether it will attempt to operate the plant if a strike occurs, either with nonunion personnel or by replacing the strikers (get legal advice on this move). If the decision is to run the plant during a strike, plans must be made to move raw materials in and finished goods out, to provide and assign personnel to production jobs, and to arrange for their food and rest if passage in and out of the plant is not feasible.

If the decision is not to operate the plant, plans must still be made for protecting plant property and for communicating with municipal agencies, employees, and the public. Personnel arrangements must be made for final payments due the strikers and decisions must be reached on whether to grant vacation pay for any part of the strike period and whether or not to continue insurance benefits.

WHAT TO DO WHEN A STRIKE OCCURS

The plant manager carries very heavy responsibilities when the plant goes on strike, and the nature of these duties will vary widely with the size of the plant, the degree of higher management involvement, and the way in which the union chooses to conduct the strike. In any strike you will be concerned, at a minimum, with the following factors.

Keep Concerned Parties Informed

As soon as you know you have a strike on your hands, advise higher management of the situation, and continue to keep them informed of developments. The next move is to put the communications plan for plant supervisory personnel into effect, so that all nonunion personnel can be instructed to assume their strike duties.

Suppliers will need to know of any cancelled deliveries or, if it has been decided to keep the plant in operation, of problems they may face in making deliveries. Customers must also be notified, but in most companies the Sales Department will handle this job.

If contact with the union representatives has been broken off, it should be resumed to establish new meeting dates for resumption of bargaining. The strikers themselves must be notified when and where to pick up the last paycheck, and should be informed of the status of their fringe benefits.

When the impact of the strike is likely to be heavy upon the local economy or the issues are of concern to the community, it may be advisable to establish contact with the news media and important public leaders. Look to the Industrial Relations Department for assistance in this area; the important point is that only one person should be authorized to speak for the company.

Protect the Plant from Possible Damage

Protection of plant and personnel is a major concern requiring immediate attention. Local police and fire authorities should be notified as soon as the strike starts. Special instructions in writing should be given to the plant guard force and to any supervisory teams working in or patrolling the plant. A responsible, accurate person should be designated on each shift to keep a written log of all incidents as they occur, including date, time, and names of people involved. This log may be very valuable to your attorney in any later legal action.

Complete Any Unfinished Operations

If the plant is to be shut down, nonunion personnel will have to complete any unfinished production operations that might result in spoiled material or damaged machines. If the plant is to run, you will be heavily occupied with putting the operations plan into effect. Arrangements may have to be made with railroads, truck lines, and utility companies for special services. In either case, the plans for housing and feeding personnel remaining in the plant will be put into action.

When It's Over

The immediate aftermath of the strike requires careful handling by plant management to minimize any bitterness or tension which may have arisen and to keep them from becoming long-lasting effects. Instruct first-line supervisors to establish a businesslike, get-back-to-work approach quickly, avoiding any tendency for groups to gather to go over recent events. The supervisors themselves should be cautioned against discussing the strike or showing their personal feelings about any of the individuals involved in it.

Chapter 13

How to Develop Effective First-Line Supervisors to Make Your Job Easier

No job in management reflects changes in the industrial scene more vividly than that of the first-line supervisor. From the earliest days when a useful qualification was to be the biggest and toughest member of the work crew, through the progressive replacement of human labor with the work of machines, and on into today's developments in automation, robotization, computerization, and other manifestations of high technology, this employee has constantly had to adapt to the changing expectations of both management and lower level employees. Corporate executives now expect the first-line supervisor to be a stronger participant in management—to understand the company's goals and how the work of his or her unit fits into them, and to be able to apply basic management principles. Today's workers want a greater say in how their work is performed, are willing to assume more responsibility for the plant's performance, and are less inclined toward blind obedience to authority.

These trends have prompted some employers to do away with the traditional foreman's job, letting workers supervise themselves (or, more accurately, their machines) aided by a floor manager with more of a support role—bringing in external help when needed (maintenance, quality control, engineering) and coordinating the flow of materials—and with less of the trappings of an authoritarian leader. But these are isolated instances, and in the majority of plants there will still be a need for the foreman-type employee who assigns work, coordinates activity, adjusts the response of the work crew to unexpected developments, and handles grievances and discipline at the first level of management.

No matter what management calls this employee, he or she is of major importance to the company, always being present at critical moments in the life of the plant—emergencies, the start-up of new processes and equipment, sudden developments in labor relations. If the first-line supervisor is not convinced of the worth and feasibility of new management plans for conducting operations and is not well trained in their implementation, they may not get very far in the plant. We have repeatedly identified in earlier chapters the compelling need to develop the first-line supervisor as a communicator, manager, and contributor to company development. This chapter deals with the job definition, recruiting, training, and motivation of this critical employee.

WHERE IT ALL STARTS: THE JOB DESCRIPTION

The logic is simple: No manager can rationally recruit for a position without a clear idea of what the prospective employee will be expected to do. The only way to develop this idea in a format that will meet all of its intended uses is for you to set down on paper exactly what you want—in other words, a written job description. Before looking at an example of a job description, let's examine its potential uses, what it should contain, and some of the pitfalls to avoid in constructing it.

Four Uses of Job Descriptions

Training. Nothing can be more helpful to an employee who is learning a job than a clear statement of the job's responsibilities and duties; when the statement is written, the employee can refer to it as often as needed.

Recruiting. The Personnel Department, an outside employment agency, or anyone assisting in the recruiting process can do a better job when they know what qualifications are needed. The prospective employee can measure her abilities against its requirements, arriving at a sounder decision on acceptance.

Performance appraisal. The first step in measuring an employee's performance is to compare it to a statement of the responsibilities of the job.

Job evaluation. A complete job description furnishes an objective basis for determining its salary and its relation on the salary scale to other jobs in the organization.

What Job Descriptions Should Contain

Objectives. The first section should contain a broad statement of the job's responsibilities and the objectives it is designed to fulfill.

Reporting relationships. State the titles of all individuals reporting to the job holder, as well as the title of the superior. Be sure to include dotted line relationships in the job description if they are shown on the organization chart.

Lateral relationships. No job description is complete unless it specifies the other organizational groups—both line and staff—with which the incumbent is expected to relate, and her cooperative responsibilities to them.

List of duties. Often the attempt is made to condense a long list of duties into a brief summarizing statement. While the objective is commendable, it is nevertheless true that a statement of all of the duties performed is necessary if the full dimensions of the job are to be revealed. The following list of categories of foreman's activities can be used to be sure all duties are included:

Production   Employee Relations

Quality   Administration:

Cost   Production Reports

Safety   Time Records

Housekeeping   Inventory Reports

Communications

What *Not* to Include

Responsibilities too generalized.

Responsibilities too narrow. Statement leaves no room for short-term growth of the job.

Personality requirements. Describe a job, not a person. By putting personality requirements ("eager, responsive, friendly") in the description you may eliminate some very capable candidates for the job or wind up with an incumbent who is frustrated because, although she gets the work done, she is penalized for not matching some personality profile.

Performance standards. Include only what is to be done, not how well it is to be done. Impossible goals such as "Must meet all production schedules" only serve to convince the supervisor that there is no way to win. It is a much better practice, as we shall see later in this chapter, to keep performance standards out of the job description and reserve them for the performance appraisal form.

Operating Example 13–1: Typical Job Description for Production Foreman. This is an example of a job description for a first-line supervisor using the principles outlined above:

SHOPCITY INDUSTRIES, INC.
POSITION DESCRIPTION

TITLE: Foreman—Production Shift   DATE: February 18, 19___

PLANT: Shopcity   DEPARTMENT: Production

I. General Objective

Supervises assigned production employees; performs administrative tasks and maintains communications associated with the activities of a production shift. Assumes responsibility for the shift's performance in safety, product quality, production output, housekeeping, and cost control; for employee relationships; and for effectiveness of communications relevant to shift performance and the attainment of plant goals.

II. Organizational Relationships

A. Reports to:	General Foreman, Production Department
B. Supervises Directly:	Hourly production employees assigned to his shift.
C. Indirectly Supervises:	None, but in emergencies assumes authority over everyone present in production area, except those directly above him in line organization.
D. Lateral Relationships:	Cooperates with other foremen and supervisors in Production, Shipping, Maintenance, Personnel, and Inspection departments whose work affects that of his shift. Cooperates with Engineering, Research, and Planning department personnel when their work is conducted in or relates to that of the Production Department.

III. Duties

Safety:	Observes plant safety rules. Instructs subordinates in safe operating procedures and plant conduct, and requires them to follow these instructions. Identifies safety hazards and takes appropriate steps to control them. Prepares equipment so that it can be safely worked on by others, and signs safety work permits. In emergencies, directs control efforts of subordinates and orders their evacuation when necessary for their protection.
Quality:	Requires subordinates to follow all provisions of operating instructions. Monitors quality of output and takes appropriate action, including shutdown of process, to prevent or limit production of off-grade material. Conducts, and assists others in conduct of, investigations to determine causes of quality defects.
Production:	Ascertains assigned production goal at start of shift. Assigns personnel and determines use of machines so as to achieve this goal. Arranges for flow of raw material and finished product. Monitors progress during shift and makes appropriate adjustments. Informs superiors when it appears that goal will not be met.
Cost:	Conducts operations so as to meet established cost standards for use of raw materials, utilities, manpower, and supplies.

	Instructs subordinates in most efficient use of machines and materials, and requires instructions to be followed. Contributes to plant cost reduction effort.
Housekeeping:	Assigns housekeeping tasks to subordinates so as to maintain production area in a neat and orderly condition. Cooperates with other shift foremen in housekeeping endeavors. Prepares production area for housekeeping inspections and serves, as assigned, on inspection teams.
Communications:	Relays appropriate information and instructions from higher management to subordinates. Passes comments and concerns of and relevant information about employees back to management. Maintains effective lateral communications with other departments whose work affects that of his shift, giving them timely notice of his requirements.
Employee Relations:	Interviews and evaluates prospective production employees. Observes and reports on morale of subordinates. Evaluates and provides ratings of their performance. Initiates disciplinary action as required. Hears and responds to first-step grievances.
Administration:	Prepares and submits shift logs, production and inventory reports, time records, and such other reports on shift activities as management requests. Prepares work orders, and work and safety permits.

WHAT TO CONSIDER WHEN RECRUITING

Key Qualifications to Look for

The plant manager has two basic questions: What are the qualifications for this job and where will I find the people to fill them? First, let's look at qualifications:

Leadership. This is the key quality, and it must be present in demonstrated or clearly potential form. You should be able to visualize the candidate you intend to promote or hire giving orders, training people, organizing work, applying plant rules or a union contract, correcting substandard performance, supervising former co-workers, and handling emergencies. If you can't find these qualities in the employee, don't put him in the job.

Experience. At least five years of industrial plant experience is indicated, and most promotees have considerably more. Don't deprive yourself of good potential candidates by requiring experience in too narrow a range; a bright candidate with good leadership qualities will pick up all but the most difficult technology very quickly.

Education. While a high school diploma is not an absolute must, especially when older people are being considered, you will want communications and mathematical skills at least equivalent to that level of education. A year or two of college would be a real plus. If your industry is highly technical in nature, you may have to require special training in the candidate's background.

Potential Candidates—Where to Look

In recruiting for the job of first-line supervisor, there is a natural tendency to promote the best production operator—after all, shouldn't the employee who has done the best job of turning out the company's product be the best one to lead others in that effort? There is no question that superior operating skill will be of great help to the new foreman, but the qualifications call for someone with good communications skills and with the ability to organize the work of others and take responsibility for their performance. If the best operator has these skills, fine; if not, it can be a costly mistake to promote that person. Now let's look at possible sources of candidates:

Within the company. Typically, a foreman is promoted from the hourly ranks of the plant work force, and for good reasons. He is familiar with the company's products, the manufacturing processes, quality requirements and problems, and the people and the rules under which they work. Training requirements will be limited to developing an understanding of the managerial process and familiarization with some administrative procedures. You will want a substantial proportion—at least 50 percent—of your foremen to have this background.

If *all* of the first-line supervisors are recruited from the hourly ranks, there is a danger that the organization will become too ingrown and unable to generate or cope with new ideas and approaches. Broaden your search within the company to include potential candidates from Quality Control, the drafting room, Accounting Department, Materials Management Department, and the pilot plant. You may be able to offer attractive opportunities to younger people in these departments, while achieving diversification of background and viewpoint in the foreman group.

Outside the company. When the supply of candidates within the company is exhausted or foremen with specialized backgrounds are needed to start new manufacturing processes or the decision has been made to broaden the field from which candidates are selected, you must look at the qualifications of candidates from outside the company. The risk is great, because you will be placing a new employee in a very sensitive position without having seen him at work. Two hints to help make the selection process successful: First, limit the candidates to those who have already attained foremanship elsewhere; it is too chancy to assume that an employee can make the vertical move to supervisory ranks at the same time she is making a lateral move to another company. Second, examine the reasons for a candidate's change of companies very closely; if they don't make sense to you, don't hire her. She may be covering up an inability to get along with those who work with her.

Transfers. Foremen have generally been regarded as creatures of their local communities, and transfers to distant plants have been uncommon. As the American population becomes more mobile, however, geography is less of an inhibiting factor to putting someone in the job best suited to her and to offering her the maximum opportunity to develop her abilities. Don't overlook transfer from a remote plant when you have a supervisory slot to fill.

College graduates. A number of companies recruit a proportion of their foremen from young college graduates coming into the company who aspire to a career in production management or engineering. The benefit is twofold: The young professionals can learn the manufacturing operation, its products, and its capacity to produce and deliver from the actual experience of helping to manage it. What they learn will be of value to them and the company in any future job they may hold. In return, they bring a fresh point of view and an analytical frame of mind to the manufacturing process, helping to keep the permanent foremen's thinking stimulated and the organization from becoming too ingrown.

Two points: You can't expect to keep these people as foremen permanently. Within two to three years you will have to move them laterally or up or you probably will lose them. And don't recruit all of your foremen from this source; you need the stabilizing effect of the long-service, nontechnical foreman. Fifty percent is a good ratio—it provides equal balance of both points of view and prevents one group from dominating the other by weight of numbers.

INTEGRATING THE FIRST-LINE SUPERVISOR INTO THE MANAGEMENT TEAM

Recognize Him as a Manager

First-line supervisors spend most of their working hours with plant employees, have probably risen from their ranks, and may still have family and social ties to them. If we are to prevent ambivalence on their part about where they belong in the organization or, worse, a feeling of isolation, management must treat them *and be perceived as treating them* as full partners in management. Here are some ways to provide this much-needed recognition:

Training. If you want first-line supervisors to perform as professional managers while keeping up with the demands of ever-changing technology, then you must provide the necessary training. This subject is so important that it is dealt with in a separate section of this chapter. Announcement of training programs should be made in such a way as to enhance the status of those enrolled in them and avoid the problem I once ran into: I had determined to send my first-line supervisors, in rotation, to a series of three-day seminars on basic management, and had selected Jim, the senior supervisor, to be the first to attend. After watching a glum face on Jim for two days, I asked one of the other supervisors if he knew what was wrong. "Of course," was the reply, "by asking Jim to be the first to take training, he thinks you feel that he is the worst supervisor of the bunch!" It took a lot of explaining, probably not completely successful, to convince Jim that I had no such idea in mind.

Compensation. Nothing the company does says more about the value it places on its foremen than the salaries it pays them. If their compensation falls below that of the surrounding area or that of the most highly paid hourly workers in the plant, their status will fall with it.

Office and desk. Supervisors should have a place to be able to answer the phone in privacy, a desk to work on and to keep important papers in, and a place to discuss individual matters with employees. If a fully walled-off office cannot be included in building plans or added to an existing structure, a good-looking partition-type office (complete with ceiling) can be inexpensively installed in the work area.

Secretarial help. Notices posted over their signature and the occasional report, letter, or memorandum which the foremen write, should be professionally typed. While a secretary is not needed, the foremen should be able to call upon this kind of help when necessary.

Foreman's Club. An organization sponsored and usually subsidized by the company exclusively for first-line supervisors can be the focus of training activities as well as a social program. Some companies provide a special building on the plant property for this purpose.

Subscriptions. Many companies buy subscriptions to bulletins and magazines published for foremen. Receiving such a publication enhances the foreman's own view of the job.

Uniforms. When the plant supplies its hourly force with work clothing, distinctive uniforms should be provided for the foremen. (Some companies have their foremen wear shirts and ties.) Most commercial laundries will supply dress shirts and attractive slacks for this purpose.

Department dinners. In smaller plants the entire Production Department and in larger plants individual departments may hold dinner meetings to discuss broad problems, review progress, or to make important announcements. The first-line supervisors should always be invited to these functions.

How to Motivate Your Foremen

By the time employees reach the level of foremen, the simple needs of food, clothing, and shelter are no longer prime motivating factors; they have advanced to a level of need for recognition, accomplishment, belonging, and self-realization. You can move to meet those needs in the following ways:

Keep score. To use a baseball analogy, your players are not likely to be motivated to give their best at the right moment in the game if they don't know what inning it is, the score, and the number of outs. The leaders of your production team in the plant should know when production quotas are met or missed, and by how much; what level of quality is being maintained; what their cost performance is compared to standards and budgets; and the frequency and severity of accidents in their departments. Be sure to make reports of all these statistics available to them.

Teach management principles. First-line supervisors can hardly be expected to be motivated to become professional managers if nobody takes the trouble to teach them what management is. Nothing that you do to make them feel a part of management will have more effect than instructing them in the fundamentals of planning, organizing, and controlling, and expecting them to apply these principles.

Involve them in plans and decision making.

- Let them make as many of the plant operating decisions as they can successfully handle
- Share corporate plans with them and bring them into management conferences at the highest appropriate level
- Let them review blueprints for engineering projects which affect their work, and consider their suggestions
- Ask them to write the operating procedure for the newly completed project or process

Every corporation has its policies, its customs, and its style of operation which may limit the degree to which you can involve the first-line supervisors in these activities. Our purpose here is not to conflict with such policies but to obtain the greatest participation by the first-line supervisors in plant management.

Reward their efforts. Of course you will think of salary increases and promotions as rewards for jobs well done and as incentives for greater achievement. But don't neglect the motivational value of sincere commendation for good work and, above all, the satisfaction of seeing ideas adopted in the plant.

Compensation Factors

Your problem in setting salary ranges for first-line supervisors breaks down into three components: What factors to consider in setting base pay, how to find out what others are paying for similar services, and hat to do about premium pay such as overtime and shift differential.

Factors affecting base pay

- Highest paid worker supervised
- Number of workers supervised
- Value of equipment and materials handled, and criticalness of operation to overall plant production
- Allowances for overtime and shift differential, if not paid separately
- Degree of supervision exercised. This can range from that of a working foreman who does little more than assigning work to fellow employees to that of a foreman exercising full administrative control over several assistants and an hourly group with a wide range of pay rates and skills

Where to get salary information

- National Surveys. The Executive Compensation Service of the American Management Association issues to its subscribers an excellent statistical survey of base and fringe compensation for supervisors and foremen, on a national basis. Another very good source of information is a study published by the

National Industrial Conference Board entitled "Compensating First-Line Supervisors in Factory and Office."

- Local surveys. Regional employers' associations, chambers of commerce, and management councils often publish local surveys that include supervisory salaries.
- Want ads. The salaries mentioned in want ads can be misleading because the full job content is not always revealed by its title. But when the same job title is advertised with salaries by a number of companies, you can get a reasonably good estimate of the range being paid.
- Other plants. Personnel departments and your counterpart manager in other plants may be willing to trade supervisory salary information with you. Expect more reluctance in revealing this kind of information than hourly rates, which are usually published in union contracts and employee handbooks anyway.
- Employment agencies. Reputable firms that place large numbers of foreman can give you very current information on salaries being paid at hiring. Beware of misunderstandings about job content in evaluating their data.

Special problems

- Overtime. This is the most difficult compensation problem, and companies have adopted a bewildering variety of schemes to handle it. Ideally, the foreman's base pay should be adjusted to compensate for the average amount of overtime worked, for two reasons: (1) It removes any personal benefit when his group works overtime; and (2) Surveys have shown that when this is the case, the amount of overtime worked by the group drops sharply.

  Other methods include calculating the foreman's hourly rate and paying him under the same rules as the workers; paying a flat rate of so many dollars per eight hours accumulated overtime; paying only for overtime scheduled in advance; and giving no pay but allowing the foreman to take equal time off at a later date.
- Shift differential. If shift differentials are paid to the hourly workers, then foremen should be paid a premium or have it included in their base pay when assigned to a night shift or placed on rotating shifts.
- Fringe benefits. Vacations, holidays, insurance plans, pensions, and sick leave are taken for granted by most industrial workers today, and you will have to offer them if you are to maintain an effective supervisory force. On the other hand, they are not likely to have much impact on the recruitment and motivation of foremen unless their provisions are exceptionally good or bad. When stock options and bonus plans are offered to management employees, make sure that first-line supervisors are included; the extent of their participation is not nearly so important as the fact that they are included in the managerial group in the eyes of the corporation.

Training

Industrial progress inevitably brings more complicated processes to the plant and higher performance standards for the managerial team. The need for training to acquire, improve, and update skills pervades the entire plant organization. Nowhere is this need more intense than at the level of the foreman, who must now be able to perform as a professional manager while supervising employees who carry out a wider variety of technically demanding tasks.

Technical training

In-house. If your corporation is large enough to have a training department capable of conducting technical courses, you have the best possible situation, because those courses can be tailored to the technology and equipment you are using. In a smaller company, you may be able to recruit very effective instructors from the engineering staff, line management, and the data processing group, who can use operating procedures and suppliers' manuals as the basis for course content.

Outside. Local colleges, technical institutes, and adult education courses at public high schools all offer training in the basic sciences, mathematics, and computers. Where there are many manufacturing plants in the area, such courses may be designed especially for first-line supervisors.

Companies that supply highly technical equipment—such as instruments, computers, and power plants—often conduct training schools in the use and maintenance of such equipment.

Managerial training

Remote. The nonprofit American Management Association as well as a growing number of private consulting firms are offering workshops, seminars, and training courses on various aspects of foremanship at regional centers throughout the United States (New York, Chicago, Dallas, Atlanta). The programs usually last from two to five days and cover such topics as the management cycle, training new workers, discipline and grievances, administering a labor contract, and motivating and evaluating hourly employees. These courses offer well-thought-out programs led by excellent instructors and give the foremen a chance to talk over common problems with peers in other companies.

Local. Employers' associations and colleges may sponsor and conduct seminars similar to those mentioned above, or they may offer regular semester courses that meet for one or two evenings a week. These programs are usually inexpensive and are often tailored to local needs.

In-house. Again, if you can call upon the services of a professional training department within your company, a very important function can be handled with very little effort on your part, yet with full assurance that the company's management philosophy is the one being taught to your foremen.

Do-it-yourself. The best system of all (though perhaps better suited to a smaller plant) is to teach the course on management techniques yourself, possibly with another senior line manager as co-chairman. While the demand on you is heavy—probably requiring two nights a week for a period of three months—the rewards are very great. The foremen will know that the material being taught is really meant to be applied in the plant because they are hearing it from the plant manager. You will develop a very deep rapport with your supervisory group, and you will learn things about your organization from the comments and discussions in the training sessions that you would never have gleaned in any other way.

GUIDELINES FOR COMMUNICATING WITH THE SUPERVISOR

Alert, interested supervisors want as much information about the company as possible: personnel changes, new product developments, corporate plans for the future, and union-management relations above their own level. You as the plant manager have rightful concerns of your own about releasing confidential information, or simply giving more information than the recipients can wisely use. Use these guidelines:

1. Some things they must know to perform their jobs, and you have no choice but to pass this information on. When information could be dangerous if lost, there are ways to make it harmless. For instance, one company uses code numbers for raw materials on its process instruction sheets; if the sheets were lost, the new owner would have no idea of what went into the product. Another company issues cost reports to the foremen, but not in terms of dollars; their copies show man-hours of labor, kilowatts of electricity, and pounds or units of supplies consumed per unit of product.

2. Some information can be revealed without harm to the corporation or anyone in it; examples are new engineering projects, high-level personnel changes, new developments in parent or subsidiary companies. Make it a habit to be the first to communicate this kind of news to your first-line supervisors.

3. Some information can be revealed only in confidence, you will have to make this clear when you disclose it. Whether you dare release such information depends upon the ability of your group to keep a secret. Test them by releasing some innocuous information as confidential and see how long it takes to get around the plant.

4. There are kinds of information which carry such great risks to the company's competitive position, or to the reputations of individuals, or which might cause needless worry to groups of employees, they simply cannot be revealed. Withholding this information is not likely to cause resentment among your foremen, especially if you have been forthright on other subjects.

Follow two cardinal rules: They must be the first to hear information that affects them personally, and it must come from the immediate superior. Second, don't equivocate. The foremen's communications problems are difficult enough, and the last thing they should have to contend with is unreliable or misleading information from you.

APPRAISING THE SUPERVISOR'S PERFORMANCE

In an earlier section we advised limiting the job description to telling *what* is to be done. Now it is time to deal with the question of *how well* it is to be done.

Performance appraisal is often thought to be an unpleasant chore. The Personnel Department annually sends the manager a printed form to complete. Since you as the manager may have had little or no input into the content of the form, you may regard the procedure as something to be gotten out of the way quickly and with as little fuss as possible. The supervisor to be rated may perceive it as a stilted process with little relationship to actual performance or to his or her future with the company. In this kind of climate very little useful communication can take place, but the situation may be corrected by developing an effective appraisal system using the following principles:

Decide what you want from the performance appraisal. It will be a combination of some or all of these factors: (a) performance improvement, (b) basis for salary increase, (c) ranking of a number of individuals performing the same job, (d) an opportunity for upward communication, (e) counseling of employees, and (f) warnings to substandard performers.

Determine the timing. Annual reviews are the most common, and the year is a long enough time period to fully evaluate a foreman's performance. Some companies adhere to a semi-annual schedule, but more frequent reviewing is not recommended. The shorter schedule is useful for recently appointed foremen or for frequent transfers and new assignments.

Establish the content. Even if you are sent a printed form to use, you can add appraisal factors to it and minimize those that do not meet your needs. When devising your own form, be sure to

Relate the categories of appraisal only to the functions in the job description you asked the supervisor to perform. The performance appraisal should not wander off into new areas he didn't know he would be rated on.

Avoid subjective or personality-oriented criteria. One rating form identifies "enthusiasm" as an appraisal factor, with "works enthusiastically" near the top of the scale, and "matter-of-fact attitude" near the bottom. I see no value and some danger in this. In my industrial experience, the "enthusiastic" man sometimes accomplishes very little, while the "matter of fact" or even dour individual gets the work done. You are after results, not happy faces or sunshine personalities.

Use as many measurable criteria as possible. The foreman will understand more clearly and you will have a more objective basis for rating when you include performance statistics on production quantity, quality percentages, frequency and severity figures on safety, and cost information.

Developing numerical standards for rating performance may seem to be an awkward and uncomfortable process, with the manager saying, "I can measure things like production output—we have plenty of records and statistics for that—but how do I put a numerical value on something like cooperation? Furthermore, if I reduce everything to numbers, won't I wind up spending all my time just keeping score?" Good questions; but there are good answers, as the following Operating Example shows. In it, three very different elements of the job description have been selected to illustrate how numerical standards can be developed for them.

Operating Example 13–2: Developing Measurable Criteria for Performance Appraisal. The Shopcity Industries plant manager who drew up the job description of Operating Example 13–1 must now develop performance appraisal standards. The Personnel Department is requiring, in the interests of uniformity, that four categories of performance be used—*Outstanding, Excellent, Good,* and *Unsatisfactory.* Looking through the job description, the manager realizes standards must be set not only for all the duties listed, but also for the Lateral Relationships section in which the foremen are told that they are expected to cooperate with others in the plant whose work affects theirs or vice versa. Here is how this manager developed measurable, numerical standards for three of the performance categories:

Performance Category 1: Cooperation

Outstanding: No incidents of failure to cooperate with other supervisors/departments and at least two instances observed by superiors or reported by other supervisors/departments of teamwork beyond the normal requirement.

Excellent: No incidents of failure to cooperate with other supervisors/departments.

Good: No more than two incidents of failure to cooperate with other supervisors/departments.

Unsatisfactory: Three or more incidents of failure to cooperate with other supervisors/departments.

Performance Category 2: Safety

Outstanding: Lost-time Accident Frequency:* 0
                         Lost-time Accident Severity:*   0
                         At least two significant contributions to the elimination of safety hazards with a lost-time accident potential. No incidents of observed breaches of safety regulations by members of shift.

Excellent: Lost-time Accident Frequency: 33 or lower
                     Lost-time Accident Severity: 217 or lower
                     At least one significant contribution to the elimination of a safety hazard with lost-time accident potential. No more than two incidents of observed breaches of safety regulations by members of shift.

Good: Lost-time Accident Frequency: 65 or lower
               Lost-time Accident Severity: 434 or lower

---

*Lost-time Accident Frequency and Severity are defined in Chapter 14.

No more than four incidents of observed breaches of safety regulations by members of shift.

Unsatisfactory: Lost-time Accident Frequency: 66 or higher
                  Lost-time Accident Severity: 435 or higher
                  Five or more observed breaches of safety regulations by members of
shift.

Performance Category 4: Production

Outstanding: Meets shift production targets at least 97 percent of the time when in control. At least one contribution to production methods which increases capacity by 1 percent or more. No observed lapses in arranging for material flow, monitoring progress, or informing superiors of likelihood that production goal would not be met.

Excellent: Meets shift production targets at least 95% of the time when in control. No more than two observed lapses in arranging for material flow, monitoring progress, or informing superiors of likelihood that production goal would not be met.

Good: Meets shift production targets at least 90 percent of the time when in control. No more than four observed lapses in arranging for material flow, monitoring progress, or informing superiors of likelihood that production goal would not be met.

Unsatisfactory: Meets shift production targets less than 90 percent of the time when in control. Five or more observed lapses in arranging for material flow, monitoring progress, or informing superiors of likelihood that production goal would not be met.

This manager had ready-made numerical criteria whenever plant record-keeping supplied him with reliable figures, as was the case for production performance. Note the inclusion of the phrase *when in control,* which avoids penalizing the supervisor unfairly when production goals are missed for reasons beyond his or her control.

Faced with the more intangible category of cooperation, this manager said, "If the supervisor is cooperative, then I should see very few examples of lack of cooperation in the course of a year." That put him in a position to use measurable standards involving only small numbers, and he decided that three such incidents would result in a rating of *Unsatisfactory,* with two and zero incidents appropriate for *Good* and *Excellent* ratings. When it came to the *Outstanding* rating, he not only demanded no failures but also wanted a positive contribution in the form of at least two instances of cooperation that went beyond normal expectations. He also applied this concept of positive contributions in the higher ratings of the safety and production categories.

How does the manager keep track of these incidents? By establishing a "drop file" for each supervisor. Whenever a positive contribution is observed or a good or bad performance noticed within the meaning of the performance appraisal, make a note and place it in the file. At the end of the year, an objective record is ready for the performance review.

Discuss the performance criteria with the supervisor at the start of the rating period. The system works best when both parties agree to the criteria, and an effort should be made to reach agreement. But at the very least, be sure the employee understands the criteria he is to be rated on before the period begins.

How to Conduct the Appraisal Interview

Notify the employee in advance of the interview and give him a blank rating form to fill out. During the interview compare his estimate of his performance with yours; where there is agreement, a sound basis for improvement exists. Where there is disagreement, you have a start on some badly needed communication.

Be sure that both parties understand that the review covers performance in the current time period only. His job is tough enough without having old sins held against him; on the other hand, he must realize that old achievements won't carry him forever.

Do not announce a salary adjustment during the interview. You want the employee's full attention on his performance; you won't get it if he is expecting you to announce a raise. Give the employee a chance to tell you how he sees the factors affecting his performance. There may be conditions beyond his control of which you are not aware.

Finally, act on your reviews. Promotions, raises, transfers, bonuses—these and other rewards should be given on the basis of performance. When this is not done, foremen will soon lose interest in the appraisal procedure, and it becomes a meaningless exercise.

Chapter 14

How to Run Effective Safety and Housekeeping Programs

In Chapter 2 we discussed how safety and housekeeping were key performance elements of the plant manager's job. These managers and their superiors recognized the impact of these responsibilities on each other and on the remaining plant functions of quality, cost, production, and employee relationships. And if these factors were not sufficient motivators, we have now entered into an era when employees, the public, and the courts hold management responsible for the long-term effects of worker exposure to toxic substances.

Stringent federal laws now affect the way plant managers conduct their operations, and the specifics of these laws will be dealt with in Chapter 15. This chapter is dedicated to the principle that it is good economic sense to run effective safety and housekeeping programs regardless of any legal requirements. In the first section we will consider all aspects of safety at the plant manager's level, including responsibility, impact on costs, the plant safety program, safety procedures, accident statistics, fire prevention, and sources of safety information. The second section deals with the reasons for and the techniques of carrying out an effective housekeeping program.

RESPONSIBILITY FOR SAFETY AND THE COST OF ACCIDENTS

Where Safety Responsibility Lies

There is no escaping the basic principle: Safety is a *line* responsibility. Staff people can offer assistance in a variety of important ways, but accident and property loss prevention is the job of the foremen, superintendents, managers, and their superiors in the manufacturing line organization. Any safety program based on delegation or dilution of this responsibility is doomed to failure.

Foremen especially must understand that they are responsible for all aspects of safety performance in their departments—observance of safety rules, training of new employees, and accident prevention. Above all, they must not be allowed to develop the notion that safety performance is the concern of the Personnel Department, the Safety Department, or "someone else" in the corporate organization.

What Accidents Cost

The humanitarian aspects of a good safety program are obvious, and any responsible manager and corporation would find them sufficient justification for the program. But neither can afford to lose sight of the impact of accidents on one of their most important performance criteria: costs.

The National Safety Council estimates that in 1985 the average cost of a disabling industrial injury—one sufficient to render the employee unable to work for at least one full day subsequent to the day of the accident—was $12,200. This figure includes workmen's compensation payments, medical costs, lost wages, administrative costs, and indirect costs. Most of these costs, with the exception of lost wages, are paid by the company; even workmen's compensation payments, which are covered by insurance, are often charged back to the company virtually dollar for dollar. For a fatality, the average cost rises to $460,000. If left to rise unchecked, costs of this magnitude would rapidly change the color of the ink in any company's bottom line; they provide all the incentive needed for managers to run an effective safety program. Here are some of the indirect, or hidden, costs which add to the dollar toll of a plant accident:

- Time lost by other workers—to help injured, discuss accident, and so on
- Downtime; lost production; off-grade production
- Cost of overtime to replace injured worker or train a new employee
- Legal costs if lawsuits follow
- Time spent by supervisors and managers on investigations and reports
- Damage to machines and equipment—repair costs and replacement rental
- Special costs to meet shipping commitments—phone calls, telegrams, air freight, other special arrangements

FOUR ELEMENTS OF THE SAFETY PROGRAM AND HOW TO PUT THEM INTO ACTION

If you take the old catch phrase for a safety program—*engineering, education, enforcement*—and add *establishment of rules*, we have the four basic components of a safety program for the plant. Here's how to put them into effect:

Provide safe buildings and equipment. When new equipment is designed or proposed for purchase, or when new buildings are to be constructed, potential safety problems should be considered at the earliest stages of design. Safety features are of two kinds: those designed to *prevent* accidents—such as machinery guards, nonslip walking surfaces, electrical grounding, automatic cutoff devices, spark suppression, pressure relief, and so on—and those designed to *minimize injury and damage* after an accident occurs—such as fire extinguishers, sprinklers, hose houses, safety showers, eye baths, fire doors, first aid equipment, emergency lights, alternate exits, fire alarm systems, and so on.

Formulate rules for safe practices. Publish the rules in writing and cover these points:

Personal protective equipment. Specify equipment to be worn all the time in work areas, such as safety shoes, hard hats, and safety glasses. Then specify equipment to be worn for special operations—welding masks, goggles, face shields, acid suits, rubber gloves, rescue harness.

Plant conduct. Forbid running, sudden loud noises, horseplay. Require attendance at safety meetings, cooperation with fire drills, and training exercises. Insist that hazards and unsafe conditions be reported.

Performance of work. Spell out the safety precautions to be followed in the operation of machinery and the transportation of materials through the plant.

Handling of hazardous materials. Identify raw materials and in-process work which pose special hazards to personnel, tell what the hazards are, and the safe methods of avoiding them.

What to do in case of accident or emergency. Instruct personnel to report all accidents to foremen. If fire, power failure, flood, or other emergency occurs, employees should be well rehearsed in the procedures you want followed—whether to leave equipment running or shut it down, whether to fight fire or evacuate immediately (see Chapter 4, pages 64-65).

Train personnel. When safe equipment has been provided and plant rules established, the never-ending job of safety training begins. It starts with the first-line supervisors, who should carefully instruct all new employees in safe work procedures. They should also be required to hold regular, short safety meetings with their groups, accenting topics relevant to their work assignment. Safety meetings for larger groups should be conducted by the plant personnel manager, safety engineer, or line superintendents and managers. These meetings can cover more general topics and can be livened by the use of motion pictures and guest speakers. Regular drills to practice evacuation, firefighting, and rescue techniques should be held. The program can be rounded out by the use of safety contests, posters, and awards as means of keeping employees' attention focused on the subject.

Enforce regulations. The quickest way for you to measure the degree of compliance with safety rules is to walk through the plant and make your own visual observations. If you discover violations, bring them to the attention of the foreman of that area for correction; never attempt to correct the erring employee yourself unless immediate injury or property damage is threatened. Accident investigations are another source of information on the degree of compliance. It is important to keep in mind that if an individual accident report is used primarily as an enforcement tool, it can lose its effectiveness. However, if a large number of accident reports reveal repeated employee failure to follow rules, you must step up education and enforcement programs. Another useful enforcement tool is the periodic safety inspection conducted by a plant committee which files a formal written report. Inspections can be made competitive among the departments as a way of stimulating interest.

WRITTEN SAFETY PROCEDURES: WHAT TO INCLUDE

Provide each operating department with its own set of safety procedures. They can be written by department superintendents (or even foremen with an aptitude for it) but should be reviewed and approved by you. Publish them in typewritten form, with the pages inserted into acetate envelopes and bound in sturdy covers. Distribute them throughout the operating areas of the plant for easy access to all operating employees.

Contents should include the general plant rules and then go on to cover the special safety hazards of the individual department—dangerous materials; precautions in the use of tools and equipment; safe handling of heat, electrical, or radioactive energy; use of vehicles; and instructions for emergencies. The procedures should not fail to set forth the safety requirements for work performed in the department by outside agencies, such as the Maintenance Department or contractors.

Figure 14-1 is an example of how the safety conditions surrounding outside work can be controlled. It is issued by the foreman of the department where the work is to be done after the necessary precautions have been taken. It authorizes the mechanic to begin work at a certain time and limits the period in which she may work. Since the foreman's authority does not extend beyond his shift, the authorization automatically terminates at the end of the shift, and the oncoming foreman countersigns or reissues it for an additional time period. The safe work permit can be made up in pads of printed forms; some plants find it handy to have it printed on the back of the Maintenance Job Order (Figure 5-2, page 79).

The issuance of separate safety procedures is not the end of the plant's effort to specify safe work practices. Every shop order and operating procedure should contain a brief statement of the safety hazards which will be encountered in the work it describes and the precautions taken to offset them. Required safety steps should be matter of factly included in the detailed instructions for performing the operation.

SAFE WORK PERMIT

Date _____

_____ is authorized to
(name of person performing work)

_____ on _____
(work to be performed)   (equipment to be worked on)
                                                                P.M.
in Department _____, Section (floor or building) _____, between _____ A.M. and
   A.M.
_____ P.M. The equipment to be worked on has been prepared (circle one or more: shut down, drained, cleaned, depressurized, disconnected, locked out, fuses removed, other _____) for maintenance work. The following safety precautions are to be observed by persons performing this work:

☐ Tank entry permit required.
☐ Fire permit required.
☐ Other _____.
☐ Other _____.   Signed _____

FIGURE 14-1: Safe Work Permit

HOW TO INVESTIGATE ACCIDENTS

Zero accidents is the goal of the plant safety program; therefore, when an accident occurs it represents a failure of the program in some aspect to some degree. The only way in which these failures can be studied and remedied is through a thorough accident investigation. Use these guidelines:

1. It is essential that the investigation be *reported in writing*. Your insurance company will provide printed forms—or you can design your own. Figure 14-2 is an example of a supervisor's accident report form.

2. *Include* the names of the injured and any witnesses; the date, time, and place of the accident; degree of injury sustained; a narrative report of exactly how the accident happened; and what machinery, tools, equipment, or vehicles were involved.

3. The investigation report should be filled out *immediately following* the accident by the foreman of the area in which it took place.

4. The investigation is *not a witch hunt*. Its objective is not to fix blame but to find preventable causes.

SUPERVISOR'S ACCIDENT REPORT

☐ Injury   ☐ Near-Miss   Date of report _____

Accident location _____ Date _____ Time _____ A.M.
                                                                  P.M.

Describe how accident took place, including personnel, machinery, tools, equipment,

and vehicles involved _____

_____

_____

Name of injured _____ Dept. _____ Badge/Clock No. _____

Describe injuries _____

_____

☐ First Aid   ☐ Treated by doctor   ☐ Taken to _____ hospital

Lost time _____ days (☐ estimated   ☐ actual). Was injured wearing or

using required safety equipment? Explain _____

_____

What action can be taken to prevent this accident from happening again? _____

_____

_____

Action ☐ has been completed   ☐ will be completed by _____ (date).

Supervisor's signature _____

FIGURE 14-2: Supervisor's Accident Report Form

5. The report form should ask for a statement by the foreman as to why the accident happened and *how it could be prevented* in the future.

6. *Include near misses,* especially where the injury could have been serious or fatal.

7. File reports in a central place where they can be *tabulated and studied.* Use them as a basis for devising safety rules and for deciding where to put emphasis in safety training.

SAFETY STATISTICS: TWO KEY METHODS

A system of scoring safety performance is needed so that managers can observe trends, compare plants, and measure the results of steps taken to reduce accidents. Actually, there are two methods currently in use in the United States, but both have the same objective—to provide measurements of *how often* accidents occur and *how serious* they are in terms of lost time.

1. OSHA Incidence Rates

Virtually all manufacturing plants in the United States come under the Occupational Safety and Health Act of 1970, and most now use the OSHA methods of reporting occupational injury and illness. As a measure of how often they occur, OSHA employs a statistic called "incidence rate" which, for any given time period, is defined by the formula

$$\text{Incidence Rate} = \frac{(\text{Number of injuries} + \text{illnesses}) \times 200{,}000}{\text{Total hours worked by all employees}}$$

When "total recordable cases" are being reported, the number within the parentheses is the sum of fatality cases; cases that result in lost workdays; and cases without lost workdays but which require termination of employment or transfer to another job, or those which involve loss of consciousness or restriction of work or motion, or those which require medical treatment by a physician or registered personnel working under the standing orders of a physician. Not included are first aid cases (minor scratches, cuts, burns, and splinters which do not ordinarily require medical care) even though treatment is provided by professional medical personnel. By substituting the appropriate numbers in the parenthesis the incidence rate for lost workday cases only, or for nonfatal cases without lost workdays, can be calculated.

To measure the seriousness of accidents and illnesses that occur, the number of cases in the formula is replaced by the number of workdays lost:

$$\text{Incidence Rate for Lost Workdays} = \frac{\text{Total lost workdays} \times 200{,}000}{\text{Total hours worked by all employees}}$$

2. Frequency-Severity Method

This is an older system which was in wide use before 1970 and is still used by some companies. It comprises two statistics defined in American Standards Code Z16.1, Method of Recording and Measuring Work Injury Experience. In this system the measure of how often accidents and occupational illnesses occur is defined by the formula:

$$\text{Frequency} = \frac{(\text{Number of disabling injuries} + \text{illnesses}) \times 1{,}000{,}000}{\text{Total employee-hours worked}}$$

Disabling injury is an injury causing death, permanent disability, or any degree of temporary total disability beyond the day of the accident.* Temporary total disability occurs when there is at least one day not including the day of the accident when the injured employee cannot perform his job effectively throughout a full shift.

The measure of seriousness of the accidents/illnesses that occur is given by the formula:

$$\text{Severity} = \frac{\text{Total lost workdays} \times 1{,}000{,}000}{\text{Total hours worked by all employees}}$$

These statistics are usually calculated on both a monthly and an annual basis. A detailed explanation of the rules used in defining disabling injuries and employee-hours can be found in an excellent presentation in *Accident Prevention Manual for Industrial Operations, Administration and Programs Volume* (8th ed., Chicago: National Safety Council, 1981) pp. 187–188.

3. Comparison of the Two Methods

An obvious difference between the two methods is the use of different constant factors in the numerators of the two formulas. If it is assumed that the average employee works 2,000 hours per year (50 weeks × 40 hours per week), then the OSHA system is basing its incidence rate on 100 employees, since 200,000 divided by 2,000 = 100. Another way of saying this is that an OSHA incidence rate of 3.8 for total lost time cases means that there were 3.8 cases during the period for every 100 employees. The frequency-severity method uses 1,000,000 in its numerator, however, and if we divide that by 2,000 we find that the rate is based on 500 employees. The OSHA incidence rate of 3.8 for total lost workday cases becomes 3.8 × 5 = 19.0 when expressed as a frequency rate for disabling injuries. This means that there were 19 cases for every 500 employees.

The OSHA formula is somewhat more flexible because incidence rates can be calculated for lost-time cases only, for those requiring medical treatment but involving no lost time, or for both. The U.S. Bureau of Labor Statistics usually reports all three in its compilations. The frequency-severity calculations, on the other hand, are limited by definition to lost-time cases, as can be seen in Operating Example 14–1.

Operating Example 14–1: How to Calculate Safety Statistics. In one calendar year a manufacturing plant's record of accidents/occupational illnesses showed the following:

14 work injuries which resulted in 38 lost workdays

3 skin rash cases which required treatment by a dermatologist but no lost workdays

---

*As defined by National Safety Council in *Accident Facts,* 1983 Edition.

52 cases treated at first aid room for minor cuts, burns, splinters, and so on

The plant had 190 employees who worked a total of 409,638 hours.

1. Calculation of OSHA Incidence Rates

$$\text{Total Recordable Cases} = \frac{(14 + 3) \times 200,000}{409,638} = 8.3$$

$$\text{Lost Workday Cases} = \frac{14 \times 200,000}{409,638} = 6.8$$

$$\text{Nonfatal Cases Without Lost Workdays} = \frac{3 \times 200,000}{409,638} = 1.5$$

$$\text{Lost Workdays} = \frac{38 \times 200,000}{409,638} = 18.6$$

2. Calculation of Frequency and Severity

$$\text{Frequency} = \frac{14 \times 1,000,000}{409,638} = 34.2$$

$$\text{Severity} = \frac{38 \times 1,000,000}{409,638} = 92.8$$

WHERE TO GET SAFETY INFORMATION

Industrial safety is a highly developed technology. Much of the work involved in making a manufacturing process safe requires the application of specialized information. You as the plant manager and those whom you designate to assist you in the development of the safety program can turn to these sources for information:

The National Safety Council. A nonprofit, nongovernmental organization chartered by Congress and dedicated to the prevention of accidental injury by the gathering and dissemination of safety information. It publishes six safety periodicals, *Accident Facts,* an annual compilation of accident statistics, and several accident prevention manuals. It conducts safety training courses at its Chicago headquarters and on-site at industrial locations, and sponsors the annual National Safety Congress. It welcomes corporations and individuals as members.

Trade associations. These industrial groups, formed to promote the general interests of their respective industries and member companies, often supply very good safety information. An outstanding example is the Chemical Manufacturer's Association, Washington, D.C., which publishes an extensive series of *Chemical Safety Data Sheets* covering the properties, hazards, and safe-handling methods for specific chemicals. There is almost sure to be a trade association that is offering safety information relevant to one or more of your plant's operations, as indicated by this very small sample: Steel Plate Fabricator's Association, Downer's Grove, Illinois; American Welding Society, Miami, Florida; Milk Industry Foundation, Washington, D.C.; Adhesives Manufacturer's Association, Chicago, Illinois; and Portland Cement Association, Skokie, Illinois.

Government agencies. Several departments of the federal government issue publications on safety topics. The Superintendent of Documents, U.S. Government Printing Office, Washington, D.C. 20402 offers Subject Bibliographies at no charge; they are lists of the various publications available. To obtain the bibliographies on industrial safety, write for SB-229, Accidents and Accident Prevention, and SB-213, Occupational Safety and Health. For a complete list of the bibliographies, ask for SB-888 and Price List 36. (Chapter 15 deals with the Occupational Safety and Health Act and the Environmental Protection Act in much greater detail.)

State agencies also issue and enforce industrial safety codes and health regulations. In some states the storage and transportation of flammable liquids is regulated by the state police. You should be familiar with all these codes and regulations, since they represent the minimum legal standards for conditions in your plant.

Insurance groups and special organizations. If your workmen's compensation insurance carrier is a large company, it probably provides a wide range of inspection, advisory, and educational services. It may also offer help through the Alliance of American Insurers, Schaumburg, Illinois, which offers a variety of safety manuals on specific topics. Your fire insurance carrier probably provides inspection and fire protection assistance through the Factory Insurance Association (FIA) in Hartford, Connecticut, or the Factory Mutual System, Norwood, Massachusetts. The American Insurance Association, New York; Underwriter's Laboratories, Northbrook, Illinois; and the National Fire Protection Association, Quincy, Massachusetts, all conduct research and issue publications on a wide variety of fire protection topics.

THREE FIRE PREVENTION MEASURES TO INITIATE

Three ingredients are required to start a fire:

- an accumulation of combustible material in solid, liquid, or gaseous form
- oxygen
- a source of ignition, usually a flame or spark caused by friction, static electricity, or electrical arcing

Since all three must be present at the same time for a fire to start, industrial fire prevention consists of preventing that from happening. Your best chance for success is achieved by attacking all three elements at once, using these techniques:

How to Prevent Accumulation of Solid Combustibles

Avoid accumulations of **solid combustible materials:** (1) by employing a minimum of wood, cloth, and flammable plastic in the design and construction of industrial buildings; and (2) by housekeeping practices that prevent the accumulation of combustible trash inside (or in dangerous proximity outside) plant buildings. Forestall spills of **flammable liquids** by rigidly controlled methods of transfer from vessel to vessel and by careful maintenance of tanks, fittings, and pipelines. Eliminate flammable vapor accumulations by adequate ventilation of confined spaces and by proper venting of storage tanks.

How to Eliminate Excess Oxygen

Eliminating oxygen is much more difficult because it is present in air at a concentration of 21 percent by volume. It can be swept from the vapor space above flammable liquids in tanks by introducing gaseous nitrogen or carbon dioxide (neither of which supports combustion), or it can be displaced from empty vessels by filling them with water or steam.

Tips on Offsetting Ignition Sources

A variety of methods are used to eliminate **sources of ignition.** Smoking or the carrying of matches and lighters is forbidden in work areas. Electric motors are of the totally enclosed type; electric and gasoline driven lift trucks are purchased with spark suppression systems. Electrical ground straps are used to dissipate a possible static potential difference between metal containers when flammable liquids are poured from one to the other. Tanks and vessels used for the storage and processing of flammables are electrically grounded to a copper plate buried in the ground. Static collector combs are installed to draw off static potential created by moving belts. Process operations which require the use of flame or which repeatedly produce sparks are carried out in isolated buildings or behind fire walls.

A significant danger of ignition arises from sparks inadvertently produced by routine maintenance and welding operations in the plant. Figures 14-3 and 14-4 illustrate the way in which this danger is controlled. Figure 14-3 is a Class B Fire Permit, which must be filled out by the production foreman of the department before any work involving the use of spark-producing tools—such as hammer and chisel, star drill, hack saw, and so on—is allowed to begin. The Class A permit shown in Figure 14-4 is used for welding and open-flame operations, and should require the signature of a department superintendent or the plant manager. In both cases the conditions under which the work is carried out are carefully controlled. The forms can be printed up in pads; fire insurance organizations may provide standardized versions at no charge. (Smaller plants may find it convenient to combine the two forms into one.)

CLASS B FIRE PERMIT
(For spark-producing tools only. Not good for
welding or open-flame work.)

Date _____

_____ (is) (are) authorized to use the spark-producing
        (Name of worker(s))
tools or equipment checked:

☐ Steel hand tool. Specify _____.   ☐ Electric tool. Specify _____.

☐ Air-driven tool. Specify _____.   ☐ Electric appliance or extension cord.

☐ Other _____.   Specify _____.

in Building _____ at _____ between _____ A.M./P.M.
                    (specific location and equipment)

and _____ A.M./P.M. These precautions must be observed.

☐ One person must be assigned as fire watch. Name _____.

☐ Flammable vapor concentration test required. Meter reading. _____.

☐ Other _____.

☐ Notify these persons before starting work: _____ , _____

        _____ , and _____.

☐ Keep tool contact area wet with water.

☐ Stop work at request of any employee.

Signed _____
                    (Foreman)

FIGURE 14-3: Class B Fire Permit

HOW TO IMPLEMENT AN AGGRESSIVE HOUSEKEEPING PROGRAM

Why Keep the Plant Clean?

The rationale for an aggressive housekeeping program is not always apparent to
plant managers and their subordinates in operations management. The pressures
of fulfilling production schedules and meeting shipment deadlines often seem to
overwhelm the available manpower, leaving no time for "cleanup." The absence
of any reference to housekeeping practices in the standard operating procedures

CLASS A FIRE PERMIT
(Required for open-flame work and welding.
Must be signed by Department Supervisor or Plant Manager.)

Date _____.

_____ (is) (are) authorized to use the open-flame and welding
(Name of worker(s))
devices checked below:

☐ Cutting torch   ☐ Blow torch

☐ Gas welder   ☐ Electric welder

☐ Lead or tar furnace   ☐ Burn debris

in Building _____ at _____ between
(specific location and equipment)
_____ A.M./P.M. and _____ A.M./P.M. These precautions must be observed:

☐ Foreman must sign before work is started _____.

☐ Stop work at request of any employee.

☐ Notify these persons before starting work: _____, _____, and

_____.

☐ Flammable vapor concentration test required. Meter reading: _____.

☐ Remove combustible materials within 35-ft. radius of work.

Lay out:
☐ Fire hose, fully pressured.

☐ Fire extinguisher, Type _____.

☐ Names of those assigned as fire watch: _____, _____, and

_____.

(Must patrol floor above and below half hour after completion of welding.)

☐ Other _____.

Signed _____.
(Department Supervisor or Plant Manager)

FIGURE 14-4: Class A Fire Permit

and shop instructions implies to plant personnel that housekeeping can wait until some spare time is available, and, since that spare time never seems to appear, the job is indefinitely postponed. These are the compelling reasons for establishing and continuing a thoroughgoing housekeeping program:

Quality control. Not every industrial process requires a "clean room" with filtered air and controlled humidity, but it is increasingly true that products which must be made under standard conditions, and the instruments and tools used in their manufacture, will not tolerate exposure to dirt and dust.

Employee morale. Employee attitudes toward their work and toward their company are significantly affected by the cleanliness of the place in which they work.

Higher management impressions. As discussed in Chapter 2, corporate officers and directors often are not experts in the process the plant is using but get their impressions (and the basis for investment decisions) from its general appearance.

External relations. Customers who have occasion to visit the plant will be favorably impressed by a high state of cleanliness and order; conversely, they will become alarmed about the integrity of your product and service if the plant is dirty and unkempt. Community relationships are also enhanced by a clean plant, and it assists the recruiting effort if your plant is known as "a good clean place to work."

Tie-in with Safety

A warehouse employee (actual case), while walking in the concrete aisle of a storage area looking for some material stored in an upper rack, stepped on a piece of wood which had broken off a shipping pallet. A heavy man, he twisted his ankle so badly he was out of work for three weeks.

Variations of this accident are needlessly repeated thousands of times each year in American industry. People may fall and injure themselves over solid pieces of debris left lying about a plant. They may slip and injure themselves on liquid spills that are not immediately cleaned up.

The threat to personnel posed by careless housekeeping readily extends to fire prevention. Accumulations of combustible trash (even small ones) provide a fuel bed for sparks which would otherwise expire on a bare surface. Lubricating oils and grease spilled on or exuding from machinery will feed a fire; if the wiping rags used to clean them are not disposed of promptly, they can start a fire by spontaneous combustion. Dried films resulting from spills of plastic emulsions or solutions, while not easily ignited, will burn fiercely once started.

Key Methods for Getting the Program Started

Use these methods to achieve and maintain a clean plant:

Establish housekeeping standards for each department and section—in writing. Your organization will never satisfy your demands for cleanliness if they don't know how clean you want the plant to be.

Train foremen and workers. Start with the employment interview. Continue with early indoctrination. Use housekeeping as a safety meeting topic. Incorporate housekeeping steps in the detailed operating procedures.

Conduct regular inspections. The most important inspection is your own. Inspections should be done frequently, and your impressions—good or bad—made known to the supervisors of the departments you visit. Set up a formal committee (rotate assignments) of foremen, supervisors, and superintendents to conduct monthly inspections and report their findings in writing to you. Hourly employees, when appropriate, can be included on this committee. Invite higher management to inspect the plant periodically to demonstrate their interest.

Use competition. The inspection report can be used to rate the departments competitively, and the winners awarded prizes and publicity in the house organ.

Management must do its part. If your employees get the impression that housekeeping is simply a form of drudgery for them, without any contribution from management, the program will fail. You must provide routine painting of buildings and work areas; effective trash removal services; tools and machines for housekeeping; prompt repair of oil, steam, and process leaks; and consideration for housekeeping problems in the engineering design of new buildings and equipment.

Safety and housekeeping are essential contributors to the plant's overall performance; without excellence in these areas the plant organization cannot fully succeed in meeting its goals for production, quality, cost, and employee relationships. Both safety and housekeeping require support from higher management, steady attention from the plant manager, and incorporation in the plant's operating procedures.

Chapter 15

Simplifying OSHA and EPA Compliance

Enactment by Congress of the National Environmental Policy Act of 1969 and the Williams–Steiger Occupational Safety and Health Act of 1970 permanently changed the legal setting in which industrial operations are conducted. Until that time a variety of state, local, and even some federal laws applied to pollution control, worker safety, and the health conditions of plant operations. Some of these laws were specific in content, others vague; some were rigorously enforced, others laxly; most reflected local concerns and conditions. Today a series of comprehensive federal laws have been and continue to be initiated, all geared to covering plant operations.

In this chapter we will examine some of these important laws and point out the basic steps the plant manager must take to keep his operation in compliance with them.

OCCUPATIONAL SAFETY AND HEALTH

Key Provisions Stipulated by Law

Before dealing with the actions to be taken to comply, let's look at the key provisions. The Occupational Safety and Health Act of 1970 does the following:

- States its purpose "To assure safe and healthful working conditions for working men and women; by authorizing enforcement of the standards developed under the Act; by assisting and encouraging the States in their efforts to assure safe and healthful working conditions; by providing for research, information, education, and training in the field of occupational safety and health; and for other purposes."

- Imposes certain duties upon employers and employees.
- Empowers the Secretary of Labor to set safety and health standards.
- Authorizes the Secretary (through his designees) to inspect and investigate safety and health conditions at the employers' premises and to require them to maintain appropriate accident and illness records.
- Establishes procedures for enforcement and penalties for noncompliance.
- Establishes the Occupational Safety and Health Review Commission and the mechanism for employers to contest citations and penalties, and for employees to contest the time allowed to correct a violation.
- Sets conditions under which individual states may assume responsibility for development and enforcement of occupational safety and health standards.
- Establishes the National Institute for Occupational Safety and Health (NIOSH) and provides for research and training activities.

The law applies to virtually every commercial and industrial establishment in the United States because it defines an employer as "a person engaged in a business affecting commerce who has employees." No minimum number of employees is required and the employer does not have to be operating in interstate commerce—only in a business which affects it. Exempted are federal, state, and local government employees, and those in industries over which other federal (and certain state) agencies exercise statutory authority to enforce regulations affecting occupational safety or health.

Employers' Responsibilities

These are quite simply stated in the Act as follows:

Sec. 5. (a) Each employer
(1) shall furnish to each of his employees employment and a place of employment which are free from recognized hazards that are causing or likely to cause death or serious physical harm to his employees;
(2) shall comply with the occupational safety and health standards promulgated under this Act.

The operating details of meeting these responsibilities are described in the next section.

HOW OSHA ENFORCES THE LAW

The law is administered by the Occupational Safety and Health Administration (OSHA) which is a part of the U.S. Department of Labor. OSHA has put in force regulations that require you to do the following:

Bring plant facilities and procedures into compliance with OSHA standards As of July 1985, OSHA had established standards for the following:

Walking-Working Surfaces

Occupational Health and Environmental Control

Personal Protective Equipment

Fire Protection

Machinery and Machine Guarding

Special Industries (paper, textiles, bakery, laundry, sawmills, logging, telecommunications, and agriculture)

Means of Egress

Hazardous Materials

General Environmental Controls

Compressed Gas and Compressed Air Equipment

Hand and Portable Powered Tools and Other Hand-Held Equipment

Commercial Diving Operations

Powered Platforms, Manlifts, and Vehicle-Mounted Work Platforms

Medical and First Aid

Materials Handling and Storage

Welding, Cutting, and Brazing

Electrical

Toxic and Hazardous Substances

These standards are revised from time to time, and new ones added. You must know the standards in order to adapt buildings, equipment, and operating procedures to meet them. They can be quite lengthy—the standard for Walking-Working Surfaces is 38 pages long. Furthermore, if your operations are in shipbuilding, longshoring, construction, or agriculture, standards other than those cited above may apply. To sort all this out, you need one or more of the following publications:

1. Appropriate volumes of the Code of Federal Regulations, available from the Superintendent of Documents, U.S. Government Printing Office, Washington, D.C. 20402. They are revised yearly, and you will want the current edition of these three volumes:

29 CFR Parts 1900 to 1910

29 CFR Parts 1911 to 1919

29 CFR Parts 1920 to end

Prices change from year to year; inquire of the Superintendent of Documents.

2. The Occupational Safety and Health Subscription Service. OSHA itself publishes a continuing subscription service which consists of a looseleaf set of standards, interpretations, regulations, and procedures which are continually updated. The volume titles and the 1984 subscription price for each are as follows:

Volume I	General Industry Standards and Interpretations	$66.00
Volume II	Maritime Standards and Interpretations	41.00
Volume III	Construction Standards and Interpretations	29.00

Volume IV	Other Regulations and Procedures	95.00
Volume V	Field Operations Manual	28.00
Volume VI	Industrial Hygiene Field Operations Manual	27.00

Most plant managers should subscribe to all but volumes II and III; order from the Superintendent of Documents, U.S. Government Printing Office, Washington, D.C. 20402.

3. Commercial subscription services such as the *Occupational Safety and Health Reporter* published by the Bureau of National Affairs, Inc., 1231 25th Street NW, Washington, D.C. 20037.

Post notices and keep records. You must post and/or keep the following notices and records as indicated in each section. Posting must be done in a prominent location.

You must post the Job Safety and Health workplace poster (OSHA 2203), shown in Figure 15-1. The wording of the text may be changed slightly from time to time, as will the name of the Secretary of Labor, but the basic message—advising employees of the law and their rights under it—remains the same.

If you have more than ten employees, you must maintain records of occupational injuries and illnesses as they occur. These forms must be maintained on a calendar-year basis but are not sent to OSHA; they must be kept available for inspection at your establishment for a period of five years. These are the two forms used:

1. Log and Summary of Occupational Injuries and Illnesses. (OSHA No. 200). Each recordable case of illness or injury is entered on one line on this form, which is reproduced in Figure 15-2. At the end of the year the number of fatalities, lost time, and nonlost-time injuries and illnesses are summarized on the form. Instructions and definitions are printed on the reverse side of OSHA No. 200, not shown here. The portion of this form to the right of the vertical dotted line—the summary section—must be posted by February 1 of the following year and kept in place until March 1.

2. Supplementary Record of Occupational Illnesses and Injuries. (OSHA No. 101). This form provides one page for the history of each accident or exposure to illness and is reproduced in Figure 15-3. OSHA No. 101 must be retained for five years but does not have to be posted.

Note: Even though you have fewer than 11 employees, you may still be required to maintain these records if you are selected by the Bureau of Labor Statistics to participate in their periodic statistical surveys.

If citations are issued by an OSHA inspector, they must be posted at or near the location of the alleged violations for three days or until the violations are abated, whichever is longer. If an employer files a petition for modification of abatement, that also must be posted. If he chooses to contest the citation, he must supply the employees' authorized representative (the union normally) with a copy; if there is no authorized representative, the notice of contest must be posted.

JOB SAFETY & HEALTH PROTECTION

The Occupational Safety and Health Act of 1970 provides job safety and health protection for workers by promoting safe and healthful working conditions throughout the Nation. Requirements of the Act include the following:

Employers

All employers must furnish to employees employment and a place of employment free from recognized hazards that are causing or are likely to cause death or serious harm to employees. Employers must comply with occupational safety and health standards issued under the Act.

Employees

Employees must comply with all occupational safety and health standards, rules, regulations and orders issued under the Act that apply to their own actions and conduct on the job.

The Occupational Safety and Health Administration (OSHA) of the U.S. Department of Labor has the primary responsibility for administering the Act. OSHA issues occupational safety and health standards, and its Compliance Safety and Health Officers conduct jobsite inspections to help ensure compliance with the Act.

Inspection

The Act requires that a representative of the employer and a representative authorized by the employees be given an opportunity to accompany the OSHA inspector for the purpose of aiding the inspection.

Where there is no authorized employee representative, the OSHA Compliance Officer must consult with a reasonable number of employees concerning safety and health conditions in the workplace.

Complaint

Employees or their representatives have the right to file a complaint with the nearest OSHA office requesting an inspection if they believe unsafe or unhealthful conditions exist in their workplace. OSHA will withhold, on request, names of employees complaining.

The Act provides that employees may not be discharged or discriminated against in any way for filing safety and health complaints or for otherwise exercising their rights under the Act.

Employees who believe they have been discriminated against may file a complaint with their nearest OSHA office within 30 days of the alleged discrimination.

Citation

If upon inspection OSHA believes an employer has violated the Act, a citation alleging such violations will be issued to the employer. Each citation will specify a time period within which the alleged violation must be corrected

The OSHA citation must be prominently displayed at or near the place of alleged violation for three days, or until it is corrected, whichever is later, to warn employees of dangers that may exist there.

Proposed Penalty

The Act provides for mandatory penalties against employers of up to $1,000 for each serious violation and for optional penalties of up to $1,000 for each nonserious violation. Penalties of up to $1,000 per day may be proposed for failure to correct violations within the proposed time period. Also, any employer who willfully or repeatedly violates the Act may be assessed penalties of up to $10,000 for each such violation.

Criminal penalties are also provided for in the Act. Any willful violation resulting in death of an employee, upon conviction, is punishable by a fine of not more than $10,000, or by imprisonment for not more than six months, or by both. Conviction of an employer after a first conviction doubles these maximum penalties.

Voluntary Activity

While providing penalties for violations, the Act also encourages efforts by labor and management, before an OSHA inspection, to reduce workplace hazards voluntarily and to develop and improve safety and health programs in all workplaces and industries. OSHA's Voluntary Protection Programs recognize outstanding efforts of this nature.

Such voluntary action should initially focus on the identification and elimination of hazards that could cause death, injury, or illness to employees and supervisors. There are many public and private organizations that can provide information and assistance in this effort, if requested. Also, your local OSHA office can provide considerable help and advice on solving safety and health problems or can refer you to other sources for help such as training.

Consultation

Free consultative assistance, without citation or penalty, is available to employers, on request, through OSHA supported programs in most State departments of labor or health.

More Information

Additional information and copies of the Act, specific OSHA safety and health standards, and other applicable regulations may be obtained from your employer or from the nearest OSHA Regional Office in the following locations:

Atlanta, Georgia
Boston, Massachusetts
Chicago, Illinois
Dallas, Texas
Denver, Colorado
Kansas City, Missouri
New York, New York
Philadelphia, Pennsylvania
San Francisco, California
Seattle, Washington

Telephone numbers for these offices, and additional area office locations, are listed in the telephone directory under the United States Department of Labor in the United States Government listing.

Washington, D.C.
1985
OSHA 2203

William E. Brock, Secretary of Labor

U.S. Department of Labor
Occupational Safety and Health Administration

Under provisions of Title 29, Code of Federal Regulations, Part 1903.2(a)(1) employers must post this notice (or a facsimile) in a conspicuous place where notices to employees are customarily posted.

FIGURE 15-1: Workplace Poster

Bureau of Labor Statistics
Log and Summary of Occupational
Injuries and Illnesses

U.S. Department of Labor

For Calendar Year 19 _____   Page ____ of ____

Form Approved
O.M.B. No. 1220-0029

Company Name

Establishment Name

Establishment Address

NOTE: This form is required by Public Law 91-596 and must be kept in the establishment for 5 years. Failure to maintain and post can result in the issuance of citations and assessment of penalties. (See posting requirements on the other side of form.)

RECORDABLE CASES: You are required to record information about every occupational death; every nonfatal occupational illness; and those nonfatal occupational injuries which involve one or more of the following: loss of consciousness, restriction of work or motion, transfer to another job, or medical treatment (other than first aid). (See definitions on the other side of form.)

Case or File Number	Date of Injury or Onset of Illness	Employee's Name	Occupation	Department	Description of Injury or Illness	Extent of and Outcome of INJURY						Type, Extent of, and Outcome of ILLNESS														
						Fatalities	Nonfatal Injuries					Type of Illness							Fatalities	Nonfatal Illnesses				
						Injury Related	Injuries With Lost Workdays				Injuries Without Lost Workdays	CHECK Only One Column for Each Illness (See other side of form for terminations or permanent transfers.)							Illness Related	Illnesses With Lost Workdays				Illnesses Without Lost Workdays
Enter a nonduplicating number which will facilitate comparisons with supplementary records.	Enter Mo./day.	Enter first name or initial, middle initial, last name.	Enter regular job title, not activity employee was performing when injured or at onset of illness. In the absence of a formal title, enter a brief description of the employee's duties.	Enter department in which the employee is regularly employed or a description of normal workplace to which employee is assigned, even though temporarily working in another department at the time of injury or illness.	Enter a brief description of the injury or illness and indicate the part or parts of body affected. Typical entries for this column might be: Amputation of 1st joint right forefinger; Strain of lower back; Contact dermatitis on both hands; Electrocution—body.	Enter DATE of death. Mo./day/yr.	Enter a CHECK if injury involves days away from work, or days of restricted work activity, or both.	Enter a CHECK if injury involves days away from work.	Enter number of DAYS away from work.	Enter number of DAYS of restricted work activity.	Enter a CHECK if no entry was made in columns 1 or 2 but the injury is recordable as defined above.	Occupational skin diseases or disorders	Dust diseases of the lungs	Respiratory conditions due to toxic agents	Poisoning (systemic effects of toxic materials)	Disorders due to physical agents	Disorders associated with repeated trauma	All other occupational illnesses	Enter DATE of death. Mo./day/yr.	Enter a CHECK if illness involves days away from work, or days of restricted work activity, or both.	Enter a CHECK if illness involves days away from work.	Enter number of DAYS away from work.	Enter number of DAYS of restricted work activity.	Enter a CHECK if no entry was made in columns 8 or 9.
(A)	(B)	(C)	(D)	(E)	(F)	(1)	(2)	(3)	(4)	(5)	(6)	(a)	(b)	(c)	(d)	(e)	(f)	(g)	(8)	(9)	(10)	(11)	(12)	(13)
					PREVIOUS PAGE TOTALS →																			
					TOTALS (Instructions on other side of form.) →																			

OSHA No. 200

Certification of Annual Summary Totals By _____ Title _____ Date _____

FOLD

OSHA No. 200   POST ONLY THIS PORTION OF THE LAST PAGE NO LATER THAN FEBRUARY 1.

FIGURE 15-2: Log and Summary of Injuries and Illnesses

Bureau of Labor Statistics
Supplementary Record of
Occupational Injuries and Illnesses

U.S. Department of Labor

This form is required by Public Law 91-596 and must be kept in the establishment for *5 years.* Failure to maintain can result in the issuance of citations and assessment of penalties.	Case or File No.	Form Approved O.M.B. No. 1220-0029

Employer

1. Name

2. Mail address *(No. and street, city or town, State, and zip code)*

3. Location, if different from mail address

Injured or Ill Employee

4. Name *(First, middle, and last)*   Social Security No.

5. Home address *(No. and street, city or town, State, and zip code)*

6. Age   7. Sex: *(Check one)*   Male ☐   Female ☐

8. Occupation *(Enter regular job title, not the specific activity he was performing at time of injury.)*

9. Department *(Enter name of department or division in which the injured person is regularly employed, even though he may have been temporarily working in another department at the time of injury.)*

The Accident or Exposure to Occupational Illness

If accident or exposure occurred on employer's premises, give address of plant or establishment in which it occurred. Do not indicate department or division within the plant or establishment. If accident occurred outside employer's premises at an identifiable address, give that address. If it occurred on a public highway or at any other place which cannot be identified by number and street, please provide place references locating the place of injury as accurately as possible.

10. Place of accident or exposure *(No. and street, city or town, State, and zip code)*

11. Was place of accident or exposure on employer's premises?   Yes ☐   No ☐

12. What was the employee doing when injured? *(Be specific. If he was using tools or equipment or handling material, name them and tell what he was doing with them.)*

13. How did the accident occur? *(Describe fully the events which resulted in the injury or occupational illness. Tell what happened and how it happened. Name any objects or substances involved and tell how they were involved. Give full details on all factors which led or contributed to the accident. Use separate sheet for additional space.)*

Occupational Injury or Occupational Illness

14. Describe the injury or illness in detail and indicate the part of body affected. *(E.g., amputation of right index finger at second joint; fracture of ribs; lead poisoning; dermatitis of left hand, etc.)*

15. Name the object or substance which directly injured the employee. *(For example, the machine or thing he struck against or which struck him; the vapor or poison he inhaled or swallowed; the chemical or radiation which irritated his skin; or in cases of strains, hernias, etc., the thing he was lifting, pulling, etc.)*

16. Date of injury or initial diagnosis of occupational illness   17. Did employee die? *(Check one)*   Yes ☐   No ☐

Other

18. Name and address of physician

19. If hospitalized, name and address of hospital

Date of report	Prepared by	Official position

OSHA No. 101 (Feb. 1981)

FIGURE 15-3: Supplementary Injury and Illness Record

If the employer petitions for variances from standards or record-keeping procedures, he must post summaries of the petitions.

What Triggers an OSHA Inspection

Using its authority under the Act, OSHA makes about 50,000 workplace inspections each year. Because it is able to inspect only one out of a hundred workplaces under its jurisdiction in a given year, OSHA uses a system of priorities in deciding who gets inspected.

Imminent danger situations. When OSHA is reasonably certain that a condition exists that may cause death or serious physical harm immediately or before normal enforcement procedures can eliminate it, they will inspect. If such a condition is found, OSHA will ask the employer to abate the hazard; if the employer fails to do so, OSHA may apply to the Federal District Court for legal action to remove it. If OSHA arbitrarily declines to bring court action, the affected employees may sue the Secretary of Labor to compel him to do so. In any event, before the OSHA inspector leaves the workplace, he will inform all affected employees of the hazard.

Fatal or multiple accidents. When there is a fatality or an accident that results in the hospitalization of five or more employees, the employer must report it to the nearest OSHA office within 48 hours. An investigation will be made to determine if standards were violated and to find ways to avoid similar accidents.

Complaints by employees. The law gives every employee the right to request an OSHA inspection if he believes that there is an imminent hazard or that there is a violation of a standard which threatens physical harm. OSHA will keep the employee's name confidential if so requested. Inspection is not automatic; OSHA will review the request and inspect only if it believes the complaint is justified or if it is in doubt; it would not inspect for obviously trivial or vindictive complaints.

High-hazard programs. When death, illness, or injury rates, or known exposure of employees to toxic substances attracts OSHA's concern, it may target specific industries on either a regional or national basis for increased inspection activity. Usually emphasis will be on those companies whose lost workday rates are higher than the national average.

Reinspections. When a company has been cited for a previous serious violation, it may be reinspected to see if the hazard has been corrected.

How Inspections Are Conducted

You should be aware of the following key points.

No notice. It is illegal for anyone to notify an employer in advance of an OSHA inspection. OSHA itself may give such notice in certain rare circumstances but only within less than 24 hours. The inspection of your plant is virtually certain to be a surprise. Remember: *You don't have to let the inspector in without a warrant.* That's a 1978 decision of the U.S. Supreme Court. Whether it is a good idea to demand a warrant is another question; the effect on employees, the union (if any), and the public should be weighed carefully and discussed with legal counsel. The effect on the inspector must also be considered; although he is not supposed to let your demand affect his judgment, he will surely be curious as to why you refuse him access. On the other hand, it is not certain that a court will honor OSHA's request for a warrant—it may not believe that OSHA has probable cause to believe that there is a violation.

Opening conference.   Upon arrival, the compliance officer will ask to see a representative of the employer, who should ask to see the officer's credentials; they will be issued by the Department of Labor, and will bear the officer's photograph and a serial number that can be verified by phone at the nearest OSHA office. As OSHA publication 2056 points out, "Anyone who tries to collect a penalty at the time of inspection, or promotes the sale of a product or service at any time, is not an OSHA compliance officer." The officer will explain the purpose of the visit and the scope of the inspection, and will provide the employer with copies of applicable standards, as well as a copy of any employee complaint. The employer is asked to provide a representative to accompany the officer on the inspection tour.

Employee representative.   The employees have a right to have a representative at the opening conference and on the inspection tour. If there is a union, it usually will designate the employee representative; if there is no union, the employees on the plant safety committee can designate the representative; if there is neither, the employees may select someone or, failing that, the compliance officer may find an employee who can represent the interest of the others. The important point is that the employer may never select the employee representative.

Inspection tour.   The compliance officer and the representatives begin a tour of the establishment, with the route and duration determined by the officer. He will be checking conditions for compliance with standards, and in doing so may take photographs and instrument readings, examine records, and talk with employees (in private if necessary) about safety conditions. He also will check on posting and record-keeping.

In the course of his work, the compliance officer may discover trade secrets of the employer; the officer is forbidden by law, with penalties of fine and imprisonment, from releasing such confidential information without authorization.

If some observed violations can be and are corrected on the spot, the compliance officer will make a record of the correction to be used later in judging the employer's good-faith effort; the correction is not, however, a bar to the issuance of a citation and proposed penalty.

Closing conference.   When the tour is completed, the compliance officer informs the employer (or his representative) of the apparent violations of standards that he has found. The employer can discuss the situation, show compliance efforts, and give information to help OSHA determine how much time should be allowed for correction. The officer will either issue or recommend the issuance of citations; in either case they must be approved by the OSHA area director. The officer does not indicate what any penalties might be; again, only the area director has the authority to assess penalties.

On-site consultation. In the early days of OSHA, employers complained that they could not get an informal inspection of their plants so they could find out what might be wrong and have a chance to correct it; once the OSHA man was in the door, he was duty-bound to record violations and recommend or issue citations for them. That is still the case, but a program has been established under which consultants—provided either by the states or hired from the private sector—will come and conduct an inspection similar to OSHA's at the request of an employer and at no cost to him. The consultant will hold opening and closing conferences, will explain the standards and point out any violations, and may give suggestions as to how to correct them. No citations will be issued, no penalties assessed, and the consultant's files will not be used to trigger an OSHA inspection. There is one catch, however: The employer has to agree to eliminate any hazardous condition found by the consultant that could cause death or serious physical harm. If the employer does not take action to eliminate such hazards within a reasonable time, the consultation project manager is required to notify OSHA. In most states you can obtain details of the program by calling the state Department of Labor or Department of Health.

Types of Penalties, Contests, and Appeals

When the compliance officer turns in the report of the plant inspection, the area director decides what citations will be issued and the proposed penalties. These are the types of violations and the possible penalties:

Other than serious. Directly related to safety and health but not likely to cause serious physical harm. Discretionary penalty of up to $1,000 for each violation but may be adjusted downward on the basis of employer's good-faith efforts to comply, size of business, and history of previous violations. When penalty falls below $50, none is proposed. (Very minor infractions were once known as *de minimis* violations.)

Serious. Substantial probability of death or serious physical harm and the employer knew, or should have known, of the hazard. Mandatory proposed penalty between $300 and $1,000 for each violation; may be adjusted downward on the basis of employer's good faith, history of previous violations, gravity of the violation, and size of business—to as low as $60. *Imminent danger situations* (see page 242) are cited and penalized as serious violations.

Willful. The employer commits an intentional and knowing violation of the Act or knows that a hazardous condition exists and makes no reasonable effort to eliminate it. Maximum penalty of $10,000 for each violation, with possible downward adjustment. If a willful violation results in the death of an employee, a court may impose a maximum fine of $10,000 or a prison term of six months or both. If the employer is convicted a second time, these penalties may be doubled.

Repeated. When any standard, regulation, rule, or order is violated, the employer may be cited for a repeated violation if he previously has been cited for a substantially similar condition (not necessarily the same piece of equipment or location in the plant). Maximum fine: $10,000 for each repeated violation. Time limit: 3 years from the date that the first citation became a final order or the date of final correction of the violation, whichever is later.

Additional violations and penalties:

- Violation of posting requirements: $1,000 maximum

- Failure to correct a violation: $1,000 maximum for each day beyond the prescribed abatement date

- Falsifying records, reports, or applications: $10,000 fine and six months in jail

- Assaulting, resisting, opposing, intimidating, or interfering with a compliance officer: $5,000 fine and imprisonment for 3 years, maximum

Following an inspection in which violations have been found, you will receive a written Citation and Notification of Penalty, which explains the exact nature of the violations found and states the proposed penalty. If you agree to the citation and penalty, you should correct the violation by the date set in the citation and pay the penalty within 15 working days of receipt of the notice. You also must notify the area director in writing of the corrective action taken.

If you disagree, you may contest in writing within 15 days of receipt of the notice of the citation, the proposed penalty, the abatement date, or any or all of them. Your contest is forwarded to the Occupational Safety and Health Review Commission (an independent federal agency which is not part of the U.S. Department of Labor), where it is assigned to an administrative law judge. The judge will schedule a hearing at which employees and the employer may be present, and which is conducted much like a trial. The administrative law judge may render a decision upholding, modifying, or eliminating any contested item of the citation or penalty. The ruling of the judge may be subjected to further review by the full Review Commission at the request of any party to the case. Finally, the Commission's ruling may be appealed to the U.S. Court of Appeals.

If you do not contest within 15 working days, the citation becomes a final order and cannot be changed by the OSHA area director. During that period, however, you may request an informal conference with the director to ask questions about the standards and the cited violations, discuss problems with correcting the violations, and negotiate an Informal Settlement Agreement. The area director is authorized to enter into such agreements which may mitigate citations and penalties.

If you are unable to meet the correction date specified in the citation, you may file a Petition for Modification of Abatement no later than one working day after the correction date. In it you must show what you have already done to comply and when you did it; how much additional time you need and why you need it; and make a statement to the effect that you have posted the petition, that you have given a copy to an authorized representative of the affected employees, and the date of the posting. The OSHA area director may grant or oppose the petition; if he opposes, it becomes a contested case before the Review Commission.

When a new standard is issued and you are unable to meet it because of the unavailability of materials, equipment, or professional/technical personnel, you may apply to OSHA for a *temporary variance* if you can present an effective program for reaching compliance as quickly as possible and can demonstrate that all available steps are being taken to safeguard employees. The temporary variance may be granted for up to one year and may be renewed twice, for six months each time. When you can prove that your existing facilities or methods of operation are at least as safe and healthful as those required by an OSHA standard, you may apply for a *permanent variance* from that standard. When applying for either type of variance, you must inform employees of the application and their right to request a hearing.

Employees' Rights

The most basic right of employees, as stated in the purpose of the Act and repeated in the employer's general duty clause, is to be provided with a safe and healthful workplace free from hazards likely to cause death or serious harm. In setting up the mechanism by which that purpose would be achieved, Congress intended that employees would be active participants and provided them with the following specific rights:

To be informed. In addition to the workplace poster, which employers are required to display, employees are entitled to review a copy of the Act and relevant OSHA standards and regulations made available by the employer at the workplace. They may request information from you on safety and health hazards in the workplace. They may review the Log and Summary of Occupational Injuries (OSHA No. 200). Citations must be posted, as well as copies of the employer's notice to contest. Employees must be notified if you apply for either a temporary or permanent variance from an OSHA standard. They have the right to see their own examination records and must be told by the employer if exposure to harmful agents has exceeded permissible levels. If test measurements are taken to determine and record employee exposure, employees have the right to be present during the testing and to examine records of the results.

To request an inspection. The employee may request an inspection anonymously if he or she believes there are hazardous conditions or violations of standards. Employees also have the right to have their authorized representative accompany the inspecting officer, to answer any questions, and to request a closing conference.

To appeal actions taken by OSHA or the employer. Employees may request an informal conference with OSHA to discuss an inspection, citation, notice of proposed penalty, employer's notice of intention to contest, or OSHA's decision not to issue a citation. Employees may not formally contest citations or amendments to them, penalties, or lack of penalties. However, they may contest the amount of time OSHA has allowed the employer to correct the violation. They may also contest within 10 working days of its receipt or posting an employer's Petition for Modification of Abatement. The contest of a citation must be within 15 working days. When an employer applies for a variance from a standard, employees have the right to testify at the variance hearing and to appeal the final decision. And, as already noted on page 242, employees may bring an action against the Secretary of Labor in the United States District Court to compel him to seek a court order providing relief in cases of imminent danger when he has arbitrarily refused to do so.

To be free from retaliation by employers for exercising their rights under the Act. Employers are forbidden to punish or discriminate against any employee for participating in OSHA conferences, inspections, or hearings; for complaining to an employer, union, or the OSHA about work hazards; for filing safety grievances; or for serving on safety committees. Discrimination could, among others, consist of firing, demoting, taking away seniority or other earned benefits, transferring to an undesirable job or shift, threatening or harassing, or singling out for punishment.

Employee responsibilities. The Act states that "Each employee shall comply with occupational safety and health standards and all rules, regulations, and orders issued pursuant to this Act which are applicable to his own actions and conduct." OSHA publications expand on this provision by telling employees to read the workplace poster, comply with applicable standards, follow all employer's safety rules (including the wearing of prescribed protective equipment), report hazardous conditions and job-related injuries and illness to the employer, cooperate with OSHA inspectors, and exercise their rights under the Act responsibly. However, there are no penalties for employees' failing to meet these responsibilities; the feeling in Congress seemed to be that the employer has enough authority in the workplace to enforce compliance with safety regulations.

CHANGING TRENDS IN OSHA

The manner in which OSHA approaches its responsibilities is subject to many influences. Although it has not amended the law in the first fifteen years of its existence, Congress can curtail or encourage specific OSHA activities through annual appropriation bills. As political administrations change in Washington, there may be greater or lesser emphasis on various aspects of the program. An outgoing administration issued a rule requiring employers to pay employees for time spent accompanying compliance officers during inspections; a subsequent administration rescinded the rule. At one time OSHA moved quickly to establish as many regulations on as many subjects as possible; at another, it stopped to review regulations it considered too cumbersome or complicated to work well. Inspections were once made in as many plants as possible in high-hazard industries, but later it was decided to skip those plants with lower than average lost workday experiences. At another time the agency exempted from routine inspections all establishments with ten or fewer employees. While the plant manager will want to keep abreast of the current stance of OSHA through trade journals, the general press, or trade associations, the principles of Chapter 14 should not be forgotten—that the company's best interests are served (financially and otherwise) by the operation of an effective safety program, regardless of any legal requirement to do so.

A precaution: Because we are dealing with federal law, much of what has been said in this chapter is quoted directly from the Act or follows closely the language used in OSHA publications—especially OSHA No. 2056, *All About OSHA*, 1982 (Revised)—in order to more clearly transmit the intention of those who wrote the law and regulations. Nevertheless, nothing said here is intended to be a legal interpretation, and professional help should be sought when such interpretation is needed.

ENVIRONMENTAL PROTECTION

Landmark Laws and How They Affect Manufacturing Plants

The body of law enacted to protect the environment is much more complex. The federal government started pollution control legislation with the Rivers and Harbors Act of 1899, which outlawed the depositing of refuse in the navigable waters of the United States without a permit from the Army Corps of Engineers. The beginning of the modern era of pollution control cannot be stated with precision, but the Clean Air Act of 1963, the Water Quality Act of 1965, the National Environmental Policy Act of 1969, and the Reorganization Plan No. 3 of 1970—which established the Environmental Protection Agency (EPA)—are all landmarks in its evolution. Congress enacted separate laws to deal with air pollution, water pollution, disposal of solid wastes, noise control, and toxic substances. Those most likely to interest and affect managers of manufacturing plants are listed below.

The National Environmental Policy Act (1969, amended in July 1975 and August 1975). This is a broad statement of national aims, making it the policy of the federal government to use all practicable means to create and maintain conditions under which people and nature can exist in productive harmony. Directs federal agencies to work and cooperate toward this end. Requires them to prepare environmental impact statements for major actions they propose to take affecting the environment. Establishes the Council on Environmental Quality in the Executive Office of the President to make policy recommendations to him, to monitor the activities of the federal government in the light of national policy, and to prepare an annual report on the condition of the environment. Affects federal agencies primarily; no direct regulations for private-sector manufacturing plants.

Reorganization Plan No. 3 of 1970. Establishes the Environmental Protection Agency and transfers various pollution control functions previously performed by other agencies to it.

Clean Air Act (1963, numerous amendments through July 1981). Basic purpose is to protect and enhance the quality of the nation's air resources. Primary responsibility for control of air pollution belongs to state and local governments, but they are provided technical and financial assistance. Establishes national research program and assists regional control programs. Requires development of national ambient air quality standards. Manufacturing managers are directly affected by sections directing the EPA administrator to promulgate standards of performance for new stationary sources of air pollution and to develop a list of hazardous air pollutants and establish emission standards for them.

Federal Water Pollution Control Act (1972, many amendments through January 1983). Also known as Clean Water Act. Establishes national goal to eliminate discharge of pollutants into navigable waters. Provides for research programs and grants to state and local governments for construction of treatment works. Requires EPA administrator to set effluent limitations and outlaws the discharge of any pollutant by any person without an EPA permit. Sets up a list of toxic pollutants, and requires the best available technology to limit or eliminate them.

Federal Insecticide, Fungicide, and Rodenticide Act (1972, amendments through December 1980). Requires registration with the EPA of any pesticide sold or distributed; classification by the administrator for general or restricted use; and certification of applicators.

Resource Conservation and Recovery Act of 1976 (amended in October and December 1980). For control of solid waste disposal (which may include solids or liquids). Requires the administrator to develop a list of hazardous wastes; to establish standards for generators, transporters, and operators of disposal facilities for such wastes; and to set up a permit system for the operation of disposal facilities.

Toxic Substances Control Act (October 1976, revised December 1981). Gives the EPA administrator authority to prohibit the use of dangerous chemicals; limit the quantities or concentrations to be manufactured, processed, or distributed; require that they be accompanied by warnings and safe use instructions; require manufacturers and processors to conduct tests and submit data; and to require advance notice of the proposed manufacture of a new chemical. Places an outright ban on PCBs (polychlorinated biphenyls).

Comprehensive Environmental Response, Compensation, and Liability Act of 1980 (Superfund) (1980, amended September 1982). Gives the President and/or the EPA administrator authority to respond to releases—imminent or actual—of hazardous substances into the environment, either on an emergency basis or over longer periods. Cleanup costs are to be paid from the Hazardous Substance Response Trust Fund, supported by a variety of taxes including those on the manufacture of certain chemicals and petroleum products, and the Post-closure Liability Trust Fund, supported by a tax on the receipt of hazardous waste at a waste disposal facility.

Other laws. There are approximately thirty federal laws dealing with the environment, and not all can be listed here. The attempt has been made to describe those that most directly affect the operations of manufacturing plants. Some others which may indirectly or directly affect the work activities of plant managers are

Water Resources Planning Act

Water Research and Development Act of 1978

National Ocean Pollution Planning Act of 1978

Marine Mammal Protection Act

Wild and Scenic Rivers Act

Endangered Species Act of 1973

Coastal Zone Management Act of 1972

Outer Continental Shelf Lands Act

Energy Supply and Environmental Coordination Act of 1974

Environmental Education Act of 1978

Safe Water Drinking Act

Ports and Tanker Safety Act of 1979

Deepwater Port Act of 1974

Marine Protection, Research, and Sanctuaries Act of 1972

Fish and Wildlife Coordination Act

Soil and Water Resources Conservation Act of 1977

Surface Mining Control and Reclamation Act of 1977

Noise Control Act of 1972

Environmental Quality Improvement Act of 1970

Environmental Research, Development, and Demonstration Authorization Act of 1980

These laws are augmented by a series of Presidential Executive Orders which direct the manner in which federal agencies will carry out certain of their provisions. Environmental legislation is not static, and Congress continually amends these laws and enacts new ones.

Common Provisions Found in the Environmental Laws

There are some common provisions which appear in similar form in most of the environmental laws:

- States are encouraged to establish their own pollution control programs, federal grants are authorized to help them do that, and federal authority may be delegated to them when they have established acceptable programs. Therefore, you may well find that you are dealing with state, rather than federal, authorities in these areas.

- Enforcement clauses provide for both civil and criminal penalties for violators. Typical maximums are fines of $25,000 per day of violation and/or one year of imprisonment.

- Employees are protected against discharge or discrimination by employers as punishment for instituting or participating in any procedure under the law.
- Federal officers (usually the EPA administrator or his designee) are granted the right to inspect the premises of pollution sources and require the owner/operator to install monitoring equipment and keep records.
- The administrator must treat as confidential any information, upon a satisfactory showing by the person submitting it, which, if made public, would divulge trade secrets.
- In situations of imminent danger, the administrator is authorized to bring suit in court to restrain polluters and to seek authority to seize hazardous materials.
- Small businesses are granted certain exemptions in several of the laws, as well as other forms of assistance.

EPA Administration and Regional Offices and Their Main Functions

The EPA is organized to handle the problems of pollution control on the basis of what is being protected—air, water, or land. This breakdown is reflected in the structure of its Washington headquarters, which is headed by an administrator. Under the administrator is an Office of the Assistant Administrator for each of the following main functions (the subfunctions are indented and each is usually headed by a deputy assistant administrator).

Air, Noise, and Radiation
- Air Quality Planning and Standards
- Mobile Source Air Pollution Control
- Noise Abatement and Control
- Radiation Programs

Water and Waste Management
- Water Planning and Standards
- Water Program Operations
- Drinking Water
- Solid Waste

Toxic Substances
- Pesticide Programs
- Chemical Control
- Testing and Evaluation
- Program Integration and Information

Enforcement

- Water Enforcement
- General Enforcement
- Mobile Source and Noise Enforcement

There are also Offices of the Assistant Administrator for Planning and Management, and for Research and Development, as well as Staff Offices for Legislation, International Activities, Environmental Review, Civil Rights, and Administrative Law Judges. When approaching the Washington office for assistance, it is a good idea to know beforehand under which function or subfunction your inquiry falls.

Regional Offices of the EPA

EPA has divided the nation into ten regions, and this list gives the states comprising each region as well as the address of each regional office:

Region I

Connecticut, Maine, Massachusetts, New Hampshire, Rhode Island and Vermont. Room 2203, John F. Kennedy Federal Building, Boston, MA 02203.

Region II

New Jersey, New York, Puerto Rico, Virgin Islands. Environmental Protection Agency, Room 1009, 26 Federal Plaza, New York, NY 10278.

Region III

Delaware, Maryland, Pennsylvania, Virginia, West Virginia, District of Columbia. Environmental Protection Agency, Curtis Building, Sixth and Walnut Streets, Philadelphia, PA 19106.

Region IV

Alabama, Florida, Georgia, Kentucky, Mississippi, North Carolina, South Carolina, Tennessee. Environmental Protection Agency, 345 Courtland Street NE, Atlanta, GA 30365.

Region V

Illinois, Indiana, Michigan, Minnesota, Ohio, Wisconsin. Environmental Protection Agency, 230 South Dearborn Street, Chicago, IL 60604.

Region VI

Arkansas, Louisiana, New Mexico, Oklahoma, Texas. Environmental Protection Agency, First International Building, 1201 Elm Street, Dallas, TX 75270.

Region VII

Iowa, Kansas, Missouri, Nebraska. Environmental Protection Agency, 324 E. 11th Street, Kansas City, MO 64106.

Region VIII

Colorado, Montana, North Dakota, South Dakota, Utah, Wyoming. Environmental Protection Agency, Lincoln Tower, 1860 Lincoln Street, Denver, CO 80295.

Region IX

Arizona, California, Hawaii, Nevada, American Samoa, Trust Territories of the Pacific Islands, Guam, Wake Island, Northern Marianas. Environmental Protection Agency, 215 Fremont Street, San Francisco, CA 94105.

Region X

Alaska, Idaho, Washington, Oregon. Environmental Protection Agency, 1200 Sixth Avenue, Seattle, WA 98101.

Most plant managers will deal with regional offices in their contacts with EPA.

The rules and regulations through which EPA administers the environmental laws are published in the Code of Federal Regulations. The Code is divided into 50 Titles, each covering a broad area subject to federal regulation. Title 40—Protection of Environment—is broken down into lettered Subchapters (A, B, C, and so on) for general topics, and further into numbered parts dealing with specific areas of regulation. For instance, the national primary ambient air quality standard for sulfur dioxide is contained in Part 50.4, and reference to it is shown as

40 CFR 50.4

(The Subchapter letters are not used in the reference numbering system, since the parts are numbered serially through the entire title.)

Selected Title 40 Sections of Interest to Plant Managers

Title 40 is divided into nine paperback volumes which are sold by the Superintendent of Documents, U.S. Government Printing Office, Washington, D.C. 20402 (prices vary by volume and over time, and can be requested at time of purchase). The following is a list of selected volumes and parts which contain information and regulations that are most likely to concern and affect plant managers.

40 CFR Parts 0 to 51

Subchapter A—General

Statement of Organization and General Information	Public Information
	Small Business

Subchapter C—Air Programs

National Primary and Secondary
Ambient Air Quality Standards

40 CFR Part 52

Approval and Promulgation of State
Implementation Plans

40 CFR Parts 53 to 80

Standards of Performance for New
Stationary Sources

Assessment and Collection of
Noncompliance Penalties by EPA

Approval and Promulgation of State
Plans for Designated Facilities and
Pollutants

EPA Approval of State
Noncompliance Penalty Program

40 CFR Parts 81 to 99

Designation of Areas for Air Quality
Planning Purposes

40 CFR Parts 100 to 149

Subchapter D—Water Programs

Designation of Hazardous Substances

Water Quality Standards

EPA-Administered Permit Programs:
The National Pollutant Discharge
Elimination System; the Hazardous
Waste Permit Program; and the
Underground Injection Control
Program

Determination of Reportable
Quantities for Hazardous Substances

State Certification of Activities
Requiring a Federal License or
Permit

Criteria and Standards for the
National Pollutant Discharge
Elimination System

Toxic Pollutant Effluent Standards

40 CFR Parts 150 to 189

Subchapter E—Pesticide Programs

Registration of Pesticide-producing
Establishments, Submission of
Pesticides Reports, and Labeling

Books and Records of Pesticide
Production and Distribution

40 CFR Parts 190 to 399

Subchapter F—Radiation Protection Programs

Environmental Radiation Protection
Standards for Nuclear Power
Operations

Environmental Protection Standards
for Uranium Mill Tailings

Subchapter G—Noise Abatement Programs

Subchapter H—Ocean Dumping

Subchapter I—Solid Wastes

Identification and Listing of Hazardous Waste

Standards Applicable to Generators of Hazardous Waste

40 CFR Parts 400 to 424

Subchapter N—Effluent Guidelines and Standards

Effluent Limitations Guidelines for Standards of Performance and Pretreatment Standards for New Sources for the Following Industries:

Dairy Products Processing

Canned and Preserved Fruits and Vegetables Processing

Sugar Processing

Cement Manufacturing

Electroplating

Plastics and Synthetics

Soap and Detergent Manufacturing

Fertilizer Manufacturing

Nonferrous Metals Manufacturing

Phosphate Manufacturing

Ferroalloy Manufacturing

General Pretreatment Regulations for Existing and New Sources of Pollution

Grain Mills

Canned and Preserved Seafood Processing

Textile Industry

Feedlots

Organic Chemicals Manufacturing

Inorganic Chemicals Manufacturing

Petroleum Refining

Iron and Steel Manufacturing

Steam Electric Power Generating

40 CFR Part 425 to end

(continuation of industry listings from previous volume)

Leather Tanning and Finishing

Rubber Manufacturing

Pulp, Paper, and Paperboard

Meat Products

Coal Mining

Mineral Mining and Processing

Ore Mining and Dressing

Paint Formulating

Ink Formulating

Pesticide Chemicals

Carbon Black Manufacturing

Hospital Point Source

Glass Manufacturing

Asbestos Manufacturing

Timber Products Processing

Builders Paper and Roofing Felt

Oil and Gas Extraction

Pharmaceutical Manufacturing

Paving and Roofing Materials (Tars and Asphalt)

Gum and Wood Chemicals Manufacturing

Explosives Manufacturing

Photographic Point Source

Subchapter R—Toxic Substances Control Act

Reporting and Record-keeping Requirements	Chemical Exports and Imports
Inventory Reporting Regulations	Chemical Information Rules
Fully Halogenated Chlorofluoro-alkanes Manufacturing, Processing, Distribution, and Use Prohibitions	Polychlorinated Biphenyls (PCBs)
	Asbestos
	Storage and Disposal of Waste Material

Because the Code of Federal Regulations is published only once a year, federal agencies need a publication in which they can promulgate new rules during the year. This need is filled by the *Federal Register*, which is published daily and sold by the Superintendent of Documents. Thus, to be sure that you have the latest ruling on a particular topic, you would first consult the most recent issue of the CFR and then check all issues of the *Federal Register*, published subsequently. The superintendent also sells a monthly *Federal Register Index*, issued in cumulative form.

It was mentioned in the previous section that the states are encouraged to establish their own programs and enforcement activities. State agencies tend to have names such as State Department of Environmental Conservation; in some states pollution control responsibilities are placed under the State Department of Health. With only rare exceptions the headquarters of the state agency is located in the capital city.

KEY REGULATIONS FOR CONTROLLING AIR EMISSIONS

The many state and federal regulations affecting air pollution are extremely complex, and there is no single manual or code that you can consult to find out exactly what rules apply to your operation. Congress repeatedly amends the Clean Air Act; EPA responds with new regulations to implement the amendments; the states revise their plans to conform; EPA may accept the state plans in whole or in part but substitutes its own regulations for the parts it does not approve; environmentalist groups challenge these laws and regulations in the courts as being too lenient, while corporations and manufacturers' associations institute suits against them for being too strict, both causing the courts to enter the picture and impose yet another set of interpretations. The best approach to thread your way through all this may be to consult local or state authorities first as to what regulations apply and then verify the answers with the regional office of EPA. To help you understand their answers, here are some landmark regulations issued by EPA to control air pollution.

National Ambient Air Quality Standards

EPA has issued primary and secondary air quality standards for the pollutants listed in Table 15-1. Primary standards set the levels necessary to protect public health; secondary standards are set to protect the public welfare from known or anticipated adverse effects of a pollutant.

TABLE 15-1: National Primary and Secondary Air Quality Standards

(FROM 40 CFR 50.2)

Pollutant	Primary Standard	Secondary Standard
Sulfur Oxides (Sulfur Dioxide)	Annual arithmetic mean: 80 micrograms per cubic meter (0.03 parts per million Maximum 24-hr concentration exceeded no more than once per year: 365 mcg per cu m (0.14 ppm)	Maximum 3-hr concentration to be exceeded no more than once per year: 1,300 micrograms per cubic meter (0.5 ppm)
Particulate Matter	Annual geometric mean: 75 mcg per cu m Maximum 24-hr concentration to be exceeded no more than once per year: 260 mcg per cu m	Annual geometric mean: 60 mcg per cu m Maximum 24-hr concentration exceeded no more than once per year: 150 mcg per cu m
Carbon Monoxide	Maximum 8-hr concentration exceeded no more than once per year: 10 milligrams per cubic meter (9 ppm) Maximum 1-hr concentration exceeded no more than once per year: 40 mg per cu m (35 ppm)	Same Same
Ozone	Maximum hourly average concentration expected to occur on no more than 1 day per year: 0.12 ppm (235 mcg per cu m)	Same
Nitrogen Dioxide	Annual arithmetic mean: 100 mcg per cu m (0.053 ppm)	Same
Lead	Maximum arithmetic mean averaged over one quarter: 1.5 mcg per cu m	Same

Nonattainment Areas and State Implementation Plans

The Clean Air Act requires the states to develop implementation plans which will bring the level of each pollutant in Table 15-1 (and any others which may be added later to the list) within the limits of the national standard. EPA assesses their progress, and for "designated areas" within each state determines whether that area meets the primary and secondary standards for each pollutant, is better than the national standards, or cannot be classified. The results are published in 40 CFR 81.300 to 81.356. No matter where your plant is in the United States or its possessions, by consulting this reference you can find out whether the area in which it is located does not meet the standard for any one of the pollutants. If so, it is a *nonattainment area* for that pollutant, and you can expect increasingly stringent state (or EPA) regulations covering emissions from existing plants in order to bring the area within the standards.

Matters become much more complicated if you plan to build a new plant in a nonattainment area or modify an existing one, thus creating a "major new source." To obtain a permit for the new source, you will need to go through the following steps:

1. Determine whether the new installation will emit, or have the potential to emit, more than 100 tons per year of any pollutant subject to regulation under the Act. If not, the following conditions do not have to be met.

2. Design the new source with controls that will provide the Lowest Achievable Emission Rate, which is defined as the lowest limit allowed in any state implementation plan, or, if less, the lowest emission rate that is actually achieved in the industry for the pollutant in question. If, however, the new source would have an allowable emission rate under the state implementation plan or new source performance standards not exceeding 50 tons per year, 1,000 pounds per day, or 100 pounds per hour, then it is exempt from this requirement.

3. Certify that all other major sources (100 tons or more per year) owned or operated by your company in the same state are in compliance with all applicable emission limitations and standards under the Act.

4. Obtain emission reductions, or "offsets," of the pollutants in question from existing sources in the area—whether owned by your company or by others—sufficient to demonstrate reasonable progress toward bringing the area into attainment. Generally, companies find it easiest to obtain offsets by reducing emissions from their own units, but there have been cases where offsets were obtained by paying for pollution control equipment to be installed in another company's plant. In yet other instances, local politicians or chambers of commerce have prevailed upon existing plants to reduce their emissions so that a new facility could be located in the area. Pollutant offsets must be of the same kind; that is, you cannot obtain permission to add a sulfur dioxide source by reducing particulate matter in an existing source.

5. Show that the offsets you have obtained more than equal the emissions from the proposed new source. Again, you are exempt from this requirement if the new source meets the 50-1,000-100 rate requirement mentioned at the end of Step 2.

Both the law and EPA regulations permit the states to adopt regulations more stringent than the federal standards (but not less stringent).

Prevention of Significant Deterioration

This set of regulations, covered in 40 CFR 51.24, is designed to prevent any worsening of air quality in those areas that are already in compliance with the national standards. Every area of the country is designated as Class I, II, or III, (unless it is already a nonattainment area). Class I areas are those with the cleanest air, such as might be found over a large national park. Class III is for highly industrialized areas, and Class II covers everything in between the two extremes. EPA regulations require that state plans permit no more increases in the concentration of particulates and sulfur dioxide than those shown in Table 15-2. (Ultimately, increments will be specified for all the regulated pollutants shown in Table 15-1.)

If you plan to build a new "major stationary source" or undertake a major modification of existing facilities in an area designated for prevention of significant deterioration, you must incorporate the Best Available Control Technology in the design and operation of the installation; provide continuous air quality monitoring data from the area for the previous year; show that the installation will not cause a violation of any national air quality standard or of any allowable increase over baseline concentrations; submit information necessary to analyze and make determinations as to the air quality impact of the proposed installation; provide an analysis of the impairment of visibility, soils, and vegetation as a result of the installation and growth associated with it; and meet all other local, state, or federal requirements. The reviewing authority will notify the EPA and other appropriate officials of the application, as well as the general public, providing them an opportunity to comment in writing or at a public hearing. You may also submit a plan for the use of innovative technology, as long as it would achieve emission reductions equal to those obtainable with Best Available Control Technology, without putting public health at risk.

A very complicated set of exemptions to these procedures is allowed in 40 CFR 51.24; in general, your stationary source may be exempt if it emits (or has the potential to emit) less than 101 tons per year of any regulated pollutant and is one of 28 classes of industrial facilities listed in the Code; emits less than 251 tons per year and is any other type of facility. A modification may be exempt if it results in a net emissions increase less than those specified in the code for 15 types of pollutants. Also, a modification may be exempt from certain parts of the procedure if it is a change in a major stationary source that existed on March 1, 1978, and the net increase in allowable emissions of each regulated pollutant after

TABLE 15–2: Allowable Increments for Area Classes

(FROM 40 CFR 51.24)

Pollutant	Maximum allowable increase (micrograms per cubic meter)
CLASS I	
Particulate matter:	
Annual geometric mean	5
24-hr maximum	10
Sulfur dioxide:	
Annual arithmetic mean	2
24-hr maximum	5
3-hr maximum	25
CLASS II	
Particulate matter:	
Annual geometric mean	19
24-hr maximum	37
Sulfur dioxide:	
Annual arithmetic mean	20
24-hr maximum	91
3-hr maximum	512
CLASS III	
Particulate matter:	
Annual geometric mean	37
24-hr maximum	75
Sulfur dioxide:	
Annual arithmetic mean	40
24-hr maximum	182
3-hr maximum	700

application of Best Available Control Technology would be less than 50 tons per year. A new stationary source or a modification may be exempt if the net emissions increase would cause air quality impacts less than the concentrations listed for 13 specified pollutants.

New Source Performance Standards

In addition to the regulations for Nonattainment Areas and Prevention of Significant Deterioration, the Clean Air Act requires that the EPA develop standards for all new sources (or modifications of existing ones) constructed after specific dates in various industrial categories. Part 60 of the Code of Federal Regulations (40 CFR 60.1, et seq., plus appendices) details such standards for the 39 industrial categories listed below, and more will be published by EPA as time goes on.

Fossil-Fired Steam Generators Incinerators

Nitric Acid Plants

Asphalt Concrete Plants

Storage Vessels for Petroleum Liquids

Secondary Brass and Bronze Ingot Production Plants

Primary Copper Smelters

Primary Lead Smelters

Wet-Process Phosphoric Acid Plants

Diammonium Phosphate Plants

Granular Triple Superphosphate Storage Facilities

Ferroalloy Production Facilities

Kraft Pulp Mills

Grain Elevators

Stationary Gas Turbines

Lead Acid Battery Manufacturing Plants

Phosphate Rock Plants

Ammonium Sulfate Manufacture

Industrial Surface Coating: Large Appliances

Asphalt Processing and Asphalt Roofing Manufacture

Pressure Sensitive Tape and Label Surface Coating Operations

Beverage Can Surface Coating Industry

Bulk Gasoline Terminals

Synthetic Fiber Production Facilities

Equipment Leaks of Volatile Organic Compounds from Onshore Natural Gas Processing Plants

Electric Utility Steam Generating Units

Portland Cement Plants

Sulfuric Acid Plants

Petroleum Refineries

Secondary Lead Smelters

Iron and Steel Plants

Sewage Treatment Plants

Primary Zinc Smelters

Primary Aluminum Reduction Plants

Superphosphoric Acid Plants

Triple Superphosphate Plants

Coal Preparation Plants

Steel Plants: Electric Arc Furnaces

Glass Manufacturing Plants

Surface Coating of Metal Furniture

Lime Manufacturing Plants

Automobile and Light-Duty Truck Surface Coating Operations

Graphic Arts Industry: Publication Rotogravure Printing

Metal Coil Surface Coating

Equipment Leaks of Volatile Organic Compounds in the Synthetic Organic Chemicals Manufacturing Industry

Flexible Vinyl and Urethane Coating and Printing

Petroleum Dry Cleaners

Wool Fiberglass Insulation Manufacturing Plants

Each standard consists of sections that give (1) definitions of the category and the date after which a facility is considered "new," (2) definitions of terms used in the standard, (3) the emissions limits for one or more pollutants, (4) rules for monitoring operations, and (5) test methods and procedures to be used in collecting and analyzing emission samples. For example, the Standards of Performance for Surface Coating of Metal Furniture applies to facilities that apply organic coatings to metal furniture and began construction, modification, or reconstruction after November 28, 1980; the Standard also limits the discharge of Volatile Organic Compounds into the atmosphere to a maximum of 0.90 kilograms per liter of coating solids applied.

National Emission Standards for Hazardous Air Pollutants

The Clean Air Act requires the EPA administrator to identify and establish emission standards for those pollutants not covered by ambient air quality standards and "which may reasonably be anticipated to result in an increase in mortality or an increase in serious irreversible, or incapacitating reversible, illness." As of mid-1986 standards had been issued for arsenic, asbestos, benzene, beryllium, beryllium rocket motor firing, mercury, radionuclides, and vinyl chloride. These standards, which apply to both new and existing sources, are couched not only in terms of emission concentrations—such as a limit of 10 parts per million for vinyl chloride in exhaust gases—but also in nonnumerical terms such as "no visible emissions to the outside air" for asbestos mills. The benzene standard is primarily an *equipment standard* which requires that benzene facilities have certain mechanical features, such as double seals on pumps and compressors and closed-loop sampling systems.

Four Regulatory Techniques That Offer More Flexibility: Bubbles, Banking, Offsets, and Netting

By now you can see that the foregoing set of regulations and laws is complex, overlapping, and highly restrictive. Concerned that its rules for industrial expansion might be so rigid as to eliminate it altogether, the EPA adopted a set of regulatory techniques to offer manufacturers more flexibility in expansion requirements. These approaches are succinctly summed up in the following excerpt from *13th Annual Report of the Council on Environmental Quality* (Washington, D.C.: U.S. Government Printing Office, p. 8):

> EPA's emissions trading policy incorporates four . . . regulatory mechanisms, all of which take advantage of market incentives to reduce air emissions at the lowest possible cost. First, EPA's bubble policy allows existing plants, or groups of plants, to be excused from imposing controls on one or more emissions sources in exchange for compensating controls on other, less costly to control, sources. Second, the netting policy excuses plants from new source review requirements usually required when they expand or modernize, if any increase in plant-wide emissions is insignificant. Third, under EPA's emissions offset policy new or modified sources in nonattainment areas may be required to secure surplus emissions restrictions which more than offset

increased emissions, thus allowing industrial growth while improving air quality. Fourth, the emissions banking policy lets firms store up emissions reductions for later use in bubble, netting, or offset transactions, or for sale to other firms that cannot achieve the same level of reductions as cheaply.

These trade-off regulations are controversial, and may undergo changes as administrations come and go in the federal government, Congress amends the law, or court challenges are mounted. In one such case, the Supreme Court has upheld EPA's "bubble" concept, which allows a plant (or group of plants, in some situations) to be regarded as having a canopy over it, with only one emission vent going to the atmosphere. If the plant installs a new source under the canopy but reduces the emissions from another source by an equivalent amount, there is no net increase to the atmosphere from the bubble and the new source may not have to go through all the approval steps otherwise required.

Five Key Types of Equipment for Controlling Air Emissions

With more than two decades of stringent air pollution control requirements behind it, industry has developed and adapted a variety of devices. These are the main types you may encounter:

1. Air filters. Usually employed in the form of "bag-houses"—large chambers formed by a steel framework and lined with cloth fabric. As air flows into the chamber and through the fabric, particulate matter is filtered out. The collected dust on the fabric has to be removed periodically.

2. Scrubbers. Rectangular chambers or cylindrical towers in which the air stream, moving vertically upward, is subjected to a water spray that removes particulates and soluble gases. A chemical solution may also be used as the spray fluid; for example, a caustic soda solution may be used which will neutralize the acid formed when sulfur dioxide is dissolved in water. A variation of the scrubber is the *packed tower,* which is filled with ceramic spheres (or other shapes); as the scrubbing fluid flows down over the spheres, it achieves better contact with the air stream flowing up through the spaces between them.

3. Cyclones. The cyclone is a cylindrical vessel with a conical bottom. Particulate-laden air enters the vessel tangentially and is given a swirling motion; the particles are thrown by centrifugal force against the wall of the cyclone and drop out through the bottom cone, while the cleaned air is discharged out the top.

4. Electrostatic precipitators. Used to remove particulates, this device causes the particles to pick up an electrical charge by subjecting them to an electrical field; the air is then passed between flat metal plates with an opposite electrical charge. The particles are held on the plates and the cleaned air passes on. When the plates become fully loaded, the unit must be shut down and cleaned.

5. Adsorption beds. Air containing hydrocarbons or chemicals with obnoxious odors is passed through an adsorbing bed, often consisting of activated charcoal. The organic chemicals are adsorbed on the surface of the carbon particles, sometimes in quantities that can be recovered.

MAJOR ASPECTS OF WATER POLLUTION CONTROL

Controlling water pollution should be a more straightforward operation for the plant manager. The requirement to obtain a permit for discharge is as old as the Rivers and Harbors Act of 1899, and is a more familiar and widely understood procedure than those for air discharge. And, although it may be difficult to reach, the ultimate national goal—elimination of *all* water pollutants—could not be any clearer. There are, however, similarities between the air and water programs—federal laws and EPA regulations set the goals and standards but encourage the states to take as much of the responsibility as they are willing or able to; there is a division between general and hazardous pollutants; and there are sets of regulations applicable to specific industries. In this section we will examine some of the major elements of the water pollution control program.

Types of Pollutants

In 40 CFR 122.2 the EPA defines "pollutant" to mean dredged spoil, solid waste, incinerator residue, filter backwash, sewage, garbage, sewage sludge, munitions, chemical wastes, biological materials, radioactive materials (unless regulated under the Atomic Energy Act), heat, wrecked or discarded equipment, rock, sand, cellar dirt, and industrial, municipal, and agricultural waste discharged into water. Various sections of the law also require EPA to set up certain classes and lists of pollutants. These are the main categories:

A. Conventional Pollutants

1. Biochemical Oxygen Demand (BOD). An indicator of the amount of organic chemical and biologic material in the effluent which can be consumed by bacteria in the receiving stream. It is a measure of the amount of oxygen the bacteria need to consume the organic pollution.

2. Total suspended solids (nonfilterable). The amount of undissolved, suspended material in the effluent stream.

3. pH. A measure of the acidity or alkalinity of the effluent. The pH scale ranges from 0 to 14; when the pH is at 7, the solution is neither acid nor alkaline but neutral. As pH decreases from 7 toward 0, the solution becomes more acidic; as it increases from 7 toward 14, it becomes more alkaline. (A more technical definition of pH: It is the negative logarithm of the hydrogen ion concentration.)

4. Fecal coliform. Bacteria found in the feces of man and animals, or similar

bacteria. Usually reported as the number of bacteria per 100 milliliters of effluent.

5. Oil and grease.

B. Toxic Pollutants

The Clean Water Act itself contains a list of toxic pollutants but instructs the EPA administrator to amend the list as he sees fit. As of July 1, 1983, the following 65 substances were on the list (from 40 CFR 401.15):

1. Acenaphthene
2. Acrolein
3. Acrylonitrile
4. Aldrin/Dieldrin
5. Antimony and compounds
6. Arsenic and compounds
7. Asbestos
8. Benzene
9. Benzidine
10. Beryllium and compounds
11. Cadmium and compounds
12. Carbon tetrachloride
13. Chlordane (technical mixture metabolites)
14. Chlorinated benzenes (other than dichlorobenzenes)
15. Chlorinated ethanes (including 1,2-dichloroethane, 1,1,1-trichloroethane, and hexachloroethane)
16. Chloroalkyl ethers (chloroethyl and mixed ethers)
17. Chlorinated naphthalene
18. Chlorinated phenols (other than those listed elsewhere; includes trichlorophenols and chlorinated cresols)
19. Chloroform
20. 2-chlorophenol
21. Chromium and compounds
22. Copper and compounds
23. Cyanides
24. DDT and metabolites
25. Dichlorobenzenes (1,2-, 1,3-, and 1,4-dichlorobenzenes)
26. Dichlorobenzidine
27. Dichloroethylenes (1,1-, and 1,2-dichloroethylene)
28. 2,4-dichlorophenol
29. Dichloropropane and dichloropropene
30. 2,4-dimethylphenol
31. Dinitrotoluene
32. Diphenylhydrazine
33. Endosulfan and metabolites
34. Endrin and metabolites
35. Ethylbenzene
36. Fluoranthene
37. Haloethers (other than those listed elsewhere; includes chlorophenylphenyl ethers, bromophenylphenyl ether, bis-(dichloroisopropyl) ether, bis-(chloroethoxy) methane and polychlorinated diphenyl ethers)
38. Halomethanes (other than those listed elsewhere; includes methylene chloride, methylchloride, methylbromide, bromoform, dichlorobromo-methane
39. Heptachlor and metabolites
40. Hexachlorobutadiene

41. Hexachlorocyclohexane	55. Polynuclear aromatic hydrocarbons (including benzanthracenes, benzopyrenes, benzofluoranthene, chrysenes, dibenzanthracenes, and indenopyrenes)
42. Hexachlorocyclopentadiene	
43. Isophorone	
44. Lead and compounds	
45. Mercury and compounds	
46. Naphthalene	56. Selenium and compounds
47. Nickel and compounds	57. Silver and compounds
48. Nitrobenzene	58. 2,3,7,8-tetrachlorodibenzo-p-dioxin (TCDD)
49. Nitrophenols (including 2,4-dinitrophenol, dinitrocresol)	
50. Nitrosamines	59. Tetrachloroethylene
51. Pentachlorophenol	60. Thallium and compounds
52. Phenol	61. Toluene
53. Phthalate esters	62. Toxaphene
54. Polychlorinated biphenyls (PCBs)	63. Trichloroethylene
	64. Vinyl chloride
	65. Zinc and compounds

"Compounds" includes both organic and inorganic compounds.

C. Hazardous Substances

The Act requires the administrator to establish a list of substances which when discharged in any quantity would present a danger to public health or welfare, including fish, shellfish, wildlife, shorelines, and beaches. In 40 CFR 116.4 the administrator designates some 300 compounds and classes of compounds as hazardous, and in 40 CFR 117 sets the "reportable quantities," the amounts which when discharged must be reported to authorities. On this list are such materials as acetaldehyde, ammonia, amyl acetate, aniline, arsenic trioxide, benzene, carbon tetrachloride, chlordane, chlorine, cresol, 2,4-D acid and ester, diazinon, ethylene dibromide, ferric sulfate, formaldehyde, hydrochloric acid, isoprene, lindane, naphthalene, nitric acid, phenol, phosphoric acid, potassium hydroxide, resorcinol, sodium hydroxide, styrene, sulfuric acid, toluene, xylene, zinc chloride, and many others. Some materials are on both this and the toxic pollutant list.

D. Nonconventional Pollutants

All those pollutants not included in any other category belong here. Examples are nitrogen, ammonia, phosphorus, sulfides, total organic carbon, and chemical oxygen demand.

National Pollutant Discharge Elimination System (NPDES)

The Clean Water Act makes the discharge of any pollutant by any person unlawful, except as provided for in the Act under permits issued by the EPA administrator or by those states with qualifying pollution control programs to which authority has been delegated. The Act also sets up the National Pollutant Discharge Elimination System, usually referred to as NPDES, which establishes the mechanism and basic requirements for issuing permits. The steps involved in obtaining a permit will be discussed in a subsequent section; this section will examine the various technology designations used in NPDES permits.

The permit will specify effluent quality limitations that are developed in one of two ways: (1) They may be based on one or more technologies that the EPA believes achieves the highest degree of control, or (2) where the EPA determines that it is necessary to protect a designated use of the receiving water. When EPA issues a technology-based permit, it severely limits the choices of the discharger, since only a small number of technologies may meet the standards. The technology designations are not precisely defined in the CFR, and presumably will change as improvements are made; these are the categories mentioned in the Code:

1. Conventional pollutants. Effluent limitations will be based on the Best Conventional Pollutant Control Technology (BCT), which was to be achieved by all industrial direct dischargers by July 1, 1984.

2. Toxic pollutants. Effluent limitations based on the Best Available Technology Economically Achievable (BAT) were to be imposed in all permits by July 1, 1984. However, if the toxic pollutant was not on the original list accompanying the Clean Water Act amendments of 1977 (but added later by the administrator), the deadline for achieving BAT is extended to three years from the date the effluent limitation was first incorporated into the permit.

3. Nonconventional pollutants. Effluent limitations based on BAT, to be achieved within three years of the date first incorporated into the permit but no later than July 1, 1987, in any case.

4. Best Management Practices (BMPs). For those plants that handle toxic pollutants, BMPs are specified to prevent pollution from surface run-off, spills, leaks, drainage from raw material storage, and sludge or waste disposal. BMPs consist of operating, maintenance, and management practices installed to prevent pollution from those sources.

Best Practicable Control Technology (BPT) is an older, less stringent control which was replaced by BAT and BCT.

Certain economic, water quality related, and thermal variances from the technology-based treatment requirements may be granted under the Act and are described in 40 CFR 125, Subparts E, F, G, and H.

EPA Effluent Guidelines

EPA is required by the Act to publish regulations providing guidelines for effluent limitations and to revise them periodically in the light of the latest scientific knowledge and available technology. EPA has done this in 40 CFR 400-424 for the following industrial point source categories:

Dairy products

Canned and preserved seafood processing

Cement manufacturing

Inorganic chemicals manufacturing

Fertilizer manufacturing

Nonferrous metals manufacturing

Ferroalloy manufacturing

Leather tanning

Rubber manufacturing

The Builders' Paper and Board Mills

Coal mining

Pharmaceutical manufacturing

Paint formulating

Pesticide chemicals

Photographic

Plastics molding and forming

Aluminum forming

Grain mills

Sugar processing

Feedlots

Electroplating

Plastics and synthetics

Petroleum refining

Phosphate manufacturing

Glass manufacturing

Timber products processing

Meat products

Oil and gas extraction

Ore mining and dressing

Ink formulating

Explosives manufacturing

Hospital

Coil coating

Copper forming

Canned and preserved fruits and vegetables processing

Textile mills

Organic chemicals manufacturing

Soap and detergent manufacturing

Iron and steel manufacturing

Steam electric power generating

Asbestos manufacturing

Pulp, paper and paperboard

Metal finishing

Mineral mining

Paving and roofing materials

Gum and wood chemicals

Carbon black

Battery manufacturing

Porcelain enameling

Electrical and electronic components

These "guidelines" (which are really regulations) set out for each industry a list of the pollutants to be controlled, showing for each the amount that may be discharged (1) in any one day, and (2) as an average of daily values for 30 consecutive days. For each industry subcategory the limitations under BPT are shown first, followed by the limitations under BAT. Finally, a stricter set of limits is given as New Source Performance Standards. These standards apply to sources that begin construction after the publishing of proposed regulations by EPA for that type of source. In return for meeting the more stringent standard, the new source discharger is protected with certain exceptions from the imposition of any more stringent standards for a period of ten years (see 40 CFR 122.29).

The guidelines also regulate the pretreatment of wastes that are discharged into a Publicly Owned Treatment Works (POTW). For each of the industrial categories mentioned, limits are not only placed on particular pollutants but the discharger is required to meet a set of general requirements laid down in 40 CFR 403. The thrust of the general regulations is to prohibit discharges that interfere either with the operation of a POTW or its ability to meet its own permit requirements and those that "pass through" POTWs and pollute the receiving waters. Specifically prohibited by this section are pollutants that create a fire or explosion hazard in the POTW, cause corrosive structural damage, are solid or viscous enough to obstruct flow, or are hot enough to inhibit biological activity. Dilution of the waste stream as a substitute for treatment is also prohibited.

A special set of effluent standards is set out in 40 CFR 129 for certain toxic pollutants—aldrin/dieldrin, DDT, polychlorinated biphenyls (PCBs), endrin, toxaphene, and benzidine. No discharges of the first three are permitted, and numerical limits are set for discharges by manufacturers of the last three.

Finally, in 40 CFR 403, Appendix D, are listed some 160 subcategories of various industries whose discharges into POTWs are exempted from regulation because the levels of pollution coming from their operations are too small to be of concern.

Five Important Questions to Consider When Obtaining and Holding a Discharge Permit

There are five major questions you should consider in the process:

1. Where to apply? You may have to apply to your state agency, since the EPA has delegated its permit authority to 35 states. To find out if your state issues permits, contact the regional EPA office; if your state does not have permit authority, you will have to apply there anyway. Even when authority is delegated to the states, the EPA retains the upper hand by requiring the state to forward a copy of every permit application, draft permit it proposes to issue, or final permit it has issued. If the EPA feels that the permit conditions do not meet its regulations, it may order a change.

2. Who applies and who signs? Anyone who discharges or proposes to discharge must obtain a permit. If the owner and operator of the facility are not the same, the operator must apply. The permit must be signed by the proprietor, general partner, or principal executive officer (of at least the level of vice-president).

3. What information is required? Complete identification of the facility and its operator; a list of all other environmental permits applied for or held; a description of the business and the activities that require it to apply for a permit; a topographic map of the area; a line drawing of the water flow and mass balances through the facility; average and intermittent flow rates; location of outfall; and characteristics of the effluent, including analyses, a list of the toxic pollutants used or expected to be used, and any other information which may reasonably be requested. If the applicant is a small business—averaging less than $100,000 annual sales—it may be exempt from supplying certain of the analytical data mentioned. New sources must apply before beginning construction. (For a more complete listing of information requirements see 40 CFR 122.21.) If the application is for a new source *and* the EPA itself is the issuing authority, the law may require EPA to prepare an environmental impact statement.

4. What must I do to keep the permit? Comply with all of its conditions. Violations can result in civil penalties of up to $100,000 per day and criminal penalties of up to $25,000 per day and/or a year in jail. Other duties are to reapply before the permit expires; halt or reduce plant activity if needed to stay in compliance; mitigate any adverse impact on the environment resulting from noncompliance; properly operate and maintain all systems for control and treatment; provide information as requested, and allow authorities to enter the premises, take samples, inspect and copy records; monitor conditions by taking samples and measurements and keeping records of these activities; submit regular reports of monitoring activities and special reports of any actual or anticipated noncompliance, including a report within 24 hours of any noncompliance that may endanger health or the environment. A permit may be revoked or modified for cause and is not transferable without notice to the regional director.

5. How long is the permit good for? The maximum term is five years, but it may be issued for a shorter period.

Some additional notes: If you wish to claim any information submitted to the EPA as confidential, stamp each page containing such information with the words "confidential business information." Confidentiality will not be extended to the identity of the applicant/permittee, the permit application, the permit itself, and effluent data.

Applicants for permits may request variances from effluent limitations for a limited variety of reasons, spelled out in 40 CFR 122.21(1).

Public hearings may be held after a draft permit has been prepared. The regional director may schedule such hearings when requested or when he feels that it is necessary to clarify issues involved in the permit decision.

Although separate applications must be submitted for permits under the various air, water, and solid waste programs, they may be consolidated for processing by the issuing authority if they all apply to the same facility or activity.

Underground Injection Control Program

This program was undertaken by EPA to carry out certain provisions of the Safe Drinking Water Act and the Resource Conservation and Recovery Act, and its regulations are set out in 40 CFR 144-149. It is designed to protect aquifers that are or may be underground sources of drinking water by regulating injection wells that may be drilled in or near them.

Any underground injection is prohibited unless authorized by permit (obtained by a procedure similar to that described in the preceding section) or allowed under rules stated in 40 CFR 144.21-144.28. The regulations classify injection wells as follows: Class I—Industrial and municipal disposal wells and wells used to inject hazardous wastes *below* the lowermost formations containing, within one-quarter mile of the well bore, an underground source of drinking water; Class II—Wells for the reinjection of fluids from oil or gas production, for enhanced recovery of oil and gas or for storage of hydrocarbons; Class III—Injection wells for extraction of minerals such as sulfur, uranium, or potash; Class IV—Wells used for disposal of hazardous or radioactive waste by injection *into* or *above* a formation that contains an underground source of drinking water within one quarter of a mile; Class V—Injection wells not included in the other classes. See 40 CFR 144.6 for an elaboration of these definitions.

Operators of injection wells are forbidden to take any action that allows the movement of fluids that contain contaminants into an underground source of drinking water. In addition to setting up the permit system and establishing the requirements for state programs, the regulations set the standards for construction, operation, monitoring, and reporting of each class of injection well.

Oil Pollution Prevention

Owners and operators of facilities for the production, distribution, or consumption of oil or oil products located where they might discharge into the navigable waters of the United States come under the regulations for oil spill prevention and countermeasures spelled out in 40 CFR Parts 112–114. Exempted are facilities subject to the regulations of the Department of Transportation or those that have underground storage capacity of no more than 42,000 gallons and aboveground storage capacity of no more than 1,320 gallons of oil in units no larger than 660 gallons. The thrust of the regulations is to require owner/operators to prepare a Spill Prevention Control and Countermeasure Plan, have it certified by a registered professional engineer, and keep it available at the site for review by the regional administrator during normal working hours. At a minimum, each plan should identify equipment with a potential for failure and predict the direction, rate of flow, and quantity of oil that could be discharged as a result of such failure; and for both onshore and offshore facilities describe the containment or diversionary structures used to prevent oil from reaching the watercourse. When it is determined that the installation of such structures is not practicable, the plan must contain oil spill contingency provisions (such as those of 40 CFR 109) and a written commitment of the manpower, equipment, and materials required to control and remove any harmful quantities of oil discharged. Further guidelines are established for facility drainage; bulk tanks; transfer, pumping, and in-plant process; tank car and truck loading and unloading; onshore and offshore oil production and transfer operations; onshore and offshore oil drilling and workover facilities; and personnel, training, and spill prevention procedures (40 CFR 112.7). These regulations require the reporting of any oil discharges that occur twice in one year and violate water quality standards or cause discoloration of the surface or deposition of a sludge or emulsion beneath the surface or on the shoreline. A single spill of more than 1,000 gallons also must be reported.

Violation of these regulations can bring a civil penalty of up to $5,000 per day. The government is authorized to clean up a spill and charge the cost to the owner or operator. If the spill resulted from willful negligence or misconduct, the government can charge the entire cost. Otherwise, there is a liability limit of $50,000,000. Acts of God, war, a third party, or negligence of the United States government are excluded. Lower limits of liability for smaller onshore facilities are prescribed; they range from $4,000 to $200,000 for aboveground storage capacities of 10 to 1,000 barrels and $5,200 to $260,000 for belowground capacities of 10 to 1,000 barrels.

Methods and Equipment for Controlling Water Pollution

The equipment, methods, and levels of treatment for water pollution are more varied and complex than those for air. These are some of the highlights:

Revise the plant process. The best treatment method of all is to revise the plant process to keep the waste out of the effluent stream. The value of the recovered material can be subtracted from the capital and operating costs of effluent treatment to create an economic offset as well as a side benefit of eliminating some of the plant's regulatory burdens. Keep in mind that many of the treatments described here only concentrate the wastes and remove them from the water; they must still be disposed of by some other means, such as incineration or burial in a sanitary landfill.

Levels of treatment. Water treatment processes are classified by the degree of pollutant removal they achieve and their complexity:

- *Primary treatment* may consist of little more than allowing suspended solids to settle out in a tank or pond, or skimming oil and grease off the surface.

- *Secondary treatment* takes the effluent from a primary treatment facility through additional purification steps; for example, adding chemicals to precipitate dissolved solids and removing the solids in a clarifier or thickener.

- *Tertiary treatment* would involve taking the process one step further, such as putting the secondary effluent through a filter for final removal of solids, or passing a toxic waste stream through a carbon adsorption bed to remove all but the very small amounts of toxic pollutants allowed by the permit.

Types of treatment. Water treatment processes are also classified by the nature of the operation carried out—physical, chemical, or biological:

- *Physical methods* include flotation, settling, clarifying, thickening, screening, filtration, adsorption, and solvent extraction.

- *Chemical methods* include oxidation, acid and alkali neutralization, ion exchange, coagulation and precipitation by the addition of chemical agents, membrane processes (reverse osmosis), and incineration.

- *Biological methods*, which include treatment with *aerobic bacteria* (which function in the presence of oxygen) and *anaerobic bacteria* (which function in the absence of oxygen). The bacteria, in the form of a biomass or activated sludge (see following) act upon dissolved pollutants, either causing them to precipitate in solid form or converting them to more stable compounds that may be less polluting or readily removed in another treatment step. *Facultative organisms* are those that can function with or without oxygen present. The term *facultative system* may also be applied to a treatment method in which an anaerobic first step is followed by an aerobic process.

Systems and equipment. These are the main types:

1. *Lagoons.* Shallow ponds dug in the earth and sized so that the retention time of wastewater flowing through them may range from hours to weeks. Used

as settling ponds and for both aerobic and anaerobic biological treatment. May have aeration equipment to maintain dissolved oxygen levels.

2. *Activated Sludge.* Probably the most frequently used wastewater treatment method. A biomass of bacteria first contacts the wastewater in a mixing/aeration tank; air or oxygen is piped in to support the process. The wastewater containing the precipitated pollutants is then pumped to a sedimentation tank where the sludge is allowed to settle out while the treated water overflows to a sewer or outfall. The sludge is sent to filters, thickeners, or centrifuges for concentration and is finally disposed of in a landfill or by incineration.

3. *Clarifiers and thickeners.* Similar devices for concentrating suspended solids, thereby producing a cleaner effluent. These are large-diameter, relatively shallow cylindrical tanks with conical bottoms and fitted with a rotating scraper arm. The solids concentrate at the bottom of the cone and are removed; the clarified effluent discharges through an overflow at the top. Clarifiers handle more dilute suspensions and are built somewhat lighter than thickeners.

4. *Filters.* Devices that remove a much higher percentage of suspended solids than clarifiers or thickeners by passing the wastewater through a *filter medium*—usually a cloth or fine-mesh metal screen. In *plate and frame filters* the filter medium is stretched over a metal frame and a number of frames are combined in a machine so that wastewater passes through them in parallel. When the cloths become caked with solids, flow is stopped, the machine opened, and the accumulated solids removed. In the *rotary vacuum filter* the filter cloth is mounted as the outer surface of a long cylindrical drum. As the drum is rotated while partially submerged in the wastewater, a vacuum is pulled on the interior of the drum, causing water to pass through the cloth while a cake of solids builds up on the outside. As the drum rotates, the cake is brought out of the water and scraped off; the cleaned cloth then goes back into the wastewater. In the *belt-press filter,* sludge is placed between two layers of filter cloth formed into a belt which passes between rollers. The water is squeezed out through the cloth and the filter cake mechanically removed.

RULES AND GUIDELINES FOR HANDLING SOLID/HAZARDOUS WASTES AND TOXIC SUBSTANCES

The three basic laws covering these topics—The Resource Conservation and Recovery Act of 1976 (replacing the Solid Waste Disposal Act); The Comprehensive Environmental Response, Compensation, and Liability Act of 1980 (Superfund); and the Toxic Substances Control Act—were outlined on pp. 249–250. This section reviews some of the rules set out by EPA in the Code of Federal Regulations to implement these laws, and provides some operating guidelines for plant managers in handling solid/hazardous wastes and toxic substances problems.

Solid Waste

Solid waste is defined in 40 CFR 257.2 as "garbage, refuse, sludge from a waste treatment plant, water supply treatment plant, or air pollution control facility and other discarded material, including solid, liquid, semisolid, or contained gaseous material resulting from industrial, commercial, mining, and agricultural operations, and from community activities . . ." Ultimately the solid waste generated by your plant is going to a waste dump, because even though you have compacted it, burned it to extract energy, or converted it chemically to reduce a hazard, you will still be left with a solid residue which must be disposed of. The waste dump may be on your plant site or it may be owned and operated by someone else. In either case it will be classed as an "open dump" or a "sanitary landfill," and the purpose of the rules in 40 CFR 240–271 is to eliminate open dumps. Yours is an open dump if it does any of the following (condensed from criteria in 40 CFR 257.3–1 through 8; see the original reference for details and definitions):

Obstructs floodplains	Contaminates underground drinking water sources
Pollutes surface water	
Distributes wastes containing cadmium or polychlorinated biphenyls (PCBs) on land used for growing food-chain crops	Places untreated sewage sludge or septic tank pumpings on agricultural land
Fails to minimize disease vectors	Burns solid waste in the open
Generates explosive gases	Creates a fire hazard
Threatens endangered species	Disposes of putrescible waste which may attract birds near an airport

Conversely, if your dump meets these criteria in a favorable way, it is classed as a sanitary landfill.

Most plants hire outside contractors to pick up and dispose of solid wastes, and the tendency is strong to forget the problem once those arrangements are made. Plant managers should, at least, apply these operating techniques: (1) Keep wastes such as paper, trash, food, and process wastes segregated at their points of origin. If they are allowed to be mixed, costly labor and equipment may be required to separate them later. (2) Look for manufacturing wastes that can be recycled back into the process. If the capital and operating costs of recycling are less than those of disposal, savings can be enjoyed for a very long time—as long as the process itself lasts. (3) Examine the solid waste stream for materials that can be sold or given to others for disposal at no cost. (4) Examine the outgoing waste personally from time to time; it probably contains some surprises.

Hazardous Waste

A solid waste is classed as hazardous if it has measurable, detectable characteristics of ignitability, corrosivity, reactivity, or toxicity, and the EPA administrator finds that it may cause an increase in mortality or serious illness, or that it poses a hazard to human health or the environment if improperly handled; all as defined in 40 CFR 261.10–261.24. A waste is also hazardous if it is one of the more than 750 materials included on three lists set out in 40 CFR 261.31–261.33. These lists classify hazardous wastes as (1) those from specific sources, such as spent pickle liquor from steel finishing operations; (2) those from nonspecific sources, such as spent solvents from degreasing operations; and (3) individual chemicals that are discarded, off-spec material, or residues from containers or spills. Be sure to monitor these lists, either through the *Federal Register* or the annual editions of the CFR, since EPA adds new items to them from time to time.

If you are a generator of hazardous wastes, you must meet the standards set out in 40 CFR 262. The first step is to determine whether or not your waste is hazardous; if it is not on the lists mentioned earlier, you may still have to test it or apply knowledge of its characteristics to see if it meets the general criteria of 40 CFR 261.20–261.24 (ignitability, reactivity, corrosivity, or toxicity). Then check to see whether you qualify for any of several possible exemptions, including that of small generator (less than 1,000 kilograms per year, provided the waste is treated or disposed of acceptably). If it is a hazardous waste, you must apply to the EPA on Form 8700-12 for an identification number before treating, storing, disposing of, transporting, or offering it for transportation.

Most plant operators prefer to send their hazardous wastes to off-site disposal facilities owned by others. If, however, you decide to operate a treatment, storage, or disposal facility of your own, you must meet the standards of 40 CFR 264, which deal with such administrative matters as financial requirements, record-keeping and reporting, preparedness and prevention, and contingency plans and emergency procedures; and with such technical and operating concerns as ground-water protections, closure and post-closure, and use and management of containers, tanks, surface impoundments, waste piles, land treatment and landfills, and incinerators. Even if you do not intend to operate a waste facility, you could inadvertently become subject to these standards if you accumulate hazardous waste for more than 90 days without an extension granted by the regional administrator. Owners and operators of hazardous waste facilities must obtain permits as outlined in 40 CFR 270.

If you send out your hazardous waste for treatment or disposal by others, you must meet the standards for generators as set out in 40 CFR 262. After determining that your waste is classified as hazardous and obtaining an identification number from EPA, you must set about packaging, labelling, and marking the shipment, and placarding the vehicle that carries it, according to the requirements of the Department of Transportation regulations in 49 CFR 172, 173, 178, and 179. Before shipment takes place, you must prepare a manifest in a sufficient number of copies to provide one for yourself, one for each transporter, one for the owner or operator of the treatment/disposal facility, and another to be returned to you by the facility. The manifest must show (1) a document number; (2) your name, address, phone number, and EPA identification number; (3) the name and EPA ID number of each transporter; (4) name, address, and EPA ID number of the disposal facility to which the waste is being sent and any alternate facility which might be designated; (5) description of the wastes as required by DOT regulations in 49 CFR 172.101 and 172.202–203; and (6) the total quantity of each waste, with the number and types of containers in which it is shipped. As the generator of the hazardous waste, you must also place a certificate on the manifest and sign it by hand, stating that the wastes are properly classified, described, packaged, marked and labeled, and are in proper condition for shipment according to EPA and DOT regulations. You must also obtain the written signature of the initial transporter and the date of his acceptance of the shipment.

There are record-keeping and reporting obligations as well. You must keep copies of the manifests for three years from the date of receipt at the disposal facility, plus the results of any tests or analyses. The three-year term is extended automatically at the request of the EPA administrator or if there is any unresolved enforcement action. By March 1 of every even-numbered year you must submit a biennial report to the regional administrator of all waste shipment activity on EPA Form 8700-13A.

Hazardous Waste Treatment

In the spectrum of possible treatments of hazardous wastes, physical methods are used primarily for volume reduction and separation, and the most widely used are adsorption, distillation, filtration, flotation, sedimentation, and solar evaporation. Among chemical treatments, precipitation is the most widely used process for volume reduction and separation, while neutralization is most often selected for detoxification. Of the thermal treatments, incineration is the most widely used to accomplish detoxification and volume reduction. Biological treatments are used for detoxification, and among them activated sludge and waste stabilization ponds are favored.

Superfund Responsibilities

If you dispose of hazardous wastes off site it is important to choose contractors very carefully, because the Superfund law confers "joint and several" liability on all three participants in the waste disposal chain—the generator, transporter, and owner/operator of the disposal facility. Even though you, as the generator, thought you had contracted away responsibility for these wastes after they left the plant, you may still be held liable for cleanup costs for release of such materials while in the hands of the other two participants, especially if they cannot be found or cannot pay.

The Comprehensive Environmental Response, Compensation, and Liability Act of 1980 (CERCLA) requires the setting up of a National Oil and Hazardous Substances Contingency Plan, and EPA sets out the regulations implementing it in 40 CFR 300. The plan is intended to cover releases, or substantial threats of releases, of hazardous substances, pollutants, or contaminants that may present imminent and substantial danger to public health or welfare. Much of the plan deals with the coordination of effort and division of responsibilities among state and federal agencies, especially the EPA and the U.S. Coast Guard. It sets up such entities as the National Response Center (NRC) at the headquarters of the Coast Guard in Washington, D.C.; a National Response Team headquartered in Edison, New Jersey; and the On-Scene Coordinator—an EPA, Coast Guard, or state official who directs federal responses under the plan. Although 40 CFR Part 300 deals with a number of important aspects of organization and operational methods, this discussion will be limited to your company's involvement as the source of a release.

Oil Discharges

If your plant is the source of an oil discharge, you must notify the NRC immediately at Coast Guard Headquarters, Washington, D.C. (telephone 202-426-2675, as of February 1987); notification also may be made by government agencies or the public. The NRC will notify the On-Scene Coordinator, who will assess the situation, and if your plant is found to be the source of the discharge, will decide if you are taking proper removal action. If so, the authorities will simply continue to monitor the progress of removal. If not and an immediate effort must be made to stop the pollution, you will be notified as to what action by you will be considered appropriate. If you do not "properly respond," you will be notified of your potential liability, which may include all costs of removal by others, the cost of assessing and restoring damaged natural resources, and the costs of a federal response.

Hazardous Substances

The same notification requirements apply if your facility discharges hazardous substances in "reportable quantities" (see Part C, Hazardous Substances, in the section on *Major Aspects of Water Pollution Control* of this chapter). Again, an assessment will be made as to whether immediate removal is necessary to control the release and mitigate its effects on health, public welfare, or the environment. This assessment includes determining whether there is a nonfederal party ready, willing, and able to undertake a proper response. If there is no such party and the release endangers human life or health or the environment, federal agencies may begin *immediate action* to control it; immediate action cannot, by law, continue for longer than six months or after the expenditure of $1 million. If an expedited but not necessarily immediate response is required, *planned removal* is undertaken. Planned removal must be requested by the governor of the state in which the release occurs, and the state must be willing to contribute 10 percent of the cost. *Remedial action* consists of steps taken to minimize permanently or prevent the release of hazardous substances into the environment. Remedial action is often involved with control of releases from the most dangerous sites; that is, the some 900 uncontrolled waste dumps on the National Priority List. Federal officials or those officials from states that have contracts with the federal government may use the Superfund to accomplish control of such releases, but they must collect and maintain documentation identifying the responsible parties and providing the necessary information to seek cost recovery from them. The law "limits" the liability of plant owners to the total of all costs of response to control a release *plus* $50 million for any damages!

Toxic Substances Control Act

Anyone who plans to manufacture or import a new chemical substance for commercial purposes in the United States must notify the EPA on Form 7710-25. A copy of this form appears as Appendix A to 40 CFR 720. The administrator may limit or prohibit the manufacture, processing, distribution in commerce, use, or disposal of new chemicals if there is insufficient data upon which to judge their safety until such data is developed. The administrator may not only take these actions against new chemicals but also against existing ones if they present an unreasonable risk of injury to health or the environment. Those who plan to export chemicals that are subject to the rules promulgated under the Act also must notify EPA under the requirements of 40 CFR 707; EPA will in turn notify the ambassador of the receiving country. EPA maintains an "inventory" list of over 60,000 chemicals in commerce in the United States, and those who plan to manufacture any chemical (not necessarily a new chemical) listed in 40 CFR 712.30 for the first time must also notify EPA. There are also reporting requirements for persons who have unpublished studies for a list of chemicals in 40 CFR 716.17 and for those who have information on any substance indicating that it presents a substantial risk to health or the environment.

There are some severe restrictions in the regulations on particular materials. In 40 CFR Part 761, there is virtually a total ban on the manufacture, processing, use, and distribution of polychlorinated biphenyls (PCBs—chemicals widely used in the past as electrical transformer oils). Container marking and record-keeping and reporting requirements are also given in this section. In Part 762 the use of fully halogenated fluoralkanes (some are sold under the trade name Freon) as aerosol propellants is prohibited, with certain exceptions. Part 763 imposes certain reporting requirements on persons who manufacture, mine, process, or import asbestos.

Ten Chemicals That Can Cause Long-Term Poisoning

Even though their primary business is not chemical manufacturing, most plants use chemicals in some way—if not as raw materials or intermediates, then as solvents, plating solutions, cleaning agents, pesticides, lubricants, surface coatings, and many more. If your plant is handling chemicals for any reason, it is important that you check the various lists of hazardous and toxic materials reproduced or referred to in both the OSHA and Environmental Protection sections of this chapter to see if they are hazardous, and to find out what regulations govern their use. As an example of the kinds of materials that are regarded as hazardous, ten "bad actors" are listed following; they tend to be insidious poisons—that is, exposure to low concentrations over long periods of time, without noticeable discomfort, can result in serious and lethal diseases such as blood and nervous system disorders, leukemia, and cancer:

acrylonitrile	cadmium
arsenic	isocyanates
asbestos	mercury
benzene	polychlorinated biphenyls
beryllium	vinyl chloride

All are regulated closely by OSHA or EPA, and if your plant is using any of them without strict controls, you should correct the situation immediately. Again, this list is only illustrative and is not intended to be an exhaustive tabulation of dangerous materials.

Economic Incentives for Controlling Pollution

At first it may seem that the cost of meeting environmental regulations is all expenditure with no financial return. That will be true in some cases, but there also will be many situations in which there will be economic returns that partly or even completely offset the investment and operating costs of the pollution controls. Here are some examples:

1. Conservation of material. If the pollutant is a raw material or intermediate or final product, then stopping losses to the environment usually means that the recovered material is cycled back into the process, and so its value is an offset to the cost of controls.

2. Conservation of energy. Materials lost as pollutants to the environment may be carrying heat or represent other investments of energy. If pollution control systems return these materials to the process, the cost of the energy in them is recovered.

3. Sale of recovered material. In those situations where the recovered pollutant cannot be returned to the process, it may nevertheless have a potential sale value, either as a raw material for another plant's process or as a neutralizing agent for someone else's wastes.

4. Development of saleable pollution control technology. This happens much more rarely, but there is a historical example. In the mid-1970s when stringent safety and environmental controls were proposed for one of the "bad actor" materials listed in the previous section, several companies predicted that they would have to close their U.S. plants because they would be too expensive to operate. After the U.S. Supreme Court upheld the regulations, one of the companies developed new technology so as to meet the requirements and keep its plants open; it now licenses the technology to plants all over the world, presumably at a profit.

Pollution Control and Public Relations

Over the last three decades the American voting public has made clear its demands for clean air and water and the reduction of industrial hazards to human health and wildlife. Companies that choose to oppose this trend—obeying the law only when and where it is enforced, becoming defensive about pollution traced to them, and maintaining a general air of truculence—are missing excellent opportunities to improve public relations.

Other companies take advantage of these opportunities by telling the public what they are doing in the way of installing pollution control systems and working toward the establishment of a "good neighbor" image for their plants. The results will be smoother relations with community authorities and the development of the plant's reputation as a good place to work, enabling it to attract the better workers in the region.

Another Precaution

The same caution advised at the end of the Occupational Safety and Health section applies here. The material presented here is intended to highlight some of the main items of interest to plant managers that is contained in the thousands of pages of law and regulation, and any legal interpretation of this material should be made with the help of qualified professionals.

PART III

Plant Facilities and Equipment

How to Operate More Reliable Mechanical, Electrical, and Process Equipment Systems

Much of any plant's equipment will be specific to the industry in which it operates; if your plant extrudes aluminum shapes, prints wallpaper, or molds plastic parts, you no doubt are using machinery unique to that industry. But some types of equipment are common to all or most manufacturing plants, and they are addressed in this chapter. In considering electrical, mechanical, fluid flow, process, heating, ventilating, and air conditioning equipment, let's deal first with some of the technical principles on which they are based and then move directly into their applications in the plant.

THE ELECTRICAL SYSTEM: HOW POWER IS RECEIVED, DISTRIBUTED, AND TRANSFORMED

From the Utility Lines

Utility companies transmit electric power at high voltages for two reasons, both of which are important as well to the transmission of power within the plant. The first is that in an electrical circuit:

$$\text{Power} = \text{Voltage} \times \text{Current}$$

Therefore, the higher the voltage, the lower the required amount of current to transmit a given amount of power. The second is that the amount of current that a wire can carry is roughly proportional to its cross-sectional area; the lower the current, the smaller the wire required to carry it. Summed up, higher voltages require less current which requires smaller wires, cutting the capital cost of the transmission installation. You can expect that the utility wires arriving at your plant boundary will be carrying voltages between 1,100 and 100,000 volts; 12,000 to 14,000 volts is a very common level.

The transmission line voltage is stepped down to lower levels for plant distribution by transformers which may be owned by the utility company, by the consumer, or they may be jointly owned. Plants with electrical systems rated at less than five million watts usually prefer to avoid the capital expense and maintenance costs of transformer ownership and favor ownership by the utility company. Plants with higher rated systems are likely to have distribution systems of their own requiring a number of transformers, and may find it more economical to own them rather than pay rental charges. The decision goes to the system which offers the lowest overall cost; to make it requires a working knowledge of what equipment the utility company will provide, rental charges and rebates, and allowances (if any) for transformer power losses.

Key Aspects of Industrial Transformers

Electricity is seldom generated at more than 20,000 volts, is mostly consumed at less than 600 volts, and yet is transmitted at levels ranging into the hundreds of thousands of volts. The job of stepping up the voltage at the generating plant and stepping it back down in the distribution system falls to the *transformer,* the most expensive device in the substation.

Construction of the transformer begins with an iron core, made up of rectangular sheets of steel with rectangular holes cut out of the center. The sheets are bolted together to form a laminated core. The alternating current wire whose voltage is to be changed is wrapped around one leg of the core to form a coil with a given number of turns; this coil which takes the incoming power is called the *primary.* The wire that is to carry the outgoing power is wrapped around the other leg of the core, to form a coil called the *secondary;* it will have a different number of turns. The alternating current in the primary coil will cause a magnetic flux in the core, which in turn induces a voltage in the secondary coil. The voltages in the two coils will have the same ratio as the number of turns in their windings. Thus, if it is desired to reduce the voltage from 2,000 to 200 and the primary winding has 1,500 turns, the secondary winding must have 150 turns. (To cut down internal energy losses, many industrial transformers have both coils wrapped around the same leg of the transformer.)

Here are some of the more important aspects of the design, application, and selection of industrial transformers:

Methods of connecting three-phase transformer coils. If the three coils of one side of a transformer are connected to a central point so as to (diagrammatically) radiate outward, this is called a Y (wye) connection. The phase wires are connected to the ends of the branches. If the coils are connected so as to form a triangle, it is called a delta (after the Greek letter Δ) connection. Other methods are the open delta or V, the T (tee), and a modification of it called the Scott connection. The remaining side of the transformer can be connected in the same or a different configuration. Figure 16–1 illustrates a transformer wired in delta connection on the primary side and in wye connection on the secondary side.

Y connections are used where it is desirable to have a fourth neutral wire. Delta connections are sometimes chosen because if the coils on one side of the triangle fail, the other two can operate as a V-connected system. All of the possible combinations are used—wye-wye, delta-delta, wye-delta, and delta-wye. The V connection allows a lower first cost because it requires only two sets of coils; later, when more power is required, the third coil can be added to complete a delta connection. The T connection also allows the handling of three-phase power with only two sets of coils. The Scott connection is used for transformation from a three-phase to a two-phase system.

Energy losses and dissipation of heat.   Of the power fed into the primary of an industrial transformer, only 95 to 99 percent is realized as output from the secondary. The missing power is converted into heat in the core and coils and must be dispersed. In *dry* type transformers the heat is carried away by the surrounding air, either by natural or forced convection; in *oil* type transformers the heat is transferred to mineral or synthetic oil in which the core and coils are immersed and then dissipated to the surrounding air through fins or tubes. Fluid-filled transformers are used for higher power ratings and voltages; the fluids used are selected for their electrical insulating properties as well as heat transfer.

Transformer ratings, installation, and special devices.   Transformers are rated in terms of kilovolt-amperes (kva), and those used for primary and secondary power distribution in industrial plants range from 50 to 50,000 kva. Dry types are usually used for indoor installations; above 15,000 volts, indoor transformers must be placed in a special vault, as must any indoor oil-filled unit. Outdoor units are set on concrete pads with wire enclosures to exclude all but authorized personnel.

As new electrical loads are added, the voltage in the secondary circuit may drop to unacceptably low levels. To avoid this, a series of two to six *taps* are provided on the primary side at voltage intervals of 2½ percent above and below the rated voltage. As new loads are added, connections are changed from tap to tap to maintain the nominal voltage. Larger transformers may have special devices to accomplish tap changes without disconnecting wires. Some transformers have internal high-voltage circuit breakers equipped with external operating handles.

Distribution Systems Within the Plant

The most commonly used electrical devices—lights, appliances, instruments, and motors—are rated at 110, 208, 220, 277, 440, and 550 volts. The distribution systems that supply these utilization voltages are usually designed to operate at slightly higher levels, such as 120, 240, and 480 volts. In-plant systems seek the same economies as long-distance transmission facilities: lowest capital cost resulting from the use of high voltages and low current. Large plants that distribute major quantities of electricity to different buildings scattered around the site often use intermediate voltages between the incoming primary and equipment utilization levels; 2,400 and 4,160 are typical values. Some limitations on maximum voltages are the ability of local maintenance forces to handle them, safety and building codes, and available voltage ratings on the larger pieces of electrical equipment.

These are the major equipment and design elements of the plant distribution systems:

Substation components. The typical substation consists of the incoming high-voltage power cables, a disconnect switch, a transformer, a bus bar to which the outgoing wires are connected, and one or more circuit breakers or fuses to protect the system against overload currents. In the simplest systems there is only one substation, and the incoming voltage from the utility company is reduced in one step to the voltage at which it will be used in the various load centers of the plant.

The ways in which substations are interconnected. Plants that use intermediate voltage distribution levels and those that have scattered load centers (buildings and process units) require a number of substations. The simplest and cheapest way of connecting them is the *radial* method, in which a direct and separate connection is made from the low-voltage side of the primary substation to each of the scattered substations. The problems with this system are a tendency toward voltage fluctuation in the isolated branch circuits and the fact that if there is a cable or transformer failure in one of the circuits, all of the loads on that circuit are dropped. If it is important to avoid these difficulties, more expensive connection systems can be used. In general they involve connecting the substations in loop circuits equipped with sophisticated circuit breaker arrangements which can isolate a defective component while the rest of the system carries the load. They go by such names as secondary selective, banked secondary radial, primary selective, and network.

Polyphase systems. In an alternating current circuit, the voltage starts at zero, increases to a peak positive value, decreases to zero, continues to decrease to a low negative value, and increases back to zero, completing one *cycle*. As the voltage changes in value, so does the current, which flows in opposite directions during each half of the cycle. The net result of all this is that power is fed into the circuit in pulses, much as a piston pump creates surges of pressure and flow in a pipeline. And just as the hydraulic engineer builds a triplex pump with three pistons operating on staggered cycles to even out the flow, the electrical engineer designs generators that produce staggered pulses of power in three phases carried by separate wires. Sometimes a fourth wire is added as a neutral to ground.

The three-phase, four-wire system is commonly used for secondary electrical distribution systems within the plant. Power loads, such as motors, are connected to the three phase wires and take the full voltage of the system. Smaller loads, such as lighting and appliances, are connected between one phase and the neutral wire and draw the full voltage divided by 1.73. For instance, in a 208/120 V system, motors and large loads are powered by three-wire connection, while lighter loads are connected across one of the phases and the neutral. In plants with large lighting loads, the 480/277 V system is popular; the 277 V circuits are used for lighting, and transformers are added to provide 120 V circuits for office machines and small appliances. This method of plant wiring is illustrated diagrammatically in Figure 16-1.

How Circuit Breakers Protect Against Damage

Very serious damage to electrical equipment and distribution systems can result from the excessively high current—known as *fault current* to the electrical designer—which accompanies the familiar "short circuit." To protect the system against fault currents *circuit breakers* are installed—devices that open the circuit and stop the flow of power when a preset level of current is exceeded. The system designer must select breakers with ratings that will permit the normal flow of current but interrupt fault currents that might damage the system. Calculation of the fault currents that may occur in different parts of a system is a complicated procedure involving the resistance, reactance, and impedance of its components.

Types. The simplest and cheapest type, with good reliability, is the *fuse;* it is available in 35 normal current ratings between 15 and 6,000 amperes. Despite their advantages, fuses should not be used if the time it takes to replace them represents an unacceptably long outage or if equipment could be damaged by one phase being out while the other two still have power.

Mechanical circuit breakers usually have two elements: a *thermal* device, which cuts out after a relatively low overload current exists for a period of time, and a *magnetic* device, which trips instantaneously when a massive "short circuit" current occurs. Some are equipped with an *automatic reclosing* feature which restores the system to power if the fault has cleared quickly; after several unsuccessful attempts to close, it locks out permanently. Models also are available to protect against low current and low voltage. Equipment manufacturers often combine circuit breakers in package units with other devices, such as disconnect switches, alarm signals, and motorized lever actuators.

Application. On branch circuits serving a number of motors, the breaker is rated at the full load current of all the motors plus 125 percent of that of the largest motor. When breakers are selected for the main and secondary branches of a distribution system, the choices represent a compromise between cost, continuity of service, full protection of the system, and the need to isolate branches with fault currents without disturbing the entire system. The three basic arrangements are the *fully rated, cascade,* and *selective systems.*

Motors—What You Need to Know About the Basics

Technical principles. Engineers define the motor as a device for converting electrical energy into mechanical energy; it is based on the fact that if an electric current is passed through a conductor placed in a magnetic field, a mechanical

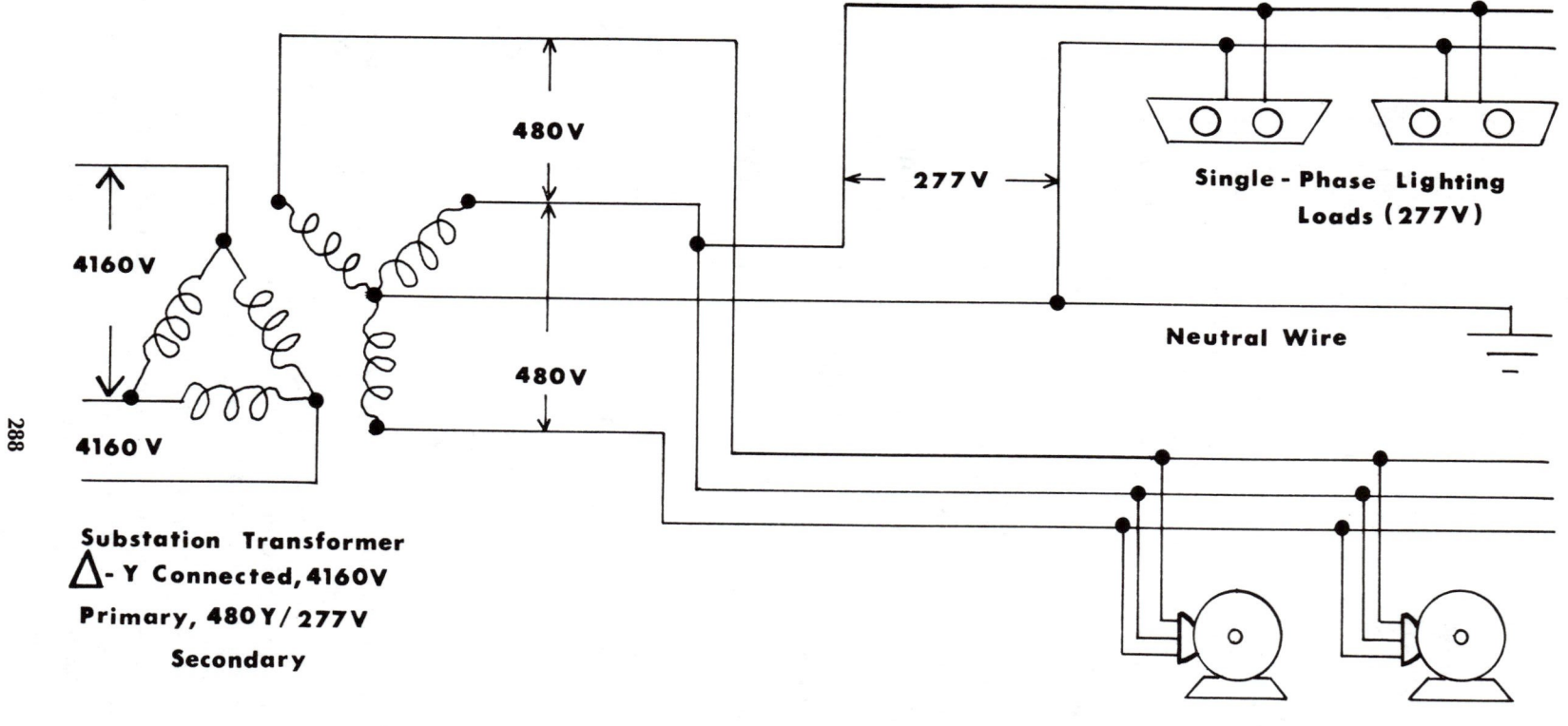

FIGURE 16-1: Three-phase, four-wire distribution system taken from secondary of substation transformer. 480 V loads are connected across phase wires, and 277 V loads are connected across one phase wire and neutral.

force will be exerted on the conductor. Industrial motors are designed for operation on direct current (DC) or alternating current (AC); the most commonly encountered industrial type is the three-phase squirrel cage induction motor. At its center is the *shaft* (whose spin represents the output of mechanical energy) on which is mounted the *rotor* (a current-carrying device that looks like a squirrel cage). The rotor-shaft assembly fits inside a hollow cylindrical *stator* consisting of insulated iron laminations in which the magnetic field is produced. The stator, in turn, fits inside a steel cylinder called the *frame;* it is fitted with *end-bells,* each of which contains a bearing to support one end of the spinning shaft.

The important operating characteristics of a motor are torque, speed, and horsepower. *Torque* is the rotational force which the motor shaft is capable of applying to the attached load; it depends on the length of the conductor, the intensity of the magnetic field, and the amount of current. The basic reference point is full-load torque at full-load speed; starting torque is usually much higher and is expressed as percentage of full-load torque. *Speed* is simply the revolutions per minute at which the shaft spins, but complicated design and selection problems arise in achieving desired speed, adjusting speed, varying speed, and in finding the right combinations of speed and torque to accommodate different types of loads. Shaft speeds of 200 to 10,000 rpm are available in industrial motors; common shaft speeds for squirrel cage induction motors are 900, 1,200 1,800, and 3,600 rpm. *Horsepower* (which represents work done per unit time) derives from the combination of applied torque and speed; it is the primary characteristic used for matching a motor to a job. Available ratings range from 1/4 to 5,000 hp, and special units have been built with ratings in excess of 100,000 hp.

Types of industrial motors available. AC motors are by far the most widely used, because alternating current is the most common form of power distribution, they have good constant speed characteristics, and are relatively inexpensive and reliable. DC motors are used when high starting torque and variable speed control are important. To utilize DC equipment most plants have to convert AC power; this is done by means of motor-generator sets, mercury-arc rectifiers (such as the ignitron), semiconductor devices (selenium and silicon rectifiers), and static inverters.

DC motors are classified as *shunt* (the field coil is connected in parallel to the armature), *series* (field in series with the armature) and *compound* (both series and parallel connection). Shunt motors operate essentially as constant-speed motors. With appropriate control devices they are readily converted to controlled-speed motors. They are used for compressors, machine drives, piston pumps, and building elevators. Series motors are used for variable-speed loads requiring high starting torque, such as cranes and traction motors. Compound motors are used for similar applications as the shunt motor, with special application to machines whose loads are applied suddenly (cutters, punch presses, and stamping machines).

AC motors are *synchronous* or *induction* types. In the synchronous motor a rotating magnetic field is excited in the stator by a polyphase current. An electromagnet on the rotor is excited by a direct current. As the poles of the magnet follow the rotating field, the rotor is turned. Synchronous motors operate at constant speed, are cheaper than other types in certain applications, and have air adjustable power factor. They are used in sizes above 25 hp to drive gas compressors, motor-generator sets, rubber mills, and pumps; very small sizes are used to drive electric clocks and instruments.

The induction motor is operated by the creation of a rotating magnetic field which induces a current in rotor winding. The *single-phase* induction motor is employed in sizes from $\frac{1}{20}$ horsepower to 25 hp, and often has a 110 V rating. The *polyphase induction* motor is the most widely used industrial motor, with standard sizes available from ½ to 500 hp, and much higher ratings as special designs. It is durable, inexpensive, essentially constant-speed, and can be modified to obtain high starting torque. The *squirrel cage* motor is the most common version. When high starting torque is required, *wound-rotor* and *double squirrel cage* types are used. (All these polyphase motors are three phase; two-phase motors are available but rarely used.) The chief disadvantage of polyphase motors is the difficulty of achieving speed control electrically, and mechanical speed reducers must be used when speed adjustment is desired.

Choosing a Motor

After the basic type has been selected, there are further choices to be made.

NEMA design types. Because the polyphase squirrel cage induction motor is the most commonly used industrial type, the National Electrical Manufacturers Association has classified these motors on the basis of the starting torque that the motor applies to the load as it is turned on and the maximum torque it reaches as it picks up the load, both expressed as percentages of full load torque. (Starting torque is also called *breakaway*, or *locked rotor* torque, and maximum torque is sometimes called *breakdown* torque.) In the following listing, NEMA Design B is shown first because it is the "standard," most often used type:

Design B. Starting torque may range from 70 percent to 275 percent of full load torque; a typical value is 150 percent. Maximum torque ranges from 175 to 300 percent, and 200 percent is a typical value. Used for general application around an industrial plant on such equipment as production machines, pumps, and fans.

Design A. Starting torque is the same as for Design B, but the maximum torque is slightly higher. Used for centrifuges and mills; may not be available "off the shelf" but only on special order.

Design C. Characterized by high starting torque which ranges from 200 percent to 250 percent. Has normal *slip* (the difference between the speed of the rotating magnetic field in the stator and that of the rotor) of 5 percent or less. Used for hard-to-start equipment such as conveyors, loaded compressors, reciprocating pumps, vibrating screens, crushers, and escalators. Maximum torque for all motors rated above 5 hp is 190 percent.

Design D. Highest starting torque—275 percent—which is also the maximum. High slip rates of 8 percent, 13 percent, and even greater. Used for hoists and cranes, elevators, and for machinery with high inertia and sudden load changes, such as punch presses and shears.

Motor enclosures. The internal parts of motors can be injured by the intrusion of liquids, dust particles, corrosive atmospheres, and moisture. NEMA has established the following classifications of enclosures for the protection of motors in ascending order of both cost and protection:

Open dripproof motors are designed to prevent entry of liquid drops or particles dropping on the motor at an angle no greater than 15 degrees from the vertical. *Splashproof* motors increase the angle to 100 degrees from vertical. *Dripproof guarded* motors are protected at the air inlet by screens which prevent large particles from entering the working parts of the motor.

Weather Protected, Type I motors are constructed to minimize the entrance of rain, snow, and airborne particles to the working parts. Available in sizes of 3 hp and up. Ventilation openings are designed to prevent the passage of a 3/4-inch diameter rod. For both indoor and outdoor use.

Weather Protected, Type II have baffled ventilating passages so that drops and particles from driving winds do not enter the working parts. Usually for outdoor installations in sizes of 300 hp and up.

Totally Enclosed Fan-Cooled (TEFC) motors are built with separate internal and external air circulating systems and therefore offer greater protection against corrosive atmospheres or ambient air that contains moisture and dirt particles. Fans may be provided for the circulation of either or both the internal and external air systems; in sizes under 3 hp there may be no fans. Used in chemical plants and other applications where dirt- and fume-laden atmospheres are prevalent. In *pipe ventilated* motors, clean air for ventilation may be brought to and removed from the motor through piping or ducts; in some applications the recirculating air may be cooled by water in a heat exchanger.

A special type of TEFC motor is the *explosionproof* motor, which is built so that if a flammable vapor or dust enters the motor enclosure and is ignited, the frame will withstand the pressure developed *and* ignition of the atmosphere outside the motor is prevented. These motors are built to withstand various levels of vapor and dust hazard as classified in the National Electrical Code: See the section on explosionproof equipment later in this chapter for the classes, groups, and divisions of hazard for which various types of explosionproof equipment are built.

Frame sizes. Through NEMA, manufacturers of motors have agreed to standardize the dimensions of motors, and for each NEMA frame designation there are 29 dimensions specified. Before replacing a motor or selecting one for installation on existing machinery, be sure to check frame sizes and critical dimensions carefully. Equipment makers will be glad to supply detailed information; bear in mind that standard frame dimensions are changed from time to time as new developments in motor technology make possible smaller units for a given horsepower rating. See Table 8 in the Appendix, and for further information consult NEMA Motor and Generator Standard, Publication MG1.

Temperature-altitude.   Insulating materials within a motor are classified by the maximum temperatures they can withstand:

Class	Degrees C
A	105
B	130
F	155
H	180

Motor nameplates are stamped with the class of insulation used in building the motor and the maximum ambient air temperature at which they are designed to be operated; the most common ambient temperature rating is 40°C (104°F). Other ratings are for temperatures in degrees Celsius of 50, 65, 90, and 115. The temperature of a motor goes up during operation, and standards have been established for maximum allowable *temperature rise* for each class of insulation. Expressed in degrees Celsius, the temperature rises for various types of motors, with Class A insulation range from 60 to 70; for Class B from 80 to 90; for Class F from 105 to 115; and for Class H from 125 to 135. These ratings hold for elevations from sea level up to 3,300 feet; above that altitude motors will experience greater temperature rises. Temperature rise has been discontinued as a rating criterion and is no longer stamped on the nameplate, having been supplanted by the ambient temperature rating and the insulation class.

Service factor.   This is the margin by which a motor may be overloaded without damage to its internal parts. If a 10-hp motor has a service factor of 1.25 stamped on the nameplate, it may be operated at $10 \times 1.25 = 12.5$ hp, as long as the other limitations on the nameplate (such as ambient temperature) are not exceeded. Totally enclosed motors have a service factor of 1.0, which means that they cannot be overloaded at all. Smaller motors tend to have higher service factors than larger ones. The values of service factor in the following table are for general purpose motors, but you should always check the nameplate before connecting a motor to an overload. And consult the manufacturer's literature before buying a motor for overload service, to be sure that you have the correct service factor:

Motor Horsepower	Service Factor at 1800 rpm
0.05 —0.125	1.4
0.167—0.333	1.35
0.5 —0.75	1.25
1.0 and Higher	1.15

Types of Choices Available for Motor Controls and Control Centers

Motor controls include devices for starting and stopping motors, protecting them against high current and low voltage; and when it is done electrically, controlling motor speed. Selection among the large variety of equipment offered is made on the basis of cost, safety, convenience, and the suitability of the control to the type of load the motor handles. These are some of the choices offered:

Across-the-line (full voltage) versus part-voltage starters. When an across-the-line starter is connected, full line voltage is immediately applied to the motor; this type is used with motors ranging in size from less than one to 1,500 horsepower, but can only be used where the driven machine can withstand the high starting torque and where a high initial surge of current will not damage the motor or upset the distribution system.

There are four types of part-voltage (also known as reduced voltage) starters used with polyphase induction motors: the *primary resistor* type, which offers very smooth acceleration on 65 percent to 85 percent of the full voltage current; the *autotransformer,* which gives next-best acceleration characteristics and the highest torque output per unit of current drawn; the *part-winding* starter, which can only be used with motors that have double windings in each phase—the cheapest of the reduced voltage methods, offering the least smooth acceleration, and operating by starting the motor on one winding and then connecting the second winding after it picks up the load; and the *wye-delta* starter, which is arranged to start the motor in Y connection but switches to delta after it is running. It offers good torque output per ampere of starting current but is not as good as the autotransformer in smoothness of acceleration.

Manual versus magnetic starters. The manual starter makes and breaks contact by means of a mechanical lever (similar to the familiar toggle switch) actuated by hand. It is limited to horsepower ratings not exceeding 7.5 and must be located near the motor.

In the magnetic starter, a pushbutton actuates a magnetic coil which closes the contacts. The pushbutton can be located near the motor, while the control mechanism can be remotely located in a more protected area. Motors above 7.5 hp are almost always equipped with magnetic starters.

Reversing versus nonreversing. In many applications it is necessary or desirable to reverse the direction of rotation of the motor. This can be accomplished in the polyphase induction motor by switching any two of the phase connections, and the reversing starter provides a mechanism to do that at the touch of a button.

Motor starters are enclosed in steel boxes, usually with a hinged lid. A popular form is the *combination starter* which contains the motor starter, short circuit protection, overload devices, and a manual disconnect. Undervoltage protection may also be provided. Thermal overload devices called *heaters* provide protection against steady overload currents that are not high enough to trip the short circuit protection.

Motor control centers are steel structures on which a number of motor control housings can be stacked from floor level to a height of about six feet. They offer the convenience of assembling all the motor controls for a plant department or area in one place, which can be away from heat, dust, moisture, or exposure to process materials. In plants that handle flammable materials, they can be placed in isolated rooms designed so that flammable vapors cannot accumulate and be ignited by a spark from the controls.

How to Raise Plant Power Factor with Motors and Capacitors

Unfortunately the equation Power = Voltage × Current is true only for DC circuits and some AC circuits under special conditions. In most AC circuits the power utilized is less than the product of the voltage and current supplied, and the ratio between them is called *power factor:*

$$\frac{\text{Power Utilized}}{\text{Voltage} \times \text{Current Supplied}} = \text{Power Factor}$$

Power factor takes on values ranging up to a maximum of 1.0 and is usually expressed as a decimal (0.80) or as a percentage (80%). (The electrical engineer further defines power factor as the cosine of the angle θ by which the voltage leads the current, and expresses the power equation thus: Power = Voltage × Current × Cosine θ.)

Power factor values above 0.90 are usually considered acceptable, and no corrective action is taken. Below this level a number of cost and operating liabilities are encountered: power is being paid for which is not utilized; in some localities power companies bill penalty charges for low power factor; voltage regulation suffers; and higher rated distribution equipment (transformers and transmission lines) is required. Stated another way, more load can be added to an existing system if low power factor is corrected.

Inductive loads create low power factor in which the voltage leads the current, and appear most often in the form of the widely used squirrel cage induction motor. On the other hand, capacitive loads (such as synchronous motors and static capacitors) cause the current to lead the voltage, and can be used of offset the inductive loads. Take these steps to uncover the cost saving opportunities in your electrical system:

1. Determine what the power factor is. Your maintenance department, engineering group, outside contractor, or possibly the power company can take voltage, ampere, and wattmeter readings to determine power factor.

2. Your electrical engineer and the power company can help you calculate the periodic cost savings as well as the additional load that can be added to the system after power factor is corrected.

3. Use these techniques to correct power factor:

   ● Install synchronous motors. If some of the motor applications are suited to the use of synchronous motors, they can be applied to offset the effect of the induction motors. Typical uses for synchronous motors are to drive motor-generator sets, gas compressors, rolling mills, pumps, and grinding mills, usually in sizes of 50 to 100 hp and up.

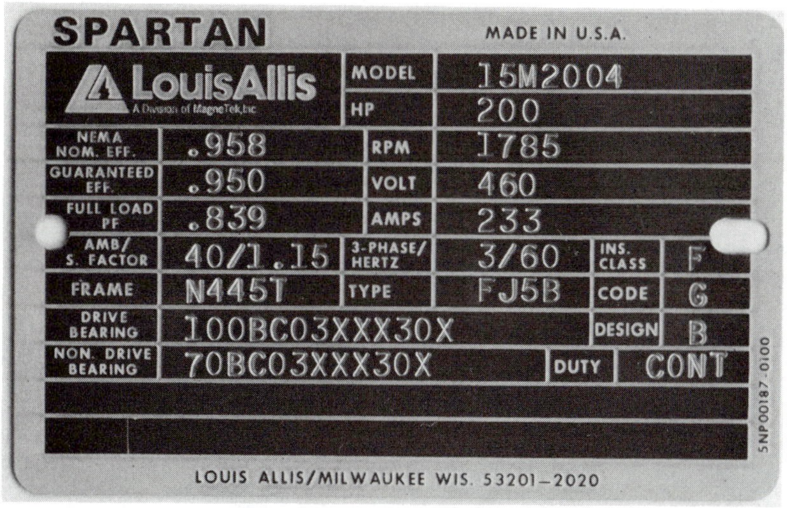

FIGURE 16-2: Industrial Motor Nameplate. (Courtesy of Louis Allis, a Division of MagneTek, Inc.) The trade name "Spartan" and the model number are manufacturer's designations. "NEMA Nominal Efficiency" refers to a standard of the National Electrical Manufacturers Association, and is the ratio of useful power output to the power input. Motor efficiency decreases slightly with age, and for this motor the manufacturer guarantees that it will not go below .950. The shaft speed is 1785 revolutions per minute (rpm). This motor is designed to operate on 460 volts and to draw 233 amperes of current at full load; under these conditions it will have a power factor of .839 (see accompanying text). "AMB/S. FACTOR-40/1.15" indicates that the motor is designed to operate in ambient temperatures not exceeding 40°C, and that it has a service factor of 1.15 (meaning that it can be overloaded by 15 percent). This is a 3-phase motor operating on 60 Hertz (cycles per second). It has Class F insulation. The frame number is 445T (see Table 8, NEMA Electric Motor Dimensions in the Appendix). The letter T used as a suffix means that standard dimensions have been established for this frame; the prefix N is a manufacturer's code. The entry FJ5B under "Type" is also a manufacturer's designation. "Code" refers to NEMA's locked-rotor kVA per horsepower classification. The letter G means that the kVA/hp for this motor is 5.6 to 6.2; from this information the starting current can be calculated. The NEMA design type is B (see page 290). This motor is built for continuous (as opposed to intermittent) duty. "Drive Bearing" refers to the end of the motor from which the drive shaft projects; "Nondrive Bearing" refers to the other end. The number entries in these two categories are standard bearing numbers of the Anti-Friction Bearing Manufacturers Association.

- Replace oversized induction motors. Process designers and plant operating personnel may like the comfort of having a motor with twice the capacity of the expected load, but a high price is paid in energy consumption because a 10-hp which is only half loaded may suffer a decrease in power factor of 10 percent to 20 percent from that experienced at full load.

- Install static capacitors. Small units can be connected at each motor or inductive load, or larger units can be installed at substations to handle entire branch circuits. The first method is preferred when the primary object is to increase the load-carrying capacity of the branch, the second when the objective is the cutting of power costs.

Are Standby Generators Needed? Four Questions to Ask

The answer is not an automatic yes. Evaluate these factors before making the decision:

What are the electrical usages?   Make a list of all the facilities and equipment that would become inoperative in a power failure:

Process Machinery	Elevators	Heating and Ventilating Units
Electric Furnaces	Boilers	Instrumentation
Illumination	Lift Truck Chargers	Data Processing
Refrigeration	Cooling Towers	Air Conditioners

What is the risk of power failure? Plant records will give the number, duration, and incurred losses of power outages in the last five years. Contact the local power company to supplement this information and to discuss the likelihood of future power failures. Combine all the available information into probabilities of occurrence and duration.

What are the consequences?   Safety and cost are the principal concerns:

Safety: Is emergency lighting required for orderly shutdown of the process and safe evacuation of personnel? Will process materials be subject to overheating, fire, or explosion? Is standby power needed for ventilating equipment to remove dangerous fumes? Will important firefighting equipment (pumps, signal systems) be knocked out of service?

Cost: Will there be damage to any equipment if the outage exceeds a certain length of time? Will in-process materials suffer quality deterioration or possibly have to be scrapped? Will personnel have to be dismissed but paid anyway?

If the answer to any of the safety questions is yes, standby equipment is clearly needed. The same answer for any of the cost questions requires a calculation of how much money is at stake in each situation.

What equipment is needed? Rarely will the combined factors of outage probability, safety hazard, and cost risk call for 100 percent standby generating capacity; instead, a few critical usages will be selected, and their total consumption in kilowatts determined.

Batteries: Storage batteries are sometimes used as sources of emergency power for lighting, communications, and alarm systems. Because they are limited to direct current and relatively low power output, they are not suitable for general supply of electricity.

Standby generators: They consist of a fuel-burning engine coupled to an electric generator. Fuel choices are gasoline, natural gas, and diesel fuel; the engines are internal combustion, diesel, reciprocating natural gas, and gas turbines. Output of standard models ranges from 1 to 1,000 kilowatts; single and three-phase current; and voltages from 110 to 4,160. All units require periodic start-ups and preventive maintenance to assure reliability in an emergency.

"Explosionproof" Equipment: What It Is and When to Use It

Electrical equipment is intrinsically spark-producing, and when used in atmospheres that may contain flammable vapors or combustible dusts, creates a serious explosion hazard. Fortunately, manufacturers of this equipment are able to supply virtually all types in explosionproof form: motors, switches, starters, lights, telephones, clocks, thermostats, forklift trucks, water coolers, refrigerators, and many kinds of instruments. Such items are built according to the standards of the National Electrical Code® (available from the National Fire Protection Association, Batterymarch Park, Quincy, MA 02269), and are designed to contain any ignition that occurs so that it cannot spread to the surrounding atmosphere.* Physical characteristics are use of rigid conduit, threaded joints, heavy enclosures, seals, and enclosure covers that have carefully machined mating surfaces and no gaskets. Explosionproof equipment is rated according to the type of hazardous atmosphere in which it is to be used, and the NEC® divides the hazards into *classes,* which distinguish the types of hazard present—for example, solvent vapors or ignitible dust; *divisions,* which describe the frequency and likelihood that the hazard will be present in a given area; and *groups,* which specify the hazardous materials and rank them according to intensity of hazard. These classifications are briefly summarized in Table 16-1.

Class I, Group D, Division 1 is the type of explosionproof equipment most often specified for oil refineries, chemical plants, and areas where solvents or lacquers are used.

Operating Example 16-1: How to Choose the Appropriate Rating of Explosionproof Equipment. A paint plant installed a new process involving the use of lacquer solvent in drums as a raw material. The contents of the drums were to be poured through open manholes into mixing tanks; the final product was removed by gravity through the bottoms of the tanks and packed into five-gallon pails. This operation would take place an average of three times per shift.

The engineers designing the new unit knew that some sort of protection against the accidental ignition of solvent fumes by electrical equipment would be needed, and they consulted the National Electrical Code® to determine in which category of hazard the new unit belonged. Because the new area would be exposed to flammable vapors in sufficient quantities to produce ignitible mixtures, it was designated as a

---

*National Electrical Code® and NEC® are registered trademarks of the National Fire Protection Association, Inc., Quincy, MA.

HAZARDOUS MATERIALS PRESENT	CLASS I Flammable vapors	DIVISION 1 Usually present	Where the explosive hazard is typified by but not limited to the presence of →	GROUPS		
				GROUP A Acetylene		GROUP B Hydrogen
				GROUP C Ethyl ether		GROUP D Gasoline Acetone Alcohol Lacquer solvent Benzene
		DIVISION 2 Occasionally present				
	CLASS II Combustible dust Electrially conducting dust	DIVISION 1 Frequency of suspension in air at least intermittent	Where combustibility is typified by but not limited to that of →	GROUPS		
				GROUP E Aluminum dust		
				GROUP F Coal dust		
		DIVISION 2 Dust accumulations		GROUP G Grain dust		
	CLASS III Ignitible fibers, but in less than combustible concentrations in air	DIVISION 1 Processing areas	Where fibers are typified by but not limited to the presence of →	(No group distinction)		
		DIVISION 2 Storage areas		Textile fibers Jute Baled waste Excelsior		

TABLE 16–1: Matrix showing relationships among hazardous area classifications of National Electrical Code®.

Class I location. The specific flammable material—lacquer solvent—classified it in Group D. And the periodic presence of the vapors as part of normal operating conditions placed it in Division 1. Therefore, when the electrical equipment was ordered for the new area, all components were specified for Class I, Group D, Division 1 service.

The purchase order or equipment contract for explosionproof equipment should require that it carry the Underwriters Laboratory label (usually a metal tag on industrial equipment) showing the class, group, and division for which it is rated. Some suppliers may represent their equipment as being "explosionproof" but not want to go through the procedure of obtaining the Underwriter's label. If you buy such equipment, you are entirely dependent on the supplier's word and are without the benefit of third-party control and inspection of the way in which the equipment is constructed.

Once installed, explosionproof equipment is effective only if it is properly maintained. Allow only qualified personnel who understand and will follow the manufacturer's instructions to disassemble the equipment. Do not attempt to install gaskets where none are provided originally. When reassembling, draw up all screwed and bolted fittings tight. Make sure that all bolts are replaced.

Tips on Evaluating Your Plant's Lighting Systems

Whether concerned with upgrading the illumination in older buildings or approving the lighting designs for new facilities, your goal is to provide adequate light of good quality for the tasks to be performed at optimum cost.

The language of lighting. The *candela* is the basic unit of light intensity and is roughly equivalent to the luminous intensity of a burning candle viewed horizontally (formerly called *candle*). It may be called *candlepower* in the aggregate; that is, 200 candelas = 200 candlepower. The *footcandle* is the illumination on a surface all points of which are one foot away from a one-candela source. *Lumen* is the quantity (as opposed to the intensity) of light emitted by a source in all directions. One lumen is the quantity of light falling on a one square foot area on the inside surface of a sphere with a radius of one foot and a one candela light source at its center.

So far we have been dealing with point sources; the brightness of an object with a substantial surface area is measured in *footlamberts*. An object which gives off (by reflection or emission) one lumen per square foot of its area has a brightness of one footlambert.

Determine how much light is needed. Illumination levels at working surfaces in various plant areas should have these minimum values, expressed in footcandles: Production areas and machine shops: 20, 50, and 100, depending on fineness of the work. Stairways: 10–20. Offices: 30, 50, or 150 depending on fineness of the work. Warehouses: 20–50. Laboratories and test areas: 50–500, depending on fineness of work. For more detailed listings of types of areas and the illumination required for them, consult the *Illuminating Engineering Society Lighting Handbook* and publications of manufacturers of lamps and fixtures.

Tie-in the lighting system with other plant systems. It has already been pointed out that in a three-phase, four-wire distribution system single-phase loads can be connected to one of the phases and to the neutral wire, drawing a voltage equal to the system voltage divided by 1.73. Thus, in a 208 V three-phase system, lamps connected across one of the phases would draw $208 \div 1.73 = 120$ volts. Lighting systems have been developed to operate at 277 V, that being the single-phase voltage from a 480 V three-phase distribution system.

For ways in which lighting systems can be planned to save energy, see Chapter 9, page 144.

Choose from available equipment types to optimize cost. *Incandescent* lamps yield about 15 lumens per watt and have the lowest initial equipment cost. But because they convert a relatively high proportion of the energy consumed to heat and are therefore costly to operate, they are used only in basements, unfrequented areas, and temporary installations. Fluorescent lamps produce about 60 lumens per watt and are the universal choice for offices, laboratories, and light manufacturing areas. In most situations they represent the best cost combination of initial and operating expenses. High-intensity discharge (HID) lamps include the mercury, metal halide, and high-pressure sodium types; they are available in sizes up to 1,000 watts and yield from 60 to 140 lumens per watt. They are more costly to buy and operate but can be used to light large areas, offer good energy efficiency, and long life. They are well adapted to industrial situations. *Luminaires* are the various reflectors, lenses, and "egg crate" devices used to enhance, diffuse, and remove objectionable glare from the lamp.

Compare lighting systems on the basis of *total annual cost;* that is, the cost of lamps, luminaires, electric power, lamp replacement, and cleaning, all reduced to a yearly base.

Group relamping is a maintenance system in which all lamps in a given area are replaced and fixtures cleaned and repaired at the same time.

OPERATING GUIDELINES FOR MECHANICAL EQUIPMENT IN THE PLANT

Steam Boilers

Here are the important features and operating guidelines for this very common piece of plant equipment:

Field erected versus packaged units. In package boilers all of the essential components—tube section, fuel burner, controls and safety devices, air fans—are assembled at the factory and mounted on a steel skid framework for support and easy handling. When delivered they need only be connected to the appropriate piping and electrical systems. If the package boiler is a *firetube* type (hot gases from the fuel combustion are passed through the tubes while the water to be heated is contained in the surrounding space) it can be obtained in capacity ratings up to 24,000 pounds per hour of steam; if it is a *watertube* type (water is inside the tubes while hot gases are passed through the surrounding space) capacity ratings up to 200,000 pounds per hour are available. Figure 16–3 shows the main external components of a packaged firetube boiler.

Field erected units are constructed on the plant site, are often custom designed to meet local conditions, and while some have been constructed with capacities as low as 30,000 lb/hr their most frequent application is in the capacities above the limits of packaged boilers, that is, over 200,000 lb/hr.

Number of "passes."   A *pass* is a one-way trip through the length of the boiler. In a four-pass firetube boiler the gases travel from the burner through a set of tubes to the other end, where direction is reversed by a baffle, and return to the front end; the process is repeated to obtain a total of four trips.

Auxiliary equipment.   A primary objective of boiler design is to extract the maximum heat value from the fuel consumed. In the *economizer* waste heat from the flue gases is used to raise the temperature of water fed to the boiler; in the *feedwater heater* the same result is obtained by using exhaust steam. The *air preheater* takes heat from the waste flue gases to raise the temperature of the air fed to the furnace, improving the efficiency of the combustion process.

To provide the required quantity of air for combustion, *forced-draft fans* supply fresh air under pressure to the furnace. In larger installations *induced-draft fans* are located just ahead of the exhaust stack to pull the flue gases through the system.

Steam is obtained from water at the boiling point temperature (212°F at 0 psi gauge; 338°F at 100 psi gauge), but in some processes it is advantageous to heat the steam to temperatures well above the boiling point. That is accomplished by means of a *superheater*, a bank of tubes containing steam which may be fired separately or, more often, is included in the boiler furnace.

Boiler ratings.   Boilers are usually specified by number of pounds per hour of steam which they generate. Because the heat content of steam varies with the temperature and pressure, those two conditions must be specified. For example, a boiler might be rated for 10,000 pounds per hour from and at 212°F and atmospheric pressure (= 0 psi gauge). This means that the boiler has an energy output equivalent to the evaporation of 10,000 pounds of water per hour into steam at the stated temperature and pressure.

Another method of boiler rating is the *boiler horsepower*. It is equivalent to the evaporation of 34.5 lb/hr of water into steam from and at 212°F and atmospheric pressure. It is also equivalent to 33,475 Btu/hr. (It should be noted that boiler horsepower has nothing to do with the standard physical definition of one horsepower, which is equal to 2,545 Btu/hr.) A boiler rated at 200 HP will have a steam capacity of 6,900 lb/hr from and at 212°F and atmospheric pressure.

Effective operation and maintenance of boilers is a matter of direct concern to the plant manager who must worry about cost efficiency, continuity of operations, and the physical safety of the plant. Make sure that your boiler operation includes these basic controls:*

---

*The basic procedures for sound boiler operation and maintenance listed here are contained in *Boiler Care Handbook*, published by the Cleaver-Brooks Division of Aqua-Chem, Inc.

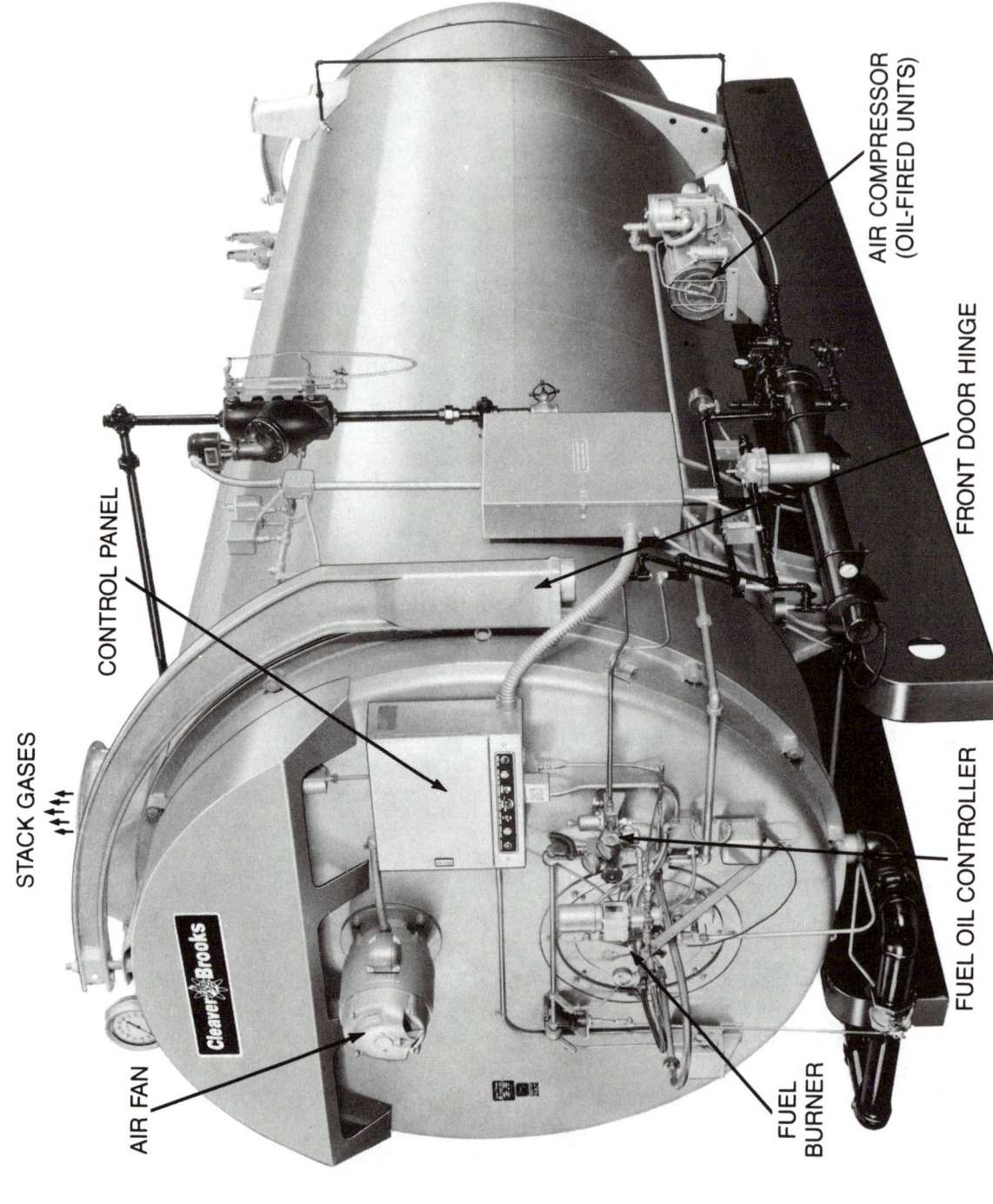

FIGURE 16-3: Packaged Firetube Boiler, Showing Essential External Operating Components (Courtesy of Cleaver-Brooks)

- Require operators to keep a written log of all pressure, temperature, liquid level, and flow gauge readings, as well as a notation of any unusual circumstances.

- Maintain chemical treatment of boiler water at specified levels (see discussion of boiler water chemistry that follows) with a program of daily testing by qualified personnel. Record results in a log book.

- Get rid of sludge formation by periodic or continuous *blowdown*—that is, draining a small proportion of the water out of the boiler.

- Analyze flue gases to achieve maximum burner efficiency. Oxygen content should not exceed 1 to 2 percent; carbon monoxide level should be zero; and carbon dioxide content should be 8.5 to 10 percent when burning gas, 12.5 to 13.8 percent when burning #6 oil—the higher the better in both cases.

- Diagnose combustion problems by monitoring stack temperature. If the temperature of the existing flue gases rises and remains above normal levels, the tube surfaces may have become clogged with soot and need cleaning. If the stack temperature exceeds the steam temperature by more than 150°F, heat is being wasted, and burner adjustment may be required.

- Avoid thermal shock by preventing sudden addition of steam load and rapid introduction of cold feedwater. Always bring a boiler up to temperature from a cold start very gradually.

- Make weekly checks of protective devices—low level cutoffs, relief valves, fuel cutoffs—to ensure that they will operate properly when needed.

Seven Key Techniques for an Effective Boiler Maintenance Program

Use these techniques for an effective maintenance program:

1. Take the boiler out of service and open it up for inspection and repair semiannually.

2. Replace all handhole and manhole gaskets and seals.

3. Inspect the waterside for scale deposits, corrosion, and mud accumulation. If scale is heavy, a chemical acid cleaning may be necessary; if corrosion is evident, chemical treatment of the water is needed; if mud accumulation is heavy, blowdown procedures and chemical treatment need adjustment.

4. Inspect tubes and tube sheet. Replace broken tubes and those showing severe corrosion. Reroll or reweld tube ends at tube sheet if they appear loose, corroded, or leaking.

5. Inspect fireside. Stack should be clean; if it is sooty, adjust air-fuel ratio. Fill in cracks and eroded spots in refractory lining. Clean burner tip and nozzle.

6. Make detailed check of protective devices. Replace any components that past history indicates will fail before next overhaul.

7. Arrange for inspection of the boiler while it is open by state, municipal, or insurance inspector.

The chemical state of water in the boiler must be carefully controlled to avoid damage to the equipment. *Dissolved oxygen* causes pitting corrosion; it can be removed physically by passing the feedwater through a *deaerator,* or scavenged chemically in the boiler by the addition of hydrazine or sodium sulfite. *Acid corrosion* is prevented by the addition of alkali chemicals to keep the pH on the alkaline side—usually around 11. *Sludge accumulation* is retarded by the addition of chemical dispersants to keep solid particles in suspension so that they can leave with the blowdown. *Scale formation* is inhibited by presoftening the raw feedwater and by the addition of sodium phosphate or organic sequestering agents to the boiler. *Condensate line corrosion* can be controlled by the addition of volatile amines to the boiler water, but this method must be reviewed carefully if the steam comes in contact with any process materials.

Boiler water chemistry is a complicated subject, and this review is not intended to provide recipes for water treatment. If your company cannot provide the technical expertise required to set up a water treatment program, a number of consulting firms can provide technical advice, chemicals, and periodic reviews of the effectiveness of treatment. Consult an industrial directory under Water Treatment Chemicals for the names of such firms providing service in your area.

Mechanical Power Transmission

The spinning shaft of an electric motor represents the usual form in which mechanical power first arrives for use in an industrial plant. But most mechanical devices cannot operate at the high speeds of the motor shafts, and in many cases cannot receive the power in alignment with the motor. Three basic types of mechanical transmission devices commonly used to overcome the twin problems of speed reduction and transfer of power between planes are the gear drive, the chain drive, and the belt drive. A fourth device, the variable speed drive, accomplishes the work of the other types and in addition allows the speed of the driven shaft to be changed without dismantling the machine. Use these guidelines for the application and operation of MPT equipment in your plant:

Gear drives. Capable of transmitting more power and operating at higher speeds than the other types, the gear drive consists of a metal housing with an input shaft and one or more output shafts. Inside the casing are gear combinations of the following types:

1. Types and application: *Spur gears* are the strongest, cheapest, noisiest, and are relatively efficient. They are universally used for moderate loads and speeds. *Helical gears* are used for higher loads and speeds, are quieter and more efficient, but more costly. *Worm gears* permit operation on intersecting axes, are good for high speed work, carry larger gear ratios, and are relatively quiet, but efficiency is low. *Bevel gears* are normally used for intersecting shafts at 90 degrees, but other angles are possible. They are relatively expensive. Figure 16-4 illustrates the most common gear types.

2. Selection criteria: Manufacturers of gear drives provide tables of service factors based on the type of application (cranes, machine tools, screw conveyors, and

 Worm Gear

 Spur Gears

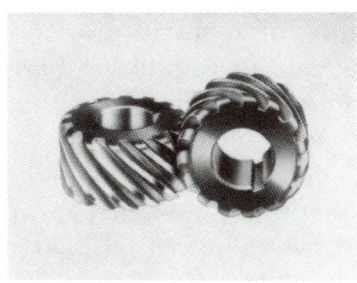 Helical Gears

 Bevel Gears

FIGURE 16–4: Four Common Types of Gears (Courtesy Akron Gear & Engineering Inc.)

so on), the uniformity of loading, and the number of hours per day of operation. The service factor is multiplied by the horsepower required at the driven machine to determine the size of the gear reducer required. Torque requirement and ambient temperature also affect the size requirement.

3. Speed ratio: The rpm of the input shaft divided by the rpm of the output shaft is the speed reduction ratio of the unit. The most commonly employed ratios are 15 to 1, 30 to 1, and 50 to 1, but many other ratios ranging from 3:1 to 500:1 are available.

4. Operation and maintenance: Gears operate under a film of oil constantly replenished by a reservoir in the casing. Be sure that this oil is the type recommended by the manufacturer and is maintained at the specified level (overoiling can cause as much damage as underoiling). Poor alignment of the gear drive shafts with connected equipment can cause bearing strain and rapid failure; check alignment periodically during preventive maintenance inspections.

Chain drives.   Falling between gear drives and belt drives in load-carrying capacity, chain drives retain the fixed speed ratios of the gear drives but escape the space limitations of the fixed housing.

1. Chain technology: *Pitch* is the distance from the centerline of one link to that of the next. Most roller chain is manufactured to specifications of the American Standard Association and is designated by ASA number; No. 40 single strand roller chain has a pitch of ½ in., while No. 200 chain has a pitch of 2½ in. Each pitch consists of a roller, a bushing, side plates, pin, and spring clip, cotter pin, or rivet. When loading or speed is too great for

a single strand chain, *multiple strand* chain is used; it is available in double, triple, or quadruple parallel strands, with specially made types up to 24 strands. *Double pitch* chain has twice the centerline distance of comparable regular chain, and the ASA number has a prefix of 20; thus ASA No. 2040 designates a chain with a pitch of 1 in., rather than the ½ in. of No. 40 chain. The double pitch costs about half as much as regular chain, can only be used at slow speeds, and is not made in multiple strands. *Self-lubricating* chain is available for sensitive operations (such as food processing) where standard lubricants are prohibited. *Sprockets* are the toothed wheels on which the chain rides; they are designed to ASA standards for tooth profile and critical dimensions. Most manufacturers stock sprockets cut to popular bore sizes but will rebore for a fee. The speed reduction of a chain drive is the ratio of the number of teeth on each of the two sprockets.

2. Design and installation: Manufacturer's catalogs usually contain design tables for the selection of chains and sprockets based on the horsepower that must be transmitted, the type of service, type of primary drive, the speed ratio, and the distance between shafts.

   Speed ratios are usually limited to 7:1 for a single drive; above that, two chain drives should be used. The optimum center distance between shafts is 30 to 50 chain pitches, but the range can be spread from 20 to 80 in special cases. The chain should be in contact with the sprocket over at least 120 degrees of arc. Idler sprockets are sometimes used to change chain direction or maintain tension; current practice is to avoid them because they require additional flexing of the chain and hasten its wear. On horizontal installations it is good practice to have the slack portion of the chain on the lower side; when the sprockets must be placed one above the other, they should be offset from the vertical by 20 to 30 degrees.

3. Operation and maintenance: There are four standard methods of chain drive lubrication, depending upon the speed and severity of service: manual, drip lubrication, oil bath, and oil stream (supplied by a circulating pump). Lubricating oil grades are SAE 20 to 50; higher viscosity lubricants may not penetrate to the rubbing surfaces.

Chain adjustment should not be too tight (excessive wear) or too loose (tends to ride up and off sprocket teeth). The chain drive should be taken out of service periodically for lubrication check, tightness adjustment, and alignment of sprockets, which should be done with a straight edge. A set of the special tools required for adjustment and repair should be available to maintenance personnel.

Belt drives: Widely used because of ease of installation, low first cost, simple maintenance, and relative convenience in making speed changes, belt drives can carry loads up to 1,500 horsepower and operate at speeds up to 12,000 feet per minute.

1. Types and application: *Flat belts* made of leather or rubber and operating on grooveless pulleys are seldom specified for power transmission applications

because of their tendency to slip and a speed limitation around 3,000 feet per minute. *V-Belt* drives are much more widely used because of greater load-carrying capacity and speeds up to 12,000 feet per minute. The V-belt has a trapezoidal cross section, the slanted edges gripping the sides of a V-shaped groove in the pulley. The top of the belt rides at the top of the groove, but the bottom of the belt does not touch the bottom of the groove.

V-Belt types and ratings are specified by the Rubber Manufacturers Association. Types 2L, 3L, 4L, and 5L are light-duty or fractional horsepower (fhp) belts, are used singly, and have hp ratings from under 0.1 to 1.1 at speeds from 200 fpm to 6,000 fpm. For higher ratings and multiple belt drives, Types A, B, C, D, and E are used; the ranges of these belts overlap, with A having hp ratings of 0.69 to 4.38 and E of 14.7 to 57.6 hp per belt at speeds between 1,200 and 6,000 fpm and various small sheave diameters. Recent advances in materials engineering have made possible a series of Narrow V-Belts designated 3V, 5V, and 8V. They cover approximately the same range as the A through E belts but can carry the same loads with fewer belts and smaller sheaves, reducing cost and space requirements. In multiple belt drives with long center distances, or subject to shock loading, individual belts may ride off the pulleys or turn over in the sheave groove; for these difficult applications, sets of two to five belts banded together at the top by a solid web are available. *V-Flat* belt drives consist of a set of V-belts, a grooved small-diameter sheave, and a flat or grooveless large pulley. This arrangement is cheaper than having both sheaves grooved and works well when center distances are short and speed ratios are high.

Synchronous belt drives (timing belts) employ a flat belt from ¼ in. to 14 in. wide with transverse rubber teeth on the inside surface. These teeth engage grooves in the surface of the pulley which are parallel to its axis. Available in ratings over 600 hp and speeds to 16,000 fpm, synchronous belt drives have the advantage of precise speed control, small space and weight requirements, and quiet operation.

2. Selection and installation. To choose the proper belts for a power application requires a series of tables and graphs found in manufacturers' catalogs. First a design horsepower is calculated by multiplying the rated horsepower of the motor by a service factor, which is derived from a table based on the type of load, torque characteristics of the driver, and continuity of service. Then a graph of design horsepower versus rpm of the faster shaft is consulted to determine the type of belt—A, B, C, 3V, 5V, and so on. Next the horsepower per belt is obtained from a table based on driver and driven pulley speeds and center distance between them. Design horsepower divided by hp per belt gives the number of belts required.

Provide an adjustable motor mount so that the belts can be installed loosely, without prying over the pulley edges. Then adjust to proper tension using an inexpensive tension tester. Check pulley alignment with a straight edge. Finally, take precautions to protect the belts from excessive heat, chemical fumes, dripping oil, or abrasive dust.

3. Operation and maintenance. Follow these rules for reliable service and extended belt life:

   a. Continue tension adjustments—within two weeks of installation and on a periodic preventive maintenance schedule thereafter. Loose belts result in poor load-pulling performance and early wear; overly tight belts may burn out from excessive heat buildup.

   b. Replace belts as matched sets. Attempts to economize by replacing part of a set results in uneven tension, erratic performance, and early wear of the new belts.

What to Look for in Couplings

These devices are used to connect two shafts rotating on the same axis line. In most industrial applications one shaft is connected to a driver (such as an electric motor or internal-combustion engine) and the other to a driven, work-performing machine (such as an agitator, hoist, pump, and so forth), giving rise to a wide range of application problems—load capacity, torque, vibration, and shaft misalignment. Use this classification to select the proper type for your application:

Rigid couplings. As the name implies, this type is built of solid metal halves, either joined in mating flange faces or in bolted longitudinal sleeves. Capable of carrying heavy loads at high speeds, they are the cheapest and least complicated mechanically but can only be used where there is *no* misalignment of the connected shafts.

Flexible couplings. The most widely used type, they are designed to overcome the three most common types of misalignment: (1) offset, in which the axes of the rotating shafts are parallel but displaced laterally; (2) angular, in which the axes are not parallel but meet at a slight angle; and (3) end-float, in which the shaft ends change position in the axial direction because of mechanical thrust or temperature change. Figure 16–5 illustrates the various types of shaft misalign-

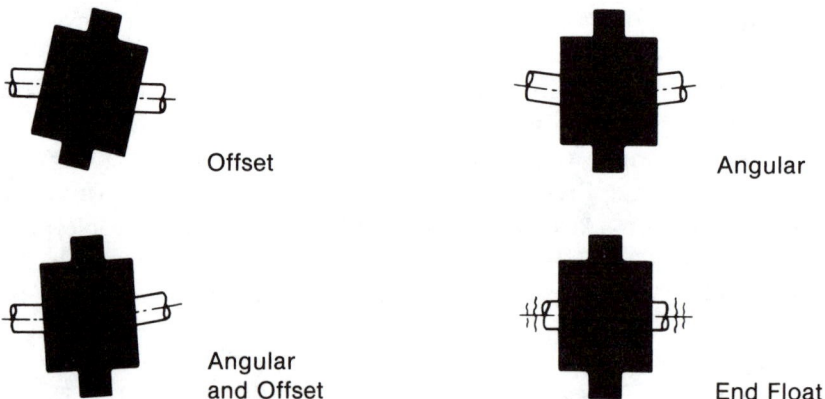

Offset

Angular

Angular and Offset

End Float

FIGURE 16–5: Types of Shaft Misalignment at Couplings (Courtesy of Falk Corporation, Subsidiary of Sundstrand Corporation.)

ment. Flexible couplings can also cushion shock loads and dampen torsional vibration.

Among the many varieties commercially available are the *chain coupling*, which has two facing sprockets joined by a length of roller chain wrapped around their circumferences. Figure 16–6 shows three types of coupling made by the Falk Corporation: (1) a *gear* coupling, in which a gear wheel is placed at the end of each shaft to be coupled and the gear wheels are engaged by the internal teeth of a surrounding rim; (2) the Falk Steelflex® coupling, in which a sinuous circular springlike grid is snapped into the grooves of two facing hubs; and (3) the Falk Torus® coupling, an elastomeric type in which a synthetic rubber ring is used to connect the two metal rings joined to the connected shafts. Not illustrated is the *universal joint*, which allows a high level (up to 30 degrees) of angular misalignment.

Fluid drives.   The basic principle of the fluid drive—transmission of the input energy of the driver to a fluid which turns a rotor connected to the load—is used to build couplings that allow enough slip for the motor to come up to speed before it has to carry the full load. The result is smoother starts and torque overload protection for the motor and the drive mechanism.

a. Gear Coupling

b. Steelflex® Coupling

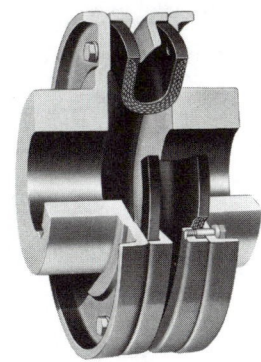

c. Torus® Coupling

FIGURE 16–6: Three Types of Falk Couplings (Courtesy of Falk Corporation, Subsidiary of Sundstrand Corporation.)

Bearings

Where the moving and stationary parts of a machine meet, a *bearing* is installed to reduce friction to a nondestructive level. The plant manager is seldom involved in the intricacies of bearing design but should understand these basic principles of application:

Type of load. A load whose direction is from the centerline of a rotating shaft toward the circumference is a *radial* load; a horizontal shaft supported by two bearings at either end always has a radial load resulting from the weight of the shaft and any wheels or devices attached to it. A load in the direction of the centerline is a *thrust* load; a vertically mounted shaft always has a thrust load at its lower end resulting from the weight of the shaft and attached devices, but many horizontal shafts carry thrust loads as well. Industrial bearings often must be designed to carry combined radial and thrust loads.

Type of friction. *Journal* bearings and *sleeve* bearings are based on sliding friction. The bearing consists of a hollow cylinder of special antifriction alloy metal in which the shaft rotates; that part of the shaft inside the bearing is called the *journal*. The shaft may also oscillate back and forth, without rotation, as in a crankshaft or piston. *Ball* bearings and *roller* bearings take advantage of the lower frictional forces inherent in rolling friction and consist of concentric rings, with the rolling element lodged between them. (See Figures 16–7 and 16–8.) Spherical balls of hardened steel are used in the raceways of ball bearings; cylindrical steel rollers are used in roller bearings, and when their length is more than four times the diameter, a *needle* bearing results.

Housing. The *pillow block* is a common form of bearing housing; circular and square *flanges* also are used. Because alignment is critical, *take-up* housings and frames are available which permit fine adjustment of the bearing position. *Self-aligning* bearings are constructed internally to withstand some initial misalignment and that due to later settling of the bearing supports.

Life rating. Manufacturers' catalogs show the "Minimum Hours Life" (also called the "B-10 Life') for each bearing at various radial loads and shaft rpm. The minimum hours life ranges from 500 to 30,000 hours and is the service time that may be expected from at least 90 percent of a group of the bearings operating under identical conditions. Average life is five times the minimum life.

Lubrication

No operation under the plant manager's jurisdiction has more impact on the performance reliability of process equipment than the lubrication program. Follow these suggestions to build an effective lubrication program:

Use the right lubricant. Comply with equipment manufacturer's instructions concerning type of lubricant and frequency of change, as shown in the operating manual or nameplate mounted on the equipment.

When it is important to reduce the number of kinds of lubricant used, or when the equipment is old and lubrication instructions are not available, try an

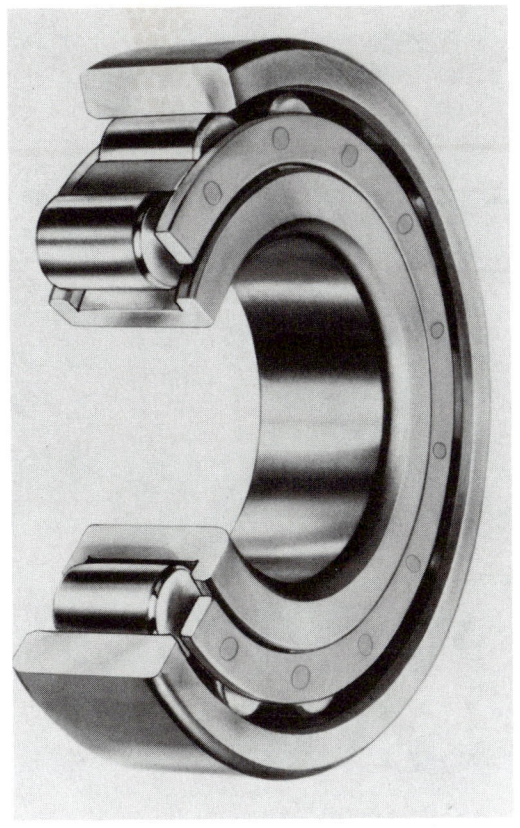

Roller Bearing

Ball Bearing

FIGURE 16–7: Rolling Friction Bearings (Courtesy of PT Components, Inc. Link-Belt Bearing Division.)

oil company survey. Most major oil companies have lubrication experts who will review your needs and recommend specific oils and greases to meet them. A word of caution here—in one industrial checkup review it was found that on three critical operations oil company recommendations were in error twice. Be sure to supply the oil company representative with all the information you have on equipment manufacturer's recommendations.

Petroleum lubricants are the most widely used type in industry; they are often compounded with animal and vegetable oils and synthetic additives. Synthetic fluids such as silicones, polyalkylene glycols, and chlorinated hydrocarbons are used when high temperatures, equipment corrosion, and process contamination must be resisted.

Service classifications for gasoline engine lubricants are ML, MM, and MS for light, moderate, and severe operating conditions; DG, DM, and DS are the corresponding designations for diesel service (American Petroleum Institute).

FIGURE 16-8: Cutaway View of Spherical Bearing Mounted in Pillow Block Housing (Courtesy of PT Components, Inc. Link-Belt Bearing Division.)

Greases are often classified by the soap base with which they are compounded—lime-base greases have good water resistance but are limited to 175° F, while soda-base greases are usable at 260° F but have poor water resistance. EP (extreme pressure) lubricants are used on hypoid gears and in bearings subject to high internal contact forces.

When it becomes necessary to change suppliers, or efficiency demands that the plant consolidate a large inventory of grease and oil types, some method of correlating the various trade-name products is needed. One way is to compare them on the basis of the grade and class designations of such organizations as the Society of Automotive Engineers (SAE) and the American Gear Manufacturers Association (AGMA).

Find the best method of getting it to the wear surface. There are four choices:

1. Manual. The simple oil can or the hand-operated grease gun, used conscientiously, will suffice for most light-duty machine lubrication.

2. Immersion. Some mechanical devices are best lubricated when they are operated in or continuously passed through an oil bath. Frequently the oil is circulated by a pump and passed through a cooler and filter.

3. Gravity feed systems. They start with an oil reservoir, which for single-point application is a small cup made of glass or plastic and for multi-point application is an oil tank. Oil is conducted to the wear point by piping, where it is applied by means of a simple drip tube, wick, brush, or vibrating rod. On multi-point systems the use of sight feed valves is common; they permit adjustment and observation of the oil flow rate.

4. Pressure systems. Similar in design to the gravity systems, this type moves oil or other lubricants out of the reservoir by air pressure or by pump, achieving a force feed. A variation is the *spray* system, in which the oil is atomized by a pressurized air stream which delivers it to the wear point as a spray.

Establish a well-defined application and checkup system. It must have these three elements:

1. Trained and motivated lubrication personnel. Classify the lubricator's job at a high enough pay rate to attract capable people. Give them detailed training in technique and responsibility in classes conducted by your lubrication engineer, maintenance superintendent, or oil company representative. Repeat this training annually or more frequently as need arises.

2. Specific instructions. The lubricator must know exactly what machines he is to lubricate, when he is to do it, and the precise lubricant to be used. Some ways of communicating this information are route sheets issued daily to the lubricators and decals or plastic tags placed on each machine to be lubricated. The computer is especially well adapted to storing the information needed to carry out a lubrication program, including a daily printout of route sheets for the lubricators.

3. Checkoff reporting. Require the lubricator to sign or initial each task performed, using the punched card, the route sheet, or the plastic tag as a permanent record. Leave space for and invite his comments on the conditions he finds at the lubrication points.

Instrumentation

Measurement of its variables is the starting point for control of a manufacturing process, and there are many commercially available instruments for measurement and control. Among the most common process variable measurements encountered in industry are

Electrical	*Physical*	*Composition*
Voltage	Count	Percent solids
Resistance	Weight	pH (Acidity-alkalinity)
Current	Thickness	Analysis (percent of one or more constituents present)
Wattage	Color	
Power Factor	Density	
Radiation	Level (Liquids in tanks, solids in bins)	
	Temperature	
	Pressure	
	Flow rate	
	Viscosity	
	Turbidity	

Sometimes a simpler measurement can be substituted for a more complicated and expensive one. An example would be interpreting the electric current drawn by the motor of an agitator stirring a liquid in a tank as an indication of the viscosity of the liquid.

If an industrial instrument only displays the measurement of a variable, it is called an indicating instrument, or *indicator*. If it records the measurement on a chart, it is a *recorder*. If it controls the variable, it is a *controller*. These functions are combined in different ways. If an instrument records and controls, it is a *recorder-controller*. If it indicates and controls, it is an *indicator-controller*. Some instruments control without indicating or recording, and are called *blind controllers*.

The control loop. Figure 16–9 illustrates how a control loop with a flow controller works. The task is to pump the liquid out of the tank at a specified flow rate in gallons per minute. The pump moves the water through a discharge pipe in which is installed a primary measuring element called an *orifice plate*. It is a metal plate with a carefully machined hole slightly smaller than the pipe diameter. As the liquid passes through the plate, the observed pressure on the

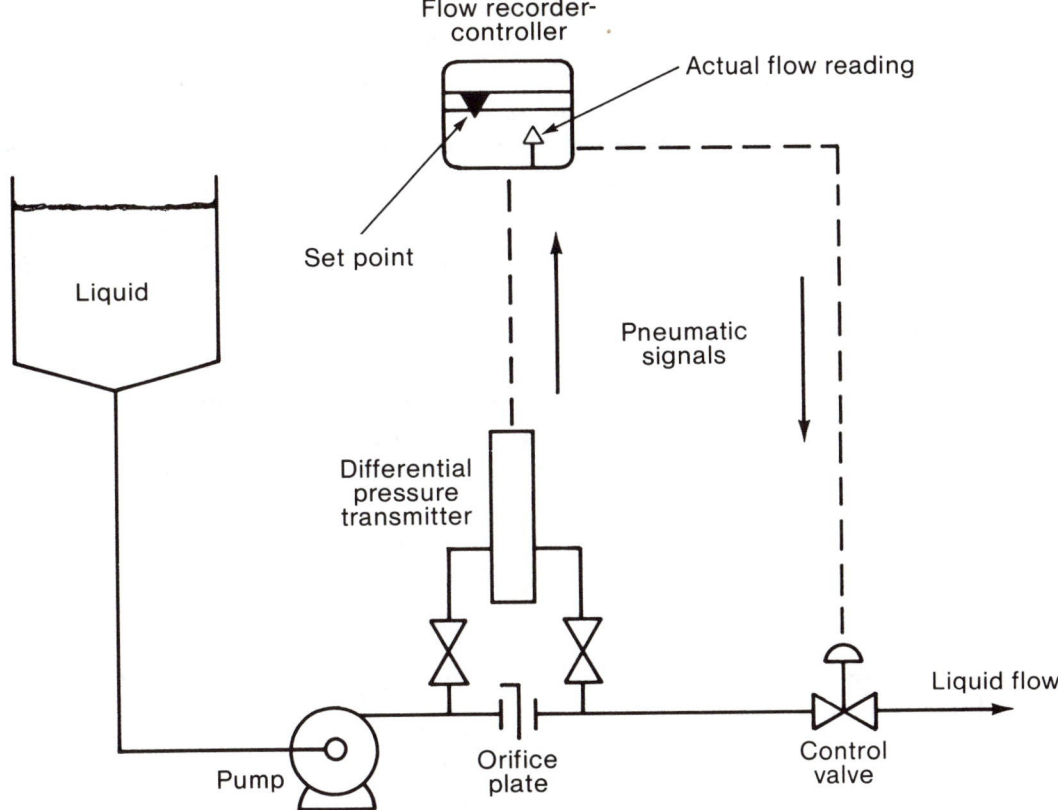

FIGURE 16-9: Instrument Control Loop

downstream side will be lower than that on the upstream side, and the difference between the two is a measure of the rate of flow. Pressure taps are placed on either side of the orifice plate and connected to a *differential pressure transmitter,* which sends a signal to the flow recorder-controller showing what the pressure difference is. At the controller, the operator has put the *set point* (black triangle) at the desired flow rate. The white triangle indicates the actual flow rate and records it on the chart with a pen. The controller compares the desired flow rate with the actual rate and sends a signal to the control valve, opening or closing it to bring the flow to the desired setting.

Control modes.   Control loops vary in the precision of control required and in characteristics that affect the way control is achieved. Controllers are equipped with different control modes to provide the precision and response time desired. In ascending order of performance and cost, these are the modes used in industrial equipment:

On-off.   This mode is the simplest and cheapest. When the measurement at the controller goes above or below the set point, the control valve opens or closes all the way. For the system shown in Figure 16-9 this would be an unacceptable mode because there would be sudden, repetitive changes in the head on the pump and a pulsating, start-stop flow in the pipe. On-off is not widely applicable to industrial situations but is used in space heating thermostats and for rough control applications such as prevention of overflow in a tank. It can be modified with a *deadband,* or *differential-gap,* which actuates the control device at settings above and below the set point. For example, if a room thermostat is set at 70 degrees, the heat would turn on at 69 and off at 71.

Proportional band. The control device moves from fully opened to fully closed over a range that is a predetermined percentage of the total span of the instrument. Assume that the control instrument in Figure 16–9 has a total span of 0 to 60 gallons per minute. If the proportional band is set at 50 percent, the control valve will move from fully opened to fully closed over a range of 30 gpm; thus, if the set point is 40 gpm, the valve will be fully open at $40 - 1/2(30) = 25$ gpm, and fully closed at $40 + 1/2(30) = 55$ gpm. Some controllers have a *proportional gain* setting instead of proportional band. It is equal to 100 divided by the proportional band expressed in percent.

Smoother control is possible with proportional band, because the valve no longer slams open or shut upon a deviation from set point but is open to a degree that depends on how large the deviation is. The disadvantage of a controller which only has proportional band, however, is that it does not return the controlled variable to the set point but lines the system out at some other value. The difference between them is called the *offset.*

Reset. If, in the example just mentioned, the controller is set at 40 gpm and a system upset occurs driving the flow rate up to 57 gpm, the instrument with proportional band only will attempt to bring the flow back to 40 gpm but may actually line out at some other value—say 49 gpm. The operator can attempt to correct the situation by lowering the set point—say to 35 gpm. That may cause the flow to line out at 42 gpm, so he resets the set point to another value, still trying to get the flow back to 40 gpm. This process is entirely too cumbersome for industrial applications and so *reset* is added to proportional band as an additional control mode. Mathematically reset *integrates* the difference between the set point and actual flow rate, and an instrument having both modes is called a *PI controller.* Reset is expressed in minutes, and represents the time required for each increment of change resulting from proportional action. Its final effect is to bring the process variable back to the set point.

Derivative. Also called *rate control,* this is usually added to an instrument that has proportional band and reset, resulting in a *PID controller.* Less frequently it is combined with proportional band alone, giving a *PD controller.*

With derivative, the *rate* of response of the control device depends upon the size of the deviation from set point; in our example, if the controller is set at 40 gpm, the control valve will be shutting much faster when the flow is 55 gpm than when it is 45 gpm. Derivative brings the system back to the set point faster than is possible with the other two modes.

Other configurations. When the output signal of a controller is not sent to a control device, such as a valve, but instead is used to position the set point of another control instrument, the arrangement is called a *cascade* system. In *duplex control* a signal from one instrument is sent to two control devices. In *ratio control* the instrument receives two signals but only controls one device; an example would be a system in which it is desired to have the flow in pipe *A* always to be one-half the flow in pipe *B*. The instrument would need to receive signals from both pipes so that it can compare the flows but would only control the flow in pipe A.

Trends. Until the 1970s most industrial control systems were pneumatic; in Figure 16-9 the signal line between the differential pressure transmitter and the controller would be a tube containing air. The transmitter would tell the instrument what the flow rate in the line is by adjusting the pressure in that line between 3 and 15 psi. The controller would compare the flow rate signal to the set point and send a 3 to 15 psi pneumatic signal to the control valve, opening it or closing it to adjust the flow. In recent years electronic instrumentation has been replacing pneumatic systems for several reasons: (1) Control signals travel through wires much faster than pneumatic signals through tubes. (2) Electronic instruments can be made smaller and cheaper than pneumatic types. (3) Electronic instruments can be more easily interfaced with computers to build highly sophisticated control systems. Electronic instruments, however, can be hazardous in plants with flammable atmospheres because of their spark-producing characteristics. But this can be overcome either by enclosing them in explosionproof enclosures or connecting them to *transducers*, devices that can receive signals from pneumatic devices located in the hazardous areas and can convert them to electrical signals for use in the control system.

Cooling Towers

The cooling tower is a device for transferring heat from an industrial process to the atmosphere using recirculated water. Figure 16-10 shows how a cooling tower system works. Cooled water from a concrete sump is pumped to the plant, where it picks up heat from a process heat exchanger, air conditioning condenser, or other device. The heated water goes to a series of spray nozzles at the top of the tower where it is broken up into droplets which "rain" down through the tower fill. A fan (or fans) at the top of the tower draws air in through the louvers at the base. The droplets fall through a tower fill, which is a latticework of wood, plastic, or concrete designed to keep the water stream broken up into droplets and to promote contact between the air and the water. As the water droplets pass downward through the rising air stream, they evaporate partially, transferring heat and moisture to the air. The rising air stream passes through drift eliminators, which screen out any droplets rising with it, and is finally discharged as hot, humid air out the top. The cooled water collects in the sump and is pumped back to the process to pick up more heat and start the cycle over again.

Figure 16-10 represents an *induced draft* tower because the air is pulled into the tower by the fan; in a *forced draft* tower the fan would be placed where one of the sets of louvers is shown in Figure 16-10, and the air pushed in. The *hyperbolic tower* (the familiar shape seen in photographs of nuclear power plants)

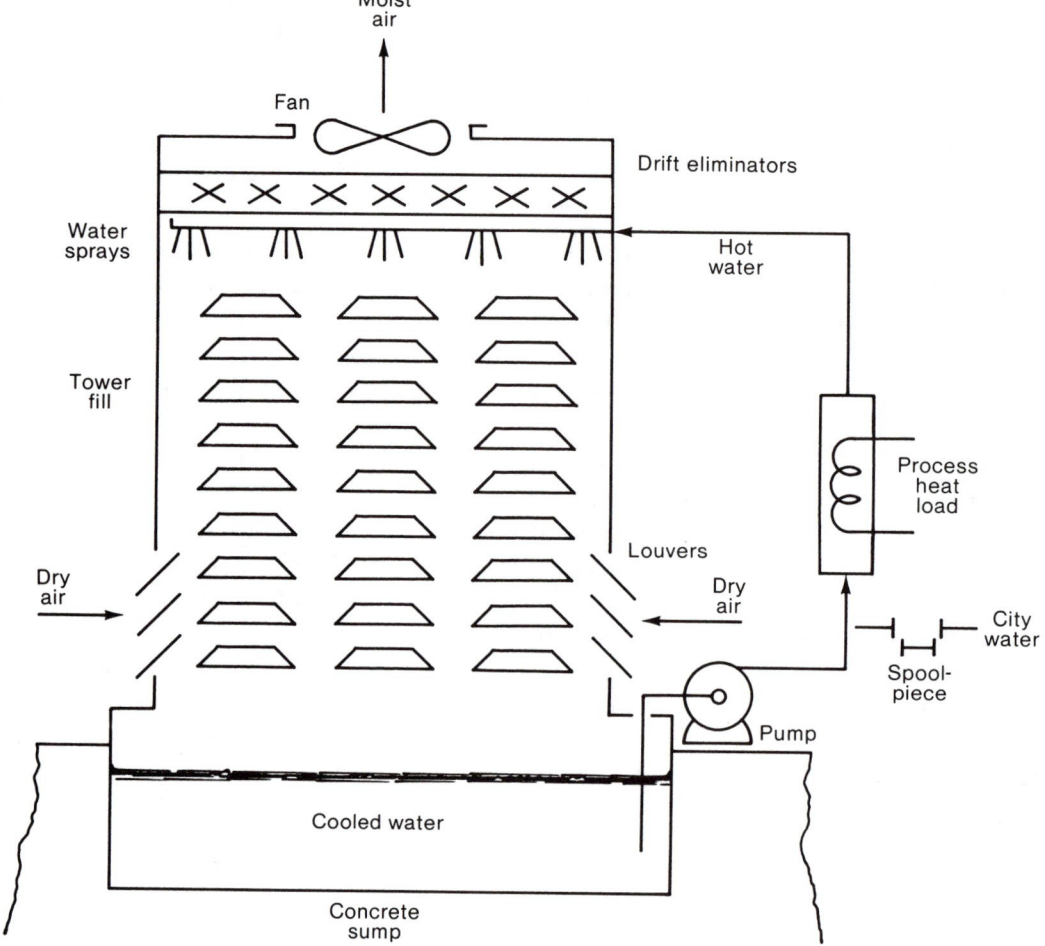

FIGURE 16–10: Cooling Tower

uses no fan at all but depends on the "chimney effect" to draw air up through the tower; although it saves the energy cost of operating the fan, it requires a much larger unit to accomplish the same amount of heat transfer. The tower of Figure 16–10 is a *counterflow* type because the air and water travel in opposite directions through it; in a *crossflow* tower the air would pass through at right angles to the falling water.

These are the important operating aspects of concern to the plant manager:

Chemical treatment. The metal surfaces of heat exchangers, pumps, and piping in the cooling system require protection against corrosion, the deposition of scale, and the accumulation of bacterial slime. Chemicals are added to the water daily to prevent these problems, and the results monitored by chemical tests. Choosing these chemicals and adjusting the amounts to be added can be a confusing process, and the best way to handle the problem is to hire a water treatment firm which will provide the chemicals as well as consulting advice on the condition of your system. Some even provide corrosion coupons, small metal strips that are installed in the water stream and removed periodically for measurement of corrosion rate.

Blowdown.   The mineral content of the recirculating water tends to build up because some of the water evaporates in the tower, but of course the minerals do not evaporate with it. When the mineral content gets too high, some of the water must be drained to the sewer and replaced by fresh water. The fresh water added is called *make-up*.

Backflow.   In many plants an alternate supply of cooling water is essential if the cooling tower system should fail for any reason (such as a power outage), and the simplest way to obtain it is to connect the city water supply to the recirculation system. Municipal water authorities will not permit a simple pipe connection with a valve, however, because of the fear of backflow, which can occur whenever the pressure in the tower system is higher than the city water pressure, allowing tower water to leak back through the valve and contaminating the city water. Usually they will require a break in the line, with a "spoolpiece" (a short length of pipe flanged at either end) available for quick installation if the city water should be needed. This type of connection is illustrated in Figure 16-10. When there would not even be sufficient time to install a spoolpiece, a *backflow preventer* may be permitted; it is a fairly expensive device offered by some valve manufacturers, which prevents backflow through a series of pressure regulators and drains. Municipal authorities may also allow a "homemade" backflow preventer: four gate valves are installed in the city water line, with three check valves alternating between them. A small drain line with an open valve at its end is installed between each check valve and its adjacent gate valve. If there is any backflow through the gate or check valves, it runs out the drains and can be seen immediately. When city water is needed for emergency cooling, the drain valves are closed and the gate valves opened.

Guidelines for Choosing Dryers

Industrial materials that require drying cover a wide variety of forms—lumber, ceramic objects, plastic films, textiles, solutions, pastes, and slurries. The liquid to be removed is usually water but can be any volatile liquid. And the final form can be the original solid object or sheet, a powder, or a granular solid.

Design and selection of dryers from the manager's point of view

1. Make sure a broad economic review is made before selecting a particular drying technique. One process equipment catalog lists 36 categories of dryers. Comparisons should include not only the substantial first cost of such equipment but energy consumption over its lifetime as well.

2. Can the dryer be included in the materials movement scheme? That is, can the material be dried while on a moving belt, in a bucket elevator, or on a screw conveyor? (See Chapter 17.)

3. Mechanical separation of the liquid from the solid is much cheaper than evaporation in a dryer. Can a settling, screening, or centrifuging step be inserted ahead of the dryer to reduce the load on it?

4. Avoid overdesign. There is no point in being able to dry wood chips to a moisture content of 1 percent if later they will reach an equilibrium moisture content of 10 percent while in contact with the air in a warehouse.

Types of dryers available. *Continuous vs. batch:* The most common of the batch units is the *tray* dryer. An insulated cabinet (usually of walk-in height) is fitted with heating coils and fans. The material to be dried is placed on trays which are mounted on wheeled carts. The carts are moved into the cabinet, the doors closed, and the material subjected to hot air flow for as long as needed to reach desired dryness. Although the first cost of this equipment is relatively low, labor cost is high, and it is limited to situations in which the material cannot tolerate agitation, in which relatively small amounts of a large number of different products are dried, or those in which long drying times are required.

The continuous dryers offer much more economical materials handling. The tray dryer concept can readily be adapted to the continuous *tunnel* dryer, in which the carts are pulled through a long drying cabinet, with the residence time calculated to match the drying cycle. The most common of the continuous types is the *rotary* dryer, which consists of a horizontal cylinder mounted to rotate around its long axis. Finlike sheet metal *flights* are attached to the interior surface. The wet feed enters at one end of the rotating cylinder, is picked up by the flights, and cascaded through the air space. Hot air is passed through the cylinder, either *concurrently* or *countercurrently* to the direction of the feed flow. *Belt* dryers are really tunnel dryers that use a conveyor belt to transport the material; the belt can contain perforations or be a screen to allow air to pass up through the material as well as over it.

Direct vs. indirect heating: All of the dryers described above are *direct heat* types, because the heat which evaporates the moisture is carried by the air (or gas) stream which comes in direct contact with the material being dried. Further illustrations of the direct heat type are the *spray* dryer, in which a solution is forced through a spray nozzle into a chamber through which hot gases flow, suspending the falling droplets until the water evaporates and a dry powder remains. Spray dryers are used for dilute solutions, heat-sensitive materials, and some types of slurries. The *fluid bed* dryer takes advantage of the fact that a mass with the properties of a fluid can be achieved by passing a gas flow through a bed of granular solids at velocities high enough to suspend or "fluidize" the particles. If the gas is heated, drying can be accomplished at the same time. Fluid bed dryers can be operated either as batch or continuous flow systems.

In *indirect heat* dryers the heat for drying is not carried by the gas flow but comes through a metal wall with which the material to be dried is kept in contact. A prime example is the *drum* dryer, which is a slowly rotating cylinder, closed off at either end to form a hollow chamber. Steam or any desired heating medium is passed through the interior of the drum. The feed is applied to the hot exterior surface, dries as it rides around the periphery, and is scraped off as a flake or

a. Tray Dryer (Batch Type).
(Courtesy of Proctor & Schwartz, Inc.)

b. Rotary Dryer (Continuous Type)
(Courtesy FMC Corp., Material Handling Systems Division.)

FIGURE 16-11: Examples of Batch and Continuous Dryers

powder by a knife-edged bar. Drum dryers are often used when it is desired to recover the solids in flake form, are readily adapted to handling viscous feeds, and are suited to solvent-recovery applications. Another type is the double-cone shaped *tumble* dryer, which takes a batchwise charge and turns end over end during the drying cycle. Heat is supplied to an external jacket. The ordinary screw conveyor is converted to a *screw flight* dryer by adding a heating jacket to the trough.

Vacuum vs. atmospheric pressure drying: Drying at less than atmospheric pressure lowers the operating temperature (a necessity for heat-sensitive materials), and facilitates the recovery of solvents. The tray, rotary drum, and tumble dryers already mentioned are adaptable to vacuum operation. Another type often equipped for vacuum operation is the *pan* dryer. It has a relatively shallow-dished circular container into which the feed flows. Heating is indirect, through a jacket, and an agitator sweeps the bottom of the pan, effecting material discharge through a side port.

Operating hints

1. Don't overdry. If the quality specification allows a moisture content of X, it is a waste of (sometimes considerable amounts of) money to dry it to one-tenth or even one-half X.

2. Schedule shutdowns. Of all the kinds of process equipment, dryers are among those that benefit most from preplanned downtime for cleaning and maintenance. Heat transfer surfaces become fouled, plastic and rubber seals in rotating elements are subject to erosion by abrasive particles and plugging by solids buildups, and air filters become plugged after so many hours of use. If these problems are not attended to *before* they cause trouble, emergency outages and accumulations of off-grade product will be the outcome *after* they become evident.

3. Monitor inlet (as well as outlet) streams. If the feed is wetter (or has other properties different) than design specifications, the dryer may be hopelessly overloaded. Operating managers then have to make the choice between shutting down and straightening out the problems in upstream equipment (decanters, centrifuges, settlers) or producing a "wet" product which will have to be redried.

MAKING THE MOST OF ROBOTS IN THE PLANT

What Robots Are

The Robot Institute of America defines the robot as "a reprogrammable multifunctional manipulator designed to move material, parts, tools, or specialized devices through variable programmed motions for the performance of a variety of tasks." This definition clearly separates robots from "hard automation" devices which are not reprogrammable but can only perform the same tasks over and over, albeit for thousands and even millions of repetitions.

There are many types and sizes of robots, but the welding robot shown in Figures 16-12 and 16-13 demonstrates some typical characteristics. Figure 16-12

FIGURE 16–12: Industrial Robot Applied to Welding Operation. Robot manufacturer supplies the welding power supply, gun, wire reels, feeders, and part positioning table. (Courtesy Cincinnati Milacron, Inc.)

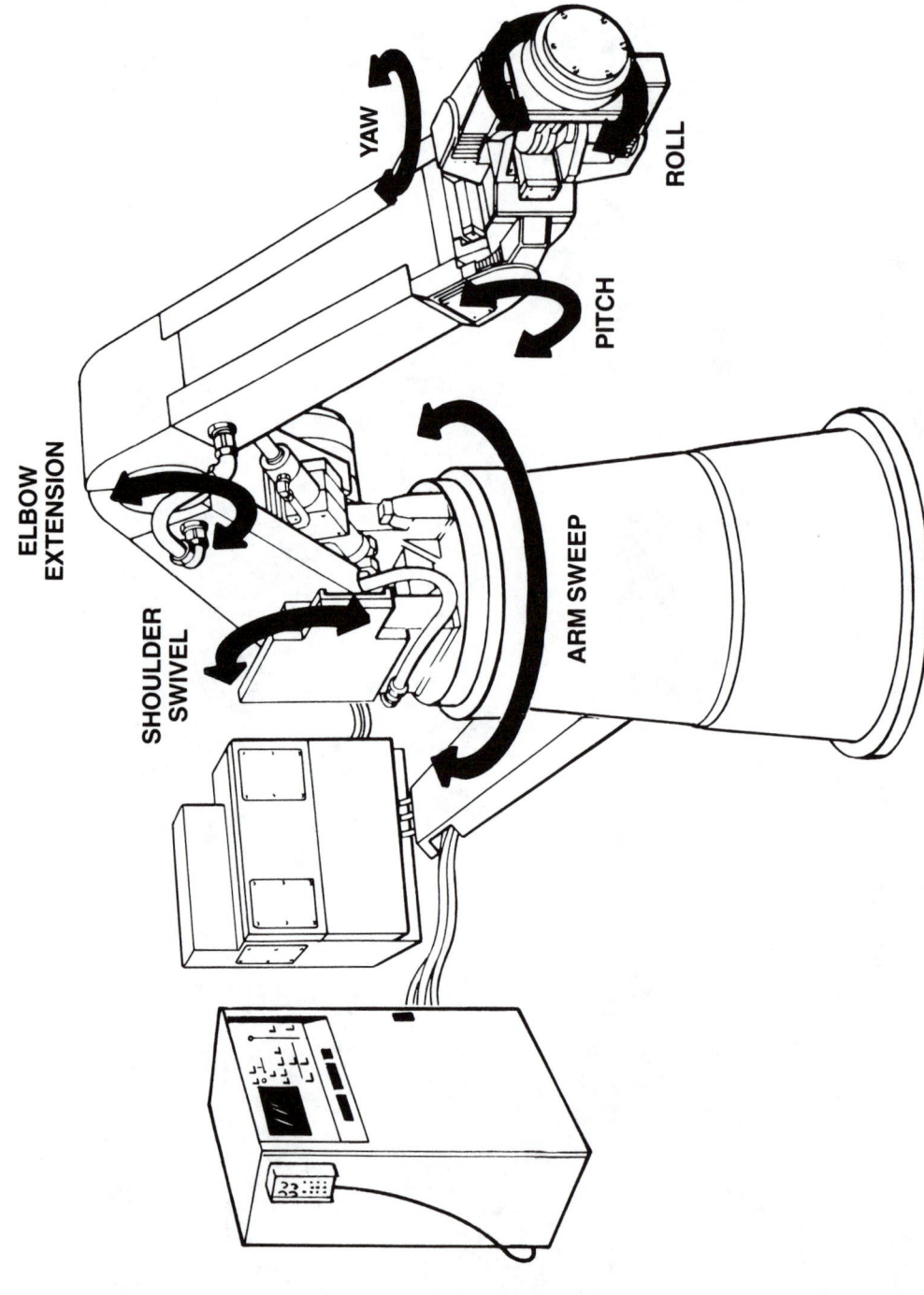

FIGURE 16-13: Diagram of Robot Shown in Figure 16-12 (but Without Welding Equipment). This is a jointed-arm, computer-controlled robot system. The boxlike unit directly behind the robot is a combined hydraulic and electric power supply. The computer control unit is at the left. (Courtesy Cincinnati Milacron, Inc.)

pictures the robot performing a welding operation. Figure 16–13 is a diagrammatic representation of the same model, but without the welding equipment. The diagram shows the robot itself, the computer control unit, and the power unit which, in this case, supplies both hydraulic and electrical power to the robot. The arm sweep, shoulder swivel, and elbow extension movements permit the robot arm to operate in three dimensions; the pitch, roll, and yaw movements of the manipulator wrist allow the *end effector* (the tool that performs the task) to be positioned in any desired attitude. The *work envelope* is the volume of space within which the robot can position the end effector. Computerized robots are capable of operating sequences involving hundreds of steps. *Sensors* are devices that tell the computer control unit where the end effector is located and may even be able to distinguish objects in the work environment.

What Robots Can Do for You

A robot will be able to do one or more of the following tasks: pick up a piece; reposition it; insert it in a machine; remove it when the machine operation is completed; grasp a tool, position it properly, and hold it while an operation is completed; place the completed piece in a container or on a pallet or conveyor for removal from the work station. It can do these things in unpleasant or hazardous atmospheres, with minimal illumination, heating, cooling, and ventilation.

The most numerous applications of robots have been in materials handling, welding, and machine loading, but they are also used in spray painting and other coatings applications, die casting, machining, assembly, and a variety of other manufacturing plant operations.

Types of Robots Available

Robots are classified on the basis of several characteristics—how they are powered, mechanical complexity, and complexity of the control system.

Power systems.   Air-powered (pneumatic) robots are used for light loads and in operations where speed is important. Hydraulically powered robots can lift heavier loads and offer greater accuracy in positioning the end effector. The best positioning accuracy and repeatability is obtained when electric motors power the robot, and they can be enclosed for protection against dusty and corrosive atmospheres.

Mechanical complexity.   The device shown in Figures 16–12 and 16–13 represents the high end of the spectrum; the articulated arm, the three axes of motion of the wrist, and the computerized control add up to a complex (and therefore versatile) system. Less complicated robots may only have straight arms which may move up and down, back and forth horizontally, or rotate about one or more axes—so that the device may end up having anywhere from two to seven axes of motion. These robots may have cylindrical or spherical work envelopes. At the low end of the spectrum is the "pick and place" robot that has only a rigid arm which it can extend to pick up a piece, raise the arm to a set angle, swivel, and drop the piece in another location. It is probably air-driven and is set in motion and stopped by triggers, limit switches, and mechanical bars.

Control complexity. The major difference is between servo controls, which provide feedback as to the location of the robot arm, and nonservo controls, which have no feedback. In the simplest nonservo types, motion along each axis is between two points, and the motion is limited by a mechanical device—such as a crossbar inserted in the moving arm.

Servo robots use a closed-loop control system consisting of a feedback device, which tells the control unit what is happening, and a computerized control unit, which processes the feedback information and tells the robot what to do about it. Feedback is provided by sensors of various types. Internal sensors tell the controller where the end of the robot arm is located in the robot's rectangular, spherical, or cylindrical coordinate system. Vision, proximity, force, and contact sensors tell the controller when it is near or is touching an object, what force is being exerted against it, and what objects are in its field of vision (the vision sensor is usually a television camera). Servo robots may be of the *point-to-point* type, which means that the robot arm will return to preset points along its axes without regard to the path followed in getting there, or the *continuous path* type, which means that the arm will always sweep along the same path it was originally "taught," as would be required in welding, spray painting, and other coating operations.

When to Use Robots

The manager considering how a manufacturing task is to be accomplished can choose hard automation, robots, or human labor. Hard automation is the choice when the operation is to be repeated thousands or even millions of times without change—a bottle-capping operation is an example. Human labor is a better choice when the products are made as individual items or in relatively small batches (less than a few hundred), when the operations are complicated, when errors must be quickly recognized and corrected to prevent damage, and when the operating environment is randomized and disorderly—that is, parts arrive at the work station mixed up in size and type or jobs are stopped and temporarily put aside while another order is worked on.

Robots fit in between these two extremes. They find application in batch-type operations where the number of parts to be worked on ranges from a few hundred to around 20,000 and when each batch may require a change in operating procedure from the previous one. Although robots may work no faster than humans, their productivity measured over time may be much better because they work unceasingly, without the need for relief periods. They are often better at accuracy and, especially, at repeatability—performing the job in precisely the same way time after time. Further, they can be used for tasks that humans find boring, tedious, or dangerous—handling materials that are hot, cold, corrosive, heavy, or radioactive; working in positions where it is difficult for a human to stand or bend; and in atmospheres that require humans to wear masks or protective clothing.

Planning the Selection and Installation of a Robot: A Two-Track Approach

The management which decides that, simply for the sake of trying them out—"we're going to install five robots next year"—is probably headed for a misapplication and problems that may leave plant personnel reluctant for a long time to try them again.

Like any other machine, robots should be used where they offer an advantage to the operation: better product quality, lower costs, or improved safety conditions. Therefore, the first step is to examine the plant's manufacturing operations to see where there may be opportunities to use robots to advantage. Once potential applications have been identified, the next step is to begin looking at those machines offered on the market that might be suitable. Robot manufacturers tend to specialize in certain types of operation—some are preeminent in painting, others in machining, and still others in materials handling. Once in negotiations with a robot vendor, you must be prepared to state what performance characteristics are required. The accuracy of positioning the end effector may range from $\pm$ 0.0005 in. to $\pm$ 0.25 in.; the repeatability of positioning the end effector may range from $\pm$ 0.0005 in. to $\pm$ 0.020 in.; arm speeds may vary from 30 to 60 in. per second; and carrying capacity ranges from less than a pound to 500 lb and on up to almost 2 tons. It must be decided whether servo or nonservo control is needed and how elaborate the sensors and computer controls must be. When a tentative supplier selection is made, it is a good idea to try to see his machine in action—preferably in another customer's plant.

Planning the actual installation proceeds on two tracks. The first involves the engineering considerations—which operation gets the first robot, setting a target date, identifying the utility connections that will be needed, deciding how raw materials and parts will arrive at the work station, and arranging for the robot supplier's technicians as well as your own to be on hand during start-up. Instead of limiting the planning to the installation of one machine, this may be a good time to review the automation of the entire manufacturing process and the changes in work flow and materials handling that will ultimately go with it.

The second track follows the human relations aspects. Operators will be understandably nervous about robots because, of all the machines management might choose to install, they most resemble human workers. The union will be wondering how many people are going to be displaced. Foremen and superintendents may worry that they will be reduced from first-line managers of people to technicians managing only a battery of machines. The situation calls for an educational program explaining management's employment philosophy, the benefits that management expects the workers to receive if robots are installed, and the dangers of failing to use them for increased productivity when the company's competitors may be using them. It will be wise, if possible, to have the first robot relieve plant operators of a dangerous, dirty, or uncomfortable task.

Economics of Purchase, Installation, and Operation

What you should expect to pay. A typical price for a robot is $60,000, but simple types may sell for $20,000 or less, and the more complicated models at

$250,000 and on up to $1 million. Installation costs, including start-up and development of control software, range from 15 percent to 500 percent of the purchase price. Operating costs, including energy and amortization of the initial costs, are about $6 an hour (which compares with some skilled labor rates at $20 per hour).

What you should expect to get back.   Fivefold productivity increases are not uncommon, and some users report much higher ratios than that—even thirtyfold. Most robots have a useful life of about eight years and will pay for themselves in one to three years; again, some may pay back in less than a year. Most users report on-line time of about 95 percent for robots. Many experience not only improvements in product quality, but what may be even more important, a greater consistency in product quality. Robots tend to use operating supplies such as welding rod and paint more efficiently than humans and require less light, heat, and ventilation.

The Future for Robots

Industrial application of robots has not proceeded as fast as predicted in the United States, and the reasons are many—potential users' ignorance of their capabilities and economic returns; reluctance to replace human workers or to face workers' opposition to the new machines; shortage of technicians within the company to utilize and maintain them; and, for smaller companies, lack of the necessary capital to acquire them. Each company will, of course, have to overcome these obstacles when a competing manufacturer begins to reap the cost, quality, and productivity advantages of installing robots.

Users have not been reluctant to tell robot manufacturers what improvements they want, and the future should see improvements in vision (ability to recognize objects through camera attachments), touch (ability to distinguish objects through tactile sensors), as well as lighter, faster, and more accurately positioned arms, standardization of computer programming, and lower initial cost. As these improvements are made, and as manufacturing managers become more aware of the potential of robots, they will be more widely used—not only in materials handling, machine loading, and welding but in assembly, machining, and applications involving plastics, textiles, and other materials including metals.

PROCESSING FLUID STREAMS

Fluid System Principles

The ability to transport fluids—liquids, slurries, or gases—from one processing unit to another is a key element in the development of a continuous processing stream. The plant manager who is interested in obtaining the most efficient fluid systems for his operations will find useful the basic design principles and the economic balances that must be struck in using them as they are outlined here.

The designer of a piping system for liquid flow uses as a basic tool this form of the Bernoulli equation:

$$Z_1 + \frac{V_1^2}{2g} + \frac{p_1}{\rho_1} + W = Z_2 + \frac{V_2^2}{2g} + \frac{p_2}{\rho_2} + F$$

The subscripts 1 and 2 refer to values of the variables at two different points in the system, usually the starting and ending points. Z is the elevation in feet above a convenient datum line established by the designer, often through the lowest point in the system. V is the linear velocity of the fluid through the piping in feet per second; g is the acceleration of gravity, a constant with the value of 32.2 feet per second squared; p is the fluid pressure, expressed in pounds per *square foot* (multiply pressure in psi by 144 to obtain pressure in psf). ρ is the density of the fluid in pounds per cubic foot. It will be noticed that when the variables in the first three terms on each side of the equation are expressed in consistent units of pounds, feet, and seconds, the units in the numerators and denominators divide out in such a way that each expression evolves in units of feet. This measurement in terms of feet is called *head*, and the three terms of the equation are *elevation head*, *velocity head*, and *pressure head*, respectively.

W represents the head that must be supplied by the pump. When it is multiplied by the flow rate in pounds per second and the resulting product divided by 550, the theoretical horsepower is obtained. Dividing this figure by the pump efficiency gives the required horsepower rating of the pump.

Before F is explained, a word is in order about the *Reynolds number*. It is the expression $DV\rho/\mu$, in which D is the pipe diameter in feet, V is the fluid velocity in feet per second, ρ is the fluid density in pounds per cubic foot, and μ is the viscosity in pounds per foot-second. When the Reynolds number takes on values below 2,000, the flow is classified as *laminar, viscous,* or *streamline*. When the Reynolds number exceeds 4,000, the flow is *turbulent*. The classification of flow and the values of the Reynolds number are important in finding F and in many other hydraulic and heat transfer calculations.

F represents the combined frictional losses in the system. There is a frictional drag between the wall of a pipe and the fluid moving inside it which produces energy losses that must be made up by the pump. The rougher the interior surface of the pipe (commercial steel pipe is rougher than copper tubing), the greater the loss. Fittings in the pipe system (valves, elbows, tees, and so forth), sudden enlargements and contractions (change from one pipe size to another), and pipe entrances and exits (for example, to or from a large tank) contribute additional energy losses to *F*. Finding *F* is a process too complicated to reproduce here, but it involves (1) calculating the Reynolds number; (2) finding the friction factor *f* from charts in handbooks on hydraulic engineering that plot *f* against Reynolds number and pipe roughness; (3) converting the number of fittings and the resistances from enlargement, contraction, entrances, and exits to equivalent lengths of straight pipe, again using information in the handbooks; and (4) determining *F* from charts that relate it to the values of *f, L,* and *V*, the fluid velocity.

The model given above is limited to noncompressible fluids (liquids) which do not undergo a temperature change. For compressible fluids (gases and vapors) more complicated equations, which take account of the change in fluid density with changes in pressure, must be used.

Four Types of Piping

Four major choices are involved in the design of a piping system: (1) optimum size, (2) appropriate material of construction, (3) best method of joining, and (4) selection of fittings.

Select optimum pipe size. Commercial pipe is made in nominal pipe sizes starting at ⅛ in. and increasing in ⅛-in. increments up to ½ in.; in ¼ in.-increments up to 1½ in.; ½-in. increments up to 4 in.; 1-in. increments up to 6 in.; and 2-in. increments up to 42 in. It is also classified according to wall thickness as Standard (STD), Extra-Strong (XS), and Double Extra-Strong (XXS). Wall thickness may also be designated by *Schedule Number*; Schedule 40 is the same as Standard for pipe sizes up to and including 10 in., and Schedule 80 is the same as Extra-Strong for sizes up to and including 8 in. For the basic dimensions of steel pipe see Table 13 in the Appendix. For a more thorough explanation of the relationship between wall thickness and schedule numbers, and for the dimensions of steel pipe expressed in both English and metric units, see American National Standard Welded and Seamless Wrought Steel Pipe, ANSI/ASME B36.10M—1985, published by the American Society of Mechanical Engineers, 345 East 47th Street, New York, N.Y. 10017. The pipe most often encountered in plant service is Standard (Schedule 40).

Choice of pipe size is based on flow velocity in feet per second (divide the flow rate in cubic feet per second by the cross-sectional area of the pipe in square feet); typical values for liquids are 5 to 15 fps, and 70 to 1,500 fps for steam. *Economic pipe diameter* is chosen on this basis: As pipe size goes up, the cost of purchase and installation increases; on the other hand, the cost of energy to move fluid through it declines, because friction losses are lower. To find the economic diameter for any particular installation: (1) plot a curve of pipe cost versus pipe size, (2) on the same plot graph energy cost versus pipe size, (3) plot a total cost line by adding the two costs for each pipe size. The economic pipe size corresponds to the lowest point on the total cost line. In actual practice this analysis may be costly to carry out and, therefore, reserved for the longer and more expensive piping runs in the plant. The piping designer also may not be able to use the economic pipe diameter because of other considerations—maximum allowable pressure drop in the system, limitations of automatic control valves, or unacceptable erosion rates caused by too high a flow velocity.

Pick the right material. Apply these criteria: cost; projected life; resistance to corrosion, temperature and shock; noncontamination of process material; heat transfer; ease of cleaning (food and chemical plants); cost of maintenance. Select from this table of available materials:

Metals	Nonmetals	Pipe linings*
Carbon steel	Concrete	Asphalt
Wrought iron	Clay	Cement
Cast iron	Asbestos cement	Wood
Brass	Graphite	Glass
Aluminum	Porcelain	Rubber
Silicon-Iron	Glass	Plastic (many types including fluorocarbon polymers, polyvinvylidene, chlorinated polyether)
Lead	Plastic	
Copper	(Many types, including polyethylene, polyvinyl chloride, and glass fiber reinforced polyester)	Metal (lead, stainless steel, aluminum, nickel and its alloys, tantalum, titanium)
Stainless steel		
Nickel-copper		
Nickel	Rubber	
Nickel-chromium	Wood	
Tin		
Titanium		
Tantalum		
Zirconium		

*Note on linings: Plastic linings may be either fused to the base pipe or inserted loose. Metal linings may be either electroplated or inserted as "clad" plates and welded to the base pipe.

Choose the best joining method. *Threaded* pipe is available in sizes up to 12 in.; although it dominates the field in sizes below 2 in., its use in larger sizes should be questioned in terms of economics, especially the labor cost of installation. Threaded joints are sealed by applying pipe dope or wrapping with Teflon tape before final tightening. *Flanged* joints are available in sizes up to 24 in. They are normally employed in sizes above 2 in. but are useful in any size when higher temperatures, higher pressures, or a need for frequent disassembly are involved. Flanges may be formed as an integral part of the pipe when it is manufactured, or they can be shipped separately and welded or screwed to the pipe in the field. Flanged joints are sealed by inserting gaskets between the flange faces and compressing them by tightening the bolts that hold the flanges together. *Welded* joints are used in long runs in larger sizes, and when the nature of the fluid requires positive leakproof joints. V-clamp joints are a newer development and use fewer bolts than a flanged joint. They are used where the lines must be opened frequently for cleaning or other reasons.

Select appropriate fittings. They may be grouped according to the functions they perform:

1. Connecting: Two pieces of pipe with external (male) threads can be connected with a *coupling*, a short pipe length with internal (female) threads. A short

pipe length with male threads is called a *nipple*. If the joint must be disassembled without disturbing adjacent pipe arrangements, a *union* is used. It has two halves that are permanently threaded to the pipe ends and joined by a single threaded connection at the center, which is easily undone with a pipe wrench.

2. Change in pipe size: When (for example) a 4-in. pipe must be connected to a 2-in. pipe, a *reducer* is used. It is a short section of pipe with the large and small connections at opposite ends; it is a *concentric reducer* if the small connection is centered on the same axis line as the large connection, and an *eccentric reducer* if it is not. A *bushing* is a single ring with an external thread of one size and an internal thread of a smaller size.

3. Change in flow direction: The common *elbow* effects a 90-degree change in direction. *Long radius elbows* have a longer arc of curvature and offer less resistance to flow; *street elbows* have an external thread at one end and an internal thread at the other; *45-degree elbows* effect change in direction at that angle. The *return bend* is U-shaped, effecting a 180-degree change in direction. The *tee* permits a 90-degree branch from the straight run. The *Y-branch*, or *lateral*, allows branching at other angles, usually 45 degrees. The *cross* provides double branching at 90 degrees. Most of the fittings mentioned are available with unequal size connections at the branches; such fittings are called *reducing tees, reducing elbows,* and so on. Pipe ends can be blocked with *caps*, which have an internal thread, or *plugs*, which have an external thread.

4. Valves: *Gate* valves are good for positive cutoff of flow but not for regulating or *throttling* flow; they should be left fully closed or fully open. *Plug cocks* offer positive flow cutoff with a quick-closing feature (usually one 90-degree turn of a handle). *Globe* valves have good throttling characteristics and positive cutoff; they are seldom used in sizes over 3 in. *Ball* valves have quick-closing, positive cutoff, and throttling features; they are often used for viscous fluids and slurries. *Butterfly* valves have good throttling characteristics and low-pressure drop; tight shutoff is available in special models. *Diaphragm* valves separate the fluid from the moving metal parts by a rubber or plastic diaphragm; they are used for corrosive and abrasive fluids at pressures up to 150 psi. *Check* valves allow flow only in one direction and have a gate or ball mechanism which seals on backpressure; basic types are *lift, swing,* and *ball* checks.

Pumps

These machines provide the driving force that moves fluids through piping; they are also discussed in the context of materials movement in Chapter 17. *Centrifugal pumps,* which are the most commonly encountered type in plant work, are really part of a larger class of variable capacity devices that include the *axial flow* pump and the *regenerative* pump. The axial flow machine has a propeller mounted on a shaft within the pump casing and imparts velocity to the fluid in the direction of the shaft. It is used when large volumes of fluid are moved against relatively low head, as in recirculation systems. The regenerative pump is also called a *turbine* pump; it moves fluid through a radial cavity at the periphery of the pump by means of vanes that are mounted on a radial disk and project into the radial cavity. Its application is the reverse of that of the axial flow types—it is used for low-volume, high-head systems. The *centrifugal* pump uses a circular impeller with spiral vanes (mounted on a spinning shaft like a wheel on an axle) which rotates inside a casing. Liquid is drawn into the eye of the impeller and discharged at the periphery. The casing is most often in the shape of a volute, which allows a smooth transformation of velocity head into pressure head.

In *positive displacement* pumps a slug of liquid is drawn into the pump, trapped in a chamber formed by the mechanism, and forced into the discharge section by some form of mechanical action. In *piston* and *plunger* pumps, liquid is drawn into a cylindrical chamber on the suction stroke and forced into the discharge line on the return power stroke. This action creates pressure pulsations in the discharge line; they can be smoothed out by mounting two or more pistons on the pump with staggered power strokes. The *triplex* pump (three pistons) is a common type.

Rotary pumps achieve a nonpulsating positive displacement by means of a continuously rotating mechanism. Typical is the *gear* pump, which has two gears mounted one above the other, so that they mesh in the center. Liquid is drawn into the pump by rotation of the gears and trapped between the gear teeth and the pump casing, which fits tightly around them. When the liquid reaches the discharge side, it is prevented from flowing back to the suction side by the meshing of the gear teeth. Other variations of the rotary pump are the *vane* pump, *screw* pump, *rotating piston*, and *lobe* pumps.

How to select a pump.   Choose a *centrifugal* pump whenever possible. This type is available in a wide variety of standard capacities, is usually lowest in first cost, has the simplest mechanism, and is easiest to install and operate. Specify a centrifugal pump *unless:*

a. The flow is outside the range of 5 gpm to 100,000 gpm.
b. Changes in flow rate caused by changes in system pressure are unacceptable.
c. Viscosity exceeds 1,000 centipoises.
d. The combination of flow rate and head requirements lies within the narrow ranges of the more specialized variable displacement pumps. Use the axial flow pump for flow rates from 1,000 to 1,000,000 gpm at heads less than 50 ft. At the other end of the scale, specify the regenerative pump for flows up to 200 gpm against heads up to 1,200 ft.

Final selection of a particular centrifugal pump for a flow system is made from curves of flow rate versus head published by manufacturers for each of their models. Examples of these curves, called *characteristics,* are given in Figure 16–14 for three pump models, A, B, and C. The characteristic shows the flow rates that will be delivered against various values of head; for example, when Pump C is

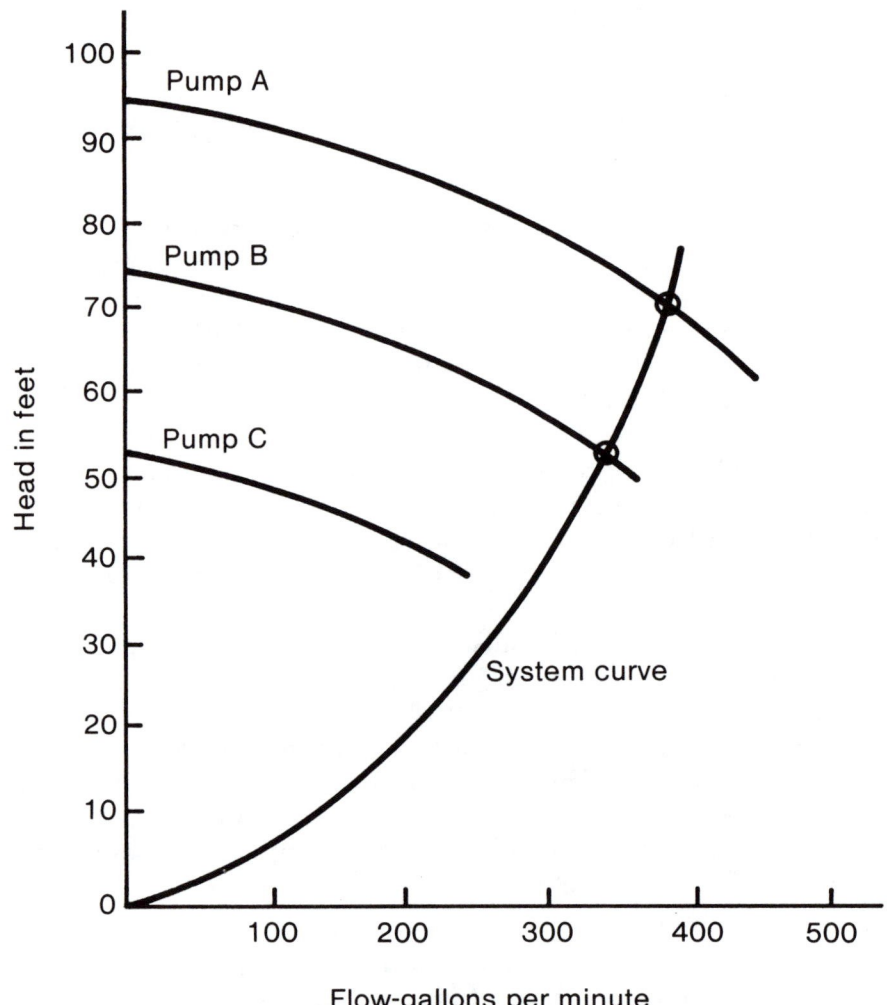

FIGURE 16-14: Pump Characteristic and System Curves

operated against a 43-ft. head, it will deliver 200 gpm. Each pump will operate at only those points that lie on its characteristic; thus, if it is desired to operate Pump C at 100 gpm, the head would have to be increased to 49 ft.

A further aid to selection is the plotting of a *system curve,* as shown in Figure 16-14. Using the equation and calculation method described on page 329, values of head required are determined for a number of flow rates in a given piping system and the results plotted on the pump curve graph. The intersection of a characteristic with the system curve represents one set of conditions at which the flow system can operate. Thus, in Exhibit 5, if the flow system can be operated at 340 gpm, it will develop a head of 53 ft.; if Pump B is operated against a head of 53 ft., it will produce a flow rate of 340 gpm. This combination of flow and head is the only one at which Pump B will operate in this system. If a higher flow rate is desired, the conditions at the intersection of the system curve and the

Pump A characteristic can be used—385 gpm at 71 ft. of head. These intersections are the only two points on the graph at which the system can operate; if other flow rates are desired, other pumps whose characteristics intersect the system curve at those flow rates would have to be obtained.

Choose a positive displacement pump when

a. Flow is less than 5 gpm.

b. Viscosity exceeds 1,000 centipoises.

c. Steady flow rate must be maintained against changes in head. Unlike the centrifugal pump, the positive displacement pump delivers at a virtually constant flow rate over a wide range of head.

d. The fluid might be injured by the high shear rate of a centrifugal pump (e.g., synthetic latex).

The centrifugal pump is usually connected directly to the motor shaft, and rotates at full motor speed. Positive displacement pumps are usually geared down to operate at lower speeds, and if a variable speed drive is used, can be adjusted to deliver accurate flows over a wide rate range. Because of their close-fitting internal parts, they should not be used with fluids containing suspended matter or those which have poor lubricating properties.

Cavitation and net positive suction head. If the pressure at the suction inlet of the pump is low enough to equal or almost equal the vapor pressure of the fluid, bubbles of vapor will form and then collapse as the fluid passes to the high-pressure side of the pump. This action is known as *cavitation*, and it can be identified by extreme vibration and noisiness. It causes erosion of the pump parts and interferes with pump performance. To overcome this problem, two kinds of net positive suction head (NPSH) must be considered: (1) The NPSH *required* by the pump. It is determined by the manufacturer and is usually plotted as a curve of required NPSH versus flow rate on the same graph as the characteristic curve of the pump. (2) The NPSH *available* at the suction inlet of the pump. Its value is the total of the elevation, pressure, and velocity heads minus the vapor pressure of the fluid. The available NPSH must equal or exceed the required NPSH if cavitation is to be avoided.

Checklist for installing, operating, and maintaining pumps

(1) When Installing:

_____Mount pump level on firm foundation or base plate.

_____Connect piping so that there is no strain on pump casing. May require flexible connection.

_____Do not connect an elbow or other change of direction fitting directly to pump casing. Fluid should have a straight run into the pump suction.

_____Locate pump as close as possible to fluid supply. Keep suction line as short as possible.

_____Check coupling for misalignment. (See p. 308.)

_____An arrow showing the proper direction of rotation will be embossed on the casing or marked on the nameplate. Check for proper rotation before starting a new pump or one that has undergone electrical repairs; wires may be reversed, causing pump to run backward.

(2) Operating:

_____Start-up. Flood casing by opening suction valve. If there is a vent cock on the casing, open it so that liquid can displace air or gas. Open discharge valve if pump is positive displacement type; if it is centrifugal type, close the discharge valve or open slightly. Check to see that all lubrication and cooling devices are in operation. Start motor; open discharge valve slowly.

_____Check for noise, vibration, overheating, and excessive motor current while pump is running. If any of these symptoms appear, take pump out of service until condition is corrected.

_____Never throttle suction valve on a pump. Never throttle discharge valve on a positive displacement pump.

_____Never run a pump dry—moving parts will wear and overheat.

(3) Maintenance:

_____Put pump on routine lubrication schedule. Make sure that oil reservoirs and grease fittings are properly supplied at all times.

_____Repack stuffing box on regular schedule; don't wait until excessive leakage or scoring of shaft takes place.

_____Store spare parts as recommended by manufacturer. Moving parts—shaft, seals, bearings—are usually on the list. If pump has a mechanical seal, stock a complete spare seal assembly for quick return of the pump to service in the event of failure.

_____On preventive maintenance inspections, check coupling alignment, tightness of baseplate bolts and piping connections, functioning of lubrication systems, and condition of packing.

_____If there is a risk of solid objects getting into the pump mechanism, install a large mesh screen or knockout pot in the suction line.

Compressors

Compressors are part of the general class of machines used to move gases from one location to another. They are differentiated from fans and blowers, which move large volumes of gas with little change in pressure, by this definition: A compressor is a device that increases the density of the gas passing between its inlet and outlet by at least 7 percent. Air and refrigerant compressors are the types most often encountered, but there are many plants that use compressors to move process gases. These guidelines for the selection, installation, and operation of compressors apply to all types.

Types and range of application

1. *Reciprocating* machines have one or more cylinders in which a sliding piston compresses and moves the gas. They are most often used for flows up to

10,000 cubic feet per minute (cfm) of inlet gas and pressures up to 10,000 pounds per square inch (psi); both limits can be exceeded by specially built machines.

2. *Rotary* compressors are positive displacement machines in which a rotating element traps a slug of gas at the inlet side, carries it around through the machine, and discharges it at the high-pressure outlet side. (The rotating element is designed to seal off the two sides of the machine from each other, so that leakage cannot occur back to the low-pressure side.) Major types are the *sliding vane*, the *single-* and *double-lobe*, the *helical screw*, and the *liquid piston*. Application is in the 10 cfm to 20,000 cfm range, and from negative pressures (vacuum) to 500 psi.

3. In the *centrifugal* compressor the gas is discharged tangentially from a high-speed rotating impeller; the action is similar to that of a centrifugal liquid pump. It is used for flows from 200 cfm to 200,000 cfm, with some machines ranging close to 1,000,000 cfm. Discharge pressures range from below atmospheric to around 5,000 psi.

4. The *axial* compressor is similar to the centrifugal compressor in that neither is a positive displacement machine but differs in that the flow is parallel to the rotating shaft and moves through a system of stationary and rotating blades. Application starts around 10,000 cfm and exceeds 1,000,000 cfm, with discharge pressures ranging from below atmospheric to 150 psi.

5. Comparative application: Reciprocating compressors are the most efficient in terms of energy consumption, and at low flows and high pressures have an advantage in purchase cost. However, they are costly to install and are subject to more frequent maintenance shutdowns. Rotary compressors have a first-cost advantage at low flows and pressures, deliver gas without pressure surges, and require no valve maintenance. Centrifugal compressors excel at handling large volumes at constant pressure, require less floor space, and are cheaper to install. Maintenance outages are less frequent but are longer in duration. Axial compressors are well adapted to constant volume applications, have some efficiency advantages over centrifugal types, but should only be used where some gas leakage is acceptable.

How to set up a compressor installation.   The enemies of reliable, low-maintenance compressor service are vibration, stress, and the presence of liquid in the system. Be sure that your design for a new compressor installation covers these key points:

Foundation. Massive enough to absorb vibration and stress. Meet or exceed compressor manufacturer's recommendations. Dissociate from building structure as much as possible.

Piping. Install traps and drains at low points for removal of liquid accumulations. Use flexible suction connections. All piping close to the compressor must be measured carefully and connected so as to avoid strain on the casing. Slope piping away from unit so that liquid cannot run back into it. Do not install shutoff valves on suction side—accidental closing can damage a compressor.

Surroundings. The mistake is often made of jamming compressor equipment into small rooms or areas crowded with other machinery. Provide horizontal room sufficient for removal of piping and dismantling of equipment, and vertical room for installation of hoisting apparatus and lubrication units.

Effective operation and maintenance.   Follow these principles for trouble-free operation:

1. Establish an operating log. Record pressures, temperatures, gas flows, cooling water rates, and oil levels.

2. Use the proper lubricant (ordinary oils may break down under the unusual heat and friction in a compressor) and use the log as a control method to make sure the lubrication program is actually carried out.

3. Check out the operation of auxiliary equipment—traps, drains, filters, and air dryers—on a daily basis. These devices must function properly to protect expensive machinery.

4. Be careful not to run the compressor outside its design limits of flow, pressure, and continuous hours of operation.

5. Repair leaks in the compressed gas system. When the compressed gas is air, leaks are easily ignored. But they incur needless power costs and can overload your machinery.

6. Inspect for mechanical vibration daily. Use an industrial stethoscope or simply train your mechanic to touch the point of a screwdriver to the casing and put his ear to the other end. He will soon learn to pick up unusual noises and will know when to shut the equipment down for preventive repair. These are relatively crude methods, but they are useful for smaller installations. Owners of larger units, or in situations where compressor failure results in costly production stoppages, usually install detection instrumentation which picks up and records acoustical and electronic signals that are recorded on a continuous chart and provide early warning of problems developing in the rotating parts of the compressor. These instruments are usually installed in the control room, and for large facilities (such as an ammonia plant), may occupy an entire panel; they normally include alarms and automatic cutoff devices.

7. Implement a preventive maintenance program. Open up the compressor to check wear, alignment, bearing condition, clearances, and corrosion effects on a quarterly to annual basis. Replace parts whose failure or excessive wear may damage other parts of the machine. Owners of machines with the automatic vibration detectors and analyzers just described may prefer to wait until the instruments show that a shutdown for repair is needed, and then make their routine parts replacement at that time.

Heat Exchangers

The simplest method of transferring heat from one fluid to another is to mix them together, and this possibility ought to be seriously considered for each heat transfer situation. This section, however, is limited to a discussion of equipment for transferring heat between two fluids that must be handled in enclosed systems and kept separate from each other.

What to specify

1. *Operating conditions.* For each fluid: the flow rate through the exchanger, the temperature in and desired temperature out, pressure, and allowable pressure drop through the equipment. In addition, the basic service of the unit: heater, cooler, evaporator, condenser, or reboiler.

2. *Physical properties of the fluids.* Density, viscosity, specific heat, thermal conductivity, and if one of the fluids is a vapor, its latent heat and the quantity and nature of any noncondensable gases that might be present. The *fouling factor* also must be known or estimated; it is a numerical measure of the degree to which the fluid can be expected to deposit unwanted solid material on the heat transfer surfaces. Values for various fluids can be obtained from equipment manufacturers or from the published standards of the Tubular Equipment Manufacturer's Association (TEMA). They range from a low of 0.0005 for steam and clean organic vapors to a high of 0.01 for polluted river water or diesel exhaust fumes.

Equipment choices.   The basic categories are *tubular* and *plate* exchangers. Of the tubular types, the simplest in construction is the *double-pipe* exchanger, which consists of a smaller pipe containing one fluid mounted concentrically inside a larger pipe, with the second fluid in the annular space. *Shell-and-tube* exchangers are the most common type and are explained in paragraph 2 following. *Spiral-tube* exchanges are constructed by winding short lengths of tubing into flat coils, stacking them close together, and connecting the inlet and outlet ends to pipe manifolds. This assembly is inserted into a compact shell that has connections for entrance and exit of the shell-side fluid. The finished unit is a very compact device whose construction overcomes thermal expansion problems and is well-suited to the handling of viscous materials.

Plate exchangers include the basic *plate-frame* unit, which consists of a series of vertical plates mounted on horizontal guide rods. The plates are gasketed around the edges and have holes at the corners for passage of the fluids. They are pressed tightly together by massive blocks tightened with a screw mechanism. If the spaces between the plates are imagined to be numbered consecutively, the plate holes are arranged so that one fluid passes through the odd-numbered spaces, while the other flows through the even-numbered spaces. This type of exchanger can readily be opened for cleaning and is often used for fluids that deposit relatively large amounts of solids. The *spiral plate* exchanger has two parallel plates wound in a spiral and enclosed in a casing. It has many of the same advantages as the spiral tube. The *plate-and-fin* exchanger has corrugated metal sheets sandwiched between flat metal plates; the "sandwiches" are stacked together, with fluids in the alternate spaces. It is widely used in very low temperature applications.

For shell-and-tube exchangers, a number of long, thin tubes are mounted inside a cylindrical shell; one fluid flows through the tubes, the other surrounds them as it passes through the shell. The ends of the tubes are fitted into circular discs called *tubesheets*. *Heads* are mounted on the tubesheets to serve as inlet and outlet reservoirs for the tubeside fluid; partitions can be installed in the heads to achieve as many passes through the tubes as desired (one to eight passes is considered "standard"). *Baffles* mounted inside the shell support the tubes and direct the flow of the shellside fluid so as to avoid dead spots. Figure 16–15 illustrates these features of a typical industrial heat exchanger.

The designer of this equipment must meet the obvious objectives of achieving

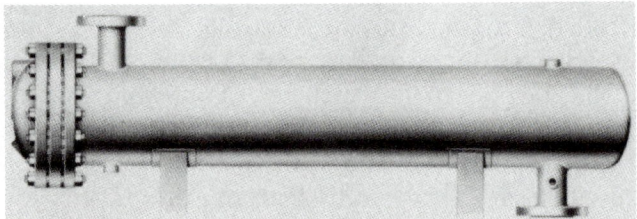

a. Photograph of U–tube heat exchanger with threaded head connections.

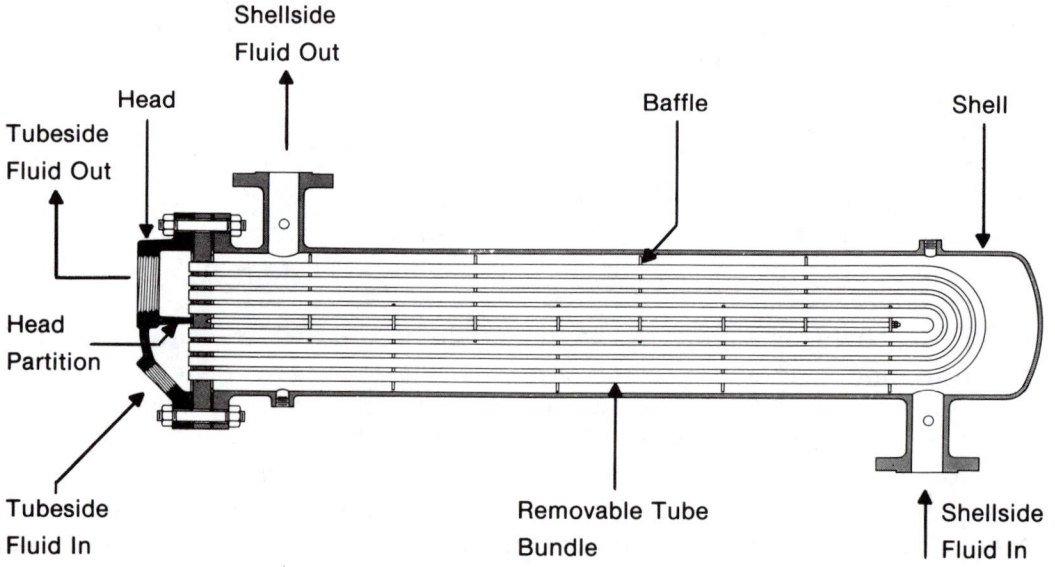

b. Diagram of above exchanger, showing internal parts.

FIGURE 16–15: Industrial Shell-and-Tube Heat Exchanger

the desired quantity of heat transfer at the lowest possible cost. She strives for the highest fluid velocities possible in order to maximize heat transfer and minimize fouling, but she must do this within the allowable pressure drops for each fluid stream. When temperature differences are large or thermal cycling frequent, the design must accommodate expansion and contraction of the components. In many cases access must be provided to the exterior of the tubes so that they can be cleaned mechanically.

There are three basic designs to meet these requirements. One is the *fixed tubesheet*, in which a tubesheet at each end of the exchanger is welded to the shell; another is the "U-tube" type, with only one tubesheet and each tube bent into a long U-shape; and the "floating head" types, in which there is one fixed tubesheet and the other is free to move back and forth in thermal expansion and contraction. Subtypes of this last group are the *pull-through floating head exchanger*, the *floating head outside packed lantern-ring exchanger*, the *floating head split backing ring* exchanger, and the *floating head outside packed stuffing box* exchanger. Features of the various designs are compared in Figure 16–16.

Operating instructions

1. Measure the performance (inlet and outlet temperatures and flow rates of both streams) while the exchanger is running well; the data will be needed for comparison when substandard performance is suspected.

2. Monitor both outlet streams for evidence of cross-contamination. If it occurs, the trouble may be a corroded tube, leaks at the tubesheet, or leaking head partition gaskets.

3. Leaking tubes can be taken out of service temporarily by tapping a soft metal plug into each end of the tube; the entire tube can be replaced at the next scheduled shutdown.

4. Arrange periodic shutdowns for cleaning of tubes and shell, replacement of head gaskets, replacement of defective tubes, and rerolling of tube ends in the tube sheet. Chemical cleaning consists of circulating solutions through the tube and shell which can dissolve solid deposits; mechanical cleaning consists of scraping and rodding, or using motorized brushes and knives to clean out tube interiors.

Vessels

Process vessels are roughly classified as *storage tanks* and *reaction kettles*. (See Chapter 17 for important considerations in the selection of tanks and the properties of process liquids.) Reaction kettles are vessels in which process fluids undergo a change in physical or chemical properties; they are typically equipped with an agitator for stirring the contents, exterior jackets or internal coils for heating and cooling, and instruments for measuring and recording temperature and pressure. Consider these points in the design and operation of both kinds of process vessels.

Type of Design	"U"-Tube	Fixed Tubesheet	Floating Head Pull-Through Bundle	Floating Head Outside Packed Lantern-Ring	Floating Head Split Backing Ring	Floating Head Outside Packed Stuffing Box
Relative Cost Increases From (A) Least Expensive through (E) Most Expensive	A	B	C	C	D	E
Provision for Differential Expansion	individual tubes free to expand	expansion joint in shell	floating head	floating head	floating head	floating head
Removable Bundle	yes	no	yes	yes	yes	yes
Replacement Bundle Possible	yes	not practical	yes	yes	yes	yes
Individual Tubes Replaceable	only those in outside row	yes	yes	yes	yes	yes
Tube Interiors Cleanable	difficult to do mechanically; can do chemically	yes, mechanically or chemically	yes, mechanically or chemically	yes, mechanically or chemically	yes, mechanically or chemically	yes, mechanically or chemically
Tube Exteriors with Triangular Pitch Cleanable	chemically only	chemically only	chemically only	chemically only	chemically only	chemically only
Tube Exteriors with Square Pitch Cleanable	yes, mechanically or chemically	chemically only	yes, mechanically or chemically	yes, mechanically or chemically	yes, mechanically or chemically	yes, mechanically or chemically
Double Tubesheet Feasible	yes	yes	no	no	no	yes
Number of Tube Passes	any practical even number possible	no practical limitations	no practical limitation (for single pass, floating head requires packed joint)	limited to single or 2 pass	no practical limitation (for single pass, floating head requires packed joint)	no practical limitation
Internal Gaskets Eliminated	yes	yes	no	yes	no	yes

FIGURE 16-16: Comparison of Various Heat Exchanger Design Features

Design criteria

1. *Density and weight.* What is the density of the process fluid? Combined weight of contents and tank when full? Should it be mounted on load cell or lever scale? Will building structure support this weight without modification?

2. *Heat transfer.* What will be the temperatures of the contents? What extremes will be reached? Will the fluid have to be heated or cooled? If so, how fast? Will the process or reaction generate heat that must be removed?

3. *Pressure.* What is the maximum pressure that will be reached in the tank? In its jacket? Will either be subject to vacuum? Has the designer provided for these pressures at the maximum temperatures?

4. *Corrosion and finish.* Will the process fluid corrode the vessel? Will the vessel material contaminate the fluid? Should the interior surface be given a special finish to minimize "skin" deposits on the walls or for sanitary cleaning?

5. *Volatility and flammability.* What is the vapor pressure of the contained fluid? At temperature extremes? Is it flammable? If so, will inert gas blanketing of the vapor space be required?

6. *Viscosity.* How "thick" is the fluid? What are the maximum and minimum viscosities encountered during processing? Have agitation and outlet nozzles been designed for the worst conditions?

Auxiliary equipment

1. Tanks. *Earth dikes* are built up around outdoor storage tanks so that surrounding areas will not be flooded if a leak occurs; if the process fluid is dangerous or expensive, *concrete pits* may be built so that it can be recovered. If more than one tank is built in a single pit, a good design rule is to size the pit to hold the contents of the largest tank plus 25 percent of the contents of the other tanks. *Dipstick nozzles* and *downpipes* permit direct measurement of the liquid level; a variety of *liquid level indicating instruments* provide indirect readings at ground level and remote stations. *Conservation vents* permit small buildups of pressure and vacuum before venting the tank to the atmosphere; they reduce vapor loss of volatile materials. *Flame arresters* (often used in combination with conservation vents) prevent flashback of ignited vapors to the interior of the tank.

2. Kettles. Pressure vessels may require *relief valves* or *rupture disks* for release of sudden pressure buildups. If visual inspection of the contents is required, *sight glasses* are mounted on manholes or nozzles in pairs—one for a light source, the other to look through. *Manholes* should be large enough to permit entry by personnel and removal of internal equipment; they may have to be fitted with *crossbars* to prevent personnel from falling in. Overhead *condensers* are used to liquefy vapors of volatile materials and return them to the vessel. *Jackets* can be of the *baffled*, *spiral*, or *dimpled* types, depending upon heat transfer and cost requirements. External *insulation* is used for heat conservation and personnel protection.

Operating precautions

1. *Inspect safety devices periodically.* Flame arresters and conservation vents can become corroded and clogged with dust after long exposure to the atmosphere. The undersides of rupture discs become coated with process materials which can alter their pressure ratings.

2. *Clean jackets annually.* Even when "city water" is used as the coolant, scale deposits will build up on the heat transfer surface. Commercial services are available to come into the plant and circulate cleaning chemicals through the jackets.

3. *Clean interior kettle surfaces on a regularly scheduled basis.* If deposits are allowed to accumulate uncontrolled, the equipment will suffer emergency outages, and cleaning will be more costly. Tank entry by personnel may be required (make sure harsh tools do not damage finished or delicate surfaces), but often solvent or solutions that react with the buildup can be found to remove deposits without tank entry.

Mixing Equipment

Process vessels usually require agitation to accomplish their objectives, which may be the blending of liquids, the dissolving or suspending of solids in liquids, the dispersion of gases in liquids, or the transfer of heat to and from liquids. Follow these steps from definition of the problem through to operation of the equipment:

How to define the mixing job. First, determine the *physical properties* of the materials being mixed: density, viscosity, and surface tension. Solubility relationships must be understood, and if solids are involved, the particle size must be known. If any of the materials are shear sensitive, the maximum allowable shear stress must be stated. When heat transfer is required, the thermal conductivity and specific heat of the mix components are essential data. Such information is available in handbooks of physical and chemical properties, in the research files of your company, from suppliers of the mixed materials, and from mixing equipment vendors.

Next, decide what *performance characteristics* must be achieved: How fast must the mixing job be accomplished? To what degree of physical or chemical conversion must it be carried? How big will the mixing vessel be? Are there any limitations on its dimensions? (Note: Give the mixing designer as much freedom as possible to determine the shape of the tank—that is, the ratio of length to diameter.) If the vessel is part of a continuous flow-through system, how much residence time is available or required? Is foaming objectionable—or desired?

Choose from available equipment. Manufacturers of mixing equipment offer a large variety of standard components; expensive, custom-designed units are rarely required. These are the basic elements of a mixing system:

1. Impeller. Selection is based on the flow pattern desired and the viscosity of the fluids. See Figure 16-17 for examples of these types: (a) The *propeller,*

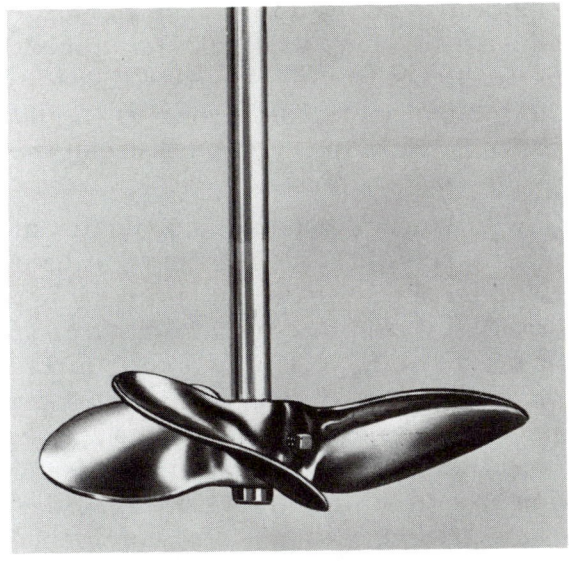

a. Propeller

b. Axial Flow Impeller

c. Flat-blade Turbine

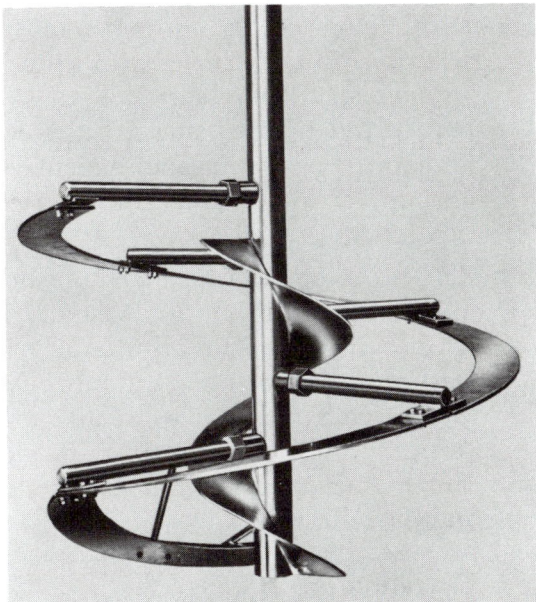

d. Helical Impeller

FIGURE 16-17: Types of Mixing Impellers
(Courtesy of Mixing Equipment Company, Inc.)

which produces axial flow—fluid motion in the same direction as the center-line of the shaft. Used for thin fluids and relatively small vessels, propeller units provide the simplest and cheapest mixer installations. (b) The *axial flow* (or *pitched paddle*) impeller is used for larger installations, but as its name implies, still gives an axial motion to the fluid. (c) The *flat-blade turbine* handles larger volumes and viscosities up to 100,000 centipoises (curved blades are sometimes used in the higher viscosity ranges), imparting a radial motion to the fluid. It is the impeller of choice when gas-liquid contacting is required. (d) The *helical* impeller is the most expensive of the group and is used for viscosities above 100,000 centipoises.

2. Shaft. The shaft must be designed to withstand the bending and vibrational forces to which it will be subjected. Cost savings in its design can be realized if a steady bearing is installed in the bottom of the tank to support the lower end, but these savings will rapidly disappear if the process fluid is not a good enough lubricant to prevent frequent failure of the bearing. Another important design consideration arises at the point where the shaft passes through the top of the tank—if there are no pressure or vapor loss problems, a simple hole in the top of the tank and a conical sheet metal collar mounted on the shaft will provide sufficient protection. For pressures up to 150 psi, *packed seals* are used; the more expensive *mechanical seals* are used for higher pressures and applications where leakage of process materials cannot be tolerated.

3. Drive. Horsepower, torque, and speed reduction are the basic criteria for selection. But the buyer also must consider flexibility for future needs (can agitator speed be changed by a simple gear replacement?), service dependability and maintenance requirements, and whether variable speed control is required (sometimes an expensive variable speed drive can be replaced by a simple two- or three-speed electric motor without real loss of process capability).

4. Baffles. An agitator mounted on the centerline of an unbaffled tank produces a swirling liquid motion, usually with a vortex forming around the shaft. This is the poorest of all mixing patterns and wasteful of power. To provide vertical as well as lateral motion, *baffles* are installed; typically, they are flat metal plates mounted vertically in the tank (length about the same as the vertical wall of the tank), positioned on 90-degree radii (width about $\frac{1}{12}$ of tank diameter), with several inches of clearance between the edge of the baffle and the tank wall.

Operating precautions

1. Don't run the agitator in an empty tank for more than a few seconds; damage to bearings and excessive shaft flexure could result.

2. Replace the packing in the stuffing box regularly; if it is allowed to "wear out," scoring of the shaft may result.

3. Keep the liquid level consistent from batch to batch. This is especially important when two (or more) impellers are mounted on the shaft and the liquid level must be maintained at a minimum distance above the upper impeller to avoid excessive foaming or shear stress.

HOW TO COORDINATE HEATING, VENTILATING, AND AIR CONDITIONING OPERATIONS

Some manufacturing operations demand close control of air quality—temperature, humidity, and dust content—in order to make an acceptable product. All manufacturing installations and their associated laboratories and offices must have adequate heat, ventilation, and possibly air conditioning for worker comfort, low labor turnover, and compliance with safety and health regulations.

While the three topics are treated separately for ease of understanding, they must be carefully coordinated in the design of any particular installation, and the material in this chapter is presented with the problems and opportunities of coordination in mind. Competent engineering work is essential in determining the needs to be met and the hardware to be used in building HVAC systems; if this important step is omitted, engineering, maintenance, and management people face long years of complaints and problems.

Space Heating Systems

Adequate building heat is the most elemental need for employee comfort, but it may also be required to prevent freezing damage to piping systems, raw materials, and products. The plant manager and the engineering staff should know how long it will take each building in the plant to cool down to unacceptable temperature levels in case of heating system failure in cold weather; they should be prepared to supply emergency heat within that time period. Whether you are considering the heating system for a new building, replacement of heating equipment in an old facility, or expansion of an existing structure, you will need to consider the following choices in design and equipment:

Centralized vs. decentralized systems. The centralized heating system is typified by the familiar home furnace which burns fuel to produce steam, hot water, or warm air. The heated fluid is circulated through pipes or conduits to radiators, registers, or similar devices to diffuse the heat at the point of need. Return pipes and conduits bring the fluid back to the furnace for reheating. In decentralized systems, each local "heater" (space heater, rooftop unit, or infra-red device) is fired by its own supply of electricity or gas.

1. Centralized systems: *Advantages* are more efficient fuel consumption, low maintenance costs, monitoring and control from one point. *Disadvantages* are slower response to sudden demand, difficulty of expansion, complete loss of heat when the system is inoperative.

2. Decentralized systems: *Advantages* are low first cost, ease of expansion, partial supply of heat when one unit is inoperative. *Disadvantages* are difficulty of access for maintenance, hazards of gas piping or high-current electrical distribution networks.

Select a fuel and the medium. Central heating systems fire coal, oil, or gas, and the choice between these fuels is based on price but modified by considerations of availability, convenience, and pollution limits.

The medium for carrying the heat of the burning fuel to the spaces to be warmed can be steam, hot water, or warm air. Steam systems are the most common in industrial space heating; piping systems are relatively simple, the fluid is moved without the aid of a pump or fan, and the amount of heat transfer surface required at the point of use is minimized by the high temperatures available and by the change from gas to liquid (each pound of steam gives up approximately 900 Btu of heat as it condenses to water). Hot water systems have the advantage of fast response to demand, quieter operation, more flexibility in piping arrangements, and less corrosion in the piping system. *High temperature hot water* systems (over 250° F) approach the economy of steam systems by requiring smaller piping and heat transfer surfaces than ordinary hot water systems while retaining their advantages. However, they do require very precise operating control to function effectively. Warm air systems are limited to smaller plants with relatively clean operations; they are inexpensive to build, have fast response to demand, and the air circulating systems can be used for ventilation in warm weather. Fuel efficiency is low, however, and if the recirculated air is contaminated by dust or odors, expensive removal devices must be installed.

Electric heat is less common in industrial plants, but the trend is up. Conditions that favor electric heating are (1) cheap electricity and special rates for heating, (2) mild outdoor temperatures, (3) buildings that are heavily insulated for other reasons, and (4) a need to avoid air pollution that might result from the burning of fossil fuels at the plant site. Electric heaters can be installed as baseboard units or placed in the air stream of central ventilating and recirculating systems, such as those required for air conditioning. Another way of applying electric heat is through infra-red units which radiate heat to localized areas that must be warmed or are used for outdoor applications such as loading docks. In buildings and offices that require large banks of fluorescent lights, the heat from these lights can be used to supplement or completely replace conventional sources of heat. Air is passed over the banks of lamps to pick up heat and is distributed to areas that must be heated.

Pick the best heater.   The apparatus that finally transfers the heat produced by the fuel to the air space where it is needed is called a "heat-emitting device," or simply a "heater." It is a key component of the heating system which affects overall performance and economy.

Two basic heat transfer devices used in many of the units described below are the *finned tube* and the *coil*. *Finned tubes* are made by mounting thin metal sheets (fins) with holes at their centers on tubing or pipe and bonding them in such a way that heat conducts readily from the tube to the fin. The total heat transfer surface of the original tube is magnified as much as twentyfold. *Coils* consist of large fins with many holes; tubing is passed back and forth through the holes in a serpentine pattern, as in an automobile radiator, and attached to the fins with a heat-conducting bond. In both types heating or cooling fluids are passed through tubes or pipes.

Heaters for centralized systems

1. *Baseboard units.* Familiar in residential construction, these devices consist of a finned tube covered by a metal enclosure with a damper on the top side for temperature control. The tubes carry steam or hot water. In industrial applications two or more units may be run side by side or mounted in stacks on a wall.

2. *Unit heaters.* (Figure 16–18.) These are compact units that can be hung from ceilings or mounted on wall brackets. The heating element is a coil supplied with steam or hot water and mounted in a finished metal cabinet. Louvers direct the air stream, which is supplied by a fan. Units mounted horizontally have the coil on the suction side of the fan; vertical units have the coil on the discharge side of the fan. An important characteristic of the unit heater is its "throw," the distance in feet from the unit at which the warm air stream is effective. Advantages are that they (a) take up no floor space; (b) have a high heat output from relatively small units; (c) may be positioned so they can be aimed at cold spots; and (d) the powered air movement helps circulation and can be used for ventilation in hot weather by simply shutting off the heat and running the fan.

3. *Cabinet convectors.* The old-fashioned cast-iron "radiator" is no longer specified for industrial heating applications, but in offices and relatively small rooms where forced air movement is not required to distribute heat, cabinet convectors can be used. They are usually wall-mounted and consist of stacks of finned tubes or coils ranging from 1½ to 3½ feet high, surrounded by close-fitting sheet-metal panels. They are effective in rooms with high heat requirements and in locations where long runs of baseboard units are impractical.

4. *Coils in central systems.* Central air conditioning systems require a network of air ducts equipped with blowers to recirculate conditioned air to and from the occupied spaces. Heated coils can be installed in these ducts and the systems used during cold weather to supply heat.

5. *Panel heaters.* Formerly referred to as *radiant heating*, this system employs coils of hot water piping embedded in floors, wall panels, and even ceilings. Advantages are (a) no loss of floor space; (b) transmission of heat at relatively low temperatures; (c) a feeling of comfort by the occupants at lower room temperatures. Disadvantages are (a) temperature control is more difficult, especially in changeable situations; (b) heat losses to the ground or outside air are greater; and (c) access to the distribution piping is more difficult.

Heaters for decentralized systems

1. *Rooftop units.* These are compact structures that are enclosed in metal cabinets and designed for mounting on the roof of the building section served. They are usually equipped for both cooling and heating, and contain an air conditioning unit for the cooling function. Heating is accomplished by the insertion of coils that may be steam or hot water heated, or the use of electric

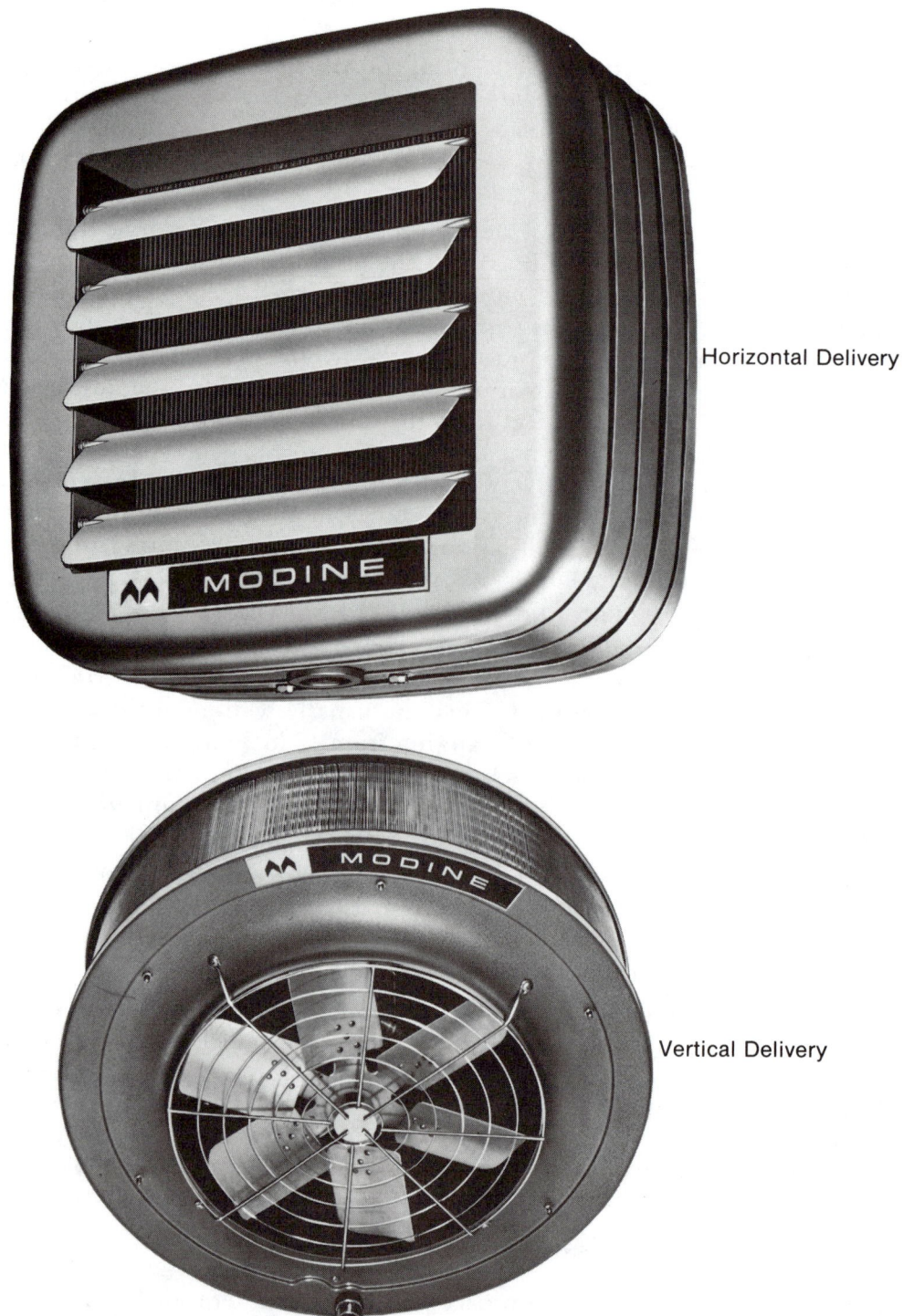

Horizontal Delivery

Vertical Delivery

FIGURE 16-18: Two Types of Unit Heaters for Use with Steam or Hot Water (Courtesy of Modine Manufacturing Company.)

or gas-fired coils. Supply and return air ducts are passed through the roof membrane. They have all the advantages previously mentioned in the section on centralized versus decentralized systems. Problems can arise, however, in continuous exposure to the weather and in damage to the roof caused by installation and maintenance activities. Commercially available sizes are rated for 70,000 to 2,500,000 Btu per hour (Btuh) of heating and 5 to 40 tons of refrigeration for cooling.

2. *Unit heaters.* Basic characteristics were discussed earlier under centralized systems. They can readily be adapted to decentralized systems by the use of electric coils or gas-fired indirect heat exchangers. Smaller electric coils consist of bare-wire resistance elements; larger units have the resistance wire embedded in refractory powder inside a finned tube. The gas-fired units require a vent to the outside for removal of combustion products; heat is transferred to the air stream from these gases by a venturitube heat exchanger.

3. *Infra-red heaters.* Because they transmit heat by radiation and therefore are not dependent upon air movement to achieve proper heat distribution, infra-red units can be used for difficult heating jobs such as high factory bays, loading docks, and outside areas where work must be performed. Electric units use the familiar infra-red lamp or quartz lamps; gas units have a ceramic grid upon which the gas flame impinges; the grid gives off its radiation when it reaches 1650° F.

4. *Fresh air heaters.* A relatively new development in space heating, these devices are the simplest of all—they simply burn gas in an open flame inserted in the incoming air stream. Because the combustion products end up in the ventilating air, the units must be designed and operated carefully to be sure that sufficient dilution is achieved. Advantages are the highest possible fuel efficiency, simplest possible machinery, and easiest installation—often no distribution ductwork is necessary.

Ventilation

Ventilation involves movement of air for human comfort or the removal of contaminants. We have seen in the foregoing section that heating entails air movement, and it would seem obvious that the need for coordinating the two is compelling. Yet in many industrial buildings the two systems have "grown" without that coordination, resulting in poor efficiency, employee discomfort and complaints, and the high cost of constant additions and corrections to the system.

Reasons for ventilation. There are many reasons to ensure proper ventilation, including the following.

1. *Human comfort.* Operating at a constant temperature of 98.6° F, the human body is a heat generator whose output (which grows with increased activity) must be transmitted to its surroundings. This transmission of heat is accomplished by *radiation* and *convection*. Radiation depends upon the temperature difference between the body and cooler objects around it, and would

take place even if air were not present (conversely, objects hotter than the body will radiate heat to it). In convection, heat is transferred from the body to a stream of cooler air moving past it; the body improves on this process by *perspiration*, with evaporation of moisture from the skin achieving additional cooling effect.

2. *Removal of toxic materials.* Gases, vapors, dusts, aerosols must be removed from the plant air if they are concentrated enough to cause injury to human beings by intense exposure for a short time or lesser exposure for extended periods.

3. *Removal of flammable vapors.* Volatile flammable liquids evaporate to form flammable (or "explosive") mixtures with air, and each material has an upper explosive limit and a lower explosive limit expressed as percentage by volume. Gasoline, for instance, has a UEL of 7.6 percent and an LEL of 1.4 percent. When materials of this type are used in industrial processes, ventilation may be required to prevent accumulations of vapor in the flammable range.

4. *Control of odors.* Many plant operations involve the use of materials which are neither toxic nor flammable, but which generate odors seriously disturbing or downright intolerable to most people. Ventilation is a key means of reducing odors to acceptable levels.

5. *Dusts.* Mineral, organic, and metal dusts may be toxic, explosive, or damaging to equipment and process materials. Ventilation of work areas is used to remove dusts from the building or to concentrate them for collection and reuse.

Types of ventilation.   Industrial buildings and offices can be ventilated by a number of methods. Choose one or a combination of these ways of accomplishing the objectives listed in the previous section:

1. *Exhaust.* Removal of contaminated air from the interior of a building to the outside atmosphere is used for general ventilation as well as for localized ventilation of areas where production processes contaminate or overheat the air.

2. *Dilution.* Hot or contaminated air can often be brought to acceptable quality levels by mixing cool, fresh air with it.

3. *Recirculation.* Because convection cooling of the body depends on air movement, it is possible to maintain a sense of comfort by moving the same air around the ventilated space in a recycling pattern. The ability to do this becomes an important cost-saving factor when the air must be heated in cold weather, or mechanically cooled in hot weather. A further advantage is that recirculated air can be passed through a cleaning system for removal of contaminants before it is returned to the occupied spaces.

4. *Cleaning.* Pollution laws may require the removal of odors, toxic material, or particulate matter before air can be exhausted to the atmosphere. The same

will be true of air which is recirculated within a building, with the addition of flammable vapors to the list. The most common devices for cleaning are filters, washers, electrostatic precipitators, absorption beds, and cyclones.

Techniques of ventilation.   Listed below are the design criteria and operating systems used to accomplish ventilating goals. Apply these methods singly or in combination to overcome your ventilating problems:

1. *Air changes.* Technical literature and manufacturer's catalog references vary widely on their recommendations for the number of air changes per hour in different types of work areas. This table gives the average of a number of sources:

Type of Space	Air Changes per Hour
Manufacturing	15
Boiler Rooms	29
Laboratories	23
Offices	11
Toilets	18
Warehouses	4

2. *Negative pressure.* When air is exhausted from a room or building at a rate faster than make-up air is supplied, the pressure drops below that of the outside atmosphere or surrounding rooms. Air will then come in through wall cracks, openings around windows and doors, or any other apertures it can find. The results are uncontrolled drafts and wide temperature differences, especially in the winter; employee complaints are not far behind. Ventilation design should always include enough make-up air to keep the pressure positive, or, as in the case of heat-producing operations, provide for controlled flow of cold air into the work space.

3. *Natural ventilation.* Two factors promote natural ventilation: one is height, and the other is the temperature difference between the inside air and the fresh air coming from the outside. For these reasons, natural ventilation tends to be limited to buildings with very high ceilings housing processes which give off a great deal of heat—in other words, heavy industry. Equipment consists of roof vents mounted at the highest point of the building and inlet louvers located near ground level. Designers usually specify the inlet louver area at one to one and one-half times that of the exhaust vent.

4. *Forced ventilation*: Local exhaust systems. Wall and ceiling fans can be installed in those plant areas where fumes, odors, dusts, and excessive heat are generated. If the conditions are not severe, they can often handle the job at low cost. In more demanding situations, the ventilation designer will specify a *hood*, a sheet metal or plastic enclosure which is placed above the work station or surrounds it on one to three sides. The hood is attached to

a ductwork through which the contaminated air is exhausted to the outside or sent to a cleaning station. Air movement is induced by a fan or blower, which may have to be explosion-proof or made of corrosion-resistant materials to meet special conditions. A key design parameter is the *capture velocity*, the linear velocity of the air at the opening of the hood, expressed in feet per minute, which is required to prevent the contaminant from escaping into the surrounding air. It varies from 100 fpm for drying ovens to 2,000 fpm for grinding operations.

5. *Forced ventilation:* Central distribution systems. Wall fans and roof ventilators are limited in their range of effectiveness, and when air must be distributed evenly over a large area, or returned to a central station for cooling or cleaning, a central air handling system must be used. These are the components and the main design considerations for its construction:

   a. *Ductwork*. Available in rectangular or circular cross-sections, it is constructed of light gauge aluminum, copper, galvanized steel, or plastic. When carrying heated or cooled air, it may be insulated to prevent unwanted heat transfer and condensation. Design is based on air velocity. If the air stream is carrying industrial dusts the minimum *transport velocity* must be maintained—3,000 to 7,000 feet per minute. When noise is a problem, much lower velocities are employed—about 1,000 fpm for offices, and 2,000 fpm for light industry plants.

   b. *Fans and blowers*. Fans are selected from manufacturers' tables which correlate speed, horsepower, flow rate, and discharge pressure for each model. Fans have characteristic curves similar to those shown in Figure 16–14, and the air duct has its own system curve similar to that described for liquid flow. The fan will only operate at the intersection of its characteristic with the system curve. If noise is a problem, it is important to choose a fan which is operating close to its maximum efficiency.

   The term "blower" is not precisely defined; flow-pressure ratings overlap fans on the one side and compressors on the other. In general, blowers are designed to deliver air at higher discharge pressures than fans, and are used to supply furnaces, air conveying systems, and heavy duty exhaust units.

   c. *Grilles and diffusers*. These devices are mounted in the ductwork at the points where it is desired to introduce air into the ventilated room. The grille is a flat frame which can be installed horizontally or vertically, and usually has adjustable vanes to direct the air stream. It may be equipped with a damper to vary the air flow. The diffuser consists of a set of concentric cones, and like the grille, may be equipped with a variable-flow damper. It is mostly used in ceiling ducts. Whichever type is chosen, it should be selected to achieve rapid and thorough mixing of the air while avoiding uncomfortable drafts (air velocities over 50 feet per minute) and disturbing temperature differentials.

   d. *Balancing the system*. Central air handling systems have many branches which vary in length, elevation, size of ducts, number of types of fittings, and volume of air to be moved. If the resistance to flow in any one branch is too high, it will not carry the desired air flow; if it is too low, it will rob other branches of their design flow rates. For systems in which it would be unwise to install adjustable dampers (such as exhaust ducts carrying heavy dusts), balancing is achieved by designing each branch so that its static pressure matches that of the main duct at the point where they meet. In systems which can use adjustable dampers, each branch is sized on desired air capacity and velocity, and the whole is balanced out by adjusting the dampers after construction.

6. *Cleaning the air.* Air brought in from the outside as well as that recirculated in a ventilating or air conditioning system can be contaminated with smoke, dust, lint, fumes, and odors. Use these devices singly or in combination to achieve acceptable air quality:

   a. *Odors.* The *activated carbon* beds adsorb odors and some gases with excellent results. *Potassium permanganate* is effective in oxidizing many odor molecules to innocuous forms. *Air washers* have limited application in removing high concentrations of water-soluble gases, but are not widely used because of the humidity they inject into the treated air.

   b. *Particles.* Generally *electrostatic air cleaners* are very effective for particles below two microns in diameter. *Viscous filters* consist of cloth or wire screen coated with oil or other viscous fluid; they are used for particle sizes over five microns. *Dry filters* may be woven or non-woven fibers of cotton, plastic, glass, asbestos, or metal. They are available as stationary panels, which can be discarded or washed for reuse after they become clogged; or in automatic roll-up units which move fresh sections into place from a continuous roll. They are available in almost any desired degree of removal efficiency and particle size. HEPA (high efficiency particulate air) filters stand at the top of the list with a removal effectiveness of up to 99.999 percent for particles down to 0.3 micron.

Air Conditioning

Air conditioning is defined as the modification of temperature, humidity, and quantity of contaminants to predetermined values and delivery to the conditioned space. Since air cleaning and distribution were discussed in the previous section, this analysis will deal primarily with temperature and humidity control. *Comfort conditioning* is aimed at producing optimum conditions for human activity; *process air conditioning* controls air quality to meet the needs of special industrial operations (machining to close tolerances, formation of certain plastic films, handling of hygroscopic materials, microassembly).

Why air conditioning?   The manager and businessman, caught between the demands of his employees for greater comfort and the necessity of justifying to his superiors the cost of installing and operating air conditioning, often finds it difficult to separate facts from emotion in arriving at a decision. Weigh these factors when making decisions and developing rationales:

1. *Employee efficiency.* Various studies have shown that employee effectiveness can be expected to drop anywhere from 7.5 percent to 28 percent at various combinations of temperature above 90° F, excessive humidity, and still air. The cost of this loss of effort should be calculated for the number of days per year on which adverse weather conditions can be expected.

2. *Employee turnover.* Your Personnel Department can work up a correlation between the rate of employee turnover and occurrence of hot humid weather. The cost of training each new employee can be calculated in terms of the hours of nonproductive time for which he must be paid, and the amount of defective output which is tolerated because he is new at the job. Combine these two to arrive at a total cost of employee turnover attributable to sultry plant conditions.

3. *Process needs.* For purposes of economic justification, process needs divide into two categories:

   a. Air conditioning essential. When materials must be handled or manufacturing operations carried out within close tolerances of temperature, humidity, and cleanliness, an air conditioning system may be essential. If so, its cost should be included in the total project expenditure required to set up the operation, and justified on an overall return on investment calculation.

   b. Air conditioning helpful. Controlled indoor climate can contribute to greater accuracy and faster processing cycles in many types of industries without being essential. Justification in such cases is based on reduced scrap rate and improved output; it should stand on its own, and be kept separate from the calculations made to determine the profitability of the process. Reliable data for these calculations are hard to come by; if a process variable (such as drying time) is involved, tests can be made in an air conditioned laboratory. Scrap rate comparisons can be made using summertime quality records and those obtained under more ideal conditions in the spring or fall.

How air conditioning works. Although the technical definition mentions only modifying air temperature, "air conditioning" always implies the ability to cool air. Cooling is accomplished by one of the three refrigeration methods described in this section, all of which come under the general heading of mechanical refrigeration. Cooling capacity of air conditioners is stated in Btuh (Btu per hour), or MBh (thousands of Btu per hour), and in *tons of refrigeration*, one ton being equivalent to heat removal of 12,000 Btuh, or 12Mbh.

Refrigerating machines are based on a simple physical phenomenon: when a liquid evaporates it creates a cooling effect by absorbing the heat required for evaporation from its surroundings. (Water has a latent heat of evaporation of about 1,000 Btu/lb; most commonly used refrigerants have latent heats between 50 and 100 Btu/lb.) When the gas is condensed back to a liquid it gives up that same latent heat, allowing the development of a *refrigeration cycle* in which heat is absorbed from the space to be cooled and rejected to outside air (or cooling water).

1. *Vapor-compression cycle.* These principles are applied in the vapor-compression refrigeration cycle illustrated in Figure 16–19. Starting with the arrow at the right side of the diagram, liquid refrigerant passes through the expansion valve, and changes to gas in the evaporator. This creates the cooling effect of the refrigerating machine. The gas then passes through the compressor, which raises the pressure sufficiently to change the gas back to a liquid in the condenser. The latent heat is released and transferred by the condenser surfaces to the outside atmosphere or to cooling water. The liquid refrigerant then goes to the expansion valve to start the cycle again.

In air conditioning machines both the condenser and the evaporator will have finned-tube coils for maximum heat transfer. One arrangement is to locate the evaporator coils directly in the space or air stream to be cooled; when this is done the cooling coils are called "DX" coils (direct expansion). Another method is to place the evaporator in a brine or other liquid coolant and circulate that to the coils in the air stream (indirect cooling).

Vapor-compression systems are by far the most commonly encountered in air conditioning practice, and are used in sizes ranging from small window units up to the largest central station installations.

2. *Absorption cycle.* No machinery with moving parts is required in this

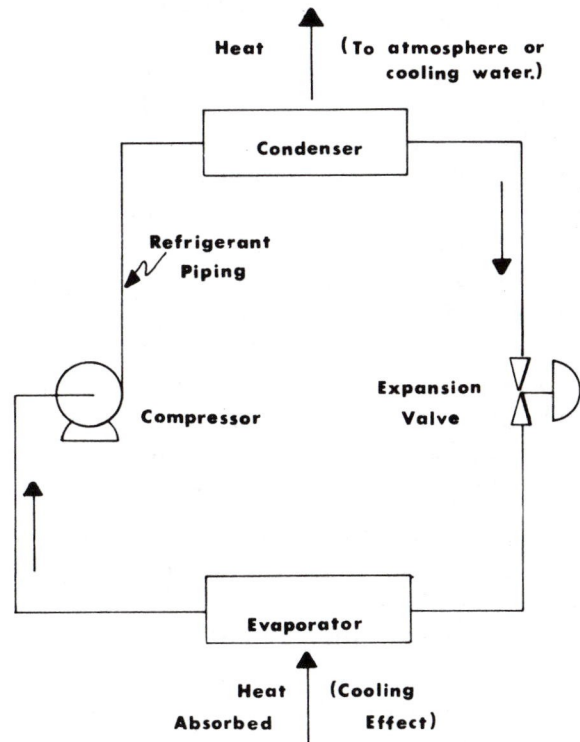

FIGURE 16–19: Vapor-compression Refrigeration Cycle

system, although some larger units may use auxiliary pumps. It is based on the principle that a concentrated solution of a chemical salt in water can absorb water vapor from the space above the liquid surface. If the vapor space of a tank containing concentrated lithium bromide solution is connected to the vapor space of a tank containing water, water vapor will be absorbed by the solution (in effect condensing out of the vapor space). Water will then evaporate from the liquid surface in the water tank (to replace the vapor removed by absorption), creating a cooling effect.

As absorption continues the concentrated salt solution becomes dilute, and must be regenerated. It is sent to a third compartment called the *generator*, where water is removed by heating the dilute solution with a steam coil, gas flame, or any other convenient method. Water vapor is driven off, liquefied in a condenser, and returned to the pure water compartment. The cooling water for the condenser is first passed through the absorber for removal of the rejected heat.

The absorption and evaporation compartments are operated under a vacuum of 29.7 inches of mercury so that the water evaporation will take place at a low enough temperature (38–40° F) to produce a useful chilling effect.

Absorption units can be built in a wide range of sizes (3 to 1,500 tons), but most applications are in sizes above 25 tons. They are especially economical when exhaust steam is available, extra boiler capacity is available during the summer months, or natural gas is plentiful and cheap. Some systems are built with ammonia, rather than pure water, as the refrigerant.

3. *Evaporative cooling.* The simplest application of the principle that evaporation causes cooling is to spray water into a moving air stream, let it evaporate, and in so doing cool the air. The difficulty with this method is that it raises the humidity of the circulated air, and thus limits its application in many parts of the United States. In most units water is collected in a sump after it falls through the air, and is recycled to the sprays by pump. In some applications it is chilled by external refrigeration before recirculation.

Despite their humidity limitations, evaporative coolers are the most economical to install and operate, and find application in industrial situations where large volumes of air must be cooled. These conditions tend to favor evaporative cooling: (a) air to be cooled is hot, but has low humidity; (b) large quantities of air are needed to cool industrial areas where processes generate much heat; (c) raw materials or the process itself requires high humidity; and (d) the space to be cooled would develop high humidity anyway—e.g., a room with open tanks containing hot water.

Choose the right equipment.   The widespread popularity of air conditioning in the United States has resulted in the availability of many types of reliable equipment. But selection must be discriminating to get the best cost advantage, maximum reliability, and satisfaction of the personnel being served. Select from these major types:

1. *Room air conditioners.* Installed in a window or through a wall, the room conditioner has its evaporator coil in the room to be cooled, and rejects heat to

the outside air through the condenser. It has fans to move air past the coils on both sides of the wall, and a dry filter to remove dust from the recirculated room air.

Sizes range from 5,000 to 34,000 Btuh. Smaller units operate on 115-volt current; above 10,000 Btuh 208 V or 230 V current is required.

Advantages of the room air conditioner are that it is readily available, easy to install, adaptable to individual preferences, and can be easily replaced when its useful life is over. Disadvantages are that it uses the highest amount of electric power per ton of refrigeration, can be costly to install if a large number of units requiring new electric outlets are involved, and can be expensive to service if a large number of units must be maintained.

2. *Unitary air conditioners.* This classification includes room air conditioners mentioned in the previous section, and rooftop units covered in the following section. The unitary air conditioner is one which has all its essential components (compressor, coils, fans, controls, filter, and condenser) factory assembled. It can be free-standing, wall or ceiling mounted, inside or outside the space to be served, connected to ductwork or discharging freely into the room. Capacities range from 2 to 60 tons.

Manufacturers have steadily increased the reliability, efficiency, and appearance of these units, and they have the advantages of being mountable in many kinds of available space and not requiring cutting through the roof.

3. *Rooftop units.* Some thirty suppliers turn out 185 models ranging from 5 to 45 ton capacity, attesting to the increasing demand for this type of unit. The factory-assembled unit contains refrigeration equipment for air cooling, a fan for air distribution, and maybe a heating system for winter use, all combined in a single cabinet designed for roof mounting. Air is transported to the conditioned space through relatively short ducts.

Rooftop units have all the advantages of decentralized systems: (a) they are readily adjustable to area needs (without having to balance a central system to varying loads), (b) they can be easily added as the building expands—a sometimes difficult problem with a central system. They also have the disadvantages: (a) decentralized units cannot match the power efficiency of a central station, (b) a large number of scattered units means a spread-out maintenance responsibility which can be costly as the units get older.

When planning a rooftop unit installation, be sure that funds are provided for a good roof cutting and patching job. Examine the building steel to see if it is heavy enough to carry the weight and vibration of the proposed unit. Review the manufacturer's design to be sure that parts exposed to the weather will resist corrosion and leakage.

4. *Central systems.* When the refrigeration load for an air conditioning system exceeds 45 tons, the built-up central station is resorted to. It is usually connected to a complex ductwork system serving areas which require different temperatures and air flow rates. Central stations may be constructed entirely from component parts, or partly constructed from packaged equipment combinations.

Figure 16-20 shows the components which may go to make up a centralized unit. Fresh air is introduced from the left side through an automatic damper, and mixed with the return air from the conditioned space. It then passes through the *filter*, which not only removes particles to improve the quality of the air for ultimate consumption, but to reduce fouling of the heat transfer coils in the central station. The *preheat coil* is used in connection with downstream water sprays, adding enough heat to be sure that the spray equipment does not freeze. It can also help carry the heating load when the central station is used as a winter air heater. The *cooling coil* is required when vapor-compression or absorption refrigeration is used, but is absent when the system employs evaporative cooling. As indicated by the diagram and described on page 357, the coil can either be of the direct expansion or indirect cooling type. The water spray can serve a number of purposes: (1) to spray upon the cooling coils, improving heat transfer between them and the air; (2) to wash out particles not screened by the filter, especially bacteria; (3) to humidify the air for some process and comfort needs; and (4) to supply the main cooling effect when the system is based on evaporative cooling. Not shown on the diagram are drift eliminators, which would be installed downstream from the sprays to catch any droplets carried by the air stream; a basin beneath the sprays to catch the water and fitted with a pump to recirculate it; and a separate chilling system to cool the recirculated water. The *reheat coil* is used to restore heat to air which has been cooled below design temperature in order to dehumidify it; like the preheat coil it can be used to help carry the heating season load. Both preheat and reheat coils can use steam or hot water. *Nonfreezing* steam coils are available for systems which must handle air below 32° F. The last component to handle the air is the *fan*, which must have sufficient capacity to move the air through the ductwork at acceptable noise levels.

5. *Control mechanisms.* Air conditioning systems are built to maintain desired ranges of temperature or humidity or both in the conditioned space. The basic control instruments are thremostats and humidistats, whose job is to monitor

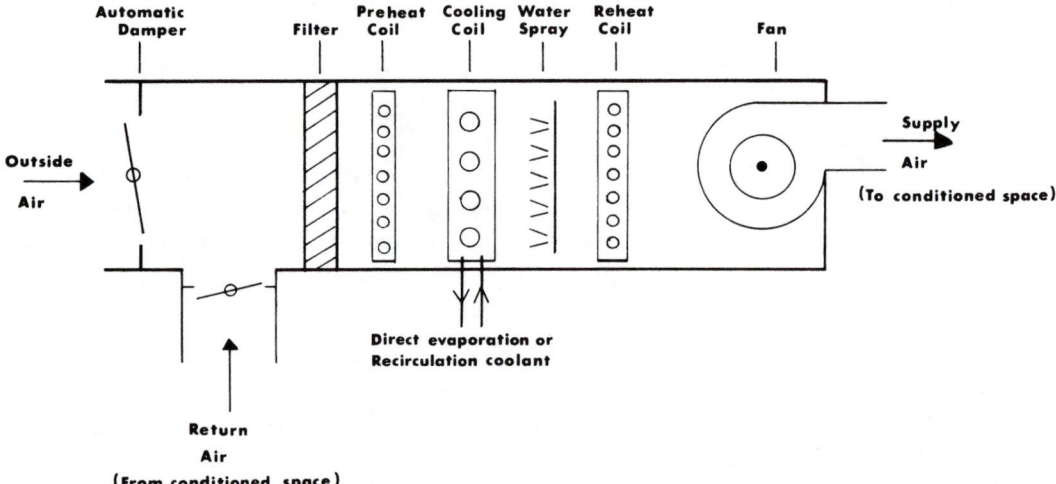

FIGURE 16-20: Components of Central Air Conditioning Station

conditions in the controlled space and signal the cooling-heating equipment to take corrective action. Beyond that the technology of automatic control becomes quite complex and lies outside the scope of this section. But you will want to keep in mind the three purposes of automatic control mechanisms:

a. To achieve design conditions. Not only is the system required to keep temperature and humidity within the design limits, but it must make changes smoothly so that personnel are not subject to drafts or sudden changes in temperature.

b. To protect equipment. Damage can occur to evaporator and condenser coils if either is allowed to operate without its fan running. Evaporator coils can freeze if chilly air is admitted at night or during cool weather. To prevent such equipment accidents, instruments should be interlocked so that damaging combinations cannot occur.

c. Achieve maximum cost efficiency. There is no point in running expensive refrigeration machinery when the temperature of room air can be reduced by simply mixing cool air from the outside with it. Conversely, when the outside air is hot maximum recirculation of inside air will reduce the refrigeration load. The automatic control network should be designed to assure maximum cost efficiency in operation of the total system.

How to set design goals. The design of an air conditioning system is accomplished in three steps: setting the desired conditions to be maintained inside, determining the extremes of outside conditions which must be met, and calculating the heat load which the system must carry.

1. *Inside conditions*

a. Air. The air circulation rate is based on the difference between the temperature of the cooled air entering the room and the desired room temperature. Although the most economical system would simply recirculate the same air over and over again, the air would soon become stale, and in most industrial applications, polluted. To overcome these problems, outside air is brought into the system, with the amount determined by local ventilation codes or tables of recommended outdoor air rates in such publications as the *Guide and Data Book* published by the American Society of Heating, Refrigerating, and Air Conditioning Engineers (ASHRAE). The average recommended rate for offices and other spaces occupied primarily by personnel is 20 cubic feet per minute of outside air for each person; it ranges from 10 to 50 cfm depending upon the type of space and the degree of smoking done by the occupants. Air distribution systems are usually designed to expose occupants to linear velocities of 15 to 35 feet per minute; office workers will complain of drafts at higher velocities. This range can be exceeded for plant personnel engaged in more active work.

b. Temperature. Office design temperature is usually 75° F; it ranges from 60° to 80° F for various manufacturing operations.

c. Humidity. Use 50 percent relative humidity for office spaces; industrial process requirements vary all the way from 20 to 80 percent.

2. Outside conditions

Dry bulb temperatures are observed on an ordinary outdoor thermometer; the *wet bulb temperature* is obtained by encasing the thermometer bulb in a cloth wick soaked with water and allowing the water to evaporate. The wet bulb temperature is always lower than the dry bulb temperature, except when the relative humidity is 100 percent; then they are equal. When both are known the relative humidity can be calculated or read from a *psychrometric chart*.

The design engineer must choose the dry bulb and wet bulb temperature extremes which can be handled by the air conditioner. The ASHRAE *Guide and Data Book* publishes tables for every state and Canadian province showing the dry bulb and wet bulb temperatures which will be exceeded 1, 2½, and 5 percent of the hours in the summer season. Installations at the 1 percent level will give closer control and fewer complaints, but will be more expensive. The reverse is true at the 5 percent design level.

3. Heat loads

The refrigeration section of an air conditioner can be thought of as a machine which has to pump heat from an indoor temperature of 75° to an outdoor temperature of, say, 95°. The question is, how much heat must be pumped? The answers are based on complicated heat transfer technology which cannot be explored here (but is covered in mechanical engineering and air conditioning texts, as well as the ASHRAE *Guide*). You, however, will want to assure yourself that the following elements have been considered in developing the design, using the most up-to-date methods:

a. External heat load. Outside air at 95° surrounding a building at 75° will transmit heat to it by convection; sun shining on the roof and walls will transmit heat by solar radiation. Heat will also be transmitted through walls and floors of adjacent buildings and rooms which are not air conditioned.

b. Internal heat load. The human body, at a temperature of 98.6° F, is a constant heat source which must be included in load calculations, taking into account the number of people occupying a conditioned space and their degree of physical activity. Electric lights, motors, and office machines contribute heat; so do manufacturing tools, machines, and processes. Internal heat loads, sometimes called *room loads*, are classified as *sensible heat* and *latent heat*. Sensible heat, such as that from a light bulb, is heat that tends to raise the temperature of the surroundings; latent heat is that associated with the evaporation of water into the air—from human perspiration, cooking, or industrial processing.

c. Makeup air and infiltration. The outside air (mentioned earlier) which must be brought in for ventilation purposes represents a heat load for the cooling system. Air which infiltrates through wall cracks, porous masonry, or the opening and closing of doors must also by included in the heat load calculations.

How to Build an Efficient Materials Movement System from Basic Concepts

Every plant is faced with the problem of how best to receive and store its raw materials, move them from step to step in the manufacturing process, store and ship them as finished goods. In many plants a critical review of the materials movement methods used will open up major opportunities for cost reduction; in every new plant design, logical planning for materials movement is essential to maximum efficiency. In developing your approach to the problems of materials movement, you should look first for cost reduction opportunities in the fuller use of space, converting to bulk handling, conducting process operations while material is moving, and applying the basic principles of materials movement to the overall flow through the plant. Next, choose the equipment most suited to the properties, quantities, and hazards of the materials to be moved. Finally, integrate internal and external movements for the greatest cost benefit. In the review of engineering design and in the selection of equipment, challenge proposed concepts until you are satisfied that the optimum selections have been made.

FUNDAMENTALS OF MATERIALS MOVEMENT

Apply these principles when evaluating existing systems of materials flow or those proposed for a new installation.

Look at the whole picture. Consider the movement of materials not as a series of discrete steps between processes but as one integrated flow system from the receipt of raw materials to the shipment of finished goods. You will then be in the best position to eliminate unnecessary steps and backtracking, utilize space to the maximum, and adjust the physical layout of the plant to all the requirements of processing and materials movement.

Combine movement with processing whenever possible. If a material must be dried, baked, coated, wetted, oiled, sorted, sealed, labeled, radiated, steamed, heated, or cooled, consider carrying out the operation while the material is in transit from one work station to another. If successful, you can telescope the time and space required for movement and processing.

Make the trips short. Arrange plant layout so that materials move directly from one processing step to the next, and reserve the shortest moves for the most difficult material conditions (the heaviest, most viscous, most fragile, most laborious), while saving the longest moves for the easiest material conditions.

Adjust speed of movement to the capacity of the process. There is no point in moving materials from Step A to Step B faster than Step B can use it; it will simply pile up and require storage space.

Make full use of vertical space. When materials can be moved overhead, the floor space below becomes available for process.

Move and store materials in bulk form whenever possible. Bulk handling offers the cheapest and fastest movement.

Whenever practicable, handle materials in fluid form. Fluid systems offer speed, safety, convenience, and low labor cost. Particulate solids can sometimes be converted to fluids by slurrying them in water or suspending them in a moving gas stream. Viscous solids often can be made thin enough to handle as fluids by raising temperature.

Utilize gravity. Look for situations where materials can be transported easily in bulk form to the upper levels of a process building and then passed downward by gravity through the process steps, using ramps, chutes, conduits, and large pipes.

Check on who is doing the work. If higher paid, skilled people are spending part of their time moving materials when this could be done by lower paid employees, change the work assignments.

Prepare for emergencies. Have a backup method of moving materials should the main system break down.

Look for opportunities to automate. Mechanized and automated equipment is available to handle any materials movement task, usually at considerable labor cost savings.

Eliminate unnecessary handling. Look for places where the material doubles back on its previous path or is picked up and set down a number of times. See if some movements can be combined with others or, better, eliminated altogether.

Don't allow mixing of parts or materials if they will have to be resegregated later on in the process.

THE BASICS OF BULK MOVEMENT

Liquid-Handling System

Even those plants that consider their operations to be totally machine-shop oriented are turning to the use of bulk and fluid processing systems to simplify operations and reduce costs. A wire-enamelling plant builds a central mixing and distribution system to control the properties of the enamel sent to each coating machine; a cigarette factory sets up bulk storage and distribution facilities for its adhesives, eliminating the handling of 55-gallon drums; a textile mill does the same thing with its bleaching chemicals. The basic considerations in developing such systems are described in this section.

A liquid-handling system has four components: pumps, piping, flow measurement and control devices, and storage tanks. The job of the systems designer is to select the least expensive combination that will handle the physical properties of the liquid to be moved.

Liquid properties. These are the important properties that must be taken into account in the design of a fluid transportation system: *Density* (water has a density of 8.33 pounds per gallon at 20° C)—usually not critical in the selection of equipment but must be taken into account in pressure and energy calculations. *Viscosity* (the consistency of a fluid—at 20° C, water has a viscosity of 1 centipoise; molasses has a viscosity of 100,000 centipoises)—significantly affects pipe size and pump selection. *Vapor pressure* (the degree of volatility—at 20° C, water has a vapor pressure of 0.34 pounds per square inch, while that of ethyl alcohol is 0.85 psi)—important to the design of the system on the suction side of the pump and to the type of tank selected. *Corrosiveness*—if the fluid is very acid or alkaline, or if it contains suspended solids whose particles are abrasive, the designer will have to choose construction materials that can withstand these conditions. Special construction materials also may be required for fluids that might become contaminated by the system. *Temperature*—as the temperature at which a fluid is handled goes up, viscosity and density usually go down. Vapor pressure rises, and corrosiveness is likely to as well. *Shear sensitivity*—some liquids, especially colloids and emulsions, are permanently damaged by violent mechanical action, such as that created by a centrifugal pump impeller. Viscosity of some fluids is reduced by mechanical action.

Tanks. The important considerations: *Materials of Construction*—carbon steel is the standard of cost and availability. More expensive metals used to meet special service requirements are aluminum, stainless steel, and copper and its alloys. When it is desirable to combine the low cost and strength of carbon steel with the corrosion resistance of more expensive metals, stainless-, nickel-, and monel-clad steel is used. Steel tanks also are lined with rubber, glass, and plastic. Tanks made of fiberglass-reinforced polyester plastic have become popular with systems designers because of their low cost, light weight, and good corrosion resistance. *Shape*—vertical cylindrical tanks occupy less floor space and make good use of overhead space but require carefully laid, level foundations. Horizontal cylindrical tanks can be supported on concrete saddles. Spherical tanks are often used for liquids with high vapor pressure. Rectangular tanks are available in smaller sizes. *Pressure rating*—under most government and insurance codes (be sure to check local regulations) a tank becomes a pressure vessel when it is designed to operate at 15 psi gauge or higher, and strict design, construction, and inspection rules apply. *Location*—most often at ground or floor level but can be elevated to conserve space or gain static pressure or buried underground to conserve space or for safety reasons.

Pumps.   Criteria for choosing between centrifugal and positive displacement pumps, and tips for their installation and operation, are presented in Chapter 16, pages 332-336.

Pipes and piping design.   Chapter 16, pages 330-332, provides the basic information needed for selecting pipe materials, sizes, and fittings. Although piping design is a large, complicated subject in itself and is usually handled by engineers, that is no bar to creative thinking at the plant level, as shown in Operating Example 17-1.

Operating Example 17-1: *Simplifying a Complex Piping System.* A chemical company had a latex storage area consisting of 9 glass-lined tanks. There was only one pipe nozzle for liquid flow on each tank—at the bottom—and all liquid flows both in and out passed through it. Because the shearing action of a pump would have destroyed the quality of the latex, all liquid movement was accomplished by air pressure on the surface of the liquids in the tanks. Each tank held a different type of latex or a different lot of the same latex, which had to be kept separate. The pipes connecting the tanks were made of glass, and all the valves had to be glass-lined, making it a costly system. The interconnecting pipes not only had to handle flows in and out of the tanks so that blends could be made from material in any combination of tanks, but there had to be pipes for bringing in latex produced in the plant and pipes to take completed blends to the Shipping Department. Connections also had to be provided for flushing the lines with water after each latex transfer. The piping system that evolved to handle these requirements became so complicated that simply to make a transfer from one tank to the one next to it required that 14 valves had to be opened, closed, or checked for correct position.

At a meeting between the area engineer and the assistant plant manager, the latter came up with the idea of setting up a system analogous to an old-fashioned telephone switchboard. Each tank would be connected directly to a central switching station by only one pipe, with only one valve on it (at the bottom of the tank). At the switching station there would be two large panel boards facing each other. The pipe from each tank would come through an opening in one of the panel boards and end there in a hose connection. A water supply pipe with a hose connection would also be provided on one of the boards. The operator would be provided with a length of hose fitted with a hose connection at each end, sufficiently long to reach between any two pipe ends on the panel boards. When a transfer was to be made, the operator simply would connect the hose to the pipe ends of the tanks involved, open only two valves, and proceed with the transfer.

The system was adopted and constructed. Not only was there a capital cost saving in the elimination of numerous and costly valves, tees, and elbows, but experience soon showed that the operators were far less prone to making transfer errors.

Flow measurement and control devices. *Displacement meters* include piston, wobble plate, and nutating disc types; they are usually equipped with digital counters which indicate total accumulated flow. *Differential pressure* meters depend on an orifice or venturi tube installed in the flow path; the differential pressure created is transmitted to a manometer, flow indicator, or recording instrument. In *rotameters* (a type of *area meter*) all the fluid is passed upward through a vertical glass tube with an etched scale. A metal float inside the tube rises to a position on the scale corresponding to the flow. All of these devices can be connected to mechanically, pneumatically, or electrically operated valves to throttle or cut off flow.

Solids Transportation System

The designer of a solids transportation system evaluates the properties of the materials to be handled and selects the most economical components for storage, movement, and flow control.

Solids properties. *Particle size*—measured in inches (for particles over ½ in. in diameter), mesh (the number of openings in one linear inch of screen; used for measurement of particles ranging from 2 mesh down to 400 mesh), and microns (one micron is equivalent to 0.001 millimeters). With most bulk solids, the larger the particle, the more free-flowing is the material. *Bulk density*—the weight in pounds of a cubic foot of the material in the state in which it will be handled. Required for the calculation of material flow rates and for the design of bin structures. *Hardness*—measured on the Mohs scale. Talc is a hardness of 1 on this scale and diamond 10. Higher hardnesses and larger particle sizes combine to create more *abrasive* materials. *Cohesiveness* is the tendency of the particles to stick to each other; it is aggravated by *hygroscopicity*, which is the tendency of the material to absorb moisture from the air. *Angle of repose* (the angle made with the horizontal by the edge of a cone-shaped pile freely built up) is important to the design of bins and conveyors, and to capacity calculations for yard storage. *Corrosiveness* requires more resistant (and therefore more expensive) materials of construction; *toxicity* can require enclosing the handling system or the addition of elaborate ventilation equipment; *explosibility* may have to be dealt with by the use of inert atmospheres and explosionproof electrical equipment.

Storage of solids. *Outdoor storage piles* offer the most economical method of storing large-volume bulk solids but are limited to those that are not affected by sunlight, rain, snow, heat, and cold. Heavy-duty trucks, cranes, and conveyors are usually needed to move materials to and from the pile. *Storage bins* can be constructed in any convenient shape (round, rectangular, cone-bottom, horizontal, vertical) and from a variety of materials (metals, wood, concrete, and brick or block walls). Bin design must take into account the angle of repose and the *angle of slide* (the minimum angle of an inclined surface that will cause the materials to flow); because solids tend to "bridge" at the outlet opening, various vibratory and aerating devices are used to keep the materials flowing at that point. *Silos* are vertical cylindrical containers with flat bottoms which rest on the ground or an indoor floor. They can be built of the same construction materials as bins and are relatively inexpensive, useful for storing materials with high angles of repose, and take advantage of overhead space.

Movement of solids. *Horizontal and inclined conveyors* include the following types: *Vibratory*—usually reserved for short runs but can be used up to 150 ft. with loadings of over 400 tons per hours. Very useful for handling hot material. *Screw*—will handle loadings in excess of 250 tons per hour and can be used up to 300 ft. Can double as mixers for the material being transported. *Continuous flow*—allowable distances and flow rates vary widely; manufacturer of equipment should be consulted for each application. When totally enclosed, protects the materials transported. A single system can have both horizontal and vertical legs. *Belt*—loads up to 5,000 tons per hour and distances exceeding 1,000 feet. High first cost but can be very economical for long runs and high flow rates. *Vertical conveyors* include these types: *Bucket elevators*—widely used for vertical lift. Low first cost. Standard capacities to 150 tons per hour. Can handle large lumps, operate at high temperatures. Subdivided into *continuous discharge, positive discharge,* and *centrifugal discharge* types. *Vertical screw*—very good in specific applications. Capacities to 150 tons per hour. Requires only a minimum of floor or ground space and support structure. *Skip hoist*—a single large bucket (up to 150 cu ft) alternately raised and lowered on a hoisting mechanism. Useful for high lifts (75–150 ft). See Figure 17–1 for various types of conveyors.

Pneumatic conveying. Based on the principle that a fast-moving stream of air in a pipeline can suspend and transport solid particles, a pneumatic conveying system consists of the bins or other storage containers to and from which the material is moved; one or more air blowers which generate the gas velocity; the pipelines through which it moves; cyclones, filters, or other devices for separating solid particles from the air at the end of the transport; and airlock valves for separating the pressurized parts of the system from the nonpressurized.

Practical design limits are up to 1½-in. particle size, 75 tons per hour carrying capacity, and 1,000-ft lengths, but every one of these "limitations" has been exceeded by wide margins in specialized installations. Pneumatic conveyors are especially useful in situations where twists and turns are required in the flow path, which could not be negotiated by mechanical conveyors. They can also be used for heating, cooling, and drying the solid. If it must be protected from oxygen, an inert gas can be used as the carrying stream.

Types of Containers to Consider Using

When shipments to customers or the handling of materials within the plant takes place in quantities too small to justify the use of bulk equipment, a large variety of containers is available for packaging both solid and liquid materials. These are the basic types:

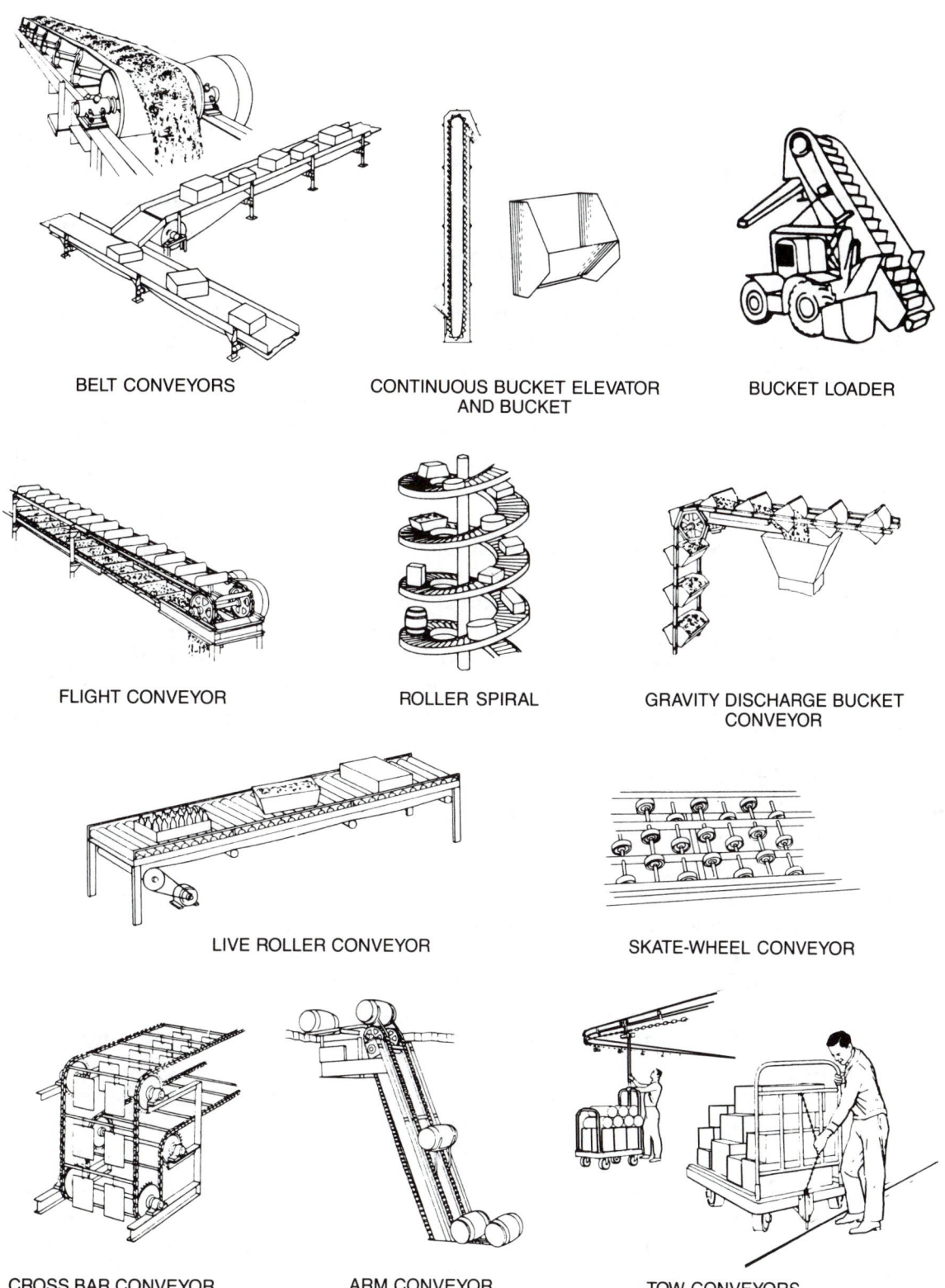

BELT CONVEYORS

CONTINUOUS BUCKET ELEVATOR AND BUCKET

BUCKET LOADER

FLIGHT CONVEYOR

ROLLER SPIRAL

GRAVITY DISCHARGE BUCKET CONVEYOR

LIVE ROLLER CONVEYOR

SKATE-WHEEL CONVEYOR

CROSS BAR CONVEYOR

ARM CONVEYOR

TOW CONVEYORS

FIGURE 17–1: Types of Solids Conveyors (Courtesy of Conveyor Equipment Manufacturers Association.)

Steel drums. Used for handling both solids and liquids. Most popular sizes are 55, 42, and 30 gallons, but other capacities are available. The *open head* type has a solid disc cover sealed at the perimeter with a gasket and a metal ring whose ends are held together by a quick-locking device or a threaded bolt and nut. The *closed head* drum cover is not removable but has one or more threaded bungs. *Basket* drums have a bung in the sidewall, usually close to the bottom. The normal steel thickness is 20 gauge for the body and 18 gauge for the heads, but heavier gauges (down to 12) may be required for corrosive liquids and lighter gauges (up to 26) can be used for solids. The cheapest drums have a bare steel interior, but fused linings of plastic, rubber, stainless steel and other metals are used for special service, as well as disposable plastic liners.

The steel drum is used when the package is exposed to the weather, requires unusual physical sturdiness, or contains hazardous materials. Its first cost is higher than that of other packages, but it has a reclamation value—it can be cleaned out and reused or sold to a drum reconditioner. The purchase of reconditioned drums is a way of achieving lower first cost.

Fiber drums. Cheaper than steel, they can be used for solids or liquids. Available in almost any desired capacity up to 75 gallons. The sidewall consists of glued layers of heavy paper; bottoms and heads are made of steel, wood, fiberboard, and plastic. Drums to be used for liquid shipments have a sprayed plastic interior lining, or they can be lined with a disposable plastic sheet.

In addition to their lower first cost, fiber drums offer lower costs for handling and shipping because they are lighter. However, there is usually no reclamation value.

Plastic drums. These are a newer development. Usually made of 100 percent high-density polyethylene, they may offer an economic alternative to lined drums for handling materials that might corrode or be contaminated by ordinary steel drums.

Paper bags. The most economical small package of all. Capacities up to 100 lb, with 50- and 80-lb sizes the most popular. Bags are rated by the weight of the paper used (50-, 60-, and 70-lb kraft) and the number of layers of "plies" (ranging from 2 to 7). Special plies of treated kraft, aluminum, or plastic are used to protect sensitive materials. More plies are needed when the material shipped is expensive or dangerous, when the distances are longer, and the number of handlings greater.

When the bag is filled, its top can be closed by sewing, pasting,heat sealing, taping, or tying with wire, or a combination of these methods. A large choice of machinery for automatically filling, weighing, and closing paper bags is available.

Portable bulk containers. Manufacturing industries have experienced an expanding need for containers larger than the steel drum but smaller than tank cars and trucks. This need has been met by a variety of containers used for both intra- and interplant shipment. They are often known as IBCs, or Intermediate Bulk Containers.

One common type is a rectangular bin ranging in capacity from 45 to 750 gallons (6 to 100 cu ft). Also called a "rigid IBC," it may be made of plastic, carbon steel, stainless steel, aluminum, or other materials. It has legs that lift it high enough off the floor so that it can be picked up with a forklift truck, and it can be stacked several layers high on other bins of the same type, without the need for racks or pallets. Capable of carrying either liquids or solids, it is fitted with a short pipe and valve at the bottom for emptying, and with an opening for filling at the top. Although the rigid IBC is a convenient, labor-saving method of storing and transporting "semi-bulk" quantities, its costs for purchase, cleaning, and freight on return trips from the customer must be considered when comparing it with other packaging methods.

Another form of portable container for solids is a large fabric bag capable of holding 4,000 pounds of material. Generally square in shape, it has built-in loops at each corner so that it can be picked up by a forklift. The fabric is usually woven of plastic fibers, and the bottom may either be solid fabric or be fitted with a pouring spout, while the top may either be completely open or closed over and fitted with a port for filling. This type is a "flexible IBC."

For liquids, a deflatable rubber bag, which roughly resembles a large air mattress, with capacities of up to several thousand gallons, is available. It is strapped to the flat bed of an ordinary truck, eliminating the need for a tank truck. For the return trip from the customer, it can be rolled up into a relatively small space.

HOW TO MOVE BULKY ITEMS

Seldom can an industrial plant move all of its materials in bulk form. Almost every plant is at some time faced with the need to transport containers and bulky single items too large to be carried by hand or too inconvenient to move by conveyor. Use these tools for such movements:

Dollies, carts, and hand trucks. Dollies are simple rectangular, triangular, or circular frames mounted on fixed or swiveled wheels or casters. (One type of circular dolly is used to support a 55-gallon drum, making it a mobile package.) Carts are made by adding bodies of wood, metal, or plastic, or simple platforms to the basic wheeled structure; they can be provided with racks and shelves or fittings to hold special types of loads.

Two-wheeled hand trucks may have a wood or tubular steel framework, with handles at the top and short forks, a platform, or other device at the bottom for supporting the load. Specialized adaptations are available for handling bags, cartons, 55-gallon drums, gas cylinders, wire reels, beverage cases, and appliances. Users of 55-gallon drums can buy a combination hand truck and tilting rack, which allows the drum to be stored indefinitely in a horizontal position for withdrawal of material.

Pallets and skids. Used for moving more than one container or item at a time, pallets are low, flat platforms that rest directly on the floor and have enough space between top and bottom layers for insertion of the forks of a lift truck. They may have a solid surface or one constructed of cross-members, and are made of boards, plywood, steel, wire mesh, and paper board. Skids are wood or metal platforms raised on metal legs at the four corners.

Bags and cartons are stacked on skids in an interlocking pattern to give load stability. Loads that will not ride well can be banded to the pallet or skid. In *shrink-wrapping*, the palletized load is enclosed in a sheet of plastic film and passed through a heated tunnel. The plastic shrinks, tightly enclosing the load. The unitized package is not only more structurally stable, but the plastic protects its contents from weather, dust, and pilferage. *Stretch-wrapping* may be a more economical variation, in which a stretchable sheet of plastic is wrapped around the sides of a palletized load by a machine that applies the proper tension to the plastic film. (Top and bottom of the load may also be covered, if desired.) If a plastic sheet is not required or desired, stretchable plastic netting may be used.

Power trucks. When the load exceeds 1,000 lb, the distance of movement 50 ft, and the height of lift more than a few inches, powered industrial trucks must be considered. A profusion of styles and features are available. (See Figure 17-2.)

1. Rider position. *Sit-down rider* trucks provide a cushioned seat for the driver and are used when the driver's sole assignment is to operate the truck. *Stand-up rider* trucks have a small platform at the center or rear of the truck for the driver, and are used when the driver is expected to leave the truck and assist with the removal of the load. *Walkie* trucks do not carry the driver at all; he walks behind the truck, guiding it with a drawbar handle on which the controls are mounted.

2. Load capacities and load centers. Forklift and platform trucks are commercially available with maximum load capacities from 1,500 to 120,000 lb. Because the lift truck carries its load outside the wheelbase, the distance between the front wheels and the center of the load must also be specified. The most common distance is 24 in., but models with load centers ranging from 14 to 48 in. are available. *Counterbalanced* trucks have a heavy weight mounted in the rear to keep the truck from tipping forward when the load is raised; *straddle* trucks have two protruding arms which remain in contact with the floor outside the forks while the load is being lifted.

3. Power source. *Electric* lift trucks are quiet, fumeless, smooth-operating. They are powered by large storage batteries which must be recharged after 8 to 12 hours of operation. *Gasoline* and *diesel engine* trucks are used for heavier loads and outdoor work. *LP Gas* trucks are used for both indoor and outdoor service, require only minimum downtime for changing gas cylinders, and can be very economical in areas where liquefied petroleum gas is inexpensive.

4. Explosionproofing and spark suppression. If the truck is to be used in areas where flammable gases and vapors or combustible dusts are likely to be present, one of the safety-rated types of trucks must be used. Underwriters' Laboratories, Inc. sets the standards for and puts its label on those trucks that meet the standards. The type designations, in ascending order of safety rating, are electric trucks—Types E, ES, EE, and EX; gasoline trucks—Types G and

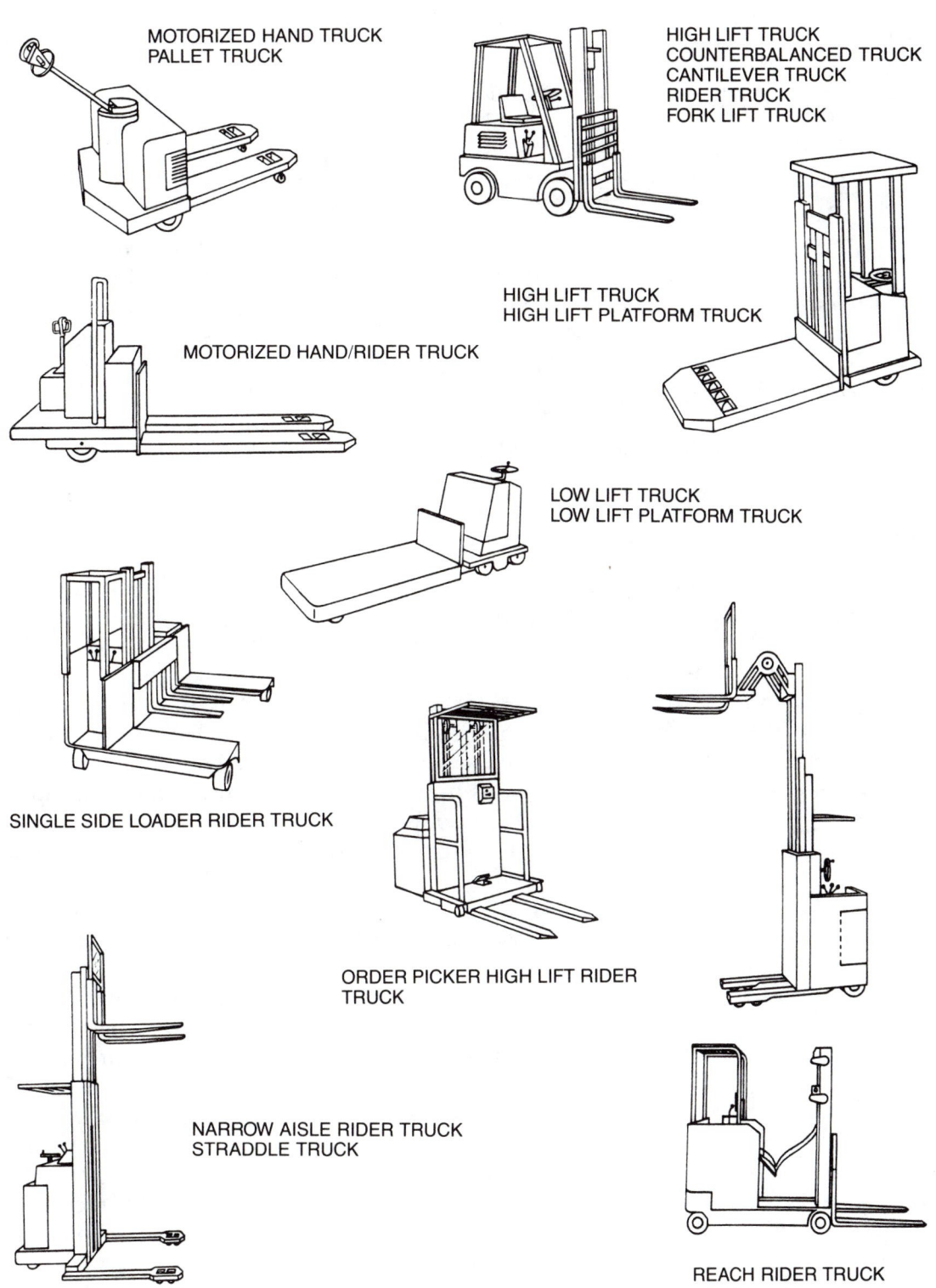

FIGURE 17–2: **Power Trucks** (from *Safety Standard for Low Lift and High Lift Trucks,* ANSI/ASME B56.1-1983. Used with permission of the publisher, The American Society of Mechanical Engineers, United Engineering Center, 345 East 47th Street, New York, NY)

GS; diesel trucks—Types D, DS, and DY; liquefied petroleum gas trucks—Types LP and LPS. Type EX is the only truck with a true explosionproof rating, that is, suitable for use in a Class I, Group D, Division 1 atmosphere (see Chapter 16, page 297, on explosionproof equipment).

5. Other design features: *maximum height* to which forks can be raised and *speed* with which they can be raised and lowered; *height of telescoping mast* raised and lowered, and *free lift*, the height to which forks can be lifted before telescoping mast begins to rise; *forward speed*—loaded and unloaded; *turning radius* and *minimum aisle width* for right-angle stacking; *mast tilt* (measured in degrees), backward and forward; *wheel types* and *sizes; gross weight*—important on upper floors and in box trailers. Don't forget to include weight of battery or gas cylinder and payload. *Special attachments*—carton clamps, drum tilters, vacuum holders, load rotators, drum and crate grabs.

Automated Storage and Retrieval Systems

For the plant that must handle its finished goods (and perhaps some of its raw materials) in packaged form, the standard warehouse configuration is a series of steel racks with storage spaces extending both horizontally and vertically. The drums, boxes, or other packages to be stored are placed on pallets, which are transported to and from the racks by forklift trucks. The height of the racks is limited by the capability of the forklift trucks; standard trucks may have a maximum lift of 10 ft. More expensive trucks with tri-lift masts may reach to 16 ft, and special high-lift masts may go as high as 27 ft, but that is about the limit. The rack spaces are numbered, and materials movements are recorded manually on paper—first, perhaps, on a transfer sheet made out by the truck operator and later in a card index file.

As the business expands, such a system may no longer suffice. Labor costs may begin to mount. A larger fleet of trucks must be purchased and maintained. Additional floor space must be acquired so that new racks can be built. As the number of storage spaces increases, so do the errors in record-keeping, and a higher percentage of labor costs may be devoted to searching for "lost" items. The proportion of goods damaged in warehouse handling usually rises during this period.

These problems may be solved by an *automated storage and retrieval system (AS/RS)*. High-rise storage racks are built to a height five or six times that of the conventional system. The aisles are narrowed, making still more storage space available. A "storage machine," a platform that moves between the racks on horizontal and vertical rails and is fitted with forks or other devices for placing and retrieving loads, replaces the forklift truck. The storage machine, which is automatically controlled, may be designed with a space for the operator to ride. The automatic control system may be driven by a computer that sends the machine to the correct space, records the movement in or out, and keeps a running inventory of the materials in stock. Some companies find this system so accurate that they no longer take an annual inventory of the warehouse.

What is available. Because the restraints on size are more economic than physical and the systems are custom-built for each project, it is not clear what the lower and upper limits of size are. However, a good idea of what customers are buying can be obtained from the following ranges of characteristics for 17 actual installations (as reported in trade journals over a recent two-year period):

RACK DIMENSIONS:
    Height   19 to 105 ft
    Width   21 to 100 ft
    Length   74 to 534 ft

NUMBER OF AISLES: 1 to 8

NUMBER OF STORAGE SPACES: 132 to 238,000

STORAGE MACHINE CAPABILITIES:
    Load Capacity   500 to 8,000 lb
    Travel Speed   210 to 500 ft per minute
    Lift/Lower Speed   20 to 120 ft per minute

COMPUTERIZATION: A central computer gives commands to the machine, records movements, and keeps inventory. Additional terminals and microprocessors may be located in other parts of the warehouse.

The industry sectors represented by these installations ranged from cosmetics to steelmaking; the manufacturer with 238,000 storage spaces makes western-style boots. Some manufacturers integrate the AS/RS with the production line, so that parts needed for assembly are automatically retrieved and brought to the production conveyor at the right time. One user even found it economical to automate the tool crib.

How to justify an AS/RS system. While the actual economics are unique to each plant, these are the basic cost factors that favor AS/RS:

1. High cost or unavailability of additional floor space for increased storage needs

2. Labor savings (reduction of warehouse labor by one half to two thirds may be possible)

3. Increased productivity (more transfers per shift)

4. Less handling-incurred damage to goods

5. Greater accuracy in placement, retrieval, and record-keeping; fewer "lost" items and "wrong" items delivered

6. Smaller inventory requirements, resulting from better accuracy and ability to move materials faster

7. Increased efficiency of production operation

EXTERNAL TRAFFIC

As the plant manager, your relationship to the external traffic function may range from complete control, in which the Traffic Department reports to you as part of the plant organization, to no control at all, in which a centralized Traffic Department arranges for all external movements and your responsibility ends at the plant door. In either of these positions, or in some intermediate relationship, you will be concerned with the following aspects of external traffic.

Coordinate with Internal Systems

Labor costs can be saved when raw materials and outgoing shipments can be handled in exactly the same condition as they arrive at the dock—for instance, when bags and drums do not have to be palletized or removed from pallets. The plant manager who has discovered cost advantages in the use of semi-bulk containers within the plant should ask the Sales Department to explore the possibility of shipping to customers in the same container. These are merely two short examples of the way in which intra- and interplant movements can be integrated to everyone's financial benefit.

Bulk Is Cheapest

The cost incentives for handling material in bulk within the plant apply to external movement as well; and water, rail, and motor lines all provide cargo carriers fully adapted to the needs of particular commodities. *Compartmented vehicles* allow several different materials to be shipped at the same time, even though no one of them is in sufficient quantity to qualify for a bulk rate on its own. All three modes of transportation offer open vehicles for the shipment of bulk solids, covered vehicles for shipment of solids that must be protected from the weather, and tanks for the shipment of liquids. There are many variations within each type of equipment, and the carriers should be consulted for specific applications.

Special Ways to Ship

When materials in transit must be refrigerated or heated, domestic rail and motor carriers offer equipment that will maintain the required temperatures. For rail shipments of easily damaged cargo, the carriers offer *damage-free* (DF) freight cars with special shock-absorbing suspensions and internal braces for stabilizing the load within the shipping compartment. In *piggy-back* shipments a truck semi-trailer is loaded, taken to a rail terminal, and placed on a railroad flatcar on which it rides to a point near its destination, and is removed and driven as a truck to the customer's plant. In *containerized shipments* a box mounted on a semi-trailer frame is loaded and sealed, hauled to a terminal where it is removed from the trailer frame, and loaded on a ship or rail car. Upon arrival at its destination terminal, it is reloaded on a truck frame and delivered to the customer.

Shipping Hazardous Materials

Both the shipper and the carrier are responsible for the proper packaging, labelling, and handling of flammable, corrosive, toxic, or otherwise hazardous materials. In 1967, responsibility for establishing and enforcing safety regulations was transferred from the Interstate Commerce Commission to the newly formed Department of Transportation. These regulations are set forth in *Code of Federal Regulations*. Title 49—Transportation, Parts 1-199, for sale by the Superintendent of Documents, U.S. Government Printing Office, Washington, D.C. 20402. See Chapter 15, page 275, for DOT regulations on the shipment of hazardous waste.

Chapter 18

How to Specify and Select the Best Buys in Plant Equipment

Throughout the life of the plant, management will make equipment changes—replacing worn-out units, updating obsolete systems, installing new production lines and processes. Because these new pieces of equipment are complicated, expensive, and have long working lives, the skill with which they are selected has an important bearing on successful operation of the plant.

The equipment selection process consists of three phases: determining what attributes are needed in the proposed equipment and developing specifications to ensure the equipment will have them; searching the marketplace to develop a list of candidates for selection; and evaluating the available equipment and suppliers to make a final choice. Once the equipment is delivered and installed, performance testing will verify the condition and capability. Throughout this process, government, industry, and technical society standards are used to ensure minimum quality, meet safety and environmental requirements, and establish a middle ground for agreement between purchaser and supplier.

In the smaller plant the plant manager is intimately involved in the selection process, while in the larger plant the engineering staff and Purchasing Department assemble the information required to make a decision. In either case you must insist that the search for the best equipment be thorough and conducted according to your standards.

HOW TO DECIDE ON WHAT YOU REALLY WANT

The choice of a major piece of equipment is a risky process; if it fails to do the job for which it was purchased, plant performance will be seriously threatened in critical areas. The manager who makes or approves selection decisions must take every action to ensure the likelihood of success. That process starts with evaluating each proposed piece of equipment against this list of characteristics and incorporating those desired into the formal specifications:

Actual performance versus design capacity. Will the equipment really produce at the "design" rate? Will capacity drop off with age, and by how much? Should it be overdesigned with a factor of 10, 20, or some other percentage?

Reliability. How often and how long must it be down for scheduled maintenance? What is the likelihood of unscheduled outages?

Simplicity of design. Fewer moving parts and fewer wearable parts (such as seals and gaskets) increase reliability.

Ease of operation. Are operating controls clearly labelled, easy to understand, convenient to reach?

Ease of maintenance. Are the parts most subject to wear easily accessible, with a minimum of disassembly required? Can repairs be made in your shop, or must the unit be shipped back to the factory?

Low cost. Have you evaluated the combination of first cost and operating cost for the life of the equipment?

Materials of construction. Are they the least expensive types that will meet the needs of the operation? Will they be subject to corrosion? Will they contaminate the product?

Standardized construction. Are parts interchangeable and readily available?

Safety and environmental requirements. Does it meet EPA and OSHA regulations? Does it comply with national technical codes? Insurance company requirements? State labor and health department regulations? Local plumbing, electrical, and construction codes?

Appearance. Very little in the way of performance can be sacrificed for appearance in the choice of industrial equipment, but an attractive design helps operator acceptance and increases the confidence of those who supply the capital funds.

SPECIFICATIONS: THE IMPORTANCE OF PUTTING IT DOWN ON PAPER

Insist that a written list of specifications be prepared before the first potential supplier is contacted; that will force your organization to clarify its thinking about what is really wanted in the equipment, and it will assure that the quotations you receive are comparable. The specifications should be

Inclusive. They should cover dimensions, output capacity, materials of construction, type and size of power train, utility connections, controls, manufacturing techniques (such as heat treating), insulation, lubrication devices, equipment auxiliaries, delivery date, and methods of performance testing.

Clear. Present them in precise terms, using the language of the trade. Vague instructions may result in the supplier using (innocently) materials of insufficient quality or of too high a quality. For example, to specify that a part be made of "stainless steel" is inadequate; both performance and cost will be quite different if "Stainless Steel Type 201" is specified rather than "Stainless Steel Type 316" or "Stainless Steel Type 316L."

Not overspecified. It is a common error to require more in equipment performance and construction than is really needed, especially when the project engineer is unfamiliar with the equipment being purchased or uses specifications taken wholesale from published standards. The results are excessive cost, unnecessarily complicated equipment, and longer delivery schedules.

Figure 18-1, which presents a detailed list of specifications for the purchase of an electric forklift truck, is an example of how extensive and complicated the development of specifications can be for a seemingly simple and relatively standard piece of industrial equipment.

WHAT THE PURCHASING DEPARTMENT DOES

As soon as the desired general attributes are translated into a definitive list of specifications, call upon the Purchasing Department to perform these important functions:

Canvass the field. No department is in a better position to develop an exhaustive list of the potential suppliers of the desired equipment.

Screen unsuitable suppliers. Purchasing people can weed out early in the search those suppliers who do not understand the specifications, whose equipment clearly does not meet the requirements, and whose performance records in delivery and quality are poor.

Define the conditions of purchase. Whether it is to be by purchase order or formal contract; delivery times, method of payment, cancellation rights, payment of freight charges, and price (when it is not determined by competitive bidding and must be negotiated).

Obtain competitive bids. This is the only way to assure that the lowest possible price is paid and should be standard practice for all major purchases. The Purchasing Department can handle this chore in a professional manner, relieving the line and technical organizations of the many details involved. No matter who handles the bids, be sure that these two important "don'ts" are observed:

Don't put any supplier with whom you do not want to do business on the bidder's list. If his bid turns out to be the lowest, you may have a great deal of explaining to do about why you want to reject it. By limiting the list to acceptable suppliers, you can confidently accept the low bid and proceed with the purchase as soon as the bids are opened.

Don't be lured into changing the specifications for one bidder. The representative of XYZ Company may suggest, "We can save some money if this stainless steel section is changed to aluminum. Why don't you let me bid it

EQUIPMENT SPECIFICATION: ELECTRIC FORKLIFT TRUCK

STYLE:	Stand up end rider, counterbalanced	**OVERALL DIMENSIONS:**	Underclearance: 2 in. min.
CAPACITY:	3,000 lb @ 24 in. load center		Length, without forks: 65 in. max.
FORKS:	Type: Standard pallet Length: 42 in.		Height (inc. overhead guard) 90 in. max.
MAST:	Type: Telescoping Collapsed Height: 83 in. max.	**WHEELS:**	Wheelbase: 30 in. Drive wheels, size: 11¼ in.
	Extended Height: 215 in. max.		Tires: 16¼ × 7 in. Steering wheels, size: 6½ in.
	Free Lift: 46 in. min. Extended Fork Height: 186 in. min.		Tires: 10½ × 5 in. Tire type: Solid, polyurethane
	Lift Speed, Loaded: 45 ft per min.	**TURNING RADIUS:**	Outside: 64 in. max.
	Lift Speed, Unloaded: 90 ft per min.		Must right-angle stack in aisle of 170 in. width
	Forward Tilt: 10 degrees	**BATTERY:**	No. of cells: 18
	Backward Tilt: 5 degrees		Ampere-Hours: 576 Voltage: 36
LEVEL SPEED:	Loaded: 4 mph, min.	**CHARGER:**	Type: Solid State Rectifer
	Unloaded: 6 mph, min.		Power Supply: 220 V, 60 cycle, 3 phase
CONTROLS:	Silicon Controlled Rectifer (SCR) type		Charge Time: 8 hrs max.
ELECTRICAL SYSTEM:	Voltage: 36	**SAFETY:**	Meets all applicable OSHA standards
	Safety Rating: Type EE (Must have UL label.)		

FIGURE 18-1: Detailed Specifications for Purchase of Electric Forklift Truck

that way?" To let him do so, of course, is to lose any valid comparison between his bid and the others. If his suggestion is acceptable, use one of these methods to take advantage of it: (1) send a formal specification change to all the bidders, (2) require all the bidders to quote on the original specifications, then invite the low bidder and the one who submitted the suggestion to rebid under the new specification.

GUIDELINES FOR EVALUATING THE EQUIPMENT PROPOSALS

At some point in the selection procedure a specific piece of equipment will be offered, either in the form of blueprints for a special design to meet your needs or as a standard item from the supplier's product line. Use these guidelines to evaluate the proposed equipment:

Compare its design features with your process experience. If you have had repeated structural failures, wearing of moving parts (such as shafts, bearings, gears, pistons, seals, and so on), motor burnouts or overload failures of any kind, check out the design details of the new equipment to be sure its parts are rugged enough to handle your service.

Ask for a performance trial. If the equipment is readily transportable, the supplier may agree to a trial on your premises on a rental basis, with the fees to be credited toward the purchase price if you decide to keep the equipment. If it is too large to be moved easily, ask the supplier if he can arrange a visit to a plant where his equipment is in operation. Or the supplier may be able to show you a test run in his plant, or allow your personnel to conduct trials on pilot-sized equipment in his laboratories.

Investigate the supplier's capacity to service the equipment at your location. Are replacement parts readily available from nearby stocks? If service personnel are required, can they reach your plant quickly? Do they enjoy a good reputation for competent work?

Talk to other owners of the equipment. The supplier may be willing to supply the names of other corporations that have bought his equipment; telephone calls to these owners will give you a good perspective on the performance history of the equipment. Bear in mind that the supplier is likely to give you the names of satisfied customers; it will take some independent digging to find not-so-satisfied purchasers.

Ask for a copy of the operating manual. Advertising claims tend to emphasize the most favorable attributes, but the operating instructions for use of the equipment reveal all of the precautions that must be taken in its use and its major service limitations. Thoroughly study this important document to discover information not otherwise available.

WARRANTIES

Equipment purchases are usually made on a tight time schedule. In the rush to get the equipment specified and on order, warranty provisions may be only considered casually or ignored altogether. If the equipment performs perfectly, no harm is done by this neglect. Your problems begin when the equipment fails to perform, and you find that the warranty does not give you the protection you assumed it contained. Be sure to consider these aspects of equipment warranty before signing the purchase order or contract:

How reliable is the supplier? The warranty is only as good as the reputation and integrity of the supplier; if she refuses to make good on defective equipment, the cost of forcing her to do so through litigation may be prohibitively expensive.

When does it start, and when does it end? Some suppliers start the warranty period when the equipment is delivered; others when it is first placed in service; still others when the purchase order is placed. It may end after a definite time period (such as ninety days or one year), after so many hours of operation, or after a fixed number of production units. If the equipment is part of a large construction project, beware that the warranty doesn't expire while it is waiting to be installed.

What does it cover? The following list of items that might be covered by a warranty is arranged roughly in order of diminishing likelihood that the supplier will agree to them:

1. Replacement of defective parts (material only)
2. Labor costs for replacement
3. Freight charges to and from supplier's plant
4. Refund of purchase price
5. Protection against patent infringement claims
6. Damage to purchaser's process materials
7. Financial losses suffered by purchaser in overhead costs and lost profits if supplier's equipment is unable to maintain normal production rate

Are all bidders providing essentially the same warranty? The supplier who agrees only to replace defective parts can submit a lower bid than the one who agrees to cover financial losses resulting from performance defects. To put all bidders on the same basis, require them to submit essentially the same warranty; when that is not practicable, be sure to take differences in their warranties into account when evaluating bid prices.

The buyer has responsibilities, too. Under most warranties the customer is required to install and operate the equipment according to the manufacturer's instructions; connect it only to approved power supplies; keep it lubricated; operate it only within design limits of output, speed, pressure, temperature, and other operating conditions; shut the equipment down and notify the supplier promptly if it does not run properly; and allow repairs to be made only by approved suppliers or personnel. Even if the warranty language does not mention these points specifically, the buyer probably weakens the claims he might have if he does not observe them.

TESTING PERFORMANCE: SIX KEY STEPS

There are three compelling reasons for conducting a formal performance trial on newly acquired equipment: to discover defects before they impair the plant operation, to prevent the original defect from causing further damage to the equipment, and to eliminate supplier's claims that the buyer contributed to equipment failure by improper operation. Include in the time schedule for equipment procurement a definite period for performance testing, and base the test procedure on this list of activities.

Step 1: Inspect before testing. As soon as the equipment is delivered, go over it for missing or broken parts and compliance with design specifications. Perform any nonoperational examinations such as leak testing, X-ray and ultrasonic tests for thickness and structural flaws, metal identification, and electrical checking of coatings, insulation, and linings.

Step 2: Have manufacturer's representative present. For large, expensive equipment purchases the representative's presence at the performance trial will probably be arranged as a matter of course, but it is a good idea to invite the supplier to send a representative even when smaller pieces of equipment are tested. She can assure her organization that test conditions were correct, foresee and prevent damage, and attest to the failure of the equipment to perform if that is the outcome.

Step 3: Follow a planned testing procedure. It can come from three sources: the manufacturer's instruction manual, developed and written by the buyer (but approved by the manufacturer), or a standard test from such organizations as the United States government (federal and military procurement specifications), technical societies, or manufacturers' and trade groups.

Step 4: Keep a written log of the test. Record all operating conditions and performance observations: speed, temperature, pressure, output, voltage, current, and flow rates—and the times at which they are observed.

Step 5: Shut down the equipment if it is not operating properly. Overheating, tripping of electrical breakers, popping of relief valves, excessive noise, inability to operate at design speeds—all indicate defects that may cause serious additional damage if the equipment continues to operate.

Step 6: Report defects promptly. The manufacturer is entitled to quick notification that his equipment is defective; if it is delayed, it increases his suspicion that the deficiency was caused by the customer's method of operation.

USE INDUSTRY STANDARDS

A wide variety of technical, trade, and insurance organizations publish equipment design and use standards, and performance test codes. Among professional society publications, the "Boiler and Pressure Vessel Code" and "Power Test Code for Steam Boilers" published by the American Society of Mechanical Engineers are well known. The American Institute of Chemical Engineers publishes "Equipment Testing Procedures, Centrifugal Pumps," "Mixing Equipment," and "Heat Exchangers," among others. Examples of industry group publications are "NEMA Standards for Motors and Generators" by the National Electric Manufacturing Association, and "Standards of the Tubular Exchangers Manufacturers Association." Contact the professional society or trade association of your industry to see if it publishes equipment specifications; your insurance carrier or a librarian can help you locate similar publications in other industries.

These technical and trade standards provide help in three basic areas of equipment procurement:

1. The industry standard can be used as one criterion for judging a proposed piece of equipment. If it meets the industry standards, a minimum level of quality is assured.

2. Specifications can be taken verbatim or adapted from the industry standards, eliminating the cost of researching and developing them independently; the purchase order or contract can quote them or simply refer to the numbered sections. But beware of copying blindly—standardized specifications may not cover all points of importance to you or handle them according to your operation's special needs.

3. Performance tests offer a neutral ground between buyer and seller on which to measure and evaluate the functioning of the new equipment. If they are to be used, they should be mentioned in the purchase order or procurement contract.

BE SURE THE TOTAL COST IS LOWEST

Up to this point it would appear that we simply have been searching for the low bidders. Their price is the best, their equipment meets the specifications, and they are on the list of suppliers with whom we are willing to do business; it only seems reasonable to assume that they win the deal.

Not necessarily so. If the low bidder's price does not include freight costs but the next higher bidder's price does, we have a new factor to consider. When the equipment is received at the plant, it must be installed. One unit may require a stronger base than another, more complicated wiring and piping hookups, or a longer production shutdown to put it in place. During its operating life, one piece of equipment may consume more electricity, steam, cooling water, or lubrication than another, or may result in more production scrap. These factors must all be considered in order to arrive at a valid comparison of the *total* costs of owning and operating each piece of equipment over its useful life.

Operating Example 18–1: Selecting the Equipment with the Lowest Total Cost. A plant manager is considering bids from two suppliers, *A* and *B*, for a piece of production equipment. Expected life of the equipment is 10 years, and interest rates are projected at 10 percent. The manager first looks at the cost of buying the equipment and having it installed. After checking the price quotations, he finds that Vendor *B* will ship freight prepaid, but Vendor *A* will ship only FOB his plant. The manager then asks the area engineer to estimate the cost of installation of each unit and comes up with the following figures for the first comparison of the offers:

	A	*B*
Price	$33,000	$36,700
Freight	1,200	–0–
Installation	3,500	2,700
First Cost	$37,700	$39,400

It appears from this analysis that Vendor A's equipment is the low-cost choice. But this manager investigates further and asks the Engineering, Maintenance, and Production departments to estimate the annual costs for each machine for electric power, maintenance (including lubrication), and scrap production losses and receives these figures:

Annual Cost of:	A	B
Electricity	$1,877	$1,612
Maintenance	768	943
Scrap	2,027	1,185
Annual Operating Costs	$4,672	$3,740

Because these numbers represent annual payments over a 10-year period, the manager decides to convert them to present worth values so that they can be added to the first costs to obtain a valid comparison of total costs. To make the present worth calculation he consults a compound interest table and finds that for interest at 10 percent and a 10-year period, the present worth, P, of a stream of annual payments each equal to R is 6.144 times R. (If the table consulted is in a financial handbook, the column of factors might be labelled "present value of annuity," rather than "present worth"; the figures are the same.) Multiplying the annual operating costs by the present worth factor of 6.144 in each case, he obtains:

Present Worth of Annual Operating Costs for 10 Years at 10 percent	A	B
For Vendor A's equipment: 6.144 × $4,672 =	$28,705	
For Vendor B's equipment: 6.144 × $3,740 =		$22,978

Now the plant manager can add these figures to the first costs and obtain:

	A	B
First Cost	$37,700	$39,400
Present Worth of Annual Operating Costs	28,705	22,978
Total Cost	$66,405	$62,378

By taking into account the annual operating costs, the manager finds that the picture has changed. What seemed to be the cheaper equipment actually would cost him more in the long run. On the basis of *total costs*, he selects Vendor B's equipment.

Chapter 19

Plant Design to Meet the Needs of Production People

Corporations build new plants for a variety of reasons: to increase production capacity, to house new processes, to get closer to raw materials supplies or finished goods markets, to eliminate or consolidate inefficient or obsolete operations, or to find a better labor market. The motives for deciding to build a new plant and its planners' forecast of changing conditions during its lifetime lead to the choice of specific design goals for the project, an area in which you can make significant contributions. In fact, if these people, with their intimate knowledge of the manufacturing process, are not brought into the planning process at an early stage, the optimum plant design is not likely to evolve.

The development of a plant design is a logical step-by-step procedure that demands the accumulation and evaluation of a large mass of information. The basic corporate motives for building a new plant, an evaluation of the business forecasting upon which the design capacity is based, and the nature of the business to be conducted at the new site all contribute to the selection of basic design goals that must be included in the subsequent steps. Site selection is primarily an economic process, but it is affected by the availability of needed materials and facilities. Once the site is chosen, the plot plan must be developed, material flow paths determined, and building types selected. Detailed design attention can then be given to provisions for utility supply, safety, and employee morale and comfort, but the design cannot be complete without early consideration of the steps that must be taken to control air and water pollution. Refurbishment of an old plant involves the same basic design techniques as the building of a new one, but compromises usually have to be reached between the ideal layout and those that are possible in the existing building.

Cost overruns are as common as they are disturbing in new plant projects, and if the cost estimate is to be reliable it must be all-inclusive, based on the most accurate data that can be obtained, and constantly subjected to critical review.

THE ROLE OF THE PLANT MANAGER'S STAFF IN PLANT DESIGN

The development and use of quality circles (Chapter 6) is basically a recognition of the fact that the people performing a job are the most familiar with it, and therefore have something to contribute to decisions about how the job is to be done. In Chapter 18, especially Operating Example 18-1, we saw that comparing only the first costs of two pieces of equipment without including a comparison of the operating costs can lead to inaccurate economic decisions.

These two ideas apply no less cogently to plant design. The plant manager's staff—interpreted broadly here as virtually everyone working in the plant—has accumulated experiences (sometimes expressed in the form of frustrations and complaints) that can be applied to the development of a better design for a new or refurbished plant. Even if the plant to be built is the first of its kind in the company and there is no in-house experience, the new production staff is likely to include some outside people whose experiences in the same industry can be valuable.

Of course, the suggestions and ideas of production people will never be included in the new plant design unless they are expressed in terms of economic advantage: either as cost savings over the life of the project or as lower initial costs. This is an area where the engineering and accounting staffs can help by translating the ideas of others into economic terms.

When to Bring Them in and What the Plant Personnel Should Do

The comments of plant personnel should be solicited as soon as the new facility is announced, and the process should be continued throughout the planning and design stages. Waiting until the engineers are well into the design work before seeking the advice of production people invites one of two adverse consequences: either costly corrections must be made to the designs already completed or the work proceeds without them, committing the new plant to less than optimum operation throughout its life.

Production personnel can contribute to the development of the new plant in two ways. The first, and most likely to generate useful comments, is the review of layout plans as they are developed. Examination of these plans by the production staff will reveal problems in the proposed design that can be eliminated on paper now, rather than in the remodeling of steel and concrete later. It is especially wise to investigate thoroughly any of their "that won't work" comments. The second contribution, to be expected less frequently, are the creative ideas that go beyond the criticism of proposed plans into entirely new concepts of equipment arrangement and plant layout. Such ideas, if valid, will need the most help from you, the plant manager, in terms of explanation, cost justification, and persuasion if they are to be adopted by the design engineers and upper management.

Of course it would be naive to expect that every comment and complaint made by production personnel can be translated into an economically justifiable revision of the new plant layout. Each idea should be examined and tested until it is proved either way—useful, or best discarded. As you elicit suggestions from your staff, you may find the following comments typical:

Production operators will have ideas stemming from their experiences with the effects of plant layout on their work—it takes too long for me to get from *A* to *B;* there is no place to store material; when I need to use a space, work station, or piece of equipment, someone else is always in the way.

Production foremen will have similar but more broadly based comments. They will be concerned about the interfaces with other departments—we produce the stuff but the Shipping Department says they have no more room, so it sits in the production aisles.

Shipping and Receiving people often feel squeezed between the flow of incoming raw materials, outgoing products, and finished goods coming from the Production Departments. They will point out how these flows may conflict with each other.

Maintenance personnel will be concerned about the accessibility of production machinery and building facilities for lubrication, repair, disassembly, and removal; they will also have suggestions about space and layout requirements in the maintenance shop, as well as storage space for spare parts.

Plant engineers will have suggestions for smoother flow of materials, integration of plant processes, and provisions for future expansion.

The *Personnel Department* will make recommendations about lunchroom, locker room, and washup facilities, as well as areas for training and employee meetings.

Quality control people will have ideas about the effect of building and production line layout on the speed and ability of inspectors to check products. If there is a testing laboratory, the staff will comment on the best ways to get samples to them and the test results back to the Production Departments.

One way to obtain suggestions is to circulate the plans to appropriate personnel and ask them to comment. That can be followed up with individual conversations, small group discussions, or even general meetings. It is better to have only one person—probably the plant manager—pass the best suggestions on to the design engineers, or if they involve additional expense, to higher management for authorization to incorporate them.

CHOICES IN PLANT DESIGN

Design Goals

In many industries plant designers must face the fact that the plant they build will outlive the original products they were designed to produce by many years, to say nothing of the sales forecasts upon which production capacities are based. The two fundamental objectives of any plant design are to build a facility that can produce the required product at the lowest cost, but beyond them there are other goals that may require emphasis in any given project:

Flexibility. A must for plants in industries whose products have short life cycles. Keep building design simple, with large unobstructed floor spaces. Provide extra strength in steel construction for heavier upper floor loading at a later date.

Expansion. Design for expansion when there is a strong likelihood that future production requirements will exceed the design capacity that can presently be justified. Leave room on the operating floors for additional machinery, and leave space around buildings for expansion. Building design should lend itself to easy extension of steel framing, sidewalls, floors, and roof.

Adaptation to transportation modes. If shipments must be received or sent by water or rail transportation, the plant design must adapt to the usually narrow range of choices for the location of the required facilities.

Minimum capital outlay. This goal is in direct conflict with the first two on this list. Provisions for expansion and flexibility may have to be dropped if conservation of capital has higher priority. Look for opportunities to save on initial expense in these areas: *installing production equipment outdoors,* a method that is readily adapted to continuous processes, and in light of increasing emphasis on automatic controls, feasible even in the colder northern sections of the United States; *review of nonprocess items,* such as fencing, landscaping, building facades, paving; and *low-cost buildings,* which tend to be single-story, one unit (rather than several buildings), and preengineered.

Location Factors

The important thing to remember is that the location decision is an *economic* decision; although intangible factors such as "labor climate" may seem to be paramount, the plant cannot succeed if it operates under substantial cost disadvantages. Consider these factors in evaluating potential plant sites:

Nearness to raw materials. Cost of transportation for inbound materials, reliability of supply, reliability of transportation.

Nearness to markets. Cost of transportation of finished goods, ease of distribution, ability to serve customers compared with that of actual and potential competitors.

Labor market. Wages and fringe benefit costs. Availability of labor both in numbers and required skills.

Availability of land. Is there enough for present *and* future requirements?

Local and state governments. Will they offer financial assistance? What are the tax rates? Will the zoning regulations affect or limit plant operations?

Transportation facilities. Rail siding available? Good trucking service? Ship and barge facilities? Air transportation for technical and administrative personnel?

Utilities. Water, steam, natural gas, electric power. Fuels for power plants.

Local hazards. Flood, earthquake, tornado, hurricane.

Environmental concerns. What will the air, water, and noise emissions from the plant be? Will it be possible to get permits for them in this location? If there are residential or retail commercial zones nearby, is the company inviting lawsuits by locating here?

Where to Look for Information

Obtain information about location factors from the following:

Government agencies. All of the states, the District of Columbia, and the Canadian provinces maintain agencies that provide information and assistance to companies considering locations within their borders. The larger cities also have industrial development agencies, and most towns (even very small ones) have a Chamber of Commerce that will supply local information.

Railroads and utility companies. Many of these companies maintain lists of potential plant sites and will gather information on those sites within the areas they serve.

Publications. Business and technical magazines (such as *Plant Engineering* and *Modern Manufacturing*) run articles from time to time on plant site selection problems and the methods used by various companies to solve them. Of special interest is the *Site Selection Handbook,* published annually by Conway Research, Inc., Atlanta, Georgia, which gives economic, demographic, and manufacturing data on the states and provinces, an index of industrial sites, and a listing of the state and local agencies and the kinds of help they offer.

Private consulting firms. A number of management, engineering, and industrial consultants will undertake detailed site selection surveys for proposed new plants. Although the cost of these services may seem high, such a firm may have a vast reservoir of information and experience to draw from and usually can take a more dispassionate view of proposed sites than company personnel.

The decision-making process comes next. The ranking of options method described in Operating Example 1-4 (page 11) is admirably suited to this kind of decision and would involve the following steps:

1. From the plant location factor list extract a set of characteristics that the site for the proposed plant *must* have; then develop a second list of characteristics that would be *desirable.*

2. Using the sources of information selected, develop as large a list as possible of potential areas and sites.

3. Screen out all those areas and sites that do not have the characteristics on the required list.

4. Eliminate the sites that have the least number of desirable characteristics.

5. Make a detailed economic study of the remaining sites, comparing annual operating costs, costs per unit of production, and return on investment for each. A very small number of sites that must be submitted for final executive decision will emerge from this comparison.

Building Arrangement and the Plot Plan

Once the site has been selected, the next step is to lay out the arrangement of buildings and facilities on a plot plan. Most of the following considerations should be explored before the land is actually purchased:

1. Determine what zoning laws and building codes apply to the site. They will affect building setbacks from the property line, the uses to which the land may be put, and the types of buildings and facilities that may be constructed. Insurance safety regulations are also a factor, affecting the minimum distance between buildings and the storage areas that contain flammable or otherwise dangerous materials.

2. Place storage areas and transportation facilities—especially railroad tracks—around the outer perimeter of the property. If placed in the center, they may create difficult and expensive problems when later expansions of process buildings are desired.

3. Place process buildings in the center of the property, with the direction of future expansion clearly defined, and room for such expansion allowed.

4. Specify the final location of buildings and heavy structures only after soil bearing tests have been made to see if there are underground impediments to construction—soil so soft that expensive footings and piling would be required, or rock formations which would require blasting.

5. Storage areas for materials that can be cheaply transported (liquids which can be pumped or solids which can be handled in bulk) should be located farther away from point of use, while nearer locations are reserved for materials more expensive to move, especially those requiring hand labor.

Equipment Layout and Materials Flow

The object is to arrive at the arrangement of process equipment and material flow paths that offers the lowest production costs. Include these considerations in developing plant layout:

1. The ideal material flow path is straight through, with minimum handling and no backtracking.

2. In a plant where the cost of moving materials is a large part of the overall production cost, the fundamental precepts of materials movement must be included in the design. See Chapter 17, page 363, for the detailed list.

3. The basic groupings of buildings and equipment are determined by the choice between process and product orientation for the manufacturing operations.

   In *process-oriented* plants each of the operations performed (boring, grinding, heat treating, plating, painting, and so on) is carried out at a given location for all of the products made. Process orientation is suited to plants that produce smaller volumes of a larger number of products and that are subject to relatively frequent product changes.

   In *product-oriented* plants each product is passed through its own production line or department and all of the steps required to produce it are carried out in sequence. Product orientation is suited to plants that manufacture large volumes of a small number of products and where products changes are infrequent. See Chapter 3, page 37, for a descriptive example contrasting product and process orientation.

4. Plant organization and plant layout have inescapable effects on each other; when one is dominant, the other must conform. See Chapter 3, page 38, for detailed considerations.

5. A pitfall in new plant design lies in the tendency to make provisions for later expansion of production capability without corresponding provisions for increased materials flow. Be sure to leave room for additional storage, conveyors, rail car spots, truck docks, and other materials handling facilities.

Types of Building Construction

Limitations on choice. Building codes, zoning regulations, cost of construction, appearance requirements, size and shape of equipment to be housed, safety requirements, insurance regulations, and time allowed for construction all affect the choice of building types.

Foundations and basements. Office and laboratory buildings may be constructed with basements to provide storage space, but manufacturing buildings are less likely to have them. The type of foundation support depends upon the load-bearing strength of the soil and the weight of the building; supports include *concrete footings, pilings* of wood, concrete or steel, and in especially soft soils, *concrete mats* which spread the load over the entire area of the building.

Floors. Almost all modern industrial buildings have reinforced concrete floors, but in special cases they are covered with wood blocks, matting of rubber or plastic, and plastic-bonded aggregates to meet special needs of worker comfort, spark control, and resistance to corrosion.

Framing. Structural steel is most commonly used for the support framework because it is cheap, strong, adaptable to a variety of building styles, and can accommodate long spans. Reinforced concrete structural members are sometimes used when heavy floor loads are required in high buildings.

Walls. The conflicting requirements are cost, appearance, fire resistance, maintenance, and insulation against heat loss. Corrugated steel is inexpensive to install but requires periodic painting and, in most locations, insulation. Concrete block is widely used, has reasonable insulating characteristics and good appearance, but still requires painting. When face brick is added to improve appearance, the cost goes up sharply. Prefabricated wall sections of steel or aluminum with factory-installed enamel coatings are low-cost and low-maintenance alternatives; insulation can be installed on the inside or a "sandwich" version can be obtained—inner and outer metal skins with insulation in the middle.

Roofs. Pitched roof construction is used when the architect or owner desires fast runoff of rain and melted snow. Flat roof construction is used when penthouses, ventilating and air conditioning equipment, dust-collecting apparatus, or other superstructures must be mounted, and when it is desired to make the fullest use of the building volume.

Number of stories. Multi-story buildings are used when unusual equipment configurations must be accommodated or you must take advantage of gravity flow to move materials or when land for expansion is not available at a site and the only direction to go is up. But in the continuing debate among engineers and architects, the one-story building has been winning out on the basis of economy, even in high-cost land areas.

Preengineered. Available in both metal and concrete, these buildings offer the economies of standard structural design and maximum use of prefabricated components, and have been a favored choice for housing operations that do not require specialized building shapes.

Utility Installations

Time deadlines and the considerable effort that goes into the design of process equipment and buildings may result in only routine attention given to ways in which steam, water, air, and electricity are supplied to the plant. But utility installations are not easily changed once the plant is built, and in many production operations the efficiency with which they are supplied can have a marked effect on the cost performance of the plant.

Water. Can the municipal supply provide the plant's full needs? Are there any flows that can be recycled? Is the plant's projected usage of water large enough to justify its own treatment plant? Are there any uses that do not require fully treated water—for instance, does the makeup supply to a cooling tower have to be drinking-water grade or would filtered or merely flocculated water do? Do the plans include acceptable devices for preventing contamination of the municipal supply with the lower grade plant waters? Is there sufficient pressure and flow in the supply of firefighting water to meet foreseeable emergencies and to obtain the lowest insurance rates?

Steam. Should steam be purchased (if available) or generated? If generated, are two or more boilers included in the plan so that the failure of one will not shut the plant down completely? Does the arrangement of buildings on the site minimize the length of distribution lines, and thereby losses? Have pressures at points of use been worked out so that contamination of the steam by the process (or vice versa, if that is worse) is avoided?

Electricity. Is it more economical to generate electricity than to buy it—especially if waste steam from the generator can be used by the process? Should co-generation be considered? (See Chapter 9, page 146.) If purchased, should standby units be provided to handle emergencies such as power outages? Should primary or secondary selective feeder systems be installed to provide backup power in case of failure in the main line? Have power factor losses been considered and capacitors provided (if needed) to minimize them? Should office and some plant space-heating be electrical? Can interior lights supply part of the space-heating load?

Air. Have all the uses for compressed air been considered in reaching the design capacity—instruments, tools, painting, pumping of liquids? Is air for any of these services required to be oil-free or moisture-free, and have separators, dryers, and separate distribution loops been provided where needed?

Personnel Facilities

The number, size, and elaborateness of these facilities depend on the number of employees in the plant and the company philosophy of industrial relations.

Food service. Very large plants may elect to install a full-fledged cafeteria complete with its own food preparation staff. Smaller plants may provide a central lunchroom with vending machine service, possibly served by an attendant during rush periods. Very small plants may provide a simple lunchroom with few embellishments other than chairs and tables. Consideration should be given to snack areas scattered around the plant to cut down the time personnel spend getting to and from lunch and coffee breaks. Under no circumstances should you allow food to be taken into the plant working areas; it is subject to contamination by all sorts of substances and, if spilled, creates an attraction for vermin.

Locker room, toilets, and showers. Be sure the locker room is built with plenty of allowance for expansion. Use lockers with sloping tops; otherwise they will collect an array of personal effects. Follow local building codes on the number of persons to one water closet; in their absence, provide one toilet for every fifteen people. Shower facilities may be required by state or local codes; if not, they should be provided for dirty, dusty, or odorous operations.

First aid room. The company doctor should decide what equipment is needed; he will probably base his decision on the speed with which an injured employee can be gotten to the hospital or a doctor's office. The first aid room, dispensary, or an elaborate medical facility should be cheerfully decorated, well lighted, and placed as far from plant noise and odors as possible.

Instructional facilities. A "classroom" fitted with a chalkboard, projection screen, and comfortable chairs will prove valuable for safety meetings and in-plant instruction.

SAFETY AND ENVIRONMENTAL CONSIDERATIONS

How to Build a Safe Plant

The plant safety program starts with the plant design: failure to incorporate sound safety principles at this stage invites injuries to personnel and damage to property for the entire life of the plant. Use this checklist of important safety provisions.

Fire prevention and control. Minimum use of combustible construction materials. Highly flammable raw materials and finished goods stored in isolated areas with suitable fire prevention devices. Fully equipped hose houses, hose stations, and appropriate types of fire extinguishers strategically distributed throughout the plant. Sprinkler system designed according to code; sprinkler heads not blocked by equipment; design based on adequate water supply.

Mechanical equipment. Moving parts covered with safety guards. Controls clearly labeled, within easy reach. Safety brakes and quick-cutoff controls on machinery likely to draw the operator in (such as a rubber mill). Automatic hand and arm withdrawal guards on machines that cut, press, or stamp.

Personnel movement. Pedestrian and vehicle traffic separated as much as possible. Walkways and stairs provided with nonskid surfaces. Ladders longer than twenty feet equipped with safety cages. Catwalks, platforms, and stairs edged with kickplates and double handrails. Outside walks, ramps, and parking areas designed with snow and ice melting devices, or at least constructed to minimize winter hazards.

Electrical. All equipment used in hazardous areas furnished with the appropriate National Electric Code rating. Multiple lockout devices provided for safe shutdown and maintenance work. Use of portable equipment and extension cords avoided wherever possible. Conductive belts and static collector brushes used on moving machinery; ground straps for transfer of flammable liquids through pipes and between containers. Distribution system grounded. Battery-operated exit and emergency lights installed for safe evacuation in power failure.

Piping and conduit. Labeled, showing contents and direction of flow. Color coding for remote identification, danger warning. Insulate hot sections within reach of personnel.

Ventilation. Adequate for comfort. Reduces concentrations of toxic, flammable, and irritating dusts and fumes to safe levels.

Housekeeping. Surfaces designed for minimum dirt accumulation and ease of cleaning. Floors sloped to drains. Floors sealed off to prevent spills from cascading downward.

Regulations. All systems must meet applicable municipal, state, and federal safety regulations and insurance safety codes. Follow published recommendations of trade associations (see Chapter 14, page 227) and OSHA requirements (see Chapter 15, pages 237–238).

Pollution Control

The range of federal pollution regulations and the techniques used to comply with them are described in Chapter 15, starting at page 248. Local regulations may be more restrictive or may deal with different pollution problems. All of them, plus the company's desire to earn a reputation as a good neighbor, may affect plant design in the following ways.

Land area. Pollution control equipment will most likely require additional square footage. Lagoons, settling ponds, and landfills will require substantial additional acreage.

Design of processes. They may have to be modified to reduce air and water pollution. The best method, if it can be used, is to recycle all of the contaminants back into the process, so that they do not appear in the emissions and effluents at all.

Drainage systems. Storm, process, and sanitary water systems probably will have to be separated and treated differently in order to meet regulations.

Noise regulations. If the new plant has a noisy operation, (1) it may have to be revised to reduce the amount of sound emitted, (2) it may have to be located in the interior of the site so as to have the least effect outside the plant boundaries, or (3) sound-absorbing features may have to be incorporated in the building design.

The bubble, netting, offset, or banking concepts described on page 262 may permit less stringent controls to be used on a point source if the resulting additional emissions can be compensated for elsewhere. That may involve trade-offs, either within the plant or with other companies in the area. These possibilities should be considered and acted upon before the pollution control designs are made final.

ESTIMATING THE COST FOR A NEW PLANT

Cost estimates for new plants frequently prove to be low, creating unpleasant surprises for those who must supply capital funds, and often resulting in the elimination or severe cutback of parts of the project. One of the contributing factors to low estimates is the failure to include all relevant cost elements. Be sure the estimate includes all the items in Table 19–1 that are applicable to the project.

Cost Information Sources

Inclusion of all costs is one essential ingredient of an accurate estimate; the other is the use of the most reliable methods of estimation available. This list of cost information sources is arranged (in the author's view) in descending order of reliability:

Contractor's firm bid. The most accurate of all cost data is the bid submitted by a reliable contractor after he has reviewed the prints and specifications for the project. We say "reliable" because some unscrupulous contractors may submit an unrealistically low bid, hoping to recoup losses by charging for "extra" items later on. Of course, the contractor's bid will not cover all of the applicable items from Table 19–1, and the remainder must still be estimated without his help.

Company files on similar construction and equipment projects. The cost data they contain must be adjusted for differences in time, geographical location, and equipment used for the process. The first two can be handled by applying cost indices appearing in *Engineering News Record*. The third is best handled by obtaining supplier quotations for the exact type of equipment specified for the new project.

Outside consultants. Consulting firms in architecture, management, engineering, and even some contractors can be retained to develop a project cost estimate.

TABLE 19-1: Cost Elements of a New Plant Project

Prefeasibility study	Utilities installation
Feasibility study	—electricity
Process license	—water
Process engineering	—steam
Detailed engineering	—compressed air
Land acquisition	—industrial gases
—purchase price	Pollution control installations
—brokerage fees	Taxes
—transfer costs	Insurance
Site preparation	Administrative costs
—grading	Start-up expenses
—drainage	Equipment supplier's technical
—fencing	services (for calibration and
—landscaping	adjustment during start-up)
—roads and sidewalks	Training of operators and
Soil testing	maintenance personnel
Piling (if needed)	Contingency[1]
Foundations	Escalation[2]
Equipment	Interest on capital funds during
—freight	construction period
Erection	Working capital[3]

[1]Contingency is a provision for unforeseen circumstances, for example, the project is delayed because a key equipment supplier cannot ship on time or, despite soil testing, additional foundation pilings are needed. Not to be confused with escalation. Usually set at 10 to 15 percent of other costs.

[2]Escalation. New plants will take several years to construct, and not all costs are incurred on the first day. Escalation funds cover the estimated inflation in costs during the life of the project.

[3]Working capital is the cost of materials in process required to fill the production "pipeline," and finished goods which must be maintained in warehouse inventory. Also included is the cost of goods shipped to customers but not paid for until 30 to 60 days later.

For this method to be successful, it is important that the agency selected has no other interest in the project; otherwise, there is a natural pressure on them to estimate low in order to keep interest in the project alive.

Cost literature. Technical libraries and even some local libraries can offer a number of books on construction cost estimating and equipment costs in specific industries; be sure to check the date of publication, because cost data published in book form may be outdated. Periodicals may publish more current cost information; the journals of the engineering societies publish cost articles from time to time, as do such general industrial periodicals as *Plant Engineering*. *Cost Engineering* is a magazine devoted to industrial equipment costs; it is published by the American Association of Cost Engineers, Morgantown, West Virginia. Also of interest is *Building Construction Cost Data* by R. S. Means, published by the National Association of Home Builders, Washington, D.C.

REFURBISHING AN OLD PLANT

There are times when the corporation feels compelled to install a new process or continue an existing process in an obsolescent building and decides to renovate the facility. Consider these factors when undertaking a refurbishment program:

Layout is a compromise. The arrangement of operating equipment aisleways, and materials handling facilities is limited by the physical structure of the existing building, and it is not always possible to achieve the optimum arrangement. Try out as many ideas for equipment layout as possible, to be sure that the best compromise has been reached.

Major physical features *can* be changed. Steel support columns can be moved provided adjustments are made in the surrounding steel structure; floors (even on upper levels) can be chopped out and repoured; mezzanines can be built, or floors chopped out to achieve a two-level bay; interior partitions and walls can be rearranged—so can exterior walls (unless, as in some older buildings, they support the structure). Changes in the basic structure of a building are expensive, however, and should be economically justified by demonstrable savings in processing or materials movement.

Look for the likely weaknesses in an old building. Modifications and repairs are often needed in these areas:

1. Roofs. May be leaking, in disrepair, and inadequately insulated.

2. Heating, ventilating, and air conditioning. Insufficient capacity, equipment obsolete or not functioning, heating not coordinated with ventilation, or ventilation not coordinated with air conditioning.

3. Windows and doors. In older buildings they tend to be small by today's standards and often are in disrepair or unattractive. Enlargement and repairs may improve appearance as well as employee morale.

4. Illumination. Insufficient light at working surfaces, obsolete types of illumination (such as incandescent lights), inadequate wiring, and broken or dirty light fixtures may all need replacement.

5. Utilities. Steam boilers may be inadequate for the load, in disrepair, or in need of replacement. Electric power mains, substations, and distribution wiring may need to be increased in capacity. Pipes and conduits for distribution of services throughout the building may be unsightly. Remove those that are not needed, hide the remainder from view wherever possible, fix leaks, repair insulation, and paint those that cannot be hidden.

6. Decor. The grim, uninviting appearance of older factory buildings can be greatly relieved by the use of today's wall colors and interior design touches (even in plants with fairly heavy industrial operations). Exterior masonry walls can be pointed, painted, and upgraded with new facia treatments, marquees, and entranceways.

Chapter 20

How to Manage
Plant Construction
Projects from
Basic Concepts
to Final Audit

The capacity, effectiveness, quality, and reliability of the plant's equipment are fundamental factors in the achievement of its manufacturing goals. Equipment does not remain static—as the plant's assignments change, the equipment must also change to maintain product output and quality and the safety and efficiency of the process. Entire new departments and processes may have to be installed, or major alterations made to existing facilities.

The plant manager is always involved in these projects and needs to understand the successive stages of their development. You can make significant contributions to the conceptual stage, in which the fundamental outlines of the project are developed; to the engineering stage, in which the precise details of construction and equipment selections are spelled out; to the decision on whether inside or outside forces are to perform the work, the selection of a contractor, and the drawing up of the contract; and to the control of the work progress. You are almost always required to prepare or approve the preparation of the economic justification for the project. You should also participate in the post-completion audit to measure actual performance against the preproject predictions.

BASIC CONCEPTS FOR DESIGNING PLANT CONSTRUCTION PROJECTS

Before any evaluation of a project can be made or any serious work begun on its design, it has to go through a conceptual stage in which the following basic questions must be answered.

How big will it be? If a building, square footage and height; if process equipment, output rating; if a materials transport facility, carrying capacity per unit time.

What will it be made of? The choice of construction and engineering materials has a significant effect on the cost of the project. Any possible corrosion or contamination effects of the product on the equipment or of the equipment on the product also must be considered.

Where will it be placed? This decision is usually made on the basis of cost and, in turn, hinges on the expense of moving materials to and from the new equipment, and the cost of running utility services to it. Movement of labor can also be a cost factor. Noneconomic considerations such as safety, sensitivity of the product to contamination, and pollution may weigh heavily in the final decision.

Should provision be made for future expansion? The present cost of providing space and capacity not immediately required is weighed against the probability of its being needed in the foreseeable future and the increased cost of providing it at a later time. The answer is influenced by the circumstances surrounding the individual project and the company's general philosophy on capital expenditures; the important point is that the question be consciously considered and resolved in the planning stage of the project.

Are there special requirements in safety, reliability, housekeeping, utility supply, pollution control, or maintenance? Any of these considerations may influence the original design concepts and can cause unwanted delay and expense if they are ignored until the project is in the late stages.

This stage requires as wide a range of thinking as possible—new ideas should be encouraged, a search for the latest equipment and methods undertaken, and if the project entails the duplication or expansion of existing facilities, improvements based on the experience gained with the old facilities incorporated. The conceptual stage can be handled by the plant's engineering staff, by outside consultants, or by a corporate central engineering department, but it should always involve the higher levels of plant management who may have original ideas of their own to contribute and who can help evaluate new ideas developed by others. It ends with the issuance of sketches and blueprints showing the major components of the project, their physical location, and the flow of materials through the process, along with a written report stating the objectives of the project, the basic design philosophy, and descriptions of the equipment and process that cannot be conveniently shown on the prints.

Key Aspects of the Feasibility Study

For most projects the steps described in the previous section are enough to get the project launched. But when the company is planning to build a new plant, enter a new line of business, or construct a very large project, a more comprehensive and detailed review is needed. This review is called a *feasibility study,* and it undertakes a thorough examination of the factors involved in the enterprise. In physical form it may run from a hundred pages or so to eight or ten volumes, but fundamentally the feasibility study seeks to answer two questions—should we do this at all, and if so, how should we go about it?

The question of whether or not to proceed is basically an economic one, and a major section of the study is an extensive financial examination of the project. It begins with estimates of annual earnings from the project for at least the first ten years of its life. Then the annual costs are added up, starting with the capital cost, which is usually converted to an annual depreciation figure, as well as any borrowing costs incurred in acquiring the capital. Operating costs come next: raw materials, freight, labor, utilities, maintenance, supplies, overhead and administration, and taxes. When the capital plus operating costs are subtracted from earnings, what is left is profit. The study then goes on to show how the estimated profits compare with the company's criteria for capital expenditures, such as return on investment (ROI), payout time, discounted cash flow, net present worth, or others. Any assumptions made about future interest rates or in developing the revenue and cost estimates should be clearly stated. If inflation is factored in, the rate should be stated, and it should be clear whether the revenue and cost projections are stated in today's dollars or are adjusted for inflation.

The result of all of this is a table that shows, year by year, the anticipated revenues, costs, and profits; it is often called the "pro forma profit and loss statement." Whatever name is used, now is the time to subject it to a series of *sensitivity analyses,* in which the numbers in any of the categories are changed in answer to "what if" questions. What if sales are 10 percent less than predicted or the price received for the product is 20 percent lower? Suppose raw material prices are 15 percent higher than estimated? The computer is usually used to convert these and other "what if" questions into profit-and-loss figures so as to come up with either *worst case* or *best case scenarios,* which give a much more realistic picture of the possible financial outcomes of the project.

In answering the question of how to develop the project, the feasibility study covers the following list of project elements, presenting the range of choices available in each:

Plant capacity.   The number of units of production to be manufactured per year. Quality grades to be produced, and an estimate of the annual amount of rework and scrap. Quantities of by-products to be produced.

Processes.   Manufacturing methods and technologies, and descriptions of how they work. Royalty payments, if needed to acquire them.

Raw materials. Availability, potential suppliers. Industry conditions that might affect continuity of supply.

General plant. Size, location, manufacturing facilities required, and "offsites," that is, utilities structures, administrative buildings, parking lots, and so on necessary to support the production complex.

Materials flow schemes. The basic arrangements and major facilities for receiving and storing raw materials, moving them through the manufacturing process, and storing the finished products.

Transportation modes. Movements of raw materials and products by rail, water, or truck, and the facilities needed to accommodate them.

Environmental questions. What laws and regulations apply and the permits needed. Process and equipment options for meeting pollution control requirements. Community relations steps that should be taken.

Completion schedule. Time required from project approval to mechanical completion, plus the period for start-up and those commissioning activities required to bring production up to design levels.

Personnel requirements. Number and types of people required to operate the new facility. How they will be recruited and trained.

For those elements that involve choices, the study should make a recommendation as to what the choice should be and should present a rationale for its position.

Smaller companies probably will hire outside consultants to perform the feasibility study, but even the larger companies with in-house capability may prefer to contract it out to preserve objectivity in the analysis of alternatives. The cost of a feasibility study will depend upon the complexity of the project; however, for a $50,000,000 project, a typical figure would be $200,000 to $500,000.

**The Design and Engineering Stage:
Two Phases**

The object of this phase is to define the project sufficiently in blueprints and specifications so that it can be submitted to contractors for firm bid prices, and once the winning bidder is selected, actually constructed. Adequate detailing at this point will prevent misunderstandings later on—in cost, in what is expected of the contractor, and in performance requirements of the equipment.

The design and engineering stage really consists of two phases: *front end*, or *process engineering*, and *detailed engineering*. In process engineering the major pieces of equipment are selected and sized, and the way in which process materials will flow between them (conveyors, piping, trucks, and so on) is determined, as well as the quantities that will flow. In detailed engineering a complete description is provided of everything to be installed—the exact shape and dimensions of equipment, the types and sizes of pipes, the fittings to be used, the shape and size of the structural members that support the conveyors, and many more. In smaller projects these two phases may be combined, but in any event the Engineering Department (or outside engineering firm) will prepare some or all of the following types of blueprints.

Flow sheets.   These are a product of the process engineering phase. The major items of equipment are depicted in outline. If they are connected by piping, it is shown as single lines; other materials flow devices are drawn in simple outline. The quantities of material entering and leaving each piece of equipment are given, as well as the temperatures and pressures prevailing in them.

Plot plans.   Essentially large-scale maps of the plant area, they show existing and proposed buildings, roads, fences, utility lines and poles, railroads, streams and ditches, parking lots, sheds and pumphouses, any other significant external feature, and the property boundary lines.

Architectural drawings.   One or more of these drawings will be prepared as determined by the size and complexity of the project:

1. Foundation plans. The subsurface structures, including piles and footings, required to support the building and construction details of the basement or first floor slab.
2. Floor plans. They show how each floor is divided into production areas, warehouse and storage, offices, lavatories, lunchrooms, locker rooms, elevator shafts, stairways, aisles, and passageways.
3. Elevations. Views of the front, sides, and rear walls of the building, showing doors, windows, and decorative features. Cross sections show the interior floors. Between them, the floor plans and elevations show how the major pieces of equipment are arranged in the building.
4. Wall sections. Vertical cross-sectional drawings of one or more of the walls of the structure. They start with the underground footings and show the construction details of the basement and upper walls, including inner and outer facings and the intersections with the several floors and roof.

Structural drawings.   They depict the structural framework that supports the building. Most modern industrial buildings have a structural skeleton of steel beams and columns, and the drawings are likely to be entitled "Steel Framing Plan."

"Mechanicals."   This is a term used by many engineering firms to include drawings showing the following types of building appurtenances:

Electrical (power supply, wiring, circuit breakers, controls, receptacles, lighting fixtures)

Fire protection (sprinkler piping, cutoff valves, hose reels, hose houses, foam units)

Piping (steam, water, compressed air, gases, and process fluids)

Heating and ventilating (air ducts, blowers, fans, radiators, space heaters, air conditioning equipment)

Instrumentation (indicators; recorders; controllers for temperature, pressure, and liquid level; alarms interlocks and cutoff devices)

For projects that involve a great deal of piping, the designer may issue "P & I diagrams," which show the location, size, and type of piping to be used, as well as the instruments to be installed for measurement and control of flow, temperature, and pressure. *Piping isometrics* are drawings that show the details of piping arrangements in three dimensions.

Detail drawings, shop drawings, and specifications. The drawings described so far usually cover too large an area to permit showing the many details of construction. In the case of a building, the front and side elevations cannot effectively show the manner in which doorcases are affixed to the walls or the exact position of the hinges. This is done in a *detail drawing,* on which may be shown the details of several items, such as doors, windows, steps, and so on.

Shop drawings are supplied by vendors to show the exact dimensions and construction features of the equipment they supply, including the location and size of bolt holes for anchoring the equipment, the position and dimensions of rotating shafts, and the size and location of flanges for attachment to piping. The weight and materials of construction used in the equipment are also specified, so that its installation can be properly engineered. Subcontractors who are building particular segments of the project may provide similar drawings showing how their work interfaces with the overall project.

Specifications are prepared by the architect or engineer to accompany each set of drawings. They give all the design details and construction procedures that cannot be described adequately on the blueprints. For instance, the specification for concrete defines the quality of the raw materials used to make it; the manner in which it is to be mixed, delivered to the site, and poured; and the laboratory and field tests that it must pass. The electrical specification on transformers gives the required current capacity, the voltage stepdown, the manner of wiring, miscellaneous electrical characteristics, and the accessories that must be supplied with them. It may also specify the manufacturer whose product is to be used or give a list of acceptable suppliers, any of which may be chosen by the contractor.

Blueprint Checklist

The plant manager is often asked to review a set of blueprints and specifications and approve them before the project proceeds into the construction stage. Unless you are very familiar with engineering practice, the task can be a confusing one because blueprints seem to present the large and the small, the important and the unimportant in equal focus.

A useful tool in this situation is the blueprint checklist, an example of which is shown in Table 20-1. This particular list covers most of the major areas of interest to a plant manager working with a project involving plant building or equipment, and can be used as is. Or it can be used as the basis of an individualized checklist you can develop to cover your special needs.

TABLE 20-1: Blueprint Checklist

☐ Building and equipment meets size and capacity requirements determined in conceptual stage.

☐ Correct suppliers and model numbers for purchased equipment.

☐ Proper materials of construction used. No prohibited materials included.

☐ Has required ratings for pressure and temperature.

☐ Meets governmental zoning, building, health and safety codes. Meets insurance requirements.

☐ Physical arrangement—major components, controls, nozzles, feed and discharge ports, motor mounts arranged properly from right to left, top to bottom, front to rear.

☐ Equipment connections—lugs, bolt holes, clamps, support frames, piping and electrical connectors properly located for attachment to building and existing equipment.

☐ Lubrication. Grease fittings, oil ports and gauges, external lubricators, pressure cylinders, auxiliary pumps provided.

☐ Equipment and building layout designed for efficient materials movement and storage.

☐ Allowance for future expansion in space allocation, structural design, and mechanical-electrical connections (if desired).

☐ Piping. Sizes, materials of construction, fittings (screwed, flanged, welded), hangers and supports, expansion loops, backflow preventers, unintended siphons.

☐ Maintenance. Machine design allows for easy replacement of wear-prone parts. Building design provides vertical and horizontal room for removal of shafts, other large components.

☐ Required air, water, and noise pollution control devices included.

☐ Proper indicating, recording, and controlling instruments provided, along with needed quality control devices and sampling connections.

☐ Specific safety devices, code and noncode included. Coupling guards, safety brakes, shields, relief valves, shear pins, fusible links, lockout devices.

☐ Housekeeping. Building and equipment constructed with minimum crevices and corners for dirt to accumulate. Surfaces easily cleaned. Trash collection and removal systems adequate.

☐ Insulation. Provided where needed to conserve heat, prevent freezing, avoid injury to people.

☐ Machine controls, valves, instruments, sight ports easily accessible from floor to catwalk.

☐ Spare units (motors, pumps, and so on). Mounts, brackets, electrical and pipe connections uniform so that one unit is usable anywhere.

☐ Blueprints coordinated with specifications. No conflicts in requirements, no areas not covered by either.

☐ Electrical layout. Proper connections to external power supply. Transformers, motors, capacitors, circuit breakers all have proper ratings for voltage, current, horsepower. Switches in accessible locations. Correct number and location of receptacles. Wires properly supported or enclosed.

In the small plant, the plant manager may be director of engineering as well; in this situation you can develop a whole series of checklists for reviewing each of the types of drawings mentioned in the previous section.

HOW TO DEVELOP THE ECONOMIC JUSTIFICATION FOR A PROJECT

As soon as the project has progressed to the stage where a firm price can be established (or very closely estimated) for its acquisition, it is ready for justification. And since it is the primary function of a business enterprise to return a profit on the money it is given to invest, nothing comes closer to the heart of the business than the way it decides to invest capital funds.

There are really two kinds of justification—noneconomic as well as economic. In *noneconomic justification,* the business authorizes the expenditure of capital funds without a definite financial return for such reasons as safety, employee morale, governmental regulation, and community relations.

But the purchase of a new production machine or the erection of a building to house a new manufacturing process must be justified on purely economic grounds, and most companies have devised uniform methods for evaluating the financial attractiveness of proposals for capital expenditure. Several of these methods are described in the two Operating Examples that follow. In the first, we will see how capital costs are added up, how the effect of the project on profit is determined, and finally how two very common and simple measures of profitability—return on investment and payback period—are calculated. In the second example, a more sophisticated form of profitability analysis—discounted cash flow—is explained.

> **Operating Example 20-1: Economic Justification of a Capital Project Using Return on Investment and Payback Period.** A plant manager proposes to purchase a piece of production equipment and have it installed by an outside contractor. Her first step in developing an economic justification is to work up an estimate of the *fixed capital cost,* listing those costs involved in the acquisition and installation of the equipment:
>
> | | |
> |---|---:|
> | 1. Purchase Price of Equipment (include freight charges and taxes) | $126,057 |
> | 2. Contractors' Charges (include subcontractors' fees for rigging, piping, electrical work, and so on) | 31,344 |
> | 3. Auxiliary Equipment (lubricators, instruments, scales, other items not included in basic purchase price) | 8,250 |
> | 4. Engineering Services (preparation of prints and specifications by outside or internal engineering groups) | 16,530 |
> | 5. Contingency (10 percent of costs up to this point) | 18,218 |
> | Fixed Capital Cost | $200,399 |
>
> *Notes*
>
>   (1) Even if the installation (Item 2) is to be carried out by plant maintenance forces rather than an outside contractor, the cost should nevertheless be estimated and included in the above list.

(2) Another item could have been added to this list, namely *escalation*. It is an estimate of the increase in costs that might take place while the project is being built. (It is different from *contingency*, which is an allowance for unexpected occurrences during the construction of the project.) Because this project was estimated to take only a few months to build, escalation was not included, but it certainly would be for a larger project taking several years to complete.

The next step is to estimate the *working capital* that will be needed—the cost of raw materials, materials in process, and finished goods inventories required to fill the "pipeline" from the beginning of the plant process to the customer's receiving docks; and the cost of accounts receivable—materials shipped to customers but not paid for until 30 to 60 days or more later. The plant manager finds these costs total $166,299 and can now state the *total investment*, the sum of fixed plus working capital:

6.	Fixed Capital Cost	$200,399
7.	Working Capital	166,299
8.	Total Investment	$366,698

With the investment costs clearly defined, it is time to evaluate the project's *effect on profit*. A capital investment can only be justified on the basis of additional profit, which it generates by producing additional goods to sell, reducing manufacturing costs on existing production, or both. The manager assumes a depreciable life of 10 years for the project; and to obtain the effect on profit, she estimates the sales revenues and operating costs for the entire plant over that period under present conditions (without the project) and proposed conditions (with the project):

		Present	*Proposed*
9.	Sales	$29,656,476	42,580,836
10.	Operating Costs	14,559,939	22,120,908
11.	Pretax Profit (Item 9 minus Item 10)	15,096,537	20,459,928
12.	Net Gain in Pretax Profit (Item 11, "Proposed" minus "Present")		$5,363,391

The profit gain from this project comes from additional sales made possible by increased production capacity. If it were a pure cost reduction project, sales figures might not be shown, and the added profit would result from lower operating costs. Although sales, cost, and profits are shown as simple line items in this example, individual companies may require extensive supporting data on their justification forms to back up these figures.

Now the manager is ready to apply two measures of profitability used by her company: return on investment (ROI) and payback period. Return on investment is the average annual profit divided by the total investment (expressed as a percentage). To obtain it, the manager first deducts the depreciation charges, which have not yet appeared as a production cost, and then subtracts taxes, as shown in the following calculations:

12.	Net Gain in Pretax Profit	$5,363,391
13.	Less Depreciation	200,399
14.	Taxable Profit	5,162,992

15. Less Income Tax at 34 percent (tax rates vary; obtain yours from   1,755,417
the Accounting Department)

16. After-tax Profit (Item 14 minus Item 15)   3,407,505

17. Average Annual Profit (Item 16 divided by 10 years)   340,750

18. Return on Investment (Average Annual Profit divided by
Total Investment)

$$\frac{340,750}{366,698} \times 100 = 92.9$$

Notes:

(1) In Item 13 only the fixed capital cost is depreciated. In this case it is fully depreciated, with no salvage value assumed. (For other methods of calculating depreciation see Operating Example 7-2.)

(2) Working capital is not depreciated, on the assumption that when the last production run is made, all of the process materials will have been converted to salable product and their costs fully recovered.

The payback period is the total investment divided by the average annual net cash flow. Net cash flows are obtained by adding the money that comes into the project (usually the sales revenue) and subtracting the money that goes out (operating costs and taxes, for example) In this case depreciation is added back to the after-tax profit to obtain net cash flow because (1) depreciation is not an actual cash outlay during the operating period, and (2) the object is to find how many years of profit will be needed to recover the cost of the project.

19. After-tax Profit (from Item 16)   3,407,505

20. Add Depreciation (from Item 13)   200,399

21. Cash Flow (Item 19 plus Item 20)   3,607,904

22. Average Annual Cash Flow   360,790
(Item 21 divided by Item 10)

23. Payback Period (Item 8 divided by Item 22)   1.0 years

With an ROI of 92.9 percent and a payback period of 1.0 years, this would seem to be an attractive investment in any company and is likely to be approved. The standard figures by which projects are accepted or rejected vary from company to company and from time to time within a company. As a general rule, smaller projects such as this will be required to have higher ROIs and shorter payback periods than larger projects, such as a new plant.

A company may employ ROI and payback period as its only criteria for capital investment decisions; it may use variations of these methods; or it may use entirely different methods. One of these is discounted cash flow (DCF), which has found wide use in recent years and is explained in Operating Example 20-2.

Operating Example 20-2: Evaluation of a Capital Investment Using Discounted Cash Flow. A corporation is considering a project with a total investment of $1,300,000, consisting of $1,100,000 in fixed capital and $200,000 in working capital, and wishes to find the discounted cash flow rate of return (DCFRR) that the project will yield. The DCFRR is the interest rate at which the sum of the present values of the annual net cash flows equals the original investment. Another way of saying this is that the DCFRR is the annual earnings rate on the investment that is represented by the cash flows *and* at which the capital investment is recovered. It is found by a trial-and-error calculation in which the annual net cash flows are estimated and their net present values calculated at various interest rates. When an interest rate is found at which the algebraic sum of the present values of all the cash flows equals zero, that is the DCFRR. In the following calculations the estimated net cash flow for each year is multiplied by the present worth factor for the interest rate being tested and the number of years into the future. For example, in Year 5 the cash flow is estimated at $326,000, and the present worth factor for 15 percent and 5 years is 0.4972; $326,000 is multiplied by 0.4972 to obtain the present value of $162,087.

		15 PERCENT TRIAL		20 PERCENT TRIAL	
Year	*Net Cash Flow*	*Present Worth Factor*	*Present Value*	*Present Worth Factor*	*Present Value*
0	−1,300,000	1.0000	−1,300,000	1.0000	−1,300,000
1	223,000	0.8696	193,921	0.8333	185,826
2	265,000	0.7561	200,367	0.6944	184,016
3	321,000	0.6575	211,058	0.5787	185,763
4	307,000	0.5718	175,543	0.4822	148,035
5	326,000	0.4972	162,087	0.4019	131,019
6	335,000	0.4323	144,821	0.3349	112,192
7	301,000	0.3759	113,146	0.2791	84,009
8	251,000	0.3269	82,052	0.2326	58,383
9	237,000	0.2843	67,379	0.1938	45,931
10	390,000 (190,000 + 200,000 recovery of working capital)	0.2472	96,408	0.1615	62,985
Net Present Value			+146,782		−101,481

We are looking for the DCFRR at which the net present value (NPV), the sum of the present value columns, equals zero. Because the NPV has a positive value, 15 percent is too low and because the NPV is negative 20 percent is too high. We could run additional trials at intermediate percentages until the NPV comes closer to 0 or we can interpolate:

$$DCFRR = \frac{146,782 - 0}{146,782 - (-101,481)} \times 5 + 15 = 18 \text{ percent}$$

Notes

(1) Net Cash Flow. The figures in this column represent the difference between the positive cash flows, such as income from sales, and the negative flows, such as operating expenses and taxes. Depreciation is *not* deducted here because it is not a part of cash flow (note that in Operating Example 20–1, lines 20 and 21, we added depreciation back to after-tax profit to obtain cash flow). The cash flow for Year 0 is negative, representing expenditures of $1,100,000 for fixed capital and $200,000 for working capital. This is the year in which the project was built; in larger projects there could be several years of negative cash flow before start-up. Of course, there can be negative cash flows during the operating years if the income is less than expenses.

In Year 10 the income minus expenses comes to $190,000, but $200,000 is added because the working capital is (at least theoretically) recovered as the plant is emptied of in-process materials on the last production day.

(2) The present worth factor can be obtained from the interest tables in financial or mathematical handbooks. Use the single payment, present worth factor (not the uniform series, present worth factor) because in the DCFRR method the annual cash flows are considered to be one-time payments occurring at the end of the year. If you cannot readily find a table with PWFs at the interest rates you need, you can easily calculate your own with a hand calculator that raises to powers (y^x) and takes reciprocals ($1/x$). For interest rate, i (expressed as a decimal fraction), and number of years, n, the PWF is $1/(1 + i)^n$. For 18 percent at 5 years, the single payment PWF is $1/(1.18)^5 = 0.4371$.

Whether or not a DCFRR of 18 percent is sufficient to proceed with the project is a question whose answer will vary from industry to industry and company to company. Your company's decision will be affected by such factors as the probability of success of the project, its size and anticipated life, the company's cost of capital, and the returns from other opportunities for investing the same capital.

HOW TO CHOOSE THE CONSTRUCTION FORCE AND CONTROL THE WORK

Who Does the Work?

For the plant manager the choice is between utilizing his own maintenance forces to complete the project or employing an outside contractor. Base the decision on these factors:

- **Skills needed** to complete the work. If they are not readily available within the plant force, the outside contractor is a must.

- **Time available** for completion. Maintenance forces must divide their time between the project and the normal maintenance needs of the plant. If the anticipated workload of the maintenance department is heavy or the allowable completion time short, it may not be the best choice.

- **Cost.** Usually, though not always, cheaper with in-house forces.

- **Union contract.** It may limit your right to use outside contractors to projects above a certain dollar amount. If the contract is silent, you may want to place jobs outside regularly in order to preserve the right to do so. During delicate stages of negotiation or times of troubled union relationships, you may wish to forego the use of outside contractors if their presence could be provocative.

Selecting and Hiring a Contractor

If the decision is to use outside work forces, the next step is to find suitable contractors. If the plant has a history of outside contracting, a number of suitable firms will be on its bidder list; if not, such sources as other plants in the area, contractors' and builders' associations, or even the telephone book must be used to develop a list of potential bidders. When evaluating a potential contractor, you should satisfy yourself on these points:

- Does he have **sufficient capacity and technical resources** to complete the job—people, equipment, know-how, experience?
- Has he done jobs **similar in scope and complexity?**
- Is he **financially sound?**
- Does he have a **good reputation** among clients for whom he performed work?

The answers to these questions can be obtained from bank references, credit information agencies such as Dun & Bradstreet, Inc., industry associations, and other plants. Develop a list of at least three or four bidders for every job; don't put on the list any contractor to whom you would not want to award the contract.

The project is now ready to send out to the acceptable contractors for bid. Because it will eventually become a part of the contract documents, use a bid form suggested by your lawyer. It should contain these elements: designation of the time and place deadline for submission of bids, scope of the work, surety bond provision, a sample copy of the contract the successful bidder will sign, insurance coverage requirements, designation of the architect or engineer (when outside consultants are used), the way copies of the blueprints and specifications can be obtained, reservation of certain rights to the owner, and the formal procedure for handling of addenda and interpretations.

If your original bidder list contained only approved contractors, you should be able to accept the lowest bid with complete confidence. (If any of the bids received seems absurdly low or high, you may want to contact the bidder to see if he fully understands the project.) The next step is preparation of the contract:

- Have your lawyer or Legal Department prepare the contract (it may be false economy to accept the bidder's offer to have the contract prepared). Standard forms for this purpose are sold by The American Institute of Architects, 1735 New York Avenue, Washington, D.C. 20006, under such titles as *Owner-Contractor Agreement—Stipulated Sum*, *General Conditions of the Contract for Construction*, and *Owner-Architect Agreement—Percentage of Construction Cost*.
- Read the contract carefully to see if you agree to all of its provisions. The plant manager particularly will want provisions that require the contractor

to maintain access to existing buildings and work areas during construction, to observe plant safety rules, and to clean up thoroughly when the work is completed.

- Be sure that the bid form and all blueprints and specifications are legally included as contract documents.

- Require the contractor to submit evidence of required insurance coverage and surety bonds before the contract is signed.

- Be sure that both signers of the contract are legally officers of their respective companies.

Control of Work Progress

Every contract will have a completion date, but it is fatuous to sit back and assume that the work will be completed on time without any further attention. Use these techniques to get the work accomplished on schedule:

- Insert a clause in the contract that requires the contractor to submit a detailed time schedule for the work as soon as the contract is signed. Be sure to discuss the requirements of this clause with each bidder before he submits his bid.

- Consider the use of bonus and penalty clauses, which require the contractor to pay the owner a fixed amount of dollars per day for every day the project is late, and the owner to pay the contractor a fixed amount (not necessarily the same) for every day the project is finished ahead of schedule. Beware of legal loopholes that invalidate the penalty side of these arrangements.

- Designate an individual to take responsibility for the on-time completion of the job—usually the plant engineer or a project engineer. Require that person to submit written reports periodically (weekly or monthly) stating what has been accomplished, where the project stands in relation to its schedule, and the plans for any slippage.

- Use diagrammatic representations of the work schedule to show progress against it. For smaller projects, a simple Gantt chart will do. (The Gantt chart is essentially a bar graph with a horizontal time line and each activity shown as a horizontal bar whose ends represent the beginning and completion times of the activity.) The Gantt chart is useful as a planning tool because it provides visual coordination of the activities that must be completed to get the project done; it is valuable as a control tool because at any given time it shows which activities should have been started, which should have been completed, and the percentage of completion of those in progress.

  Larger projects may use more elaborate methods, such as Critical Path Programming or Program Evaluation and Review Technique (PERT). In the diagrams used for these methods, important events—such as the start or finish of critical activities—are represented as circles connected by lines that designate the activity required to reach them. A time value is given to each line, and when all the circles have been connected by lines in logical sequence, the longest time path through the network can be discerned. This is the critical path, and the succession of activities on it are those that must be closely controlled by management if the project is to be completed on schedule. The PERT system is described more fully in Chapter 4, pp. 59–62, and Figure 4–3. Although that description is based on a single-unit manufacturing situation, it is equally applicable to project scheduling, for which it is widely used.

- Frequent personal inspection of the work. If the contractor only has two men working on the job when he should have six, or if his materials are stockpiled in a disorganized mess, personal inspection is the quickest way to spot the problem and personal contact the quickest way to get him to correct the deficiencies.

THE POST-COMPLETION AUDIT: THREE MAIN PARTS

Much can be learned from the corporate experience of completing a capital project, but only if the results are reviewed objectively and recorded for future use. That is the purpose of the post-completion audit. It has three basic parts:

1. A comparison of the actual cost of the project with the predicted cost. If the two figures are not close, the audit should delve into the reasons for a substantial overrun or underrun in such a way that they can be avoided in future projects.

2. An analysis of the progress of the project compared to the original schedule. If it was late in completion, the causes should be identified, and any obvious ways of overcoming them in subsequent projects should be discussed. The idea here is not to find scapegoats but to examine all the events affecting the project's progress and separate the good from the bad. Even if the project was completed on time, this analysis may lead to ways of shortening the schedule for the next project.

3. A comparison of the actual cost savings or new profits generated by the project with those predicted by the economic justification. Of course, it may take months or years after the project is in operation for this data to come in. Once available, however, it can be used to calculate the actual return on investment, payback period, and discounted cash flow rate of return.

In addition to pointing the way to better project handling in the future, the post-completion audit offers other benefits to the corporation: project originators tend to submit more careful cost and return estimates if they know their projects will be audited later; if the projects submitted by a particular plant or department are consistently over- or underestimated, higher management can adjust to this fact in its decision making; and unexpected deviations in the corporate profit and loss statement may be explained by the actual (as opposed to predicted) performance of large projects.

Chapter 21

A Guide to
Computer Applications
in Manufacturing

For most plant managers the completely automated, computer-controlled factory is still in the future. Yet very few plant managers have not had at least some contact with computerized information in their daily work—schedules, production reports, quality records, cost reports, inventory records, and others. They can all count on a continuing upward trend in plant computerization, brought about by two very strong forces:

1. The ever-expanding capabilities of computers. Once thought of by plant managers as being limited to producing payrolls and cost reports, computers have developed an astounding array of capabilities in product design and engineering, in inventory control and reporting, in robotics and machine control, and in the integration of manufacturing operations. The computer industry has managed to accomplish all this while steadily lowering prices, so that a desktop computer today not only does what it took a roomful of equipment to do twenty years ago, but does it at a fraction of the price.

2. Competition. Factory automation has not grown as rapidly as predicted in the United States, nor as fast as in some other industrialized countries. But American companies cannot lag behind forever; in domestic and international markets they must compete with manufacturers from less developed countries with cheap labor, and from industrialized countries that have advanced further into computerized operations. Squeezed by these competitive pressures, American manufacturers will have to adopt new technologies if they are to survive.

What is it about computers that makes them such a valuable tool in manufacturing? One characteristic is infallible memory—they can store vast amounts of data indefinitely, and recall it without error. Another is the ability of the computer to *manipulate* data, that is, sort data (alphabetize, list by location, quantity, value, serial number, date) and perform calculations (multiply, divide, add, subtract, raise to powers, take roots) thousands of times per second. A third is less obvious, but nonetheless real: computerizing the compilation and analysis of business information imposes the same logic on all activities of the company, leaving no place for inefficient processes and unprofitable products to hide.

The computer industry is large and growing, its products many and confusing. This chapter provides a short explanation of the basics of computers and the ways in which they are applied to manufacturing operations.

SOME COMPUTER BASICS

The Binary Numbering System

Despite the complexity of the tasks it performs and its amazing capabilities in calculation and memory, the computer is at bottom a device which can recognize whether or not electric current is flowing in any of its circuits, or whether or not any of its cores is magnetized—in short, it recognizes "on" and "off." If you let "off" equal 0 and "on" equal 1, you have the basis of the *binary numbering system* used by computers. To understand how this works, however, requires us to think about the way numbers are used. The familiar decimal system is a *base ten* system; that is, any number may be thought of as being constructed from successive powers of ten ($10^0=1$, $10^1=10$, $10^2=100$, $10^3=1,000$, $10^4=10,000$, and so on). If you are asked how the number 136 is constructed, you might say that it consists of six in the 1's column, three in the 10's column, and one in the 100's column. Another way of saying this is

$$
\begin{array}{rcll}
6 \times 10^0 = 6 \times 1 & = & 6 \\
3 \times 10^1 = 3 \times 10 & = & 30 \\
1 \times 10^2 = 1 \times 100 & = & \underline{100} \\
& & 136
\end{array}
$$

Base ten and the decimal system which is based on it are very convenient for use in our daily lives, especially in our denominations of money. But it doesn't work very well in a computer; it is very difficult to instruct a computer through a series of "on-off" positions that you want six in the 1's column, or three in the 10's column. A much better system for the computer is *base two*, in which numbers are constructed from successive powers of 2: $2^0=1$, $2^1=2$, $2^2=4$, $2^3=8$, $2^4=16$, and so on. If you were to line up eight powers of 2, placing a 0 or 1 next to each to indicate "on-off," then you could construct your number this way:

$$
\begin{array}{lll}
 & \textit{On-off} \\
 & \textit{Position} \\
2^0 = 1 & 0 \\
2^1 = 2 & 0 \\
2^2 = 4 & 0 \\
2^3 = 8 & 1 & = 8 \\
2^4 = 16 & 0 \\
2^5 = 32 & 0 \\
2^6 = 64 & 0 \\
2^7 = 128 & 1 & = \underline{128} \\
 & & \quad\; 136
\end{array}
$$

The series of 1's and 0's by which the desired number is obtained constitutes a *binary code;* if you take the 2^7 position first, the binary code for 136 is 10001000. In computer work each on-off position is called a *bit*. The eight on-off positions taken together constitute a *byte* (there are also 6-bit bytes, 16-bit bytes and 32-bit bytes).

In the preceding example, if all of the positions are at 0, the number obtained is 0; if all are at 1, the number obtained is 255. This means that all of the possible combinations of 1 and 0 in the binary code will yield 256 decimal numbers. These numbers are *not used* as such in the computer, but are used to represent letters of the alphabet, the digits from 0 to 9, punctuation marks, symbols, arithmetic symbols ($+$, $-$, $=$, etc.) and computer functions. Thus, the binary code 01010100 represents the decimal number 84, which in turn stands for the letter T; binary code 00110100 represents 52, which in turn stands for the digit 4. (These are ASCII—American Standard Code for Information Interchange—designations; there are other coding systems.) When you press the letter T on the keyboard, the computer receives the one-byte coded message 01010100.

Hardware and Software

These are probably best defined by analogy. If you consider an old-fashioned player piano, the hardware is the piano itself, a collection of keys, strings, hammers and a sounding board. The software is the piano roll—a long strip of paper with punched holes. When fed into the piano, it "instructs" the machine to play the appropriate notes, creating the music. Of course, a human being is required to select a roll, feed it into the piano, and pump the pedals to make it play.

Computer hardware consists of the physical components of the machines. In the familiar personal computer setup you would recognize the keyboard, the computer "box" itself, the display screen, and the printer as hardware. (The nature and functions of hardware are discussed more thoroughly in the next section.)

Software consists of all the instructions and programs supplied to the computer to make it carry out the desired operations. When your company's computerized payroll was set up, a programmer instructed the computer to establish a memory file for each employee with his or her name, rate of pay, position grade, number of tax exemptions, and so forth. Next a program was set up so that for each employee, at two-week intervals, the number of days worked or taken as vacation or sick leave, changes in pay or tax status, and so on are entered. The program tells the computer how to use the data entered and that already contained in the memory file to calculate the amount due the employee and print the check. (Keep in mind that the software is not the check itself nor the payroll data supplied; rather it is the set of program instructions that causes the check to be printed from the data supplied.)

Users of microcomputers, who are not likely to have a human programmer available, can purchase prepackaged software systems such as Lotus 1-2-3™ or dBASE III.®* Such systems consist of a disk which sets the program up on your machine, and an instruction manual which tells you how to establish files, enter data, and manipulate them.

Languages

If the computer can only receive instructions and information in the form of eight-bit bytes coded in 1 or 0, there must be some way of bridging the gap between that and the instructions you would like to give it, such as "multiply all the lengths in Column L by the widths in Column W and display the resulting areas in Column A." The answer is *computer languages,* and although you as a plant manager are not likely to be called upon to work directly with computer languages, it is useful to have a rudimentary idea of how they work.

Actually, a computer can be programmed by using the eight-bit binary code alone, and instructions entered this way are said to be in *machine language.* This is the coding which the machine understands, but using it to program is a difficult and tedious task because the human mind does not readily comprehend a string of eight 1's and 0's as meaning anything in particular. Machine language is appropriate, nevertheless, when the program is short and it is desired to make maximum use of the capabilities of the machine. (Higher level languages represent a compromise between ease of use and lower utilization of the computer's capacity.) Machine languages are different for each make and model of computer because the manufacturer installs different circuitry in them. The machine language for one computer cannot be used on another make or model.

To get away from having to program the computer in eight-bit binary code, *assembly language,* the next higher level language, is used. The language is created by assigning words to the binary codes; for instance, the word "add" would correspond to the binary code which tells the machine to carry out addition. By doing the same for the other codes, which tell the computer to store, retrieve, and perform operations on the information supplied to it, a language of simple words is built up. Using the language requires an *assembler program* to convert the words into binary codes which can be read by the machine. The assembler program is different for each type of computer and is usually supplied by the

*Lotus 1-2-3 is a trademark of Lotus Development Corp. dBASE III is a registered trademark of Ashton-Tate.

manufacturer. Assembly languages are therefore considered to be low-level languages.

High-level computer languages offer a much greater degree of flexibility by freeing the programmer from having to know the machine language of the computer on which the program is to be run. The translation from language to machine code is done by a *compiler,* which is designed to accept the expressions of the universal language. There are many high-level languages, but three of the most commonly used are BASIC (Beginner's All-purpose Symbolic Instruction Code), COBOL (Common Business Oriented Language), and FORTRAN (Formula Translation). COBOL was designed to handle business information at both ends of the computer process—in the entry of data and in the reports generated from the data—in formats understandable to business people. FORTRAN was developed to handle scientific notation, equations, tables, and calculations used by mathematicians, engineers, and scientists.

High-level languages have two additional advantages. Their statements and instructions look more like regular English than those of the low-level languages. They also allow a reduction in the number of instructions required to accomplish a computer task. In the earlier example of obtaining the areas of rectangles, a low-level language would have to tell the computer to load the width and the length, multiply them, and store the answer, in three distinct steps. Using a high-level language, the compiler can take the single instruction to multiply the length times the width to find the area, and translate it into the required three machine language instructions. This reduces the amount of work the programmer must do, a valuable feature when long programs are to be written.

HARDWARE, PERIPHERALS, AND TYPES OF COMPUTERS

The hardware of any computer consists of five elements: an *input device,* which receives information and instructions; a *memory unit,* which stores information, and instructions; a *control unit,* which regulates the flow of information through the computer and the program operations that are performed on it; an *arithmetic unit,* which performs addition, subtraction, and so forth on numerical data; and an *output device* that displays the results of the information processing in a form intelligible to humans (paper printout or lighted screen), or as a signal to another device such as a machine controller. The control and arithmetic units are usually grouped together as the *central processing unit,* or CPU. Figure 21-1 diagrams the relationships of these elements.

There are a number of input devices for entering data into a computer—keyboard, punched cards, punched paper tape, magnetic tape and disks, and several types of "readers" that can interpret optical characters, marks, bar codes, and magnetic ink characters (such as those used by banks on checks and deposit slips). Output devices include the cathode ray tube or CRT (similar to a television screen), printers (which produce hard copy "printouts"), punched cards, and magnetic tapes and disks. The various tape drives, readers, card punches, and printers are known as "peripheral hardware," or "peripherals."

As a plant manager, you are most likely to encounter the computer types and

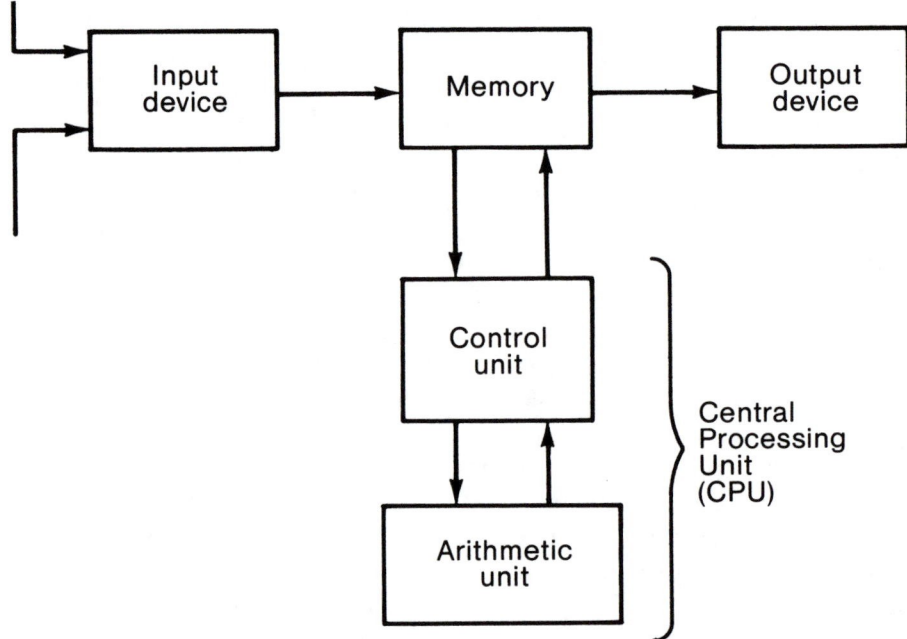

FIGURE 21-1: Computer Hardware Elements

sizes listed below, but with the striking increases in machine capacity and steady reductions in price characteristic of this industry, the dividing lines between the types are increasingly less clear.

Mainframe Computer

This is usually the largest computer the company owns in terms of capital cost and processing power. Its memory capacity is in the millions of characters, its calculating speed is measured in millions per second, and its cost at least hundreds of thousands, but more likely millions, of dollars. It is equipped to handle—and probably was delivered with—a variety of peripherals. On it are stored the company's most widely used data bases—financial and accounting information, personnel records and payroll data, sales and production records. In addition to routine tasks such as payroll preparation and monthly accounting statements, these machines turn out management reports on production, sales, budget performance, and profit. Because of their high calculating speed and large memories, they may also be used for research and engineering work.

Minicomputers

The next step down in the computer hierarchy, these machines are likely to have memory capacity below one million characters, and calculating speeds ranging from 1,000 to 100,000 per second. On the high end, its price is not likely to exceed $250,000, but at the low end it overlaps the microcomputer prices by a considerable amount. The minicomputer is typically located in a department or manufacturing plant of the corporation, and processes data specific to that department's needs, as opposed to the more generalized data of the mainframe. It will have fewer peripheral devices than the mainframe, and fewer users.

Microcomputers

This group includes the personal computer, or "PC," as well as certain smaller machines used for industrial process control. Typical memory capacities are 64,000 (64K) characters, 128K, and up to a million with special software. Calculating speeds range from 10 to 100,000 calculations per second. Peripherals for business use usually consist of a keyboard, CRT screen, and printer. A system made up of these items plus the computer can be purchased for less than $10,000, including the software packages needed to make it work. Special software packages and other peripherals (described in *CAD/CAM,* a later section of this chapter) adapt the microcomputer to scientific and engineering uses.

Programmable Controllers

Many industrial machines—welders, grinders, conveyors, centrifuges, to mention a few—perform their work through a series of operating steps, just as a domestic washing machine performs its work through fill, agitate, drain, and spin cycles. In the past, electromechanical controllers using wired circuits, timers, and relays have been used to direct the machines through their operating cycles. While these devices were adequate for unchanging, repetitive control functions, their programs could not be altered without rewiring or rebuilding the controllers.

Replacement of the electromechanical systems with computers has resulted in the *programmable controller,* a device whose program can be altered or replaced instantly. The computer component is usually in the micro- or mini-size range. Input devices include a keyboard and CRT screen, which allow the programmer to make changes and to see displayed the logic system being created. Additional input devices receive signals from the machines being controlled to the effect that an operation has been completed, or that a preset liquid level, temperature, pressure, or part count has been reached. Output signals from the controller instruct production machines to start or stop operating steps and cycles, to change the set points of control instruments, or to open and close control valves.

Because programmable controllers must often be installed on the production floor, they are built to withstand such shop conditions as dusty atmospheres, vibration, temperature extremes, and humidity.

COMPUTERIZED MATERIALS HANDLING AND INVENTORY: THREE LEVELS TO CONSIDER

How much inventory to carry is an age-old question in manufacturing. It costs money to carry inventory, so the less the better. On the other hand, too little inventory of raw materials or finished goods impairs our ability to serve customers quickly, and therefore competitively. Applying the computer to inventory control allows us to get closer to the best answer to this problem at three levels of sophistication.

Operate the Same System Faster

In a plant with no computer, inventory information is obtained from a "paper trail." Bills of lading, warehouse receipts, forklift operators' logs, and similar paper records are collected at the end of a shift or operating day and sent to a central office where clerks enter the data on master logs or material cards. These records are used by production managers wanting to know if they have enough raw material on hand to begin producing an order, and by purchasing staff to take action when a reorder point has been reached. Economic order quantity is computed on a desk calculator, and a purchase order is prepared by a typist. To obtain the dollar value of the inventory, accounting clerks enter the cost of each item, and run extensions on a calculator.

The central office operations described above can be greatly speeded up by putting the master records on a computer. Information from the plant is collected as usual, but the clerks now enter it into the computer, where the calculations of net material available, economic order quantity, reorder point, and dollar value proceed instantly. Purchase orders are printed out automatically. The current status of the inventory is available to managers as soon as the data are entered.

Either a minicomputer or a micro can handle such a system for an inventory numbering hundreds or thousands of items. While this step in computerization provides information more quickly and at less labor cost than the manual system, it does not fully utilize the powers of the computer to control and optimize inventory. To paraphrase one cynic, unless the inventory control philosophy is changed completely, the computer simply multiplies the number of bad decisions that managers can make in a given time.

Introduce Material Resource Planning (MRP)

This is a system that brings warehousing stocking and inventory control much closer to the manufacturing process. Because it requires a great many calculations, it demands, and is in fact an outgrowth of, the use of computers.

MRP starts with the master production schedule—the quantity scheduled to be produced in a month, a week, or even a day. The computer is preprogrammed to calculate the effects of the scheduled production on raw material and parts inventory, and on purchasing. If the product to be made requires 50 square feet of steel sheet, 0.19 gallons of paint, and two subassemblies each consisting of a 0.10 HP electric motor and a 10:1 gear box, the computer "explodes" these requirements from the master schedule, and compares them with inventory on hand. If there is enough inventory, the computer "reserves" it for this production order; if not, purchase orders are generated automatically, with delivery dates set to meet the production schedule. The computer will also identify material on hand which has been reserved for another order; managers can then make a priority judgment. All of this may be done "on-line," that is, information on inventory movements is not held up until the end of a shift or working day, but is entered into the computer as soon as the movements take place. Calculations are performed instantly, providing management at any moment with a complete up-to-date inventory of actual and reserved materials on hand.

With such powerful tools as these, the amount of inventory carried by a manufacturing plant can be reduced drastically along with the labor costs of keeping track of it. Users of MRP report that they can reduce inventory levels by as much as 50 percent, while enjoying other benefits including more accurate inventories and improved customer service.

The ultimate achievement in raw material inventory reduction is to reduce it to zero, and a system which attempts to do that is called Just-in-Time Manufacturing, or JIT. It involves having suppliers deliver material within hours of the time it is needed in production. This system has been successfully applied in Japan (it is called *kanban* there), where automobile manufacturers take several deliveries a day of parts that are sent to the assembly line almost immediately upon arrival. Very large reductions in inventory, the space required to store it, and the costs of carrying it are possible. JIT is most adaptable to products made in large numbers on assembly lines. In the United States, where distances between suppliers and manufacturers are much greater than in Japan, plants have been able to schedule material deliveries within one to three days of projected usage.

The power of the mainframe may be needed for MRP systems that control very large quantities of materials which move frequently. In less demanding situations, the minicomputer or a combination of it and the microcomputer are sufficient. Both MRP and JIT can be part of a larger scheme of automated manufacturing, which is discussed later in this chapter.

Operate the Warehouse Machinery

In the discussion of automated storage and retrieval systems (AS/RS) in Chapter 17, p. 374, it was noted that they are often controlled by computers. Almost any degree of automation desired can be reached by combining AS/RS systems with computers. At one level of automation, a human order picker rides a platform which moves horizontally and vertically throughout the warehouse. A computer terminal on the platform receives instructions from a minicomputer which tell the order picker what material is needed and automatically positions the platform at the proper storage location. The order picker removes the specified material and records the movement on the terminal. This recording step can be further automated by the use of bar codes printed on the material container, and "light pens," which are wands fitted with optical devices connected to the computer terminal by an electric cord. When the light pen is run across the bar code a record of the movement is automatically made by the computer, which is not only keeping track of the order being assembled but is maintaining a perpetual inventory of the warehouse as well. Complete automation is achieved by eliminating the human order picker and installing a computer-controlled picking head on the moving platform.

Computers are also used to control automatic conveying systems that move finished goods from production areas to the warehouse, and from the warehouse to shipping areas. The conveyors can be arranged in lanes to accommodate automatic sorting operations, such as making up a customer shipment. Bar codes on the containers are read by optical scanners as they pass by on the arrival conveyor, and the containers are directed by the computer into the proper lane.

Warehouse computers are usually minicomputers; units mounted on moving platforms or handling smaller tasks in the warehouse are microcomputers or their components. Warehouse computers may be connected into the corporate network, receive instructions from and transmitting information to an MRP computer or the company's mainframe. Users of computer-controlled automated warehouse systems report productivity increases of 40 to 50 percent, and reductions in errors as high as 80 percent.

CAD/CAM

These initials refer to *computer-aided design* and *computer-aided manufacturing;* sometimes *computer-aided engineering* is added, resulting in the expression CAD/CAE/CAM. Their functions overlap to a degree, and they tend to be lumped together in the expression "CAD/CAM."

CAD uses the computer to produce an engineering drawing from which a product can be manufactured or a project built. The final drawing may be quite complex, but the designer builds it up from simple geometric elements stored in the computer's data base—points, lines, circles, triangles, rectangles. These shapes are brought up on the screen and combined or "subtracted" from each other to form new shapes. Curves and shapes not derivable from the standard figures of geometry can be drawn on the screen using a light pen, or on a plotter board using a "mouse."

CAD offers important advantages over the older method of having drawings completed manually by draftsmen. Drawings are produced much more cheaply and much faster. The designer can reduce, enlarge, or rotate the image, and view it in three dimensions. A large number of design configurations can be tried out until the best one is found; a similar number of design "trials" would be prohibitively expensive in manual drafting. Users also report improved accuracy in their drawings. Figure 21-2 is an example of a drawing produced by CAD.

CAE, computer-aided engineering, takes the design process a step further. The design engineer wants answers to a variety of questions: If the object on the screen is made of a specified material, how much will it weigh? Where is its center of gravity? Will moving parts interfere with each other? Does the design meet code standards imposed by the company, trade associations, or government? When certain stresses are applied will the resulting strains exceed the strength of the object's components? A CAE system provides answers to questions such as these from its engineering database, and offers another useful feature: if the company uses one component in a number of different products, the characteristics of that component can be stored in the engineering data base and incorporated into new designs as needed.

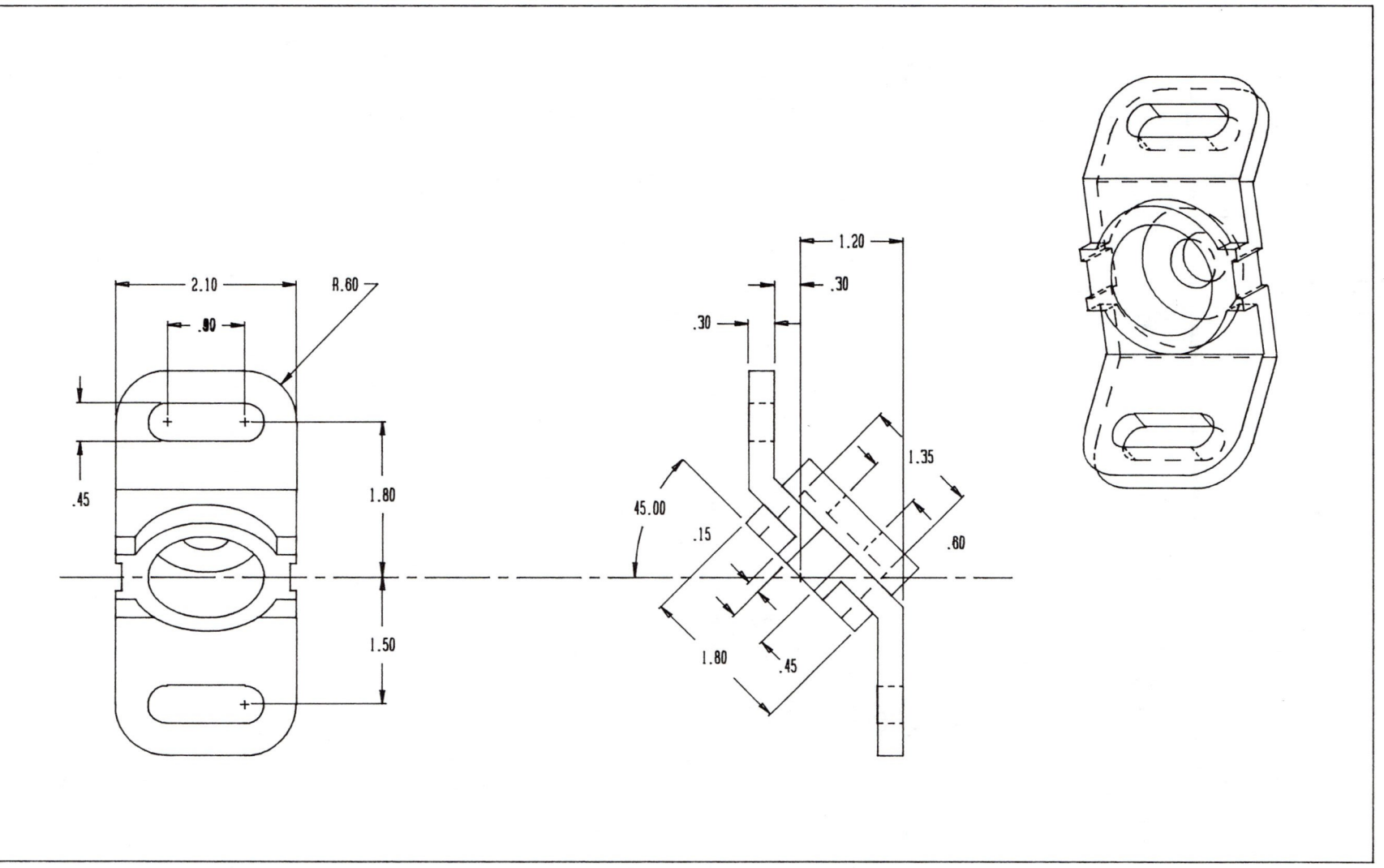

FIGURE 21-2: Engineering Drawing Produced by CAD. (Courtesy of Micro Control Systems, Inc.)

CAM takes over when the product design is completed. Its first contribution is to provide a list of the parts and materials needed to make a production run. For each unit to be produced, the computer calculates such items as the number of square feet of steel, the length of aluminum wire, the quantities and types of screws and fasteners required to build the product, and feeds this information to the inventory control or MRP system (described in the preceding section of this chapter). Working from the design developed in CAD, and using information in its data base concerning the capabilities of the various production machines, it develops a flow chart to route the product through the plant, and generates a production schedule. After production begins, CAM keeps track of the order as it proceeds through the plant, and if the production machines are computer-controlled, issues instructions to them for fabricating the product.

CAD/CAM Hardware

The components are assembled into a *workstation,* and include a central processing unit (the "computer"), a display terminal, and the input and output devices described later in this section. Figure 21-3 is an illustration of a CAD/CAM workstation.

CAD/CAM operations place heavy demands on the computer in terms of memory and speed of computation. The independent workstation is normally powered by a minicomputer, which may be either a 16-bit or 32-bit machine. Additional capacity is obtained by connecting the minicomputer to the mainframe, or by using auxiliary storage devices such as magnetic tapes. For the most sophisticated and powerful systems the *supercomputer,* a newer development to serve this market, is available, with 10 times the computational speed and 20 times the memory capacity of conventional machines. Prices are on the order of $10 million for the most capable of these machines, but drop to under a $1 million when less memory and lower computational speed are acceptable. On the lower end of the scale, CAD/CAM software packages for microcomputers have become available as those machines have increased in processing capability.

Input devices include a keyboard for entering instructions expressed in words or numbers, such as graph or drawing coordinates. To make the drawings an *electronic tablet* and stylus pen are used. With the pen, the designer selects standard shapes from a menu on the tablet or draws his own sketches which are transferred to the screen. For drawing directly on the screen a "light pen" is used. On some graphics terminals a drawing may be generated by the movement of a cursor on the screen. The cursor may be controlled by thumbwheels, one for up-and-down movement, the other for side to side; by a "joystick" or vertical lever controller, similar to that used in computer games; or by the directional arrows on the keyboard. Another input device, the *digitizer,* is used for copying existing two-dimensional drawings into the computer memory. It consists of a large (perhaps 20 square feet) electronic board fitted with a tracking arm, which "reads" the lines and symbols of the drawing and stores them in coded form in the computer. The drawings can be edited while in the computer, and later reprinted through an output device.

FIGURE 21-3: Microcomputer-based CAD/CAM Workstation. (Courtesy of Micro Control Systems, Inc.)

The display screen is an essential component among the output devices. It is one end of a CRT or cathode ray tube (similar to the picture tube of a television set), but the buyer of CAD/CAM hardware should keep in mind that there are several types of CRT available for graphics display, and that they have different performance characteristics. While an explanation of the technical differences is beyond the scope of this book, it is important to know that there may have to be trade-offs among such capabilities as picture quality, color, the ability to remove a line without reproducing the entire drawing, and animation. Paper drawings are produced by a *plotter,* a device with a drawing pen mounted on a movable head, which moves back and forth across the paper and draws lines where instructed by the computer. There are two main types: the flat-bed plotter, which holds a single sheet of paper on a flat board; and the drum plotter, which pulls the paper over a rotating drum for a supply roll. The pen is mounted on a head which moves back and forth across the paper as it passes over the rotating drum. Paper drawings produced by the workstation are much larger and more accurately dimensioned than the image on the display screen.

CAD/CAM Software

Because it takes many more commands to get a digital computer to generate a three-dimensional drawing of an object than, say, to run a payroll, computer graphics software is complex and highly specialized. The application program for producing drawings of machined parts will be very different from that for designing electrical circuits. Not all graphics programs can be run on all types of computers, and the buyer is once again advised to select the software first and then find the hardware to run it on. Software packages vary widely in capability and price. The simplest will produce only two-dimensional drawings in black and white, while the more expensive versions will turn out three-dimensional projections in color. Some produce drawings only in a "wire-frame" mode, which depicts the object by lines representing its edges and giving it the appearance of having been constructed from wires. Other software systems yield a "solid model" drawing, including shading of the surfaces which gives a very realistic appearance.

MACHINE AND PROCESS CONTROL

Application of computers to control manufacturing differs between the two basic types of industry: (1) the mechanical fabrication industries in which machine tools shape solid materials—quite often metals—into products or components of products, and (2) the continuous process industries in which bulk solids or fluids are put through a series of process steps to change them chemically or physically (examples are paper mills and oil refineries).

Mechanical Fabrication

Automation of machines that perform such functions as drilling, reaming, turning, boring, grinding, broaching, and threading began in the 1950s with the development of *numerical control*, or NC. In this system a paper tape with punched holes instructs an electromechanical controller to put the machine tool through a series of operations automatically and in sequence. If the machine has an automatic tool changer, the taped instructions can include tool changes which are carried out much more quickly than would be possible with manual changes. NC raises production capacity, reduces labor cost, improves quality, and, because the machine can be so precisely controlled, permits more complicated shapes to be machined than would be possible with only manual control.

The computer is used to improve the NC system in several ways. The first is to computerize the tape preparation. Consider this process when there is no computer. The tape is prepared in a special punching machine which is operated from a keyboard; typed instructions appear as punched holes in the tape. The typist works from a sheet of instructions prepared by the designer, who has manually performed the geometric calculations necessary to position the machine tool so that it cuts, drills, and grinds in the proper locations and to the desired depths. If the machining task is complicated these calculations are lengthy and prone to error. Computerization of this process increases productivity and accuracy, and is accomplished by inserting a computer ahead of the tape puncher. The designer, working with special software packages and using a special high-level language (such as APT, *Automatically Programmed Tools*), enters only the basic instructions required to accomplish the machining program. The computer performs the detailed calculations necessary to guide the machine, and automatically instructs the punching machine to produce a properly coded tape. For the design of simple objects a microcomputer may be sufficient for this service; more complicated shapes may require the power of a minicomputer, or processing time on a mainframe.

An even more powerful system is created when computerized NC part programming is combined with CAD. As the designer develops an object on the display screen, he or she can generate the machining instructions required to produce it. If the design creates impossible, difficult, or expensive machining conditions, it can be revised immediately.

The second way in which the computer improves NC control is to replace the electromechanical controller. There are two methods of accomplishing this: CNC, or *Computer Numerical Control*, and DNC, or *Direct Numerical Control*.

In CNC the punched tape is still used. The computer is inserted between the tape reader and the machine tool controls. The tape is used only once; after one pass through the reader its instructions are stored in the computer's memory. This eliminates the need to retrieve the tape from a file every time the particular part is to be made. The instructions are sent directly to the machine tool from the computer. Replacing the "hard-wired" circuits of the electromechanical controller with the "soft-wired" circuits of the computer offers much greater latitude in changing machine tool instructions, in fine-tuning the control system, and in adopting entirely new control schemes. Minicomputers have been used for this service, but microcomputers are seen more often as they become more powerful. CNC computers are usually supplied by the maker of the machine tool, and are built into it. Figure 21-4 is an illustration of a CNC machine.

In DNC a central computer is used to control a number of machines. The punched tape is no longer used, and the central computer sends its directions to the machine's tools either through their own CNC computers, or, if they are not so equipped, through a specially designed machine control unit, or MCU. Instructions for machining various objects and parts are stored in the central computer's memory and fed to the machine tools as needed. Each machine may be making a different part at any one time, or they may all be making the same part. This system requires two-way communication—each machine tool must be able to tell the central computer when it has completed an order, when it is ready for more work, the number and types of pieces it has produced, how long it has been in operation, and whether any of its tools are broken. This information enables the central computer to make the most efficient use of the machines available, virtually eliminating idle time waiting for instructions (a common occurrence in manually controlled shops).

FIGURE 21-4: CNC Chucker and Bar Machine. Built-in computer control and display screen is at right. (Courtesy of Hardinge Brothers, Inc.)

Continuous Processes

Oil refineries and paper mills have already been cited as examples of this industry; others are chemical, food processing, water treatment, cement, plastics, paint, and soap and detergent plants. They use process equipment as described in Chapter 16—heat exchangers, reaction vessels, dryers, pumps, and compressors—as well as distillation columns, refrigeration units, furnaces, and kilns. Automatic control of process equipment has always been important to this industry for its advantages in upgrading product quality, smoothing production operations, and reducing production costs. In fact, some of the larger installations of the process industries, such as petrochemical complexes, would not be possible without automatic control.

The computer is advancing automatic control of continuous processes to new levels of accuracy, speed of response, and sophistication of control schemes. Computers are employed at three levels in process control.

The control instruments themselves. In the discussion of trends in instrumentation in Chapter 16 (p. 317) it was pointed out that electronic instruments are replacing pneumatic instruments in many industrial control applications. Not only do they provide faster response and more reliable operation, but they are more readily adapted to computer control. If even tighter control is desired than would be possible with a standard instrument, a *microprocessor* can be built into it. The microprocessor is a silicon chip that contains in its microscopic circuitry all the essential components of a CPU—arithmetic, logic, and control. It has a built-in set of instructions, thus dedicating the instrument to a particular purpose. Its ability to perform calculations on data coming from the process to be controlled makes it much more adaptable to changes in the characteristics of the process. Microprocessors may be built into some control instruments without the buyer being aware that they are there.

Control of process equipment and groups of equipment. In conventional process control, the variable to be controlled is usually measured after it has passed through the equipment. Consider a heat exchanger with the process fluid entering and leaving through the tubes, and being heated by steam admitted to the shell through a control valve. The temperature sensing element is placed in the process fluid outlet pipe and reports the temperature back to the control instrument. If the flow rate is suddenly changed, or if the temperature of the cold feed to the exchanger fluctuates, the outlet sensor does not recognize that something is wrong until off-temperature fluid comes out of the exchanger. The instrument opens or closes the steam valve to correct the situation, but may over- or undershoot the desired temperature if feed conditions suddenly return to normal.

Introducing a computer into this situation permits much better control. The temperature sensor is moved to the cold feed inlet pipe, and a flow meter is installed there. The steam flow rate is also measured and controlled. The feed temperature and flow rate are fed into the computer, which is programmed to solve the heat transfer equation applicable to the system. The computer calculates what the outlet temperature will be if nothing is done. The control mechanism makes the necessary steam valve adjustment *before* the process system is upset, resulting in much closer control of the outlet temperature.

This principle can be applied to the control of groups of process equipment. In a petrochemical plant, for instance, a battery of distillation columns presents very complex control problems. Composition and flow rates of feed, overhead, and bottoms product streams must be measured, along with pressures, temperatures, and liquid levels. All these variables must be considered before process control adjustments can be made. No operators or supervisor can keep in their heads all of the complex relationships between these variables, so they do the best they can in conventional control—make sure the products are in specification, keep column temperatures as close to standard values as possible, and cope with upsets using a mixture of experience and intuition.

Computer control changes the situation significantly. Product analyses can be taken every few minutes, and the information entered into the computer along with readings of the other process variables (temperature, pressure, etc.). Engineers enter the equations which correlate these variables into the computer prior to operation. This allows *predictive control,* in which the computer orders changes in the setpoints of the various control instruments before upsets occur, effectively preventing them. Computer control in situations of this type pays for itself rapidly through increased production capacity, higher and more consistent product quality, and energy savings.

Computerized plant control. Using the computer for overall plant control takes place on two levels. The first is simply an extension of the control of groups of equipment described above. If the product of Department A is the feed to Department B, then process upsets in A will adversely affect operations in B. By stabilizing operations in Department A, computerized controls contribute to smoother operation in the downstream units. As with smaller groups of equipment, engineers can program the equations and models that describe the entire plant process into the computer, letting it calculate the effects of changes in important variables and compensating for them.

But the computer offers something beyond expanded automatic control. Many process plants strive to optimize profit by adjusting the slate of products they make and the size of production runs to current business factors—raw material availability and cost, sales projections for each product, prices that the products are expected to command, and the cost of energy. (A very simple example occurs in an oil refinery which obtains from crude oil a chemical that can either be sold as a raw material for polyester fiber, or mixed with gasoline to improve its octane. The decision as to what to do with it is based on factors similar to those just enumerated.) While it is conceivable that an optimum operations model can be drawn up manually and run periodically on desk calculators, the only practical approach is to establish a *computerized operations center.* A complex plant optimization model is constructed and programmed into the computer. Costs and other factors are fed in daily (or as often as desired), and the output consists of instructions to plant management as to the feed rates, product slates, and energy management strategies it should use to maximize plant profitability.

COMPUTERS IN THE MAINTENANCE SHOP

In Chapter 5 we saw that running an effective maintenance program requires good record-keeping in such areas as work order initiation and recording, job scheduling, conducting a preventive (and predictive) maintenance program, maintaining inventories of supplies and tools, and measuring maintenance department performance. The computer is an excellent, and increasingly indispensable, tool for handling these record-keeping chores.

The hardware needed for computerizing the maintenance operation can be quite simple. For a department of less than 200 mechanics and technicians a microcomputer equipped with a printer is probably sufficient. Larger operations may require the capacity of a minicomputer. Connection to the mainframe is not recommended; the machine is too remote, its usage too formalized, and it is not always instantly available.

There are many software packages commercially available for maintenance management, but you should exercise care in choosing one. Prices may exceed $20,000. Follow the same steps you would in any other "computerizing" operation: (1) decide how you want to run the operation—what records will be kept and how they will be used, (2) find the software that will permit you to establish the desired records *and* manipulate them, that is, make the various calculations and comparisons you need to run the department efficiently. Above all, put the maintenance manager in charge of the program; a system developed by any other group is bound to soon sit idle.

What Your Computerized Maintenance System Should Include

Your computerized maintenance system should provide at least the following capabilities:

Work order control. Originators may continue to use a paper work order but the Maintenance Department enters it into the computer as soon as it is received, making a permanent record of the essential information—the department (or cost center) requesting help, the machine to be repaired, the work to be done (replace coupling, tighten bolts, or "find out what is wrong"), whether the request is for routine work or an emergency, and the maintenance section and supervisor to whom it is assigned.

Information needed for planning and scheduling the work is entered upon receipt by the supervisor: crafts or skills required to do the work (mechanical, electrical, pipefitting, etc.), quantities and types of parts needed, special tools that must be reserved from the central toolroom, estimated time to complete the job, and estimated labor and material costs.

After the job is completed the actual quantities of parts, supplies, and labor and their costs are recorded, becoming part of the machine's maintenance history.

Inventory and tool control. The maintenance system is really no different from the production inventory system described earlier in this chapter, except that it is likely to be smaller. The computerized system must be able to show the quantity of each item of maintenance stores on hand, items on order with expected date of receipt, and any reservation of parts, tools, or supplies for other jobs. It must also display the location and cost of each item. A smoothly functioning and effective inventory module is prerequisite for making the rest of the system work.

Work scheduling. The computer format for scheduling should show, at a minimum, the jobs to be performed, the number and types of personnel assigned to them, and the dates and hours during which they are expected to be completed. Using the information already compiled in the work order and inventory modules, the scheduler can verify that the craft skills, tools, parts and supplies needed to perform the job will be available at the scheduled time.

Preventive maintenance. Your system should allow you to schedule preventive maintenance work automatically. In one type of module, you prepare a standard work order for each PM activity you wish to carry it out, adding the interval at which you want to do the work. The work order is stored in the computer, and the scheduling module calls it out at the desired times.

Search, query, and reports.   The real power of the computer you have bought or are buying lies in its ability to search large amounts of data and select specific items of interest, perform calculations on them, and generate reports based on them. Not all maintenance software packages provide as much capability as you may want. Before purchasing a software program be sure that at the very least it will be able to search your maintenance files to provide you with such items as

- Equipment history (sometimes called "nameplate tracking"). For any piece of plant equipment, a list of all the repair, emergency, and preventive maintenance work done on it, displaying the dates, nature of the work, cost, and the causes of failures.

- Inventory groups. You should be able to call up on display all of a general class of items in stock, for instance motors. This feature can be very useful when you have an emergency and are willing to install a 2 hp motor to replace a failed $1\frac{1}{2}$ hp motor until the correct size can be obtained.

- Scheduled personnel. You might want to look at all the future work scheduled for millwrights to see if you have any workers with this skill available for an upcoming job.

- Management reports. You will want a system that is able to provide you and higher management with the reports you need to manage the maintenance operation effectively. If you have chosen some of the ratios mentioned in Chapter 5 as indexes of maintenance performance—emergency hours to total hours, actual job time to standard job time, or maintenance costs to total plant cost—your system should be able to extract the information from your computerized files and give you these ratios for any specified time period.

- Correlations of data specific to your company and operations. If you are constructing them manually now, you will want to be sure that the system you buy will be able to provide them.

PUTTING IT ALL TOGETHER:
COMPUTER INTEGRATED MANUFACTURING

The previous sections of this chapter show how the computer is applied to the different plant functions: product and raw materials inventory, product design, engineering, scheduling and monitoring manufacturing operations, control of process machinery, and management of the maintenance function. Each of these functions has an impact on some or all of the others, and manufacturing managers soon realized that if the computer improves them separately, it can as well be applied to coordinating them for further upgrading of plant performance. If the information accumulated in each of the functional models is funneled into one location, the manager will have access to the very latest information on the status of production equipment, orders in process, materials available and on order, and even the availability of operating personnel. Any manager working from such a base will make better decisions, and be able to make them more quickly.

At the corporate level managers are concerned with the broad strategies of new product introduction, marketing campaigns, corporate profitability, addition or reduction of personnel, and the starting up and shutting down of facilities. Just as at the plant level, managers will make better decisions if they have complete, accurate, and up-to-date information on the status of the company's facilities, operations, and market position. Information of that quality can be obtained through a hierarchy of computers sending data from the plants to a central corporate computer.

Computer integrated manufacturing also implies a high degree of automation in the plant. Although a completely automated, computer-controlled manufacturing process requiring almost no human attention is not in the immediate future for most plant managers, a step in that direction can be taken with what one executive calls "existing islands of automation." This refers to two or three machining centers which are already computer-controlled. They can be combined into a *flexible manufacturing system* (FMS) by adding automated conveyors to move parts; robots to pick parts from the conveyors, place them in the machines, retrieve them when work is completed, and place them on an outgoing conveyor; and a control computer that decides what parts are to be made, on which machines, and in what order. The computer can be programmed to divert parts away from a machine that has a broken tool to another that can do the work. An FMS is especially well adapted to producing items in batches that are too small to utilize a dedicated production line capable of making only one product, and too large to be made in a specialty shop. With several flexible manufacturing systems running well, the plant is in a position to go on to higher levels of computer-controlled operation and coordination.

CIM is implemented through the installation of a series of modular systems which, although they are acquired one at a time, are intended to be interconnected ultimately. The modules may consist of either software packages designed to be run on certain commercially available computers, or, if they are supplied by computer manufacturers such as Honeywell, Hewlett-Packard, and IBM, may consist of special hardware-software combinations. The CIM packages offered vary somewhat in content, but most will offer a slate of modules similar to the following.

Master production schedule planning. This is the highest level of corporate planning in the system, and the one that looks farthest into the future—usually a year or more. It is derived from two major inputs: the long-range sales forecast and the corporate business plan. The computer uses them to identify the resources needed to operate the business—materials, factory capacity, personnel, and finances. A master schedule of company-wide production is developed to meet market demands while operating within the business plan. Most systems allow corporate management to try out different plans to see which one adjusts the company's resources most profitably to projected demand. Because the master production plan extends so far into the future, it must be continually updated and changed in the light of new information.

Material requirements planning. Mentioned earlier in the section on materials handling and inventory, MRP can be applied at the corporate level. Once the master schedule is firmed up, the MRP module goes to work to see if the needed materials are or will be on hand, and if not, places orders to obtain them. If they cannot be acquired in time to meet the planned schedule, the computer informs management. Production orders to the plants are given "planned" and "released" status in this system.

Inventory management. This is the base upon which the MRP system is built. This module keeps detailed records of the materials inventory, including location, stock level, movements in and out, and value. It is installed before the MRP module, and subsequently is connected to it.

Plant scheduling. As soon as the corporate master production schedule is firmed the production schedules can be set for the manufacturing plants. This module breaks the orders down for scheduling in the various production units, schedules the dates for beginning and completion of production runs, determines the number of shifts needed, and informs management of any resource shortage or facilities use conflict that will interfere with meeting the schedule.

Plant monitoring and control. This module keeps track of the progress of an order through the plant, and alerts management to impending failures in meeting deadlines. It also keeps track of the actual usage of labor, material, and other cost items.

Plant maintenance. This system was described in a previous section of this chapter. Its major contribution to computer integrated management is to send up information on the nonavailability of machines for future scheduling because of repair or preventive maintenance.

CIM systems may also include modules for forecasting customer demands, cost planning and control, and customer order servicing.

Hardware requirements may include all three major types of computer—micro, mini, and mainframe. Before purchasing a system find out exactly what you will get for your money, what it will do for you, and how much expert assistance the seller will provide for installing it. If you are introducing CIM to an existing plant it is better to add the modules one at a time, allowing personnel to get used to computerized methods gradually, and to see how effective they are before proceeding to new levels. For a new plant it may be better to start out with the entire system, implementing a new philosophy of management at once while avoiding the need to change over later; a prerequisite to this, however, is extensive training of plant personnel before start-up.

Tables—Appendix

TABLE 1: Decimal Equivalents of Fractions

64ths	64ths	32nds	16ths	9ths	8ths	7ths	6ths	4ths	Fractions with Denominators 11-19	
1 .01562	33 .5156	1 .03125	1 .0625	1 .1111	1 .1250	1 .1428	1 .1667	1 .2500	1/11	.09091
3 .04688	35 .5469	3 .09375	3 .1875	2 .2222	3 .3750	2 .2857	2 .3333	2 .5000	1/12	.08333
5 .07812	37 .5781	5 .1562	5 .3125	3 .3333	5 .6250	3 .4286	3 .5000	3 .7500	1/13	.07692
7 .1094	39 .6094	7 .2188	7 .4375	4 .4444	7 .8750	4 .5714	4 .7500		1/14	.07143
9 .1406	41 .6406	9 .2812	9 .5625	5 .5555		5 .7143	5 .8333		1/15	.06667
11 .1719	43 .6719	11 .3438	11 .6875	6 .6667		6 .8571			1/16	.06250
13 .2031	45 .7031	13 .4062	13 .8125	7 .7778					1/17	.05882
15 .2344	47 .7344	15 .4688	15 .9375	8 .8889					1/18	.05556
17 .2656	49 .7656	17 .5312							1/19	.05263
19 .2969	51 .7969	19 .5938								
21 .3281	53 .8281	21 .6562								
23 .3594	55 .8594	23 .7188								
25 .3906	57 .8906	25 .7812								
27 .4219	59 .9219	27 .8438								
29 .4531	61 .9531	29 .9062								
31 .4844	63 .9844	31 .9688								

TABLE 2: General Conversion Factors

A	Atmosphere (Standard)	=	33.93	feet of water @ 60°F.
	Atmosphere (Standard)	=	29.92	inches of mercury @ 32°F.
	Atmosphere (Standard)	=	760.0	millimeters of mercury @ 0°C.
	Atmosphere (Standard)	=	14.696	pounds per square inch
B	Barrel	=	5.6146	cubic feet
	Barrel	=	42.0	gallons
	Barrel of water @ 60°F.	=	0.1588	metric ton
	Barrel (36° A.P.I.)	=	0.1342	metric ton
	Barrel per hour	=	0.0936	cubic feet per minute
	Barrel per hour	=	0.700	gallon per minute
	Barrel per hour	=	2.695	cubic inches per second
	Barrel per day	=	0.02917	gallon per minute
	British Thermal Unit	=	252.	calories
	British Thermal Unit	=	0.2931	Int. Watt Hours
	British Thermal Unit	=	0.2932	watt hour (abs.)
	B.T.U. per minute	=	0.02359	horse-power
	British Thermal Unit	=	778.57	foot pounds
C	Calorie	=	.003968	British Thermal Units
	Centimeter	=	0.3937	inch
	Centimeter of mercury	=	0.1934	pounds per square inch
	Cubic centimeter	=	0.06102	cubic inch
	Cubic foot	=	0.1781	barrel
	Cubic foot	=	7.4805	gallons
	Cubic foot	=	0.02832	cubic meter
	Cubic foot per minute	=	10.686	barrels per hour
	Cubic foot per minute	=	28.800	cubic inches per second
	Cubic foot per minute	=	7.481	gallons per minute
	Cubic inch	=	16.387	cubic centimeters
	Cubic meter	=	6.2898	barrels
	Cubic meter	=	35.314	cubic feet
	Cubic meter	=	1.308	cubic yards
	Cubic yard	=	4.8089	barrels
	Cubic yard	=	46,656.	cubic inches
	Cubic yard	=	0.7646	cubic meter
F	Foot	=	30.48	centimeters
	Foot	=	0.3048	meter
	Foot	=	0.3600	vara (Texas)
	Foot of water @ 60°F.	=	0.4331	pound per square inch
	Foot per second	=	0.68182	mile per hour
	Foot pound	=	0.001284	British Thermal Unit
	Foot pound per second	=	0.001818	horse-power
G	Gallon (U.S.)	=	0.02381	barrel
	Gallon (U.S.)	=	0.1337	cubic foot
	Gallon (U.S.)	=	231.000	cubic inches
	Gallon (U.S.)	=	3.785	liters
	Gallon (U.S.)	=	0.8327	gallon (Imperial)
	Gallon (Imperial)	=	1.2009	gallons (U.S.)
	Gallon (Imperial)	=	277.274	cubic inches
	Gallon per minute	=	1.429	barrels per hour
	Gallon per minute	=	0.1337	cubic foot per minute
	Gallon per minute	=	34.296	barrels per day
	Grain (Avoirdupois)	=	0.06480	gram
	Grain per gallon	=	17.118	parts per million
	Grain per gallon	=	142.86	pounds per million gals.
	Grain per gallon	=	0.017118	gram per liter
	Gram	=	15.432	grains
	Gram	=	0.03527	ounce
	Gram per liter	=	58.415	grains per gallon
H	Horse-power	=	42.39	B.T.U.'s per minute
	Horse-power	=	33,000.	foot-pounds per minute
	Horse-power	=	550.	foot-pounds per second
	Horse-power	=	1.014	horse-power (metric)
	Horse-power	=	0.7457	kilowatt (abs.)

	Horse-power	=	.7455	kilowatt (int.)
	Horse-power hour	=	2,543.	British Thermal Units
I	Inch	=	2.540	centimeters
	Inch of mercury @ 32°F.	=	1.133	feet of water @ 39.1°F.
	Inch of mercury @ 32°F.	=	0.4912	pound per square inch
	Inch of water @ 60°F.	=	0.0361	pound per square inch
K	Kilogram	=	2.2046	pounds
	Kilogram per square cm.	=	14.223	pounds per square inch
	Kilogram per square mm.	=	1,422.32	pounds per square inch
	Kilometer	=	3,281.	feet
	Kilometer	=	0.6214	mile
	Kilowatt	=	1.3415	horse-power
L	Link (Surveyor's)	=	7.92	inches
	Liter	=	0.2642	gallon
	Liter	=	1.0567	quarts
M	Meter	=	3.281	feet
	Meter	=	39.37	inches
	Mile	=	5,280.	feet
	Mile	=	1.609	kilometers
	Mile per hour	=	1.4667	feet per second
O	Ounce	=	437.5	grains
	Ounce	=	28.3495	grams
P	Part per million	=	0.058415	grain per gallon
	Part per million	=	8.345	pounds per million gals.
	Pound	=	7,000.	grains
	Pound	=	0.4536	kilogram
	Pound per cubic inch	=	27.680	gm. per cu. cm.
	Pound per square inch	=	2.309	feet of water @ 60°F.
	Pound per square inch	=	2.0360	inches of mercury @ 32°F.
	Pound per square inch	=	51.713	millimeters of mercury @ 32°F.
	Pound per square inch	=	0.0703	kilogram per sq. cent.
	Pound per million gals.	=	0.00700	grain per gallon
	Pound per million gals.	=	0.11983	part per million
Q	Quart (Liquid)	=	0.946	liter
S	Square centimeter	=	0.1550	square inch
	Square foot	=	0.0929	square meter
	Square foot	=	0.1296	square vara (Texas)
	Square inch	=	6.452	square centimeter
	Square kilometer	=	0.3861	square mile
	Square meter	=	10.76	square feet
	Square mile	=	2.590	square kilometers
T	Temp. Centigrade	=	5/9 (Temp. Fahr. −32)	
	Temp. Fahrenheit	=	9/5 Temp. Cent. +32	
	Temp. Absolute C.	=	Temp. °C. +273	
	Temp. Absolute F.	=	Temp. °F. +460	
	Therm	=	100,000 B.T.U.	
	Ton (Long)	=	2,240.	pounds
	Ton (Metric)	=	2,205.	pounds
	Ton (Short or Net)	=	2,000.	pounds
	Ton (Metric)	=	1.102	ton (short or net)
	Ton (Metric)	=	1,000.	kilograms
	Ton (Metric)	=	6.303	barrels of water @ 60°F.
	Ton (Metric)	=	7.454	barrels (36° A.P.I.)
	Ton (Short or Net)	=	0.907	ton (metric)
W	Watt-hour (Int.)	=	3.4115	British Thermal Units
	Watt-hour (abs.)	=	3.4103	British Thermal Units
Y	Yard	=	0.9144	meter

Barrel, above, always means oil barrel = 42 gallons.
Gallon, unless otherwise noted, means U.S. gallon.

British Thermal Unit = 1054.1 absolute joules.
British Thermal Unit per pound = 5/9 (cal./gram.)
British Thermal Unit per pound per °F. = calorie per gram per °C.

TABLE 3: Metric Conversion

English-Metric		Metric-English	
		Length	
1 inch	2.540 centimeters	1 centimeter	.3937 inch
1 foot	.3048 meters	1 meter	39.37 inches
1 yard	.9144 meters	1 meter	3.281 feet
1 mile	1.609 kilometers	1 kilometer	.6214 mile
		Area	
1 square inch	6.452 square cm.	1 square cm.	.1550 sq. inch
1 square foot	.09290 square m.	1 square m.	10.76 sq. feet
1 square yard	.8361 square m.	1 square m.	1.196 sq. yards
1 acre	4,047 square m.	1 hectare	2.471 acres
1 square mile	259.0 hectares	1 sq. kilometer	.3861 sq. mile
(1 hectare equals 10,000 sq. meters and 0.1 sq. kilometers.)			
		Volume: Liquid	
1 ounce	29.57 cubic cm.	1 cubic cm.	.03381 ounce
1 quart	.9464 liters	1 liter	1.057 quarts
1 gallon	3.785 liters	1 liter	.2642 gallon
(Ounces, quarts, and gallons are U.S. measure; 1 liter equals 1,000 cu cm)			
		Volume: Dry	
1 cubic inch	16.39 cubic cm.	1 cubic cm.	.06102 cu in.
1 cubic foot	.02832 cubic m.	1 cubic m.	35.31 cu ft
1 cubic yard	.7646 cubic m.	1 cubic m.	1.308 cu yd
1 dry quart	1.101 liters	1 hectoliter	2.838 bushels
1 bushel	35.24 liters	(1 hectoliter equals 100 liters)	
		Mass	
1 ounce (avoir.)	28.35 grams	1 gram	.03527 oz. (avoir.)
1 pound	453.6 grams	1 kilogram	2.205 lbs.
1 short ton (2,000 lbs)	907.2 kilograms	1 metric ton (1,000 kg)	1.102 short tons
1 long ton (2,240 lbs)	1,106 kilograms	1 metric ton	.9842 long tons

TABLE 3: Metric Conversion (continued)

English-Metric		Metric-English	
Energy			
1 foot-pound	.1383 kg-meter	1 calorie	4.184 joules
1 kilowatt-hour	3.600×10^6 joules	1 calorie	1.162×10^{-6} kWh
1 Btu	252.2 calorie	1 joule	.7376 foot-pound
1 Btu	1055.1 joules	1 calorie	3.966×10^{-3} Btu
Power			
1 ft-lb/second	1.356 watts	1 watt	3.413 Btu/hr
1 horsepower	745.7 watts	1 metric hp	542.5 ft-lb/sec
1 horsepower	1.014 metric hp	1 kilowatt	1.341 horsepower
Pressure			
1 psi (lb/sq in)	6895 pascals	1 pascal	1.450×10^{-4} psi
1 atmosphere	101325 pascals	1 bar	14.50 psi
1 atmosphere	760 mm mercury	1 pascal	2.593×10^{-4} in mercury
1 atmosphere	10.34 meters of water	1 bar	33.49 ft water

(Mercury at 0° C and water at 15° C)

[1 pascal = 1 newton per square meter; 1 newton = .1020 kg(force)]

HOW TO USE THE TEMPERATURE CONVERSION TABLE

1. Find the temperature you desire to convert in the boldface column in the center; its Celsius equivalent will be in the left-hand column, and the Fahrenheit equivalent in the right-hand column.

2. The formulas for temperature conversion are

$$\text{deg F} = 1.8 \text{ deg C} + 32$$
$$\text{deg C} = (\text{deg F} - 32)/1.8$$

3. Temperature span: One degree Celsius is equivalent to 1.8 degrees Fahrenheit; one degree Fahrenheit is equivalent to .5556 degrees Celsius.

4. Absolute temperature scales. For certain heat transfer and thermodynamic calculations, the *absolute temperature* scales are used. Absolute zero on the Celsius scale is −273.2 degrees; to convert to Kelvin add 273.2 to the Celsius value. Absolute zero on the Fahrenheit scale is −459.7 degrees; to convert to degrees Rankine add 459.7 to the Fahrenheit value.

TABLE 4: Temperature Conversion

Deg C		Deg F	Deg C		Deg F	Deg C		Deg F	Deg C		Deg F
−273.2	−459.7		−3.3	26	78.8	24.4	76	168.8	177	350	662
−268	−450		−2.8	27	80.6	25.0	77	170.6	182	360	680
−240	−400		−2.2	28	82.4	25.6	78	172.4	188	370	698
−212	−350		−1.7	29	84.2	26.1	79	174.2	193	380	716
−184	−300		−1.1	30	86.0	26.7	80	176.0	199	390	734
−170	−273.2	−459.7	−0.6	31	87.8	27.2	81	177.8	204	400	752
−157	−250	−418	0.0	32	89.6	27.8	82	179.6	210	410	770
−129	−200	−328	+0.6	33	91.4	28.3	83	181.4	215	420	788
−101	−150	−238	1.1	34	93.2	28.9	84	183.2	221	430	806
−73.3	−100	−148	1.7	35	95.0	29.4	85	185.0	226	440	824
−45.6	−50	−58.0	2.2	36	96.8	30.0	86	186.8	232	450	842
−40.0	−40	−40.0	2.8	37	98.6	30.6	87	188.6	238	460	860
−34.4	−30	−22.0	3.3	38	100.4	31.1	88	190.4	243	470	878
−28.9	−20	−4.0	3.9	39	102.2	31.7	89	192.2	249	480	896
−23.3	−10	+14.0	4.4	40	104.0	32.2	90	194.0	254	490	914
−22.8	−9	15.8	5.0	41	105.8	32.8	91	195.8	260	500	932
−22.2	−8	17.6	5.6	42	107.6	33.3	92	197.6	288	550	1022
−21.7	−7	19.4	6.1	43	109.4	33.9	93	199.4	315	600	1112
−21.1	−6	21.2	6.7	44	111.2	34.4	94	201.2	343	650	1202
−20.6	−5	23.0	7.2	45	113.0	35.0	95	203.0	371	700	1292
−20.0	−4	24.8	7.8	46	114.8	35.6	96	204.8	399	750	1382
−19.4	−3	26.6	8.3	47	116.6	36.1	97	206.6	426	800	1472
−18.9	−2	28.4	8.9	48	118.4	36.7	98	208.4	454	850	1562
−18.3	−1	30.2	9.4	49	120.2	37.2	99	210.2	482	900	1652
−17.8	0	32.0	10.0	50	122.0	37.8	100	212.0	510	950	1742
−17.2	1	33.8	10.6	51	123.8	43.3	110	230	538	1000	1832
−16.7	2	35.6	11.1	52	125.6	48.9	120	248	593	1100	2012
−16.1	3	37.4	12.2	53	127.4	54.4	130	266	648	1200	2192
−15.6	4	39.2	12.2	54	129.2	60.0	140	284	704	1300	2372
−15.0	5	41.0	12.8	55	131.0	65.6	150	302	760	1400	2552
−14.4	6	42.8	13.3	56	132.8	71.1	160	320	815	1500	2732
−13.9	7	44.6	13.9	57	134.6	76.7	170	338	871	1600	2912
−13.3	8	46.4	14.4	58	136.4	82.2	180	356	927	1700	3092
−12.8	9	48.2	15.0	59	138.2	87.8	190	374	982	1800	3272
−12.2	10	50.0	15.6	60	140.0	93.3	200	392	1038	1900	3452
−11.7	11	51.8	16.1	61	141.8	98.9	210	410	1093	2000	3632
−11.1	12	53.6	16.7	62	143.6	100.0	212	413	1149	2100	3812
−10.6	13	55.4	17.2	63	145.4	104	220	428	1204	2200	3992
−10.0	14	57.2	17.8	64	147.2	110	230	446	1260	2300	4172
−9.4	15	59.0	18.3	65	149.0	116	240	464	1316	2400	4352
−8.9	16	60.8	18.9	66	150.8	121	250	482	1371	2500	4532
−8.3	17	62.6	19.4	67	152.6	127	260	500	1427	2600	4712
−7.8	18	64.4	20.0	68	154.4	132	270	518	1482	2700	4892
−7.2	19	66.2	20.6	69	156.2	138	280	536	1538	2800	5072
−6.7	20	68.0	21.1	70	158.0	143	290	554	1593	2900	5252
−6.1	21	69.8	21.7	71	159.8	149	300	572	1649	3000	5432
−5.6	22	71.6	22.2	72	161.6	154	310	590			
−5.0	23	73.4	22.8	73	163.4	160	320	608			
−4.4	24	75.2	23.3	74	165.2	165	330	626			
−3.9	25	77.0	23.9	75	167.0	171	340	644			

TABLE 5: Circumferences and Areas of Circles

Diam.	Circum.	Area	Diam.	Circum.	Area	Diam.	Circum.	Area	Diam.	Circum.	Area
1/64	0.0491	0.0002	3	9.4248	7.0686	8	25.1327	50.265	16	50.2655	201.06
1/32	0.0982	0.0008	1/16	9.6211	7.3662	1/8	25.5254	51.849	1/8	50.6582	204.22
1/16	0.1964	0.0031	1/8	9.8175	7.6699	1/4	25.9181	53.456	1/4	51.0509	207.39
3/32	0.2945	0.0059	3/16	10.0138	7.9798	3/8	26.3108	55.088	3/8	51.4436	210.60
1/8	0.3927	0.0123	1/4	10.2102	8.2958	1/2	26.7035	56.745	1/2	51.8363	213.82
5/32	0.4909	0.0192	5/16	10.4065	8.6179	5/8	27.0962	58.426	5/8	52.2290	217.08
3/16	0.5890	0.0276	3/8	10.6029	8.9462	3/4	27.4889	60.132	3/4	52.6217	220.35
7/32	0.6872	0.0376	7/16	10.7992	9.2806	7/8	27.8816	61.862	7/8	53.0144	223.65
1/4	0.7854	0.0491	1/2	10.9956	9.6211	9	28.2743	63.617	17	53.4071	226.98
9/32	0.8836	0.0621	9/16	11.1919	9.9678	1/8	28.6670	65.397	1/8	53.7998	230.33
5/16	0.9817	0.0767	5/8	11.3883	10.321	1/4	29.0597	67.201	1/4	54.1925	233.71
11/32	1.0799	0.0928	11/16	11.5846	10.680	3/8	29.4524	69.029	3/8	54.5852	237.10
3/8	1.1781	0.1105	3/4	11.7810	11.045	1/2	29.8451	70.882	1/2	54.9779	240.53
13/32	1.2763	0.1296	13/16	11.9773	11.416	5/8	30.2378	72.760	5/8	55.3706	243.98
7/16	1.3745	0.1503	7/8	12.1737	11.793	3/4	30.6305	74.662	3/4	55.7633	247.45
15/32	1.4726	0.1726	15/16	12.3700	12.177	7/8	31.0232	76.589	7/8	56.1560	250.95
1/2	1.5708	0.1964	4	12.5664	12.566	10	31.4159	78.540	18	56.5487	254.47
17/32	1.6690	0.2217	1/16	12.7627	12.962	1/8	31.8086	80.516	1/8	56.9414	258.02
9/16	1.7672	0.2485	1/8	12.9591	13.364	1/4	32.2013	82.516	1/4	57.3341	261.59
19/32	1.8653	0.2769	3/16	13.1554	13.772	3/8	32.5940	84.541	3/8	57.7268	265.18
5/8	1.9635	0.3068	1/4	13.3518	14.185	1/2	32.9867	86.590	1/2	58.1195	268.80
21/32	2.0617	0.3382	5/16	13.5481	14.607	5/8	33.3794	88.664	5/8	58.5122	272.45
11/16	2.1598	0.3712	3/8	13.7445	15.033	3/4	33.7721	90.763	3/4	58.9049	276.12
23/32	2.2580	0.4057	7/16	13.9408	15.466	7/8	34.1648	92.886	7/8	59.2976	279.81
3/4	2.3562	0.4418	1/2	14.1372	15.904	11	34.5575	95.033	19	59.6903	283.53
25/32	2.4544	0.4794	9/16	14.3335	16.349	1/8	34.9502	97.205	1/8	60.0830	287.27
13/16	2.5525	0.5185	5/8	14.5299	16.800	1/4	35.3429	99.402	1/4	60.4757	291.04
27/32	2.6507	0.5591	11/16	14.7262	17.257	3/8	35.7356	101.62	3/8	60.8684	294.83
7/8	2.7489	0.6013	3/4	14.9226	17.721	1/2	36.1283	103.87	1/2	61.2611	298.65
29/32	2.8471	0.6450	13/16	15.1189	18.190	5/8	36.5210	106.14	5/8	61.6538	302.49
15/16	2.9452	0.6903	7/8	15.3153	18.665	3/4	36.9137	108.43	3/4	62.0465	306.35
31/32	3.0434	0.7371	15/16	15.5116	19.147	7/8	37.3064	110.75	7/8	62.4392	310.24
1	3.1416	0.7854	5	15.7080	19.635	12	37.6991	113.10	20	62.8319	314.16
1/16	3.3379	0.8866	1/16	15.9043	20.129	1/8	38.0918	115.47	1/8	63.2246	318.10
1/8	3.5343	0.9940	1/8	16.1007	20.629	1/4	38.4845	117.86	1/4	63.6173	322.06
3/16	3.7306	1.1075	3/16	16.2970	21.135	3/8	38.8772	120.28	3/8	64.0100	326.05
1/4	3.9270	1.2272	1/4	16.4934	21.648	1/2	39.2699	122.72	1/2	64.4026	330.06
5/16	4.1233	1.3530	5/16	16.6897	22.166	5/8	39.6626	125.19	5/8	64.7953	334.10
3/8	4.3197	1.4849	3/8	16.8861	22.691	3/4	40.0553	127.68	3/4	65.1880	338.16
7/16	4.5160	1.6230	7/16	17.0824	23.221	7/8	40.4480	130.19	7/8	65.5807	342.25
1/2	4.7124	1.7671	1/2	17.2788	23.758	13	40.8407	132.73	21	65.9734	346.36
9/16	4.9087	1.9175	9/16	17.4751	24.301	1/8	41.2334	135.30	1/8	66.3661	350.50
5/8	5.1051	2.0739	5/8	17.6715	24.850	1/4	41.6261	137.89	1/4	66.7588	354.66
11/16	5.3014	2.2365	11/16	17.8678	25.406	3/8	42.0188	140.50	3/8	67.1515	358.84
3/4	5.4978	2.4053	3/4	18.0642	25.967	1/2	42.4115	143.14	1/2	67.5442	363.05
13/16	5.6941	2.5802	13/16	18.2605	26.535	5/8	42.8042	145.80	5/8	67.9369	367.28
7/8	5.8905	2.7612	7/8	18.4569	27.100	3/4	43.1969	148.49	3/4	68.3296	371.54
15/16	6.0868	2.9483	15/16	18.6532	27.688	7/8	43.5896	151.20	7/8	68.7223	375.83
2	6.2832	3.1416	6	18.8496	28.274	14	43.9823	153.94	22	69.1150	380.13
1/16	6.4795	3.3410	1/8	19.2423	29.465	1/8	44.3750	156.70	1/8	69.5077	384.46
1/8	6.6759	3.5466	1/4	19.6350	30.680	1/4	44.7677	159.48	1/4	69.9004	388.82
3/16	6.8722	3.7583	3/8	20.0277	31.919	3/8	45.1604	162.30	3/8	70.2931	393.20
1/4	7.0686	3.9761	1/2	20.4204	33.183	1/2	45.5531	165.13	1/2	70.6858	397.61
5/16	7.2649	4.2000	5/8	20.8131	34.472	5/8	45.9458	167.99	5/8	71.0785	402.04
3/8	7.4613	4.4301	3/4	21.2058	35.785	3/4	46.3385	170.87	3/4	71.4712	406.49
7/16	7.6576	4.6664	7/8	21.5984	37.122	7/8	46.7312	173.78	7/8	71.8639	410.97
1/2	7.8540	4.9087	7	21.9911	38.485	15	47.1239	176.71	23	72.2566	415.48
9/16	8.0503	5.1572	1/8	22.3838	39.871	1/8	47.5166	179.67	1/8	72.6493	420.00
5/8	8.2467	5.4119	1/4	22.7765	41.282	1/4	47.9093	182.65	1/4	73.0420	424.56
11/16	8.4430	5.6727	3/8	23.1692	42.718	3/8	48.3020	185.66	3/8	73.4347	429.13
3/4	8.6394	5.9396	1/2	23.5619	44.179	1/2	48.6947	188.69	1/2	73.8274	433.74
13/16	8.8357	6.2126	5/8	23.9546	45.664	5/8	49.0874	191.75	5/8	74.2201	438.36
7/8	9.0321	6.4918	3/4	24.3473	47.173	3/4	49.4801	194.83	3/4	74.6128	443.01
15/16	9.2284	6.7771	7/8	24.7400	48.707	7/8	49.8728	197.93	7/8	75.0055	447.69

**(Reprinted from Dodge General Engineering Catalog by special permission
of Dodge Manufacturing Division, Reliance Electric Co.)**

TABLE 5: Circumferences and Areas of Circles (continued)

Diam.	Circum.	Area	Diam.	Circum.	Area	Diam.	Circum.	Area	Diam.	Circum.	Area
24	75.3982	452.39	32	100.531	804.25	40	125.664	1256.6	48	150.796	1809.6
1/8	75.7909	457.11	1/8	100.924	810.54	1/8	126.056	1264.5	1/8	151.189	1819.0
1/4	76.1836	461.86	1/4	101.316	816.86	1/4	126.449	1272.4	1/4	151.582	1828.5
3/8	76.5763	466.64	3/8	101.709	823.21	3/8	126.842	1280.3	3/8	151.975	1837.9
1/2	76.9690	471.44	1/2	102.102	829.58	1/2	127.235	1288.2	1/2	152.367	1847.5
5/8	77.3617	476.26	5/8	102.494	835.97	5/8	127.627	1296.2	5/8	152.760	1857.0
3/4	77.7544	481.11	3/4	102.887	842.39	3/4	128.020	1304.2	3/4	153.153	1866.5
7/8	78.1471	485.98	7/8	103.280	848.83	7/8	128.413	1312.2	7/8	153.545	1876.1
25	78.5398	490.87	33	103.673	855.30	41	128.805	1320.3	49	153.938	1885.7
1/8	78.9325	495.79	1/8	104.065	861.79	1/8	129.198	1328.3	1/8	154.331	1895.4
1/4	79.3252	500.74	1/4	104.458	868.31	1/4	129.591	1336.4	1/4	154.723	1905.0
3/8	79.7179	505.71	3/8	104.851	874.85	3/8	129.983	1344.5	3/8	155.116	1914.7
1/2	80.1106	510.71	1/2	105.243	881.41	1/2	130.376	1352.7	1/2	155.509	1924.4
5/8	80.5033	515.72	5/8	105.636	888.00	5/8	130.769	1360.8	5/8	155.902	1934.2
3/4	80.8960	520.77	3/4	106.029	894.62	3/4	131.161	1369.0	3/4	156.294	1943.9
7/8	81.2887	525.84	7/8	106.421	901.26	7/8	131.554	1377.2	7/8	156.687	1953.7
26	81.6814	530.93	34	106.814	907.92	42	131.947	1385.4	50	157.080	1963.5
1/8	82.0741	536.05	1/8	107.207	914.61	1/8	132.340	1393.7	1/8	157.472	1973.3
1/4	82.4668	541.19	1/4	107.600	921.32	1/4	132.732	1402.0	1/4	157.865	1983.2
3/8	82.8595	546.35	3/8	107.992	928.06	3/8	133.125	1410.3	3/8	158.258	1993.1
1/2	83.2522	551.55	1/2	108.385	934.82	1/2	133.518	1418.6	1/2	158.650	2003.0
5/8	83.6449	556.76	5/8	108.778	941.61	5/8	133.910	1427.0	5/8	159.043	2012.9
3/4	84.0376	562.00	3/4	109.170	948.42	3/4	134.303	1435.4	3/4	159.436	2022.8
7/8	84.4303	567.27	7/8	109.563	955.25	7/8	134.696	1443.8	7/8	159.829	2032.8
27	84.8230	572.56	35	109.956	962.11	43	135.088	1452.2	51	160.221	2042.8
1/8	85.2157	577.87	1/8	110.348	969.00	1/8	135.481	1460.7	1/8	160.614	2052.8
1/4	85.6084	583.21	1/4	110.741	975.91	1/4	135.874	1469.1	1/4	161.007	2062.9
3/8	86.0011	588.57	3/8	111.134	982.84	3/8	136.267	1477.6	3/8	161.399	2073.0
1/2	86.3938	593.96	1/2	111.527	989.80	1/2	136.659	1486.2	1/2	161.792	2083.1
5/8	86.7865	599.37	5/8	111.919	996.87	5/8	137.052	1494.7	5/8	162.185	2093.2
3/4	87.1792	604.81	3/4	112.312	1003.8	3/4	137.445	1503.3	3/4	162.577	2103.3
7/8	87.5719	610.27	7/8	112.705	1010.8	7/8	137.837	1511.9	7/8	162.970	2113.5
28	87.965	615.75	36	113.097	1017.9	44	138.230	1520.5	52	163.363	2123.7
1/8	88.357	621.26	1/8	113.490	1025.0	1/8	138.623	1529.2	1/8	163.756	2133.9
1/4	88.750	626.80	1/4	113.883	1032.1	1/4	139.015	1537.9	1/4	164.148	2144.2
3/8	89.143	632.36	3/8	114.275	1039.2	3/8	139.408	1546.6	3/8	164.541	2154.5
1/2	89.535	637.94	1/2	114.668	1046.3	1/2	139.801	1555.3	1/2	164.934	2164.8
5/8	89.928	643.55	5/8	115.061	1053.5	5/8	140.194	1564.0	5/8	165.326	2175.1
3/4	90.321	649.18	3/4	115.454	1060.7	3/4	140.586	1572.8	3/4	165.719	2185.4
7/8	90.713	654.84	7/8	115.846	1068.0	7/8	140.979	1581.6	7/8	166.112	2195.8
29	91.106	660.52	37	116.239	1075.2	45	141.372	1590.4	53	166.504	2206.2
1/8	91.499	666.23	1/8	116.632	1082.5	1/8	141.764	1599.3	1/8	166.897	2216.6
1/4	91.892	671.96	1/4	117.024	1089.8	1/4	142.157	1608.2	1/4	167.290	2227.0
3/8	92.284	677.71	3/8	117.417	1097.1	3/8	142.550	1617.0	3/8	167.683	2237.5
1/2	92.677	683.49	1/2	117.810	1104.5	1/2	142.942	1626.0	1/2	168.075	2248.0
5/8	93.070	689.30	5/8	118.202	1111.8	5/8	143.335	1634.9	5/8	168.468	2258.5
3/4	93.462	695.13	3/4	118.596	1119.2	3/4	143.728	1643.9	3/4	168.861	2269.1
7/8	93.855	700.98	7/8	118.988	1126.7	7/8	144.121	1652.9	7/8	169.253	2279.6
30	94.248	706.86	38	119.381	1134.1	46	144.513	1661.9	54	169.646	2290.2
1/8	94.640	712.70	1/8	119.773	1141.0	1/8	144.906	1670.9	1/8	170.039	2300.8
1/4	95.033	718.69	1/4	120.166	1149.1	1/4	145.299	1680.0	1/4	170.431	2311.5
3/8	95.426	724.64	3/8	120.559	1156.6	3/8	145.691	1689.1	3/8	170.824	2322.1
1/2	95.819	730.62	1/2	120.951	1164.2	1/2	146.084	1698.2	1/2	171.217	2332.8
5/8	96.211	736.62	5/8	121.344	1171.7	5/8	146.477	1707.4	5/8	171.609	2343.5
3/4	96.604	742.64	3/4	121.737	1179.3	3/4	146.869	1716.5	3/4	172.002	2354.3
7/8	96.997	748.69	7/8	122.129	1186.9	7/8	147.262	1725.7	7/8	172.395	2365.0
31	97.389	754.77	39	122.522	1194.6	47	147.655	1734.9	55	172.788	2375.8
1/8	97.782	760.87	1/8	122.915	1202.3	1/8	148.048	1744.2	1/8	173.180	2386.6
1/4	98.175	766.99	1/4	123.308	1210.0	1/4	148.440	1753.5	1/4	173.573	2397.5
3/8	98.567	773.14	3/8	123.700	1217.7	3/8	148.833	1762.7	3/8	173.966	2408.3
1/2	98.960	779.31	1/2	124.093	1225.4	1/2	149.226	1772.1	1/2	174.358	2419.2
5/8	99.353	785.51	5/8	124.486	1233.2	5/8	149.618	1781.4	5/8	174.751	2430.1
3/4	99.746	791.73	3/4	124.878	1241.0	3/4	150.011	1790.8	3/4	175.144	2441.1
7/8	100.138	797.98	7/8	125.271	1248.8	7/8	150.404	1800.1	7/8	175.536	2452.0

TABLE 5: Circumferences and Areas of Circles (continued)

Diam.	Circum.	Area	Diam.	Circum.	Area	Diam.	Circum.	Area	Diam.	Circum.	Area
56	175.929	2463.0	64	201.062	3217.0	72	226.195	4071.5	80	251.327	5026.5
1/8	176.322	2474.0	1/8	201.455	3229.6	1/8	226.587	4085.7	1/8	251.720	5042.3
1/4	176.715	2485.0	1/4	201.847	3242.2	1/4	226.980	4099.8	1/4	252.113	5058.0
3/8	177.107	2496.1	3/8	202.240	3254.8	3/8	227.373	4114.0	3/8	252.506	5073.8
1/2	177.500	2507.2	1/2	202.633	3267.5	1/2	227.765	4128.2	1/2	252.898	5089.6
5/8	177.893	2518.3	5/8	203.025	3280.1	5/8	228.158	4142.5	5/8	253.291	5105.4
3/4	178.285	2529.4	3/4	203.418	3292.8	3/4	228.551	4156.8	3/4	253.684	5121.2
7/8	178.678	2540.6	7/8	203.811	3305.6	7/8	228.944	4171.1	7/8	254.076	5137.1
57	179.071	2551.8	65	204.204	3318.3	73	229.336	4185.4	81	254.469	5153.0
1/8	179.463	2563.0	1/8	204.596	3331.1	1/8	229.729	4199.7	1/8	254.862	5168.9
1/4	179.856	2574.2	1/4	204.989	3343.9	1/4	230.122	4214.1	1/4	255.254	5184.9
3/8	180.249	2585.4	3/8	205.382	3356.7	3/8	230.514	4228.5	3/8	255.647	5200.8
1/2	180.642	2596.7	1/2	205.774	3369.6	1/2	230.907	4242.9	1/2	256.040	5216.8
5/8	181.034	2608.0	5/8	206.167	3382.4	5/8	231.300	4257.4	5/8	256.433	5232.8
3/4	181.427	2619.4	3/4	206.560	3395.3	3/4	231.692	4271.8	3/4	256.825	5248.9
7/8	181.820	2630.7	7/8	206.952	3408.2	7/8	232.085	4286.3	7/8	257.218	5264.9
58	182.212	2642.1	66	207.345	3421.2	74	232.478	4300.8	82	257.611	5281.0
1/8	182.605	2653.5	1/8	207.738	3434.2	1/8	232.871	4315.4	1/8	258.003	5297.1
1/4	182.998	2664.9	1/4	208.131	3447.2	1/4	233.263	4329.9	1/4	258.396	5313.3
3/8	183.390	2676.4	3/8	208.523	3460.2	3/8	233.650	4344.5	3/8	258.789	5329.4
1/2	183.783	2687.8	1/2	208.916	3473.2	1/2	234.049	4359.2	1/2	259.181	5345.6
5/8	184.176	2699.3	5/8	209.309	3486.3	5/8	234.441	4373.8	5/8	259.574	5361.8
3/4	184.569	2710.9	3/4	209.701	3499.4	3/4	234.834	4388.5	3/4	259.967	5378.1
7/8	184.961	2722.4	7/8	210.094	3512.5	7/8	235.227	4403.1	7/8	260.359	5394.3
59	185.354	2734.0	67	210.487	3525.7	75	235.619	4417.9	83	260.752	5410.6
1/8	185.747	2745.6	1/8	210.879	3538.8	1/8	236.012	4432.6	1/8	261.145	5426.9
1/4	186.139	2757.2	1/4	211.272	3552.0	1/4	236.405	4447.4	1/4	261.538	5443.3
3/8	186.532	2768.8	3/8	211.665	3565.2	3/8	236.798	4462.2	3/8	261.930	5459.6
1/2	186.925	2780.5	1/2	212.058	3578.5	1/2	237.190	4477.0	1/2	262.323	5476.0
5/8	187.317	2792.2	5/8	212.450	3591.7	5/8	237.583	4491.8	5/8	262.716	5492.4
3/4	187.710	2803.9	3/4	212.843	3605.0	3/4	237.976	4506.7	3/4	263.108	5508.8
7/8	188.103	2815.7	7/8	213.236	3618.3	7/8	238.368	4521.5	7/8	263.501	5525.3
60	188.496	2827.4	68	213.628	3631.7	76	238.761	4536.5	84	263.894	5541.8
1/8	188.888	2839.2	1/8	214.021	3645.0	1/8	239.154	4551.4	1/8	264.286	5558.3
1/4	189.281	2851.0	1/4	214.414	3658.4	1/4	239.546	4566.4	1/4	264.679	5574.8
3/8	189.674	2862.9	3/8	214.806	3671.8	3/8	239.939	4581.3	3/8	265.072	5591.4
1/2	190.066	2874.8	1/2	215.199	3685.3	1/2	240.332	4596.3	1/2	265.465	5607.9
5/8	190.459	2886.6	5/8	215.592	3698.7	5/8	240.725	4611.4	5/8	265.857	5624.5
3/4	190.852	2898.6	3/4	215.984	3712.2	3/4	241.117	4626.4	3/4	266.250	5641.2
7/8	191.244	2910.5	7/8	216.377	3725.7	7/8	241.510	4641.5	7/8	266.643	5657.8
61	191.637	2922.5	69	216.770	3739.3	77	241.903	4656.6	85	267.035	5674.5
1/8	192.030	2934.5	1/8	217.163	3752.8	1/8	242.295	4671.8	1/8	267.428	5691.2
1/4	192.423	2946.5	1/4	217.555	3766.4	1/4	242.688	4686.9	1/4	267.821	5707.9
3/8	192.815	2958.5	3/8	217.948	3780.0	3/8	243.081	4702.1	3/8	268.213	5724.7
1/2	193.208	2970.6	1/2	218.341	3793.7	1/2	243.473	4717.3	1/2	268.606	5741.5
5/8	193.601	2982.7	5/8	218.733	3807.3	5/8	243.866	4732.5	5/8	268.999	5758.3
3/4	193.993	2994.8	3/4	219.126	3821.0	3/4	244.259	4747.8	3/4	269.392	5775.1
7/8	194.386	3006.9	7/8	219.519	3834.7	7/8	244.652	4763.1	7/8	269.784	5791.9
62	194.779	3019.1	70	219.911	3848.5	78	245.044	4778.4	86	270.177	5808.8
1/8	195.171	3031.3	1/8	220.304	3862.2	1/8	245.437	4793.7	1/8	270.570	5825.7
1/4	195.564	3043.5	1/4	220.697	3876.0	1/4	245.830	4809.0	1/4	270.962	5842.6
3/8	195.957	3055.7	3/8	221.090	3889.8	3/8	246.222	4824.4	3/8	271.355	5859.6
1/2	196.350	3068.0	1/2	221.482	3903.6	1/2	246.615	4839.8	1/2	271.748	5876.5
5/8	196.742	3080.3	5/8	221.875	3917.5	5/8	247.008	4855.2	5/8	272.140	5893.5
3/4	197.135	3092.6	3/4	222.268	3931.4	3/4	247.400	4870.7	3/4	272.533	5910.6
7/8	197.528	3104.9	7/8	222.660	3945.3	7/8	247.793	4886.2	7/8	272.926	5927.6
63	197.920	3117.2	71	223.053	3959.2	79	248.186	4901.7	87	273.319	5944.7
1/8	198.313	3129.6	1/8	223.446	3973.1	1/8	248.579	4917.2	1/8	273.711	5961.8
1/4	198.706	3142.0	1/4	223.838	3987.1	1/4	248.971	4932.7	1/4	274.104	5978.9
3/8	199.098	3154.5	3/8	224.231	4001.1	3/8	249.364	4948.3	3/8	274.497	5996.0
1/2	199.491	3166.9	1/2	224.624	4015.2	1/2	249.757	4963.9	1/2	274.889	6013.2
5/8	199.884	3179.4	5/8	225.017	4029.2	5/8	250.149	4979.5	5/8	275.282	6030.4
3/4	200.277	3191.9	3/4	225.409	4043.3	3/4	250.542	4995.2	3/4	275.675	6047.6
7/8	200.669	3204.4	7/8	225.802	4057.4	7/8	250.935	5010.9	7/8	276.067	6064.9

TABLE 5: Circumferences and Areas of Circles (concluded)

Diam.	Circum.	Area
88	276.460	6082.1
1/8	276.853	6099.4
1/4	277.246	6116.7
3/8	277.638	6134.1
1/2	278.031	6151.4
5/8	278.424	6168.8
3/4	278.816	6186.2
7/8	279.209	6203.7
89	279.602	6221.1
1/8	279.994	6238.6
1/4	280.387	6256.1
3/8	280.780	6273.7
1/2	281.173	6291.2
5/8	281.565	6308.8
3/4	281.958	6326.4
7/8	282.351	6344.1
90	282.743	6361.7
1/8	283.136	6379.4
1/4	283.529	6397.1
3/8	283.921	6414.9
1/2	284.314	6432.6
5/8	284.707	6450.4
3/4	285.100	6468.2
7/8	285.492	6486.0
91	285.885	6503.9
1/8	286.278	6521.8
1/4	286.670	6539.7
3/8	287.063	6557.6
1/2	287.456	6575.5
5/8	287.848	6593.5
3/4	288.241	6611.5
7/8	288.634	6629.6
92	289.027	6647.6
1/8	289.419	6665.7
1/4	289.812	6683.8
3/8	290.205	6701.9
1/2	290.597	6720.1
5/8	290.990	6738.2
3/4	291.383	6756.4
7/8	291.775	6774.7
93	292.168	6792.9
1/8	292.561	6811.2
1/4	292.954	6829.5
3/8	293.346	6847.8
1/2	293.739	6866.1
5/8	294.132	6884.5
3/4	294.524	6902.9
7/8	294.917	6921.3
94	295.310	6939.8
1/8	295.702	6958.2
1/4	296.095	6976.7
3/8	296.488	6995.3
1/2	296.881	7013.8
5/8	297.273	7032.4
3/4	297.666	7051.0
7/8	298.059	7069.6
95	298.451	7088.2
1/8	298.844	7106.9
1/4	299.237	7125.6
3/8	299.629	7144.3
1/2	300.022	7163.0
5/8	300.415	7181.8
3/4	300.807	7200.6
7/8	301.200	7219.4
96	301.593	7238.2
1/8	301.986	7257.1

Diam.	Circum.	Area
1/4	302.378	7276.0
3/8	302.771	7294.9
1/2	303.164	7313.8
5/8	303.556	7332.8
3/4	303.949	7351.8
7/8	304.342	7370.8
97	304.734	7389.8
1/8	305.127	7408.9
1/4	305.520	7428.0
3/8	305.913	7447.1
1/2	306.305	7466.2
5/8	306.698	7485.3
3/4	307.091	7504.5
7/8	307.483	7523.7
98	307.876	7543.0
1/8	308.269	7562.2
1/4	308.661	7581.5
3/8	309.054	7600.8
1/2	309.447	7620.1
5/8	309.840	7639.5
3/4	310.232	7658.9
7/8	310.625	7678.3
99	311.018	7697.7
1/8	311.410	7717.1
1/4	311.803	7736.6
3/8	312.196	7756.1
1/2	312.588	7775.6
5/8	312.981	7795.2
3/4	313.374	7814.8
7/8	313.767	7834.4
100	314.159	7854.0
1/4	314.945	7893.3
1/2	315.730	7932.7
3/4	316.515	7972.2
101	317.301	8011.8
1/4	318.086	8051.6
1/2	318.872	8091.4
3/4	319.657	8131.3
102	320.442	8171.3
1/4	321.228	8211.4
1/2	322.013	8251.6
3/4	322.799	8291.9
103	323.584	8332.3
1/4	324.369	8372.8
1/2	325.155	8413.4
3/4	325.940	8454.1
104	326.726	8494.9
1/4	327.511	8535.8
1/2	328.296	8576.6
3/4	329.082	8617.8
105	329.867	8659.0
1/4	330.653	8700.3
1/2	331.438	8741.7
3/4	332.223	8783.2
106	333.009	8824.7
1/4	333.794	8866.4
1/2	334.580	8908.2
3/4	335.365	8950.1
107	336.150	8992.0
1/4	336.936	9034.1
1/2	337.721	9076.3
3/4	338.507	9118.5
108	339.292	9160.9
1/4	340.077	9203.3
1/2	340.863	9245.9

Diam.	Circum.	Area
3/4	341.648	9288.6
109	342.433	9331.3
1/4	343.219	9374.2
1/2	344.004	9417.1
3/4	344.790	9460.2
110	345.575	9503.3
1/4	346.360	9546.6
1/2	347.146	9589.9
3/4	347.931	9633.3
111	348.717	9676.9
1/4	349.502	9720.5
1/2	350.287	9764.3
3/4	351.073	9808.1
112	351.858	9852.0
1/4	352.644	9896.1
1/2	353.429	9940.2
3/4	354.214	9984.4
113	355.000	10,028.7
1/4	355.785	10,073.2
1/2	356.570	10,117.7
3/4	357.356	10,162.3
114	358.141	10,207.0
1/4	358.927	10,251.9
1/2	359.712	10,296.8
3/4	360.497	10,341.8
115	361.283	10,386.9
1/4	362.069	10,432.1
1/2	362.854	10,477.4
3/4	363.639	10,522.8
116	364.425	10,568.3
1/4	365.210	10,613.9
1/2	365.995	10,659.6
3/4	366.781	10,705.4
117	367.566	10,751.3
1/4	368.352	10,797.3
1/2	369.137	10,843.4
3/4	369.922	10,889.6
118	370.708	10,935.9
1/4	371.493	10,982.3
1/2	372.279	11,028.8
3/4	373.064	11,075.3
119	373.849	11,122.0
1/4	374.635	11,168.8
1/2	375.420	11,215.7
3/4	376.206	11,262.7
120	376.991	11,309.7
1/4	377.776	11,356.9
1/2	378.562	11,404.2
3/4	379.347	11,451.5
121	380.133	11,499.0
1/4	380.918	11,546.6
1/2	381.703	11,594.2
3/4	382.489	11,642.0
122	383.274	11,689.9
1/4	384.060	11,737.8
1/2	384.845	11,785.9
3/4	385.630	11,834.0
123	386.416	11,882.3
1/4	387.201	11,930.6
1/2	387.987	11,979.1
3/4	388.772	12,027.6
124	389.557	12,076.3
1/4	390.343	12,125.0
1/2	391.128	12,173.9

Diam.	Circum.	Area
3/4	391.914	12,222.8
125	392.699	12,271.8
1/4	393.484	12,321.0
1/2	394.270	12,370.2
3/4	395.055	12,419.5
126	395.841	12,469.0
1/4	396.626	12,518.5
1/2	397.411	12,568.1
3/4	398.197	12,617.9
127	398.982	12,667.7
1/4	399.768	12,717.6
1/2	400.553	12,767.6
3/4	401.338	12,817.7
128	402.124	12,868.0
1/4	402.909	12,918.3
1/2	403.695	12,968.9
3/4	404.480	13,019.2
129	405.265	13,069.8
1/4	406.051	13,120.5
1/2	406.836	13,171.3
3/4	407.621	13,222.2
130	408.407	13,273.2
1/4	409.192	13,324.3
1/2	409.978	13,375.5
3/4	410.763	13,426.8
131	411.549	13,478.2
1/4	412.334	13,529.7
1/2	413.119	13,581.3
3/4	413.905	13,633.0
132	414.690	13,684.8
1/4	415.476	13,736.7
1/2	416.261	13,788.6
3/4	417.046	13,840.7
133	417.832	13,892.9
1/4	418.617	13,945.2
1/2	419.402	13,997.6
3/4	420.188	14,050.0
134	420.973	14,102.6
1/4	421.759	14,155.3
1/2	422.544	14,208.0
3/4	423.329	14,260.9
135	424.115	14,313.9
1/4	424.900	14,366.9
1/2	425.686	14,420.1
3/4	426.471	14,473.4
136	427.257	14,526.7
1/4	428.042	14,580.2
1/2	428.827	14,633.7
3/4	429.613	14,687.4
137	430.398	14,741.1
1/4	431.184	14,795.0
1/2	431.969	14,848.9
3/4	432.754	14,903.0
138	433.540	14,957.1
1/4	434.325	15,011.4
1/2	435.110	15,065.7
3/4	435.896	15,120.1
139	436.681	15,174.7
1/4	437.467	15,229.3
1/2	438.252	15,284.0
3/4	439.037	15,338.9
140	439.823	15,393.8
1/4	440.608	15,448.8
1/2	441.394	15,504.0
3/4	442.180	15,559.2

452 Appendix

TABLE 6: Weights of Materials and Angle of Repose

Material	Average Wt. per Cu. Ft., Pounds	Angle of Repose	Material	Average Wt. per Cu. Ft., Pounds	Angle of Repose
Acid Phosphate, fertilizer	60	....	Cocoa Nibs	35-40	30-45°
Air, 60° F—14.7 PSIA	0.0765	....	Cocoanut, meal	32	....
Alfalfa, ground	16	45° & Up	Cocoanut, shredded	20-25	45° & Up
Alum, lumpy	50-60	30-45°	Coffee, fresh beans	30-40	30-45°
Alum, pulverized	45-50	30-45°	Coffee, roasted beans	22-30	Up to 30°
Alumina	60	30-45°	Coke, loose	23-32	30-45°
Aluminum, solid mass	165	....	Coke, pulverized	25-35	45° & Up
Aluminum Oxide	70-120	Up to 30°	Coke, petroleum calcined	35-45	30-45°
Ammonium Sulfate	45-60	....	Concrete, cinder with Portland cement	112	....
Apples	40	....	Concrete, gravel & sand with Portland cement	150	....
Asbestos, shredded	20-25	45° & Up	Copper Ore	120-150	30-45°
Asbestos, solid	153	....	Copper, cast	542	....
Asbestos Brake Lining, molded	178	....	Copper, rolled	556	....
Asbestos Brake Lining, woven	110	....	Cork, solid	15	....
Ash, American White, dry (wood)	38	....	Cork, ground	5-15	45° & Up
Ashes, dry	35-40	45° & Up	Corn, on cob	45	....
Ashes, wet	45-50	45° & Up	Corn, shelled	45	Up to 30°
Ashes, gas producer, saturated	78	....	Corn, grits	40-45	30-45°
Ashes, soft coal	35-45	40°	Cottonseed, dry, de-linted	35	30-45°
Asphalt, crushed	45	30-45°	Cottonseed, dry, not de-linted	18-25	45° & Up
Asphaltum	87.3	....	Cottonseed cake, lumpy	40-45	30-45°
Bagasse	7.5	45° & Up	Cottonseed, hulls	12	45° & Up
Bakelite, powder	30-40	45° & Up	Cottonseed, meal	35-40	30-45°
Bakelite, molded	82-88	....	Cottonseed, meats	40	30-45°
Baking Powder	40-50	30-45°	Cryolite	90-110	30-45°
Bark, wood, refuse	10-20	45° & Up	Cullet	80-120	30-45°
Barley	38	Up to 30°	Culm	45-50	....
Baryte, crushed	180	....	Cypress	29	....
Basalt	184	....	Dolomite, solid	181	....
Batch, glass	90-100	30-45°	Dolomite, pulverized	46	....
Bauxite, crushed	75-85	30-45°	Dolomite, lumpy	90-100	30-45°
Beans, castor, whole	36	Up to 30°	Earth, common dry	70-80	30-45°
Beans, cocoa	37	....	Earth, moist	75-85	30-45°
Beans, navy	48-54	Up to 30°	Earth, fullers dry	30-35	23°
Beans, soy	45	Up to 30°	Elm, dry	35	....
Beets	45	....	Feldspar, solid	160	....
Bentonite, crude	34-40	45° & Up	Feldspar, lumps	85-95	....
Bones, pulverized	50-60	....	Feldspar, dust	75-80	45°
Borax, fine	50-55	30-45°	Fibre, hard	87	....
Bran	16	30-45°	Fir	24-33	....
Brass, cast	519	....	Fish, scrap	40-50	....
Brass, rolled	534	....	Fish, meal	35-40	45° & Up
Brewers Grain	25-30	45° & Up	Flaxseed, whole	45	Up to 30°
Brick, best pressed	150	....	Flour, wheat	35-40	45° & Up
Brick, common hard	125	....	Fluorspar, solid	200	....
Brick, fire	137	....	Fluorspar, lumps	80-110	45° & Up
Brick, soft inferior	100	....	Fluorspar, dust	80-95	45° & Up
Brickwork, fine	140	....	Foundry, refuse	60-80	....
Bronze, copper 8, tin 1	546	....	Foundry, sand, loose	80-90	....
Buckwheat	40-42	Up to 30°	Foundry, sand, rammed	100-110	....
Calcium Carbide	70-80	30-45°	Garbage, average	30	....
Carbon, black pellets	25	Up to 30°	Glass, window or plate	161	....
Carbon, powder	4-6	....	Glass, batch	90-100	30-45°
Carbon, solid	134	....	Glass, broken	80-100	....
Cedar, red	35	....	Glue, animal, flaked	35	....
Cement, bulk	75-85	....	Glue, vegetable, powdered	40	....
Cement, clinker	75-95	....	Gluten, meal	39	30-45°
Cement, Portland (376 lbs. net per bar.)	90-100	30-45°	Granite, solid	150-170	....
Cement, slurry	90	....	Granite, lumps	96	30-45°
Cement mortar, Portland 1:2½	135	....	Graphite, flake	40	30-45°
Chalk, lumpy	82-95	45° & Up	Gravel, dry, round or sharp	90-100	30-40°
Chalk, fine	65-75	45° & Up	Gravel, wet	100-120	....
Chalk, solid	156	....	Greenstone, crushed, loose	107	....
Charcoal, wood	15-30	....	Gypsum, solid	142	....
Cherry wood, dry	42	....	Gypsum, lumps	90-100	30-45°
Chestnut wood, dry	41.2	....	Gypsum, ground	75-80	....
Chocolate, powder	40	....	Gypsum, pulverized	60-80	45° & Up
Chromium ore	125-140	30-45°	Hay, loose	5	....
Cinders, (coal, ashes and clinkers)	40	25-40°	Hay, pressed	24	....
Clay, potter's dry	100-120	....	Hemlock, dry	25	....
Clay, dry in lumps	65	25-45°	Hickory, dry	53	....
Coal, Anthracite, solid	94	....	Hops, moist	35	45° & Up
Coal, Anthracite, loose	52-57	30-45°	Ice, solid	57.4	....
Coal, Bituminous, solid	84	....	Ice, crushed	35-40	Up to 30°
Coal, Bituminous, loose or slack	43-50	30-45°	Ilmenite	144	30-45°

(Reprinted from Dodge General Engineering Catalog by special permission of Dodge Manufacturing Division, Reliance Electric Co.)

TABLE 6: Weights of Materials and Angle of Repose (continued)

Material	Average Wt. per Cu. Ft., Pounds	Angle of Repose	Material	Average Wt. per Cu. Ft., Pounds	Angle of Repose
Iron Ore	120-180	....	Rosin	67	....
Iron, cast gray	450	....	Rubber, caoutchouc	59	....
Iron, cast ductile	444	....	Rubber, manufactured	95	....
Iron, wrought	480	....	Rubber, scrap (ground)	25-35	45° & Up
Iron, borings	130-200	....	Rye	42-45	Up to 30°
Lead, commercial	710	....	Salt cake	80-95	30-45°
Lead, red	230	....	Salt, coarse	45-55	30-45°
Lead Ore, crushed	180-270	....	Salt, fine	70-80	30-45°
Lead, white pigment	250-260	....	Saltpeter	70-80	30-45°
Lignite, air dried	45-55	30-45°	Sand, wet	110-130	45° & Up
Lignum Vitae, dry	41-83	....	Sand, dry	90-110	34°
Lime, briquettes	60	....	Sand, loose, foundry	80-100	30-45°
Lime, burned pebble	53-56	45° & Up	Sand, rammed	100-110	....
Lime, quick, crushed	64	....	Sand, voids full of water	110-130	15-30°
Lime, hydrated	20-40	30-45°	Sandstone, quarried and piled	82-86	....
Limestone, solid	165	....	Sawdust	10-25	....
Limestone, loose	100	....	Scale, rolling mill	125-160	....
Limestone, pulverized	85-90	45° & Up	Sewage, sludge	40-50	....
Linseed, whole	45-50	Up to 30°	Shales, solid	162	....
Linseed, meal	28-40	30-45°	Shales, broken	85-100	30-45°
Locust, dry	44	....	Silica, flour	80	....
Magnesite, solid	188	....	Slag, solid	160-180	....
Magnesium, solid	109	....	Slag, furnace, granulated	60-65	30-45°
Magnesium Sulfate, crystal	70	....	Slag, Birmingham	80-95	....
Mahogany, Spanish, dry	53	....	Slate, solid	165-175	....
Mahogany, Honduras, dry	35	....	Slate, fine ground	80-90	30-45°
Malt	20-22	30-45°	Slate, flakes	70-85	....
Manganese, solid	475	....	Snow, fresh fallen	5-12	....
Manganese Ore	125-140	....	Snow, compacted by rain	15-50	....
Manganese Oxide	120	....	Soap, solid	50	....
Manure	25	....	Soap, chips	5-15	30-45°
Maple, dry	49	....	Soap, flakes	5-15	30-45°
Marble, crushed	90-95	30-45°	Soap, powder	20-25	30-45°
Marl	79	30-45°	Soda Ash, heavy	55-65	30-45°
Masonry, granite or limestone	165	....	Soda Ash, light	20-35	30-45°
Mercury, 32° F.	849	....	Sodium Aluminate, ground	72	....
Mica, solid	181	....	Sodium Nitrate, ground	70-80	....
Mica, ground	75-80	30-45°	Soybeans, whole	45-50	Up to 30°
Milk, malted	25-35	45° & Up	Spruce, California, dry	28	....
Milk, powdered	28	45° & Up	Starch, powdered	25-45	....
Molybdenum Ore, powdered	107	....	Steel, solid	489.6	....
Mortar, wet	150	....	Steel, chips	100-150	30-45°
Oak, live, dry	59	....	Steel, turnings	60-120	45° & Up
Oak, red	32-45	....	Sugar, brown	45	....
Oats	26-28	32°	Sugar, powdered	45-55	....
Oats, rolled	19	30-45°	Sugar, granulated	50-55	30-45°
Oil Cake	48-50	....	Sugar, raw cane	55-65	45° & Up
Oil, linseed	58.8	....	Sugarbeet Pulp, dry	12-15	....
Oil, petroleum	55	....	Sugarbeet Pulp, wet	24-45	....
Oyster Shells, ground	53	30-45°	Sugarcane, knifed	15-18	45° & Up
Paper, writing and wrapping	65-90	....	Sulphur, solid	125	....
Paraffine	45	....	Sulphur, lumps	80-85	30-45°
Peanuts, shelled	35-45	30-45°	Sulphur, dust	50-70	30-45°
Peanuts, not shelled	15-20	30-45°	Sycamore, dry	37	....
Pebbles	90-100	....	Talc, solid	165-170	....
Petroleum, coke	35-45	....	Talc, granulated	50-65	....
Phosphate, rock	200	30-45°	Tanbark, ground	55	....
Phosphate, sand	90-100	30-45°	Tankage	50-70	....
Pine, White, dry	26	....	Tar	69-75	....
Pine, Yellow Northern, dry	34	....	Tin, cast	459	....
Pine, Yellow Southern, dry	45	....	Tobacco, scraps	15-25	45° & Up
Pitch	72	....	Tobacco, stems	16-25	45° & Up
Potash	80	....	Traprock, compact	187	....
Potassium Chloride	120-130	30-45°	Traprock, crushed	95-110	30-45°
Potatoes, white	48	....	Turf	20-30	....
Pumice, ground	40-45	45° & Up	Walnut, black, dry	38-42	....
Pyrites, pellets	120-130	30-45°	Water, pure	62.4	....
Quartz, solid	165	....	Water, sea	64.08	....
Quartz, lumps	95-100	....	Wheat	48	28°
Quartz, sand	70-80	....	Wheat, cracked	40-45	30-45°
Redwood, California, dry	26-30	....	Wood Chips	10-30	45° & Up
Resin, synthetic, crushed	30-40	....	Wood Flour	16-35	....
Rice, hulled and polished	45-48	Up to 30°	Zinc, calcines	75-80	30-45°
Rice, rough	36	30-45°	Zinc, cast	443	....
Rice Grits	42-45	30-45°	Zinc Ore, granular	160	....
Rip-rap	80-105	....	Zinc Oxide	10-35	45° & Up

TABLE 7: Properties of Saturated Steam*

Absolute Pressure Psi**	Temperature Deg F	Specific Volume of Vapor cu ft/lb	Enthalpy, Btu/lb		
			Saturated Liquid	Evaporation	Saturated Vapor
1	101.7	333.6	69.70	1036.3	1106.0
5	162.2	73.52	130.13	1001.0	1131.1
10	193.2	38.42	161.17	982.1	1143.3
14.696	212.0	26.80	180.07	970.3	1150.4
15	213.0	26.29	181.11	969.7	1150.8
20	228.0	20.09	196.16	960.1	1156.3
25	240.1	16.30	208.42	952.1	1160.6
30	250.3	13.75	218.82	945.3	1164.1
35	259.3	11.90	227.91	939.2	1167.1
40	267.2	10.50	236.03	933.7	1169.7
45	274.4	9.401	243.36	928.6	1172.0
50	281.0	8.515	250.09	924.0	1174.1
55	287.1	7.787	256.30	919.6	1175.9
60	292.7	7.175	262.09	915.5	1177.6
65	298.0	6.655	267.5	911.6	1179.1
70	302.9	6.206	272.61	907.9	1180.6
75	307.6	5.816	277.43	904.5	1181.9
80	312.0	5.472	282.02	901.1	1183.1
85	316.2	5.168	286.39	897.8	1184.2
90	320.3	4.896	290.56	894.7	1185.3
95	324.1	4.652	294.56	891.7	1186.2
100	327.8	4.432	298.40	888.8	1187.2
110	334.8	4.049	305.66	883.2	1188.9
120	341.2	3.728	312.44	877.9	1190.4
130	347.3	3.455	318.81	872.9	1191.7
140	353.0	3.220	324.82	868.2	1193.0
150	358.4	3.015	330.51	863.6	1194.1
160	363.5	2.834	335.93	859.2	1195.1
170	368.4	2.675	341.09	854.9	1196.0
180	373.1	2.532	346.03	850.8	1196.9
190	377.5	2.404	350.79	846.8	1197.6
200	381.8	2.288	355.36	843.0	1198.4
225	391.8	2.042	366.09	833.8	1199.9
250	401.0	1.844	376.00	825.1	1201.1
275	409.4	1.680	385.21	816.9	1202.1
300	417.3	1.543	393.84	809.0	1202.8
350	431.7	1.326	409.69	794.2	1203.9
400	444.6	1.161	424.0	780.5	1204.5
450	456.3	1.032	437.2	767.4	1204.6
500	467.0	0.9278	449.4	755.0	1204.4
600	486.2	0.7698	471.6	731.6	1203.2
700	503.1	0.6554	491.5	709.7	1201.2
800	518.2	0.5687	509.7	688.9	1198.6
900	532.0	0.5006	526.6	668.8	1195.4
1000	544.6	0.4456	542.4	649.4	1191.8
1500	596.2	0.2765	611.6	556.3	1167.9
2000	635.8	0.1878	671.7	463.4	1135.1
2500	668.1	0.1307	730.6	360.5	1091.1
3000	695.4	0.0858	802.5	217.8	1020.3
3206.2	705.4	0.0503	902.7	0	902.7

*Excerpted from *Thermodynamic Properties of Steam,* J.H. Keenan and F.G. Keyes (New York: John Wiley & Sons, Inc., 1936) by permission of the publishers.

**Subtract 14.696 psi to obtain gage pressure.

TABLE 8: NEMA Electric Motor Dimensions

The following tables and diagrams are reprinted from ANSI/NEMA Standards Publication/No. MG-1-1978 (R 1981), Revision No. 8 (1984), with the permission of the National Electrical Manufacturers Association (NEMA). ANSI stands for American National Standards Institute.

The information reproduced here was selected to cover the most commonly used type of industrial motor—the polyphase, squirrel cage, NEMA design B. The dimensions shown in Part c. below are for the foot-mounted type of frame only. Users of Table 8. should recognize that there are many other types of motors and generators described in the publication referred to above, as well as other frame configurations.

a. Frame designations for polyphase, squirrel-cage, designs A and B, horizontal and vertical motors, 60 hertz, class B insulation system, open type, 1.15 service factor, 575 volts and less*

Hp	Speed, rpm			
	3600	1800	1200	900
½	. . .	. . .	. . .	143T
¾	. . .	. . .	143T	145T
1	. . .	143T	145T	182T
1½	143T	145T	182T	184T
2	145T	145T	184T	213T
3	145T	182T	213T	215T
5	182T	184T	215T	254T
7½	184T	213T	254T	256T
10	213T	215T	256T	284T
15	215T	254T	284T	286T
20	254T	256T	286T	324T
25	256T	284T	324T	326T
30	284TS	286T	326T	364T
40	286TS	324T	364T	365T
50	324TS	326T	365T	404T
60	326TS	364TS†	404T	405T
75	364TS	365TS†	405T	444T
100	365TS	404TS†	444T	445T
125	404TS	405TS†	445T	. . .
150	405TS	444TS†	. . .	. . .
200	444TS	445TS†	. . .	. . .
250‡	445TS	. . .	. . .	. . .

*The voltage rating of 115 volts applies only to motors rated 15 horsepower and smaller.
†When motors are to be used with V-belt or chain drives, the correct frame size is the frame size shown but with the suffix letter S omitted. For the corresponding shaft extension dimensions, see MG 1-11.31 in NEMA Standards Publication No. MG 1-1978 (R 1981).
‡The 250 horsepower rating at the 3600 rpm speed has a 1.0 service factor.
NOTE—See MG 1-11.31 in NEMA Standards Publication No. MG 1-1978 (R 1981) for the dimensions of the frame designations.

b. Dimension Lettering for Foot-mounted Machines—Side View

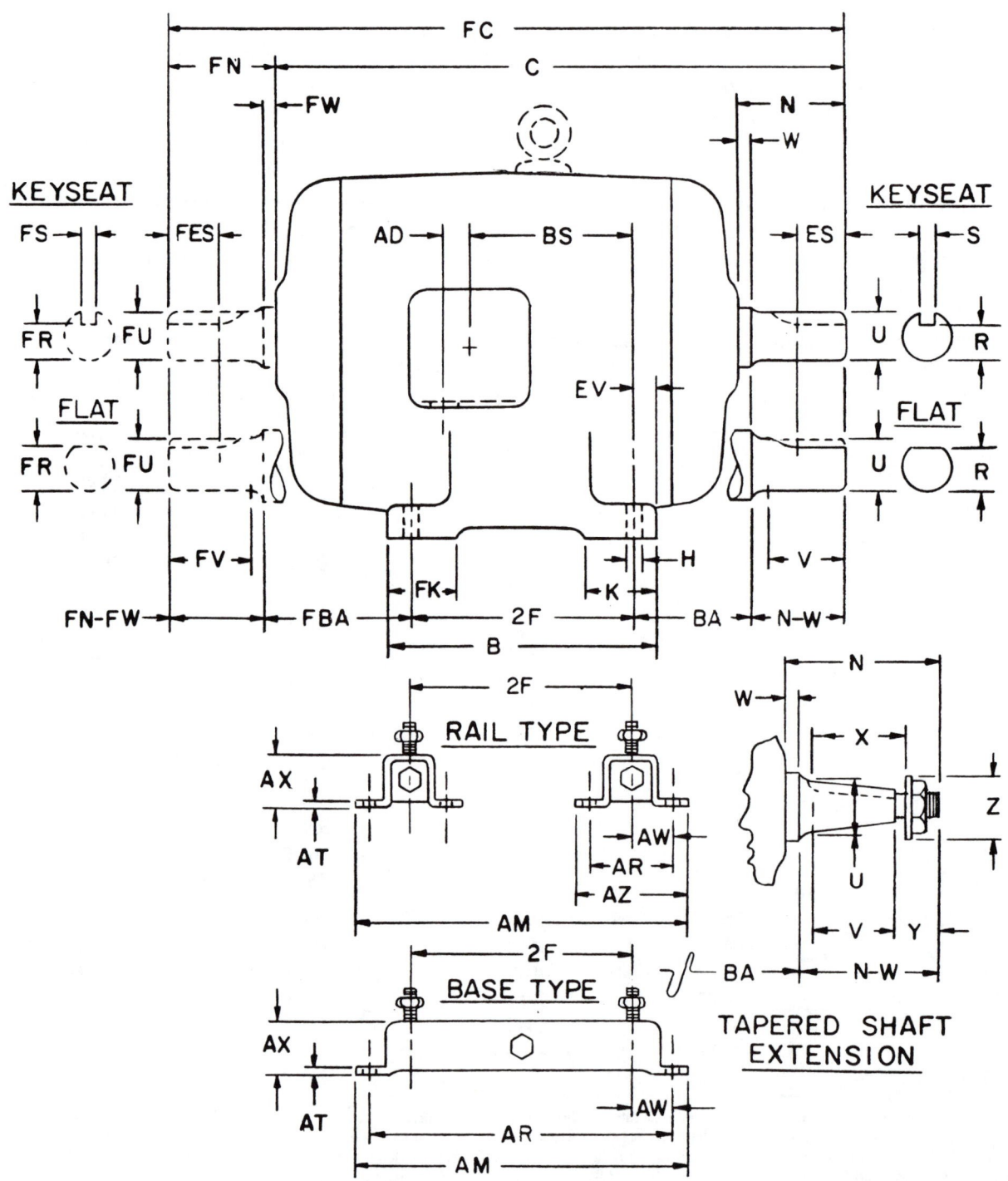

c. Dimension Lettering (continued)—Drive End View

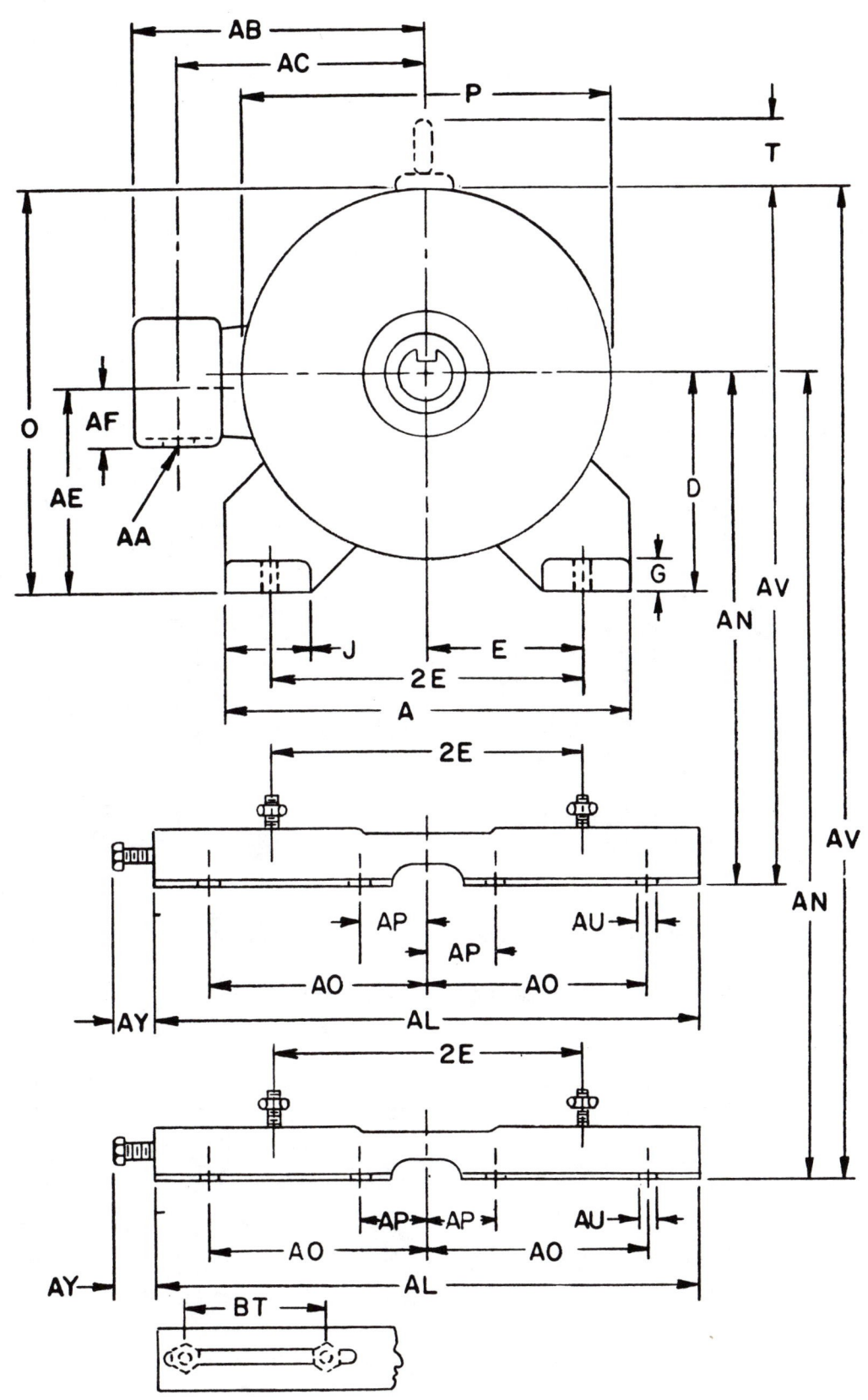

d. MG 1-11.31 Dimensions for Alternating-current Foot-mounted Motors and Generators with Single Straight-shaft Extension

Frame Designation	A Max	B Max	D*	E†	2F†	BA	H†	U	N–W	V Min	Keyseat R	ES Min	S	AA Min‡
42	. . .	. . .	2.62	1.75	1.69	2.06	0.28 slot	0.3750	1.12	. . .	0.328	. . .	flat	. . .
48	. . .	. . .	3.00	2.12	2.75	2.50	0.34 slot	0.5000	1.50	. . .	0.453	. . .	flat	. . .
48H	. . .	. . .	3.00	2.12	4.75	2.50	0.34 slot	0.5000	1.50	. . .	0.453	. . .	flat	. . .
56	. . .	. . .	3.50	2.44	3.00	2.75	0.34 slot	0.6250	1.88	. . .	0.517	1.41	0.188	. . .
56H	. . .	. . .	3.50	2.44	5.00	2.75	0.34 slot	0.6250	1.88	. . .	0.517	1.41	0.188	. . .
143T	7.0	6.0	3.50	2.75	4.00	2.25	0.34 hole	0.8750	2.25	2.00	0.771	1.41	0.188	¾
145T	7.0	6.0	3.50	2.75	5.00	2.25	0.34 hole	0.8750	2.25	2.00	0.771	1.41	0.188	¾
182T	9.0	6.5	4.50	3.75	4.50	2.75	0.41 hole	1.1250	2.75	2.50	0.986	1.78	0.250	¾
184T	9.0	7.5	4.50	3.75	5.50	2.75	0.41 hole	1.1250	2.75	2.50	0.986	1.78	0.250	¾
213T	10.5	7.5	5.25	4.25	5.50	3.50	0.41 hole	1.3750	3.38	3.12	1.201	2.41	0.312	1
215T	10.5	9.0	5.25	4.25	7.00	3.50	0.41 hole	1.3750	3.38	3.12	1.201	2.41	0.312	1
254T	12.5	10.8	6.25	5.00	8.25	4.25	0.53 hole	1.625	4.00	3.75	1.416	2.91	0.375	1¼
256T	12.5	12.5	6.25	5.00	10.00	4.25	0.53 hole	1.625	4.00	3.75	1.416	2.91	0.375	1¼
284T	14.0	12.5	7.00	5.50	9.50	4.75	0.53 hole	1.875	4.62	4.38	1.591	3.28	0.500	1½
284TS	14.0	12.5	7.00	5.50	9.50	4.75	0.53 hole	1.625	3.25	3.00	1.416	1.91	0.375	1½
286T	14.0	14.0	7.00	5.50	11.00	4.75	0.53 hole	1.875	4.62	4.38	1.591	3.28	0.500	1½
286TS	14.0	14.0	7.00	5.50	11.00	4.75	0.53 hole	1.625	3.25	3.00	1.416	1.91	0.375	1½
324T	16.0	14.0	8.00	6.25	10.50	5.25	0.66 hole	2.125	5.25	5.00	1.845	3.91	0.500	2
324TS	16.0	14.0	8.00	6.25	10.50	5.25	0.66 hole	1.875	3.75	3.50	1.591	2.03	0.500	2
326T	16.0	15.5	8.00	6.25	12.00	5.25	0.66 hole	2.125	5.25	5.00	1.845	3.91	0.500	2
326TS	16.0	15.5	8.00	6.25	12.00	5.25	0.66 hole	1.875	3.75	3.50	1.591	2.03	0.500	2
364T	18.0	15.2	9.00	7.00	11.25	5.88	0.66 hole	2.375	5.88	5.62	2.021	4.28	0.625	3
364TS	18.0	15.2	9.00	7.00	11.25	5.88	0.66 hole	1.875	3.75	3.50	1.591	2.03	0.500	3
365T	18.0	16.2	9.00	7.00	12.25	5.88	0.66 hole	2.375	5.88	5.62	2.021	4.28	0.625	3
365TS	18.0	16.2	9.00	7.00	12.25	5.88	0.66 hole	1.875	3.75	3.50	1.591	2.03	0.500	3
404T	20.0	16.2	10.00	8.00	12.25	6.62	0.81 hole	2.875	7.25	7.00	2.450	5.65	0.750	3
404TS	20.0	16.2	10.00	8.00	12.25	6.62	0.81 hole	2.125	4.25	4.00	1.845	2.78	0.500	3
405T	20.0	17.8	10.00	8.00	13.75	6.62	0.81 hole	2.875	7.25	7.00	2.450	5.65	0.750	3
405TS	20.0	17.8	10.00	8.00	13.75	6.62	0.81 hole	2.125	4.25	4.00	1.845	2.78	0.500	3
444T	22.0	18.5	11.00	9.00	14.50	7.50	0.81 hole	3.375	8.50	8.25	2.880	6.91	0.875	3
444TS	22.0	18.5	11.00	9.00	14.50	7.50	0.81 hole	2.375	4.75	4.50	2.021	3.03	0.625	3
445T	22.0	20.5	11.00	9.00	16.50	7.50	0.81 hole	3.375	8.50	8.25	2.880	6.91	0.875	3
445TS	22.0	20.5	11.00	9.00	16.50	7.50	0.81 hole	2.375	4.75	4.50	2.021	3.03	0.625	3
440	. . .	. . .	11.00	9.00	**	7.50	. . .	. . .	. . .	. . .	. . .	. . .	. . .	. . .
500	. . .	. . .	12.50	10.00	**	8.50	. . .	. . .	. . .	. . .	. . .	. . .	. . .	. . .

All dimensions in inches.

* Frames 42 to 56H, inclusive—The tolerance on the D dimension for rigid base motors shall be + 0.00 inch, − 0.06 inch. Frames 143T to 326TS, inclusive—The tolerance on the D dimension for rigid base motors shall be + 0.00 inch, − 0.03 inch. Frames 364T to 500, inclusive—The tolerance on the D dimension for rigid base motors shall be + 0.00 inch, − 0.06 inch. No tolerance has been established for the D dimension of resilient mounted motors.

† Frames 42 to 56H, inclusive—The tolerance for the 2F dimension shall be ± 0.03 inch and for the H dimension (width of slot) shall be + 0.02 inch, − 0 inch.

Frames 143T to 500, inclusive—The tolerance for the 2E and 2F dimensions shall be ± 0.03 inch and for the H dimension shall be + 0.05 inch, − 0 inch.

‡ For dimensions of clearance holes, see MG 1-4.04.

** For the 2F dimension and corresponding third (and when required the fourth) digit in the frame series, see MG 1-11.01.B and Table 11-1.

Note I—For the meaning of the letter dimensions, see MG 1-4.01 and Figures 4-1 and 4-2.

Note II—For tolerances on shaft extension diameters and keyseats, see MG 1-4.05.

Note III—It is recommended that all machines with keyseats cut in the shaft extension for pulley, coupling, pinion, and so forth, be furnished with a key unless otherwise specified by the purchaser. (Approved as Authorized Engineering Information 3-8-1983.)

Note IV—Frames 42 to 56H, inclusive—If the shaft extension length of the motor is not suitable for the application, it is recommended that deviations from this length be in 0.25-inch increments. (Approved as Authorized Engineering Information 3-8-1983.)

458

**TABLE 9: Sheet Steel Gage Numbers and Equivalent Thicknesses
(Courtesy of American Iron and Steel Institute.)**

HOT ROLLED AND COLD ROLLED SHEET		HOT DIPPED ZINC COATED (GALVANIZED) SHEET	
Manufacturer's Standard Gage No.	Thickness Equivalent, Inch	Galvanized Sheet Gage No.	Thickness Equivalent, Inch
3	0.2391	8	0.1681
4	.2242	9	.1532
5	.2092	10	.1382
6	.1943	11	.1233
7	.1793	12	.1084
8	.1644	13	.0934
9	.1495	14	.0785
10	.1345	15	.0710
11	.1196	16	.0635
12	.1046	17	.0575
13	.0897	18	.0516
14	.0747	19	.0456
15	.0673	20	.0396
16	.0598	21	.0366
17	.0538	22	.0336
18	.0478	23	.0306
19	.0418	24	.0276
20	.0359	25	.0247
21	.0329	26	.0217
22	.0299	27	.0202
23	.0269	28	.0187
24	.0239	29	.0172
25	.0209	30	.0157
26	.0179	31	.0142
27	.0164	32	.0134
28	.0149		

This table is for information only. The products are commonly specified to decimal thickness, not to gage number. From *Steel Products Manual*, Sheet Steel, Carbon, High Strength Low Alloy and Alloy Coils and Cut Lengths. American Iron and Steel Institute, Washington, D.C. October 1979.

TABLE 10: Carbon Steel Wire Rod Sizes and Wire Gages
(Courtesy of American Iron and Steel Institute.)

SIZES OF WIRE RODS*

Inch Fraction	Decimal Equivalent in.	Inch Fraction	Decimal Equivalent in.
7/32	0.219	31/64	0.484
15/64	0.234	1/2	0.500
1/4	0.250	33/64	0.516
17/64	0.266	17/32	0.531
9/32	0.281	35/64	0.547
19/64	0.297	9/16	0.562
5/16	0.312	37/64	0.578
21/64	0.328	19/32	0.594
11/32	0.344	39/64	0.609
23/64	0.359	5/8	0.625
3/8	0.375	41/64	0.641
25/64	0.391	21/32	0.656
13/32	0.406	43/64	0.672
27/64	0.422	11/16	0.688
7/16	0.438	45/64	0.703
29/64	0.453	23/32	0.719
15/32	0.469	47/64	0.734

*Consult the producer for other available sizes.

TABLE 10: Carbon Steel Wire Rod Sizes and Wire Gages (continued)

STEEL WIRE GAGE

Gage No.	Decimal Equivalent in.	Gage No.	Decimal Equivalent in.
7/0	0.490	9	0.148
6/0	0.462	9½	0.142
5/0	0.430	10	0.135
4/0	0.394	10½	0.128
3/0	0.362	11	0.120
2/0	0.331	11½	0.113
1/0	0.306	12	0.106
1	0.283	12½	0.099
1½	0.272	13	0.092
2	0.262	13½	0.086
2½	0.253	14	0.080
3	0.244	14½	0.076
3½	0.234	15	0.072
4	0.225	15½	0.067
4½	0.216	16	0.062
5	0.207	16½	0.058
5½	0.200	17	0.054
6	0.192	17½	0.051
6½	0.184	18	0.048
7	0.177	18½	0.044
7½	0.170	19	0.041
8	0.162	19½	0.038
8½	0.155	20	0.035

From *Steel Products Manual*, Wire Rods, Carbon Steel. American Iron and Steel Institute, Washington, D.C. March 1984.

TABLE 11: Tank Volumes
Capacities of Vertical Cylinders

Diameter Ft	In	Gallons per Ft of Height	Diameter Ft	In	Gallons per Ft of Height	Diameter Ft	In	Gallons per Ft of Height
1	—	5.9	5	6	177.7	10	—	587.5
1	6	13.2	5	8	188.6	10	6	647.7
2	—	23.5	5	10	199.9	11	—	710.9
2	6	36.7	6	—	211.5	11	6	777.0
3	—	52.9	6	2	223.4	12		846.0
3	2	58.9	6	4	235.7	13		992.9
3	4	65.3	6	6	248.2	14		1152
3	6	72.0	6	8	261.1	15		1322
3	8	79.0	6	10	274.3	16		1504
3	10	86.3	7	—	287.9	17		1698
4	—	94.0	7	2	301.8	18		1904
4	2	102.0	7	4	316.0	19		2121
4	4	110.3	7	6	330.5	20		2350
4	6	119.0	7	8	345.3	21		2591
4	8	128.0	7	10	360.5	22		2844
4	10	137.2	8	—	376.0	23		3108
5	—	146.9	8	6	424.5	24		3384
5	2	156.8	9	—	475.9	25		3672
5	4	167.1	9	6	530.2			

Contents of Horizontal Tanks (Flat Ends)

Gallons per Foot of Length

Diam Ft	\multicolumn{10}{c}{Depth of Liquid, Inches}									
	6	12	18	24	30	36	42	48	54	60
3	5.8	15.4	26.4	37.4	47.1	52.9	—	—	—	—
4	6.8	18.4	32.2	47.0	61.8	75.6	87.2	94.0	—	—
5	7.6	20.8	37.0	54.9	73.4	92.0	109.8	126.0	139.2	146.9
6	8.4	23.2	41.3	61.6	83.4	105.8	128.1	149.9	170.2	188.3
7	9.1	25.2	45.2	67.9	92.3	117.9	143.9	170.0	195.6	220.0
8	9.8	27.2	48.7	73.5	100.4	128.8	158.2	188.0	217.8	247.2
9	10.4	28.9	52.1	78.7	107.9	138.7	171.2	204.3	238.0	271.6
10	11.0	30.6	55.2	83.6	114.9	148.2	183.3	219.5	256.4	293.8

Diam Ft	\multicolumn{10}{c}{Depth of Liquid, Inches}									
	66	72	78	84	90	96	102	108	114	120
6	203.1	211.5	—	—	—	—	—	—	—	—
7	242.6	262.7	278.8	287.9	—	—	—	—	—	—
8	275.6	302.5	327.2	348.9	366.2	376.0	—	—	—	—
9	304.7	337.2	368.0	397.2	423.8	447.0	465.5	475.9	—	—
10	331.1	368.1	404.3	439.3	472.7	503.9	532.3	557.0	576.6	587.5

TABLE 12: Corrosion Resistance of Metals

LEGEND

A = EXCELLENT
B = GOOD
C = FAIR
D = NOT SUITABLE
E = EXPLOSIVE
I = IGNITES
• = INFORMATION NOT AVAILABLE

No.	Chemicals	% Concentration	°F Temperature	Carbon Steel	Copper	Red Brass	Muntz	Admiralty	Copper Silicon	90-10 Cupro-Nickel	70-30 Cupro-Nickel	Aluminum	304 Stainless Steel	316 Stainless Steel	Nickel	Monel	Inconel	Hastelloy	Titanium	Zirconium	Tantalum	No.
1.	Acetaldehyde	100	70	A	E	E	E	E	E	E	E	A	A	A	A	A	A	A	B	•	A	1.
2.	Acetic Acid (Aerated)	100	70	D	D	D	D	D	D	D	C	C	B	A	A	D	A	B	A	A	A	2.
3.	Acetic Anhydride	100	70	D	B	C	D	C	B	B	B	A	B	B	B	B	B	B	A	A	B	3.
4.	Acetone	100	70	A	A	A	A	A	A	A	A	A	A	A	B	A	A	B	A	•	A	4.
5.	Acetylene	100	70	A	E	E	E	E	E	E	E	A	A	A	A	A	A	A	A	•	A	5.
6.	Aluminum Chloride	10	70	D	D	D	D	D	D	D	D	D	D	D	D	C	B	D	A	A	A	6.
7.	Aluminum Hydroxide	10	70	B	B	B	B	B	B	B	B	B	B	B	B	B	B	B	•	•	B	7.
8.	Ammonia (Anhydrous)	100	70	A	A	A	A	A	A	A	A	A	A	B	A	B	A	B	A	•	A	8.
9.	Ammonium Chloride	10	70	D	D	D	D	D	D	D	D	D	C	B	B	B	B	B	A	•	A	9.
10.	Ammonium Sulfate	10	70	C	C	C	C	C	C	C	C	C	D	C	C	C	B	B	A	A	A	10.
11.	Ammonium Sulfite	10	70	D	B	B	B	D	B	B	B	B	B	C	C	C	D	D	D	•	A	11.
12.	Amyl Acetate	100	70	B	A	A	C	A	B	A	A	A	A	A	A	A	A	B	A	•	A	12.
13.	Aniline	100	70	A	D	D	D	D	D	D	D	D	D	A	A	B	B	B	B	•	A	13.
14.	Aroclor	100	70	B	A	A	A	A	A	A	A	A	B	B	A	A	A	A	A	•	A	14.
15.	Barium Chloride	30	70	B	B	B	D	C	B	B	B	B	B	B	B	B	B	B	A	A	A	15.
16.	Benzaldehyde	100	70	B	B	B	B	B	B	B	B	B	B	B	B	B	B	B	A	•	A	16.
17.	Benzene	100	70	A	A	A	A	A	A	A	A	B	B	B	B	B	B	B	A	•	A	17.
18.	Benzoic Acid	10	70	D	B	B	B	B	B	B	B	B	B	B	B	B	B	B	A	•	A	18.
19.	Boric Acid	10	70	D	B	B	B	B	B	B	B	B	C	A	A	B	B	B	A	•	A	19.
20.	Butadiene	100	70	A	A	A	A	A	A	A	A	A	A	A	A	A	A	A	A	•	A	20.
21.	Butane	100	70	A	A	A	A	A	A	A	A	A	A	A	A	A	A	A	A	•	A	21.
22.	Butanol	100	70	A	A	A	A	A	A	A	A	A	A	A	A	A	A	A	A	•	A	22.
23.	Butyl Acetate	100	70	A	B	B	B	B	B	B	B	A	B	B	B	A	B	A	B	•	A	23.
24.	Butyl Chloride	100	70	A	A	A	A	A	A	A	A	A	A	A	A	A	A	A	A	•	A	24.
25.	Calcium Chloride	20	70	B	B	B	D	C	B	B	B	B	C	B	A	A	A	B	A	A	A	25.
26.	Calcium Hydroxide	10	70	B	B	B	B	B	B	B	B	D	B	B	B	B	B	B	A	•	A	26.
27.	Carbon Dioxide (Wet)	100	70	C	C	C	C	C	C	C	C	B	A	A	A	A	A	A	A	•	A	27.
28.	Carbon Tetrachloride (Dry)	100	70	B	B	B	B	B	B	B	B	B	B	B	A	A	A	B	A	A	A	28.
29.	Carbonic Acid	100	70	C	C	C	C	C	C	C	C	B	B	B	B	C	A	A	A	•	A	29.
30.	Chlorine Gas (Dry)	100	70	B	B	B	B	B	B	B	B	C	B	B	B	B	A	B	I	A	A	30.
31.	Chloroform (Dry)	100	70	B	B	B	B	B	B	B	B	B	B	B	A	A	B	B	A	A	A	31.
32.	Chromic Acid	20	70	D	D	D	D	D	D	D	D	D	C	B	D	D	B	B	B	A	A	32.
33.	Citric Acid	20	70	D	C	C	D	C	C	C	C	A	C	B	B	B	A	C	A	A	A	33.
34.	Creosote	100	70	B	B	B	B	B	B	B	B	B	B	B	B	B	B	B	A	•	A	34.
35.	Dibutylphthalate	100	70	A	A	A	A	A	A	A	A	B	B	B	B	B	B	B	A	•	A	35.
36.	Dichlorobenzene	100	70	B	B	B	B	B	B	B	B	B	B	B	B	B	B	B	B	•	A	36.
37.	Dichlodifluoromethane (F-12)	100	70	A	A	A	A	A	A	A	A	A	A	B	B	B	B	A	A	•	A	37.
38.	Diethanolamine	100	85	A	B	B	B	B	B	B	B	A	A	A	A	A	A	A	A	•	A	38.
39.	Diethyl Ether	100	70	B	B	B	B	B	B	B	B	B	B	B	B	B	B	B	A	•	A	39.
40.	Diethylene Glycol	100	70	A	B	B	B	B	B	B	B	B	A	A	B	B	B	B	A	•	A	40.
41.	Diphenyl	100	160	B	B	B	B	B	B	B	B	A	B	B	B	B	B	B	A	•	A	41.
42.	Diphenyl Oxide	100	85	B	B	B	B	B	B	B	B	B	B	B	B	B	B	B	A	•	A	42.

TABLE 12: Corrosion Resistance of Metals (continued)

LEGEND
A = EXCELLENT
B = GOOD
C = FAIR
D = NOT SUITABLE
E = EXPLOSIVE
I = IGNITES
● = INFORMATION NOT AVAILABLE

No.	Chemicals	% Conc.	°F Temp.	Carbon Steel	Copper	Red Brass	Muntz	Admiralty	Copper Silicon	90-10 Cupro-Nickel	70-30 Cupro-Nickel	Aluminum	304 Stainless Steel	316 Stainless Steel	Nickel	Monel	Inconel	Hastelloy	Titanium	Zirconium	Tantalum	No.
43.	Ethane	100	70	A	A	A	A	A	A	A	A	A	A	A	A	A	A	A	A	●	A	43.
44.	Ethanolamine	100	70	B	B	B	B	B	B	B	B	B	A	B	B	B	B	B	B	●	A	44.
45.	Ether	100	70	B	B	B	B	B	B	B	B	B	B	B	B	B	B	B	A	●	A	45.
46.	Ethyl Acetate (Dry)	100	70	B	B	B	B	B	B	B	B	B	B	B	B	B	B	B	A	●	A	46.
47.	Ethyl Alcohol	100	70	B	B	B	B	B	B	B	B	B	B	B	B	B	B	A	A	A	A	47.
48.	Ethyl Ether	100	70	B	B	B	B	B	B	B	B	B	B	B	B	B	B	B	A	●	A	48.
49.	Ethylene	100	70	A	A	A	A	A	A	A	A	A	A	A	A	A	A	A	A	●	A	49.
50.	Ethylene Glycol	100	70	B	B	B	B	B	B	B	B	B	B	B	B	B	B	B	A	●	A	50.
51.	Fatty Acids	100	400	D	D	D	D	D	D	D	D	A	D	A	B	C	B	A	B	●	A	51.
52.	Ferric Chloride	20	70	D	D	D	D	D	D	D	D	D	D	D	D	D	D	B	A	D	A	52.
53.	Ferric Sulfate	10	70	D	D	D	D	D	D	D	D	D	B	B	D	D	D	A	A	●	A	53.
54.	Ferrous Sulfate	10	70	D	B	B	B	D	B	B	B	B	B	B	D	D	D	B	A	●	A	54.
55.	Formaldehyde	50	200	D	B	B	B	B	B	B	B	C	B	B	B	B	B	B	B	●	A	55.
56.	Furfural	100	70	B	B	B	D	B	B	B	B	B	B	B	B	B	B	B	A	●	A	56.
57.	Glycerine	100	70	A	A	A	A	A	A	A	A	A	A	A	A	A	A	A	A	●	A	57.
58.	Hexane	100	70	A	A	A	A	A	A	A	A	A	A	A	A	A	A	A	A	●	A	58.
59.	Hydrochloric Acid (Aerated)	38	70	D	D	D	D	D	D	D	D	D	D	D	D	D	D	B	D	D	A	59.
60.	Hydrofluoric Acid (Aerated)	40	70	D	C	D	D	D	D	D	D	C	D	D	D	D	C	D	A	D	D	60.
61.	Iodine	20	70	D	D	D	D	D	D	D	D	D	D	D	D	D	D	B	D	●	A	61.
62.	Isopropanol	100	70	A	B	B	B	B	B	B	B	B	B	B	B	B	B	B	A	●	A	62.
63.	Lactic Acid	50	70	D	B	B	D	C	B	B	B	D	B	A	B	C	A	A	A	A	A	63.
64.	Linseed Oil	100	70	A	B	B	B	B	B	B	B	B	A	A	B	B	B	B	A	●	A	64.
65.	Lithium Chloride	30	200	B	B	B	D	B	B	B	B	D	B	A	A	A	A	A	●	●	A	65.
66.	Lithium Hydroxide	10	200	B	B	B	D	B	B	B	B	D	B	B	B	B	B	B	●	●	A	66.
67.	Magnesium Chloride	30	70	B	B	B	D	C	B	B	B	C	B	B	A	B	A	A	A	A	A	67.
68.	Magnesium Hydroxide	10	70	B	B	B	B	B	B	B	B	D	B	B	B	B	B	B	A	●	B	68.
69.	Magnesium Sulfate	30	200	B	B	B	B	B	B	B	B	C	A	A	B	B	B	A	A	A	A	69.
70.	Methane	100	70	A	A	A	A	A	A	A	A	A	A	A	A	A	A	A	A	A	A	70.
71.	Methallyamine	100	70	C	B	B	B	B	B	B	B	B	B	B	B	C	B	B	B	●	A	71.
72.	Methyl Alcohol	100	70	B	B	B	B	B	B	B	B	B	B	B	A	B	A	A	A	A	A	72.
73.	Methyl Chloride (Dry)	100	70	A	A	A	A	A	A	A	A	E	A	A	B	B	B	B	A	●	A	73.
74.	Methylene Chloride (Dry)	100	70	B	B	B	B	B	B	B	B	B	B	B	B	B	B	B	B	●	A	74.
75.	Monochlorobenzene (Dry)	100	70	B	B	B	B	B	B	B	B	A	B	B	A	A	A	B	B	●	A	75.
76.	Monochlorodifluoro Methane (F-22)	100	70	A	A	A	A	A	A	A	A	A	A	A	A	A	A	A	A	●	A	76.
77.	Monoethanolamine	100	200	B	B	B	B	B	B	B	B	B	B	B	B	B	B	●	●	●	A	77.

TABLE 12: Corrosion Resistance of Metals (continued)

LEGEND
A = EXCELLENT
B = GOOD
C = FAIR
D = NOT SUITABLE
E = EXPLOSIVE
I = IGNITES
• = INFORMATION NOT AVAILABLE

No.	Chemicals	% Concentration	°F Temperature	Carbon Steel	Copper	Red Brass	Muntz	Admiralty	Copper Silicon	90-10 Cupro-Nickel	70-30 Cupro-Nickel	Aluminum	304 Stainless Steel	316 Stainless Steel	Nickel	Monel	Inconel	Hastelloy	Titanium	Zirconium	Tantalum	No.
78.	Naphtha	100	70	A	B	B	B	B	B	B	B	A	B	B	B	B	B	B	B	•	A	78.
79.	Naphthalene	100	70	A	B	B	B	B	B	B	B	B	A	A	A	A	A	B	B	•	A	79.
80.	Nickel Chloride	20	70	D	B	B	D	B	B	B	B	D	B	B	D	B	D	A	A	A	A	80.
81.	Nickel Sulfate	10	200	D	B	B	D	B	B	B	B	D	B	B	B	B	B	B	B	A	A	81.
82.	Nitric Acid	50	200	D	D	D	D	D	D	D	D	D	B	B	D	D	D	D	A	B	A	82.
83.	Nitrous Acid	10	70	D	D	D	D	D	D	D	D	D	B	B	D	D	D	•	•	•	A	83.
84.	Oleic Acid	100	70	B	B	B	C	B	B	B	B	B	B	B	A	A	A	B	B	B	B	84.
85.	Oxalic Acid	10	70	D	B	B	C	B	B	B	B	C	B	B	C	B	B	B	D	B	A	85.
86.	Perchloric Acid (Dry)	100	70	D	D	D	D	D	D	D	D	B	B	B	D	D	D	•	•	•	A	86.
87.	Perchloroethylene	100	70	A	B	B	C	B	B	B	B	B	B	B	B	A	A	•	A	•	A	87.
88.	Phenol	10	120	B	B	B	B	B	B	B	B	A	B	B	B	A	B	A	A	•	A	88.
89.	Phosphoric Acid (Aerated)	50	200	D	D	D	D	D	D	D	D	D	B	B	D	D	B	A	C	D	B	89.
90.	Phthalic Anhydride	100	300	B	B	B	B	B	B	B	B	B	B	B	B	B	B	B	B	•	A	90.
91.	Potassium Bicarbonate	30	200	B	B	B	C	B	B	B	A	D	B	B	B	B	B	B	A	•	A	91.
92.	Potassium Carbonate	40	200	B	B	B	B	B	B	B	B	D	B	B	B	B	B	B	A	•	A	92.
93.	Propylene Glycol	100	70	B	B	B	B	B	B	B	B	B	B	B	B	B	B	B	A	•	A	93.
94.	Pyridine	100	70	A	B	B	B	B	B	B	B	B	B	B	B	B	B	B	B	•	A	94.
95.	Silver Chloride	10	70	D	D	D	D	D	D	D	D	D	D	D	D	D	C	B	B	•	A	95.
96.	Silver Nitrate	10	70	D	D	D	D	D	D	D	D	D	B	B	D	D	B	B	A	A	A	96.
97.	Sodium Acetate	10	70	D	B	B	B	B	B	B	B	C	B	B	B	B	B	B	B	•	A	97.
98.	Sodium Hydroxide	50	300	D	D	D	D	D	D	D	D	D	D	D	A	B	B	B	B	B	D	98.
99.	Sodium Nitrate	40	70	B	B	B	C	B	B	B	B	B	A	A	B	B	A	B	A	•	A	99.
100.	Sodium Sulfate	10	200	B	B	B	B	B	B	B	B	A	B	A	B	B	B	B	A	•	A	100.
101.	Sulfur Dioxide (Dry)	100	300	B	B	B	C	B	B	B	B	B	B	B	B	B	B	B	A	•	A	101.
102.	Sulfuric Acid (Aerated)	60	200	D	D	D	D	D	D	D	D	D	D	D	D	D	D	B	D	A	A	102.
103.	Toluene	100	200	A	A	A	A	A	A	A	A	A	A	A	A	A	A	A	A	A	A	103.
104.	Trichloroethylene (Dry)	100	150	B	B	B	C	B	B	B	B	B	B	B	A	A	B	A	A	A	A	104.
105.	Turpentine	100	70	B	B	B	B	B	B	B	B	B	B	B	B	B	B	B	B	•	A	105.
106.	Vinyl Chloride (Dry)	100	70	A	B	B	D	C	B	B	B	A	B	A	A	A	A	A	A	•	A	106.
107.	Water (Fresh)	100	70	C	A	A	A	A	A	A	A	B	A	A	A	A	A	A	A	A	A	107.
108.	Water (Sea)	100	70	C	B	B	C	A	B	A	A	B	A	A	B	A	B	B	A	A	A	108.
109.	Xylene	100	200	B	A	A	A	A	A	A	A	B	A	A	A	A	A	A	A	A	A	109.
110.	Zinc Chloride	10	70	D	D	D	D	D	D	D	D	C	B	B	B	A	D	B	A	A	A	110.
111.	Zinc Sulfate	20	70	D	B	B	D	B	B	B	B	D	B	A	B	B	A	B	A	•	A	111.

TABLE 13: Steel Pipe Dimensions[1]

Nominal Pipe Size, in.	Outside Diameter, in.	Wall Thickness, in.	Inside Diameter, in.	Inside Cross-sectional Area, sq. in.
Standard (STD)[2]				
1/8	0.405	0.068	0.269	0.0568
1/4	0.540	0.088	0.364	0.104
3/8	0.675	0.091	0.493	0.191
1/2	0.840	0.109	0.622	0.304
3/4	1.050	0.113	0.824	0.533
1	1.315	0.133	1.049	0.864
1¼	1.660	0.140	1.380	1.496
1½	1.900	0.145	1.610	2.036
2	2.375	0.154	2.067	3.356
2½	2.875	0.203	2.469	4.788
3	3.500	0.216	3.068	7.392
3½	4.000	0.226	3.548	9.887
4	4.500	0.237	4.026	12.730
5	5.563	0.258	5.047	20.006
6	6.625	0.280	6.065	28.890
8	8.625	0.322	7.981	50.027
10	10.750	0.365	10.020	78.854
12	12.750	0.375	12.000	113.097
14	14.000	0.375	13.250	137.886
16	16.000	0.375	15.250	182.654
18	18.000	0.375	17.250	233.705
20	20.000	0.375	19.250	291.039
22	22.000	0.375	21.250	354.656
24	24.000	0.375	23.250	424.557
26	26.000	0.375	25.250	500.740
28	28.000	0.375	27.250	538.207
30	30.000	0.375	29.250	671.957
32	32.000	0.375	31.250	766.990
34	34.000	0.375	33.250	868.307
36	36.000	0.375	35.250	975.906

[1]First three columns extracted from American National Standard Welded and Seamless Wrought Steel Pipe, ANSI/ASME B36.10M-1985, with the permission of the publisher, The American Society of Mechanical Engineers, 345 East 47th Street, New York, NY 10017.

[2]Same as Schedule 40 for pipe sizes up to and including 10-in.

TABLE 13: Steel Pipe Dimensions (continued)

Nominal Pipe Size, in.	Outside Diameter, in.	Wall Thickness, in.	Inside Diameter, in.	Inside Cross-sectional Area, sq. in.

Nominal Pipe Size, in.	Outside Diameter, in.	Wall Thickness, in.	Inside Diameter, in.	Inside Cross-sectional Area, sq. in.
Extra Strong (XS)[3]				
1/8	0.405	0.095	0.215	0.0363
1/4	0.540	0.119	0.302	0.0716
3/8	0.675	0.126	0.423	0.140
1/2	0.840	0.147	0.546	0.234
3/4	1.050	0.154	0.742	0.432
1	1.315	0.179	0.957	0.719
1¼	1.660	0.191	1.278	1.283
1½	1.900	0.200	1.500	1.767
2	2.375	0.218	1.939	2.953
2½	2.875	0.276	2.323	4.238
3	3.500	0.300	2.900	6.605
3½	4.000	0.318	3.364	8.888
4	4.500	0.337	3.826	11.497
5	5.563	0.375	4.813	18.194
6	6.625	0.432	5.761	26.067
8	8.625	0.500	7.625	45.664
10	10.750	0.500	9.750	74.662
12	12.750	0.500	11.750	108.434
14	14.000	0.500	13.000	132.732
16	16.000	0.500	15.000	176.714
18	18.000	0.500	17.000	226.980
20	20.000	0.500	19.000	283.529
22	22.000	0.500	21.000	346.360
24	24.000	0.500	23.000	415.476
26	26.000	0.500	25.000	490.874
28	28.000	0.500	27.000	572.555
30	30.000	0.500	29.000	660.520
32	32.000	0.500	31.000	754.768
34	34.000	0.500	33.000	855.298
36	36.000	0.500	35.000	962.113

[3]Same as Schedule 80 for pipe sizes up to and including 8-in.

Index